Brief Contents

Writing First
with Readings

Paragraphs and Essays

Writing First with Readings

Paragraphs and Essays

Sixth Edition

Laurie G. Kirszner
University of the Sciences, Emeritus

Stephen R. Mandell
Drexel University

Bedford / St. Martin's
Boston ◆ New York

For Bedford/St. Martin's

Vice President, Editorial, Macmillan Higher Education Humanities: Edwin Hill
Editorial Director for English and Music: Karen S. Henry
Executive Editor, Developmental English: Vivian Garcia
Developmental Editors: Karrin M. Varucene; Jonathan Douglas
Senior Production Editor: Harold Chester
Production Supervisor: Samuel Jones
Senior Marketing Manager: Christina Shea
Copy Editor: Jamie Nan Thaman
Indexer: Kirsten Kite
Photo Researcher: Julie Tesser
Text Design: Jerilyn Bockorick
Cover Design: Donna Lee Dennison
Cover Art: A Stack of Books, © Jorg Greuel / Getty Images
Composition: Cenveo Publisher Services
Printing and Binding: RR Donnelley and Sons

Manufactured in the United States of America.

9 8 7 6 5 4
f e d c b a

For information, write: Bedford/St. Martin's, 75 Arlington Street, Boston, MA 02116
(617-399-4000)

ISBN 978-1-4576-6783-1 (paperback)
ISBN 978-1-4576-8603-0 (loose-leaf edition)

Acknowledgments

Preface

In college, writing comes first. In fact, as soon as students set foot in a classroom, they are asked to write—to take notes, to complete assignments, to write essays, to take exams. For this reason, writing also comes first in *Writing First with Readings: Paragraphs and Essays*.

Our years in the classroom have taught us that students learn to write best by writing, so unlike other books of its kind, *Writing First* makes writing integral both to the writing process chapters *and* to the grammar chapters. Each of these chapters is built around a Write First sequence of prompts that gets students writing on the first page and guides them in revising their writing as they move through the chapter.

Our goals in this edition of *Writing First* remain the same as they were when we wrote the first edition: to motivate students to improve their writing and to give them the tools they need to do so. With the help of feedback from instructors and students who have used past editions, we have worked hard to make this edition even more motivating and instructive. Specifically, we have fine-tuned the Write First strand, adding new, engaging chapter-opening visuals and revising writing prompts to allow for flexibility in the topics students use to practice their writing. We have also added more in-depth coverage of the writing process. This coverage offers new instruction and exercises, which help students understand and think critically about the criteria for selecting strong supporting points; enhanced coverage of the revision process, including guidelines for productive conferences and peer review; and streamlined student case studies, which guide students through the writing process, step-by-step, using their own writing.

In addition, with LaunchPad Solo for *Writing First with Readings*, we bring the book's instruction into an online, interactive space, where students can continue their practice of key grammatical and mechanical concepts. Also included in the LaunchPad Solo are several e-readings to provide instructors with choice and flexibility in the readings they assign to students. LaunchPad Solo is available to package with this book. Please see the inside back cover for more information on LaunchPad Solo.

Organization

Writing First with Readings has a flexible organization that permits instructors to teach various topics in the order that works best for them and their students. The book is divided into three sections, which are color coded to help students and instructors more easily navigate the book:

- **Writing Paragraphs and Essays,** Chapters 2–16, is a comprehensive discussion of the writing process.

- **Revising and Editing Your Writing,** Chapters 17–35, is a thorough review of sentence skills, grammar, punctuation, and mechanics.

- **Becoming a Critical Reader,** Chapters 36 and 37, introduces students to critical-reading skills and includes nineteen professional essays (four of which are available online), each illustrating a particular pattern of development.

Features

Central to the text is our philosophy that students best learn to write by working with their own writing. This philosophy is supported by innovative features designed to make students' writing practice meaningful, productive, and enjoyable.

TEST helps students write and revise. This unique self-assessment tool, introduced in Chapter 2 and revisited throughout the text, helps students check their paragraphs and essays for unity, support, and coherence. By applying TEST to their writing, students can quickly see where their drafts need more work.

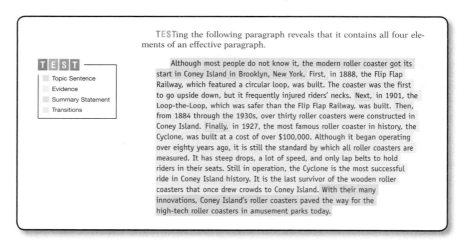

TESTing the following paragraph reveals that it contains all four elements of an effective paragraph.

TEST
- Topic Sentence
- Evidence
- Summary Statement
- Transitions

Although most people do not know it, the modern roller coaster got its start in Coney Island in Brooklyn, New York. First, in 1888, the Flip Flap Railway, which featured a circular loop, was built. The coaster was the first to go upside down, but it frequently injured riders' necks. Next, in 1901, the Loop-the-Loop, which was safer than the Flip Flap Railway, was built. Then, from 1884 through the 1930s, over thirty roller coasters were constructed in Coney Island. Finally, in 1927, the most famous roller coaster in history, the Cyclone, was built at a cost of over $100,000. Although it began operating over eighty years ago, it is still the standard by which all roller coasters are measured. It has steep drops, a lot of speed, and only lap belts to hold riders in their seats. Still in operation, the Cyclone is the most successful ride in Coney Island history. It is the last survivor of the wooden roller coasters that once drew crowds to Coney Island. With their many innovations, Coney Island's roller coasters paved the way for the high-tech roller coasters in amusement parks today.

Write First activities engage and motivate students. An activity at the beginning of each chapter asks students to begin writing immediately by responding to a chapter-opening visual and prompt. An end-of-chapter prompt sends students back to their initial writing to apply the new skills they have learned and to create a final draft.

Students get the writing and grammar help they need—in a clear, step-by-step format. Eleven chapters on paragraph writing and three on essay writing cover the writing process and nine patterns of development. Each chapter includes a student-focused case study and an abundance of clear examples and engaging exercises. Chapter 16, Using Research in Your Writing, guides students through the steps of writing a research paper.

Instruction and activities emphasize critical reading and thinking. With a full chapter on reading critically and a set of questions based on critical reading and thinking for each professional reading at the back of the book, *Writing First* helps students build these essential skills.

Grammar coverage is thorough yet accessible. Nineteen chapters dedicated to sentence structure and grammar clearly and concisely convey the rules and conventions of English grammar.

New to This Edition

LaunchPad Solo for *Writing First with Readings.* Throughout this textbook you will see icons in the margins indicating when additional online content is available through our LaunchPad Solo platform.

- LearningCurve, innovative adaptive online quizzes, lets students learn at their own pace, with a game-like interface that keeps them engaged. Quizzes are keyed to grammar instruction in the book. Instructors can also check in on each student's activity in an online gradebook.

- Additional multiple-choice grammar exercises offer students even more practice with their most challenging grammar concepts. The exercises are auto-gradable and report directly to the instructor's grade book.

- Also included in the LaunchPad Solo are several e-readings to provide instructors with choice and flexibility in the readings they assign to students.

Please see the inside back cover for more information on LaunchPad Solo.

21a Recognizing Parallel Structure

Parallelism is the use of matching words, phrases, clauses, and sentence structure to highlight similar ideas in a sentence. When you use parallelism, you are telling readers that certain ideas are related and have the same level of importance. By repeating similar grammatical patterns to express similar ideas, you create sentences that are clearer, more concise, and easier to read.

🅔 macmillanhighered.com
/writingfirst
LearningCurve > Parallelism;
Additional Grammar Exercises
> Recognizing Parallel
Structure

A streamlined chapter structure keeps students focused on their own writing. The hallmark Write First strand throughout the patterns chapters now includes more engaging chapter-opening visuals and writing prompts that allow for flexibility in the topics students use to practice their writing.

Expanded guidance for developing paragraphs includes new instruction and exercises that help students understand and think critically about the criteria for choosing strong supporting points. Students will be able to develop those points to fully support a paragraph's topic sentence.

Enhanced coverage of the revision process, including guidelines for productive conferences and peer review, empowers students to read their own work critically and enables them to tackle one of the more challenging steps in the writing process.

Streamlined student case studies, using real student models, serve not only to teach by example but also to guide students through the writing process, step-by-step, as they draft and revise their own writing.

Support for Instructors and Students

Writing First is accompanied by comprehensive teaching and learning support.

📖 Print   💻 Online   💿 CD-ROM

Student Resources

Free with a New Print Text

💻 **LaunchPad Solo for *Writing First with Readings*, Sixth Edition,** at **macmillanhighered.com/writingfirst**, provides students with interactive and adaptive grammar exercises and several e-readings. Please see the inside back cover for more information on LaunchPad Solo. Free when packaged with the print text. Package ISBN: 978-1-319-00574-0.

💻 ***Re:Writing 3*,** at **bedfordstmartins.com/rewriting**, provides new open online resources with videos and interactive elements to engage students in new ways of writing. You'll find tutorials about using common digital writing tools, an interactive peer review game, Extreme Paragraph Makeover, and more—all for free and for fun.

📖 ***The Bedford/St. Martin's Planner*** includes everything students need to plan and use their time effectively, with advice on preparing schedules and to-do lists plus blank schedules and calendars (monthly and weekly). The planner fits easily into a backpack or purse, so students can take it everywhere. **Free** when packaged with the print text. Package ISBN: 978-1-4576-9963-4

📖 ***From Practice to Mastery*** (study guide for the Florida Basic Skills Exit Tests) gives students all the resources they need to practice for—and pass—the Florida tests in reading and writing. It includes pre- and post-tests, abundant practices, many examples, and clear instruction in all the skills covered on the exams. **Free** when packaged with the print text. Package ISBN: 978-1-4576-9964-1

Premium

💻 **SkillsClass** provides students with a dynamic, interactive online course space preloaded with LearningCurve quizzes, exercises, diagnostics, video tutorials, and writing and commenting tools, plus guidance and practice in reading and study skills. SkillsClass helps students stay focused and lets instructors see how they are progressing. It is available at a significant discount when packaged with the print text. To learn more about SkillsClass, visit **yourskillsclass.com**. For access card: ISBN: 978-1-4576-2346-2

💻 **WritingClass** provides students with a dynamic, interactive online course space preloaded with exercises, diagnostics, video tutorials, writing and commenting tools, and more. WritingClass helps students stay focused and lets instructors see how they are progressing. It is available at a significant discount when packaged with the print text. To learn more about WritingClass, visit **yourwritingclass.com**. For access card: ISBN: 978-0-312-57385-0

📖 ***The Bedford/St. Martin's Textbook Reader*, Second Edition,** by Ellen Kuhl Repetto, gives students practice in reading college textbooks across the curriculum. This brief collection of chapters from market-leading introductory college textbooks can be packaged inexpensively with *Writing First*. Beginning with a chapter on college success, *The Bedford/St. Martin's Textbook Reader* also includes chapters from current texts on composition, mass communication, history, psychology, and environmental science. Comprehension questions and tips for reading success guide students in reading college-level materials efficiently and effectively. Package ISBN: 978-1-319-00300-5

Free Instructor Resources

The Instructor's Annotated Edition of *Writing First with Readings* contains answers to all grammar practice exercises as well as many of the exercises throughout the reading and writing instructional chapters, in addition to numerous teaching ideas, reminders, and cross-references useful to teachers at all levels of experience. ISBN: 978-1-4576-8156-1

Classroom Resources and Instructor's Guide for Writing First, Sixth Edition, offers advice for teaching developmental writing as well as chapter-by-chapter pointers for using *Writing First* in the classroom. It contains answers to all of the book's grammar exercises, sample syllabi, additional teaching materials, and full chapters on collaborative learning. To download, go to **macmillanhighered.com/writingfirst/catalog**.

***Testing Tool Kit: Writing and Grammar Test Bank* CD-ROM** allows instructors to create secure, customized tests and quizzes from a pool of nearly two thousand questions covering forty-seven topics. It also includes ten prebuilt diagnostic tests. ISBN: 978-0-312-43032-0

Teaching Central at macmillanhighered.com/teachingcentral offers the entire list of Bedford/St. Martin's print and online professional resources in one place. You will find landmark reference works, sourcebooks on pedagogical issues, award-winning collections, and practical advice for the classroom.

Bedford Bits is our award-winning weekly blog in which a host of Bedford authors—including Andrea Lunsford, Emily Isaacs, Susan Naomi Bernstein, and Elizabeth Wardle—bring you new ideas for the classroom. Join the conversation at **bedfordbits.com**.

e-Book Options

The Bedford e-Book to Go for *Writing First with Readings* includes the same content as the print book and provides an affordable, tech-savvy PDF e-book option for students. Learn more about Bedford e-Books to Go at **macmillanhighered.com/ebooks**—where you can also learn more about other e-book versions of *Writing First with Readings* in a variety of formats including Kindle, CourseSmart, Barnes & Noble Nook-Study, Know, CafeScribe, or Chegg.

Ordering Information

To order any of the ancillaries for *Writing First with Readings*, contact your local Bedford/St. Martin's sales representative, e-mail **sales_support@ bfwpub.com**, or visit our website at **macmillanhighered.com**.

Acknowledgments

In our work on *Writing First*, we have benefited from the help of a great many people.

We are grateful to Sally Gearhart of Santa Rosa Junior College, who used her experience and expertise to contribute valuable suggestions for improvement to Chapter 32, Grammar and Usage for ESL Writers.

We thank Linda Crawford of McLennan Community College, Katherine Canter of Bluegrass Community and Technical College, and Mary Dubbé of Thomas Nelson Community College, who wrote and revised essential sections of the instructor's manual.

Instructors throughout the country have contributed suggestions and encouragement at various stages of the book's development. For their collegial support, we thank Tiffany Baker, *Bluegrass Community and Technical College*; Lisa Bates, *Moraine Valley Community College*; Candace Boeck, *San Diego State University*; Gricelle Cano, *Houston Community College*; Katherine Canter, *Bluegrass Community and Technical College*; William Carney, *Cameron University*; Carol Eisenhower, *Sierra College*; Jane Ellingwood, *Eastern Maine Community College*; Kathleen Gandy, *Centenary College*; Yolanda Gonzalez, *McLennan Community College*; Martha Goodwin, *Bergen Community College*; M. Elizabeth Grooms, *Cameron University*; Ronald Harvey, *Lane Community College*; Scarlett Hill, *Brookhaven College*; Timothy Jones, *Oklahoma City Community College*; Anna Joy, *Sacramento City College*; Jenn Kepka, *Lane Community College*; Charlotte Laughlin, *McLennan Community College*; Jill Maggs, *University of Rio Grande and Rio Grande Community College*; Jim McKeown, *McLennan Community College*; Barbara McNellis, *Moraine Valley Community College*; Aubrey Moncrieffe, *Housatonic Community College*; Beth Penney, *Monterey Peninsula College*; Sherry Rankin, *Jackson State University*; Angela Rhodes, *Rio Hondo College*; Mark Silvia, *Southeast Community College*; Ann Smith, *Modesto Junior College*; Cathleen Stevenson, *Tarrant County College*; Kristen Tilbury, *Delta Community College*; and David Waller, *McLennan Community College*.

At Bedford/St. Martin's, we thank founder and former president Charles Christensen, former president Joan Feinberg, and former editor in chief Nancy Perry, who believed in this project and gave us support and encouragement from the outset. We thank Denise Wydra, Karen Henry, Alexis Walker, and Edwin Hill for overseeing this edition. We are also grateful to Shuli Traub, Elise Kaiser, Samuel Jones, and Harold Chester, for ably guiding the book through production, and to Lucy Krikorian, for once again overseeing the book's design. Many thanks also go to Christina Shea, senior marketing manager. And finally, we thank our fantastic editor, Karrin Varucene, for all her hard work on this project. Her energy, insight, and intelligence are truly impressive.

It almost goes without saying that *Writing First* could not exist without our students, whose work inspired the sample sentences, paragraphs, and essays in this book. We thank all of them, past and present, who allowed us to use their work.

We are grateful in addition for the continued support of our families. Finally, we are grateful for the survival and growth of the writing partnership we entered into when we were graduate students. We had no idea then of the wonderful places our collaborative efforts would take us. Now, we know.

Laurie G. Kirszner
Stephen R. Mandell

A Note to Students

As both teachers and former students, we know how demanding college can be and how hard it is to juggle academic assignments with work and family responsibilities. We also know that you don't want to waste your time. That is why in *Writing First* we make information easy to find and use, and include many features to help you become a better writer.

Boxes

Preview boxes. Each chapter starts with a list of key concepts that will be discussed in the chapter. Looking at these boxes before you begin the chapter will give you an overview of what's to come.

Writing prompt boxes. Most chapters start with a Write First activity, accompanied by a visual, that asks you to begin writing about a topic. Later in the chapter, a TEST-Revise-Edit-Proofread prompt guides you to fine-tune your writing.

FYI boxes. Throughout the book, purple-outlined boxes labeled "FYI" (For Your Information) highlight useful information, explain key concepts, and offer tips for using technology.

Grammar-in-Context boxes. Throughout the writing chapters, boxes identify key grammar issues. These boxes will help you understand how particular grammatical concepts are relevant to your writing.

---

grammar in context

Exemplification

When you write an exemplification paragraph, always use a comma after the transitional word or phrase that introduces an example.

> For example, Burma became Myanmar in 1989.

> For instance, the Gold Coast changed its name to Ghana in 1957.

> Finally, Zimbabwe gave up its British name after winning independence.

For information on using commas with transitional words and phrases, see 33b.

For more practice with comma usage, complete the LearningCurve Commas activity at **macmillanhighered.com/writingfirst**.

Checklists

Self-Assessment Checklists. Chapters 2 and 13 include Self-Assessment Checklists that enable you to measure your understanding of basic paragraph and essay structure.

Review Checklists. All grammar chapters and some of the writing chapters end with a summary of the most important information in the chapter. Use these checklists to review material for quizzes or to remind yourself of key points.

TEST Checklists. All paragraph development chapters and each section of the essay development chapter end with a checklist that helps you check your writing for the four TEST elements.

TESTing a cause-and-effect essay

Thesis Statement Unifies Your Essay

☐ Does your introduction include a **thesis statement** that indicates your main idea and makes clear whether your essay will focus on causes or effects?

Evidence Supports Your Essay's Thesis Statement

☐ Does all your **evidence**—examples and details—support your thesis, or should some be deleted?

☐ Do you identify and explain all causes or effects relevant to your topic, or do you need to add any?

☐ Do you arrange causes and effects to indicate which are more important than others?

☐ Does each body paragraph identify and explain one particular cause or effect (or several closely related causes or effects)?

Summary Statement Reinforces Your Essay's Unity

☐ Does your conclusion include a **summary statement** that reinforces your essay's thesis?

Transitions Add Coherence to Your Essay

☐ Do you include **transitions** that introduce each of your causes or effects and make your essay's cause-and-effect connections clear?

Contents

15 Patterns of Essay Development 183

Unit 4 Research

16 Using Research in Your Writing 243

REVISING AND EDITING YOUR WRITING

Unit 5 Writing Effective Sentences

17 Writing Simple Sentences   269 🄴

18 Writing Compound Sentences   278 🄴

19 Writing Complex Sentences   290 🄴

🄴 **LearningCurve** activities and additional multiple-choice grammar exercises are available for the topics in this chapter. Visit **macmillanhighered.com/writingfirst**.

🄴 **LearningCurve** activities and additional multiple-choice grammar exercises are available for the topics in this chapter. Visit **macmillanhighered.com/writingfirst**.

Unit 6 Solving Common Sentence Problems

e **LearningCurve** activities and additional multiple-choice grammar exercises are available for the topics in this chapter. Visit **macmillanhighered.com/writingfirst**.

ᴇ **LearningCurve** activities and additional multiple-choice grammar exercises are available for the topics in this chapter. Visit **macmillanhighered.com/writingfirst**.

e **LearningCurve** activities and additional multiple-choice grammar exercises are available for the topics in this chapter. Visit **macmillanhighered.com/writingfirst**.

Unit 8 Understanding Punctuation and Mechanics

33 Using Commas   481 🄴

34 Using Apostrophes   495 🄴

35 Understanding Mechanics   502 🄴

🄴 **LearningCurve** activities and additional multiple-choice grammar exercises are available for the topics in this chapter. Visit **macmillanhighered.com/writingfirst**.

BECOMING A CRITICAL READER

Unit 9 Reading Essays

36 Reading Critically   516

37 Readings for Writers   533

🄴 This e-reading is available online at **macmillanhighered.com/writingfirst**.

Writing First with Readings

Paragraphs and Essays

1 Academic Writing and Success

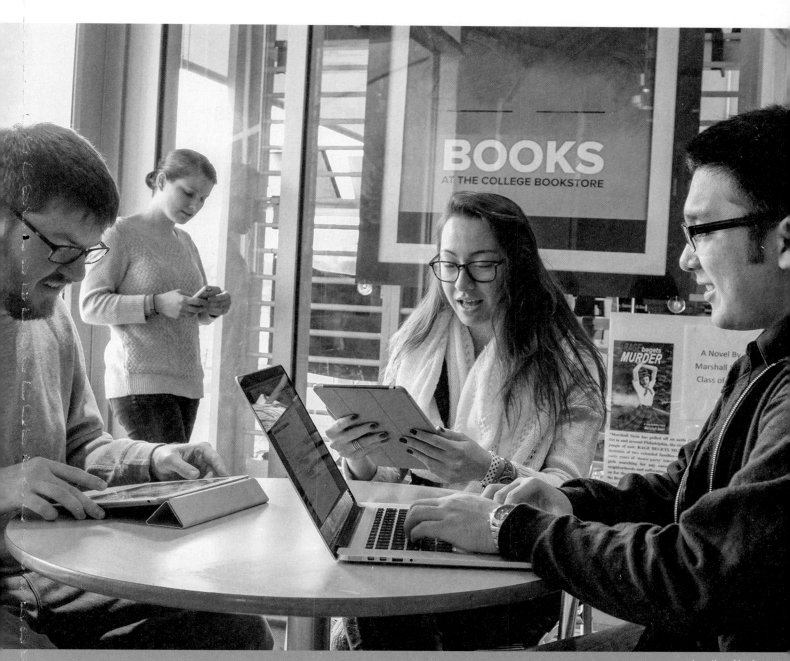

Jonathan Ugol

write first

Most of us write every day. Look through some of your own recent emails, social media posts, and texts. To whom are you writing? What reasons do you have for writing? What different styles of writing do you use? Write for a few minutes about your personal writing habits.

In this chapter, you will learn strategies for

- understanding academic writing (1a)
- managing day-to-day college life (1b)
- managing your time (1c)
- taking notes (1d)
- completing homework assignments (1e)
- taking exams (1f)
- maintaining academic honesty (1g)

1a Academic Writing Strategies

This text places writing first because writing is essential to success in college and beyond. Most people agree that the best way to learn to write is by writing. In a sense, then, you are already something of an expert when it comes to writing; after all, you have been writing for years—not just for your classes but also in your everyday life. For example, on your Facebook page, you write and update your profile, post and respond to comments, and send messages; you probably text, tweet, and email every day. In these situations, you write fluently, confidently, and concisely, without self-consciousness, because you know your audience and you know what you want to say. Now, it is time to learn how to translate those skills, and that confidence, into the writing you do in an academic context.

Academic writing is different from the informal, casual kinds of writing you do every day. Here are some important tips to keep in mind when writing in an academic setting (anything from a final paper submitted for a grade or an email to an instructor or an administrator).

1. *Use an appropriate tone.* College writing tends to be more formal than personal communications. For example, "textspeak," abbreviations, and shorthand are not acceptable in college writing assignments, and spontaneous bursts of words are acceptable only in the very roughest of first drafts or activities, such as freewriting, brainstorming, clustering, and journal writing (see 2b).
2. *Know your audience.* In an academic setting, the audience for your writing is usually a college instructor or your classmates. You cannot assume, as you do when writing to your friends, that these readers will always know exactly what you mean or understand the context for your comments. In your college writing, you need to provide convincing support for your ideas and opinions, and you need to express them clearly so that your audience will understand exactly what you are saying.
3. *Follow the conventions of standard English grammar.* Academic writing needs to be grammatically correct and free of errors in sentence structure, punctuation, and mechanics. Your college writing also must follow certain formal conventions and formats; you cannot produce shapeless, slang-filled, punctuation-free documents and expect your readers to figure out what you mean.

The following two examples illustrate the differences between informal writing and academic writing.

Text to a friend

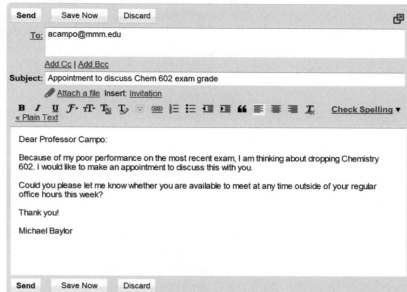

Email to an academic advisor

FYI

Using Email

Although you may not use email much in your personal communications, your instructors will likely use it to communicate with their students. For this reason, you should check your school email account regularly for schedule or assignment updates. When you contact your instructors by email, you should be sure to include a specific subject line to let them know what the message is about, and your message should get to the point right away.

To succeed in college, you need to learn to write well—and you will learn skills and strategies for writing well as you go through this book. In the rest of this chapter, you will learn some practical strategies for making the most of your college education.

1b Day-to-Day Strategies

As you get busier and busier, you may find it difficult to keep everything under control. Here are some strategies to help you as you move through the semester.

1. ***Find a place to study.*** As a college student, you will need your own private place to work and study. If possible, this space should be a quiet place with good lighting, a comfortable chair, a clean work surface, storage for supplies, and so on.

FYI

Checking Your Computer Skills

Don't wait until you have an assignment due to discover that your computer skills need improvement. Be sure your basic computer skills are at the level you need for your work and that you understand how to access course sites and to use the online materials you need for your classes. If you need help, get it right away. Your school's computer lab, writing center, and library are good places to turn for help.

WORD POWER

priorities things considered more important than others

2. *Set up a bookshelf.* Keep your textbooks, calculator, supplies, and everything else you use regularly for your coursework in one place—ideally, in your own workspace. That way, when you need something, you will know exactly where it is.

3. *Set up a study schedule.* Try to identify thirty- to forty-five-minute blocks of free time before, between, and after classes. Set this time aside for review. Remember, studying should be part of your regular routine, not something you do only the night before an exam.

4. *Establish priorities.* It is very important to understand what your priorities are. Before you can establish priorities, however, you need to know which assignments are due first, which ones can be done in steps, and which tasks or steps will be the most time consuming. Then, you have to decide which tasks are most pressing. For example, studying for a test to be given the next day is more pressing than reviewing notes for a test scheduled for the following week. Finally, you need to decide which tasks are more important than others. For example, studying for a midterm is more important than studying for a quiz, and the midterm for a course you are in danger of failing is more important than the midterm for a course in which you are doing well. Remember, you cannot do everything at once; you need to know what must be done immediately and what can wait.

5. *Check your email.* Check your school email account regularly—if possible, several times a day. If you miss a message, you may miss important information about changes in assignments, canceled classes, or rescheduled quizzes. (If your classes have course web pages, check those as well.)

6. *Schedule conferences.* Try to meet with each of your instructors during the semester, even if you are not required to do so. You might schedule one conference during the second or third week of the semester and another a week or two before a major exam or paper is due. Your instructors will appreciate and respect your initiative.

7. *Become familiar with the student services available on your campus.* There is nothing wrong with getting help from your school's writing center or tutoring center or from the center for disability services (which serves students with learning disabilities as well as physical challenges), the office of international students, or the counseling center, as well as from your advisor or course instructors. You should take advantage of all the available services you need.

FYI

Asking for Help

Despite all your careful planning, you may still run into trouble. For example, you may miss an exam and have to make it up, you may miss several classes in a row and fall behind in your work, you may have trouble understanding the material in one of your courses, or a family member may get sick. Do not wait until you are overwhelmed to ask for help. If you have an ongoing personal problem or a family emergency, let your instructors and the dean of students know immediately.

1c   Time-Management Strategies

Learning to manage your time is very important for success in college. Here are some strategies you can adopt to make this task easier.

1. ***Use an organizer.*** New electronic tools are constantly being developed to help you stay organized. For example, Schoolbinder, a free online organizer, can help you manage your time and create a study schedule. If you have trouble blocking out distractions when you are studying, a site like StudyRails can be helpful. For a small monthly fee, this site will help you plan a study schedule and alert you to when it's time to focus on schoolwork. It can also be programmed to block your go-to recreational sites during hours when you should be studying.

    You can use the calendar function on your smartphone to keep track of deadlines and appointments. At the beginning of the semester, enter key pieces of information from each course syllabus—for example, the date of every quiz and exam and the due date of every paper as you learn of them—and continue to add assignments and deadlines. In addition, enter such information as days when a class will be canceled or will meet in the computer lab or in the library, reminders to bring a particular book or piece of equipment to class, and appointments with instructors or other college personnel.

2. *Use a calendar.* Buy a large wall calendar, and post it where you will see it every morning—on your desk; on the refrigerator; or wherever you keep your phone, keys, and ID. At the beginning of the semester, fill in important dates, such as school holidays, work commitments, exam dates, and due dates for papers and projects. When you return from classes each day, update the calendar with any new information you have entered into your organizer.

3. *Plan ahead.* If you think you will need help from a writing center tutor to revise a paper that is due in two weeks, don't wait until day thirteen to make an appointment; all the tutoring slots may be filled by then. To be safe, make an appointment about a week in advance.

4. *Learn to enjoy downtime.* When you have a free minute, take time for yourself—and don't feel guilty about it.

1d Note-Taking Strategies

Learning to take notes in a college class takes practice, but taking good notes is essential for success in college. Here are some basic guidelines that will help you develop and improve your note-taking skills.

During Class

1. *Come to class.* If you miss class, you miss notes—so come to class, and come on time. Sit where you can see the board or screen and hear the instructor. Do not feel you have to sit in the same spot every day; change your seat until you find a location that is comfortable for you.

2. *Develop a system of shorthand to make note taking faster and more efficient.* You can use texting abbreviations and even symbols in your notes, but remember not to use such abbreviations in your college writing.

3. *Date your notes.* Begin each class by writing the date at the top of the page. Instructors frequently identify material that will be on a test by dates. If you do not date your notes, you may not know exactly what to study.

4. *Know what to write down.* You cannot possibly write down everything an instructor says. If you try, you will miss a lot of important information. Listen carefully *before* you write, and listen for cues to what is important. For example, sometimes the instructor will tell you that something is important or that a particular piece of information will be on a test. If the instructor emphasizes an idea or underlines it on the board, you should do the same in your notes.

5. *Include examples.* Try to include an example for each important concept introduced in class—something that will help you remember what the instructor was talking about. (If you do not have time to include examples as you take notes during class, add them when you review your notes.) For instance, if your world history instructor is explaining

nationalism, you should write down not only a definition but also an example, such as "Germany in 1848."

6. ***If you take notes by hand, write legibly and use helpful signals.*** Use blue or black ink for your note taking, but keep a red or green pen handy to highlight important information, jot down announcements (such as a change in a test date), note gaps in your notes, or question confusing points. Do not take notes in pencil, which is hard to read and not as permanent as ink.

7. ***Ask questions.*** If you do not hear (or do not understand) something your instructor said, or if you need an example to help you understand something, *ask!* Do not, however, immediately turn to another student for clarification. Instead, wait to see if the instructor explains further or if he or she pauses to ask if anyone has a question. If you are not comfortable asking a question during class, make a note of the question and ask the instructor—or send an email—after class.

After Class

1. ***Review your notes.*** After every class, try to spend ten or fifteen minutes rereading your notes, filling in gaps and examples while the material is still fresh in your mind. You might also recopy or retype important information from your notes to reinforce what you have learned.

2. ***Copy announcements*** (such as quiz dates) onto your calendar.

3. ***Enter reminders*** (for example, a note to schedule a conference before your next paper is due) into your organizer.

4. ***Write questions*** you want to ask the instructor at the top of the next blank page in your class notebook.

Before the Next Class

1. ***Reread your notes.*** Leave time to skim the previous class's notes just before each class. This strategy will get you oriented for the next class and will remind you of anything that needs clarification or further explanation. (You might want to give each day's notes a title so you can remember the topic of each class. This strategy can help you find information when you study.)

2. ***Ask for help.*** Call or email a classmate if you need to fill in missing information; if you still need help, see the instructor during his or her office hours, or come to class early to ask your question before class begins.

1e   Homework Strategies

Doing homework is an important part of your education. Homework gives you a chance to practice your skills and measure your progress. If you are having trouble with the homework, chances are you are having trouble with the course. Ask the instructor or teaching assistant for help *now*; do not wait until the day before the exam. Here are some tips for getting the most out of your homework.

1. ***Write down the assignment.*** Do not expect to remember your assignment. If you are not exactly sure what you are supposed to do, check with your instructor or with another student.

2. ***Do your homework, and do it on time.*** Teachers assign homework to reinforce classwork, and they expect homework to be done on a regular basis. It is easy to fall behind in college, but trying to do three—or five—nights' worth of homework in one night is not a good idea.

3. ***Be an active reader.*** Get into the habit of highlighting and annotating your textbooks and other material as you read. (See Chapter 36 for information on becoming an active reader.)

4. ***Join study groups.*** A study group of three or four students can be a valuable support system for homework as well as for exams. If your schedule permits, review homework assignments or class notes with other students regularly. In addition to learning information, you will learn different strategies for doing assignments.

1f   Exam Strategies

Preparation for an exam should begin well before the exam is announced. In a sense, you begin this preparation on the first day of class.

Before the Exam

1. ***Attend every class.*** Regular attendance in class—where you can listen, ask questions, and take notes—is the best possible preparation for exams. If you do have to miss a class, arrange to copy—and read—another student's notes *before the next class* so that you will be able to follow the discussion.

2. ***Keep up with the reading.*** Read every assignment, and read it before the class in which it will be discussed. If you do not, you may have trouble understanding what is going on in class.

3. ***Take careful notes.*** Take careful, thorough notes, but be selective. If you can, compare your notes on a regular basis with those of other students in the class; working together, you can fill in gaps or correct errors. Establishing a buddy system will also force you to review your notes regularly instead of just on the night before the exam.

4. ***Study on your own.*** When an exam is announced, adjust your study schedule—and your priorities—so that you have time to review everything. (This is especially important if you have more than one exam in a short period of time.) Over a period of several days, review all your material (class notes, readings, and so on), and then review it again. Make a note of anything you do not understand, and keep track of topics you need to review. Try to predict the most likely questions, and—if you have time—practice answering them.

5. ***Study with a group.*** If you can, set up a study group. Studying with others can help you understand the material better. However, do not come to group sessions unprepared and expect to get all the information you need from the other students. You must first study on your own.

6. ***Make an appointment with your instructor.*** Make a conference appointment with the course instructor or teaching assistant a few days before the exam. Bring to this meeting any specific questions you have about course content and about the format of the upcoming exam. (Be sure to review all your study material before the conference.)

7. *Review the material one last time.* The night before the exam is not the time to begin your studying; it is the time to review. When you have finished your review, get a good night's sleep.

During the Exam

By the time you walk into the exam room, you will already have done all you could to get ready for the test. Your goal now is to keep the momentum going and not do anything to undermine all your hard work.

FYI

Taking Essay Exams

If an exam question asks you to write an essay, remember that what you are really being asked to do is write a **thesis-and-support essay**. Chapter 13 tells you how to do this.

1. *Read through the entire exam.* Be sure you understand how much time you have, how many points each question is worth, and exactly what each question is asking you to do. Many exam questions call for just a short answer—*yes* or *no, true* or *false*. Others ask you to fill in a blank with a few words, and still others require you to select the best answer from among several choices. If you are not absolutely certain what kind of answer a particular question calls for, ask the instructor or the proctor *before* you begin to write.
2. *Budget your time.* Once you understand how much each section of the exam and each question are worth, plan your time and set your priorities, devoting the most time to the most important questions. If you know you tend to rush through exams, or if you find you often run out of time before you get to the end of a test, you might try checking your progress when about one-third of the allotted time has passed (for a one-hour exam, check after twenty minutes) to make sure you are pacing yourself appropriately.
3. *Reread each question.* Carefully reread each question *before* you start to answer it. Underline the **key words**—the words that give specific information about how to approach the question and how to phrase your answer. (These key words are listed in the FYI box on page 10.)

   Remember, even if everything you write is correct, your response is not acceptable if you do not answer the question. If a question asks you to *compare* two novels, writing a *summary* of one of them will not be acceptable.
4. *Brainstorm to help yourself recall the material.* If you are writing a paragraph or an essay, look frequently at the question as you brainstorm. Quickly write down all the relevant points you can think of— what the textbook had to say, your instructor's comments, and so on. The more information you can think of now, the more you will have to choose from when you write your answer.
5. *Write down the main idea.* Looking closely at the way the question is worded and at your brainstorming notes, write a sentence that states the main idea of your answer. If you are writing a paragraph, this

sentence will be your **topic sentence**; if you are writing an essay, it will be your **thesis statement**.

6. ***List your key supporting points.*** You do not want to waste your limited (and valuable) time making a detailed outline, but an informal outline that lists just your key points is worth the little time it takes. An informal outline will help you plan a clear direction for your paragraph or essay.

7. ***Draft your answer.*** You will spend most of your time actually writing the answers to the questions on the exam. Follow your outline, keep track of time, and consult your brainstorming notes when you need to—but stay focused on your writing.

8. ***Reread, revise, and edit.*** When you have finished drafting your answer, reread it carefully to make sure it says everything you want it to say—and that it answers the question.

FYI

Key Words

Here are some words that can help you decide how to approach an exam question that calls for a paragraph or an essay.

analyze	give examples	illustrate
argue	identify	recount
compare	identify or explain	summarize
contrast	causes, origins,	support
define	contributing	take a stand
demonstrate	factors	trace
describe	identify or explain	
evaluate	results, effects,	
explain	outcomes	

Model Essay Exam

The following essay exam was written by a student in an introductory psychology class in response to the following question:

Define and explain one of the following concepts related to memory: retrieval, flashbulb memories, déjà vu, false memories. *Be sure to give examples from the text, class discussion, or your own experiences to support the points you make.*

Déjà Vu

INTRODUCTION

Definition of term

Memory is a group of mental processes that allow people to form, store, and retrieve information. Memory concepts include retrieval, the process of recovering stored information; flashbulb memories, very specific remembered images or details of a vivid, rare, or important personal event; and false memories, recollections that are distorted or that recall things that never happened. Perhaps the most interesting memory concept is déjà vu. Déjà vu is a French phrase meaning "already seen." Déjà vu is a feeling that one has experienced something before but is unable to remember when or where. When people experience déjà vu, they find it impossible to explain the feeling of familiarity, so people often think it must somehow be related to the paranormal. However, déjà vu can actually be explained scientifically, through concepts related to memory.

— Thesis statement

Researchers and scientists have discovered several characteristics of déjà vu. It seems to occur most commonly in young adults ages twenty to twenty-four, and the older we get, the less often we tend to have feelings of déjà vu. Researchers have also found that feelings of déjà vu most commonly occur later in the day, when a person is tired or under emotional stress, and when a person is around other people. Most often a feeling of déjà vu is triggered by something that is seen—for example, a coffee mug in a specific place on a desk with an open book next to it. Something about the placement of the items and the specific pages of the open book seem very familiar, but the observer cannot explain why. Sometimes déjà vu can also be triggered by something a person smells, hears, or touches. For example, a case recorded by two researchers focuses on a blind man who experienced déjà vu when he zipped up his jacket while listening to a certain song.

Characteristics of déjà vu

When a feeling of déjà vu is triggered, a person is often confused by it. Something seems so familiar, but the person is unable to explain why. Because it is difficult and even impossible to give a logical explanation for the feeling of familiarity, people sometimes think the feeling must be related to the paranormal. For example, a person may think something seems very familiar because he or she has experienced it in a past life or because it is going to happen in the near future. These and other paranormal explanations are not grounded in science.

Misperceptions about déjà vu

Many scientific explanations for déjà vu have been proposed. For example, some scientists believe that déjà vu is a disruption in source memory. In other words, a person has forgotten the source of the memory related to the feeling of déjà vu. For example, someone might experience déjà vu while walking down a street he or she has never been down before and seeing a house that looks familiar. The person is sure that he or she has never seen that house before, but maybe a picture of the house appeared in the real estate section of the local newspaper and the person forgot having seen it there. Several other scientific explanations for déjà vu have been proposed, but although scientists have spent a great deal of time studying this concept, they do not agree on any one explanation for it.

Scientific explanations for déjà vu

Déjà vu is something most people have experienced. Although many know what it feels like, it is difficult to explain. This may make déjà vu seem to be something otherworldly, but there are actually many possible scientific explanations for the feeling of déjà vu, all grounded in memory-related research.

CONCLUSION

1g Strategies for Maintaining Academic Honesty

Academic honesty—the standard for truth and fairness in work and behavior—is very important in college. Understanding academic honesty goes beyond simply knowing that it is dishonest to cheat on a test. To be sure you are conforming to the rules of academic honesty, follow these guidelines.

- Don't reuse papers you wrote in high school. The written work you are assigned in college is designed to help you learn, and your instructors expect you to do the work for the course when it is assigned.
- Don't copy information from a book or article or paste material from a website directly into your papers. Using someone else's words or ideas without proper acknowledgment constitutes **plagiarism**, a very serious offense.
- Don't ask another student (or a friend or family member) to help you write or revise a paper. If you need help, ask your instructor or a writing center tutor.
- Don't allow another student to copy your work on a test.
- Don't allow another student to turn in a paper you wrote (or one you helped him or her write).
- Don't work with other students on a take-home exam unless your instructor gives you permission to work collaboratively.
- Never buy a paper from a website. Even if you edit it, it is still not your own work.

think about your writing

Look back at your response to the Write First prompt on page 1. Now that you have read this chapter, what have you learned about the writing you will be doing in college? Add this information to your response.

review checklist

Academic Writing and Success

- [ ] Mastering academic writing is important for college success. (See 1a.)
- [ ] Certain day-to-day strategies can help you adjust to college life. (See 1b.)
- [ ] Learning to manage your time is a key part of college success. (See 1c.)
- [ ] Learning to take good notes is essential for success in your college courses. (See 1d.)
- [ ] Doing homework assignments gives you a chance to practice your skills and assess your academic progress. (See 1e.)
- [ ] Preparation for an exam should begin well before the exam is announced. (See 1f.)
- [ ] Understanding academic honesty is a key part of a college education. (See 1g.)

2 Understanding the Writing Process

write first

Today's college students may find themselves in either a traditional classroom or a career-oriented setting. What do you think is the primary purpose of college—to give students a general education or to prepare them for specific careers? Think about this question as you read the pages that follow.

In this chapter, you will learn to

- focus on your assignment, purpose, and audience (2a)
- find ideas to write about (2b)
- identify your main idea and write a topic sentence (2c)
- choose supporting points (2d)
- develop supporting points (2e)
- make an outline (2f)
- draft, TEST, revise, edit, and proofread your paragraph (2g–2j)

A **paragraph** is a group of sentences that is unified by a single main idea. The **topic sentence** states the main idea, and the rest of the sentences in the paragraph provide **evidence** (examples and details) to support the main idea. The sentences in a paragraph are linked by **transitions**—words and phrases (such as *also* and *for example*) that show how ideas are related. At the end of the paragraph, a **summary statement** reinforces the main idea.

Paragraph Structure

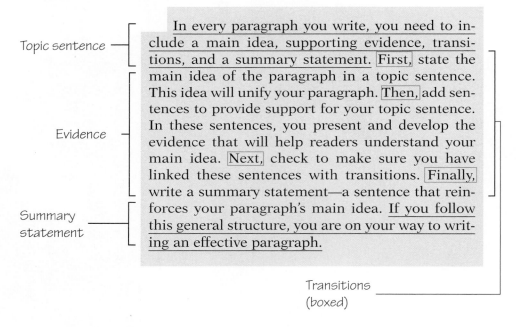

Topic sentence

Evidence

Summary statement

Transitions (boxed)

In every paragraph you write, you need to include a main idea, supporting evidence, transitions, and a summary statement. First, state the main idea of the paragraph in a topic sentence. This idea will unify your paragraph. Then, add sentences to provide support for your topic sentence. In these sentences, you present and develop the evidence that will help readers understand your main idea. Next, check to make sure you have linked these sentences with transitions. Finally, write a summary statement—a sentence that reinforces your paragraph's main idea. If you follow this general structure, you are on your way to writing an effective paragraph.

The first letters of these four elements—**T**opic sentence, **E**vidence, **S**ummary statement, and **T**ransitions—spell TEST. Whenever you write a paragraph, you should TEST it to make sure it is complete.

FYI

The first sentence of a paragraph is **indented**, starting about half an inch from the left-hand margin. Every sentence begins with a capital letter and, in most cases, ends with a period. (Sometimes a sentence ends with a question mark or an exclamation point.)

PRACTICE

2-1   Bring two paragraphs to class—one from a newspaper or magazine article and one from a textbook. Compare your paragraphs with those brought in by other students. What features do all your paragraphs share? How do the paragraphs differ from one another?

> ### The Writing Process
>
> Writing is a **process**, a series of steps that begins in your college classes when you get an assignment.
>
> **Step 1: Planning**
> You start by thinking about what you want to say and finding ideas to write about. Then, you identify the main idea you want to get across.
>
> **Step 2: Organizing**
> Once you have material to write about, you arrange the points that support your main idea in an order that makes sense to you.
>
> **Step 3: Drafting**
> When you have decided how to arrange your ideas, you write a draft.
>
> **Step 4: TESTing and Revising**
> When you finish your draft, you TEST it to make sure it includes all the elements of an effective paragraph, and then continue revising your draft until you are satisfied with it.
>
> **Step 5: Editing and Proofreading**
> Finally, you edit and proofread.

The five steps in the writing process are explained and illustrated in the pages that follow.

STEP 1: PLANNING

2a   Focusing on Your Assignment, Purpose, and Audience

In college, a writing task usually begins with an assignment that gives you a topic to write about. Instead of jumping in headfirst and starting to write, take time to consider some questions about your **assignment** (*what* you are expected to write about), your **purpose** (*why* you are writing), and your **audience** (*for whom* you are writing). Answering these questions at this point will save you time in the long run.

Questions about Assignment, Purpose, and Audience

Assignment

- What is your assignment? Is it included on your course syllabus or posted on the class web page?
- Do you have a word or page limit?
- When is your assignment due?
- Will you be expected to work on your assignment only at home, or will you be doing some work in class?
- Will you be expected to work on your own or with others?
- Will you be allowed to revise before you hand in your assignment?
- Will you be allowed to revise after your assignment is graded?
- Does your instructor require a particular **format**?

Purpose

- Are you expected to express your personal reactions—for example, to tell how you feel about a piece of music or a news event?
- Are you expected to present information—for example, to answer an exam question, describe a process in a lab report, or summarize a story or an essay you have read?
- Are you expected to argue for or against a position on a controversial issue?

Audience

- Who will read your paper—just your instructor or other students as well?
- How much will your readers know about your topic?
- Will your readers expect you to use **formal** or **informal** language?

WORD POWER

format specified arrangement of elements in a document—for example, where to type your name, the date, and the course number

formal language language that is grammatically precise and uses words familiar to an educated audience

informal language language that is used in conversation and personal email; may include contractions and slang

PRACTICE

2-2   Each of the following writing tasks has a different audience and purpose. Think about how you would approach each task. (Use the Questions about Assignment, Purpose, and Audience listed above to help you decide on the best strategy.) Be prepared to discuss your ideas with your class or in a small group.

1. For the other students in your writing class, a description of your best or worst educational experience

2. For the instructor of an education course, a discussion of your first day of high school

3. An email to your community's school board in which you try to convince members to make two or three changes that you believe would improve the schools you attended (or those your children might attend)

4. A thank-you note to a work supervisor—either past or current—telling what you appreciate about his or her guidance and how it has helped you develop and grow as an employee

5. A letter to a restaurant where you received poor service and were served terrible food, describing your experience and suggesting ways the service and food could be improved

2b   Finding Ideas to Write About

Once you know what, why, and for whom you are writing, you can begin the process of finding material to write about. This process is different for every writer.

In this chapter, you will be following the writing process of Stella Drew, a student in an introductory writing course, who was given the following assignment.

Should community service—unpaid work in the community—be a required part of the college curriculum? Write a paragraph in which you answer this question.

Before she drafted her paragraph, Stella used a variety of strategies to find ideas to write about. The pages that follow illustrate the four strategies her instructor asked the class to try.

- Freewriting
- Brainstorming
- Clustering
- Journal writing

WORD POWER

curriculum all the courses required by a school

FYI

Keep in mind that you do not have to use all four strategies every time you write a paragraph. Try out the various strategies, and see which ones work best for you.

Freewriting

When you **freewrite**, you write for a set period of time—perhaps five minutes—without stopping. Your goal is to relax and let ideas flow without worrying about whether or not they are related—or even make sense. (If you have trouble thinking of something to say, keep repeating the last word of your freewriting until something else comes to mind.) Sometimes you can freewrite without a topic in mind, but at other times you will focus your attention on a particular topic. This strategy is called **focused freewriting**.

When you finish freewriting, read what you have written. Then, underline any ideas you think you might be able to use. If you find an idea you want to explore further, freewrite again, using that idea as a starting point.

Stella's focused freewriting on the topic of whether or not community service should be a required part of the college curriculum appears on the next page.

Community service. Community service. Sounds like what you do instead of going to jail. Service to the community—service in the community. Community center. College community—community college. Community service—I guess it's a good idea to do it—but when? In my spare time—spare time—that's pretty funny. So after school and work and all the reading and studying I also have to do <u>service</u>? Right. And what could I do anyway? Work with kids. Or homeless people. Old people? Sick people? Or not people—maybe animals. Or work for a political candidate. Does that count? But when would I do it? Maybe other people have time, but I don't. OK idea, could work—but not for me.

Stella's freewriting

PRACTICE

2-3   Reread Stella's freewriting on the topic of community service for college students. If you were advising her, which of her ideas would you suggest she explore further? Underline these ideas in her freewriting, and be prepared to discuss your suggestions with the class or in a small group.

freewrite

Write (or type) for at least five minutes on the following topic: What is the primary purpose of college—to give students a general education or to prepare them for specific careers?

When you are finished, reread your freewriting, and underline any ideas you think you might be able to use in your paragraph.

FYI

To practice freewriting, open your word-processing program, but turn off the monitor. You can still type, but you won't be able to see what you're writing. This will help you to experience genuine freewriting.

Brainstorming

When you **brainstorm**, you quickly record all the ideas about your topic that you can think of. Unlike freewriting, brainstorming is sometimes written in list form and sometimes scattered all over the page. You don't have to use complete sentences; single words or phrases are fine. You can underline, star, or box important points. You can also ask questions, draw arrows to connect ideas, and even draw pictures or diagrams.

Here are Stella's brainstorming notes on community service.

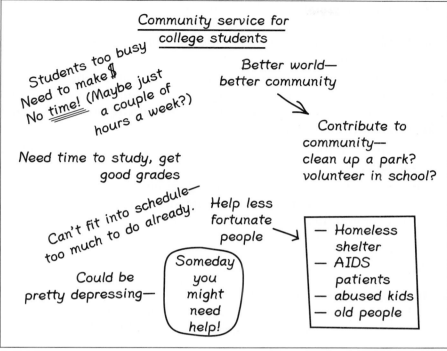

Stella's brainstorming notes

PRACTICE

2-4 Reread Stella's brainstorming notes on community service. How is her brainstorming similar to her freewriting on the same subject (p. 18)? How is it different? If you were advising Stella, which ideas would you suggest she write more about? Which ideas should she cross out? Be prepared to discuss your suggestions with the class or in a small group.

brainstorm

On a sheet of paper or on your computer, brainstorm about your assignment: What do you think is the primary purpose of college—to give students a general education or to prepare them for specific careers? (Begin by writing your topic, "The purpose of college," at the top of the page.)

When you have finished, look over what you have written. Did you come up with any new ideas as you brainstormed that you did not discover while freewriting?

FYI

Usually you brainstorm on your own, but at times you may find it helpful to do **collaborative brainstorming**, working with other students to find ideas. Sometimes your instructor may ask you and another student to brainstorm together. At other times, the class might brainstorm as a group while your instructor writes down the ideas you think of. However you brainstorm, your goal is the same: to come up with as much material about your topic as you can.

PRACTICE

2-5 Working as a class or in a group of three or four students, practice collaborative brainstorming, following these steps.

- First, decide as a group on a topic for brainstorming. (Your instructor may assign a topic.)

- Next, choose one person to write down ideas on a blank sheet of paper or on the board. (If your group is large enough, you might choose two people to write down ideas, and have them compare notes at the end of the brainstorming session.)

- Then, discuss the topic informally, with each person contributing at least one idea.

- Finally, review the ideas that have been written down. As a group, try to identify interesting connections among ideas, and suggest ideas that might be explored further.

Clustering

Clustering, sometimes called *mapping*, is another strategy that can help you find ideas to write about. When you cluster, you begin by writing your topic in the center of a sheet of paper. Then, you branch out, writing

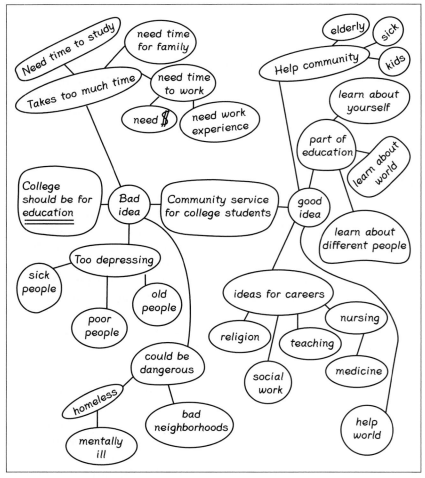

Stella's cluster diagram

related ideas on the page in groups, or clusters, around the topic. As you add new ideas, you circle them and draw lines to connect the ideas to one another and to the topic at the center. (These lines will look like a spider-web or like spokes of a wheel or branches of a tree.) As you move from the center to the corners of the page, your ideas will get more and more specific.

Sometimes one branch of your cluster exercise will give you all the material you need. At other times, you may decide to write about the ideas from several branches, or to choose one or two ideas from each branch. If you find you need additional material after you finish your first cluster exercise, you can cluster again on a new sheet of paper, this time beginning with a topic from one of the branches.

See Stella's cluster diagram on the topic of community service for college students on page 20.

PRACTICE
2-6   Look closely at Stella's cluster diagram on community service for college students. How is it similar to her brainstorming on the same subject (p. 19)? How is it different? If you were advising Stella, which branches of the cluster diagram would you tell her to develop further? Why? Would you add any branches? Be prepared to discuss your suggestions with the class or in a small group.

make a cluster diagram

Write your topic ("The purpose of college") in the center of a blank sheet of unlined paper. Circle the topic, and then branch out with specific ideas and examples, continuing to the corners of the page if you can.

When you have finished, identify the branches and ideas that you could develop further. Then, add as many new details and branches as you can.

Keeping a Journal

A **journal** is a notebook or a computer file in which you keep an informal record of your thoughts and ideas. In a journal, you can reflect, question, summarize, or even complain. Your journal is also a place where you record ideas about your assignments and note possible ideas to write about. Here you can try to resolve a problem, restart a stalled project, argue with yourself about your topic, or comment on a draft. You can also try out different versions of sentences; list details or examples; or keep a record of interesting things you read, see, or hear.

Journal writing works best when you write regularly, ideally at the same time each day, so that it becomes a habit. Once you have started making regular entries in your journal, take the time every week or so to go back and reread what you have written. You may find material you want to explore in further journal entries—or even an idea for a paper.

FYI

Journal Writing

Here are some subjects you can write about in your journal.

- *Your schoolwork*   You can explore ideas for writing assignments, reflect on what you have learned, and ask questions about concepts you are having trouble understanding.

- *Your job*   You can record job-related successes and frustrations, examine conflicts with coworkers, or review how you handled problems on the job. Reading over these entries can help you understand your strengths and weaknesses and become a more effective employee.

- *Your ideas about current events*   Expressing your opinions in your journal can be a good way to explore your reactions to social or political issues. Your journal entries may encourage you to write to your local or school newspaper or to public officials—and even to become involved in community projects or political activities.

- *Your impressions of what you see*   Many writers carry their journals with them everywhere so they can record any interesting or unusual things they observe. You can later incorporate these observations into essays or other pieces of writing.

- *Aspects of your personal life*   Although you may not want to record the intimate details of your life if your instructor plans to collect your journal, writing about relationships with family and friends, personal problems, hopes and dreams, and so on can help you develop a better understanding of yourself and others.

Here is Stella's journal entry on the topic of community service for college students.

I'm not really sure what I think about community service. I guess I think it sounds like a good idea, but I still don't see why we should have to do it. I can't fit anything else into my life. I guess it would be possible if it was just an hour or two a week. And maybe we could get credit and a grade for it, like a course. Or maybe it should just be for people who have the time and want to do it. But if it's not required, will anyone do it?

Stella's journal entry

write a journal entry

For your first journal entry, write down your thoughts about the topic you have been working on in this chapter: the purpose of college.

2c Identifying Your Main Idea and Writing a Topic Sentence

When you think you have enough material to write about, it is time to identify your **main idea**—the idea you will develop in your paragraph.

To find a main idea for your paragraph, begin by looking over what you have already written. As you read through your freewriting, brainstorming, clustering, or journal entries, look for the main idea that your material seems to support. The sentence that states this main idea and gives your writing its focus will be your paragraph's **topic sentence**.

The topic sentence is usually the first sentence of your paragraph, and it is important because it tells both you and your readers what the focus of your paragraph will be. An effective topic sentence has three characteristics.

1. *A topic sentence is a complete sentence.* There is a difference between a *topic* and a *topic sentence*. The **topic** is what the paragraph is about. A **topic sentence**, however, is a complete sentence that includes a subject and a verb and expresses a complete thought. This sentence includes both a topic and the writer's idea about the topic.

TOPIC	Community service for college students
TOPIC SENTENCE	Community service should be required for all students at our school.

2. *A topic sentence is more than just an announcement of what you plan to write about.* A topic sentence makes a point about the topic the paragraph discusses.

ANNOUNCEMENT	In this paragraph, I will explain my ideas about community service.
TOPIC SENTENCE	My ideas about community service changed after I started to volunteer at a soup kitchen for homeless people.

3. *A topic sentence presents an idea that can be discussed in a single paragraph.* If your topic sentence is too broad, you will not be able to discuss it in just one paragraph. If your topic sentence is too narrow, you will not be able to say much about it.

TOPIC SENTENCE TOO BROAD	Students all over the country participate in community service, making important contributions to their communities.
TOPIC SENTENCE TOO NARROW	Our school has a community service requirement for graduation.
EFFECTIVE TOPIC SENTENCE	Our school's community service requirement has had three positive results.

When Stella Drew reviewed her notes, she saw that they included two different kinds of ideas: ideas about the value of doing community service, and ideas about the problems it presents. The material on the value of community service seemed more convincing, so she decided that her paragraph should support a community service requirement. She stated her main idea in a topic sentence.

> Community service is so important that college students should be required to do it.

When Stella thought about how to express her topic sentence, she knew it had to be a complete sentence, not just a topic, and that it would have to make a point, not just announce what she planned to write about. When she reread the topic sentence she had written, she felt confident that it did these things. Her topic sentence was neither too broad nor too narrow, and it made a statement she could support in a paragraph.

PRACTICE

2-7 Reread the following items. Put a check mark next to each one that has all three characteristics of an effective topic sentence. Be prepared to explain why some items are effective topic sentences while others are not.

Examples

Speaking two languages, an advantage in today's workplace _____

Our school should not abandon the foreign language requirement. ____✓____

1. The new farmers' market makes it easier for people in the neighborhood to buy fresh produce. _____

2. Eating a balanced diet with plenty of proteins and carbohydrates _____

3. In this paragraph, I will look at the disadvantages of a large high school. _____

4. The best size for high schools: not too large, not too small. _____

5. Participation in sports is important for children because it teaches them how to compete.

6. The history of sports goes back to before the earliest civilizations.

_____

7. Spending a quiet evening at home can have several advantages.

_____

8. Television, the most popular leisure activity in the United States

_____

PRACTICE

2-8   Decide whether each of the following statements could be an effective topic sentence for a paragraph. If a sentence is too broad, write _too broad_ in the blank following the sentence. If the sentence is too narrow, write _too narrow_ in the blank. If the sentence is an effective topic sentence, write _OK_ in the blank.

> **Example:**   Unfortunately, many countries in today's world are
>
> involved in conflicts. _too broad_

1. Deciding what to do in life is a difficult task for many young people.

_____

2. A college career counselor can help students decide what kind of work they would like to do. _____

3. The college career counseling office has three full-time employees and two part-time employees. _____

4. Safe driving reduces the number of accidents and saves lives. _____

5. Different countries, and even different states, have different rules of the road. _____

6. Texting while driving greatly increases the chance of an accident.

_____

7. Some students are much happier with their college experience than are other students. _____

8. Joining a study group is a good way for students who commute to get to know other students. _____

9. Flu shots are especially important for people in certain high-risk groups. _____

10. Flu shots occasionally result in soreness in the area where the shot was given. _____

identify your main idea, and write a topic sentence

Look over the work you have done so far, and try to identify the main idea your material seems to support. Do you think college should give students a general education or prepare them for specific careers? Write a topic sentence that expresses your main idea on the lines below.

Topic sentence: _____

_____

STEP 2: ORGANIZING

2d   Choosing Supporting Points

After you have stated your paragraph's main idea in a topic sentence, you will need to provide specific **evidence** (examples and details) to **support** your main idea.

When you choose points to support your topic sentence, make sure they are *relevant*, *distinct*, and *specific*.

1. **Relevant** points are directly related to your main idea.

   TOPIC SENTENCE   College is necessary because it teaches students important skills for their future careers.

   SUPPORTING POINTS

   - Students learn to write in college, and knowing how to write well is important for any job.
   - Students learn to think critically in college, and knowing how to think critically is necessary for almost any career.
   - ~~Choosing a career path is difficult.~~

   The third supporting point is not relevant because it does not support the topic sentence. (It does not provide an example of how skills learned in college will help students in their future careers.)

2. **Distinct** points are different from other points you plan to use.

   TOPIC SENTENCE   College is necessary because it teaches students important skills for their future careers.

   SUPPORTING POINTS

   - Students learn to write in college, and knowing how to write well is important for any job.

■ Students learn to think critically in college, and knowing how to think critically is necessary for almost any career.

■ ~~College writing courses will prepare students to write on the job.~~

The third point is not distinct because it is saying the same thing as the first point.

3. **Specific** points communicate exactly what you want to say; they are not general or vague.

to write in college, and knowing how to write well is important for

■ Students learn ~~things in college that will help them in~~ any job.

The original point is not specific because it does not tell what "things" students learn. The revision clarifies the point the writer is using to support the topic sentence.

As she continued to work on her paragraph, Stella listed several points from her notes that she thought she could write about. After she read through her list of points, she crossed out those that did not support her topic sentence or that overlapped with other points. She decided that the remaining two points would give her enough material to write about in her paragraph.

TOPIC SENTENCE   Community service is so important that college students should be required to do it.

■ ~~Community service helps people.~~

■ ~~Some community service activities could be boring.~~

■ ~~Community service can help the world.~~

■ Community service helps the community.

■ ~~College students are busy.~~

■ ~~Community service takes a lot of time.~~

■ ~~Community service might not relate to students' majors.~~

■ ~~Community service can be upsetting or depressing.~~

■ Community service can be part of a student's education.

PRACTICE
2-9   In each of the following two cases, the topic sentence and a tentative list of supporting points have been provided. Read each list of points carefully, and consider whether the points support the topic sentence. Cross out any points that are not relevant, distinct, and specific.

1. *Topic Sentence:* Even though some fans may object, professional sports teams should abandon their Indian logos and nicknames.

   ■ Indian logos and nicknames are offensive to many people.

   ■ Indian logos and nicknames misrepresent Indians and perpetuate troubling stereotypes.

WORD POWER
perpetuate to cause to last for a long time

- Some Indian tribes have given teams official permission to use tribal names or symbols.

- Many high school and college teams have already abandoned their Indian names and logos.

- Some sports teams change their names when they move to a different city.

- Tradition is not a strong enough reason to keep racist names and logos.

- Change is difficult, but fans will get used to new names and logos.

- Many people dislike teams' Indian nicknames and logos.

- Changing a name or a logo is not a big deal.

- Team names and logos that are disrespectful of other races and cultures are unacceptable.

2. *Topic Sentence:* The government should ban unpaid internships because they are unfair.

- Internships can be hard to find.

- Employers benefit financially from interns' free labor.

- Many unpaid interns do boring, menial work and gain few valuable job skills.

- Some students are just looking to boost their résumés and do not mind working for free.

- The government has a responsibility to protect workers from being exploited.

- Without government involvement, few employers will offer to pay their interns.

- Employers are taking advantage of their interns' unpaid work.

- A lot of unpaid interns do not benefit much from their internship experiences.

- Low-income interns cannot afford to work without pay as wealthier students can.

- Nobody wants to work for free.

- Interns do not have enough power to negotiate with employers for paid positions.

choose supporting points

Review your freewriting, brainstorming, clustering, and journal writing to find the points that can best support your topic sentence. Write your topic sentence on the lines below; then, list your supporting points.

Topic sentence: _____

_____

Supporting points:

- _____

- _____

- _____

Check carefully to make sure each point on your list supports your topic sentence. Cross out any points that are not relevant, distinct, and specific.

2e   Developing Supporting Points

Now that you have identified points that support your main idea, you need to **develop** them, explaining them more fully and making clear how they relate to your topic sentence. One way to develop your points is to provide examples. To come up with examples, ask yourself *how? why?* or *what?* for each point.

After Stella chose the two points she was going to use to support her main idea, she went back and added examples to develop each point.

SUPPORTING POINT	EXAMPLES
Community service helps the community. (How? In what specific ways?)	— *Volunteers can help feed the homeless.* — *They can work with the elderly.* — *They can tutor in schools.*
Community service can be part of a student's education. (How?)	— *Students can learn about themselves and others.* — *Students can learn about their community and the world.* — *Students can discover what they want to do for a career.*

develop your supporting points

Review your list of supporting points, and then list examples you can use to develop each point. If you like, you can make a chart like the one above to help you arrange your supporting points.

2f   Making an Outline

After you have decided which points to use to support your topic sentence and chosen examples to develop each point, your next step is to make an informal **outline**. You do this by arranging your supporting points in the order in which you plan to discuss them in your paragraph.

When Stella thought she had listed enough examples to develop the two points she would discuss in her paragraph, she made the following informal outline.

Outline

Topic sentence: Community service is so important that college students should be required to do it.

- Community service helps the community.
  — Volunteers can help feed the homeless.
  — Volunteers can work with the elderly.
  — Volunteers can tutor students.

- Community service can be part of a student's education.
  — Students can learn about themselves.
  — Students can learn about others.
  — Students can learn about their community.
  — Students can learn about the world.
  — Students can discover what they want to do for a career.

Stella's informal outline

make an outline

Look over your supporting points, and decide which ones you want to include in your paragraph. Then, make an informal outline that arranges your supporting points in the order in which you plan to write about them.

STEP 3: DRAFTING

2g   Drafting Your Paragraph

Once you have written a topic sentence for your paragraph, selected the points you will discuss, and arranged them in the order in which you plan to write about them, you are ready to write a first draft.

In a **first draft**, your goal is to get your ideas down on paper. Begin your paragraph with a topic sentence that states the paragraph's main idea. Then, following your informal outline, write or type without worrying about correct wording, spelling, or punctuation. If a new idea occurs to you, write it down. Don't worry about whether it fits with the other ideas. Your goal is not to produce a perfect piece of writing but simply to create a working draft. Later on, when you revise, you will have a chance to rethink ideas and rework sentences. Because you will be making changes to this first draft, you should print a copy with wide margins, extra space between lines, and extra blank lines in places where you might need to add material.

When you have finished your first draft, don't make any changes right away. Take a break (overnight if possible), and think about something—anything—else. Then, return to your draft, and read it with a fresh eye.

Here is the first draft of Stella's paragraph on the topic of community service for college students. Note that she included a brief working title to help her focus on her topic.

Community Service

Community service is so important that college students should be required to do it. When college students do community service, they spend their time doing good for someone or for the community. Working in a homeless shelter, doing chores for senior citizens, and tutoring children are all examples of community service. Community service activities like these are good for the community, and they can be more fulfilling for students than playing sports or participating in school activities. Community service can be an important part of a college education. Students can learn a lot about themselves and others and can discover what they want to do with their lives. Community service can also make the world a better place.

Stella's first draft

PRACTICE

2-10   Reread the first draft of Stella's paragraph. Working in a group of three or four students, make a list of changes that you think Stella should make. For example, what should she add? What should she cross out? Have one member of your group write down all your suggestions, and be prepared to exchange ideas with the class.

draft your paragraph

Write a first draft of your paragraph about the purpose of a college education. Be sure you state your main idea in the topic sentence and support the topic sentence with specific evidence. If you like, you can add a working title.

STEP 4: TESTING AND REVISING

2h   TESTing Your Paragraph

When you have finished your draft, you are ready to revise it. Your first step is to "test" what you have written to make sure it includes all the elements of an effective paragraph. You do this by asking the following **TEST** questions.

T ▪ **Topic sentence**—Does your paragraph have a topic sentence that states its main idea?

E ▪ **Evidence**—Does your paragraph include specific points that support your topic sentence? Are these points developed with evidence (examples and details)?

S ▪ **Summary statement**—Does your paragraph end with a statement that reinforces its main idea?

T ▪ **Transitions**—Does your paragraph include transitional words and phrases that show readers how your ideas are related?

If your paragraph includes these four **TEST** elements, you are off to a very good start. If it does not, you will need to add whatever is missing.

When Stella reread her draft, she **TEST**ed it to take a quick inventory of her paragraph.

▪ She decided that her **topic sentence** clearly stated her main idea.
▪ She thought she needed more **evidence** to support her topic sentence.
▪ She noticed that her paragraph had no **summary statement**.
▪ She realized she needed to add **transitions** to connect her ideas.

2i   Revising Your Paragraph

Revision is the process of reseeing, rethinking, reevaluating, and rewriting your work. Revision involves much more than substituting one word for another or correcting a comma here and there. It means moving sentences, adding words and phrases, and even changing the direction or emphasis of your ideas.

Using a Self-Assessment Checklist

To get the most out of the revision process, you should carefully reread your draft, using the following Self-Assessment Checklist to guide your revision.

self-assessment checklist

Revising Your Paragraph

- [ ] Is your topic sentence clearly worded?

- [ ] Do you have enough evidence to support your topic sentence, or do you need to look back at your notes or try another strategy to find additional supporting material?

- [ ] Do you need to explain anything more fully or more clearly?

- [ ] Do you need to add or delete examples or details?

- [ ] Does every sentence say what you mean?

- [ ] Can you combine any sentences to make your writing smoother?

- [ ] Should you move any sentences?

- [ ] Are all your words necessary, or can you cut some?

- [ ] Should you change any words to make them more specific?

- [ ] Does your paragraph end with a summary statement that reinforces its main idea?

Using Peer Review

Sometimes you revise on your own, but at other times—with your instructor's permission—you may be able to get feedback (in the form of oral or written comments) from your classmates. The process of giving and receiving constructive feedback is called **peer review**. Peer review is most productive if you know how to make helpful comments and how to use the comments you get from your peers.

> **WORD POWER**
>
> **peer** someone with equal standing; an equal

Guidelines for Peer Review

Giving Feedback

- **Be positive.** Remember that your purpose is to help other students improve their writing.

- **Be tactful.** Be sure to emphasize the good points about the writing. Mention one or two things the writer has done particularly well before you offer your suggestions for improvement.

- **Be specific.** Offer concrete suggestions about how the writer could do better. A general comment like "You need more support" is not as helpful as a more specific comment like "You need support for the point you make in the fourth sentence."

(continued)

(continued from previous page)

- **Be involved.** If you are giving feedback orally instead of in writing, make sure you interact with the writer. Ask questions, listen to responses, and explain your comments.
- **Look at the big picture.** Don't focus on issues such as spelling and punctuation, which the writer will correct at the editing and proofreading stage. At this stage, the clarity of the topic sentence (or the thesis statement for an essay), the effectiveness of the support, and the organization of ideas are much more important.
- **Be thorough.** When possible, write down and explain your comments, either on a form your instructor provides or in the margins of the draft you are reviewing. (If you are reviewing another student's writing electronically, you can use the Comment function in Microsoft Word's Track Changes tool to insert your feedback.)

Using Feedback

- **Be open-minded.** Receive your peers' comments with an open mind. They might notice something important that you missed, and they might help you see something from a different angle.
- **Be selective.** It is up to you to carefully evaluate the suggestions from your peers and decide whether or not their advice will strengthen your draft. Remember, not every suggestion is worth following, but every one is worth considering.

One effective strategy to use when you are reviewing the work of your classmates is to TEST their writing. Just as you TEST your own drafts, you can use TEST to guide your peer review and to help you stay focused on the big picture. Here are the questions you should ask yourself as you review other students' work and make comments.

- **T** ■ **Topic sentence**—Does this paragraph have a topic sentence that states its main idea? If the answer is no, remind your classmate to include a topic sentence that clearly states the main idea of the paragraph.

- **E** ■ **Evidence**—Does this paragraph include specific points that support the topic sentence? Are these points developed with evidence (examples and details)? If the answer to these questions is no, alert the writer to this issue and suggest the kinds of examples and details that he or she might add to better support the topic sentence.

- **S** ■ **Summary statement**—Does this paragraph end with a statement that reinforces its main idea? If the answer is no, remind your classmate to add a summary statement that clearly reinforces the main idea of the paragraph.

- **T** ■ **Transitions**—Does this paragraph include transitional words and phrases that show readers how ideas are related? If the answer is no, point out specific areas where the relationship between ideas is particularly unclear.

Classmates in Stella's peer-review group used TEST to make suggestions for revision, working on an electronic draft of Stella's paragraph as part of a homework assignment. Their comments on her first draft, inserted using the Comment function of Microsoft Word's Track Changes tool, follow.

Community Service

Community service is so important that college students should be required to do it. When college students do community service, they spend their time doing good for someone or for the community. Working in a homeless shelter, doing chores for senior citizens, and tutoring children are all examples of community service. Community service activities like these are good for the community, and they can be more fulfilling for students than playing sports or participating in school activities. Community service can be an important part of a college education. Students can learn a lot about themselves and others and can discover what they want to do with their lives. Community service can also make the world a better place.

Comment [RK1]: Can title be more specific? What will paragraph be about?

Comment [AJ1]: Good topic sentence!

Comment [RK2]: Good examples

Comment [RK3]: Add examples here?

Comment [AJ2]: TEST element missing—you need a summary statement

Stella's peer-reviewed draft

Guided by her TEST responses and the Self-Assessment Checklist, as well as by comments from her peer-review group, Stella revised her paragraph, writing her changes in by hand on her typed draft.

Community Service *Why* *Should Be Required*

Community service is so important that college students should be

required to do it. When college students do community service, they spend

their time *helping a person or organization in their communities.* ~~doing good for someone or for the community. Working~~ *For example, they can work* in a homeless

shelter, *s do* ~~doing~~ chores for senior citizens, *or tutor or mentor at-risk* ~~and tutoring~~ children. ~~are all exam-~~

~~ples of community service.~~ Community service activities like these are good for

the community, and they *are also good for the students who give their time. This work* can be more fulfilling ~~for students~~ than playing

sports or participating in school activities. Community service can *also* be an im-

portant part of a college education. Students can learn a lot about themselves

~~and others and~~ *, about their communities, about different kinds of people, and about their world. They* can discover what they want to do with their lives. ~~Community~~

~~service can also make the world a better place.~~ *even* *For example, working in a*

school can lead a student to a career as a teacher. For all these reasons, community

service should be a required part of the college curriculum.

Stella's revised draft with handwritten revisions

As she made her revisions, Stella did not worry about being neat. She crossed out words, added material, and changed sentences and words. When she felt her revision was complete, she was ready to move on to edit and proofread her paragraph.

TEST and revise your paragraph

TEST the first draft of your paragraph to make sure it includes all four elements of an effective paragraph: **T**opic sentence, **E**vidence, **S**ummary statement, and **T**ransitions. (If any elements are missing, plan to add them as you revise.) Then, continue revising your paragraph, using the Self-Assessment Checklist on page 33 (and, if your instructor allows it, feedback from peer review) to guide you.

STEP 5: EDITING AND PROOFREADING

2j   Editing and Proofreading Your Paragraph

When you **edit**, you check for correct grammar, punctuation, mechanics, and spelling. Then, you go on to **proofread** carefully for typographical errors that your spell checker may not identify, checking to make sure that you have indented the first sentence of your paragraph and that every sentence begins with a capital letter and ends with a period. Finally, you check your essay's **format** to make sure it satisfies your instructor's requirements.

Remember, editing is a vital step in the writing process. Many readers will not take your ideas seriously if your paragraph contains grammatical or mechanical errors. You can use the following checklist to guide your editing.

self-assessment checklist

Editing and Proofreading Your Paragraph

- [ ] Are all your sentences complete and grammatically correct?
- [ ] Do all your subjects and verbs agree?
- [ ] Have you used the correct verb tenses?
- [ ] Are commas used where they are required?
- [ ] Have you used apostrophes correctly?
- [ ] Have you used other punctuation marks correctly?
- [ ] Have you used capital letters where they are required?
- [ ] Are all words spelled correctly?

For help with grammar, punctuation, mechanics, and spelling, see Units 5–8 of this text.

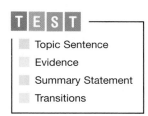

Before Stella edited her paragraph, she typed in the changes she made on her first draft and printed out a revised copy. Then, she checked grammar, punctuation, mechanics, and spelling. Finally, she proofread for typos. The final version of her paragraph follows.

|T|E|S|T|
- Topic Sentence
- Evidence
- Summary Statement
- Transitions

Why Community Service Should Be Required

Community service is so important that college students should be required to do it. When college students do community service, they spend their time helping a person or organization in their communities. For example, they can work in homeless shelters, do chores for senior citizens, or tutor or mentor at-risk children. Community service activities like these are good for the community, and they are also good for the students who give their time. This work can be more fulfilling than playing sports or participating in school activities. Community service can also be an important part of a college education. Students can learn a lot about themselves, about their communities, about different kinds of people, and about their world. They can even discover what they want to do with their lives. For example, working in a school can lead a student to a career as a teacher. For all these reasons, community service should be a required part of the college curriculum.

(Margin labels: Topic sentence; Evidence; Summary statement)

PRACTICE

2-11   Reread the final draft of Stella's paragraph about community service for college students and compare it with her first draft (p. 31). Then, working in a group of three or four students, answer the following questions about her revision. (Be prepared to discuss your responses to these questions with the class.)

1. Why do you think Stella did not revise her paragraph's topic sentence? Do you agree with her decision?

2. What new supporting material did Stella add to her paragraph? Can you think of any new material she *should* have added?

3. What did Stella cross out? Why do you think she deleted this material? Do you think she should cross out any additional material?

4. Why do you think Stella added "For example" and "also" to her final draft?

5. In her revision, Stella added a sentence at the end of the paragraph. Do you think this sentence is necessary? Why or why not?

edit and proofread your paragraph

Now that you have **TEST**ed and revised your paragraph, you should go on to edit it, checking grammar, punctuation, mechanics, and spelling. Then, proofread carefully for typos. When you are satisfied with your paragraph, print it out.

review checklist

Understanding the Writing Process

- [ ] Before you start to write, consider your assignment, purpose, and audience. (See 2a.)

- [ ] Use freewriting, brainstorming, clustering, and journal writing to help you find ideas. (See 2b.)

- [ ] Identify your main idea, and write a topic sentence. (See 2c.)

- [ ] Choose points to support your main idea. (See 2d.)

- [ ] Develop your supporting points with evidence. (See 2e.)

- [ ] Make an informal outline by arranging your points in the order in which you plan to discuss them. (See 2f.)

- [ ] Write a first draft of your paragraph. (See 2g.)

- [ ] TEST your paragraph. (See 2h.)

- [ ] Revise your paragraph. (See 2i.)

- [ ] Edit and proofread your paragraph. (See 2j.)

3 TESTing Your Paragraphs

Photography: Lara Schneider

write first

These pictures show a student's closet before (left) and after (right) she organized it. How do you organize your own closet (or your desk, furniture, or other items in your room)? Does everything have its place, or do you arrange items more randomly? Write a paragraph about how you organize a space of your own.

As you learned in Chapter 2, you should TEST every paragraph after you finish drafting, before you revise. TESTing will tell you whether or not your paragraph includes all the elements of an effective paragraph.

T opic sentence
E vidence
S ummary statement
T ransitions

TESTing the following paragraph reveals that it contains all four elements of an effective paragraph.

TEST

☐ Topic Sentence
☐ Evidence
☐ Summary Statement
☐ Transitions

> Although most people do not know it, the modern roller coaster got its start in Coney Island in Brooklyn, New York. First, in 1888, the Flip Flap Railway, which featured a circular loop, was built. The coaster was the first to go upside down, but it frequently injured riders' necks. Next, in 1901, the Loop-the-Loop, which was safer than the Flip Flap Railway, was built. Then, from 1884 through the 1930s, over thirty roller coasters were constructed in Coney Island. Finally, in 1927, the most famous roller coaster in history, the Cyclone, was built at a cost of over $100,000. Although it began operating over eighty years ago, it is still the standard by which all roller coasters are measured. It has steep drops, a lot of speed, and only lap belts to hold riders in their seats. Still in operation, the Cyclone is the most successful ride in Coney Island history. It is the last survivor of the wooden roller coasters that once drew crowds to Coney Island. With their many innovations, Coney Island's roller coasters paved the way for the high-tech roller coasters in amusement parks today.

WORD POWER

innovation something newly invented; a new way of doing something

3a TESTing for a Topic Sentence

The first thing you do when you TEST a paragraph is look for a **topic sentence (T)**. An effective paragraph focuses on a single main idea, and it includes a topic sentence that states this main idea.

A paragraph is **unified** when all of its sentences support the main idea stated in the topic sentence. When you revise, you can make your paragraphs unified by crossing out sentences that do not support your topic sentence and, if necessary, adding sentences that do.

The following paragraph is not unified because it includes sentences that do not support the paragraph's topic sentence. (These sentences have been crossed out.)

The weak economy has led many people to move away from the rural Ohio community where I was raised. Over the years, farmland has become more and more expensive. Years ago, a family could buy each of its children twenty-five acres on which they could start farming. Today, the price of land is so high that the average farmer cannot afford to buy this amount of land, and those who choose not to farm have few alternatives. ~~After I graduate, I intend to return to my town and get a job there. Even though many factories have moved out of the area, I think I will be able to get a job. My uncle owns a hardware store, and he told me that after I graduate, he will teach me the business. I think I can contribute something to both the business and the community.~~ Young people just cannot get good jobs anymore. Factories have moved out of the area and taken with them the jobs that many young people used to get after high school. As a result, many eighteen-year-olds have no choice but to move away to find employment.

The following revised paragraph is unified. It discusses only the idea that is stated in the topic sentence.

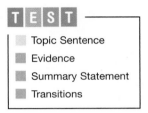

The weak economy has led many people to move away from the rural Ohio community where I was raised. Over the years, farmland has become more and more expensive. Years ago, a family could buy each of its children twenty-five acres on which they could start farming. Today, the price of land is so high that the average farmer cannot afford to buy this amount of land, and those who choose not to farm have few alternatives. Young people just cannot get good jobs anymore. Factories have moved out of the area and taken with them the jobs that many young people used to get after high school. As a result, many eighteen-year-olds have no choice but to move away to find employment.

PRACTICE 3-1 The following paragraph is not unified because some sentences do not support the topic sentence. First, underline the topic sentence. Then, cross out any sentences that do not support the topic sentence.

Although many people still get down on one knee to propose, others have found more creative ways to pop the question. Using Jumbotrons, computer games, or even zero-gravity chambers, some people are making the moment truly memorable. Last year, one English graffiti artist asked his girlfriend to marry him by spray-painting his proposal on the side of a building. In 2011, a man used the Sunday crossword puzzle in the *Washington Post* to propose to his girlfriend. As she completed the puzzle, she saw that the answers to several of the clues spelled out her name and a question. Weddings are also becoming more unusual. Some couples are choosing to get married while skydiving or riding bicycles. One couple recently got married in a shark tank. Several brave people have also proposed on television. By buying ad space and recording a brief video clip, they appear on the screen during a favorite show. People are clearly using their imaginations to ask this age-old question in unexpected ways.

PRACTICE
3-2   The following paragraph has no topic sentence. Read it carefully, and then choose the most appropriate topic sentence from the list that follows the paragraph.

While continuing to make its famous interlocking plastic bricks, Lego has created a number of popular video games, such as *Lego Racer* and *Lego Star Wars*. The company also shares ownership of four Legoland amusement parks and owns dozens of retail stores in Europe and North America. In 2014, Lego released a feature film. Meanwhile, the company makes products using licensed characters from other movies, such as the Harry Potter series, and has its own television series on the Cartoon Network. The Lego Group also offers special programs to accompany its products. For example, the Lego Group has developed an educational branch, Lego Education, which sponsors competitions for students and provides lesson plans and professional development for educators. With such wide-ranging programs and merchandise, the company will likely continue to thrive.

Put a check mark next to the topic sentence that best expresses the main idea of the paragraph above.

1. The Lego Group has been very successful in the video game market.

    _____

2. Because of a decline in sales, the Lego Group is now pursuing the education market. _____

3. Today, the Lego Group is much more than just a manufacturer of children's construction toys. _____

4. The founder of the Lego Group, a Danish man named Ole Kirk Christiansen, had a passion for making children's toys. _____

5. By diversifying its products and services, the Lego Group has spread itself too thin. _____

PRACTICE
3-3   The following paragraphs do not have topic sentences. Think of a topic sentence that expresses each paragraph's main idea, and write it on the lines above the paragraphs.

Example: *Possible answer: Rock and roll originated in African-American music* *but was reinterpreted by white performers.*

Early 1950s African-American musicians included performers such as Johnny Ace, Big Joe Turner, and Ruth Brown. Groups like the Drifters and the Clovers were also popular. By the mid-1950s, white performers such as Bill Haley and the Comets, Jerry Lee Lewis, and Elvis Presley were imitating African-American music. Their songs had a beat and lyrics that appealed to a white audience. Eventually, this combination of black and white musical styles became known as rock and roll.

1. _____

_____

First, you have to find a suitable job to apply for. Once you decide to apply, you have to put together your résumé and send it to your potential employer. Then, when you are invited in for an interview, you need to decide what you are going to wear. At the interview, you need to speak slowly and clearly and answer all questions directly and honestly. After the interview, you need to send a note to the person who interviewed you, thanking him or her. Finally, if everything goes well, you will get an email or a phone call offering you the job.

2. _____

_____

There are no written records left by the Native Americans themselves. Most of the early European settlers in North America were more interested in staying alive than in writing about the Native Americans. In addition, as the westward expansion took place, the Europeans encountered the Native Americans in stages, not all at once. Also, the Native Americans spoke at least fifty-eight different languages, which made it difficult for the Europeans to speak with them. Most important, by the time scholars decided to study Native American culture, many of the tribes no longer existed. Disease and war had wiped them out.

3b TESTing for Evidence

The next thing you do when you TEST a paragraph is to make sure you have enough **evidence (E)** to support the main idea stated in your topic sentence.

Evidence consists of the examples and details that support your statements. To make a convincing point, you need to support it with evidence. For example, it is one thing to say that gun violence has torn your neighborhood apart, but it is much more effective to follow this general statement with examples of specific incidents of gun violence in your community. The same is true when you describe something you have observed. You could, for example, say that a certain area of campus is peaceful. This statement means little to readers, however, unless you follow it with the details—the tall trees, the grass, the silence—that explain what you mean.

A paragraph is **well developed** when it includes enough evidence to explain and support its main idea. The following paragraph does not include enough evidence to support its main idea.

Although pit bulls have a bad reputation, they actually make good pets. Part of their problem is that they can look frightening. Actually, though, pit bulls are no worse than other breeds of dogs. Even so, the bad publicity they get has given them a bad reputation. Pit bulls really do not deserve their bad reputation, though. Contrary to popular opinion, pit bulls can (and do) make friendly, affectionate, and loyal pets.

The following revised paragraph now includes enough evidence to support the main idea stated in the topic sentence.

Although pit bulls have a bad reputation, they actually make good pets. Part of their problem is that they can look frightening. Their wide, powerful jaws; short muscular legs; and large teeth are ideally suited for fighting, and they were bred for this purpose. In addition, some pit bulls—especially males—can be very aggressive toward both people and other dogs. Actually, though, pit bulls are no worse than other breeds of dogs. As several recent newspaper articles have pointed out, the number of reported bites by pit bulls is no greater than the number of bites by other breeds. In fact, some breeds, such as cocker spaniels, bite more frequently than pit bulls. Even so, the bad publicity they get has given them a bad reputation. Pit bulls really do not deserve their bad reputation, though. The problem is that whenever a pit bull attacks someone, the incident is reported on the evening news. Contrary to popular opinion, pit bulls can (and do) make friendly, affectionate, and loyal pets.

Note: Length alone is no guarantee that a paragraph includes enough supporting evidence for your main idea. A long paragraph that consists of one generalization after another will still not include enough support for the topic sentence.

T E S T
- Topic Sentence
- Evidence
- Summary Statement
- Transitions

Evidence added

Evidence added

Evidence added

PRACTICE

3-4   Underline the specific supporting evidence in the following paragraph.

Hearing people have some mistaken ideas about the deaf community. First, some hearing adults think that all deaf people consider themselves disabled and would trade anything not to be "handicapped." Hearing people do not realize that many deaf people do not consider themselves handicapped and are proud to be part of the deaf community, which has its own language, customs, and culture. Second, many hearing people think that all deaf people read lips, so there is no need to learn sign language to communicate with them. However, lip reading—or speech reading, as deaf people call the practice—is difficult. Not all hearing people say the same words in the same way, and facial expressions can also change the meaning of the words. If hearing people make more of an attempt to understand the deaf culture, communication between them will improve.

PRACTICE

3-5 Provide two or three specific pieces of evidence (examples or details) to support each of the following topic sentences.

1. When it comes to feeding a family, there are several alternatives to fast food.

   • _____

   • _____

   • _____

2. A romantic relationship with a coworker can create serious problems.

   • _____

   • _____

   • _____

3. Choosing the right career is harder than I thought it would be.

   • _____

   • _____

   • _____

PRACTICE

3-6 The paragraph that follows does not include enough supporting evidence. Suggest some examples and details that might help the writer develop his or her topic sentence more fully.

Young adults who move back in with their parents after college face many challenges. Feeling dependent on one's parents after living away from home can be frustrating. Living at home can restrict a person's freedom. Also, some parents can be overbearing and treat the young graduate as if he or she is a child. Of course, the success of the living situation depends on how well the college graduate and his or her parents communicate. Despite these drawbacks, living at home for a while after college can make sense.

3c TESTing for a Summary Statement

The third thing you do when you TEST a paragraph is to make sure it ends with a **summary statement (S)**—a sentence that reinforces your paragraph's main idea. By reminding readers what your paragraph is about, a summary statement helps to further **unify** your paragraph.

The following paragraph has no summary statement.

> Overpopulation is one of the biggest concerns for scientists. In 1900, there were 1.6 billion people on earth, a quarter of today's population. At that time, life expectancy was also much shorter than it is now. By 2000, the world's population had grown to over 6 billion, and today, the average life expectancy worldwide is almost sixty-five years. The low death rate, combined with a high birth rate, is adding the equivalent of one new Germany to the world's population each year. According to a United Nations study, if present trends continue, by 2050 the world's population will be between 7.3 and 10.5 billion— so large that much of the world may be either malnourished or starving.

The summary statement in the following revised paragraph reinforces the paragraph's main idea and brings the paragraph to a close.

> Overpopulation is one of the biggest concerns for scientists. In 1900, there were 1.6 billion people on earth, a quarter of today's population. At that time, life expectancy was also much shorter than it is now. By 2000, the world's population had grown to over 6 billion, and today, the average life expectancy worldwide is almost sixty-five years. The low death rate, combined with a high birth rate, is adding the equivalent of one new Germany to the world's population each year. According to a United Nations study, if present trends continue, by 2050 the world's population will be between 7.3 and 10.5 billion—so large that much of the world may be either malnourished or starving. Given these increases, it is no wonder that scientists who study population are worried.

▪ Topic Sentence
▪ Evidence
▪ Summary Statement
▪ Transitions

PRACTICE

3-7 Read the following paragraph, which does not include a summary statement. Then, on the lines below the paragraph, write a summary statement that adds unity to the paragraph by reinforcing the main idea stated in the topic sentence. Be careful not to use the wording of the topic sentence.

> Founded more than fifty years ago, NASCAR has become one of the most successful spectator sports in the world. In December 1947, Bill France formed the National Association for Stock Car Auto Racing (NASCAR). The first NASCAR race was held at Daytona Beach's auto race-course in 1948. From this modest start, France turned NASCAR into a highly successful business. Attendance grew 8.2 percent during 1997, and 2,102,000 fans attended the thirty-one NASCAR events in 1998. This was the first time that NASCAR attendance topped the two million mark. Then, in 2007, NASCAR negotiated a new multimillion-dollar television deal with Fox Sports/Speed, TNT, and ABC/ESPN. As a result, these networks now televise NASCAR's most popular events.

_____

_____

3d TESTing for Transitions

The final thing you do when you TEST a paragraph is make sure it includes **transitions (T)** that connect ideas in a clear, logical order.

Transitional words and phrases create **coherence** by indicating how ideas are connected in a paragraph—for example, in *time order*, *spatial order*, or *logical order*. By signaling the order of ideas in a paragraph, these words and phrases make it easier for readers to follow your discussion.

- You use **time** signals to show readers the order in which events occurred.

    In 1883, my great-grandfather came to this country from Russia.

- You use **spatial** signals to show readers how people, places, and things stand in relation to one another. For example, you can move from top to bottom, from near to far, from right to left, and so on.

    Next to my bed is a bookcase that also serves as a room divider.

- You use **logical** signals to show readers how ideas are connected. For example, you can move from the least important idea to the most important idea or from the least familiar idea to the most familiar idea.

    Certain strategies can help you do well in college. First, you should learn to manage your time effectively.

Because transitional words and phrases create coherence, a paragraph without them can be difficult to understand. You can avoid this problem by checking to make sure you have included all the words and phrases that you need to link the ideas in your paragraph.

Frequently Used Transitional Words and Phrases

SOME WORDS AND PHRASES THAT SIGNAL TIME ORDER

after	finally	phrases that
afterward	later	include dates
at first	next	(for example,
before	now	"In June,"
during	soon	"In 1904")
earlier	then	
eventually	today	

SOME WORDS AND PHRASES THAT SIGNAL SPATIAL ORDER

above	in front	on the left
behind	inside	on the right
below	in the center	on top
beside	near	over
in back	next to	under
in between	on the bottom	

(continued)

(continued from previous page)

SOME WORDS AND PHRASES THAT SIGNAL LOGICAL ORDER

also	in fact
although	last
as a result	moreover
consequently	next
even though	not only . . . but also
first . . . second . . . third	one . . . another
for example	similarly
for instance	the least important
furthermore	the most important
however	therefore
in addition	

The following paragraph has no transitional words and phrases to link ideas.

During his lifetime, Jim Thorpe faced many obstacles. Thorpe was born in 1888, the son of an Irish father and a Native American mother. He was sent to the Carlisle Indian School in Pennsylvania. Pop Warner, the legendary coach at Carlisle, discovered Thorpe. Thorpe left Carlisle to play baseball for two seasons in the newly formed East Carolina minor league. He returned to Carlisle, played football, and was named to the All-American team. Thorpe went to the Olympic Games in Stockholm, where he won two gold medals. Thorpe's career took a dramatic turn for the worse when a sportswriter who had seen him play baseball in North Carolina exposed him as a professional. The Amateur Athletic Union stripped him of his records and medals. Thorpe died in 1953. The International Olympic Committee returned Thorpe's Olympic medals to his family in 1982. Ironically, only in death was Thorpe able to overcome the difficulties that had frustrated him while he was alive.

The following revised paragraph is coherent because it includes transitional words and phrases that connect its ideas.

TEST
- Topic Sentence
- Evidence
- Summary Statement
- Transitions

During his lifetime, Jim Thorpe faced many obstacles. Thorpe was born in 1888, the son of an Irish father and a Native American mother. In 1904, he was sent to the Carlisle Indian School in Pennsylvania. The next year, Pop Warner, the legendary coach at Carlisle, discovered Thorpe. Thorpe left Carlisle in 1909 to play baseball for two seasons in the newly formed East Carolina minor league. In 1912, he returned to Carlisle, played football, and was named to the All-American team. Thorpe then went to the Olympic Games in Stockholm, where he won two gold medals. The next year, however, Thorpe's career took a dramatic turn for the worse when a sportswriter who had seen him play baseball in North Carolina exposed him as a professional. As a result, the Amateur Athletic Union stripped him of his records and medals. Thorpe died in 1953. After years of appeals, the International Olympic Committee returned Thorpe's Olympic medals to his family in 1982. Ironically, only in death was Thorpe able to overcome the difficulties that had frustrated him while he was alive.

PRACTICE

3-8 Read the following paragraph carefully. Then, select transitional words and phrases from the accompanying alphabetized list, and write them in the appropriate blanks. When you have finished, reread your paragraph to make sure that it is coherent.

TRANSITIONS

after	for centuries
at first	however
before	in fact
by 1904	in 1897

The history of Jell-O is full of surprising setbacks. _____ Jello became "America's Most Famous Dessert," gelatin struggled for attention. _____, people experimented with the substance, but no one could make it appealing. By adding flavored syrup _____, Pearle B. Wait was the first to make gelatin taste good. Wait's wife, May, named the product Jell-O. _____, Wait could not market his new creation and ended up selling the company for $450 in 1899. _____, the next owner, Orator Francis Woodward, had the same problem. _____, he had supposedly tried to sell the company for even less money. _____ failing to find a buyer, Woodward started a major marketing campaign. He advertised in magazines and gave out free Jell-O cookbooks. _____, Jell-O was finally on its way to becoming the country's best-known dessert.

TEST · Revise · Edit · Proofread

Review the paragraph you drafted in response to the Write First prompt on page 39. TEST your paragraph to make sure it includes a topic sentence, evidence, a summary statement, and transitions, and revise your draft accordingly. Then, edit and proofread your paragraph.

EDITING PRACTICE

TEST and revise the following paragraph to make sure it is **unified**, **well developed**, and **coherent**. Begin by underlining the topic sentence. Then, cross out any sentences that do not support the topic sentence. If necessary, add evidence (details and examples) to support the topic sentence. Next, decide whether you need to make any changes to the paragraph's summary statement. (If the paragraph includes no summary statement, write one.) Finally, add transitional words and phrases where they are needed.

In 1979, a series of mechanical and human errors in Unit 2 of the nuclear generating plant at Three Mile Island, near Harrisburg, Pennsylvania, caused an accident that changed the nuclear power industry. A combination of stuck valves, human error, and poor decisions caused a partial meltdown of the reactor core. Large amounts of radioactive gases were released into the atmosphere. The governor of Pennsylvania evacuated pregnant women from the area. Other residents then panicked and left their homes. The nuclear regulatory agency claimed that the situation was not really dangerous and that the released gases were not a health threat. Activists and local residents disagreed with this. The reactor itself remained unusable for more than ten years. Large demonstrations followed the accident, including a rally of more than 200,000 people in New York City. Some people came just because the day was nice. By the mid-1980s, as a result of the accident at Three Mile Island, new construction of nuclear power plants in the United States had stopped.

COLLABORATIVE ACTIVITY

In a newspaper or magazine, find an illustration or photograph that includes a lot of details. Then, write a paragraph describing what you see. (Include enough details so that readers will be able to "see" it almost as clearly as you can.) Decide on a specific spatial order—from top to bottom or from left to right, for example—that makes sense to you, and follow this order as you organize the details in your paragraph. Finally, trade paragraphs with another student, and offer suggestions that could improve his or her paragraph.

review checklist

TESTing Your Paragraphs

☐ A topic sentence states a paragraph's main idea. (See 3a.)

☐ A paragraph should include enough evidence—examples and details—to support its main idea. (See 3b.)

☐ A paragraph should end with a summary statement that reinforces its main idea and helps to unify the paragraph. (See 3c.)

☐ A paragraph should include transitional words and phrases that indicate how ideas are connected. (See 3d.)

4 Exemplification

Student Services

FIRST FLOOR
Dean of Students
Disability Services
Student Affairs

SECOND FLOOR
Writing Center
Career Development
Advising

THIRD FLOOR
Counseling and Wellness Center
Center for International Students
Student Life

Jonathan Ug

write first

Most colleges have a student services center, where students can get information and advice on making the most of the programs and support the school provides. Brainstorm to develop a list of the programs and services your school offers (or should offer) to help students adjust to college. (If you prefer, you may choose a topic from the list on the following page.) You will return to your topic and review your brainstorming later in the chapter when you write your exemplification paragraph.

In this chapter, you will learn to write an exemplification paragraph.

PREVIEW

additional topics for exemplification

Effective (or ineffective) teachers
Qualities that make a great athlete
Challenges that older students face
A challenging job
Things you can't do without

In Chapters 2 and 3, you learned how to write effective paragraphs. In Chapters 4 through 12, you will learn different ways of organizing your ideas within paragraphs. Understanding these patterns of paragraph development can help you organize ideas and become a more effective, more confident writer.

4a Exemplification Paragraphs

What do we mean when we tell a friend that an instructor is *good* or that a football team is *bad*? What do we mean when we say that a movie is *boring* or that a particular war was *wrong*? To clarify general statements like these, we use **exemplification**—that is, we give **examples** to illustrate a general idea. In daily conversation and in school, you use specific examples to help explain your ideas.

GENERAL STATEMENT	SPECIFIC EXAMPLES
Today is going to be a hard day.	Today is going to be a hard day because I have a math test in the morning, a lab quiz in the afternoon, and work in the evening.

GENERAL STATEMENT	SPECIFIC EXAMPLES
My car is giving me problems.	My car is burning oil and won't start on cold mornings. In addition, it needs a new set of tires.

An **exemplification paragraph** uses specific examples to explain or clarify a general idea. Personal experiences, class discussions, observations, conversations, and readings can all be good sources of examples. (For information about writing exemplification essays, see 15a.)

When you **TEST** an exemplification paragraph, make sure it follows these guidelines.

T ■ An exemplification paragraph should begin with a **topic sentence** that states the paragraph's main idea.

E ■ An exemplification paragraph should present **evidence**—in the form of examples—that supports and clarifies the general statement made in the topic sentence. Examples should be arranged in **logical order**—for example, from least to most important or from general to specific. The number of examples you need depends on your topic sentence. A broad statement will probably require more examples than would a relatively narrow one.

S An exemplification paragraph should end with a **summary statement** that reinforces the paragraph's main idea.

T An exemplification paragraph should include **transitions** that introduce the examples and connect them to one another and to the topic sentence.

Paragraph Map: Exemplification

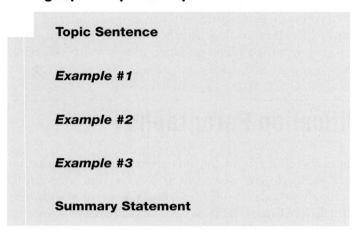

Topic Sentence

Example #1

Example #2

Example #3

Summary Statement

Model Paragraph: Exemplification

The following paragraph uses several examples to support the idea that some countries change their names for political reasons.

T E S T
Topic Sentence
Evidence
Summary Statement
Transitions

Examples presented in logical order

New Government, New Name

When countries change their names, it is often for political reasons. Sometimes a new government decides to change the country's name to separate itself from an earlier government. For example, Burma became Myanmar when a military government took over in 1989. Cambodia has had several name changes as well. After a coup in 1970, it was called the Khmer Republic. Then, in 1975, under Communist rule, it became Kampuchea. Gaining independence from another nation is another reason for a country to change its name. For instance, in 1957, after gaining independence from Great Britain, the Gold Coast became Ghana. Another name change occurred when the French Sudan became Mali. After gaining independence from France in 1960, it decided to reject its colonial past. Finally, Zimbabwe gave up its former British name, Rhodesia, several years after winning independence. These name changes can be confusing, but they reveal the changing political climate of the countries in which they occur.

—Kim Seng (student)

Some Transitional Words and Phrases for Exemplification		
also	furthermore	the most important
finally	in addition	example
first . . . second . . .	moreover	then
(and so on)	one example . . .	the next example
for example	another example	
for instance	specifically	

grammar in context

Exemplification

When you write an exemplification paragraph, always use a comma after the transitional word or phrase that introduces an example.

> For example, Burma became Myanmar in 1989.

> For instance, the Gold Coast changed its name to Ghana in 1957.

> Finally, Zimbabwe gave up its British name after winning independence.

For information on using commas with transitional words and phrases, see 33b.

:e: For more practice with comma usage, complete the LearningCurve Commas activity at **macmillanhighered.com/writingfirst**.

Analyzing an Exemplification Paragraph

Read the following exemplification paragraph; then, follow the instructions in Practice 4-1.

Jobs of the Future

    College students should take courses that prepare them for the careers that will be in demand over the next ten years. For example, the health-care field will have tremendous growth. Hundreds of thousands of medical workers—such as home-care aides, dental hygienists, and registered nurses—will be needed. Also, there will be an ongoing demand for workers who can operate and repair the specialized machines used in hospitals, labs, and other medical settings. In addition, a wide range of "green" jobs will become available as many industries work to strengthen their environmental policies. For example, construction workers, architects, and landscapers will be needed to create eco-friendly living and working spaces. Finally, education will be an attractive area for job seekers in the coming years. Many new teachers, especially those who are experienced with e-learning, will be needed to replace the teachers who retire during the next ten years. Students who know what jobs will be available can prepare themselves for the future.

—Bill Broderick (student)

PRACTICE
4-1

1. Underline the topic sentence of the paragraph above.

2. List the specific examples the writer uses to support his topic sentence. The first example has been listed for you.

health-care jobs

_____

_____

3. Circle the transitional words and phrases that the writer uses to connect ideas in the paragraph.

4. Underline the paragraph's summary statement.

PRACTICE
4-2

Following are four possible topic sentences for exemplification paragraphs. List three or four examples you could use to support each topic sentence. For example, if you were writing a paragraph about how difficult the first week of your new job was, you could mention waking up early, getting to know your coworkers, and learning new routines.

1. Getting a student loan can be difficult.

2. Internships give students valuable opportunities to develop job skills.

3. Good advice is sometimes difficult to get.

4. Some reality television shows insult the intelligence of their viewers.

4b Case Study: A Student Writes an Exemplification Paragraph

Here is how one student, Sarah Herman, wrote an exemplification paragraph.

When Sarah was asked to write a paragraph about a challenging job, she had little difficulty deciding what to focus on. She had just finished a summer job waiting tables in a beach community on the New Jersey shore—by far the most challenging job she had ever had. Once Sarah decided to focus her paragraph on this difficult work experience, she drafted the following topic sentence.

TOPIC SENTENCE Waiting tables at the Jersey shore was the most challenging job I ever had.

identify your main idea, and write a topic sentence

Look back at the brainstorming you did in response to the Write First prompt on page 52, and choose several programs or services to write about. Then, draft a topic sentence that communicates the main idea your paragraph will discuss.

_____

_____

After Sarah drafted her topic sentence, she listed several examples of why she had found her job waiting tables to be so challenging.

Restaurant too big

Boss disrespectful

No experience

Kitchen chaotic

Customers rude

Tips bad

list examples

List some examples that can support your topic sentence and help you develop your exemplification paragraph about programs or services that your school offers (or should offer) to help students adjust to college life.

_____

_____

_____

_____

Next, Sarah eliminated the examples on her list that she thought did not directly support her topic sentence. Then, she made an **informal outline**, arranging the remaining examples in the order in which she thought she could discuss them most effectively—in this case, from the least important to the most important example.

TOPIC SENTENCE
Waiting tables at the Jersey shore was the most challenging job I ever had.
1. No experience
2. Customers rude
3. Tips bad
4. Boss disrespectful

make an outline

Create an informal outline for your paragraph by arranging your list of examples in a logical order—for instance, from the least important to the most important example. Make sure you include only those examples that directly support your topic sentence.

Using her informal outline as a guide, Sarah wrote the following draft of her paragraph.

Waiting tables at the Jersey shore was the most challenging job I ever had. I had little experience as a food server. The first day of work was so bad that I almost quit. The customers were rude. All they wanted was to get their food as fast as possible so they could get back to the beach or the boardwalk. They were often impolite and demanding. The tips were bad. It was hard to be pleasant when you knew that the people you were waiting on were probably going to leave you a bad tip. Finally, the owner of the restaurant did not show us any respect. He often yelled at us, saying that if we didn't work harder, he would fire us. He never did, but his constant threats didn't do much to help our morale.

draft your paragraph

Using your informal outline as a guide, draft your exemplification paragraph.

When she finished her draft, Sarah scheduled a conference with her instructor, who suggested that her paragraph would be stronger if she made some of her examples more specific. For example, what experience did she have that made her want to quit? Exactly how were customers rude? Her instructor also reminded her that she needed to TEST her paragraph. As she TESTed her paragraph, Sarah assessed her draft.

- She checked her **topic sentence** and decided that it was effective.
- When she evaluated her **evidence**, she realized she needed to add more examples and details and delete irrelevant materials.

- She noticed that she did not have a **summary statement**, so she planned to add one at the end of her paragraph.
- She decided she needed to add more **transitions** to make it easier for readers to follow her discussion.

After TESTing her paragraph, Sarah continued revising her draft. The final draft, below, which has been edited and proofread, includes all the elements that Sarah looked for when she TESTed her paragraph.

Why I'll Never Wait Tables Again

Waiting tables at the Jersey shore was the most challenging job I ever had. First, I had never worked in a restaurant before, so I made a lot of mistakes. Once, I forgot to bring salads to a table I waited on. A person at the table complained so loudly that the owner had to calm him down. I was so frustrated and upset that I almost quit. Second, the customers at the restaurant were often rude. All they wanted was to get their food as fast as possible so they could get back to the beach or the boardwalk. They were on vacation, and they wanted to be treated well. As a result, they were frequently very demanding. No one ever said, "excuse me," "please," or "thank you," no matter what I did for them. Third, the tips were usually bad. It was hard to be pleasant when you knew that the people you were waiting on were probably going to leave you a bad tip. Finally, the owner of the restaurant never showed his workers any respect. He would yell at us, saying that if we didn't work harder, he would fire us. He never did, but his constant threats didn't do much to help our morale. Even though I survived the summer, I promised myself that I would never wait tables again.

T E S T	
	Topic Sentence
	Evidence
	Summary Statement
	Transitions

TEST · Revise · Edit · Proofread

Look back at the draft of your exemplification paragraph. Using the TEST checklist on page 60, evaluate your paragraph to make sure it includes a topic sentence, evidence, a summary statement, and transitions, and revise your draft accordingly. Finally, edit and proofread your paragraph.

TESTing an exemplification paragraph

T opic Sentence Unifies Your Paragraph

☐ Do you have a clearly worded **topic sentence** that states your paragraph's main idea?

☐ Does your topic sentence state an idea that can be supported by examples?

E vidence Supports Your Paragraph's Topic Sentence

☐ Does all your **evidence**—the examples you present—support your paragraph's main idea?

☐ Do you need to add more examples?

S ummary Statement Reinforces Your Paragraph's Unity

☐ Does your paragraph end with a **summary statement** that reinforces your main idea?

T ransitions Add Coherence to Your Paragraph

☐ Do you use **transitions** to introduce each example your paragraph discusses?

☐ Do you need to add transitions to make your paragraph clearer and to help readers follow your ideas?

5 Narration

write first

These four panels are from Lynda Barry's book *One! Hundred! Demons!*, a graphic story about the author's childhood. Look at the panels, and then brainstorm to identify some experiences that you could discuss in a paragraph about a difficult period in your own childhood. (If you prefer, you may choose a topic from the list on the following page.) You will return to your topic and review your brainstorming later in the chapter when you write your narrative paragraph.

additional topics for narration

A difficult choice
An embarrassing situation
A dangerous experience
An experience that had an impact on you
An instance of injustice

5a Narrative Paragraphs

Narration is writing that tells a story. For example, a narrative paragraph could tell how an experience you had as a child changed you, how the life of Martin Luther King Jr. is inspiring, or how the Battle of Gettysburg was the turning point in the Civil War. (For information about writing narrative essays, see 15b.)

When you TEST a **narrative paragraph**, make sure it follows these guidelines.

T ▪ A narrative paragraph should begin with a **topic sentence** that states its main idea, letting readers know why you are telling a particular story.

E ▪ A narrative paragraph should present **evidence**—events and details—in **time order**, usually in the order in which the events actually occurred. Effective narrative paragraphs include only those events that tell the story and avoid irrelevant information that could distract or confuse readers.

S ▪ A narrative paragraph should end with a **summary statement** that reinforces the paragraph's main idea.

T ▪ A narrative paragraph should include **transitions** that connect events to one another and to the topic sentence.

Paragraph Map: Narration

Topic Sentence

Event #1

Event #2

Event #3

Summary Statement

Model Paragraph: Narration

The student writer of the following paragraph presents a series of events to support the idea that the fashion designer Chloe Dao had a difficult life.

T E S T

☐ Topic Sentence
☐ Evidence
☐ Summary Statement
☐ Transitions

Overnight Success

Chloe Dao had to overcome a lot of difficulties to become a successful fashion designer. When Dao was a baby, her parents decided to leave her native country, Laos, and come to the United States. Unfortunately, the Viet Cong captured her and her family as they tried to cross the border. They were sent to a refugee camp, where they stayed for four years. In 1979, when she was eight, Dao and her family were allowed to come to the United States. Once they arrived, they had to earn enough money to live on. Dao's mother worked three jobs. On the weekends, the entire family ran the snack bar at a flea market. Finally, they saved enough money to open a dry-cleaning business. When she was twenty, Dao moved to New York to attend school. After she graduated, she got a job as production manager for designer Melinda Eng. Eventually, she opened a boutique, where she featured clothes that she designed. Her big break came in 2006 when she was chosen as the winner on the reality show *Project Runway*. Although Chloe Dao may appear to be an "overnight success," she had to struggle to get where she is today.

—Christine Clark (student)

Events arranged in time order

Some Transitional Words and Phrases for Narration

after	first . . . second . . . third	specific days or dates (for
as	immediately	example, "On Saturday,"
as soon as	later	"In 2006")
at this point	later on	suddenly
before	meanwhile	then
by the time	next	two hours (days, months,
earlier	now	years) later
eventually	once	until
finally	soon	when

---

grammar in context

Narration

When you write a narrative paragraph, you tell a story. As you become involved in your story, you might begin to string events together without proper punctuation. If you do, you will create a **run-on**.

INCORRECT (RUN-ON)   Dao's mother worked three jobs on the weekends, the entire family ran a snack bar at a flea market.

(continued)

(continued from previous page)

> CORRECT   Dao's mother worked three jobs. On the weekends, the
>   entire family ran the snack bar at a flea market.

For information on how to identify and correct run-ons, see Chapter 23.

> :e For more practice with run-ons, complete the LearningCurve Run-Ons activity at
> **macmillanhighered.com/writingfirst**.

Analyzing a Narrative Paragraph

Read this narrative paragraph; then, follow the instructions in Practice 5-1.

Two men who risked their lives in the 1904 Harwick mine disaster were the
inspiration for the Hero Fund, a charity that awards money to heroes and their
families. The Harwick mine disaster began with a small explosion near the entry to
the Harwick mine in Pennsylvania. This small explosion immediately caused a chain
reaction in which more and more coal dust was stirred up and ignited. Then, a
strong blast sent materials and even a mule flying out of the mine shaft. Ten hours later,
a rescue party led by Selwyn Taylor went down into the mine. The rescue party
found only one survivor, but Taylor believed more men might still be alive deep
within the mine. As he advanced, however, Taylor was overcome by fumes.
The following day, another rescue worker, Daniel Lyle, was also overcome by
fumes while searching for survivors. Neither Taylor nor Lyle found any survivors,
and both men died as a result of their efforts. Three months after the mine disaster, Pittsburgh steelmaker Andrew Carnegie founded the Hero Fund to provide
financial assistance to the families of those injured or killed while performing
heroic acts. The Hero Fund continues to honor people like Selwyn Taylor and Daniel
Lyle, ordinary people who take extraordinary risks to save others' lives.

—Kevin Smiley (student)

**PRACTICE
5-1**

1. Underline the topic sentence of the paragraph above.

2. List the major events discussed in the paragraph. The first
   event has been listed for you.

   A small explosion occurred near the entry to the mine.

   _____

   _____

_____

_____

_____

3. Circle the transitional words and phrases that the writer uses to link events in time.

4. Underline the paragraph's summary statement.

PRACTICE

5-2 Following are four possible topic sentences for narrative paragraphs. List three or four events that could support each topic sentence. For example, if you were recalling a barbecue that turned into a disaster, you could tell about burning the hamburgers, spilling the soda, and forgetting to buy paper plates.

1. One experience made me realize that I was no longer as young as I thought.

2. The first time I _____, I got more than I bargained for.

3. I didn't think I had the courage to _____, but when I did, I felt proud of myself.

4. I remember my reactions to one particular event very clearly.

5b   Case Study: A Student Writes a Narrative Paragraph

Here is how one student, Todd Kinzer, wrote a narrative paragraph. When Todd's instructor asked students to write a paragraph about an experience that had a great impact on them, Todd began by listing some experiences that he could write about.

> Accident at camp—realized I wasn't as strong as I thought I was
>
> Breaking up with Lindsay—that was painful
>
> Shooting the winning basket in my last high school game—sweet
>
> The last Thanksgiving at my grandparents' house—happy and sad

As Todd looked over the experiences on his list, he realized that he could write about all of them. He decided, however, to focus on the last Thanksgiving he spent at his grandparents' house. This occasion was especially meaningful to him because his grandfather had died shortly after the holiday.

Todd began by freewriting on his topic. He typed whatever came into his mind about the dinner, without worrying about spelling, punctuation, or grammar. Here is Todd's freewriting paragraph.

Thanksgiving. Who knew? I remember the smells when I woke up. I can see Granddad at the stove. We were all happy. He told us stories about when he was a kid. I'd heard some of them before, but so what? I loved to hear them. We ate so much I could hardly move. They say turkey has something in it that puts you to sleep. We watched football all afternoon and evening. I still can't believe Granddad is dead. I guess I have the topic for my paragraph.

freewrite

Look back at the brainstorming you did in response to the Write First prompt on page 61. Choose one experience from your notes, and then freewrite about that experience. Be sure to write nonstop, without worrying about spelling, punctuation, or grammar.

After he finished freewriting, Todd arranged the main events he planned to write about in an informal outline that reflected the order in which they occurred.

Grandfather cooking

Grandfather told stories

Sat down for Thanksgiving dinner

Watched football on TV

make an outline

Create an informal outline for your paragraph by arranging the events you remember from your childhood experience in the order in which they occurred. (Keep in mind that you will add details to develop these events when you draft your paragraph.)

Using his informal outline as a guide, Todd drafted the following paragraph.

Last Thanksgiving, my grandparents were up early. My grandfather stuffed the turkey, and my grandmother started cooking the other dishes. When I got up, I could smell the turkey in the oven. The table was already set for dinner, so we ate breakfast in the kitchen. My grandfather told us about the Thanksgivings he remembered from when he was a boy. When we sat down for dinner, a fire was burning in the fireplace. My grandmother said grace. My grandfather carved the turkey, and we all passed around dishes of food. For dessert, we had pecan pie and ice cream. After dinner, we watched football on TV. When I went to bed, I felt happy. This was my grandfather's last Thanksgiving.

draft your paragraph

Using your informal outline as a guide, draft your narrative paragraph.

Todd knew his draft needed a lot of work. Before he wrote the next draft, he tried to recall what other things had happened that Thanksgiving. He also tried to decide which idea was the most important and what additional supporting information could make his paragraph stronger. Todd sent his draft to his instructor as an email attachment, and his instructor returned the draft along with her comments. After considering his instructor's suggestions and TESTing his paragraph, Todd decided to make the following changes as he revised his draft.

- He decided that he needed to add a **topic sentence** that stated his paragraph's main idea.
- He decided that he needed to add more details and examples and to delete irrelevant sentences so that all his **evidence** would support his main idea.
- He decided to write a stronger **summary statement**.
- He decided that he needed to add **transitions** to indicate the time order of the events in his paragraph.

When he finished his revisions, Todd edited his paragraph, checking grammar, punctuation, mechanics, and spelling, and proofread carefully for typos. The final draft includes all the elements Todd looked for when he TESTed his paragraph.

Thanksgiving Memories

This past Thanksgiving was happy and sad because it was the last one I would spend with both my grandparents. The holiday began early. At five o'clock in the morning, my grandfather woke up and began to stuff the turkey. About an hour later, my grandmother began cooking corn pie and pineapple casserole. At eight o'clock, when I got up, I could smell the turkey cooking. While we ate breakfast, my grandfather told us about Thanksgivings he remembered when he was a boy. Later, my grandfather made a fire in the fireplace, and we sat down for dinner. After my grandmother said grace, my grandfather carved and served the turkey. The rest of us passed around dishes of sweet potatoes, mashed potatoes, green beans, asparagus, cucumber salad, relish, cranberry sauce, apple butter, cabbage salad,

T E S T
- Topic Sentence
- Evidence
- Summary Statement
- Transitions

stuffing, and, of course, corn pie and pineapple casserole. For dessert, my grandmother served pecan pie with scoops of ice cream. After dinner, we turned on the TV, and the whole family watched football all evening. That night, I remember thinking that life couldn't get much better. Four months later, my grandfather died in his sleep. For my family and me, Thanksgiving would never be the same.

TEST · Revise · Edit · Proofread

Look back at the draft of your narrative paragraph. Using the TEST checklist below, evaluate your paragraph to make sure it includes a topic sentence, evidence, a summary statement, and transitions, and revise your draft accordingly. Finally, edit and proofread your paragraph.

TESTing a narrative paragraph

T opic Sentence Unifies Your Paragraph

☐ Do you have a clearly worded **topic sentence** that states your paragraph's main idea?

☐ Does your topic sentence give readers an idea of why you are telling the story?

E vidence Supports Your Paragraph's Topic Sentence

☐ Do you include enough information about the events you discuss?

☐ Does all your **evidence**—events and details—support your paragraph's main idea?

☐ Do you need to include more events or details in your narrative?

S ummary Statement Reinforces Your Paragraph's Unity

☐ Does your paragraph end with a **summary statement** that reinforces your main idea?

T ransitions Add Coherence to Your Paragraph

☐ Do your **transitions** indicate the time order of events in your paragraph?

☐ Do you need to add transitions to make your paragraph clearer and to help readers follow your ideas?

6 Description

Jonathan Ugol

write first

This is a picture of what many people would consider an ideal vacation spot.
Brainstorm to develop a list of places that you would like to visit on vacation.
(If you prefer, you may choose a topic from the list on the following page.)
You will return to your topic and review your brainstorming later in the
chapter when you write your descriptive paragraph.

In this chapter, you will learn to write a descriptive paragraph.

additional topics for description

> Your workplace
> An unusual person
> Your dream house
> Someone you admire
> A useful gadget or tool

6a Descriptive Paragraphs

In a personal email, you may describe a new boyfriend or girlfriend. In a biology lab manual, you may describe the structure of a cell. In a report for a nursing class, you may describe a patient you treated.

When you write a **description**, you use words to paint a picture for your readers. With description, you use language that creates a vivid impression of what you have seen, heard, smelled, tasted, or touched. The more details you include, the better your description will be. (For information about writing descriptive essays, see 15c.)

The following description is flat because it includes very few descriptive details.

FLAT   Today, I saw a beautiful sunrise.

In contrast, the following passage is full of descriptive details that convey the writer's impression of the scene. This revised description relies on sight (*glowed red*; *turned slowly to pink, to aqua, and finally to blue*), touch (*the soft sandy beach*; *felt the cold water*), and sound (*heard the waves hit the shore*) to create a vivid picture.

VIVID   Early this morning, as I walked along the soft sandy beach, I saw the sun rise slowly out of the ocean. At first, the ocean glowed red. Then, it turned slowly to pink, to aqua, and finally to blue. As I stood watching the sun, I heard the waves hit the shore, and I felt the cold water swirl around my toes. For a moment, even the small gray-and-white birds that hurried along the shore seemed to stop and watch the dazzling sight.

When you **TEST** a **descriptive paragraph**, make sure it follows these guidelines.

T ■ A descriptive paragraph should begin with a **topic sentence** that conveys the main idea or general impression you want to communicate in your paragraph—for example, "The woods behind my house may seem ordinary, but to me, they are beautiful" or "The old wooden roller coaster is a work of art."

E ■ A descriptive paragraph should present **evidence**—descriptive details—that supports the topic sentence. Details should be presented in a clear **spatial order** that reflects the order in which you observed the person, place, or thing you are describing. For example, you can move from near to far or from top to bottom.

S ■ A descriptive paragraph should end with a **summary statement** that reinforces the paragraph's main idea.

T ■ A descriptive paragraph should include **transitions** that connect details to one another and to the topic sentence.

Paragraph Map: Description

Topic Sentence

Detail #1

Detail #2

Detail #3

Summary Statement

Model Paragraph: Description

The student writer of the following paragraph uses descriptive details to support the idea that the Lincoln Memorial is a monument to American democracy.

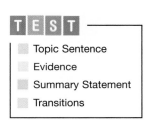

T E S T
▢ Topic Sentence
▢ Evidence
▢ Summary Statement
▢ Transitions

The Lincoln Memorial

The Lincoln Memorial was built to celebrate American democracy. In front of the monument is a long marble staircase that leads from a reflecting pool to the memorial's entrance. Thirty-six columns—which symbolize the thirty-six states reunited after the Civil War—surround the building. Inside the building are three rooms. The first room contains the nineteen-foot statue of Lincoln. Seated in a chair, Lincoln looks exhausted after the long Civil War. One of Lincoln's hands is a fist, showing his strength, and the other is open, showing his kindness. On either side of the first room are the two other rooms. Carved on the wall of the second room is the Gettysburg Address. On the wall of the third room is the Second Inaugural Address. Above the Gettysburg Address is a mural showing an angel freeing the slaves. Above the Second Inaugural Address is another mural, which depicts the people of the North and the South coming back together. As its design shows, the Lincoln Memorial was built to celebrate both the sixteenth president and the nation's struggle for democracy.

—Nicole Lentz (student)

Descriptive details arranged in spatial order

> ### Some Transitional Words and Phrases for Description
>
> | | | |
> |---|---|---|
> | above | in back of | spreading out |
> | at the edge | in front of | surrounding |
> | at the entrance | inside | the first . . . the second |
> | behind | nearby | the least important . . . |
> | below | next to | the most important |
> | between | on | the next |
> | beyond | on one side . . . on the | to the right . . . to the left |
> | down | other side | under |
> | farther | outside | |
> | in | over | |

grammar in context

Description

When you write a descriptive paragraph, you sometimes use **modifiers**—words and phrases that describe other words in the sentence. A modifier should be placed as close as possible to the word it is supposed to modify. If you place a modifying word or phrase too far from the word it modifies, you create a **misplaced modifier** that will confuse readers.

CONFUSING (MISPLACED MODIFIER) Seated in a chair, the long Civil War has clearly exhausted Lincoln. (Was the Civil War seated in a chair?)

CLEAR Seated in a chair, Lincoln looks exhausted after the long Civil War.

For information on how to identify and correct misplaced modifiers, see Chapter 27.

Analyzing a Descriptive Paragraph

Read this descriptive paragraph; then, follow the instructions in Practice 6-1.

Gen's Lunches

My friend Gen's lunches are as original as they are delicious. Nearly every day, Gen prepares a bento box, or traditional Japanese lunch. Today, she has brought an oval baby blue bento box. In the center of the box are three flattened rice balls that Gen calls onigiri. Using strips and dots of nori seaweed, she has given her onigiri adorable eyes and smiles. Using molded deli meat, she has even added pink circles to the cheeks. Surrounding the rice balls are small portions of tasty foods. For example, above the rice to the left are three breaded and fried zucchini strips that shine with golden oil. Directly above the rice sit two peeled hard-boiled eggs; I can just imagine their yummy crumbly yellow yolks. A deli-meat flower perches on each egg, and a cherry tomato snuggles nearby. Above the rice to the right nestle three wedges of sweet winter squash. The contrast between their bright orange flesh and their striped green rinds is very pleasing. Gen's bento boxes always make me hungry, but it's hard to watch her eat her lovely creations—especially the sweet onigiri with their smiling faces.

PRACTICE
6-1

1. Underline the topic sentence of the paragraph above.

2. In a few words, summarize the main idea of the paragraph.

_____

3. What are some of the details the writer uses to describe Gen's bento box lunch? The first detail has been listed for you.

_oval baby blue box_____

_____

_____

_____

_____

_____

4. Circle the transitional words and phrases that the writer uses to lead readers from one detail to another.

5. Underline the paragraph's summary statement.

PRACTICE
6-2

Each of the following topic sentences states a possible main idea for a descriptive paragraph. For each, list three details that could help convey the main idea. For example, to support the idea that sitting in front of a fireplace is relaxing, you could describe the crackling of the fire, the pine scent of the smoke, and the changing colors of the flames.

1. The most valuable possession I own is _____.

2. The most beautiful place I ever visited is _____.

3. One look at my instructor told me that this was going to be an interesting semester.

4. One of my favorite stores to shop at is _____.

5. My neighborhood is full of distinctive sounds and smells.

6b Case Study: A Student Writes a Descriptive Paragraph

Here is how one student, Jared Lopez, wrote a descriptive paragraph. When Jared was asked to write a descriptive paragraph about someone he admired, he decided to write about his uncle Manuel, who had been a father figure to him.

Because he was very familiar with his paragraph's subject, Jared did not have to brainstorm or freewrite to find material to write about. Instead, he immediately started to list the features of his uncle that he considered the most memorable.

Looks friendly

Hands

Dark eyes

Distinguished looking

Tall

list details

Choose a vacation spot from the brainstorming you did in response to the Write First prompt on page 69, and then list the details that best describe your vacation spot.

_____

_____

_____

After reviewing the list of features he planned to discuss, Jared arranged the features in an informal outline in the order in which he planned to discuss them.

Tall

Dark eyes

Looks friendly

Distinguished looking

Hands

make an outline

Create an informal outline for your paragraph by arranging the details you listed in the order in which you plan to discuss them.
You might arrange them in the order in which you observe them—for example, from far to near—or, as Jared did, from least to most important.

Jared decided to begin his paragraph with a general description of his uncle Manuel and then move on to concentrate on his uncle's most distinctive feature: his hands. Here is the first draft of Jared's paragraph.

> My uncle's name is Manuel, but his friends call him Manny. He is over six feet tall. Uncle Manny's eyes are dark brown, almost black. They make him look very serious. When he laughs, however, he looks friendly. His nose is long and straight, and it makes Uncle Manny look very distinguished. Most interesting to me are Uncle Manny's hands. Even though he hasn't worked as a stonemason since he opened his own construction company ten years ago, his hands are still rough and scarred. They are large and strong, but they can be gentle, too.

draft your paragraph

Using your informal outline as a guide, draft your descriptive paragraph.

After a conference with his instructor, Jared TESTed his paragraph.

- He decided that he needed to add a **topic sentence** that stated the main idea of his description.
- He decided that he needed to add more descriptive details to give readers more **evidence** of his uncle's strength and gentleness.
- He decided that he needed to add a stronger **summary statement** to unify his paragraph.
- He decided to include more **transitions** to move readers from one part of his description to the next.

Then, Jared continued revising his paragraph. The final edited and proofread draft that follows includes all the elements Jared looked for when he TESTed his paragraph.

T E S T
- ☐ Topic Sentence
- ☐ Evidence
- ☐ Summary Statement
- ☐ Transitions

My Uncle Manny

    My uncle Manuel is a strong but gentle person who took care of my mother and me when my father died. Manuel, or "Manny" as his friends and family call him, is over six feet tall. This is unusual for a Mexican of his generation. The first thing most people notice about my uncle Manny is his eyes. They are large and dark brown, almost black. They make him look very serious. When he laughs, however, the sides of his eyes crinkle up and he looks warm and friendly. Another thing that stands out is his nose, which is long and straight. My mother says it makes Uncle Manny look strong and distinguished. The most striking thing about Uncle Manny is his hands. Even though he hasn't worked as a stonemason since he opened his own construction company ten years ago, his hands are still rough and scarred from carrying stones. No matter how much he tries, he can't get rid of the dirt under the skin of his fingers. Uncle Manny's hands are big and rough, but they are also gentle and comforting. To me, they show what he really is: a strong and gentle man.

TEST · Revise · Edit · Proofread

Look back at the draft of your descriptive paragraph. Using the TEST checklist below, evaluate your paragraph to make sure it includes a topic sentence, evidence, a summary statement, and transitions, and revise your draft accordingly. Finally, edit and proofread your paragraph.

TESTing a descriptive paragraph

Topic Sentence Unifies Your Paragraph

☐ Do you have a clearly worded **topic sentence** that states your paragraph's main idea—the general impression you want to convey?

☐ Does your topic sentence identify the person, place, or thing you will describe in your paragraph?

Evidence Supports Your Paragraph's Topic Sentence

☐ Does all your **evidence**—descriptive details—support your paragraph's main idea?

☐ Do you have enough descriptive details, or do you need to include more?

Summary Statement Reinforces Your Paragraph's Unity

☐ Does your paragraph end with a **summary statement** that reinforces your main idea?

Transitions Add Coherence to Your Paragraph

☐ Do your **transitions** lead readers from one detail to the next?

☐ Do you need to add transitions to make your paragraph clearer and to help readers follow your ideas?

7 Process

write first

This picture shows a screen from the popular game *Angry Birds*, an app that so far has been downloaded over two billion times. Brainstorm to develop a list of games you know well and could explain to others. (If you prefer, you may choose a topic from the list on the following page.) You will return to your topic and review your brainstorming later in the chapter when you write your process paragraph.

In this chapter, you will learn to write a process paragraph.

PREVIEW

additional topics for process

How to apply for financial aid
How to shop online for bargains
A process you perform every day
How to find an apartment
How to prepare for a storm or another natural disaster

7a Process Paragraphs

When you describe a **process**, you tell readers how something works or how to do something. For example, you could explain how the optical scanner at the checkout counter of a food store works, how to hem a pair of pants, or how to set up an email account on a smartphone. A **process paragraph** tells readers how to complete a process by listing steps in time order. (For information about writing process essays, see 15d.)

When you **TEST** a process paragraph, make sure it follows these guidelines.

T ■ A process paragraph should begin with a **topic sentence** that identifies the process you are explaining and the point you want to make about it (for example, "Parallel parking is easy once you know the secret" or "By following a few simple steps, you can design a résumé that will get noticed").

E ■ A process paragraph should discuss all the steps in the process, one at a time. These steps should be presented in strict **time order**— the order in which they occur. A process paragraph should present enough **evidence**—examples and details—to explain the steps and make the process clear to readers.

S ■ A process paragraph should end with a **summary statement** that reinforces the paragraph's main idea.

T ■ A process paragraph should include **transitions** that connect the steps in the process to one another and to the topic sentence.

Paragraph Map: Process

Topic Sentence

Step #1

Step #2

Step #3

Summary Statement

There are two types of process paragraphs: *process explanations* and *instructions*.

Model Paragraph: Process Explanations

In a **process explanation**, your purpose is to help readers understand how something works or how something happens—for example, how a hurricane forms or how to do a database search. With a process explanation, you do not expect readers to perform the process.

In the following process explanation paragraph from a psychology exam, the writer explains the four stages children go through when they acquire language.

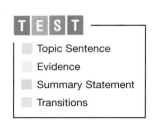

TEST

- Topic Sentence
- Evidence
- Summary Statement
- Transitions

Steps presented in time order

> Children go through four distinct stages when they learn language. The first stage begins as soon as infants are born. By crying, they let people know when they need something or if they are in pain. The second stage begins when children are about a year old and are able to communicate with single words. For example, a child will use the word *food* to mean anything from "I'm hungry" to "feed the dog." The third stage begins at about twenty months. During this stage, children begin to use two-word sentences, such as "dada car" (for "This is dada's car"). Finally, at about thirty months, children begin to learn the rules that govern language. They learn how to form simple sentences, plurals, and the past tense of verbs. No matter what language they speak, all children follow the same process when they learn language.
>
> —Jennifer Gulla (student)

Model Paragraph: Instructions

When you write **instructions**, your purpose is to give readers the information they need to perform a task or an activity—for example, to fill out an application, to operate a piece of machinery, or to help someone who is choking. Because you expect readers to follow your instructions, you address them directly, using **commands** to tell them what to do (*check* the gauge . . . *pull* the valve).

In the following paragraph, the writer gives a humorous set of instructions on how to get food out of a defective vending machine.

TEST

- Topic Sentence
- Evidence
- Summary Statement
- Transitions

Step-by-step instructions presented in time order

Man vs. Machine

> There is a foolproof method of outsmarting a vending machine that refuses to give up its food. First, approach the vending machine coolly. Make sure you don't seem frightened or angry. The machine will sense these emotions and steal your money. Second, be polite. Say hello, compliment the machine on its selection of goodies, and smile. Be careful. If the machine thinks you are trying to take advantage of it, it will steal your money. Third, if the machine steals your money, remain calm. Ask nicely to get the food you paid for. Finally, it is time to get serious. Hit the side of the vending machine with your fist. If this doesn't work, lower your shoulder and throw yourself at the machine. (A good kick or two might also help.) When the machine has had enough, it will drop your snack, and you can grab it. If you follow these few simple steps, you should have no trouble walking away from vending machines with the food you paid for.
>
> —Adam Cooper (student)

Some Transitional Words and Phrases for Process		
after that, after this	first	subsequently
as	immediately	the first (second, third) step
as soon as	later	then
at the same time	meanwhile	the next step . . . the last step
at this point	next	when
during	now	while
finally	once	
	soon	

grammar in context

Process

When you write a process paragraph, you may find yourself making **illogical shifts** in tense, person, and voice. If you shift from one tense, person, or voice to another without good reason, you may confuse readers.

CONFUSING (ILLOGICAL SHIFT) First, the vending machine should be approached coolly. Make sure you don't seem frightened or angry. (illogical shift from passive to active voice)

CLEAR First, approach the vending machine coolly. Make sure you don't seem frightened or angry. (consistent use of active voice)

For information on how to avoid illogical shifts in tense, person, and voice, see Chapter 26.

For more practice with shifts in tense and voice, complete the LearningCurve Verbs and Active and Passive Voice activities at **macmillanhighered.com/writingfirst**.

Analyzing a Process Paragraph

Read this process paragraph; then, follow the instructions in Practice 7-1.

An Order of Fries

I never realized how much work goes into making French fries until I worked at a potato-processing plant in Hermiston, Oregon. The process begins with freshly dug potatoes being shoveled from trucks onto conveyor belts leading into the plant. During this stage, workers pick out any rocks that may have been dug up with the potatoes because these could damage the automated peelers. After the potatoes have gone through the peelers, they travel on a conveyor belt through the "trim line." Here, workers cut out any bad spots, being careful not to waste potatoes by trimming too much. Next, the potatoes are sliced by automated cutters and then deep-fried for about a minute. After this, they continue along a conveyor belt to the "wet line." Here, workers again look for bad spots, and they throw away any rotten pieces. At this point, the potatoes go to a second set of fryers for three minutes before being moved to subzero freezers for ten minutes. Then, it's on to the "frozen line" for a final inspection. The inspected fries are weighed by machines and then sealed into five-pound plastic packages, which are weighed again by workers who also check that the packages are properly sealed. Finally, the bags are packed into boxes and made ready for shipment to various restaurants across the western United States. This process goes on twenty-four hours a day to bring consumers the French fries they enjoy so much.

—Cheri Rodriguez (student)

PRACTICE

7-1

1. Underline the topic sentence of the paragraph above.

2. Is this a process explanation or instructions? _____

   How do you know? _____

3. List the steps in the process. The first step has been listed for you.

   The potatoes are unloaded, and the rocks are sorted out. _____

   _____

   _____

   _____

   _____

   _____

   _____

4. Circle the transitional words and phrases that the writer uses to move readers from one step to the next.

5. Underline the paragraph's summary statement.

PRACTICE

7-2   Following are four possible topic sentences for process paragraphs. List three or four steps that explain the process each topic sentence identifies. For example, if you were explaining the process of getting a job, you could list preparing a résumé, looking at ads in newspapers or online, writing a job-application letter, and going on an interview. Make sure each step follows logically from the one that precedes it.

1. Getting the lowest prices when you shop is not a simple process.

2. Getting the most out of a student-teacher conference requires some preparation.

3. Cage-training a puppy can be a tricky process.

4. Choosing the perfect outfit for a job interview can be challenging.

7b Case Study: A Student Writes a Process Paragraph

Here is how one student, Manasvi Bari, wrote a process paragraph. When Manasvi was assigned to write a paragraph in which she explained a process she performed every day, she decided to write about how to get a seat on a crowded subway car. To make sure she had enough to write about, she made the following list of possible steps she could include.

Don't pay attention to heat

Get into the train

Get the first seat

Look as if you need help

Get to a pole

Don't travel during rush hour

Choose your time

Be alert

Squeeze in

After looking over her list, Manasvi crossed out steps she didn't think were essential to the process she wanted to describe.

~~Don't pay attention to heat~~

Get into the train

Get the first seat

Look as if you need help

~~Get to a pole~~

~~Don't travel during rush hour~~

~~Choose your time~~

Be alert

Squeeze in

list the steps in the process

Choose one game from the brainstorming you did in response to the Write First prompt on page 78, and then list the steps you need to discuss in order to explain how to play the game. (Assume that your readers know nothing about the game you are describing.)

_____

_____

_____

_____

_____

Now, cross out any steps you don't think readers will need in order to understand how to play the game.

Once she had decided on her list of steps, Manasvi made an informal outline, arranging the steps in the order in which they should be performed.

Get into the train

Be alert

Get the first seat

Squeeze in

Look as if you need help

make an outline

Create an informal outline for your paragraph by arranging the steps for playing your game in the order in which they should be performed.

At this point, Manasvi thought she was ready to begin writing her paragraph. Here is her draft.

When the train arrives, get into the car as fast as possible. Be alert. If you see an empty seat, grab it and sit down immediately. If there is no seat, ask people to move down, or squeeze into a space that seems too small. If none of this works, you'll have to use some imagination. Look helpless. Drop your books, and look as if the day can't get any worse. Sometimes a person will get up and give you a seat. If this strategy doesn't work, stand near someone who looks as if he or she is going to get up. When the person gets up, jump into the seat as fast as you can. Don't let the people who are getting on the train get the seat before you do.

draft your paragraph

Using your informal outline as a guide, draft your process paragraph.

Manasvi showed the draft of her paragraph to a writing center tutor. Together, they TESTed her paragraph and made the following decisions.

- They decided that she needed to add a **topic sentence** that identified the process and stated the point she wanted to make about it.
- They decided that her **evidence**—the examples and details that described the steps in her process—was clear and complete.
- They decided that she needed to add a **summary statement** that reinforced the point of the process.
- They decided that she needed to add **transitions** that helped readers follow the steps in the process.

Based on these decisions, Manasvi continued revising her paragraph. The final edited and proofread draft includes all the elements Manasvi looked for when she TESTed her paragraph.

Surviving Rush Hour

T E S T

☐ Topic Sentence
☐ Evidence
☐ Summary Statement
☐ Transitions

Anyone who takes the subway to school in the morning knows how hard it is to find a seat, but by following a few simple steps, you should be able to get a seat almost every day. First, when the train arrives, get into the car as fast as possible. Be alert. As soon as you see an empty seat, grab it and sit down immediately. Meanwhile, if there is no seat, ask people to move down, or try to squeeze into a space that seems too small. If none of this works, the next step is to use some imagination. Look helpless. Drop your books, and look as if the day can't get any worse. Sometimes a person will get up and give you a seat. Don't be shy. Take it, and remember to say thank you. Finally, if this strategy doesn't work, stand near someone who looks as if he or she is going to get up. When the person gets up, jump into the seat as fast as you can. By following these steps, you should be able to get a seat on the subway and arrive at school rested and relaxed.

TEST · Revise · Edit · Proofread

Look back at the draft of your process paragraph. Using the TEST checklist below, evaluate your paragraph to make sure it includes a topic sentence, evidence, a summary statement, and transitions, and revise your draft accordingly. Finally, edit and proofread your paragraph.

TESTing a process paragraph

Topic Sentence Unifies Your Paragraph

☐ Do you have a clearly worded **topic sentence** that states your paragraph's main idea?

☐ Does your topic sentence identify the process you will discuss?

☐ Does your topic sentence indicate whether you will be explaining a process or giving instructions?

Evidence Supports Your Paragraph's Topic Sentence

☐ Have you included all the steps in the process?

☐ Have you included enough **evidence**—examples and details—to explain the steps and make the process clear to readers?

☐ If your paragraph is a set of instructions, have you included all the information readers need to perform the process?

Summary Statement Reinforces Your Paragraph's Unity

☐ Does your paragraph end with a **summary statement** that reinforces your main idea?

Transitions Add Coherence to Your Paragraph

☐ Do your **transitions** move readers from one step in the process to the next?

☐ Do you need to add transitions to make your paragraph clearer and to help readers follow your ideas?

8 Cause and Effect

AP Photo/MTV

write first

Look at this picture of a teen mother with her infant son. Then, freewrite to decide on a particular event that caused you to grow up in a hurry. (If you prefer, you may choose a topic from the list on the following page.) You will return to your topic and review your freewriting later in the chapter when you write your cause-and-effect paragraph.

additional topics for cause and effect

Why a particular video went viral
The reasons you decided to attend college
A decision that changed your life
How an event affected you
Why students drop out of high school

8a Cause-and-Effect Paragraphs

Why is the cost of college so high in the United States? How does smoking affect a person's health? What would happen if the city increased its sales tax? How dangerous is the flu? All these questions have one thing in common: they try to determine the causes or effects of an action, an event, or a situation.

A **cause** is something or someone that makes something happen. An **effect** is something brought about by a particular cause.

CAUSE		EFFECT
Increased airport security	→	Long lines at airports
Weight gain	→	Health problems
Seat belt laws passed	→	Traffic deaths reduced

A **cause-and-effect paragraph** examines or analyzes reasons and results. It helps readers understand why something happened or is happening, or shows how one thing affects another. (For information about writing cause-and-effect essays, see 15e.)

When you TEST a cause-and-effect paragraph, make sure it follows these guidelines.

T ■ A cause-and-effect paragraph should begin with a **topic sentence** that tells readers whether the paragraph is focusing on causes or on effects—for example, "There are several reasons why the cost of gas is so high" (causes) or "Going to the writing center has given me confidence as well as skill as a writer" (effects).

E ■ A cause-and-effect paragraph should present **evidence**—examples and details—to support the topic sentence and explain each cause and effect. Causes or effects should be arranged in **logical order**—for example, from least to most important.

S ■ A cause-and-effect paragraph should end with a **summary statement** that reinforces the paragraph's main idea.

T ■ A cause-and-effect paragraph should include **transitions** that connect causes or effects to one another and to the topic sentence.

Paragraph Map: Cause and Effect

Topic Sentence

Cause (or effect) #1

Cause (or effect) #2

Cause (or effect) #3

Summary Statement

Model Paragraph: Causes

The following paragraph focuses on **causes**.

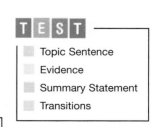

T E S T
- Topic Sentence
- Evidence
- Summary Statement
- Transitions

Why Young People Don't Vote

There are several reasons why young adults do not often vote in national elections. The first reason is that many young people are just not interested in politics. They are busy getting an education or working, and they do not take the time to think about politics or which candidate to vote for. Another reason is that they do not think their vote is important. They think that because millions of people are voting, their vote will not have an effect on the outcome of an election. A third reason is that many young people do not think the candidates are speaking to them. They do not think that national issues such as capital gains taxes, Social Security, and Medicare have much to do with them. Finally, many young people are turned off by politics and politicians. As far as they are concerned, politicians just want to get elected and will say anything to get votes. Until these issues are addressed, many young people will continue to stay away from the polls.

—Moniquetta Hall (student)

Causes arranged in logical order

Model Paragraph: Effects

The following paragraph focuses on **effects**.

T E S T
- Topic Sentence
- Evidence
- Summary Statement
- Transitions

The Negative Effects of Climate Change

Climate change caused by global warming would have several negative effects. One effect would be an increase in the number of intense storms. Large hurricanes and other types of storms would damage property and kill many people. Another effect would be a rise in sea level. As the earth warms, the polar ice would melt and raise the level of the earth's oceans. Coastal

Effects arranged in logical order

Effects arranged in
logical order

cities and low-lying areas would probably be flooded. Still another effect would be the spread of certain kinds of diseases. Many diseases, now found only in warm areas, would spread to areas that were once cool but then became warm. Malaria and yellow fever, for example, could become as common in the United States as they are in Africa and Southeast Asia. Finally, climate change associated with global warming would affect agriculture. Farming areas, such as the Midwest, where American farmers grow corn and wheat, would become dry. As a result, there would be food shortages, and many people could go hungry. No one knows for certain what will happen, but if global warming continues, our lives will certainly be affected.

—Jackie Hue (student)

Some Transitional Words and Phrases for Cause and Effect

accordingly	moreover	the first (second, third)
another cause	since	reason
another effect	so	the most important cause
as a result	the first (second,	the most important effect
because	third, final) cause	therefore
consequently	the first (second,	
finally	third, final) effect	
for		
for this reason		

grammar in context

Cause and Effect

When you write a cause-and-effect paragraph, you should be careful not to confuse the words *affect* and *effect*. *Affect* is a verb meaning "to influence." *Effect* is a noun meaning "result."

One ~~affect~~ *effect* would be an increase in the number of intense storms.

(*effect* is a noun)

No one knows for certain what will happen, but if global warming continues, our lives will certainly be ~~effected~~ *affected*.

(*affect* is a verb)

For more information on effect *and* affect, *see 22g.*

Analyzing a Cause-and-Effect Paragraph

Read this cause-and-effect paragraph; then, follow the instructions in Practice 8-1.

The Decline of Orphanages in the United States

There are several reasons for the decline of U.S. orphanages after World War II. First, people discovered that children who are not hugged and snuggled fail to thrive. As a result, "child rescue" groups were formed to bring the warmth of families to children. Second, although the U.S. government supported many orphanages, religious groups ran many others. Some politicians distrusted this relationship between religious groups and orphans; after all, the United States has a tradition of separation of church and state. Finally, the government saw that it was less expensive to give financial assistance to poor parents than to maintain large orphanages. Consequently, a program called Aid to Dependent Children, which was part of the 1935 Social Security Act, was established to support children in their own homes. In 1960, the program was expanded to include children in foster care. For these reasons, orphanages are seldom seen in the United States today.

PRACTICE

1. Underline the topic sentence of the paragraph above.
2. List the words that tell you the writer is moving from one cause to another in the paragraph.

_____

3. List the causes the writer describes. The first cause has been listed for you.

   People discovered that children who are not hugged and snuggled fail to thrive.

   _____

   _____

   _____

4. Circle the transitional words and phrases that the writer uses to identify causes.
5. Underline the paragraph's summary statement.

PRACTICE

8-2   Following are four possible topic sentences for cause-and-effect paragraphs. For each topic sentence, list the effects that could result from the cause identified in the topic sentence. For example, if you were writing a paragraph about the effects of excessive drinking on campus, you could list low grades, health problems, and vandalism.

1. Having a baby can change your life.

2. Being bilingual has many advantages.

3. College has made me a different person.

4. Impulse buying can have negative effects on a person's finances.

PRACTICE

8-3   List three causes that could support each of the following topic sentences.

1. The causes of teenage obesity are easy to identify.

2. Chronic unemployment can have many causes.

3. The high cost of college tuition is not easy to explain.

4. There are several reasons why professional athletes' salaries are so high.

8b   Case Study: A Student Writes a Cause-and-Effect Paragraph

Here is how one student, Sean Jin, wrote a cause-and-effect paragraph. When Sean was asked to write a cause-and-effect paragraph for his composition class about how a particular event affected him, he had no trouble thinking of a topic. Because a debate was currently going on in his hometown about building a Walmart Superstore there, he decided to write a paragraph discussing the effects that such a store would have on the local economy.

Sean's instructor told the class that the main problem to watch for in planning a cause-and-effect paragraph is to make sure that a **causal relationship** exists—that one event actually causes another. In other words, just because one event follows another closely in time, students should not assume that the second event was caused by the first.

With this advice in mind, Sean brainstormed to develop a list of possible effects a Walmart would have on his small town. Here is Sean's list of effects.

Provides new jobs

Offers low-cost items

Pays low wages

Pushes out small businesses

list effects

Choose one event from the freewriting you did in response to the Write First prompt on page 87. Then, brainstorm to develop a list of the specific effects the event has had on you.

_____

_____

_____

_____

After reviewing his list of effects, Sean drafted a topic sentence that introduced his topic and communicated the point he wanted to make about it. Here is Sean's topic sentence.

Walmart can have good and bad effects on a small town.

write a topic sentence

Review your list of effects, and then draft a topic sentence for your cause-and-effect paragraph.

_____

_____

Next, Sean made an informal outline that arranged the effects on his list in a logical order. This outline helped him check to make sure he had included enough examples to explain each effect and to support his topic sentence. Here is Sean's outline.

Good effects

Provides new jobs
   –Store needs many employees
   –Many people out of work in rural town and need jobs

Offers low-cost items
   –Families on a budget can buy things they usually can't afford
   –Walmart prices lower than most other stores' prices

Bad effects

Pays low wages
   –Walmart pays less than other stores

Pushes out small businesses
    –Forces many small businesses to close
    –Local businesses can't match low prices or wide selection

make an outline

Create an informal outline for your paragraph by arranging your list of effects in a logical order—for example, from least to most important.

After completing his outline, Sean wrote the following draft of his paragraph.

> Walmart can have good and bad effects on a small town. It provides jobs. A large store needs a lot of employees. So, many people from the area will be able to find work. Walmart's prices are low. Families that don't have much money may be able to buy things they can't afford to buy at other stores. Not all of Walmart's effects are positive. Walmart pays employees less than other stores. Walmart provides jobs, but those jobs don't pay very much. When Walmart comes into an area, many small businesses are forced to close. They just can't match Walmart's prices or stock as much merchandise as Walmart can.

draft your paragraph

Using your informal outline as a guide, draft your cause-and-effect paragraph.

When he finished his draft, Sean went to the writing center and met with a tutor. After going over his draft with the tutor and TESTing his paragraph, Sean made the following decisions.

- He decided that he needed to sharpen his **topic sentence** to tie his discussion of Walmart to the small town in which he lived.
- He decided to provide more **evidence** to support his topic sentence— for example, what exactly does Walmart pay its salespeople?
- He realized that he needed to add a **summary statement** to reinforce his main idea.
- He decided to add **transitions** to identify positive and negative effects.

Now Sean was ready to continue revising his paragraph. The final edited and proofread draft includes all the elements Sean looked for when he TESTed his paragraph.

Walmart Comes to Town

When Walmart comes to a small town like mine, it can have good and bad effects. The first and most positive effect is that it provides jobs. A large Walmart Superstore needs a lot of employees, so many people will be able to find work. In my rural town, over 15 percent of the people are out of work. Walmart could give these people a chance to improve their lives. Another positive effect that Walmart can have is to keep prices low, so families on tight budgets will be able to buy things they cannot afford to buy at other stores. My own observations show that many items at a local Walmart are cheaper than those at other stores. Not all of Walmart's effects are positive, however. One negative effect Walmart can have is that it can actually lower wages in an area. My aunt, a longtime employee, says that Walmart pays beginning workers between $8 and $10 an hour. This is less than they would get in stores that pay union wages. Another negative effect Walmart can have is to drive other, smaller businesses out. When Walmart comes into an area, many small businesses are forced to close. They just cannot match Walmart's prices or selection of merchandise. It is clear that although Walmart can have a number of positive effects, it can also have some negative ones.

T E S T

- Topic Sentence
- Evidence
- Summary Statement
- Transitions

TEST · **Revise · Edit · Proofread**

Look back at the draft of your cause-and-effect paragraph. Using the TEST checklist below, evaluate your paragraph to make sure it includes a topic sentence, evidence, a summary statement, and transitions, and revise your draft accordingly. Finally, edit and proofread your paragraph.

TESTing a cause-and-effect paragraph

Topic Sentence Unifies Your Paragraph

☐ Do you have a clearly worded **topic sentence** that states your paragraph's main idea?

☐ Does your topic sentence identify the cause or effect on which your paragraph will focus?

Evidence Supports Your Paragraph's Topic Sentence

☐ Do you need to add any important causes or effects?

☐ Do you need to explain your causes or effects more fully?

☐ Does all your **evidence**—examples and details—support your paragraph's main idea?

(continued)

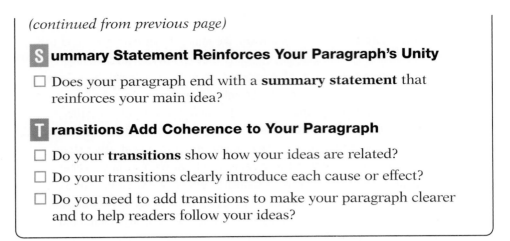

(continued from previous page)

Summary Statement Reinforces Your Paragraph's Unity

☐ Does your paragraph end with a **summary statement** that reinforces your main idea?

Transitions Add Coherence to Your Paragraph

☐ Do your **transitions** show how your ideas are related?

☐ Do your transitions clearly introduce each cause or effect?

☐ Do you need to add transitions to make your paragraph clearer and to help readers follow your ideas?

9 Comparison and Contrast

	OLD WORDS	NEW MEANINGS
GREEN	yellow + blue	good for the planet
FRIEND	a person you know	a random person
ORGANIC	living matter	made naturally in a factory

© Maria Scrivan www.mariascrivan.com

write first

This chart shows old words that have acquired new meanings. Brainstorm to develop a list of three or four words that you think have acquired new meanings. (You can also do an Internet search with the terms "old words, new meanings.") Then, make your own chart that lists the old and new meaning of the words you have listed. (If you prefer, you may choose a topic from the list on the following page.) You will return to your topic and review your brainstorming later in the chapter when you write your comparison-and-contrast paragraph.

additional topics for comparison and contrast

Two popular television personalities
Men's and women's attitudes toward
    marriage, shopping, or conversation
Two cars you would consider buying
Two websites
Two people, places, or objects

9a Comparison-and-Contrast Paragraphs

When you buy something—for example, a hair dryer, a smartphone, a computer, or a car—you often comparison-shop, looking at various models to determine how they are alike and how they are different. In other words, you *compare and contrast*. When you **compare**, you consider how things are similar. When you **contrast**, you consider how they are different. A **comparison-and-contrast paragraph** can examine just similarities, just differences, or both similarities and differences. (For information on writing comparison-and-contrast essays, see 15f.)

When you TEST a comparison-and-contrast paragraph, make sure it follows these guidelines.

T ■ A comparison-and-contrast paragraph should begin with a **topic sentence** that tells readers whether the paragraph is going to discuss similarities, differences, or both. The topic sentence should also make clear the main point of the comparison—why you are comparing or contrasting the two subjects (for example, "The writers Toni Morrison and Maya Angelou have similar ideas about race and society" or "My parents and I have different ideas about success").

E ■ A comparison-and-contrast paragraph should include enough **evidence**—examples and details—to make the similarities and differences clear to readers. A comparison-and-contrast paragraph should discuss the same or similar points for both subjects, one by one. Points should be arranged in **logical order**—for example, from least to most important.

S ■ A comparison-and-contrast paragraph should end with a **summary statement** that reinforces the paragraph's main idea.

T ■ A comparison-and-contrast paragraph should include **transitions** that connect the two subjects being compared and link the points you make about each subject.

There are two kinds of comparison-and-contrast paragraphs: *subject-by-subject comparisons* and *point-by-point comparisons*.

Subject-by-Subject Comparisons

In a **subject-by-subject comparison**, you divide your comparison into two parts and discuss one subject at a time. In the first part of the paragraph, you discuss all your points about one subject. Then, in the second part, you discuss the same (or similar) points about the other subject. (In each part of the paragraph, you discuss the points in the same order.) A subject-by-subject comparison is best for paragraphs in which you do not discuss too many points.

Paragraph Map: Subject-by-Subject Comparison

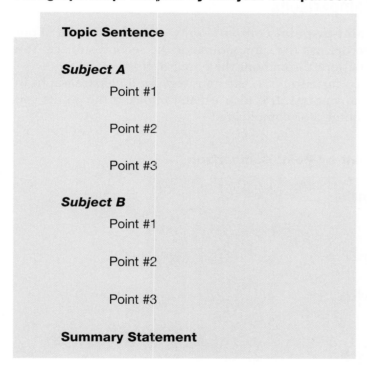

Topic Sentence

Subject A
  Point #1

  Point #2

  Point #3

Subject B
  Point #1

  Point #2

  Point #3

Summary Statement

Model Paragraph: Subject-by-Subject Comparison

The writer of the following paragraph uses a subject-by-subject comparison to compare two places to eat on campus.

Eating on Campus

Food trucks are a good alternative to the campus cafeteria. Eating in the cafeteria takes a lot of time. Students have to go into a building, wait in line, walk down some stairs, and find a table. In addition, the cafeteria usually has a limited variety of food, with only two or three different hot meals and some prepackaged sandwiches. The food is cooked in advance, and after sitting on a steam tray for a few hours, it is dry and lukewarm. Finally, food in the cafeteria costs a lot. Students who are not on a food

T E S T

☐ Topic Sentence
☐ Evidence
☐ Summary Statement
☐ Transitions

Subject A:
Eating in the school cafeteria

Subject B:
Eating at the food trucks

plan can easily spend seven or eight dollars for dinner. In contrast, the food trucks are much quicker than the cafeteria. Most food trucks serve a meal in less than five minutes. If the weather is nice, students can sit anywhere on campus and eat. Another difference is that the food trucks offer a lot of choices. Some of the trucks, such as the ones that sell Chinese food, even sell platters. Unlike cafeteria food, the food from the trucks is fresh and hot most of the time. A final difference is that meals from a food truck usually cost less than five dollars. This is a big savings, especially if a student is on a tight budget. For this reason, the food trucks are often a better choice than the cafeteria.

—Dan Lindt (student)

Point-by-Point Comparisons

When you write a **point-by-point comparison**, you discuss a point about one subject and then discuss the same point for the second subject. You use this alternating pattern throughout the paragraph.

A point-by-point comparison is a better strategy for long paragraphs in which you discuss many points. It is also a better choice if the points you are discussing are technical or complicated.

Paragraph Map: Point-by-Point Comparison

Topic Sentence

Point #1
    Subject A

    Subject B

Point #2
    Subject A

    Subject B

Point #3
    Subject A

    Subject B

Summary Statement

Model Paragraph: Point-by-Point Comparison

In the following paragraph, the writer uses a point-by-point-comparison to compare two characters in a short story.

Two Sisters

Although they grew up together, Maggie and Dee, the two sisters in Alice Walker's short story "Everyday Use," are very different. Maggie, who was burned in a fire, is shy and has low self-esteem. When she walks, she shuffles her feet and looks down at the ground. Her sister Dee, however, is confident and outgoing. She looks people in the eye when she talks to them and is very opinionated. Maggie and Dee also have different attitudes toward life. Maggie never complains or asks for anything more than she has. She has remained at home with her mother in rural Georgia. In contrast, Dee has always wanted nicer things. She has gone away to school and hardly ever visits her mother and Maggie. The biggest difference between Maggie and Dee is their attitude toward tradition. Although Maggie values her family's rural American traditions, Dee values her African heritage. Maggie cherishes her family's handmade quilts and furniture, hoping to use them with her own family. In contrast, Dee sees the handmade objects as things to be displayed and shown off, not used every day. The many differences between Maggie and Dee add conflict and tension to the story.

—Margaret Caracappa (student)

T E S T
- Topic Sentence
- Evidence
- Summary Statement
- Transitions

Point 1: Different personalities

Point 2: Different attitudes toward life

Point 3: Different attitudes toward tradition

Some Transitional Words and Phrases for Comparison and Contrast

although	one difference . . . another difference
but	one similarity . . . another similarity
even though	on the contrary
however	on the one hand . . . on the other hand
in comparison	similarly
in contrast	though
like	unlike
likewise	whereas
nevertheless	

---

grammar in context

Comparison and Contrast

When you write a comparison-and-contrast paragraph, you should express the points you are comparing in **parallel** terms to highlight their similarities or differences.

NOT PARALLEL Although Maggie values her family's rural American traditions, the African heritage of her family is the thing that Dee values.

PARALLEL Although Maggie <u>values</u> her family's rural American <u>traditions</u>, Dee <u>values</u> her African <u>heritage</u>.

For more information on revising to make ideas parallel, see Chapter 21.

e For more practice with parallelism, complete the LearningCurve Parallelism activity at **macmillanhighered.com/writingfirst.**

Analyzing a Comparison-and-Contrast Paragraph

Read this comparison-and-contrast paragraph; then, follow the instructions in Practice 9-1.

Virtual and Traditional Classrooms

Taking a course online is very different from taking a course in a traditional classroom. One difference is that students in an online course have more flexibility than do students in a traditional course. They can do their schoolwork at any time, scheduling it around other commitments, such as jobs and childcare. Students in a traditional course, however, must go to class at a specific time and place. Another difference is that students in an online course can feel isolated from the teacher and other students because they never actually come into physical contact with them. Students in a traditional classroom, however, are able to connect with the teacher and their classmates because they interact with them in person. A final difference is that in an online course, students use email or a discussion board to discuss course material. A student who is a slow typist or whose Internet connection is unreliable is clearly at a disadvantage. In a traditional course, most of the discussion takes place in the classroom, so technology is not an issue. Because online and traditional courses are so different, students must think carefully about which type of course best fits their needs.

—William Hernandez (student)

PRACTICE

1. Underline the topic sentence of the paragraph above.

2. Does this paragraph deal mainly with similarities or differences? How do you know? _____

   _____

3. Is this paragraph a subject-by-subject or a point-by-point comparison? How do you know? _____

   _____

4. List some of the contrasts the writer describes. The first contrast has been listed for you.

   When it comes to their schedules, students in an online course have more flexibility

   than do students in a traditional course.

_____

_____

_____

_____

_____

5. Circle the transitional words and phrases the writer uses to move from one point of comparison to the next.

6. Underline the paragraph's summary statement.

PRACTICE
9-2   Following are three possible topic sentences for comparison-and-contrast paragraphs. For each topic sentence, list three or four similarities or differences between the two subjects. For example, if you were writing a paragraph comparing health care provided by a local clinic with health care provided by a private doctor, you could discuss the cost, the length of waiting time, the quality of care, and the frequency of follow-up visits.

1. My mother (or father) and I are very different (or alike).

2. My friends and I have different views on _____.

3. Two of my college instructors have very different teaching styles.

9b   Case Study: A Student Writes a Comparison-and-Contrast Paragraph

Here is how one student, Jermond Love, wrote a comparison-and-contrast paragraph. When Jermond was asked by his composition instructor to compare two people, places, or objects, he began by brainstorming to find a topic. When he reviewed his brainstorming notes, he decided that the following topics looked most promising.

Football and soccer

American and Caribbean cooking

The differences between my brother and me

Life in Saint Croix versus life in New York City

After considering each of these topics, Jermond decided to write about the differences between life in Saint Croix—the Caribbean island where he was raised—and life in New York City, where he now lived. He listed various points that he thought he could compare and contrast. Then, he crossed out the ones he didn't want to write about.

Size

~~Economy~~

~~Businesses~~

Lifestyle

~~Politics~~

~~Education~~

~~Music~~

~~Agriculture~~

~~Sports~~

~~Living conditions~~

~~Industry~~

~~Traditions~~

After thinking about the relative sizes of Saint Croix and New York City as well as their respective lifestyles, Jermond brainstormed again to identify some specific differences that he could discuss in his paragraph.

Population: 60,000 versus over 8 million

Laid-back versus hurried lifestyle

Christiansted and Frederiksted versus five boroughs

Friendly versus not always friendly

yellow + blue

list differences

Look over the brainstorming activity you did in response to the Write First prompt on page 97, and then cross out the word pairs that you do not want to discuss in your paragraph. On the lines below, list the word pairs you plan to discuss.

_____

_____

_____

_____

After reviewing his list of differences, Jermond drafted the following topic sentence. This sentence told readers that he was going to focus on differences, and it also identified the main point he was going to make in his comparison-and-contrast paragraph.

TOPIC SENTENCE   Life in Saint Croix is very different from life in New York City.

---

write a topic sentence

Review your list of words with new meanings, and then draft a topic sentence for your comparison-and-contrast paragraph.

_____

_____

good for the planet

At this point, Jermond created the following informal outline, presenting his ideas in the order in which he was going to discuss them in his paragraph.

Size
    Saint Croix
        Small size
        Small population
        Christiansted and Frederiksted
    New York City
        Large size
        Large population
        Five boroughs

Lifestyle
    Saint Croix
        Laid-back
        Friendly
    New York City
        In a hurry
        Not always friendly

Jermond thought that a point-by-point organization would be easier for his readers to follow than a subject-by-subject organization. With this organization, readers would be able to keep track of his comparison as he discussed each of his points, one at a time.

a person you know

make an outline

Decide whether you will write a subject-by-subject or point-by-point comparison. Then, use the appropriate format (see the paragraph maps on pages 99 and 100) to help you create an outline for your comparison-and-contrast paragraph. Before you begin, decide on the order in which you will present your points—for example, from least to most important. (For a subject-by-subject comparison, begin by deciding which subject you will discuss first.)

Using his informal outline as a guide, Jermond drafted his paragraph. Here is his draft.

Life in Saint Croix is very different from life in New York City. Saint Croix is much smaller than New York City. Saint Croix has a total population of about 60,000 people. The two main towns are Christiansted and Frederiksted. New York City is very large. Its residents are crowded into five boroughs. The lifestyle in Saint Croix is different from the lifestyle of New York City. In Saint Croix, almost everyone operates on "island time." Everyone is friendly. People don't see any point in getting anyone upset. In New York City, most people are always in a hurry. They don't take the time to slow down and enjoy life. As a result, people can seem unfriendly. They don't take the time to get to know anyone. I hope when I graduate I can stay in New York City but visit my home in Saint Croix whenever I can.

living matter

draft your paragraph

Using your informal outline as a guide, draft your comparison-and-contrast paragraph.

Jermond put his paragraph aside for a day and then reread it. Although he was generally satisfied with what he had written, he thought that his draft could be improved. To help students revise their paragraphs, his instructor divided students into peer-review groups and asked them to read and discuss each other's paragraphs. After working with a classmate on his draft—first **TEST**ing it and then discussing ways he might revise it—Jermond made the following decisions.

- He decided that his **topic sentence** was clear and specific.

- He saw that he needed more **evidence**—examples and details—to help his readers understand the differences between his two subjects.

- He decided to change his **summary statement** because it didn't clearly reinforce the idea in his topic sentence.

- Finally, he decided that he needed to add **transitional words and phrases** that would show when he was moving from one subject to another.

As Jermond revised his paragraph, he added background about Saint Croix. (The classmate who read his draft had pointed out that many people in the class would not know anything about the island.) The final edited and proofread draft includes all the elements Jermond looked for when he TESTed his paragraph.

Saint Croix versus New York City

Life in Saint Croix is very different from life in New York City. One difference between Saint Croix and New York is that Saint Croix is much smaller than New York. Saint Croix, the largest of the United States Virgin Islands, has a population of about 60,000. The two main towns on the island are Christiansted, with a population of about 3,000, and Frederiksted, with a population of only about 830. Unlike Saint Croix, New York City is large. It has a population of over 8 million crowded into the five boroughs of Manhattan, Brooklyn, the Bronx, Queens, and Staten Island. My neighborhood in Brooklyn is more than twice the size of Christiansted and Frederiksted combined. Another difference between Saint Croix and New York City is their lifestyles. Life in Saint Croix is slower than life in New York. In Saint Croix, almost everyone operates on "island time." Things get done, but people don't rush to do them. When workers say "later," they can mean "this afternoon," "tomorrow," or even "next week." No one seems to mind, as long as the job gets done. People don't see any point in getting anyone upset. In New York, however, most people are always in a hurry. They don't take the time to slow down and enjoy life. Everything is fast—fast food, fast cars, fast Internet access. As a result, people can seem unfriendly. Although Saint Croix and New York City are so different, life is interesting in both places.

T	E	S	T

- Topic Sentence
- Evidence
- Summary Statement
- Transitions

TEST · Revise · Edit · Proofread

Look back at the draft of your comparison-and-contrast paragraph. Using the TEST checklist on page 108, evaluate your paragraph to make sure it includes a topic sentence, evidence, a summary statement, and transitions, and revise your draft accordingly. Finally, edit and proofread your paragraph.

made naturally in a factory

TESTing a comparison-and-contrast paragraph

T opic Sentence Unifies Your Paragraph

☐ Do you have a clearly worded **topic sentence** that states your paragraph's main idea?

☐ Does your topic sentence indicate whether you are focusing on similarities or on differences?

E vidence Supports Your Paragraph's Topic Sentence

☐ Does all your **evidence**—examples and details—support your paragraph's main idea?

☐ Do your examples and details show how your two subjects are alike or different?

☐ Do you need to discuss additional similarities or differences?

S ummary Statement Reinforces Your Paragraph's Unity

☐ Does your paragraph end with a **summary statement** that reinforces your main idea?

T ransitions Add Coherence to Your Paragraph

☐ Do your **transitions** indicate whether you are focusing on similarities or on differences?

☐ Do transitional words and phrases lead readers from one subject or point to the next?

☐ Do you need to add transitions to make your paragraph clearer and to help readers follow your ideas?

10 Classification

AP Photo/Kathy Willens

write first

This picture shows fans at a football game. Look at the picture, and then brainstorm to identify the categories of fans you often see at a particular sporting event. (If you prefer, you may choose a topic from the list on the following page.) You will return to your topic and review your brainstorming later in the chapter when you write your classification paragraph.

additional topics for classification

Types of friends
Part-time jobs
Parents or children
Types of teachers
Ways people give back to their communities

10a Classification Paragraphs

When you **classify**, you sort items (people, things, ideas) into categories or groups. You classify when you organize bills into those you have to pay now and those you can pay later, or when you sort the clothes in a dresser drawer into piles of socks, T-shirts, and underwear.

In a **classification paragraph**, you tell readers how items can be sorted into categories or groups. Each category must be **distinct**. In other words, none of the items in one category should also fit into another category. For example, you would not classify novels into mysteries, romances, and e-books because both mystery novels and romance novels could also be e-books. (For information about writing classification essays, see 15g.)

When you **TEST** a classification paragraph, make sure it follows these guidelines.

T ▪ A classification paragraph should begin with a **topic sentence** that introduces the subject of the paragraph. It may also identify the categories you will discuss (for example, "Before you go camping, you should sort the items you are thinking of packing into three categories: absolutely necessary, potentially helpful, and not really necessary").

E ▪ A classification paragraph should discuss one category at a time and should include enough **evidence**—examples and details—to explain each category and show how it is distinct from the other categories. The categories should be arranged in **logical order**— for example, from least to most important or from smallest to largest.

S ▪ A classification paragraph should end with a **summary statement** that reinforces the paragraph's main idea.

T ▪ A classification paragraph should include **transitions** to introduce the categories you discuss and connect them to one another and to the topic sentence.

Paragraph Map: Classification

> **Topic Sentence**
>
> *Category #1*
>
> *Category #2*
>
> *Category #3*
>
> **Summary Statement**

Model Paragraph: Classification

The writer of the following paragraph classifies bosses into three distinct groups.

T E S T

- Topic Sentence
- Evidence
- Summary Statement
- Transitions

Types of Bosses

I've had three kinds of bosses in my life: the uninterested boss, the supervisor, and the micromanager. The first type is an uninterested boss. This boss doesn't care what workers do as long as they do the job. When I was a counselor at summer camp, my boss fell into this category. As long as no campers (or worse yet, parents) complained, he left you alone. He never cared if you followed the activity plan for the day or gave the kids an extra snack to keep them quiet. ⎫ First type of boss

The second type of boss is the supervisor. This kind of boss will check you once in a while and give you helpful advice. You'll have a certain amount of freedom but not too much. When I was a salesperson at the Gap, my boss fell into this category. She helped me through the first few weeks of the job and encouraged me to do my best. At the end of the summer, I had learned a lot about retail business and had good feelings about the job. ⎬ Second type of boss

The last, and worst, type of boss is the micromanager. This kind of boss gets involved in everything. My boss at Taco Bell was this kind of person. No one could do anything right. There was always a better way to do anything you tried to do. If you rolled a burrito one way, he would tell you to do it another way. If you did it the other way, he would tell you to do it the first way. This boss never seemed to understand that people need praise every once in a while. Even though the supervisor expects a lot and makes you work, it is clear to me that this boss is better than the other types. ⎬ Last type of boss

—Melissa Burrell (student)

Some Transitional Words and Phrases for Classification

one kind . . . another kind	the first group . . . the last group
one way . . . another way	the first type . . . the second type
the first (second, third) category	the most (or least) important group
	the next part

grammar in context

Classification

When you write a classification paragraph, you may list the categories you are going to discuss. If you use a **colon** to introduce your list, make sure that a complete sentence comes before the colon.

INCORRECT Bosses can be divided into: the uninterested boss, the supervisor, and the micromanager.

CORRECT I've had three kinds of bosses in my life: the uninterested boss, the supervisor, and the micromanager.

For more information on how to use a colon to introduce a list, see 35d.

Analyzing a Classification Paragraph

Read this classification paragraph; then, follow the instructions in Practice 10-1.

Unusual Smartphone Applications

Generally, there are three kinds of unusual smartphone applications: those that are harmlessly entertaining, those that are surprisingly useful, and those that are deadly serious. The first kind is harmlessly entertaining. The purpose of the odd apps in this category is to be amusing, silly, or fun. People enjoy using them to do unimportant things, such as "pop" bubble wrap, blow out birthday candles, or add steam to their photos. Goofy apps like iMilk, which creates a virtual glass of milk that tilts when you pretend to drink it, fall into this first category. The second kind of unusual app is also odd but surprisingly useful, helping people accomplish various tasks. For example, Guitar Toolkit helps users tune their guitars and find chords, and Cubecheater helps users find the fastest solution to a Rubik's Cube puzzle. Also in this category is iStutter, an app that trains stutterers to speak with more fluency. The third kind of unusual app is the deadly serious kind, which can actually help save lives. Often, this kind of app is available only to select groups, not to the general public. For example, trained minesweepers use the PETAL app for the iPhone to help them determine the size and shape of land mines. Another example is the U.S. Army's specialized app for training soldiers to launch missiles. Although they are certainly not equally important, each of these three kinds of apps has its uses.

—Emily Bentz (student)

PRACTICE 10-1

1. Underline the topic sentence of the paragraph above.

2. What is the subject of the paragraph? _____

3. What three categories does the writer describe?

_____

_____

_____

4. Circle the transitional phrases the writer uses to introduce the three categories.

5. Underline the paragraph's summary statement.

PRACTICE 10-2

List items for each of the following groups; then, sort the items into three or four categories.

1. All the items on your desk

2. Buildings on your college campus

3. Websites you visit

4. The various parts of a piece of equipment you use for a course or on the job

10b   Case Study: A Student Writes a Classification Paragraph

Here is how one student, Corey Levin, wrote a classification paragraph. For a college composition course, Corey participated in a service-learning project at a local Ronald McDonald House, a charity that houses families of seriously ill children receiving treatment at nearby hospitals. He met several professional athletes there and was surprised to learn that many of them regularly donate time and money to charity.

When Corey was asked by his composition instructor to write a paragraph about what he had learned from his experience, he decided to write a paragraph that classified the ways in which professional athletes give back to their communities. Based on his experience, he was able to come up with the following three categories.

Starting charitable foundations

Guidance

Responding to emergencies

list categories

Look back at the brainstorming you did in response to the Write First prompt on page 109, and cross out any categories that you do not plan to discuss. List the remaining categories—the ones that you will discuss in your classification paragraph—on the lines below.

_____

_____

_____

Corey then made an informal outline, listing examples to develop each of the three categories.

Starting charitable foundations
    Michael Jordan
    Troy Aikman

Guidance
    Shaquille O'Neal
    The Philadelphia 76ers

Responding to emergencies
    Ike Reese
    Vince Carter

make an outline

Create an informal outline for your paragraph by arranging the categories of sports fans in the order in which you will discuss them and listing examples to develop each of your categories.

After completing his informal outline, Corey drafted the following topic sentence for his paragraph.

High-profile athletes find many ways to give back to their communities.

write a topic sentence

Review your list of categories, and then draft a topic sentence for your classification paragraph.

_____

_____

Then, using his informal outline as a guide, Corey wrote the following draft of his paragraph.

> High-profile athletes find many ways to give back to their communities. Many athletes as well as teams do a lot to help people. I met some of them when I volunteered at the Ronald McDonald House. For example, Michael Jordan and the Chicago Bulls built a Boys and Girls Club on Chicago's West Side. Troy Aikman set up a foundation that builds playgrounds for children's hospitals. Shaquille O'Neal's Shaq's Paq provides guidance for inner-city children. The Philadelphia 76ers visit schools and have donated over five thousand books to local libraries. Ike Reese, formerly with the Atlanta Falcons, collects clothing and food for families that need help. Vince Carter of the Orlando Magic founded the Embassy of Hope Foundation. It distributes food to needy families at Thanksgiving and hosts a Christmas party for disadvantaged families.

draft your paragraph

Using your informal outline as a guide, draft your classification paragraph.

Following his instructor's suggestion, Corey emailed his draft to a classmate for feedback. In her email reply to Corey, his classmate TESTed his paragraph and made the following suggestions.

- Keep the **topic sentence** the way it is. "Many ways" shows you're writing a classification paragraph.
- Add more specific **evidence**. Give examples of each category of "giving back" to support the topic sentence. You also need to explain the athletes' contributions in more detail.
- Add a **summary statement** to sum up the paragraph's main idea.
- Add **transitions** to introduce the three specific categories you're discussing.

Corey kept these comments in mind as he revised his paragraph. The final edited and proofread draft includes all the elements Corey's classmate looked for when she TESTed his paragraph.

Giving Back

> High-profile athletes find many ways to give back to their communities. One way to give back is to start a charitable foundation to help young fans. For example, Michael Jordan and the Chicago Bulls built a Boys & Girls Club on Chicago's West Side. In addition, Troy Aikman set up a foundation that builds playgrounds for children's hospitals. Another way athletes give back to their communities is by mentoring, or giving guidance to young people.

T E S T

- Topic Sentence
- Evidence
- Summary Statement
- Transitions

Many athletes work to encourage young people to stay in school. Shaquille O'Neal's Shaq's Paq, for example, provides guidance for inner-city children. The Philadelphia 76ers visit schools and have donated over five thousand books to local libraries. One more way athletes can contribute to their communities is to respond to emergencies. Football player Ike Reese, formerly with the Atlanta Falcons, collects clothing and food for families that need help. Basketball player Vince Carter founded the Embassy of Hope Foundation. It distributes food to needy families at Thanksgiving and hosts a Christmas party for disadvantaged families. These are just some of the ways that high-profile athletes give back to their communities.

TEST · Revise · Edit · Proofread

Look back at the draft of your classification paragraph. Using the **TEST** checklist below, evaluate your paragraph to make sure it includes a topic sentence, evidence, a summary statement, and transitions, and revise your draft accordingly. Finally, edit and proofread your paragraph.

TESTing a classification paragraph

Topic Sentence Unifies Your Paragraph

☐ Do you have a clearly worded **topic sentence** that states your paragraph's main idea?

☐ Does your topic sentence identify the categories you will discuss?

Evidence Supports Your Paragraph's Topic Sentence

☐ Does all your **evidence**—examples and details—support your paragraph's main idea?

☐ Do your examples and details explain each category and indicate how each is distinct from the others?

☐ Do you need to include more examples or details?

Summary Statement Reinforces Your Paragraph's Unity

☐ Does your paragraph end with a **summary statement** that reinforces your main idea?

Transitions Add Coherence to Your Paragraph

☐ Do your **transitions** clearly indicate which categories are more important than others?

☐ Do you need to add transitions to make your paragraph clearer and to help readers follow your ideas?

11 Definition

Vegan (vē′gən) n.

A vegan is someone who tries to live without exploiting animals, for the benefit of animals, people and the planet.

Vegans eat a plant-based diet, with nothing coming from animals; no meat, fish, milk, eggs or honey.

Vegan lifestyle avoids leather, wool, silk & other animal products for clothing or any other purpose as much as possible.

Photo by Emily Behrendt

write first

Read the definition of the word *vegan* printed on the shopping bag pictured here, and consider how this definition could be developed further. Then, brainstorm to identify some words you have encountered in your college courses for which you could write one-paragraph definitions. (If you prefer, you may choose a topic from the list on the following page.) You will return to your topic and review your brainstorming later in the chapter when you write your definition paragraph.

additional topics for definition

A negative quality, such as *jealousy*

A type of person, such as a *show-off*

A controversial term, such as *right to life, affirmative action,* or *social justice*

A goal in life, such as *happiness* or *success*

11a Definition Paragraphs

During a conversation, you might say that a friend is stubborn, that a stream is polluted, or that a neighborhood is dangerous. In order to make yourself clear, you have to define what you mean by *stubborn*, *polluted*, or *dangerous*. Like conversations, academic assignments may involve definition. In a history paper, for example, you might have to define *imperialism*; on a biology exam, you might be asked to define *mitosis*.

A **definition** tells what a word means. When you want your readers to know exactly how you are using a specific term, you define it.

When most people think of definitions, they think of the **formal definitions** they see in a dictionary. Formal definitions have a three-part structure.

- The term to be defined
- The general class to which the term belongs
- The things that make the term different from all other items in the general class to which the term belongs

TERM	CLASS	DIFFERENTIATION
Ice hockey	is a game	played on ice by two teams on skates who use curved sticks to try to hit a puck into the opponent's goal.
Spaghetti	is a pasta	made in the shape of long, thin strands.

A single-sentence formal definition is often not enough to define a specialized term (*point of view* or *premeditation*, for example), an abstract concept (*happiness* or *success*, for example), or a complicated subject (*stem-cell research*, for example). In these cases, you may need to expand the basic formal definition by writing a definition paragraph. In fact, a **definition paragraph** is an expanded formal definition. (For information about writing definition essays, see 15h.)

When you TEST a definition paragraph, make sure it follows these guidelines.

T ▪ A definition paragraph should begin with a formal definition in the **topic sentence**.

E ▪ A definition paragraph does not follow any one pattern of development; in fact, it may define a term by using any of the patterns discussed in this text. For example, a definition paragraph may explain a concept by *comparing* it to something else or by giving *examples*. For this reason, your discussion of each category should include **evidence**—examples and details—that is appropriate for the pattern of development you use.

S ▪ A definition paragraph should end with a **summary statement** that reinforces the paragraph's main idea.

T ▪ A definition paragraph should include **transitions** that are appropriate for the pattern or patterns of organization you use.

Here is one possible structure for a definition paragraph. Notice that this paragraph uses a combination of **narration** and **exemplification**.

Paragraph Map: Definition

Topic Sentence

Point #1
　Narrative

Point #2
　Example

　Example

Point #3
　Example

　Example

Summary Statement

T E S T
- Topic Sentence
- Evidence
- Summary Statement
- Transitions

Model Paragraph: Definition

The writer of the following paragraph uses narration and exemplification to define the term *business casual*.

Business Casual

Business casual is a dress code that is followed in many professional workplaces. Until recently, men and women dressed formally for work. For example, men wore dark suits and plain ties while women wore dark jackets and skirts. In the 1990s, however, the rise of technology companies in Silicon Valley made popular a new style of work attire, called *business casual*. Today, business casual is the accepted form of dress in many businesses. For men, this usually means wearing a collared shirt with no tie and khaki pants, sometimes with a sports jacket and loafers. For women, it means wearing a skirt or pants with a blouse or collared shirt. Women can wear low heels or flats. High-tech companies can be even more informal. They may even allow employees to wear jeans and T-shirts to work. Although business casual may be the new norm, every company has its own standards for what is acceptable.

—Chase Durbin (student)

Narrative — [first part]

Examples of men's business casual

Examples of women's business casual

Some Transitional Words and Phrases for Definition

after	like
also	often
as a result	one characteristic . . . another
even so	characteristic
for example	one way . . . another way
however	sometimes
in addition	specifically
in particular	the first kind . . . the second kind
instead	today
in the 1990s (or another time)	until recently

grammar in context

Definition

A definition paragraph often includes a formal definition of the term or concept you are going to discuss. When you write your formal definition, be careful not to use the phrases *is where* or *is when*.

Business casual is ~~when employees wear informal attire~~ a dress code that is followed in many professional workplaces. ~~to work.~~

Analyzing a Definition Paragraph

Read this definition paragraph; then, follow the instructions in Practice 11-1.

Loans That Change Lives

Microloans are small loans given to people who live in extreme poverty. The idea for such loans originated in 1974, when a Bangladeshi economist loaned $27 to a group of local women. The women used the loan to purchase bamboo to make furniture. After they sold the furniture, they repaid the loan and kept a small profit for themselves. As a result of this experience, the economist created a bank for microloans. Similar microcredit banks now exist throughout the world. For example, microcredit banks can be found in Bosnia, Peru, Ethiopia, and Russia. Microloans are different from ordinary loans because they are not awarded on the basis of credit history or financial means; instead, they are based on trust. A microcredit bank trusts a borrower to make money even if he or she has no or little income at the time of the loan. Some people see microloans as a wonderful opportunity for poor businesspeople; others criticize microloans because they can encourage governments to reduce their support for the poor. Even so, microloans have helped countless people all over the world lift themselves out of poverty.

PRACTICE

1. Underline the topic sentence of the paragraph above.

2. What is the subject of this definition? _____

3. What is the writer's one-sentence definition of the subject?

_____

4. List some of the specific information the writer uses to define the subject. The first piece of information has been listed for you.
   Microloans originated in Bangladesh in 1974.

   _____

   _____

   _____

5. Circle the transitional words and phrases the writer uses.

6. What patterns of development does the writer use in the definition? List them here.

   _____

7. Underline the paragraph's summary statement.

PRACTICE

11-2   Following are four possible topic sentences for definition paragraphs. Each topic sentence includes an underlined word. In the space provided, list two possible patterns of development you could use to develop a definition of the underlined word. For example, you could define the word *discrimination* by giving examples (exemplification) and by telling a story (narration).

1. During the interview, the job candidate made a <u>sexist</u> comment.

   Possible strategy: _____

   Possible strategy: _____

2. <u>Loyalty</u> is one of the chief characteristics of golden retrievers.

   Possible strategy: _____

   Possible strategy: _____

3. More than forty years after President Johnson's Great Society initiative, we have yet to eliminate <u>poverty</u> in the United States.

   Possible strategy: _____

   Possible strategy: _____

4. The problem with movies today is that they are just too <u>violent</u>.

   Possible strategy: _____

   Possible strategy: _____

11b Case Study: A Student Writes a Definition Paragraph

Here is how one student, Lorraine Scipio, wrote a definition paragraph. On a history exam, Lorraine was asked to write a one-paragraph definition of the term *imperialism*. Lorraine had studied for the exam, so she knew what imperialism was. Because she wanted to make sure that she did not leave anything out of her definition (and because she had a time limit), she quickly listed some supporting examples and details on the inside front cover of her exam book. Then, she crossed out two items that did not seem relevant.

A policy of control

Military

~~Lenin~~

Establish empires

Cultural superiority

Raw materials and cheap labor

Africa, etc.

~~Cultural imperialism~~

Nineteenth-century term

---

list examples and details

Review the brainstorming you did in response to the Write First prompt on page 117, and choose a word to define. Then, list the examples and details that can best help you develop a definition of that word.

_____

_____

_____

_____

Now, cross out the items on your list that do not seem relevant to your definition.

After reviewing her list of examples and details, Lorraine drafted the following topic sentence.

The goal of imperialism is to establish an empire.

---

write a topic sentence

Review your list of examples and details, and then draft a topic sentence for your definition paragraph. Include a formal definition of the term you are defining.

_____

_____

Next, Lorraine made an informal outline, quickly arranging her supporting examples and details in the order in which she planned to write about them.

Establish empires

Nineteenth-century term

Cultural superiority

Africa, etc.

Raw materials and cheap labor

A policy of control

Military

make an outline

Create an informal outline for your paragraph by arranging your examples and details in the order in which you plan to discuss them.

Referring to the material on her list, Lorraine wrote the following draft of her definition paragraph. Notice that she uses several different patterns to develop her definition.

The goal of imperialism is to establish an empire. The imperialist country thinks that it is superior to the country it takes over. It justifies its actions by saying that it is helping the other country. But it isn't. Countries such as Germany, Belgium, Spain, and England have been imperialist in the past—especially in nineteenth-century Africa. The point of imperialism is to take as much out of the occupied countries as possible. Often, imperialist countries sent troops to occupy other countries and to keep order. As a result, imperialism kept the people in occupied countries in poverty and often broke down local governments and local traditions.

draft your paragraph

Using your informal outline as a guide, draft your definition paragraph. Remember, you can use any of the patterns of development discussed in Unit 2 of this text to help you define your term. Begin by identifying the term. Then, you can describe it, give examples, tell how it works, explain its purpose, consider its history or future, or compare it with other similar terms.

After she finished her draft, Lorraine reread it quickly, **TEST**ing her paragraph to make sure it answered the exam question. Then, she made the following revisions.

- Because the exam question asked for a definition, she rewrote her **topic sentence** as a formal definition.

- She strengthened her **evidence**, explaining her supporting examples and details more fully. She also deleted some vague statements that did not support her topic sentence.

- She added **transitional words and phrases** to make the connections between her ideas clearer.

- She added a **summary statement** to reinforce the negative effects of imperialism.

Lorraine made her revisions directly on the draft she had written, crossing out unnecessary information and adding missing information. She also edited her paragraph for grammar, punctuation, and mechanical errors. Then, because she had some extra time, she neatly rewrote her paragraph and proofread it before handing in her exam.

Lorraine's revised, edited, and proofread paragraph appears here. (Because this is an exam answer, she does not include a title.) Notice that the final draft includes all the elements Lorraine looked for when she TESTed her paragraph.

Imperialism is the policy by which one country takes over the land or the government of another country. In the nineteenth century, the object of imperialism was to establish an empire. The imperialist country thought that it was superior to the country it took over. It justified its actions by saying that it was helping the other country. For instance, countries such as Germany, Belgium, Spain, and England followed their imperialist ambitions in Africa when they claimed large areas of land. The point of imperialism was to take as much out of the occupied countries as possible. For example, in South America and Mexico, Spain removed tons of gold from the areas it occupied. It made the natives slaves and forced them to work in mines. In order to protect their interests, imperialist countries sent troops to occupy the country and to keep order. As a result, imperialism kept the people in occupied countries in poverty and often broke down local governments and local traditions. Although European imperialism occasionally had benefits, at its worst it brought slavery, disease, and death.

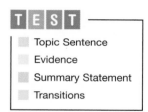

T E S T
- Topic Sentence
- Evidence
- Summary Statement
- Transitions

FYI

Writing Paragraph Answers on Exams

When you write a paragraph-length answer on an exam, you do not have much time to work, so you need to be well prepared. Know your subject well, and memorize important definitions. You may have time to write an outline, a rough draft, and a final draft, but you will have to work quickly. Your final draft should include all the elements of a good paragraph: a topic sentence, supporting details, transitions, and a summary statement.

TEST · Revise · Edit · Proofread

Look back at the draft of your definition paragraph. Using the TEST checklist below, evaluate your paragraph to make sure it includes a topic sentence, evidence, a summary statement, and transitions, and revise your draft accordingly. Finally, edit and proofread your paragraph.

TESTing a definition paragraph

Topic Sentence Unifies Your Paragraph

☐ Do you have a clearly worded **topic sentence** that states your paragraph's main idea?

☐ Does your topic sentence identify the term you are defining?

Evidence Supports Your Paragraph's Topic Sentence

☐ Does all your **evidence**—examples and details—support your paragraph's main idea?

☐ Do you need to add more examples or details to help you define your term?

Summary Statement Reinforces Your Paragraph's Unity

☐ Does your paragraph end with a **summary statement** that reinforces your main idea?

Transitions Add Coherence to Your Paragraph

☐ Are your **transitions** appropriate for the pattern (or patterns) of development you use?

☐ Do you need to add transitions to make your paragraph clearer and to help readers follow your ideas?

12 Argument

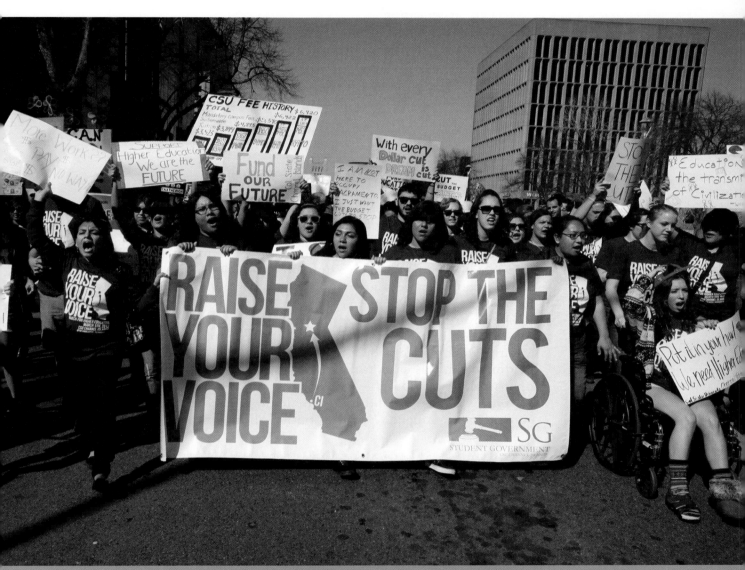

AP Photo/Rich Pedroncelli

write first

Many teachers and students, like those seen in this photo, expressed their displeasure at the rising cost of education at a demonstration that took place in Sacramento, California, in 2012. Brainstorm to develop a list of political issues that interest you. Review your brainstorming, choose one issue, and then write a journal entry exploring your thoughts on this issue. (If you prefer, you may choose a topic from the list on the following page.) You will return to your journal entry later in the chapter when you write your argument paragraph.

additional topics for argument

Online education
Campus security
Banning cell phones in class
School speech codes
College debt

12a   Argument Paragraphs

When most people hear the word *argument*, they think of heated exchanges on television interview programs. These discussions, however, are more like shouting matches than arguments. True **argument** involves taking a well-thought-out position on a **debatable topic**—a topic about which reasonable people may disagree (for example, "Should teenagers who commit felonies be tried as adults?").

In an **argument paragraph**, you take a position on an issue, with the purpose of persuading readers that your position has merit. You attempt to convince people of the strength of your ideas by presenting **evidence**—in this case, facts and examples. In the process, you address opposing ideas, and if they are strong, you acknowledge their strengths. If your evidence is solid and your logic is sound, you will present a convincing argument. (For information about writing argument essays, see 15i.)

FYI

Evidence

You can use two kinds of **evidence** in your argument paragraphs: *facts* and *examples*.

1. A **fact** is a piece of information (such as "Alaska officially became a state in 1959") that can be verified. If you make a statement, you should be prepared to support it with facts—using statistics, observations, or statements that are generally accepted as true.

2. An **example** is a specific illustration of a general statement. To be convincing, an example should clearly relate to the point you are making.

When you TEST an argument paragraph, make sure it follows these guidelines.

T ▪ An argument paragraph should begin with a **topic sentence** that clearly states your position. Using words like *should*, *should not*, or *ought to* in your topic sentence will make your position clear to your readers.

> The federal government <u>should</u> lower taxes on gasoline.

> The city <u>ought to</u> spend 20 percent of its budget on helping businesses convert to sustainable energy sources.

E ▪ An argument paragraph should present points that support the topic sentence in **logical order**. For example, if your purpose is to argue in favor of placing warning labels on unhealthy snack foods, you should give reasons—arranging them from least to most important—why this policy should be instituted. Each of these points should then be supported with **evidence**—facts and examples.

An argument paragraph should also address and **refute** (argue against) opposing arguments. By showing that an opponent's arguments are weak, inaccurate, or misguided, you strengthen your own position. If an opposing argument is particularly strong, you may want to **concede** (accept) its strengths and then point out its weaknesses or shortcomings.

S ▪ An argument paragraph should end with a **summary statement** that reinforces the paragraph's main idea—the position you take on the issue.

T ▪ An argument paragraph should include **transitions** to connect the points you are making to one another and to the topic sentence.

Paragraph Map: Argument

Topic Sentence

Point #1

Point #2

Point #3

*Opposing Argument #1
(plus refutation)*

*Opposing Argument #2
(plus refutation)*

Summary Statement

Model Paragraph: Argument

The following paragraph argues in favor of an emergency notification system for college students.

Point 1 and support

Point 2 and support

Opposing argument 1 (plus refutation)

Opposing argument 2 (plus refutation)

Why Our School Should Set Up an Emergency Notification System

Our school should set up an emergency notification system that would deliver an instant message to students' cell phones in a campus crisis. The first reason why we should set up an emergency notification system is that it is needed. Currently, it takes an hour or two to inform the whole campus of something—for example, that school is closing because of bad weather or that a school event has been canceled. Another reason why we should set up an emergency notification system is that it will make our campus safer by warning students if a crime takes place on campus. For example, when a shooting took place in 2007 on the campus of Virginia Tech, the school was unable to warn students to evacuate the campus. The result was that more than thirty people were killed. An emergency notification system might have saved the lives of many of these people. One objection to a text-messaging emergency notification system is that email notification works just as well. However, although many students check their email once or twice a day, most students carry cell phones and read text messages whenever they get them. Another objection is that some students do not have cell phones. The same system that delivers text messages to students, however, could also deliver messages to digital message boards around campus. Because communicating with students in a crisis situation can save lives, our school should set up an emergency notification system.

—Ashley Phillips (student)

Some Transitional Words and Phrases for Argument

accordingly	first . . . second . . .	moreover
admittedly	for example	nevertheless
after all	for instance	nonetheless
also	for this reason	of course
although	granted	one . . . another
because	however	on the one hand . . .
certainly	in addition	on the other hand
consequently	in conclusion	since
despite	indeed	the first reason
even so	in fact	therefore
even though	in summary	thus
finally	meanwhile	to be sure

grammar in context

Argument

When you write an argument paragraph, you should use both **compound sentences** and **complex sentences**. By doing this, you not only show the relationship between ideas but also eliminate choppy sentences.

> **COMPOUND SENTENCE** An emergency notification system will help all of us *, and it* communicate ~~better. It~~ will ensure our school's safety.
>
> **COMPLEX SENTENCE** *Because communicating* ~~Communicating~~ with students in a crisis situation can save lives. ~~Our~~ *, our* school should set up an emergency notification system.

For more information on how to create compound sentences, see Chapter 18. For more information on how to create complex sentences, see Chapter 19.

Analyzing an Argument Paragraph

Read this argument paragraph; then, follow the instructions in Practice 12-1.

Why We Need Full-Body Scanners

Because of their advantages, airport full-body scanners are a necessary tool in the fight against terrorism. One reason why airport scanners are necessary is that the federal government needs a quick and effective way of screening passengers. Because of their ease of operation, whole-body scanners accomplish this goal. Well over a million people fly throughout the United States each day. A single airport scanner is capable of screening thousands of people a day and is much faster than other methods of screening. Another reason why airport scanners are necessary is that they provide an additional layer of security. For example, scanners are able to detect both metallic and nonmetallic items that are taped to the body. In other words, scanners will detect both weapons and bomb materials that metal detectors might miss. People who oppose scanners say that they are unsafe. However, the literature that the government distributes at airports makes it clear that airport scanners expose passengers to less radiation than they experience when they fly at high altitudes. Opponents also point out that scanners violate the Constitution's guarantee of privacy because they show a three-dimensional image of a person's naked body. To deal with this objection, the

Transportation Security Administration has made sure that the TSA officer who operates a scanner never sees the images of the person being scanned. He or she sees only a screen that indicates whether the person has successfully cleared the screening. In addition, the images themselves are deleted immediately after a person has left the screening area. Given the recent attempts that terrorists have made to attack the United States, airport scanners are a useful and effective way of keeping people safe when they fly.

—Carl Manni (student)

PRACTICE

12-1

1. Underline the topic sentence of the paragraph above.

2. What issue is the subject of the paragraph?

_____

3. What is the writer's position?

_____

4. What specific points does the writer use to support his topic sentence?

_____

_____

5. List some evidence (facts and examples) that the writer uses to support his points. The first piece of evidence has been listed for you.

   A single full-body scanner is capable of screening thousands of people a day.

_____

_____

_____

6. What other evidence could the writer have used?

_____

_____

_____

7. What opposing arguments does he mention?

_____

_____

8. How does he refute these arguments?

_____

_____

9. Circle the transitional words and phrases the writer uses to move readers through his argument.

10. Underline the paragraph's summary statement.

PRACTICE
12-2 Following are four possible topic sentences for argument paragraphs. List two or three points that could support each topic sentence. For example, if you were arguing in support of laws requiring motorcycle riders to wear safety helmets, you could say helmets cut down on medical costs and save lives.

1. High school graduates should perform a year of public service before going to college.

2. All student athletes should be paid a salary by their college or university.

3. College students caught cheating should be expelled.

4. The U.S. government should forgive all federal student loans.

PRACTICE
12-3 Choose one of the topic sentences from Practice 12-2. Then, list two types of evidence that could support each point you listed. For example, if you said that wearing safety helmets saves lives, you could list "accident statistics" and "statements by emergency room physicians."

_____

_____

PRACTICE
12-4 List opposing arguments for the topic sentence you selected for Practice 12-3. Then, list the weaknesses of each of these arguments.

Opposing argument #1: _____

Weaknesses: _____

Opposing argument #2: _____

Weaknesses: _____

12b Case Study: A Student Writes an Argument Paragraph

Here is how one student, Phillip Zhu, wrote an argument paragraph for his composition class on an issue that interested him. Because he was taking a course in computer ethics, he decided to write about an issue that had been discussed in class: the way many employers now search social-networking sites, such as Facebook, to find information about job applicants.

Phillip had already formed an opinion about the issue, so he was ready to write the following topic sentence that expressed his position.

Employers should not use social-networking sites to find information about job applicants.

write your topic sentence

Look back at the journal entry you wrote in response to the Write First prompt on page 127. Determine your position on the political issue you chose to write about, and then draft a topic sentence that clearly states the position you will take in your argument paragraph.

_____

_____

Phillip then listed the following points that he could use to support his topic sentence.

Social-networking sites should be private

People exaggerate on social-networking sites

Posts meant to be funny

No one warns applicant

Expect limited audience

Employers can misinterpret what they find

Employers going where they don't belong

Not an accurate picture

Not fair

Not meant to be seen by job recruiters

list your supporting points

Review your topic sentence, and list as many points as you can in support of your position on the issue. Then, look back at your journal entry to find evidence to support your points.

_____

_____

_____

_____

After identifying his three most important supporting points, Phillip arranged them into an informal outline.

Social-networking sites should be private
    Expect limited audience
    Employers going where they don't belong

People exaggerate on social-networking sites
    Not meant to be seen by job recruiters
    No one warns applicant

Employers can misinterpret what they find
    Posts meant to be funny
    Not an accurate picture
    Not fair

make an outline

Create an informal outline for your paragraph by arranging the points that support your position in the order you think will be most convincing to your readers—for example, from the least important point to the most important point. Under each point, list the evidence (facts and examples) you will use as support.

Once Phillip finished his informal outline, he tried to think of possible arguments against his position because he knew he would have to consider and refute these opposing arguments in his paragraph. He came up with two possible arguments against his position.

1. Employers should be able to find out as much as they can.

2. Applicants have only themselves to blame.

list opposing arguments

Review your informal outline, and then list one or more possible arguments against your position on the lines below.

_____

_____

_____

Now, try to think of ways in which these opposing arguments are weak or inaccurate.

Phillip then wrote the following draft of his paragraph.

Employers should not use social-networking sites to find information about job applicants. For one thing, social-networking sites should be private. By visiting these sites, employers are going where they do not belong. People also exaggerate on social-networking sites. They say things that are not true, and they post things on the sites they would not want job recruiters to see. No one ever tells applicants that recruiters search these sites, so they feel safe posting all kinds of material. Employers can misinterpret what they read, especially posts that are meant to be funny. Employers and recruiters need to get as much information as they can. They should not use unfair ways to get this information. Applicants have only themselves to blame for their problems. They need to be more careful about what they put up online. This is true, but most applicants don't know that employers will search social-networking sites.

draft your paragraph

Guided by your informal outline and your list of opposing arguments, draft your argument paragraph. Begin your paragraph with a topic sentence that clearly states the position you are taking on the issue.

After finishing his draft, Phillip scheduled a conference with his instructor. Together, they went over his paragraph and **TEST**ed it. They agreed that Phillip needed to make the following revisions.

- They decided he needed to make his **topic sentence** more specific and more forceful.
- They decided he should add more **evidence** (facts and examples) to his discussion. For example, what social-networking sites is he talking about? Which are restricted? How do employers gain access to these sites?
- They decided he needed to delete irrelevant discussion blaming job applicants for their problems.
- They decided he should add **transitional words and phrases** to clearly identify the points he is making in support of his argument and also to identify the two opposing arguments he discusses.
- They decided he needed to add a strong **summary statement** to reinforce his position.

As Phillip revised his paragraph, he was guided by these decisions. The final edited and proofread draft includes all the elements Phillip looked for when he **TEST**ed his paragraph.

Unfair Searching

Employers should not use social-networking sites, such as MySpace and Facebook, to find information about job applicants. First, social-networking sites should be private. People who use these sites do not expect employers to access them. However, some employers routinely search social-networking sites to find information about job applicants. Doing this is not right, and it is not fair. By visiting these sites, employers are going where they do not belong. Another reason employers should not use information from social-networking sites is that people frequently exaggerate on them or say things that are not true. They may also post statements and pictures on the sites that they would not want job recruiters to see. Because no one ever tells applicants that recruiters search these sites, they feel safe posting embarrassing pictures or making exaggerated claims about drinking or sex. Finally, employers can misinterpret the material they see. As a result, they may reject a good applicant because they take seriously what is meant to be a joke. Of course, employers need to get as much information about a candidate as they can. They should not, however, use unfair tactics to get this information. In addition, prospective employers should realize that the profile they see on a social-networking site does not accurately represent the job applicant. For these reasons, employers should not use social-networking sites to do background checks.

T E S T

☐ Topic Sentence
☐ Evidence
☐ Summary Statement
☐ Transitions

TEST · **Revise · Edit · Proofread**

Look back at the draft of your argument paragraph. Using the TEST checklist below, evaluate your paragraph to make sure it includes a topic sentence, evidence, a summary statement, and transitions, and revise your draft accordingly. Finally, edit and proofread your paragraph.

TESTing an argument paragraph

T opic Sentence Unifies Your Paragraph

☐ Do you have a clearly worded **topic sentence** that states your paragraph's main idea?

☐ Does your topic sentence state your position on a debatable issue?

E vidence Supports Your Paragraph's Topic Sentence

☐ Does all your **evidence** support your paragraph's main idea?

☐ Have you included enough facts and examples to support your points, or do you need to add more?

☐ Do you summarize and refute opposing arguments?

(continued)

(continued from previous page)

S ummary Statement Reinforces Your Paragraph's Unity

☐ Does your paragraph end with a strong **summary statement** that reinforces your main idea?

T ransitions Add Coherence to Your Paragraph

☐ Do you use **transitions** to let readers know when you are moving from one point to another?

☐ Do you use transitional words and phrases to indicate when you are addressing opposing arguments?

☐ Do you need to add transitions to make your paragraph clearer and to help readers follow your ideas?

13 Writing an Essay

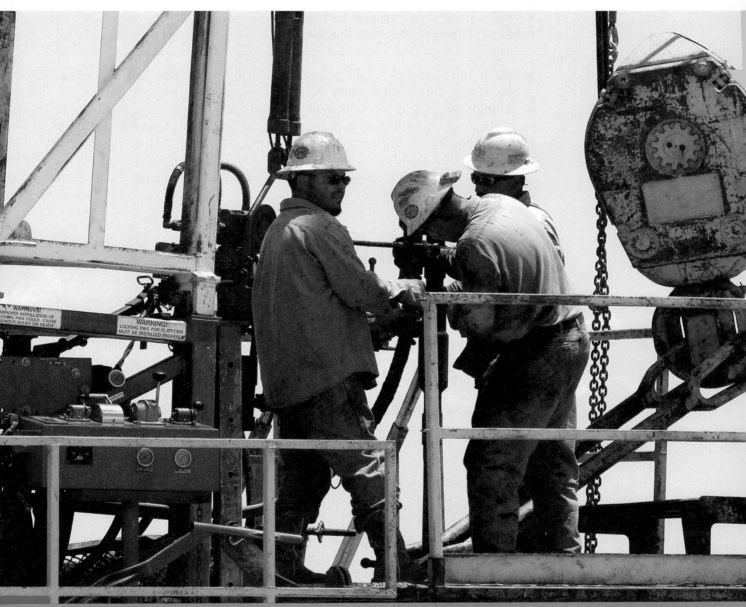

AP Photo/Sue Ogrocki

write first

Most people would agree that oil rig workers, like the ones pictured here, have a very challenging job. Think about the most difficult job you've ever had. This is the topic you will be writing about as you go through this chapter. (If you have never had a job, you may write about a specific task that you disliked or about a difficult job that a friend or relative has had.)

In this chapter, you will learn to

- understand essay structure (13a)
- move from assignment to topic (13b)
- find ideas to write about (13c)
- state your thesis (13d)
- choose supporting points (13e)
- make an outline (13f)
- draft your essay (13g)
- TEST and revise your essay (13h–13i)
- edit and proofread your essay (13j–13k)

Much of the writing you do in school will be more than just one paragraph. Often, you will be asked to write an **essay**—a group of paragraphs on a single subject. When you write an essay, you follow the same process you follow when you write a paragraph: you begin by planning and then move on to organizing your ideas, drafting, TESTing and revising, and editing and proofreading.

In this chapter, you will see how the strategies you learned for writing paragraphs can help you write essays.

STEP 1: PLANNING

13a Understanding Essay Structure

Understanding the structure of a paragraph can help you understand the structure of an essay. In a paragraph, the main idea is stated in a **topic sentence**, and the rest of the paragraph supports this main idea with **evidence** (details and examples). **Transitional words and phrases** help readers follow the discussion. The paragraph ends with a **summary statement** that reinforces the main idea.

Paragraph

> The **topic sentence** states the main idea of the paragraph.
> **Evidence** supports the main idea.
> **Transitional words and phrases** show the connections between ideas.
> A **summary statement** reinforces the main idea of the paragraph.

The structure of an essay is similar to the structure of a paragraph.

- The essay's first paragraph—the *introduction*—begins with opening remarks that create interest and closes with a **thesis statement**. This thesis statement, like a paragraph's topic sentence, presents the main idea. (For more on introductions, see 14a.)

■ The *body* of the essay contains several paragraphs that support the thesis statement. Each body paragraph begins with a topic sentence that states the main idea of the paragraph. The other sentences in the paragraph support the topic sentence with **evidence** (details and examples).

■ **Transitional words and phrases** lead readers from sentence to sentence and from paragraph to paragraph.

■ The last paragraph—the *conclusion*—ends the essay. The conclusion includes a **summary statement** that reinforces the thesis. It ends with concluding remarks. (For more on conclusions, see 14b.)

The first letters of these four key elements—thesis statement, evidence, summary statement, and transitions—spell TEST. Just as you did with paragraphs, you can TEST your essays to see whether they include all the elements of an effective essay.

Many of the essays you will write in college will have a **thesis-and-support** structure.

Essay

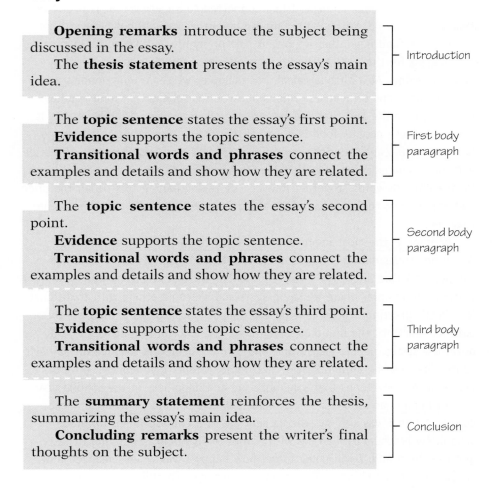

Opening remarks introduce the subject being discussed in the essay.

The **thesis statement** presents the essay's main idea.

Introduction

The **topic sentence** states the essay's first point.

Evidence supports the topic sentence.

Transitional words and phrases connect the examples and details and show how they are related.

First body paragraph

The **topic sentence** states the essay's second point.

Evidence supports the topic sentence.

Transitional words and phrases connect the examples and details and show how they are related.

Second body paragraph

The **topic sentence** states the essay's third point.

Evidence supports the topic sentence.

Transitional words and phrases connect the examples and details and show how they are related.

Third body paragraph

The **summary statement** reinforces the thesis, summarizing the essay's main idea.

Concluding remarks present the writer's final thoughts on the subject.

Conclusion

The following essay by Jennifer Chu illustrates the structure of an essay. (Note that transitional words and phrases are shaded.)

Becoming Chinese American

Introduction

Although I was born in Hong Kong, I have spent most of my life in the United States. However, my parents have always made sure that I did not forget my roots. They always tell stories of what it was like to live in Hong Kong. To make sure my brothers and sisters and I know what is happening in China, my parents subscribe to Chinese cable TV. When we were growing up, we would watch the celebration of the Chinese New Year, the news from Asia, and Chinese movies and music videos. As a result, even though I am an American, I value many parts of traditional Chinese culture.

Thesis statement

Topic sentence (states essay's first point)

First body paragraph

Evidence (supports topic sentence)

The Chinese language is an important part of my life as a Chinese American. Unlike some of my Chinese friends, I do not think the Chinese language is unimportant or embarrassing. First, I feel that it is my duty as a Chinese American to learn Chinese so that I can pass it on to my children. In addition, knowing Chinese enables me to communicate with my relatives. Because my parents and grandparents do not speak English well, Chinese is our main form of communication. Finally, Chinese helps me identify with my culture. When I speak Chinese, I feel connected to a culture that is over five thousand years old. Without the Chinese language, I would not be who I am.

Topic sentence (states essay's second point)

Second body paragraph

Evidence (supports topic sentence)

Chinese food is another important part of my life as a Chinese American. One reason for this is that everything we Chinese people eat has a history and a meaning. At a birthday meal, for example, we serve long noodles and buns in the shape of peaches. This is because we believe that long noodles represent long life and that peaches are served in heaven. Another reason is that to Chinese people, food is a way of reinforcing ties between family and friends. For instance, during a traditional Chinese wedding ceremony, the bride and the groom eat nine of everything. This is because the number nine stands for the Chinese words "together forever." By taking part in this ritual, the bride and groom start their marriage by making Chinese customs a part of their life together.

Topic sentence (states essay's third point)

Third body paragraph

Evidence (supports topic sentence)

Religion is the most important part of my life as a Chinese American. At various times during the year, Chinese religious festivals bring together the people I care about the most. During Chinese New Year, my whole family goes to the temple, where we say prayers and welcome others with traditional New Year's greetings. After leaving the temple, we all go to Chinatown and eat dim sum until the lion dance starts. As the colorful lion dances its way down the street, people beat drums and throw firecrackers to drive off any evil spirits that may be around. Later that night, parents give children gifts of money in red envelopes that symbolize joy and happiness in the coming year.

Summary statement (reinforces essay's thesis)

Conclusion

My family has taught me how important it is to hold on to my Chinese culture. When I was six, my parents sent me to a Chinese-American grade school. My teachers thrilled me with stories of Fa Mulan, the Shang Dynasty, and the Moon God. I will never forget how happy I was when I realized how special it is to be Chinese. This is how I want my own children to feel. I want them to be proud of who they are and to pass their language, history, and culture on to the next generation.

PRACTICE

13-1   Following is an essay organized according to the diagram on page 141. Read the essay, and then answer the questions that follow.

Enhanced Water

Flavored, or "enhanced," water has grown in popularity since it was introduced in the late 1990s. Most enhanced waters are owned by soft drink companies like Coca-Cola and Pepsi. Although these companies have spent millions of dollars trying to convince consumers that enhanced water is better than ordinary water, this is just not true.

There is no question that our bodies need fluid to stay hydrated. In fact, most experts say that people should drink about 64 ounces (eight cups) of water per day. Only athletes and people who are involved in strenuous activities, such as hiking, need to drink significantly more water. These individuals may benefit from the salt and carbohydrates found in sports drinks like Gatorade, but they are the exception. People who exercise at a normal rate, for about an hour a day, usually need only a few additional cups of plain water to restore lost fluids.

Despite marketing claims, it is not clear that enhanced water is more healthful than regular water. The labels on most enhanced water drinks, such as VitaminWater and SoBe Lifewater, make health claims that have not been scientifically proven. For instance, the label on VitaminWater's drink "Defense" implies that its vitamins and minerals will prevent a person from getting sick. Scientists generally agree, however, that there is no magic formula for preventing illness. Another example of a misleading claim appears on the label on SoBe's strawberry-kiwi-flavored "Calm-o-mile" drink, which lists herbs that are supposed to relieve stress. However, the amount of herbs found in this drink is too small to provide any health benefits. Moreover, many enhanced water drinks actually contain ingredients that the body does not need—for example, caffeine, artificial flavors and colors, and sugar or artificial sweeteners.

In addition to making questionable marketing claims, manufacturers of enhanced waters present nutritional information in a confusing way. For example, just a quick glance at the label for a SoBe Lifewater drink would lead someone to believe that a serving has 40 calories, 16 grams of carbohydrates, and 10 grams of sugar. These amounts may sound reasonable, but a closer look at the label reveals that each 20-ounce bottle actually contains two and a half servings. In other words, a person who drinks the whole bottle is actually consuming 100 calories, 40 grams of carbohydrates, and 25 grams of sugar—more carbohydrates and sugar than in a glazed doughnut.

In most cases, regular tap water is all people need to stay healthy and hydrated. The drink manufacturers ignore this fact, saying that enhanced water is lower in calories and sugar than non-diet soft drinks. They also say that, although the herbs and vitamins in their drinks may not have proven health benefits, at least they are not harmful. Finally, the drink manufacturers claim that their products get people to drink more fluids. Although all these claims are partially true, consumers do not need the ingredients in enhanced water or its extra cost.

1. Underline the essay's thesis statement.

2. Underline the topic sentence of each body paragraph.

3. What point does the first body paragraph make? What evidence supports this point?

   _____

   _____

   _____

   _____

   _____

4. What point does the second body paragraph make? What evidence supports this point?

   _____

   _____

   _____

   _____

5. What point does the third body paragraph make? What evidence supports this point?

   _____

   _____

6. What transitions does the essay include? How do they connect the essay's ideas?

   _____

   _____

   _____

   _____

7. Where in the conclusion does the writer restate the essay's thesis? Underline this statement.

13b Moving from Assignment to Topic

Many essays you write in college begin as **assignments** given to you by your instructors. Before you focus on any assignment, however, you should take time to think about your **purpose** (what you want to accomplish by writing your essay) and your **audience** (the people who will read your essay). Once you have considered these issues, you are ready to move on to thinking about the specifics of your assignment.

The following assignments are typical of those you might be given in a composition class.

- Discuss some things you would change about your school.
- What can college students do to improve the environment?
- Discuss an important decision you made during the past few years.

Because these assignments are so general, you need to narrow them before you can start to write. What specific things would you change? Exactly what could you do to improve the environment? Answering these questions will help you narrow these assignments into **topics** that you can write about.

ASSIGNMENT	TOPIC
Discuss some things you would change about your school.	Three things I would change to improve the quality of life on campus
What can college students do to improve the environment?	The campus recycling project

Jared White, a student in a first-year composition course, was given the following assignment.

ASSIGNMENT

Discuss an important decision you made during the past few years.

Jared narrowed this assignment to the following topic:

TOPIC

Deciding to go back to school

In the rest of this chapter, you will be following Jared's writing process.

PRACTICE

13-2   Decide whether the following topics are narrow enough for an essay of four or five paragraphs. If a topic is suitable, write *OK*. If it is not, write a revised version of the same topic that is narrow enough for a brief essay.

Examples

Successful strategies for quitting smoking ___*OK*___

Horror movies ___*1950s Japanese monster movies*___

1. Violence in American public schools _____

_____

2. Ways to improve your study skills _____

_____

3. Using pets as therapy for nursing-home patients _____

_____

4. Teachers _____

_____

5. Safe ways to lose weight _____

_____

decide on a topic

Look back at the Write First prompt on page 139. To narrow this assignment to a topic you can write about, you need to decide which difficult job to focus on. Begin by listing several jobs you could discuss.

FYI

Visit the Study Guides and Strategies website (studygs.net /writing/prewriting.htm) to learn how to use one of the graphic organizers or to find other information about the writing process.

13c   Finding Ideas to Write About

Before you start writing about a topic, you need to find out what you have to say about it. Sometimes ideas will come to you easily. More often, you will need to use specific strategies—such as *freewriting*, *brainstorming*, or *journal writing*—to help you come up with ideas.

Freewriting

When you **freewrite**, you write for a fixed period of time without stopping. When you do **focused freewriting**, you write with a topic in mind. Then, you read what you have written and choose ideas you think you can use.

The following focused freewriting was written by Jared White on the topic "Deciding to go back to school."

> *Deciding to go back to school. When I graduated high school, I swore I'd never go back to school. Hated it. Couldn't wait to get out. What was I thinking? How was I supposed to support myself? My dad's friend needed help. He taught me how to paint houses. I made good money, but it was boring. I couldn't picture myself doing it forever. Even though I knew I was going to have to go back to school, I kept putting off the decision. Maybe I was lazy. Maybe I was scared—probably both. I had this fear of being turned down. How could someone who had bad grades all through high school go to college? Also, I'd been out of school for six years. And even if I did get in (a miracle!), how would I pay for it? How would I live? Well, here I am—the first one in my family to go to college.*

Jared's freewriting

PRACTICE

13-3   Reread Jared White's freewriting. If you were advising Jared, which ideas would you tell him to explore further? Why?

freewrite

Choose two of the difficult jobs you listed, and freewrite about each of them. Then, choose one of the jobs to write about. Circle the ideas about this job that you would like to explore further in an essay.

Brainstorming

When you **brainstorm** (either individually or with others in a group), you write down (or type) all the ideas you can think of about a particular topic. After you have recorded as much material as you can, you look over your notes and decide which ideas are useful and which ones are not.

Here are Jared's brainstorming notes about his decision to go back to school.

Deciding to Go Back to School
Money a problem
Other students a lot younger
Paying tuition—how?

(continued)

(continued from previous page)

No one in family went to college

Friends not in college

Couldn't see myself in college

Considered going to trade school

Computer programmer?

Grades bad in high school

Time for me to grow up

Wondered if I would get in

Found out about community college

Admission requirements not bad

Afraid—too old, looking silly

Took time to get used to routine

Found other students like me

Like studying

Jared's brainstorming notes

**PRACTICE
13-4**   Reread Jared's brainstorming notes. Which ideas would you advise him to explore further? Why?

brainstorm

Review your freewriting. Then, brainstorm about the job for which you have found the most interesting ideas. What ideas about this job did you get from brainstorming that you did not get from freewriting?

Keeping a Journal

When you keep a **journal**, you keep an informal record of your thoughts and ideas. As you learned in Chapter 2, your journal can be a notebook or a computer file. In your journal, you record your thoughts about your assignments, identify ideas you want to explore further, and keep notes about things you read or see. After rereading your journal entries, you can decide to explore an idea further in another journal entry or to use material from a specific entry in an essay.

Following is an entry in Jared's journal that he eventually used in his essay about returning to school.

> *When I was working as a house painter, I had a conversation that helped convince me to go to college. One day, I started talking to the guy whose house I was painting. I told him that I was painting houses until I figured out what I was going to do with the rest of my life. He asked me if I had considered going to college. I told him that I hadn't done well in high school, so I didn't think college was for me. He told me that I could probably get into the local community college. That night I looked at the community college's website to see if going to college might be a good idea.*

Jared's journal entry

write journal entries

Write at least two journal entries for the topic you have been exploring for this chapter: the hardest job you ever had. Which of your entries do you want to explore further? Which could you use in your essay?

13d Stating Your Thesis

After you have gathered information about your topic, you need to decide on a thesis for your essay. You do this by reviewing the ideas from your brainstorming, freewriting, and journal entries and then asking, "What is the main point I want to make about my topic?" The answer to this question is the **thesis** of your essay. You express this point in a **thesis statement**: a single sentence that clearly expresses the main idea that you will discuss in the rest of your essay.

When Jared looked over the notes he had accumulated, he saw that his brainstorming had given him so much to work with that he didn't need to use the material he'd come up with in his journal entries. At this point, he reviewed his brainstorming notes, crossing out several points that he thought would not support his thesis.

TOPIC	THESIS STATEMENT
Three things I would change to to improve the quality of life on campus	If I could change three things improve the quality of life on campus, I would expand the food choices, decrease class size in first-year courses, and ship some of my classmates to the North Pole.
The campus recycling	The recycling project recently project begun on our campus should be promoted more actively.

Like a topic sentence in a paragraph, a thesis statement in an essay tells readers what to expect. An effective thesis statement has two important characteristics.

1. *An effective thesis statement makes a point about a topic, expressing the writer's opinion or unique view of the topic. For this reason, it must do more than state a fact or announce what you plan to write about.*

   STATEMENT OF FACT   Many older students are returning to school.

   ANNOUNCEMENT   In this essay, I will discuss older students going back to school.

A statement of fact is not an effective thesis statement because it gives you nothing to develop in your essay. After all, how much can you say about the *fact* that many older students are returning to school? Likewise, an announcement of what you plan to discuss gives readers no indication of the position you will take on your topic. Remember, an effective thesis statement makes a point.

2. *An effective thesis statement is clearly worded and specific.*

   VAGUE THESIS STATEMENT   Returning to school is difficult for older students.

A vague thesis statement gives readers no sense of the ideas the essay will discuss. It does not say, for example, *why* returning to school is difficult for older students. Remember, an effective thesis statement is specific.

FYI

Evaluating Your Thesis Statement

Once you have a thesis statement, you need to evaluate it to determine if it is effective. Asking the following questions will help you decide.

- Is your thesis statement a complete sentence?

- Does your thesis statement clearly express the main idea you will discuss in your essay?

- Is your thesis statement specific and focused? Does it make a point that you can cover within your time and page limits?

- Does your thesis statement make a point about your topic—not just state a fact or announce what you plan to write about?

- Does your thesis statement avoid vague language?

- Does your thesis statement avoid statements like "I think" or "In my opinion"?

After freewriting, brainstorming, and reviewing his journal entries, Jared decided on a topic and wrote the following effective thesis statement for his essay.

EFFECTIVE THESIS STATEMENT   Although I realized it would be difficult in some ways, I decided that if I really wanted to attend college full-time, I could.

Jared knew that his thesis statement had to be a complete sentence that made a point about his topic and that it should be both clearly worded and specific. When he reviewed his thesis statement, he felt sure that it satisfied these criteria and expressed an idea he could develop in his essay.

PRACTICE

13-5   In the space provided, indicate whether each of the following items is a statement of fact (*F*), an announcement (*A*), a vague statement (*VS*), or an effective thesis (*ET*).

Examples

My drive to school takes more than an hour. _____*F*_____

I hate my commute between home and school. _____*VS*_____

1. Students who must commute a long distance to school are at a disadvantage compared to students who live close by. _____

2. In this paper, I will discuss cheating. _____

3. Schools should establish specific policies to discourage students from cheating. _____

4. Cheating is a problem. _____

5. Television commercials are designed to sell products. _____

6. I would like to explain why some television commercials are funny. _____

7. Single parents have a rough time. _____

8. Young people are starting to abuse alcohol and drugs at earlier ages than in the past. _____

9. Alcohol and drug abuse are both major problems in our society. _____

10. Families can do several things to help children avoid alcohol and drugs. _____

PRACTICE

13-6 Rewrite the following vague thesis statements to make them effective.

Example

My relatives are funny.

Rewrite: _My relatives think they are funny, but sometimes their humor_

can be offensive.

1. Online courses have advantages.

2. Airport security is more trouble than it is worth.

3. Athletes are paid too much.

4. Many people get their identities from their cars.

5. Cheating in college is out of control.

PRACTICE

13-7 Read the following groups of statements. Then, write a thesis statement that could express the main point of each group.

1. Thesis statement: _____

_____

- *Gap year* is a term that refers to a year that students take off before they go to college.
- Many college students spend most of their time studying and socializing with their peers.
- Studies show that high school students who take a year off before they go to college get better grades.
- Many students take community-service jobs in order to broaden their interests and to increase their social awareness.

2. Thesis statement: _____

_____

- Some people post too much personal information on social-networking sites.
- Child predators frequently use social-networking sites to find their victims.
- Some experts believe that people can become addicted to social-networking sites.
- Employers have fired employees because of information they have seen on their employees' social-networking sites.

3. Thesis statement: _____

_____

- A student at Indiana University at Bloomington was able to create her own major in environmental ethics.

- Drexel University has begun recruiting students who would design their own majors.
- Some students get bored with traditional majors that force them to choose from a rigid list of courses.
- Many employers are impressed with students who design their own majors.

state your thesis

Review your freewriting, brainstorming, and journal entries. Then, write a thesis statement for your essay.

STEP 2: ORGANIZING

13e   Choosing Supporting Points

Once you have decided on a thesis statement, look over your freewriting, brainstorming, and journal entries again. Identify **evidence** (details and examples) that best supports your thesis.

Jared made the following list of possible supporting points about his decision to go back to school. When he reviewed his list, he crossed out several points that he thought would not support his thesis.

Deciding to Go Back to School: Pros and Cons

Money a problem

Other students a lot younger

Paying tuition—how?

No one in family went to college

Friends not in college

Couldn't see myself in college

~~Considered going to trade school~~

~~Computer programmer?~~

Grades bad in high school

Wondered if I would get in

Found out about community college

Admission requirements not bad

Afraid—too old, looking dumb

~~Took time to get used to routine~~

(continued)

(continued from previous page)

Found other students like me

Like studying

Jared's list of supporting points

PRACTICE

13-8 Review Jared's list of supporting points. Do you see any crossed-out points that you think he should have kept? Do you see any other points he should have crossed out?

13f Making an Outline

After you have selected the points you think will best support your thesis, make an **informal outline**. Begin by arranging your supporting points into groups. Then, arrange the groups in the order in which you will discuss them (for example, from general to specific, or from least to most important). Arrange the supporting points for each group in the same way. (As you construct your outline, you will probably think of additional ideas.) This informal outline can guide you as you write.

When Jared looked over his list of supporting points, he saw that they fell into three groups of excuses for not going back to school: not being able to pay tuition, not being a good student in high school, and not being able to picture himself in college. He arranged his points under these three headings, adding some new ideas as he thought of them, to create the following informal outline.

Excuse 1: Not being able to pay tuition

Needed to work to live

Didn't have much money saved

Found out about community college (low tuition)

Found out about grants, loans

Excuse 2: Not being a good student in high school

Got bad grades in high school: wasn't motivated and didn't work

Looked into admission requirements at community college—doable!

Made a commitment to improve study habits

Excuse 3: Not being able to picture myself in college

No college graduates in family

Friends not in college

Afraid of being too old, looking dumb

Found other students like me

Found out I like studying

Jared's informal outline

PRACTICE

13-9 Look over Jared's informal outline. Do you think his arrangement is effective? Can you suggest any other ways he might have arranged his points?

FYI

Preparing a Formal Outline

An **informal outline**—like the one Jared prepared—is usually all you need to plan a short essay. However, some writers—especially when they are planning a longer, more detailed essay—prefer to use formal outlines.

Formal outlines use a combination of numbered and lettered headings to show the relationships among ideas. For example, the most important (and most general) ideas are assigned a Roman numeral; the next most important ideas are assigned capital letters. Each level develops the idea above it, and each new level is indented.

Here is a formal outline of the points that Jared planned to discuss in his essay.

Thesis statement: Although I realized it would be difficult in some ways, I decided that if I really wanted to attend college full-time, I could.

I. Difficulty: Money
   A. Needed to work to live
   B. Didn't have much money saved
   C. Found out about community college (low tuition)
   D. Found out about grants/loans
II. Difficulty: Academic record
   A. Got bad grades in high school
      1. Didn't care
      2. Didn't work
   B. Found out about reasonable admission requirements at community college
   C. Committed to improving study habits
III. Difficulty: Imagining myself as a student
   A. Had no college graduates in family
   B. Had no friends who went to college
   C. Felt anxious
      1. Too old
      2. Out of practice at school
   D. Found other students like me
   E. Discovered I like studying

make an outline

Review the freewriting, brainstorming, and journal entries you wrote. Then, list the points you plan to use to support your thesis statement. Cross out any points that do not support your thesis statement. Finally, group the remaining points into an informal outline that will guide you as you write.

STEP 3: DRAFTING

13g   Drafting Your Essay

After you have decided on a thesis for your essay and have arranged your supporting points in the order in which you will discuss them, you are ready to draft your essay.

At this stage of the writing process, you should not worry about spelling or grammar or about composing a perfect introduction or conclusion. Your main goal is to get your ideas down so that you can react to them. Remember that the draft you are writing will be revised, so leave extra space between lines as you type. Follow your outline, but don't hesitate to depart from it if you think of new points.

As you draft your essay, be sure that it has a **thesis-and-support** structure—that it states a thesis and supports it with evidence. Include a **working title**—a temporary title that you will revise later to accurately reflect the content of your completed essay. This working title will help you focus your ideas.

Following is the first draft of Jared's essay.

Going Back to School

I was out of school for six years after I graduated from high school. The decision to return to school was one I had a lot of difficulty making. I had been around enough to know that without more education, I'd never get anywhere in life, but I always found reasons for not taking the plunge. However, after a lot of thinking, I realized that my reasons for not going to college were just excuses. Although I realized it would be difficult in some ways, I decided that if I really wanted to attend college full-time, I could.

My first excuse for not going to college was that I couldn't afford to go to school full-time. I had worked since I finished high school, but I hadn't put much money away. I kept wondering how I would pay for books and tuition. I needed to support myself and pay for rent, food, and car expenses. I was working as a house painter, and a house I was painting belonged to a college instructor. Painting wasn't hard work, but it was boring. I'd start in the morning and work without a break until lunch. We began talking. When I told him about my situation, he told me I should look at our local community college. He also told me about some loans and grants I'd probably be able to apply for. I went online and looked at the college's website. I found out that tuition was one hundred dollars a credit, less than I thought it would be. If I got just one of the grants he mentioned, I might be able to make it.

Now that I had taken care of my first excuse, I had to deal with my second—that I hadn't been a good student in high school. When I was a teenager, I didn't care much about school. School bored me to death. Probably as a result, I got bad grades. Now that I was considering going back to school, though, I wondered what price I would have to pay for my laziness and immaturity. The answer to this question was not as bad as I thought it would be. According to the community college's website, all I needed to be admitted was a high school diploma and county residence. I would have to take some placement tests, but I would be judged on my ability, not my high school grades. I knew I could do better if I made a real effort to study harder and smarter. The website was easy to navigate, and I had no problem finding information.

I had a hard time picturing myself in college. No one in my family had ever gone to college. My friends were just like me; they all went to work right after high school. I had no role model or mentor who could give me advice. I thought I was just too old for college. After all, I was probably at least six years older than most of the students. How would I be able to keep up with the younger students in the class? I hadn't opened a textbook in years, and I'd never really learned how to study. Most of my fears disappeared during my first few weeks of classes. I saw a lot of students who were as old as I was, and some were even older. Studying didn't seem to be a problem, either. I actually enjoyed learning. History, which had put me to sleep in high school, suddenly became interesting. So did math and English. It soon became clear to me that I was going to like being in college.

Going to college as a full-time student has changed my life, both personally and financially. I am no longer the same person I was in high school. I allowed laziness and insecurity to hold me back. Now, I have options that I didn't have before. When I graduate from community college, I plan to transfer to the state university and get a four-year degree.

Jared's first draft

PRACTICE

13-10   Reread Jared's first draft. What changes would you suggest? What might he have added? What might he have deleted? Which of his supporting details and examples do you find most effective?

draft your essay

Draft an essay about your most difficult job. When you finish your draft, give your essay a working title.

STEP 4: TESTING AND REVISING

When you revise your essay, you do not simply correct errors; instead, you resee, rethink, reevaluate, and rewrite your work. Some of the changes you make—such as adding, deleting, or rearranging sentences or even whole paragraphs—will be major. Others will be minor—for example, adding or deleting words or phrases.

Before you begin revising, put your essay aside for a while. This "cooling-off" period allows you to see your draft more objectively when you return to it. When you are ready to revise, keep in mind that the revision process is usually not an orderly one. It is a good idea, therefore, to revise on hard copy rather than on a computer screen. On hard copy, you are able to see a full page—or even two or three pages next to each other—as you revise. Revising on hard copy also gives you more options for interacting with your draft: you can draw arrows, underline, cross out, and write above lines and in the margins. When you have finished, you can type your changes into your document. Be careful, though, not to permanently delete sentences or paragraphs until you are certain you do not need them. Instead, move unwanted material to the end of your draft—or save multiple, dated drafts.

13h   TESTing Your Essay

Just as you **TEST** your paragraphs as you begin revising, you should also **TEST** your essays. **TEST**ing will tell you whether your essay includes the basic elements it needs to be effective.

T hesis Statement
E vidence
S ummary Statement
T ransitions

TESTing for a Thesis

The first thing you do when you **TEST** your essay is to make sure it has a clear **thesis statement (T)** that identifies the essay's main idea. By stating the main idea, your thesis statement helps to unify your essay.

When Jared **TEST**ed the draft of his essay, he decided that his thesis statement clearly stated his main idea. (His marginal note appears below.)

T **E** **S** **T**
- Thesis Statement
- Evidence
- Summary Statement
- Transitions

Jared's Introduction

I was out of school for six years after I graduated from high school. The decision to return to school was one I had a lot of difficulty making. I had been around enough to know that without more education, I'd never get anywhere in life, but I always found reasons for not taking the plunge. However, after a lot of thinking, I realized that my reasons for not going to college were just excuses. Although I realized it would be difficult in some ways, I decided that if I really wanted to attend college full-time, I could.

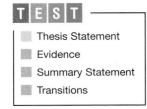

Thesis clearly states what I want to say about going to college.

TESTing for Evidence

The next thing you do when you TEST your essay is to check your **evidence** (E) to make sure that the body of your essay includes enough examples and details to support your thesis. Remember that without evidence, your essay is simply a series of unsupported general statements. A well-developed essay includes enough evidence to explain, illustrate, and clarify the points you are making.

When Jared TESTed his draft for evidence, he decided that he should add more examples and details in his body paragraphs and delete some irrelevant ones. (His marginal notes appear below.)

Jared's Body Paragraphs

My first excuse for not going to college was that I couldn't afford to go to school full-time. I had worked since I finished high school, but I hadn't put much money away. I kept wondering how I would pay for books and tuition. I needed to support myself and pay for rent, food, and car expenses. I was working as a house painter, and a house I was painting belonged to a college instructor. Painting wasn't hard work, but it was boring. I'd start in the morning and work without a break until lunch. We began talking. When I told him about my situation, he told me I should look at our local community college. He also told me about some loans and grants I'd probably be able to apply for. I went online and looked at the college's website. I found out that tuition was one hundred dollars a credit, less than I thought it would be. If I got just one of the grants he mentioned, I might be able to make it.

Now that I had taken care of my first excuse, I had to deal with my second—that I hadn't been a good student in high school. When I was a teenager, I didn't care much about school. School bored me to death. Probably as a result, I got bad grades. Now that I was considering going back to school, though, I wondered what price I would have to pay for my laziness and immaturity. The answer to this question was not as bad as I thought it would be. According to the community college's website, all I needed to be admitted was a high school diploma and county residence. I would have to take some placement tests, but I would be judged on my ability, not my high school grades. I knew I could do better if I made a real effort to study harder and smarter. The website was easy to navigate, and I had no problem finding information.

I had a hard time picturing myself in college. My friends were just like me; they all went to work right after high school. I had no role model or mentor who could give me advice. I thought I was just too old for college. After all, I was probably at least six years older than most of the students. How would I be able to keep up with the younger students in the class? I hadn't opened a textbook for years, and I'd never really learned how to study. Most of my fears disappeared during my first few weeks of classes. I saw a lot of students who were as old as I was, and some were even older. Studying didn't seem to be a problem, either. I actually enjoyed learning. History, which had put me to sleep in high school, suddenly became interesting. So did math and English. It soon became clear to me that I was going to like being in college.

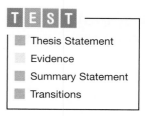

- Thesis Statement
- Evidence
- Summary Statement
- Transitions

Are details about painting necessary?

Add more about how I thought I could cover the tuition.

Give examples of boredom.

Are details about website relevant?

Evidence seems OK here

TESTing for a Summary Statement

The third thing you do when you TEST your essay is to look at your conclusion and make sure that it includes a **summary statement (S)**. Most often, your conclusion will begin with this statement, which reinforces your essay's thesis. By reinforcing your thesis, this summary statement helps to **unify** your essay.

When Jared TESTed his draft for a summary statement, he thought that his summary statement adequately reinforced the main idea of his essay. (His marginal note appears below.)

T E S T
- Thesis Statement
- Evidence
- Summary Statement
- Transitions

Conclusion is kind of short, but summary statement is OK.

Jared's Conclusion

Going to college as a full-time student has changed my life, both personally and financially. I am no longer the same person I was in high school. I allowed laziness and insecurity to hold me back. Now, I have options that I didn't have before. When I graduate from community college, I plan to transfer to the state university and get a four-year degree.

TESTing for Transitions

The last thing you do when you TEST your essay is to make sure that it includes **transitions (T)**—words and phrases that connect your ideas. Make sure you have included all the transitions you need to tell readers how one sentence (or paragraph) is connected to another. Including transitions makes your essay **coherent**, with its sentences arranged in a clear, logical sequence that helps readers understand your ideas.

By linking sentences and paragraphs, transitions emphasize the relationship between ideas and help readers understand your essay's logic. By reminding readers of what has come before, transitions prepare readers for new information and help them understand how it fits into the discussion. In this sense, transitions are the glue that holds the ideas in your essay together.

Transitions are categorized according to their function. For example, they may indicate **time order** (*first, second, now, next, finally,* and so on), **spatial order** (*above, behind, near, next to, over,* and so on), or **logical order** (*also, although, therefore, in fact,* and so on). (For a full list of transitions, see 3d.)

When Jared TESTed his draft for transitions, he realized that although he had included some transitional words and phrases, he needed to add more of them to connect his ideas. (His marginal notes appear below and on the following pages.)

Jared's Thesis + Body Paragraphs

Although I realized it would be difficult in some ways, I decided that if I really wanted to attend college full-time, I could.

My first excuse for not going to college was that I couldn't afford to go to school full-time. I had worked since I finished high school, but I hadn't put much money away. I kept wondering how I would pay for books and tuition. I needed to support myself and pay for rent, food, and car expenses. I was working as a house painter, and a house I was painting belonged to a college instructor. Painting wasn't hard work, but it was boring. I'd start in the morning and work without a break until lunch. We began talking. When I told him

Need to show relationship between ideas in this paragraph.

about my situation, he told me I should look at our local community college. He also told me about some loans and grants I'd probably be able to apply for. I went online and looked at the college's website. I found out that tuition was one hundred dollars a credit, less than I thought it would be. If I got just one of the grants he mentioned, I might be able to make it.

Now that I had taken care of my first excuse, I had to deal with my second—that I hadn't been a good student in high school. When I was a teenager, I didn't care much about school. School bored me to death. Probably as a result, I got bad grades. Now that I was considering going back to school, though, I wondered what price I would have to pay for my laziness and immaturity. The answer to this question was not as bad as I thought it would be. According to the community college's website, all I needed to be admitted was a high school diploma and county residence. I would have to take some placement tests, but I would be judged on my ability, not my high school grades. I knew I could do better if I made a real effort to study harder and smarter. The website was easy to navigate, and I had no problem finding information.

I had a hard time picturing myself in college. No one in my family had ever gone to college. My friends were just like me; they all went to work right after high school. I had no role model or mentor who could give me advice. I thought I was just too old for college. After all, I was probably at least six years older than most of the students. How would I be able to keep up with the younger students in the class? I hadn't opened a textbook in years, and I'd never really learned how to study. Most of my fears disappeared during my first few weeks of classes. I saw a lot of students who were as old as I was, and some were even older. Studying didn't seem to be a problem, either. I actually enjoyed learning. History, which had put me to sleep in high school, suddenly became interesting. So did math and English. It soon became clear to me that I was going to like being in college.

Add better transition between these two paragraphs.

Add transition here.

TEST

- [ ] Thesis Statement
- [x] Evidence
- [x] Summary Statement
- [ ] Transitions

TEST your essay

TEST your draft to make sure it includes all the elements of an effective essay. If any elements are missing, add them.

13i   Revising Your Essay

Once you have **TEST**ed your essay, there are a number of additional strategies you can use as you continue to revise. The following chart lists these revision strategies and explains the advantages of each one.

STRATEGIES FOR REVISING

STRATEGY	ADVANTAGES
FACE-TO-FACE CONFERENCE WITH INSTRUCTOR	▪ Provides one-to-one feedback that can't be obtained in the classroom ▪ Builds a student-teacher relationship ▪ Enables students to collaborate with their instructors ▪ Allows students to ask questions they might not ask in a classroom setting
WRITING CENTER	▪ Offers students a less formal, less stressful environment than an instructor conference ▪ Enables students to get help from trained tutors (both students and professionals) ▪ Provides a perspective other than the instructor's ▪ Offers specialized help to students whose first language is not English
PEER REVIEW	▪ Enables students working on the same assignment to share insights with one another ▪ Gives students the experience of writing for a real audience ▪ Gives students several different readers' reactions to their work ▪ Enables students to benefit from the ideas of their classmates
ELECTRONIC COMMUNICATION WITH INSTRUCTOR	▪ Enables students to submit email questions before a draft is due ▪ Gives students quick answers to their questions ▪ Enables instructors to give feedback by annotating drafts electronically ▪ Enables students to react to their instructor's responses when they have time ▪ Eliminates time spent traveling to instructor's office
REVISION CHECKLIST	▪ Gives students a tool that enables them to revise in an orderly way ▪ Enables students to learn to revise independently ▪ Enables students to focus on specific aspects of their writing

FYI

Getting the Most Out of a Conference

If you need help at any point in the writing process, you can get it from your instructor or from a tutor in your school's writing center. Following these guidelines will help you get the most out of your conference.

- Make an appointment in advance, either by phone or by email.
- Arrive on time; instructors and tutors often schedule several appointments in a row, and if you are late, you may miss your appointment entirely.
- Bring a copy of your assignment.
- Bring all drafts and prewriting notes for the assignment you are working on.
- Bring a list of specific questions you would like the instructor or tutor to answer.
- Pay attention, ask your questions, and be sure you understand the answers.
- Write the instructor's or tutor's suggestions directly on your latest draft.
- Schedule a follow-up appointment if necessary.

Remember, your instructor or tutor will answer questions and make recommendations, but he or she will *not* revise or edit your work for you. That is your job.

self-assessment checklist

Revising Your Essay

- [ ] Does your essay have an introduction, a body, and a conclusion?
- [ ] Does your introduction include a clearly worded thesis statement that states your essay's main idea?
- [ ] Does each body paragraph have a topic sentence?
- [ ] Does each topic sentence introduce a point that supports the thesis?
- [ ] Does each body paragraph include enough examples and details to support the topic sentence?
- [ ] Are your body paragraphs unified, well developed, and coherent?
- [ ] Does your conclusion include a concluding statement that restates your thesis or sums up your main idea?

When Jared finished **TEST**ing his essay, he decided to arrange a conference with his instructor to discuss further revisions. He made sure to follow the guidelines in the FYI box above in order to get the most out of the conference. After the conference, Jared continued revising his essay, using the Self-Assessment Checklist on page 163 to guide him.

Jared's revised first draft, with his handwritten revisions, appears on the following pages.

<del>Going Back to School</del> Starting Over

The other day, my sociology instructor mentioned that half the students enrolled in college programs across the country are twenty-five or older. His remark caught my attention because I am one of those students.

I was out of school for six years after I graduated from high school. The decision to return to school was one I had a lot of difficulty making. I had been around enough to know that without more education, I'd never get anywhere in life, but I always found reasons for not taking the plunge. However, after a lot of thinking, I realized that my reasons for not going to college were just excuses. Although I realized it would be difficult in some ways, I decided that if I really wanted to attend college full-time, I could.

My first excuse for not going to college was that I couldn't afford to go to school full-time. I had worked since I finished high school, but I hadn't put much money away. I kept wondering how I would pay for books and tuition. I also needed to support myself and pay for rent, food, and car expenses. The solution to my problem came unexpectedly. I was working as a house painter, and a house I was painting belonged to a college instructor. <del>Painting wasn't hard work, but it was boring. I'd start in the morning and work without a break until lunch.</del> During a lunch break, we began talking. When I told him about my situation, he told me I should look at our local community college. He also told me about some loans and grants I'd probably be able to apply for. Later, I went online and looked at the college's website. I found out that tuition was one hundred dollars a credit, less than I thought it would be. If I got just one of the grants he mentioned, I might be able to make it.

The money I'd saved, along with what I could make painting houses on the weekends, could get me through.

In class, I would stare out the window or watch the second hand on the clock move slowly around. I never bothered with homework. School just didn't interest me.

Now that I had taken care of my first excuse, I had to deal with my second—that I hadn't been a good student in high school. When I was a teenager, I didn't care much about school. In fact, school <del>School</del> bored me <del>to death</del>. Probably as a result, I got bad grades. Now that I was considering going back to school, though, I wondered what price I would have to pay for my laziness and immaturity. The answer to this question was not as bad as I thought it would be. According to the community college's website, all I needed to be admitted was a high school diploma and county residence. I would have to take some placement tests, but I would be judged on my ability, not my high school grades. I knew I could do better if I made a real effort to study harder and smarter. ~~The website was easy to navigate, and I had no problem finding information.~~

My biggest problem still bothered me:
∧ I had a hard time picturing myself in college. No one in my family had ever gone to college. My friends were just like me; they all went to work right after high school. I had no role model or mentor who could give me advice. Besides,
∧ I thought I was just too old for college. After all, I was probably at least six years older than most of the students. How would I be able to keep up with the younger students in the class? I hadn't opened a textbook in years, and I'd never really learned how to study. However, most ~~Most~~
∧ of my fears disappeared during my first few weeks of classes. I saw a lot of students who were as old as I was, and some were even older. Studying didn't seem to be a problem, either. I actually enjoyed learning. For example, history,
~~History,~~ which had put me to sleep in high school, suddenly became interesting.
∧ So did math and English. It soon became clear to me that I was going to like being in college.

Going to college as a full-time student has changed my life, both personally and financially. I am no longer the same person I was in high school. In the past,
∧ I allowed laziness and insecurity to hold me back. Now, I have options that I didn't have before. When I graduate from community college, I plan to transfer to the state university and get a four-year degree. The other day, one of my instructors asked me if I had ever considered becoming a teacher. The truth is, I never had, but now I might. I'd like to be able to give students like me the tough, realistic advice I wish someone had given me.

PRACTICE

13-11   Working in a group of three or four students, answer the following questions.

- What kind of material did Jared add to his draft?
- What did he delete?
- Why do you think he made these changes?
- Do you agree with the changes he made?

Be prepared to discuss your reactions to these changes with the class.

revise your essay

Using one or two of the additional revision strategies from the chart on page 162, continue revising your essay.

STEP 5: EDITING AND PROOFREADING

13j Editing Your Essay

When you **edit** your essay, you check grammar and sentence structure. Then, you look at punctuation, mechanics, and spelling. As you edit, think carefully about the questions in the following Self-Assessment Checklist. (If you have not already chosen a final title for your essay, this is a good time to do so.)

self-assessment checklist

Editing Your Essay

EDITING FOR COMMON SENTENCE PROBLEMS

- Have you avoided run-ons? (See Chapter 23.)

- Have you avoided sentence fragments? (See Chapter 24.)

- Do your subjects and verbs agree? (See Chapter 25.)

- Have you avoided illogical shifts? (See Chapter 26.)

- Have you avoided misplaced and dangling modifiers? (See Chapter 27.)

EDITING FOR GRAMMAR

- Are your verb forms and verb tenses correct? (See Chapters 28 and 29.)

- Have you used nouns and pronouns correctly? (See Chapter 30.)

- Have you used adjectives and adverbs correctly? (See Chapter 31.)

EDITING FOR PUNCTUATION, MECHANICS, AND SPELLING

- Have you used commas correctly? (See Chapter 33.)

- Have you used apostrophes correctly? Have you avoided contractions, which are usually too informal for college writing? (See Chapter 34.)

- Have you used capital letters where they are required? (See 35a.)

- Have you used quotation marks correctly where they are needed? (See 35b.)

13k Proofreading Your Essay

When you proofread, you check for typos, proper formatting, and anything you might have missed while you were editing. Remember that your spell checker and grammar checker are helpful, but they can also introduce errors into your essay. As you proofread, be sure to double-check the spelling of any words whose spelling you are unsure of. It is also a good idea to print your essay and proofread on hard copy because it is easy to miss typos and other small errors on a computer screen. After you have checked for typos and other lingering errors, check your essay's format.

The **format** of an essay is the way it looks on a page—for example, the size of the margins, the placement of page numbers, and the amount of space between lines. Most instructors expect you to follow a certain format when you type an essay. The model essay format illustrated below is commonly used in composition classes. Before you hand in an essay, you should make sure that it follows this model (or the format your instructor requires.)

Essay Format Sample

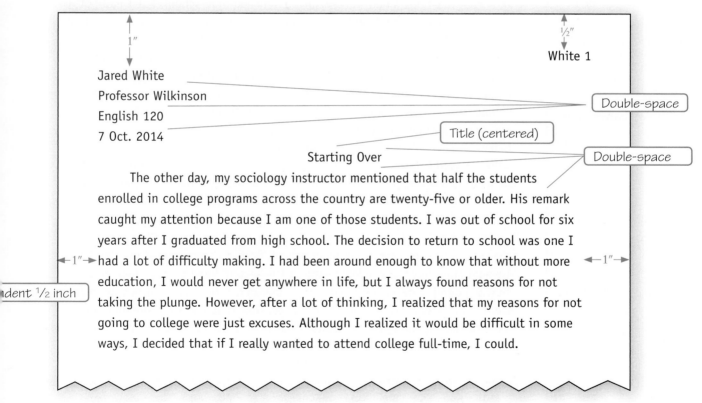

1"

½"

White 1

Jared White

Professor Wilkinson   Double-space

English 120

7 Oct. 2014

Title (centered)

Starting Over   Double-space

　　The other day, my sociology instructor mentioned that half the students enrolled in college programs across the country are twenty-five or older. His remark caught my attention because I am one of those students. I was out of school for six years after I graduated from high school. The decision to return to school was one I had a lot of difficulty making. I had been around enough to know that without more education, I would never get anywhere in life, but I always found reasons for not taking the plunge. However, after a lot of thinking, I realized that my reasons for not going to college were just excuses. Although I realized it would be difficult in some ways, I decided that if I really wanted to attend college full-time, I could.

1"→ ←1"→

dent ½ inch

Note: The bottom margin of each page should be one inch.

　　When his revisions were complete, Jared edited and proofread his essay, deleting all the contractions, which he thought made his serious essay sound too informal. The final version of his essay appears on pages 168–169. (Marginal annotations have been added to highlight key features of his essay.) Note that the final draft includes all the elements Jared looked for when he **TEST**ed his essay.

T E S T

- Thesis Statement
- Evidence
- Summary Statement
- Transitions

Jared White

Professor Wilkinson

English 120

7 Oct. 2014

Starting Over

Introduction

The other day, my sociology instructor mentioned that half the students enrolled in college programs across the country are twenty-five or older. His remark caught my attention because I am one of those students. I was out of school for six years after I graduated from high school. The decision to return to school was one I had a lot of difficulty making. I had been around enough to know that without more education, I would never get anywhere in life, but I always found reasons for not taking the plunge. However, after a lot of thinking, I realized that my reasons for not going to college were just excuses. Although I realized it would be difficult in some ways, I decided that if I really wanted to attend college full-time, I could.

Topic sentence (first point)

Examples and details

Body paragraphs

My first excuse for not going to college was that I could not afford to go to school full-time. I had worked since I finished high school, but I had not put much money away. I kept wondering how I would pay for books and tuition. I also needed to support myself and pay for rent, food, and car expenses. The solution to my problem came unexpectedly. I was working as a house painter, and a house I was painting belonged to a college instructor. During a lunch break, we began talking. When I told him about my situation, he told me I should look at our local community college. He also told me about some loans and grants I would probably be able to apply for. Later, I went online and looked at the college's website. I found out that tuition was one hundred dollars a credit, less than I thought it would be. If I got just one of the grants he mentioned, I might be able to make it. The money I had saved, along with what I could make painting houses on the weekends, could get me through.

Topic sentence (second point)

Examples and details

Now that I had taken care of my first excuse, I had to deal with my second—that I had not been a good student in high school. When I was a teenager, I did not care much about school. In fact, school bored me. In class, I would stare out the window or watch the second hand on the clock move slowly around. I never bothered with homework. School just did not interest me. Probably as a result, I got bad grades. Now that I was considering going back to school, though, I wondered what price I would have to pay for my laziness and immaturity. The answer to this question was not as bad as I thought it would be. According to the community college's website, all I needed to be admitted was a high school diploma and county residence. I would have to take some placement tests, but I would be judged on my ability, not my high school grades. I knew I could do better if I made a real effort to study harder and smarter.

Topic sentence (third point)

My biggest problem still bothered me: I had a hard time picturing myself in college. No one in my family had ever gone to college. My friends were just like me; they all went to work right after high school. I had no role model or mentor who could give me advice. Besides, I thought I was just too old for college. After all, I was probably at least six years older than most of the students. How would I be able to keep up with the younger students in the class? I had not opened a textbook in years, and I had never really learned how to study. However, most of my fears disappeared during my first few weeks of classes. I saw a lot of students who were as old as I was, and some were even older. Studying did not seem to be a problem, either. I actually enjoyed learning. For example, history, which had put me to sleep in high school, suddenly became interesting. So did math and English. It soon became clear to me that I was going to like being in college.

Going to college as a full-time student has changed my life, both personally and financially. I am no longer the same person I was in high school. In the past, I allowed laziness and insecurity to hold me back. Now, I have options that I did not have before. When I graduate from community college, I plan to transfer to the state university and get a four-year degree. The other day, one of my instructors asked me if I had ever considered becoming a teacher. The truth is, I never had, but now I might. I would like to be able to give students like me the tough, realistic advice I wish someone had given me.

Examples and details

Body paragraphs

Conclusion

PRACTICE

13-12 Reread the final draft of Jared White's essay. Working in a group of three or four students, answer these questions.

■ Do you think this draft is an improvement over his first draft (shown on pages 156–157)?

■ What other changes could Jared have made?

Be prepared to discuss your group's answers with the class.

edit and proofread your essay

Edit your draft, using the Self-Assessment Checklist on page 166 to guide you. Then, proofread your essay for typos and other small errors. Finally, make sure your essay's format follows your instructor's guidelines.

EDITING PRACTICE

1. The following student essay is missing its thesis statement and topic sentences and has no summary statement. First, write an appropriate thesis statement on the lines provided. (Make sure your thesis statement clearly communicates the essay's main idea.) Then, fill in the topic sentences for the second, third, and fourth paragraphs. Finally, add a summary statement in the conclusion.

Preparing for a Job Interview

A lot of books and many websites give advice on how to do well on a job interview. Some recommend practicing your handshake, and others suggest making eye contact. This advice is useful, but not many books tell how to get mentally prepared for an interview. [Thesis statement:] _____

_____

_____

_____

[Topic sentence for the second paragraph:] _____

_____

_____

_____

Feeling good about how you look is important, so you should probably wear a dress or skirt (or, for males, a jacket and tie) to an interview. Even if you will not be dressing this formally on the job, try to make a good first impression. For this reason, you should never come to an interview dressed in jeans or shorts. Still, you should be careful not to overdress. For example, wearing a suit or a dressy dress to an interview at a fast-food restaurant might make you feel good, but it could also make you look as if you do not really want to work there.

[Topic sentence for the third paragraph:] _____

_____

_____

Going on an interview is a little like getting ready to compete in a sporting event. You have to go in with the right attitude. If you think you are not going to be successful, chances are that you will not be. So, before you go on any interview, spend some time building your confidence. Tell yourself that you can do the job and that you will do well in the interview. By the time you get to the interview, you will have convinced yourself that you are the right person for the job.

[Topic sentence for the fourth paragraph:] _____

_____

_____

Most people go to an interview knowing little or nothing about the job. They expect the interviewer to tell them what they will have to do. Most interviewers, however, are impressed by someone who has taken the time to do his or her homework. For this reason, you should always do some research before you go on an interview—even for a part-time job. Most of the time, your research may be nothing more than a quick look at the company's website, but this kind of research really pays off. Being able to talk about the job can give you a real advantage over other candidates. Sometimes the interviewer will be so impressed that he or she will offer you a job on the spot.

[Summary statement:] _____

_____

_____

Of course, following these suggestions will not guarantee that you get a job. You still have to do well at the interview itself. Even so, getting mentally prepared for the interview will give you an advantage over people who do almost nothing before they walk in the door.

2. Now, using the topic sentence on the following page, write another body paragraph that you could add to the preceding essay. (This new paragraph will go right before the essay's conclusion.)

Another way to prepare yourself mentally is to anticipate and answer some typical questions interviewers ask.

_____

_____

_____

_____

COLLABORATIVE ACTIVITY

Working in a group, come up with thesis statements suitable for essays on three of the following topics.

Living on a budget	Gun safety
Social-networking sites	Drawbacks of online dating
Safe driving	Patriotism
Sustainable energy	Community service
Honesty	Preparing for a test

Then, exchange your group's three thesis statements with those of another group. Choose the best one of the other group's thesis statements. A member of each group can then read the thesis statement to the class and explain why the group chose the thesis statement it did.

review checklist

Writing an Essay

- [ ] Most essays have a thesis-and-support structure. The thesis statement presents the main idea, and the body paragraphs support the thesis. (See 13a.)

- [ ] Begin by focusing on your assignment, purpose, and audience to help you find a topic. (See 13b.)

- [ ] Find ideas to write about. (See 13c.)

- [ ] Identify your main idea, and develop an effective thesis statement. (See 13d.)

- [ ] List the points that best support your thesis, and arrange them in the order in which you plan to discuss them, creating an informal outline of your essay. (See 13e and 13f.)

- [ ] Write your first draft, making sure your essay has a thesis-and-support structure. (See 13g.)

- [ ] TEST and revise your essay. (See 13h and 13i.)

- [ ] Edit and proofread your essay. (See 13j and 13k.)

14 Introductions and Conclusions

AP Photo/Jae C. Hong

write first

This picture shows firefighters battling a wildfire in the Southern California mountains. Like the oil rig workers pictured on page 139, these firefighters also have very difficult jobs. Think about what this picture suggests about the work they do, and then print out a copy of the essay you wrote for Chapter 13. At the end of this chapter, you will work on revising the introduction and conclusion of your essay.

In this chapter, you will learn to
- write an introduction (14a)
- choose a title (14a)
- write a conclusion (14b)

When you draft an essay, you usually spend the most time on the **body** because it is the section in which you develop your ideas. A well-constructed essay, however, is more than a series of body paragraphs. It also includes an **introduction** and a **conclusion**, both of which contribute to the essay's overall effectiveness.

14a   Introductions

An **introduction** is the first thing people see when they read your essay. If your introduction is interesting, it will make readers want to read further. If it is not, readers may get bored and stop reading.

Your introduction should be a full paragraph that moves from general to specific ideas. It should begin with some general **opening remarks** that will draw readers in to your essay. The **thesis statement**, a specific sentence that presents the main idea of your essay, usually comes at the end of the introduction. The following diagram illustrates the shape of an introduction.

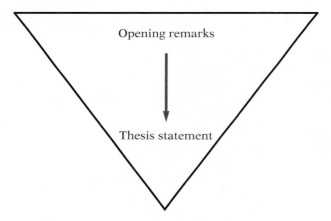

Here are some options you can experiment with when you write your introductions. (In each of the sample introductory paragraphs that follow, the thesis statement is underlined and labeled.)

Beginning with a Narrative

You can begin an essay with a narrative drawn from your own experience or from a current news event.

> On the first day my sister and I attended school in America, our parents walked us directly to the entrance of our new classroom. Even though she barely spoke any English, Mom tried earnestly to teach us how to ask for permission to use the bathroom: "Can I go to the bathroom?" Like parrots, she had us repeat

this question over and over. At the time, neither of us realized that the proper way of asking for permission is "May I go to the bathroom?" This grammar slip did not matter, though, because we forgot the question as soon as our parents left. Reluctantly, we entered the classroom, more timid than two mice trying not to awaken a sleeping cat. <u>We didn't know yet that going to school where English was the only language spoken would prove to be very difficult.</u>

Thesis statement

—Hilda Alvarado (student)

Beginning with a Question (or a Series of Questions)

Asking one or more questions at the beginning of your essay is an effective strategy. Because readers will expect you to answer the questions, they will want to read further.

Is it worth giving up a chance to go to college to make a respectable salary today? "For me it was," says Mario Sarno, general manager of Arby's store #219. At nineteen years of age, Mario looks like a salesman. He is of medium height and build and has an outgoing personality that makes him stand out. As general manager, Mario is responsible for maintaining the fast-food environment and to ensure that customers are happy. At the age of seventeen, Mario was noticed by an Arby's corporate supervisor and was promoted to manager. <u>Mario's positive experience suggests that students should consider the advantages of going directly into the job market.</u>

Thesis statement

—Lucus J. Anemone (student)

Beginning with a Definition

A definition at the beginning of your essay can give readers important information. As the following introduction shows, a definition can help explain a complicated idea or a confusing concept.

"Getting inked" is how many people refer to the act of getting a tattoo. Although some people may see it as a form of torture, tattooing is an art form that dates back hundreds of years. The craft has been more formally defined as the practice of permanently marking the skin through punctures or incisions, which receive various dyes or pigments. <u>Although Polynesian in origin, tattooing has a rich history in the United States.</u>

Thesis statement

—Kristen L. McCormack (student)

Beginning with a Quotation

An appropriate saying or some interesting dialogue can draw readers in to your essay.

According to the comedian Jerry Seinfeld, "When you're single, you are the dictator of your own life. . . . When you're married, you are part of a vast decision-making body." In other words, before you can do anything when you are married, you have to talk it over with someone else. These words kept going through my mind as I thought about asking my girlfriend to marry me.

Thesis statement

The more I thought about Seinfeld's words, the more I put off asking. <u>I never thought about the huge price that I would pay for this delay.</u>

—Dan Brody (student)

Beginning with a Surprising Statement

You can begin your essay with a surprising or unexpected statement. Because your statement takes readers by surprise, it catches their attention.

Thesis statement

Some of the smartest people I know never went to college. In fact, some of them never finished high school. They still know how to save 20 percent on the price of a dinner, fix their own faucets when they leak, get discounted prescriptions, get free rides on a bus to Atlantic City, use public transportation to get anywhere in the city, and live on about twenty-two dollars a day. Some people would call them old and poor, but I would call them survivors who have learned to make it through life on nothing but a Social Security check. <u>These survivors are my grandparents' friends, and they have taught me many things I cannot learn in school.</u>

—Sean Ragas (student)

FYI

What to Avoid in Introductions

When writing an introduction, avoid the following.

- Beginning your essay by announcing what you plan to write about

  PHRASES TO AVOID

  This essay is about . . .
  In my essay, I will discuss . . .

- Apologizing for your ideas

  PHRASES TO AVOID

  Although I don't know much about this subject . . .
  I might not be an expert, but . . .

FYI

Choosing a Title

Every essay should have a **title** that suggests the subject of the essay and makes people want to read it. Here are a few tips for properly formatting your title.

- Capitalize all words except for articles (*a, an, the*), prepositions (*at, to, of, around,* and so on), and coordinating conjunctions (*and, but,* and so on), unless they are the first or last word of the title.

■ Do not underline or italicize your title or enclose it in quotation marks. Do not type your title in all capital letters.

■ Center the title at the top of the first page. Double-space between the title and the first line of your essay.

As you consider a title for your paper, think about the following options.

■ *A title can highlight a key word or term that appears in the essay.*
Don't Call Me a Hot Tamale
Fish Cheeks

■ *A title can be a straightforward announcement or a command.*
No, I Do Not Want to Pet Your Dog
Tweet Less, Kiss More

■ *A title can establish a personal connection with readers.*
The Men We Carry in Our Minds
How Facebook Is Making Friending Obsolete

■ *A title can be a familiar saying or a quotation from your essay itself.*
Slice of Life
I Want a Wife

PRACTICE

14-1   Look through the student essays in Chapter 15, and find one introduction you think is particularly effective. Be prepared to explain the strengths of the introduction you choose.

PRACTICE

14-2   Using the different options for creating titles discussed in the FYI box on pages 176–177, write two titles for each of the essays described below.

1. A student writes an essay about three people who disappeared mysteriously: Amelia Earhart, aviator; Ambrose Bierce, writer; and Jimmy Hoffa, union leader. In the body paragraphs, the student describes the circumstances surrounding their disappearances.

_____

_____

2. A student writes an essay describing the harmful effects of steroids on student athletes. In the body paragraphs, he shows the effects on the heart, brain, and other organs.

_____

_____

3. A student writes an essay explaining why she joined the Navy Reserve. In the body paragraphs, she discusses her need to earn money for college tuition, her wish to learn a trade, and her desire to see the world.

_____

_____

14b Conclusions

Because your conclusion is the last thing readers see, they often judge your entire essay by its effectiveness. For this reason, conclusions should be planned, drafted, and revised carefully.

Like an introduction, a **conclusion** should be a full paragraph. It should begin with a **summary statement** that reinforces the essay's main idea, and it should end with some general **concluding remarks**. The following diagram illustrates the general shape of a conclusion.

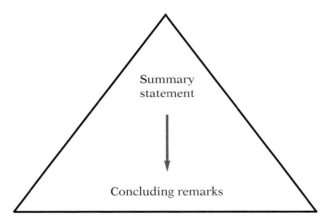

Here are some options you can experiment with when you write your conclusions. (In each of the sample concluding paragraphs that follow, the summary statement is underlined and labeled.)

Concluding with a Narrative

A narrative conclusion can bring an event discussed in the essay to a logical, satisfying close.

Summary statement

> I went to Philadelphia with my boys to share the thing my father and I had shared—a love of history. Unfortunately, they were more interested in horse-and-buggy rides, overpriced knickknacks, the tall buildings, and parades. As we walked into Independence Hall, though, I noticed that the boys became quiet. They felt it. They felt the thick historical air around us. I watched them look around as the guide painted a vivid picture of the times and spoke of the marches down Broad Street and the clashing of ideas as our forefathers debated and even fought for freedom. I felt my husband behind me and took my eyes off of my boys to turn to the left; I could almost see my father. I almost whispered out loud to him, "We were here."
>
> —Shannon Lewis (student)

Concluding with a Recommendation

Once you think you have convinced readers that a problem exists, you can make recommendations in your conclusion about how the problem should be solved.

Solutions for the binge-drinking problem on college campuses are not easy, but both schools and students need to acknowledge the problem and to try to solve it. Schools that have an alcohol-free policy should aggressively enforce it, and schools that do not have such a policy should implement one. In addition, students should take responsibility for their actions and resolve to drink responsibly. No one should get hurt or die from drinking too much, but if something does not change soon, many more students will.

Summary statement

—April Moen (student)

Concluding with a Quotation

A well-chosen quotation—even a brief one—can be an effective concluding strategy. In the following paragraph, the quotation reinforces the main idea of the essay.

I'll never forget the day I caught the ball on a penalty kick, winning the game for my team. My opponent's foot made contact with the ball, and everything around me fell silent. The ball came at me, hurtling over my head toward the top right of the goal. As I dived to catch it, I closed my eyes. The ball smacked into my hands so hard I thought it must have split my gloves. When I opened my eyes, I realized that I had caught the ball and saved the game for our team. The crowd cheered wildly, and my team surrounded me as I got to my feet. As the celebration died down, my coach walked up to me and, as I handed him the game-winning ball, said, "To the playoffs we go!"

Summary statement

—Jacob Kinley (student)

Concluding with a Prediction

This type of conclusion not only sums up the thesis but also looks to the future.

Whether people like it or not, texting is not going to go away anytime soon. This generation and future generations are going to use "text speak" and become even more comfortable with communicating via text messages. Texting has already had a large impact on today's world. In fact, texting has helped put the written word back into our lives, making people more comfortable with the skill of writing. & it's a fast, EZ way 2 communic8.

Summary statement

—Courtney Anttila (student)

FYI

What to Avoid in Conclusions

When writing a conclusion, avoid the following.

- Introducing new ideas; your conclusion should sum up the ideas you discuss in your essay, not open up new lines of thought
- Apologizing for your opinions, ideas, or conclusions; apologies will undercut your readers' confidence in you

(continued)

(continued from previous page)

PHRASES TO AVOID

At least that is my opinion . . .
I could be wrong, but . . .

■ Using unnecessary phrases to announce your essay is coming to a close.

PHRASES TO AVOID

In summary, . . .
In conclusion, . . .

PRACTICE

14-3   Look at the student essays in Chapter 15, and locate one conclusion you think is particularly effective. Be prepared to explain the strengths of the conclusion you choose.

TEST · Revise · Edit · Proofread

Look back at the essay you wrote for Chapter 13. TEST what you have written one more time. Then, revise your introduction and conclusion accordingly. Make sure your introduction creates interest, prepares readers for the essay to follow, and includes a clear thesis statement. Then, make sure your conclusion includes a summary statement and general concluding remarks. Finally, make sure your essay has an appropriate and effective title.

EDITING PRACTICE

The following student essay has an undeveloped introduction and conclusion. Decide what introductory and concluding strategies would be best for the essay. Then, rewrite both the introduction and the conclusion. Finally, suggest an interesting title for the essay.

————————

This essay is about three of the most dangerous jobs. They are piloting small planes, logging, and fishing.

Flying a small plane can be dangerous. For example, pilots who fly tiny planes that spray pesticides on farmers' fields do not have to comply with the safety rules for large airplanes. They also have to fly very low in order to spray the right fields. This leaves little room for error. Also, pilots of air taxis and small commuter planes die in much greater numbers than airline pilots do. In some places, like parts of Alaska, there are long distances and few roads, so many small planes are needed. Their pilots are four times more likely to die than other pilots because of bad weather and poor visibility. In general, flying a small plane can be very risky.

Another dangerous job is logging. Loggers are always at risk of having parts of trees or heavy machinery fall on them. Tree trunks often have odd shapes, so they are hard to control while they are being transported. As a result, they often break loose from equipment that is supposed to move them. In addition, weather conditions, like snow or rain, can cause dangers. Icy or wet conditions increase the risk to loggers, who can fall from trees or slip when they are sawing a tree. Because loggers often work in remote places, it is very hard to get prompt medical aid. For this reason, a wound that could easily be treated in a hospital may be fatal to a logger.

Perhaps the most dangerous occupation is working in the fishing industry. Like loggers, professional fishermen work in unsafe conditions. They use heavy machinery to pull up nets and to move large amounts of fish. The combination of icy or slippery boat decks and large nets and cages makes the job unsafe. The weather is often very bad, so fishermen are at risk of falling overboard during a storm and drowning. In fact, drowning is the most common cause of death in this industry. Also, like logging, fishing is done far from medical help, so even minor injuries can be very serious.

In conclusion, piloting small planes, logging, and fishing are three of the most dangerous occupations.

COLLABORATIVE ACTIVITY

Find a magazine or newspaper article that interests you. Cut off the introduction and conclusion, and bring the body of the article to class. Ask your group to decide on the best strategies for introducing and concluding the article. Then, collaborate on writing new opening and closing paragraphs and an interesting title.

review checklist

Introductions and Conclusions

☐ The introduction of your essay should include opening remarks and a thesis statement. (See 14a.) You can begin an essay with any of the following options.

A narrative	A quotation
A question	A surprising statement
A definition	

☐ Your title should suggest the subject of your essay and make people want to read further. (See 14a.)

☐ The conclusion of your essay should include a summary statement and some general concluding remarks. (See 14b.) You can conclude an essay with any of the following options.

A narrative	A quotation
A recommendation	A prediction

15 Patterns of Essay Development

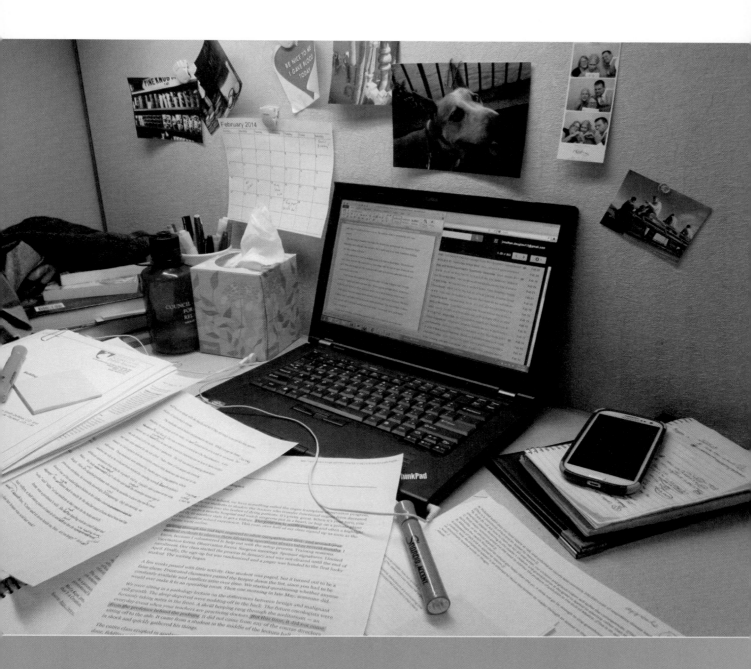

In this chapter, you will learn to organize your essays according to different patterns of development:

- exemplification (15a)
- narration (15b)
- description (15c)
- process (15d)
- cause and effect (15e)
- comparison and contrast (15f)
- classification (15g)
- definition (15h)
- argument (15i)

As you learned in Chapters 4 through 12, writers have a variety of options for developing ideas within a paragraph. These options include *exemplification, narration, description, process, cause and effect, comparison and contrast, classification, definition,* and *argument.* When you write an essay, you can use these same patterns of development to help you organize your material.

In your college courses, different assignments and writing situations call for different patterns of essay development.

- If an essay exam question asked you to compare two systems of government, you would use *comparison and contrast.*
- If an English composition assignment asked you to write about a childhood experience, you would use *narration.*
- If a section of a research paper on environmental pollution called for examples of dangerous waste-disposal practices, you would use *exemplification.*

The skills you learned for writing paragraphs can also be applied to writing essays.

15a Exemplification Essays

Exemplification illustrates a general statement with one or more specific examples. An **exemplification essay** uses specific examples to support a thesis. (For information about writing exemplification paragraphs, see Chapter 4.)

When you TEST an **exemplification** essay, make sure it includes all these elements.

T ■ **Thesis Statement**—The introduction of an exemplification essay should include a clear **thesis statement** that identifies the essay's main idea—the idea the examples will support.

E ■ **Evidence**—The body paragraphs should present **evidence**—fully developed examples that support the thesis. Each body paragraph should be introduced by a topic sentence that identifies the example or group of related examples that the paragraph will discuss.

S ■ **Summary Statement**—The conclusion of an exemplification essay should include a summary statement that reinforces the essay's thesis.

T ■ **Transitions**—An exemplification essay should use appropriate **transitional words and phrases** to connect examples within paragraphs and between one paragraph and another.

Moving from Assignment to Thesis

The wording of your assignment may suggest that you write an exemplification essay. For example, you may be asked to *illustrate* or to *give examples*. Once you decide that your assignment calls for exemplification, you need to develop a thesis that reflects this purpose.

ASSIGNMENT	THESIS STATEMENT
Education Should children be taught only in their native languages or in English as well? Support your answer with examples of specific students' experiences.	The success of students in a bilingual third-grade class suggests the value of teaching elementary school students in English as well as in their native languages.
Literature Does William Shakespeare's *Othello* have to end tragically? Illustrate your position with references to specific characters.	Each of the three major characters in *Othello* contributes to the play's tragic ending.
Composition Discuss the worst job you ever had, including plenty of specific examples to support your thesis.	My summer job at a fast-food restaurant was my worst job because of the endless stream of rude customers, the many boring tasks I had to perform, and my manager's insensitivity.

Organizing an Exemplification Essay

In an exemplification essay, each body paragraph can develop a single example or discuss several related examples. The topic sentence should introduce the example (or group of related examples) that the paragraph will discuss. Each example you select should clearly support your thesis.

Essay Map: *One Example per Paragraph*

Introduction (includes thesis statement)

First example ⎤

Second example ⎬ Evidence

Third example ⎦

Conclusion (includes summary statement)

Essay Map: *Several Related Examples per Paragraph*

Introduction (includes thesis statement)

First group of examples ⎤

Second group of examples ⎬ Evidence

Third group of examples ⎦

Conclusion (includes summary statement)

Transitions in Exemplification Essays

Transitional words and phrases should introduce your examples and indicate how one example is related to another. For a list of transitional words and phrases that are frequently used in exemplification, see page 55.

Case Study: A Student Writes an Exemplification Essay

Kyle Sims, a student in a first-year writing course, was asked to write an essay about a popular hobby or interest. Kyle imagined that most of his classmates would write about topics like video games or team sports, and while he knew a lot about team sports, his knowledge came from being a spectator, not a participant. After considering his options, he decided to write about extreme sports.

Once he had settled on a topic, Kyle did some **freewriting**. When he read over his freewriting, he saw that he had come up with three kinds of information: ideas about the dangers of extreme sports, the challenges they present, and the equipment they require. He then wrote a **thesis statement** that identified the three points he wanted to make about extreme sports. After **brainstorming** about each of these points, he had enough material for a first draft.

As he wrote his **first draft**, Kyle devoted one paragraph to each point, using examples to develop his body paragraphs. When he finished his draft, he **TEST**ed it. He was satisfied with his thesis, which told readers what points he was going to make about extreme sports and also conveyed the idea that they were not like ordinary sports. His summary statement seemed logical and appropriate. However, realizing that his readers might not know much about extreme sports, Kyle decided that he needed to add more examples to illustrate the wide range of extreme sports and more transitions to lead readers from one example to the next.

As Kyle **revised** his draft, he added examples and transitions, and he rewrote his topic sentences so that they clearly identified the three points he wanted to make about extreme sports. After he finished his revision, he **edited** and **proofread** carefully and made sure his essay met his instructor's **format** requirements.

The following final draft includes all the elements Kyle looked for when he **TEST**ed his essay.

T E S T
- Thesis Statement
- Evidence
- Summary Statement
- Transitions

Model Exemplification Essay

Read Kyle's finished essay, and complete the tasks in Practice 15-1.

Going to Extremes

1   For years, sports like football, baseball, and basketball have been popular in cities, suburbs, and small rural towns. For some young people, however, these sports no longer seem exciting, especially when compared to "extreme sports," such as snowboarding and BMX racing. Extreme sports are different from more familiar sports because they are dangerous, they are physically challenging, and they require specialized equipment.

Introduction

2   First, extreme sports are dangerous. For example, snowboarders take chances with snowy hills and unpredictable bumps. They zoom down mountains at high speeds, which is typical of extreme sports. In addition, snowboarders and skateboarders risk painful falls as they do their tricks. Also, many extreme sports, like rock climbing, bungee jumping, and skydiving, are performed at very high altitudes. Moreover, the bungee jumper has to jump from a very high place, and there is always a danger of getting tangled with the bungee cord. People who participate in extreme sports accept—and even enjoy—these dangers.

Topic sentence (introduces first point)

Examples

3   In addition, extreme sports are very difficult. For instance, surfers have to learn to balance surfboards while dealing with wind and waves. Bungee jumpers may have to learn how to do difficult stunts while jumping off a high bridge or a dam. Another example of the physical challenge of extreme sports can be found in BMX racing. BMX racers have to learn to steer a lightweight bike on a dirt track that has jumps and banked corners. These extreme sports require skills that most people do not naturally have. These special skills have to be learned, and participants in extreme sports enjoy this challenge.

Topic sentence (introduces second point)

Examples

Body paragraphs

4   Finally, almost all extreme sports require specialized equipment. For example, surfers need surfboards that are light but strong. They can choose epoxy boards, which are stronger, or fiberglass boards, which are lighter. They can choose shortboards, which are shorter than seven feet and are easier to maneuver, or they can use longboards, which are harder and slower to turn in the water but are easier to learn on. Also, surfers have to get special wax for their boards to keep from slipping as they are paddling out into the water. For surfing in cold water, they need wetsuits that trap their own body heat. Other extreme sports require different kinds of specialized equipment, but those who participate in them are willing to buy whatever they need.

Topic sentence (introduces third point)

Examples

5   Clearly, extreme sports are very different from other sports. Maybe it is because they are so different that they have become so popular in recent

Conclusion

years. Already, snowboarding, BMX racing, and other extreme sports are featured in the Olympics. The Summer and Winter X Games are televised on ESPN and ABC, and sports like BMX racing, snowboarding, surfing, and snowmobiling get national attention on these programs. With all this publicity, extreme sports are likely to become even more popular—despite their challenges.

PRACTICE
15-1

1. Restate Kyle's thesis in your own words.

2. What three points about extreme sports does Kyle make in the topic sentences of his body paragraphs?

3. What examples of extreme sports does Kyle give in paragraph 1? What examples of dangers does he give in paragraph 2? In paragraph 4, Kyle discusses surfing, giving examples of the equipment surfers need. List this equipment.

4. Is Kyle's introduction effective? How else might he have opened his essay?

5. Paraphrase Kyle's summary statement.

6. What is this essay's greatest strength? What is its greatest weakness?

grammar in context

Exemplification

When you write an exemplification essay, you may introduce your examples with transitional words and phrases like *First* or *In addition*. If you do, be sure to use a comma.

First, extreme sports are dangerous.

In addition, extreme sports are very difficult.

Finally, almost all extreme sports require specialized equipment.

For information on using commas with introductory phrases and transitional words and phrases, see 33b.

[e] For more practice with comma usage, complete the LearningCurve Commas activity at **macmillanhighered.com/writingfirst**.

Step-by-Step Guide: Writing an Exemplification Essay

Now, you are ready to write an exemplification essay on one of the following topics (or a topic of your choice).

TOPICS

Reasons to start (or not to start) college right after high school
The three best products ever invented
What kinds of people or images should appear on U.S. postage stamps? Why?
Advantages (or disadvantages) of being a young parent
Athletes who really are role models
Four items students need to survive in college
What messages do rap or hip-hop artists send to listeners?
Study strategies that work
Traits of a good employee
Three or four recent national or world news events that gave you hope

As you write your essay, follow these steps.

1. Planning
   - Make sure your topic calls for exemplification.
   - Find ideas to write about.
   - Identify your main idea, and write a thesis statement.

2. Organizing
   - Choose and develop examples to support your thesis.
   - Arrange your supporting examples in a logical order, making an informal outline if necessary.

3. Drafting
   - Draft your essay.

4. TESTing and Revising
   - TEST your essay, referring to the TESTing an Exemplification Essay checklist that follows below.
   - Revise your essay, referring to the Self-Assessment Checklist on page 163 and the Strategies for Revising chart on page 162.

5. Editing and Proofreading
   - Edit your essay, referring to the Self-Assessment Checklist on page 166.
   - Proofread your essay, and make sure it follows the proper format.

TESTing an exemplification essay

Thesis Statement Unifies Your Essay

☐ Does your introduction include a **thesis statement** that clearly states your essay's main idea?

Evidence Supports Your Essay's Thesis Statement

☐ Do you have enough **evidence**—fully developed examples—to support your thesis?

☐ Do all your examples support your thesis, or should some be deleted?

(continued)

(continued from previous page)

Summary Statement Reinforces Your Essay's Unity

☐ Does your conclusion include a **summary statement** that reinforces your essay's thesis?

Transitions Add Coherence to Your Essay

☐ Do you include **transitions** that move readers from one example to the next?

15b Narrative Essays

Narration tells a story, usually presenting a series of events in chronological (time) order, moving from beginning to end. A **narrative essay** can tell a personal story, or it can recount a recent or historical event or a fictional story. (For information about writing narrative paragraphs, see Chapter 5.)

When you **TEST** a **narrative** essay, make sure it includes all these elements.

T ■ **Thesis Statement**—The introduction of a narrative essay should include a **thesis statement** that communicates the main idea—the point the story is making.

E ■ **Evidence**—The body paragraphs should tell the story, one event at a time, with each event providing **evidence**—examples and details—to support the thesis. Events are usually presented in chronological (time) order.

S ■ **Summary Statement**—The conclusion of a narrative essay should include a **summary statement** that reinforces the essay's main idea.

T ■ **Transitions**—Throughout a narrative essay, **transitional words and phrases** should connect events in time, showing how one event leads to the next.

Moving from Assignment to Thesis

The wording of your assignment may suggest that you write a narrative essay. For example, you may be asked to *tell, trace, summarize events,* or *recount*. Once you decide that your assignment calls for narration, you need to develop a thesis statement that reflects this purpose.

ASSIGNMENT	THESIS STATEMENT
Composition Tell about a time when you had to show courage even though you were afraid.	In extraordinary circumstances, a person can exhibit great courage and overcome fear.

American history Summarize the events that occurred during President Franklin Delano Roosevelt's first one hundred days in office.	Although many thought they were extreme, the measures enacted by Roosevelt during his first one hundred days in office were necessary to fight the economic depression.
Political science Trace the development of the Mississippi Freedom Democratic Party.	As the Mississippi Freedom Democratic Party developed, it found a voice that spoke for equality and justice.

Organizing a Narrative Essay

When you write a narrative essay, you can discuss one event or several in each paragraph of your essay.

Essay Map: *One Event per Paragraph*

Introduction (includes thesis statement)

First event

Second event — Evidence

Third event

Conclusion (includes summary statement)

Essay Map: *Several Events per Paragraph*

Introduction (includes thesis statement)

First group of events

Second group of events — Evidence

Third group of events

Conclusion (includes summary statement)

Transitions in Narrative Essays

Sometimes, to add interest to your narrative, you may decide not to use exact chronological order. For example, you might begin with the end of your story and then move back to the beginning to trace the events that led to this outcome. However you arrange the events, carefully worded topic sentences and clear transitional words and phrases will help readers follow your narrative. For a list of transitional words and phrases that are frequently used in narration, see page 63.

Case Study: A Student Writes a Narrative Essay

Elaina Corrato, a returning student who was older than most of her classmates, wasn't sure how to proceed when her writing instructor gave the

WORD POWER

milestone an important event; a turning point

class an assignment to write about a milestone in their lives. The first topic that came to mind was her recent thirtieth birthday, but she was reluctant to reveal her age to her classmates. However, when she learned that no one except her instructor would read her essay, she decided to write about this topic.

Elaina began by rereading entries she had made in her **writing journal** in the days before and after her birthday as well as on the day itself. Even before she began to write, she saw that her essay would be a narrative that traced her reactions to the events she experienced on that day.

As she **drafted** her essay, Elaina was careful to discuss events in the order in which they occurred and to include transitional words and phrases to move her discussion smoothly from one event to the next. When she TESTed her essay, however, Elaina saw at once that she had not stated a thesis or included a summary statement to reinforce her main idea.

At this point, Elaina emailed her draft to her instructor and asked him for revision suggestions. (Her instructor offered this option to students whose off-campus work commitments made it difficult for them to schedule face-to-face conferences.) He explained that her thesis should not be just a general overview of the day's events; instead, it should make a point about how those events affected her. With this advice, Elaina found it was not difficult to write a thesis that expressed how she felt about turning thirty. Once she had a **thesis statement**, she was able to add a summary statement that reinforced her main idea, ending her essay on an optimistic note. With all the required elements in place, she went on to further **revise** her essay. Finally, she **edited** and **proofread** her essay and checked her **format**.

The final draft that follows includes all the elements Elaina looked for when she TESTed her essay.

TEST

Thesis Statement
Evidence
Summary Statement
Transitions

Model Narrative Essay

Read Elaina's finished essay, and complete the tasks in Practice 15-2.

Reflections

Introduction

Turning thirty did not bother me at all. My list of "Things to Do before 1
I Die" was far from complete, but I knew I had plenty of time to do them.
In fact, turning thirty seemed like no big deal to me. If anything, it was a
milestone I was happy to be approaching. Unfortunately, other people had
different ideas about this milestone, and eventually their ideas made me
rethink my own.

Topic sentence (introduces first group of events)

As the big day approached, my family kept teasing me about it. My sister 2
kept asking me if I felt any different. She couldn't believe I wasn't upset, but
I didn't pay any attention to her. I was looking forward to a new chapter
in my life. I liked my job, I was making good progress toward my college
degree, and I was healthy and happy. Why should turning thirty be a problem?
So, I made no special plans for my birthday, and I decided to treat it as just
another day.

Events and details

Body paragraphs

Topic sentence (introduces second group of events)

My birthday fell on a Saturday, and I enjoyed the chance to sleep in. 3
After I got up and had breakfast, I did my laundry and then set out for the
supermarket. I rarely put on makeup or fixed my hair on Saturdays. After all,
I didn't have to go to work or to school. I was only running errands in the

neighborhood. Later on, though, as I waited in line at the deli counter, I caught sight of my reflection in the mirrored meat case. At first, I thought it wasn't really me. The woman staring back at me looked so old! She had bags under her eyes, and she even had a few gray hairs. I was so upset by my reflection that on my way home I stopped and bought a mud mask—guaranteed to make me look younger.   *Events and details*

4   As I walked up the street toward my house, I saw something attached to the front railing. When I got closer, I realized that it was a bunch of black balloons. There was also a big sign that said "Over the Hill" in big black letters. I'd been trying to think about my birthday in positive terms, but my family seemed to have other ideas. Obviously, it was time for the mud mask.

Topic sentence (introduces third group of events)

Events and details

5   After quickly unloading my groceries, I ran upstairs to apply the mask. The box promised a "rejuvenating look," and that was exactly what I wanted. I spread the sticky brown mixture on my face, and it hardened instantly. As I sat on my bed, waiting for the mask to work its magic, I heard the doorbell ring. Then, I heard familiar voices and my husband calling me to come down, saying that I had company. I couldn't answer him. I couldn't talk (or even smile) without cracking the mask. At this point, I retreated to the bathroom to make myself presentable for my friends and family. This task was not easy.

Topic sentence (introduces fourth group of events)

— **Body paragraphs**

Events and details

6   When I managed to scrub off the mud mask, my face was covered with little red pimples. Apparently, my sensitive skin couldn't take the harsh chemicals. At first, I didn't think the promise of "rejuvenated" skin was what I got. I had to admit, though, that my skin did look a lot younger. In fact, when I finally went downstairs to celebrate my birthday, I looked as young as a teenager—a teenager with acne.

Topic sentence (introduces fifth group of events)

Events and details

7   Despite other people's grim warnings, I discovered that although turning thirty was a milestone, it wasn't a game-changer. I learned a lot that day, and I learned even more in the days that followed. What I finally realized was that I couldn't ignore turning thirty, but having a thirtieth birthday didn't have to mean that my life was over.

Conclusion

PRACTICE
15-2

1. Restate Elaina's thesis statement in your own words.

2. What specific events and details support Elaina's thesis? List as many as you can.

3. Do you think paragraph 2 is necessary? How would Elaina's essay be different without it?

4. Paraphrase Elaina's summary statement. Do you think her summary statement effectively reinforces her essay's main idea?

5. What is this essay's greatest strength? What is its greatest weakness?

grammar in context

Narration

When you write a narrative essay, you tell a story. When you get caught up in your story, you might sometimes find yourself stringing a list of incidents together without proper punctuation, creating a **run-on**.

INCORRECT   As the big day approached, my family kept teasing me about it, my sister kept asking me if I felt any different.

CORRECT   As the big day approached, my family kept teasing me about it. My sister kept asking me if I felt any different.

For information on how to identify and correct run-ons, see Chapter 23.

:e: For more practice with run-ons, complete the LearningCurve Run-Ons activity at **macmillanhighered.com/writingfirst**.

Step-by-Step Guide: Writing a Narrative Essay

Now, you are ready to write a narrative essay on one of the following topics (or a topic of your choice).

TOPICS

The story of your education
Your idea of a perfect day
The plot summary of a terrible book or movie
A time when you had to make a split-second decision
Your first confrontation with authority
An important historical event
A day on which everything went wrong
A story from your family's history
Your employment history, from first to most recent job
A biography of your pet

As you write your essay, follow these steps.

1. Planning
   - Make sure your topic calls for narration.
   - Find ideas to write about.
   - Identify your main idea, and write a thesis statement.

2. Organizing
   - Choose events and details to support your thesis.
   - Arrange events in chronological order, making an informal outline if necessary.

3. Drafting
  - Draft your essay.

4. TESTing and Revising
  - TEST your essay, referring to the TESTing a Narrative Essay checklist below.
  - Revise your essay, referring to the Self-Assessment Checklist on page 163 and the Strategies for Revising chart on page 162.

5. Editing and Proofreading
  - Edit your essay, referring to the Self-Assessment Checklist on page 166.
  - Proofread your essay, and make sure it follows the proper format.

TESTing a narrative essay

Thesis Statement Unifies Your Essay

☐ Does your introduction include a **thesis statement** that clearly states your essay's main idea?

Evidence Supports Your Essay's Thesis Statement

☐ Does all your **evidence**—events and details—support your thesis, or should some be deleted?

☐ Do you include enough specific details to make your narrative interesting?

☐ Are the events you discuss arranged in clear chronological (time) order?

Summary Statement Reinforces Your Essay's Unity

☐ Does your conclusion include a **summary statement** that reinforces your essay's thesis?

Transitions Add Coherence to Your Essay

☐ Do you include enough **transitions** to make the sequence of events clear to your reader?

15c   Descriptive Essays

Description tells what something looks, sounds, smells, tastes, or feels like. A **descriptive essay** uses details to give readers a clear, vivid picture of a person, place, or object.

When you describe a person, place, object, or scene, you can use **objective description**, reporting only what your senses of sight, sound, smell, taste, and touch tell you ("The columns were two feet tall and made of white marble"). You can also use **subjective description**, conveying your attitude or your feelings about what you observe ("The columns were tall and powerful looking, and their marble surface seemed as smooth as ice"). Many essays combine these two kinds of description.

FYI

Figures of Speech

Descriptive writing, particularly subjective description, is frequently enriched by **figures of speech**—language that creates special or unusual effects.

- A **simile** uses *like* or *as* to compare two unlike things.

  Her smile was like sunshine.

- A **metaphor** compares two unlike things without using *like* or *as*.

  Her smile was a light that lit up the room.

- **Personification** suggests a comparison between a nonliving thing and a person by giving the nonliving thing human traits.

  The sun smiled down on the crowd.

When you TEST a **descriptive** essay, make sure it includes all these elements.

T ■ **Thesis Statement**—A descriptive essay should include a **thesis statement** that expresses the essay's main idea.

E ■ **Evidence**—The body paragraphs should include **evidence**—descriptive details that support the thesis. Details should be arranged in spatial order—for example, from far to near or from top to bottom.

S ■ **Summary Statement**—The conclusion of a descriptive essay should include a **summary statement** that reinforces the essay's thesis.

T ■ **Transitions**—A descriptive essay should include **transitional words and phrases** that connect details and show how they are related.

Moving from Assignment to Thesis

The wording of your assignment may suggest that you write a descriptive essay. For example, it may ask you to *describe* or to *tell what an object looks like*. Once you decide that your assignment calls for description, you need to develop a thesis statement that reflects this purpose.

ASSIGNMENT	THESIS STATEMENT
Composition Describe a room that was important to you when you were a child.	Pink-and-white striped wallpaper, tall shelves of cuddly stuffed animals, and the smell of Oreos dominated the bedroom I shared with my sister.
Scientific writing Describe a piece of scientific equipment.	The mass spectrometer is a complex instrument, but every part is ideally suited to its function.
Art history Choose one modern painting, and describe its visual elements.	The disturbing images crowded together in Pablo Picasso's *Guernica* suggest the brutality of war.

Organizing a Descriptive Essay

When you plan a descriptive essay, you focus on selecting details that help your readers see what you see, feel what you feel, and experience what you experience. Your goal is to create a single **dominant impression**—a central theme or idea to which all the details relate—for example, the liveliness of a street scene or the quiet of a summer night. This dominant impression unifies the description and gives readers an overall sense of what the person, place, object, or scene looks like (and perhaps what it sounds, smells, tastes, or feels like).

You can arrange details in a descriptive essay in many different ways. For example, you can move from least to most important details, from top to bottom (or from bottom to top or side to side), or from far to near (or near to far). Each of your essay's body paragraphs may focus on one key characteristic of the subject you are describing or on several related descriptive details.

Essay Map: *Least to Most Important*

Introduction (includes thesis statement)

Least important details

More important details } Evidence

Most important details

Conclusion (includes summary statement)

Essay Map: *Top to Bottom/ Far to Near*

Introduction (includes thesis statement)

Details at top/ distant details

Details in middle/ closer details } Evidence

Details at bottom/ closest details

Conclusion (includes summary statement)

Transitions in Descriptive Essays

As you write, use transitional words and phrases to connect details and show how they work together to create a full picture for readers. (Many of these useful transitions indicate location or distance.) For a list of transitional words and phrases that are frequently used in description, see page 72.

Case Study: A Student Writes a Descriptive Essay

All the students in James Greggs's first-year composition course were also enrolled in sociology, psychology, or education courses with service-learning requirements that reinforced course content. For this reason, James's composition instructor asked that the students' descriptive essays focus on a person, a setting, or an item related to their service-learning experiences.

Although James was enjoying his service-learning project—building a deck for elderly residents of a trailer home—he had trouble deciding which aspect of this project to write about. Although he was required to keep a **journal** for the service-learning component of his sociology class, he realized that his entries focused on his own reactions and included few objective details. He finally settled on writing a description of the deck his team built for the trailer home.

Consulting photos he had taken of the building site and diagrams he had prepared of the trailer, James wrote a **first draft**, arranging his material from far (the field in which the trailer sat) to near (the trailer itself and the deck he helped build).

When James **TEST**ed his draft, he saw that his essay had no thesis statement—no sentence that tied all the details together to indicate the main idea he wanted his description to convey. At this point, he emailed his instructor for help, but she reminded him that he had missed her deadline for scheduling appointments, and she recommended that he make an appointment with a tutor in the writing center.

James's writing center tutor suggested that his essay would be more interesting and convincing if his thesis tied the objective details of the project to his conclusions about its value. What did his class contribute? What did they learn? Was the project worth the trouble? She also reviewed his draft with him, suggesting places where he could expand or clarify his description. Because his assignment called for a descriptive essay, not a process essay, she recommended that he delete material that summarized the steps his group followed as they built the deck. Finally, she reminded him that he would need to write a summary statement to reinforce his thesis.

As James **revised** his draft, he incorporated his tutor's suggestions and added both a thesis statement and a summary statement. He also added transitional words and phrases to move readers through his description, added more detail, and deleted irrelevant material. Then, he **edited** and **proofread** his essay and checked his **format**.

The following final draft includes all the elements James looked for when he **TEST**ed his essay.

Model Descriptive Essay

Read James's finished essay, and complete the tasks in Practice 15-3.

Building and Learning

T E S T

☐ Thesis Statement
☐ Evidence
☐ Summary Statement
☐ Transitions

Introduction

1   Throughout the United States, houses reflect not only the lives of the people who live in them but also the diversity of the American population. Some are large and elaborate, others are modest but well maintained, and still others are in need of repair. Unfortunately, most college students know little about homes other than those in their own neighborhood. I, too, was fairly sheltered until I participated in a service-learning project for my sociology class. For this project, I, along with some classmates, added a deck to a trailer that was the home of three elderly sisters living on Social Security and disability. It was hard work, but my experience convinced me that all college students should be required to do some kind of service-learning project.

2   The trailer we worked on was located at the end of a small dirt road about thirty minutes from campus. Patches of green and brown grass dotted the land around the trailer, and in the far right-hand corner of the property stood three tall poplar trees. Although the bushes in front of the trailer were trimmed, the woods behind the trailer were beginning to overrun the property. (We were told that members of a local church came once a month to trim the hedges and cut back the trees.) Dominating the right front corner of the lawn, a circular concrete basin looked like a large birdbath. The basin housed a white well pipe with a rusted blue cap. About thirty feet to the left of the concrete basin stood a telephone pole and a bright red metal mailbox.

Topic sentence (introduces first group of details)

Descriptive details

3   Like the property on which it stood, the trailer was well maintained. It was approximately thirty-five feet long and seven feet high; it rested on cinderblocks, which raised it about three feet off the ground. Under the trailer was an overturned white plastic chair. The trailer itself was covered with sheets of white vinyl siding that ran horizontally, except for the bottom panels on the right side, which ran vertically. The vinyl panels closest to the roof were slightly discolored by dirt and green moss.

Topic sentence (introduces second group of details)

Body paragraphs

Descriptive details

4   At the left end of the trailer was a small window—about two feet wide and one foot high. Next to the window was a dark red aluminum door outlined in green trim. It had one window at eye level divided by metal strips into four small sections. The number "24" in white plastic letters was glued to the door below this window. To the right of the door was a lightbulb in a black ceramic socket. Next to the light was a large window that was actually two vertical rows of three windows, each the same size as the small window on the left. Further to the right were two smaller windows. Each of these small windows tilted upward and was framed with silver metal strips. On either side of each of these windows was a pair of green metal shutters.

Topic sentence (introduces third group of details)

Descriptive details

5   The deck we built replaced three wooden steps that had led up to the trailer. A white metal handrail stood on the right side of these steps. It had been newly painted and was connected to the body of the trailer by a heart-shaped piece of metal. In front of the steps, two worn gray wooden boards led to the road.

Topic sentence (introduces fourth group of details)

Descriptive details

Topic sentence
(introduces fifth
group of details)

Descriptive details

6   Building the deck was hard work, but the finished deck provided a much better entranceway than the steps did and also gave the trailer a new look. The deck was not very large—ten feet by eight feet—but it extended from the doorway to the area underneath the windows immediately to the right of the door. We built the deck out of pressure-treated lumber so that it wouldn't rot or need painting. We also built three steps that led from the deck to the lawn, and we surrounded the deck with a wooden railing that ran down the right side of the steps. After we finished, we bought two white plastic chairs at a local thrift store and put them on the deck.

Conclusion

7   Now that I look back at the project, I believe that activities like this should be part of every student's college education. Both the residents of the trailer and our class benefited from the service-learning project. The residents of the trailer were happy with the deck because it gave them a place to sit when the weather was nice. They also liked their trailer's new look. Those of us who worked on the project learned that a few days' work could make a real difference in other people's lives.

**PRACTICE
15-3**

1. Paraphrase James's thesis statement.

2. What determines the order in which James arranges the elements of his description?

3. What details does James provide to describe the property, the trailer, and the deck?

4. What kinds of signals do James's transitions give readers? Do you think he includes enough transitions? Where could he add more?

5. This essay is primarily an objective description. Does it include any subjective details?

6. What is this essay's greatest strength? What is its greatest weakness?

grammar in context

Description

When you write a descriptive essay, you may use **modifiers**—words and phrases that describe other words in the sentence—to create a picture of your subject. If you place a modifying word or phrase too far from the word it is supposed to describe, you create a potentially confusing **misplaced modifier**.

CONFUSING   Next to the window outlined in green trim was a dark red aluminum door. (Was the window outlined in green trim?)

CLEAR   Next to the window was a dark red aluminum door outlined in green trim.

For information on how to identify and correct misplaced modifiers, see Chapter 27.

Step-by-Step Guide: Writing a Descriptive Essay

Now, you are ready to write a descriptive essay on one of the following topics (or a topic of your choice).

TOPICS

An abandoned building

A person or fictional character who makes you laugh (or frightens you)

Your room (or your closet or desk)

A family photograph

A historical site or monument

An advertisement

An object you cherish

Someone whom everyone notices

Someone whom no one notices

The home page of a website you visit often

As you write your essay, follow these steps.

1. Planning
   - Make sure your topic calls for description.
   - Find ideas to write about.
   - Decide what dominant impression you want to convey.
   - Write a thesis statement that identifies your main idea.

2. Organizing
   - Choose details that help to convey your dominant impression.
   - Arrange your details in an effective order, making an informal outline if necessary.

3. Drafting
   - Draft your essay.

4. TESTing and Revising
   - TEST your essay, referring to the TESTing a Descriptive Essay checklist that follows below.
   - Revise your essay, referring to the Self-Assessment Checklist on page 163 and the Strategies for Revising chart on page 162.

5. Editing and Proofreading
   - Edit your essay, referring to the Self-Assessment Checklist on page 166.
   - Proofread your essay, and make sure it follows the proper format.

TESTing a descriptive essay

T hesis Statement Unifies Your Essay

☐ Does your introduction include a **thesis statement** that communicates your essay's main idea?

☐ Does your introduction identify the subject of your description?

(continued)

(continued from previous page)

Evidence Supports Your Essay's Thesis Statement

☐ Does all your **evidence**—descriptive details—support the dominant impression communicated by your thesis, or should some be deleted?

☐ Do you describe your subject in enough detail, or do you need to add details to create a more vivid picture?

☐ Are your supporting details arranged in an effective order within your essay and within paragraphs?

Summary Statement Reinforces Your Essay's Unity

☐ Does your conclusion include a **summary statement** that reinforces your essay's thesis?

Transitions Add Coherence to Your Essay

☐ Do you include **transitions** that introduce your details and move readers smoothly from one aspect of your subject to another?

15d Process Essays

A **process** is a series of chronological steps that produces a particular result. **Process essays** explain the steps in a procedure, telling how something is (or was) done. A process essay can be organized as either a *process explanation* or a set of *instructions*. (For information about writing process paragraphs, see Chapter 7.)

When you TEST a **process** essay, make sure it includes all these elements.

T ▪ **Thesis Statement**—A process essay should include a **thesis statement** that expresses the essay's main idea, identifying the process you will explain and telling why it is important or why you are explaining it.

E ▪ **Evidence**—The body paragraphs should provide **evidence**—examples and details—that explains all the steps in the process and supports the essay's thesis. Each paragraph's topic sentence should identify the step (or group of related steps) that the paragraph will explain. Steps should be presented in strict chronological (time) order.

S ▪ **Summary Statement**—The conclusion of a process essay should include a **summary statement** that reinforces the essay's thesis.

T ▪ **Transitions**—A process essay should include **transitional words and phrases** that link the steps in the process and show how they are related.

Moving from Assignment to Thesis

The wording of your assignment may suggest that you write a process essay. For example, you may be asked to *explain a process*, *give instructions*, *give directions*, or *give a step-by-step account*. Once you decide that your assignment calls for process, you need to develop a thesis statement that reflects this purpose.

ASSIGNMENT	THESIS STATEMENT
American government Explain the process by which a bill becomes a law.	The process by which a bill becomes a law is long and complex, involving numerous revisions and a great deal of compromise.
Pharmacy practice Summarize the procedure for conducting a clinical trial of a new drug.	To ensure that drugs are safe and effective, scientists follow strict procedural guidelines for testing and evaluating each new drug.
Technical writing Write a set of instructions for applying for a student internship in a government agency.	If you want to apply for a government internship, you need to follow several important steps.

If your purpose is simply to help readers understand a process, not actually perform it, you will write a process explanation. **Process explanations**, like the first two examples in the chart above, often use present tense verbs ("Once a bill *is* introduced in Congress" or "A scientist first *submits* a funding application") to explain how a procedure is generally carried out. However, when a process explanation describes a specific procedure that was completed in the past, it uses past tense verbs ("The next thing I *did*").

If your purpose is to enable readers to actually perform the steps in a process, you will write instructions. **Instructions**, like the technical writing example in the chart, always use present tense verbs in the form of commands to tell readers what to do ("First, *meet* with your adviser").

Organizing a Process Essay

Whether your essay is a process explanation or a set of instructions, you can either devote a full paragraph to each step of the process or group a series of minor steps together in a single paragraph.

As you write your process essay, discuss each step in the order in which it is performed, making sure your topic sentences clearly identify each step or group of steps. (If you are writing instructions, you may also include reminders or warnings that readers might need to know when performing the process.)

Essay Map: *One Step per Paragraph*

- Introduction (includes thesis statement)
- *First step in process*
- *Second step in process* — Evidence
- *Third step in process*
- Conclusion (includes summary statement)

Essay Map: *Several Steps per Paragraph*

- Introduction (includes thesis statement)
- *First group of steps*
- *Second group of steps* — Evidence
- *Third group of steps*
- Conclusion (includes summary statement)

Transitions in Process Essays

Transitions are extremely important in process essays because they enable readers to follow the sequence of steps in the process and, in the case of instructions, to perform the process themselves. For a list of transitional words and phrases that are frequently used in process, see page 81.

Case Study: A Student Writes a Process Essay

Jen Rossi, a student in a first-year writing course, was given the following assignment.

> Write a set of instructions for a process that you are very familiar with but that your classmates probably do not know much about. Be sure your readers will be able not just to understand the process but also to perform the steps themselves.

When she considered what she might want to write about, Jen rejected familiar process topics like following a recipe or performing a household repair. Instead, she decided to explain how to sell items at a flea market. She knew a lot about this topic, but she still needed to **brainstorm** to get all the steps down on paper. Next, she **listed the steps**, arranging them in chronological order and checking to make sure that no step was missing. When she **drafted** her essay, she made sure she identified each step with transitional words and phrases.

Jen's biggest challenge was developing a **thesis statement**. Before she wrote her draft, she came up with a tentative thesis—"Selling at a flea market is a process that requires a number of steps"—but she knew this sentence was only a placeholder. Her thesis statement told readers what she planned to write about, but it didn't tell them why she was explaining this process or how she felt about it.

When she TESTed her draft, she saw that although she had a tentative thesis and plenty of support, she had not included a summary statement. She quickly jotted down a placeholder sentence—"These are the steps in selling at a flea market"—that she could revise when she revised her thesis statement.

With the help of classmates in her **peer-review** group, Jen revised her thesis statement and summary statement so that they both communicated her essay's main idea: that following a process can establish a routine to make flea-market selling easier. She also added a few more examples (for instance, examples of heavy and small items in paragraph 5 and examples of small and large items in paragraph 7) in response to suggestions from her classmates. Once she made these revisions, she went on to **edit** and **proofread** her essay and check her **format**.

The final draft that follows includes all the elements Jen looked for when she TESTed her essay.

Model Process Essay

Read Jen's finished essay, and complete the tasks in Practice 15-4.

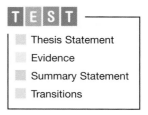

T E S T
- Thesis Statement
- Evidence
- Summary Statement
- Transitions

For Fun and Profit

1   Selling items at a flea market can be both fun and profitable. In fact, it can lead to a hobby that will be a continuing source of extra income. Your first flea market can take a lot of work, but establishing a routine will make each experience easier and more rewarding than the last one.

Introduction

2   The first step in the process is to call to reserve a spot at the flea market. If possible, try to get a spot near the entrance, where there is a lot of foot traffic. Once you have your spot, recruit a helper—for example, one of your roommates—and get to work.

Topic sentence (identifies first step)

Examples and details

3   The next step is sorting through all the items you've managed to accumulate. Your helper will come in handy here, encouraging you to sell ugly or useless things that you may want to hold on to. Make three piles—keep, sell, and trash—and, one by one, place each item in a pile. (Before you decide to sell or discard an item, check with roommates and family members to make sure you aren't accidentally throwing out one of their prized possessions.)

Topic sentence (identifies second step)

Body paragraphs

Examples and details

4   Next, price the items for sale. This can actually be the hardest step in the process. It's always difficult to accept the fact that you might have to set a low price for something that has sentimental value for you (a giant-sized stuffed animal, for example). It can be just as hard to set a high price on the ugly lamp or old record album that might turn out to be someone's treasure. In all likelihood, you will return from your first flea market with a lot of unsold items. You will also probably realize, too late, that you sold some items too cheaply. (Don't worry; you won't make these mistakes again.)

Topic sentence (identifies third step)

Examples and details

5   The next step is packing up items to be sold. You may want to borrow a friend's truck or van for the heavy, bulky items (boxes of books or dishes, for example). The small items (knickknacks, silk flowers, stray teaspoons) can be transported by car.

Topic sentence (identifies fourth step)

Examples and details

Topic sentence
(identifies fifth step)
Body paragraphs
Examples and details
Topic sentence
(identifies sixth step)

Examples and details

Topic sentence
(identifies
seventh step)

Examples and details

The final steps in your preparation take place on the day before the   6
event. Borrow a couple of card tables. Then, go to the bank and get lots of
dollar bills and quarters, and collect piles of newspaper and grocery bags.
Now, your planning is complete, and you are ready for the big day.

On the day of the flea market, get up early, and (with your trusty helper's   7
assistance) load your vehicle. When you arrive at the site where the event is
to be held, have your helper unload the car. Meanwhile, set things up, placing
small items (such as plates or DVDs) on the card tables and large items (such
as your parents' old lawnmower) on the ground near the tables.

Now, the actual selling begins. Before you can even set up your tables,   8
people will start picking through your items, offering you cash for picture
frames, pots and pans, and old video games. Don't panic! Try to develop a
system: one of you can persuade buyers that that old meat grinder or vase is
just what they've been looking for; the other person can negotiate the price
with prospective buyers. Then, while one of you wraps small items in the
newspapers or bags you brought, the other person can take the money and
make change.

Conclusion

Finally, at the end of the day, the process will come to an end. Now,   9
count your money. (Don't forget to give a share to your helper.) Then,
load all the unsold items into your vehicle, and bring them back home.
The process ends when you store the unsold items in the back of your
closet, ready to pack them all up again and follow the same routine for
the next flea market.

PRACTICE
15-4
1. Restate Jen's thesis statement in your own words.

2. What identifies Jen's essay as a set of instructions rather than a process explanation?

3. Review the transitional words and phrases that link the steps in the process. Are any other transitions needed? If so, where?

4. List the major steps in the process of selling at a flea market. Does Jen present these steps in strict chronological order?

5. Paraphrase Jen's summary statement. Do you think she needs to revise this sentence so it more clearly reinforces her thesis statement?

6. What is the essay's greatest strength? What is its greatest weakness?

grammar in context

Process

When you write a process essay, you may have problems keeping tense, person, and voice consistent throughout. If you shift from one tense, person, or voice to another without good reason, you will confuse your readers.

CONFUSING   Make three piles—keep, sell, and trash—and, one by one, each item should be placed in a pile. (shift from active to passive voice and from present to past tense)

CLEAR   Make three piles—keep, sell, and trash—and, one by one, place each item in a pile. (consistent voice and tense)

For information on how to avoid illogical shifts in tense, person, and voice, see Chapter 26.

e For more practice with shifts in tense and voice, complete the LearningCurve Verbs and Active and Passive Voice activities at **macmillanhighered.com/writingfirst**.

Step-by-Step Guide: Writing a Process Essay

Now, you are ready to write a process essay on one of the following topics (or a topic of your choice).

TOPICS

An unusual recipe
Finding an apartment
Applying for a job
Getting dressed for a typical Saturday night
A religious ritual or cultural ceremony
A task you often do at work
A do-it-yourself project that didn't get done
Your own writing process
A self-improvement program (past, present, or future)
Applying for financial aid

As you write your essay, follow these steps.

1. Planning
   - Make sure your topic calls for process.
   - Decide whether you want to explain a process or write instructions.
   - Find ideas to write about.
   - Identify your main idea, and write a thesis statement.

2. Organizing
   - Identify the most important steps in the process.
   - List the steps in chronological order, making an informal outline if necessary.

3. Drafting
   - Draft your essay.

4. **TEST**ing and Revising
   - **TEST** your essay, referring to the **TEST**ing a Process Essay checklist below.
   - Revise your essay, referring to the Self-Assessment Checklist on page 163 and the Strategies for Revising chart on page 162.

5. Editing and Proofreading
   - Edit your essay, referring to the Self-Assessment Checklist on page 166.
   - Proofread your essay, and make sure it follows the proper format.

TESTing a process essay

T hesis Statement Unifies Your Essay

☐ Does your introduction include a **thesis statement** that expresses your essay's main idea, identifying the process you will explain and indicating why you are writing about it?

E vidence Supports Your Essay's Thesis Statement

☐ Does all your **evidence**—examples and details—support your thesis, or should some be deleted?

☐ Do you identify and explain every step that readers will need to understand (or perform) the process? Should any steps in the process be deleted?

☐ Are the steps in the process given in strict chronological order?

☐ If you are writing instructions, have you included all necessary warnings or reminders?

S ummary Statement Reinforces Your Essay's Unity

☐ Does your conclusion include a **summary statement** that reinforces your essay's thesis?

T ransitions Add Coherence to Your Essay

☐ Do you include **transitions** that introduce your steps and clearly show how the steps in the process are related?

15e Cause-and-Effect Essays

A **cause** makes something happen; an **effect** is a result of a particular cause or event. **Cause-and-effect essays** identify causes or predict effects. (For information about writing cause-and-effect paragraphs, see Chapter 8.)

When you TEST a **cause-and-effect** essay, make sure it includes all these elements.

T ▪ **Thesis Statement**—The introduction of a cause-and-effect essay should include a **thesis statement** that communicates the essay's main idea and indicates whether it will focus on causes or on effects.

E ▪ **Evidence**—The body paragraphs should include **evidence**—examples and details—to illustrate and explain the causes or effects you examine. The topic sentence of each paragraph should identify the cause or effect the paragraph will discuss.

S ▪ **Summary Statement**—The conclusion of a cause-and-effect essay should include a **summary statement** that reinforces the essay's thesis.

T ▪ **Transitions**—A cause-and-effect essay should include **transitional words and phrases** that make clear which causes lead to which effects.

Moving from Assignment to Thesis

The wording of your assignment may suggest that you write a cause-and-effect essay. For example, the assignment may ask you to *explain why, predict the outcome, list contributing factors, discuss the consequences,* or tell what *caused* something else or how something is *affected* by something else. Once you decide that your assignment calls for cause and effect, you need to develop a thesis statement that reflects this purpose.

ASSIGNMENT	THESIS STATEMENT
Women's studies What factors contributed to the rise of the women's movement in the 1970s?	The women's movement of the 1970s had its origins in the peace and civil rights movements of the 1960s.
Public health Discuss the possible long-term effects of smoking.	In addition to its well-known negative effects on smokers themselves, smoking also causes significant problems for those exposed to secondhand smoke.
Media and society How has the Internet affected the lives of those who have grown up with it?	The Internet has created a generation of people who learn differently from those in previous generations.

A cause-and-effect essay can focus on causes or on effects. When you write about causes, be sure to examine *all* relevant causes. You should emphasize the cause you consider the most important, but do not forget to consider other causes that may be significant. Similarly, when you write about effects, consider *all* significant effects of a particular cause, not just the first few you think of.

If your focus is on finding causes, as it is in the first assignment on page 209, your introductory paragraph should identify the effect (the women's movement). If your focus is on predicting effects, as it is in the second and third assignments, you should begin by identifying the cause (smoking, the Internet).

Organizing a Cause-and-Effect Essay

In the body of your essay, you will probably devote a full paragraph to each cause (or effect). You can also group several related causes (or effects) together in each paragraph.

Essay Map: *Identifying Causes*

Introduction (includes thesis statement that identifies effect)

First cause

Second cause

⎫ Evidence

Third (and most important) cause

Conclusion (includes summary statement)

Essay Map: *Predicting Effects*

Introduction (includes thesis statement that identifies cause)

First effect

Second effect

⎫ Evidence

Third (and most important) effect

Conclusion (includes summary statement)

Transitions in Cause-and-Effect Essays

Transitions are important in cause-and-effect essays because they establish causal connections, telling readers that A caused B and not the other way around. They also make it clear that events have a *causal* relationship (A *caused* B) and not just a *sequential* relationship (A *came before* B). Remember, when one event follows another, the second is not necessarily the result of the first. For example, an earthquake may occur the day before you fail an exam, but that doesn't mean the earthquake caused you to fail. For a list of transitional words and phrases that are frequently used in cause-and-effect, see page 90.

Case Study: A Student Writes a Cause-and-Effect Essay

In an orientation course for first-year education majors, Andrea DeMarco was asked to write a personal essay about an event that changed her life. The wording of the assignment indicated to Andrea that her essay would have a cause-and-effect structure. She remembered writing a cause-and-effect paragraph, in response to a composition assignment, about how her parents' separation had led her to grow up quickly. Now, she thought she could develop some of the ideas she had explored in that paragraph into an essay.

Before she wrote her first draft, Andrea talked to her older sister and brother to see what they remembered about the separation. As they spoke, Andrea **took notes** so she wouldn't forget any details. Armed with her siblings' and her own memories, as well as the paragraph she'd written earlier, Andrea **drafted** her essay.

In her draft, she included a **thesis statement**—"My parents' separation made everything different"—that echoed the wording of the assignment. As she wrote, she was careful to include transitional words and phrases like *because* and *as a result* to make the cause-and-effect emphasis clear and to distinguish between the cause (the separation) and its effects. Her summary statement also reinforced the cause-and-effect emphasis of her essay.

When Andrea **TEST**ed her draft, she saw that it included all the required elements—thesis statement, evidence, summary statement, and transitions—so she continued **revising** her draft. When she finished her revisions, she **edited** and **proofread** her essay and checked her **format**.

The final draft that follows includes all the elements Andrea looked for when she **TEST**ed her essay.

Model Cause-and-Effect Essay

Read Andrea's finished essay, and answer the questions in Practice 15-5.

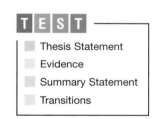

- Thesis Statement
- Evidence
- Summary Statement
- Transitions

How My Parents' Separation Changed My Life

1   Until I was eight, I lived the perfect all-American life with my perfect all-American family. I lived in a suburb of Albany, New York, with my parents; my sister and brother; and our dog, Daisy. We had a Ping-Pong table in the basement, a barbecue in the backyard, and two cars in the garage. My dad and mom were high school teachers, and every summer we took a family vacation. Then, it all changed. My parents' separation made everything different.

2   One day, just before Halloween, when my sister was twelve and my brother was fourteen (Daisy was seven), our parents called us into the kitchen for a family conference. We didn't think anything was wrong at first; they were always calling these annoying meetings. We figured it was time for us to plan a vacation, talk about household chores, or be nagged to clean our rooms. As soon as we sat down, though, we knew this was different. We could tell Mom had been crying, and Dad's voice cracked when he told us the news. They were separating—they called it a "trial separation"—and Dad was moving out of our house.

Introduction

Topic sentence (identifies first effect)

Examples and details

—*Body paragraphs*

Topic sentence (identifies second effect)	After that day, everything seemed to change. Every Halloween we always had a big jack-o'-lantern on our front porch. Dad used to spend hours at the kitchen table cutting out the eyes, nose, and mouth and hollowing out the insides. That Halloween, because he didn't live with us, things were different. Mom bought a pumpkin, and I guess she was planning to carve it up. But she never did, and we never mentioned it. It sat on the kitchen counter for a couple of weeks, getting soft and wrinkled, and then it just disappeared.
Examples and details Body paragraphs	
Topic sentence (identifies third effect)	Other holidays were also different because Mom and Dad were not living together. Our first Thanksgiving without Dad was pathetic. Christmas was different, too. We spent Christmas Eve with Dad and our relatives on his side and Christmas Day with Mom and her family. Of course, we got twice as many presents as usual. I realize now that both our parents were trying to make up for the pain of the separation. The worst part came when I opened my big present from Mom: Barbie's Dream House. This was something I had always wanted. Even at eight, I knew how hard it must have been for Mom to afford it. The trouble was, I had gotten the same thing from Dad the night before.
Examples and details	
Topic sentence (identifies fourth effect)	The separation affected each of us in different ways. The worst effect of my parents' separation was not the big events but the disruption in our everyday lives. Dinner used to be a family time, a chance to talk about our day and make plans. But after Dad left, Mom seemed to stop eating. Sometimes she would just have coffee while we ate, and sometimes she wouldn't eat at all. She would microwave some frozen thing for us or heat up soup or cook some hot dogs. We didn't care—after all, now she let us watch TV while we ate—but we did notice.
Examples and details	
Topic sentence (identifies fifth effect)	Other parts of our routine changed, too. Because Dad didn't live with us anymore, we had to spend every Saturday and every Wednesday night at his apartment, no matter what else we had planned. Usually, he would take us to dinner at McDonald's on Wednesdays, and then we would go back to his place and do our homework or watch TV. That wasn't too bad. Saturdays were a lot worse. We really wanted to be home, hanging out with our friends in our own rooms in our own house. Instead, we had to do some planned activity with Dad, like go to a movie or a hockey game.
Examples and details	
Conclusion	As a result of what happened in my own family, it is hard for me to believe any relationship is forever. By the end of the school year, my parents had somehow worked things out, and Dad was back home again. That June, at a family conference around the kitchen table, we made our summer vacation plans. We decided on Williamsburg, Virginia, the all-American vacation destination. So, things were back to normal, but I wasn't, and I'm still not. Now, ten years later, my mother and father are all right, but I still worry they'll split up again. And I worry about my own future husband and how I will ever be sure he's the one I'll stay married to.

Paragraph numbers: 3, 4, 5, 6, 7

PRACTICE
15-5

1. Restate Andrea's thesis statement in your own words. Does this statement identify a cause or an effect?

2. List the specific effects of her parents' separation that Andrea identifies.

3. Review the transitional words and phrases Andrea uses to make causal connections clear to her readers. Do you think she needs more of these transitions? If so, where?

4. Is Andrea's relatively long concluding paragraph effective? Why or why not? Do you think it should be shortened or divided into two paragraphs?

5. Is Andrea's straightforward title effective, or should she have used a more creative or eye-catching title? Can you suggest an alternative?

6. What is this essay's greatest strength? What is its greatest weakness?

grammar in context

Cause and Effect

When you write a cause-and-effect essay, you may have trouble remembering the difference between *affect* and *effect*.

The worst ~~affect~~ *effect* of my parents' separation was not the big events but the disruption in our everyday lives. (*effect* is a noun)

The separation ~~effected~~ *affected* each of us in different ways. (*affect* is a verb)

For information on affect *and* effect, *see Chapter 22.*

Step-by-Step Guide: Writing a Cause-and-Effect Essay

Now, you are ready to write a cause-and-effect essay on one of the following topics (or a topic of your choice).

TOPICS

A teacher's positive (or negative) effect on you
Why you voted a certain way in a recent election (or why you did not vote)
How your life would be different if you dropped out of school (or quit your job)
How a particular invention has changed your life
Why texting is so popular
A movie or book that changed the way you look at life
How a particular season (or day of the week) affects your mood
How having a child would change (or has changed) your life

As you write your essay, follow these steps.

1. Planning
   - Make sure your topic calls for cause and effect.
   - Decide whether your essay will focus on causes or effects.
   - Find ideas to write about.
   - Identify your main idea, and write a thesis statement.

2. Organizing
   - Choose causes or effects to support your thesis.
   - Arrange causes and effects in an effective order, making an informal outline if necessary.

3. Drafting
   - Draft your essay.

4. TESTing and Revising
   - TEST your essay, referring to the TESTing a Cause-and-Effect Essay checklist that follows.
   - Revise your essay, referring to the Self-Assessment Checklist on page 163 and the Strategies for Revising chart on page 162.

5. Editing and Proofreading
   - Edit your essay, referring to the Self-Assessment Checklist on page 166.
   - Proofread your essay, and make sure it follows the proper format.

TESTing a cause-and-effect essay

Thesis Statement Unifies Your Essay

☐ Does your introduction include a **thesis statement** that indicates your main idea and makes clear whether your essay will focus on causes or effects?

Evidence Supports Your Essay's Thesis Statement

☐ Does all your **evidence**—examples and details—support your thesis, or should some be deleted?

☐ Do you identify and explain all causes or effects relevant to your topic, or do you need to add any?

☐ Do you arrange causes and effects to indicate which are more important than others?

☐ Does each body paragraph identify and explain one particular cause or effect (or several closely related causes or effects)?

Summary Statement Reinforces Your Essay's Unity

☐ Does your conclusion include a **summary statement** that reinforces your essay's thesis?

Transitions Add Coherence to Your Essay

☐ Do you include **transitions** that introduce each of your causes or effects and make your essay's cause-and-effect connections clear?

15f Comparison-and-Contrast Essays

Comparison identifies similarities, and **contrast** identifies differences. **Comparison-and-contrast essays** explain how two things are alike or how they are different. (For information about writing comparison-and-contrast paragraphs, see Chapter 9.)

When you TEST a **comparison-and-contrast** essay, make sure it includes all these elements.

T ▪ **Thesis Statement**—The introduction of a comparison-and-contrast essay should include a **thesis statement** that communicates the essay's main idea, telling readers what two items you are going to compare or contrast and whether you are going to emphasize similarities or differences.

E ▪ **Evidence**—The body paragraphs should include **evidence**—examples and details—that supports the thesis statement. The topic sentence of each paragraph should identify the similarity or difference the paragraph will examine, and the examples and details should explain the similarity or difference.

S ▪ **Summary Statement**—The conclusion of a comparison-and-contrast essay should include a **summary statement** that reinforces the essay's thesis.

T ▪ **Transitions**—A comparison-and-contrast essay should include **transitional words and phrases** to help readers move from point to point and from subject to subject.

Moving from Assignment to Thesis

The wording of your assignment may suggest that you write a comparison-and-contrast essay—for example, by asking you to *compare, contrast, discuss similarities,* or *identify differences.* Once you decide that your assignment calls for comparison and contrast, you need to develop a thesis statement that reflects this purpose.

ASSIGNMENT	THESIS STATEMENT
Philosophy What basic similarities do you find in the beliefs of Henry David Thoreau and Martin Luther King Jr.?	Although King was more politically active, both he and Thoreau strongly supported the idea of civil disobedience.
Nutrition How do the diets of native Japanese and Japanese Americans differ?	As they become more and more assimilated, Japanese Americans consume more fats than native Japanese do.
Literature Contrast the two sisters in Alice Walker's short story "Everyday Use."	Unlike Maggie, Dee—her more successful, better-educated sister—has rejected her family's heritage.

Organizing a Comparison-and-Contrast Essay

When you organize a comparison-and-contrast essay, you can choose either a *point-by-point* or a *subject-by-subject* arrangement. A **point-by-point** comparison alternates between the two subjects you are comparing or contrasting, moving back and forth from one subject to the other. A **subject-by-subject** comparison treats its two subjects separately, first fully discussing one subject and then moving on to consider the other subject. In both kinds of comparison-and-contrast essays, the same points are discussed in the same order for both subjects.

Essay Map: *Point-by-Point Comparison*   **Essay Map:** *Subject-by-Subject Comparison*

Transitions in Comparison-and-Contrast Essays

The transitional words and phrases you use in a comparison-and-contrast essay tell readers whether you are focusing on similarities or on differences. Transitions also help move readers through your essay from one subject to the other and from one point of comparison or contrast to the next. For a list of transitional words and phrases that are frequently used in comparison-and-contrast, see page 101.

Case Study: A Student Writes a Comparison-and-Contrast Essay

Nisha Jani, a student in a first-year writing course, was given the following assignment.

Some people claim that males and females are so different that at times they seem to belong to two different species. Do you agree, or do you think males and females are more alike than different? Write an essay that supports your position.

When Nisha read this assignment, the key words *different* and *alike* told her that the assignment called for a comparison-and-contrast essay. After **brainstorming**, she decided to write about the differences between boys and girls—specifically, middle school boys and girls. She didn't want to write a serious essay, and she thought she could use humor if she wrote about the habits of two typical seventh graders. When she drafted a **thesis statement** for her essay, Nisha made sure that it focused on differences: "The typical boy and girl lead very different lives."

Once she had a thesis statement, she **listed** some of the most obvious differences between male and female seventh graders. When she reviewed the ideas on her list, she decided to follow her two subjects (Johnny and Jane) through a typical school day, and this decision led her to structure her essay as a point-by-point comparison that would contrast boys' and girls' behavior at different points of their day.

When Nisha thought she had enough material to write about, she **wrote a draft** of her essay. TESTing her draft showed her that she had included all the required elements, so she felt ready to schedule a **conference** with her instructor. After the conference, she **revised her thesis statement** to make it a bit more specific, added more examples and details, sharpened her summary statement so that it reinforced her essay's main idea, and added more transitions to make the contrast between her two subjects clearer. After she finished these revisions, she **edited** and **proofread** her essay and checked her **format**.

The final draft that follows includes all the elements Nisha looked for when she TESTed her essay.

Model Comparison-and-Contrast Essay

Read Nisha's finished essay, and complete the tasks in Practice 15-6.

T E S T

- Thesis Statement
- Evidence
- Summary Statement
- Transitions

Another Ordinary Day

1   "Boys are from Jupiter and get stupider / Girls are from Mars and become movie stars / Boys take a bath and smell like trash / Girls take a shower and smell like a flower." As simple playground songs like this one suggest, the two sexes are very different. As adults, men and women have similar goals, values, and occupations, but as children and teenagers, boys and girls often seem to belong to two different species. In fact, from the first moment of the day to the last, the typical boy and girl lead very different lives.

Introduction

2   The sun rises, and the alarm clock signals the beginning of another day for Johnny and Jane, two seventh-grade classmates. Johnny, an average thirteen-year-old boy, wakes up late and has to hurry. He throws on his favorite jeans, a baggy T-shirt, and a baseball cap. Then, he has a hearty high-cholesterol breakfast and runs out of the house to school, usually forgetting some vital book or homework assignment. Jane, unlike Johnny,

Topic sentence (identifies first difference)

Body paragraphs

Examples and details

wakes up early and takes her time. She takes a long shower and then blow-dries her hair. For Jane, getting dressed can be a very difficult process, one that often includes taking everything out of her closet and calling friends for advice. After she makes her decision, she helps herself to some food (probably low- or no-fat) and goes off to school, making sure she has with her everything she needs.

Topic sentence (identifies second difference)

School is a totally different experience for Johnny and Jane. Johnny   3
will probably sit in the back of the classroom with a couple of other guys, throwing paper airplanes and spitballs. These will be directed at the males they do not like and the females they think are kind of cute. (However, if their male friends ever ask the boys about these girls, they will say girls are just losers and deny that they like any of them.) On the opposite side of the classroom, however, Jane is focused on a very different kind of activity. At first, it looks as if she is carefully copying the algebra notes that the teacher is putting on the board, but her notes have absolutely nothing to do with algebra. Instead, she is writing about boys, clothes, and other topics that are much more important to her than the square root of 121. She proceeds to fold the note into a box or other creative shape, which can often put origami to shame. As soon as the teacher turns her back, the note is passed, and the process begins all over again.

Examples and details

Body paragraphs

> **WORD POWER**
>
> **origami** the Japanese art of folding paper into shapes representing flowers or animals

Topic sentence (identifies third difference)

Lunch, a vital part of the school day, is also very different for Johnny and   4
Jane. On the one hand, for Johnny and his friends, it is a time to compare baseball cards, exchange sports facts, and of course tell jokes about every bodily function imaginable. In front of them on the table, their trays are filled with pizza, soda, fries, and chips, and this food is their main focus. For Jane, on the other hand, lunch is not about eating; it is a chance to exchange the latest gossip about who is going out with whom. The girls look around to see what people are wearing, what they should do with their hair, and so on. Jane's meal is quite a bit smaller than Johnny's: it consists of a small low-fat yogurt and half a bagel (if she feels like splurging, she will spread some cream cheese on the bagel).

Examples and details

Topic sentence (identifies fourth difference)

After school, Johnny and Jane head in different directions. Johnny   5
rushes home to get his bike and meets up with his friends to run around and play typical "guy games," like pick-up basketball or touch football. Johnny and his friends play with every boy who shows up, whether they know him or not. They may get into physical fights and arguments, but they always plan to meet up again the next day. In contrast to the boys, Jane and her friends are very selective. Their circle is a small one, and they do everything together. Some days, they go to the mall (they will not necessarily buy anything there, but they will consider the outing productive anyway because they will have spent time together). Most days, though, they just talk, with the discussion ranging from school to guys to lipstick colors. When Jane gets home, she will most likely run to the phone and talk for hours to the same three or four girls.

Examples and details

Conclusion

At the age of twelve or thirteen, boys and girls do not seem to have   6
very much in common. Given this situation, it is amazing that boys and girls grow up to become men and women who interact as neighbors, friends, and coworkers. What is even more amazing is that so many grow up to share lives and raise families together, treating each other with love and respect.

PRACTICE
15-6

1. Restate Nisha's thesis statement in your own words.

2. Does Nisha's opening paragraph identify the subjects she will discuss? Does it tell whether she will focus on similarities or on differences?

3. Nisha's essay is a point-by-point comparison. What four points does she discuss for each of her two subjects?

4. Review the topic sentences in Nisha's body paragraphs. What part of the day does each topic sentence identify?

5. Review the transitional words and phrases Nisha uses to move readers from one subject (Johnny) to the other (Jane). Do you think these transitions are effective, or should they be revised to make the contrast clearer?

6. What is this essay's greatest strength? What is its greatest weakness?

grammar in context

Comparison and Contrast

When you write a comparison-and-contrast essay, be sure to present the points you are comparing or contrasting in **parallel** terms to highlight their similarities or differences.

> ┌─PARALLEL─┐
> Johnny, an average thirteen-year-old boy, wakes up late and has to hurry.
>
> ┌──PARALLEL──┐
> Jane, unlike Johnny, wakes up early and takes her time.

For information on revising to make ideas parallel, see Chapter 21.

> 🄴 For more practice with parallelism, complete the LearningCurve Parallelism activity at **macmillanhighered.com/writingfirst**.

Step-by-Step Guide: Writing a Comparison-and-Contrast Essay

Now, you are ready to write a comparison-and-contrast essay on one of the following topics (or a topic of your choice).

TOPICS

Two coworkers
Two movie heroes
How you expect your life to be different from the lives of your parents
Men's and women's ideas about their body images
Two ways of studying for an exam
Risk takers and people who play it safe
Country and city living (or, compare suburban living with either)

Two popular magazines (features, ads, target audiences, pictures)
Leaders and followers
Designer products and counterfeit products
Optimists and pessimists

As you write your essay, follow these steps.

1. Planning
   - Make sure your topic calls for comparison and contrast.
   - Find ideas to write about.
   - Decide whether you want to discuss similarities or differences.
   - Identify your main idea, and write a thesis statement.

2. Organizing
   - Identify specific points of comparison or contrast to support your thesis.
   - Decide whether to structure your essay as a point-by-point or subject-by-subject comparison.
   - Arrange your points in a logical order, making an informal outline if necessary.

3. Drafting
   - Draft your essay.

4. TESTing and Revising
   - TEST your essay, referring to the TESTing a Comparison-and-Contrast Essay checklist that follows.
   - Revise your essay, referring to the Self-Assessment Checklist on page 163 and the Strategies for Revising chart on page 162.

5. Editing and Proofreading
   - Edit your essay, referring to the Self-Assessment Checklist on page 166.
   - Proofread your essay, and make sure it follows the proper format.

TESTing a comparison-and-contrast essay

Thesis Statement Unifies Your Essay

☐ Does your introduction include a **thesis statement** that expresses your main idea, identifying the two subjects you will compare and indicating whether your essay will examine similarities or differences?

Evidence Supports Your Essay's Thesis Statement

☐ Do you discuss all significant points of comparison or contrast that apply to your two subjects, explaining each similarity or difference using specific examples and details?

□ Does all your **evidence**—examples and details—support your thesis, or should some be deleted?

□ Have you treated similar points for both of your subjects?

□ Is your essay's organization consistent with either a point-by-point comparison or a subject-by-subject comparison?

S ummary Statement Reinforces Your Essay's Unity

□ Does your conclusion include a **summary statement** that reinforces your essay's thesis, reminding readers what your two subjects are and how they are alike or different?

T ransitions Add Coherence to Your Essay

□ Do you include **transitions** that introduce each of your points of comparison or contrast and move readers from one subject or point to another?

15g Classification Essays

Classification is the act of sorting items into appropriate categories. **Classification essays** divide a whole (your subject) into categories, sorting various items into these categories. (For information about writing classification paragraphs, see Chapter 10.)

When you **TEST** a **classification** essay, make sure it includes all these elements.

T ▪ **Thesis Statement**—The introduction of a classification essay should include a **thesis statement** that communicates the essay's main idea and indicates what the essay will classify.

E ▪ **Evidence**—The body paragraphs should provide **evidence**—examples and details—to support the thesis statement. The topic sentence of each paragraph should identify the category it will discuss, and the examples and details should explain the category and differentiate it from other categories.

S ▪ **Summary Statement**—The conclusion of a classification essay should include a **summary statement** that reinforces the essay's thesis.

T ▪ **Transitions**—A classification essay should include **transitional words and phrases** to show how categories are related to one another and to the thesis.

Moving from Assignment to Thesis

The wording of your assignment may suggest that you write a classification essay. For example, you may be asked to consider *kinds*, *types*, *categories*, *components*, *segments*, or *parts of a whole*. Once you decide that your assignment calls for classification, you need to develop a thesis statement that reflects this purpose.

ASSIGNMENT	THESIS STATEMENT
Business What kinds of courses are most useful for students planning to run their own businesses?	Courses dealing with accounting, management, and computer science offer the most useful skills for future business owners.
Biology List the components of blood, and explain the function of each.	Red blood cells, white blood cells, platelets, and plasma have distinct functions.
Education Classify elementary school children according to their academic needs.	The elementary school population includes special-needs students, students with reading and math skills at or near grade level, and academically gifted students.

Organizing a Classification Essay

As a rule, each paragraph of a classification essay examines a separate category—a different part of the whole. For example, a paragraph could focus on one kind of course in the college curriculum, one component of the blood, or one type of child. Within each paragraph, you discuss the individual items you have put into a particular category—for example, accounting courses, red blood cells, or gifted students. If you consider some categories less important than others, you may decide to discuss those minor categories together in a single paragraph, devoting full paragraphs only to the most significant categories.

Essay Map: *One Category in Each Paragraph*

- Introduction (thesis statement identifies whole and its major categories)
- *First category*
- *Second category* — Evidence
- *Third category*
- Conclusion (includes summary statement)

Essay Map: *Major Categories in Separate Paragraphs; Minor Categories Grouped Together*

- Introduction (thesis statement identifies whole and its major categories)
- *Minor categories*
- *First major category* — Evidence
- *Second (and more important) major category*
- *Third (and most important) major category*
- Conclusion (includes summary statement)

Transitions in Classification Essays

In a classification essay, topic sentences identify the category or categories discussed in each paragraph. Transitional words and phrases signal movement from one category to the next and may also tell readers which categories you consider more (or less) important. For a list of transitional words and phrases that are frequently used in classification, see page 111.

Case Study: A Student Writes a Classification Essay

Rob O'Neal, a student in a first-year writing course, was given the following assignment.

> Write a classification essay focusing on a type of consumer product—for example, smartphones, jeans, mountain bikes, or hair gels. Discuss three or four categories of the product you select, examining the same features for each category.

At first, Rob was overwhelmed by the possibilities; after all, he was a consumer, and there were many products to choose from. Stuck in traffic on his way home from school, he started noticing the names of the different cars around him and thinking about all the different models he had learned to identify when he was younger and fascinated by everything related to cars. At this point, he realized that he could write his essay about cars, classifying them on the basis of the kinds of names they had.

When Rob got home, he **brainstormed**, listing all the car names he could think of. Then, he made a **cluster diagram** to help him sort all the names into categories. When he looked over his diagram, he saw that he could organize the car names he had listed into three categories: those that suggest exciting destinations, those that suggest toughness, and those that suggest exploration and discovery. Identifying these three categories led him to a **thesis statement** for his essay: "The names auto manufacturers choose for their cars appeal to Americans' deepest desires."

When he **drafted** his essay, Rob developed each branch of his cluster diagram into one of his body paragraphs and wrote topic sentences that clearly identified and defined each category. When he TESTed his essay, he saw that it included all the required elements, but he still wasn't completely satisfied with his draft. To help him plan his revision, he made a **writing center appointment** and went over his draft with a tutor. She advised him to add more examples of each kind of car name as well as more transitional words and phrases to help readers move smoothly through his essay. When he finished making the revisions suggested by his tutor (as well as some he decided on himself), he went on to **edit** and **proofread** his essay and checked his **format**.

The final draft that follows includes all the elements Rob looked for when he TESTed his essay.

Model Classification Essay

Read Rob's finished essay, and complete the tasks in Practice 15-7.

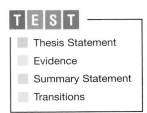

T E S T
- Thesis Statement
- Evidence
- Summary Statement
- Transitions

Introduction

Topic sentence
(identifies first category)

Examples and details

Topic sentence
(identifies second category)

Examples and details

Body paragraphs

Topic sentence
(identifies third category)

Examples and details

Conclusion

Selling a Dream

The earliest automobiles were often named after the men who manufactured   1
them—Ford, Studebaker, Nash, Olds, Chrysler, Dodge, Chevrolet, and so on. Over
the years, however, American car makers began competing to see what kinds
of names would sell the most cars. Many car names seem to have been chosen
simply for how they sound: Alero, Corvette, Neon, Probe, Caprice. Many others,
however, are designed to sell specific dreams to consumers. Americans always
seem to want to be, do, and become something different. They want to be tough
and brave, to explore new places, to take risks. The names auto manufacturers
choose for their cars appeal to Americans' deepest desires.

Some American cars are named for places people dream of traveling to.   2
Park Avenue, Malibu, Riviera, Seville, Tahoe, Yukon, Aspen, and Durango are
some names that suggest escape—to New York City, California, Europe, the
West. Other place names—Sebring, Daytona, and Bonneville, for example—
are associated with the danger and excitement of car racing. And then there is
the El Dorado, a car named for a fictional paradise: a city of gold.

Other car names convey rough and tough, even dangerous, images.   3
Animal names fall into this category, with models like Ram, Bronco, and
Mustang suggesting powerful, untamed beasts. The "rough and tough"
category also includes car names that suggest the wildness of the Old West:
Wrangler and Rodeo, for example. Because the American auto industry was
originally centered near Detroit, Michigan, where many cities have Indian
names, cars named for the cities where they are manufactured inherited
these names. Thus, cars called Cadillac, Pontiac, and Cherokee recall the
history of Indian nations, and these, too, might suggest the excitement of
the untamed West.

The most interesting car names in terms of the dream they sell, however,   4
were selected to suggest exploration and discovery. Years ago, some car names
honored real explorers, like DeSoto and LaSalle. Now, model names only sell an
abstract idea. Still, American car names like Blazer, Explorer, Navigator, Journey,
Mountaineer, Expedition, Caravan, and Voyager (as well as the names of foreign
cars driven by many Americans, such as Nissan's Pathfinder and Quest and
Honda's Passport, Pilot, and Odyssey) have the power to make drivers feel they
are blazing new trails and discovering new worlds—when in fact they may
simply be carpooling their children to a soccer game or commuting to work.

Most people take cars for granted, but manufacturers still try to make   5
consumers believe they are buying more than just transportation. Today, however,
the car is just an ordinary piece of machinery, a necessity for many people.
Sadly, the automobile is no longer seen as the amazing invention it once was.

PRACTICE
15-7

1. Restate Rob's thesis statement in your own words.

2. What three categories of car names does Rob discuss in his essay?

3. Is Rob's treatment of the three categories similar? Does he present the same kind of information for each kind of car name?

4. How do Rob's topic sentences move readers from one category to the next? How do they link the three categories?

5. Do you think Rob should have included additional examples in each category? Should he have included any additional categories?

6. What is this essay's greatest strength? What is its greatest weakness?

grammar in context

Classification

When you write a classification essay, you may want to list the categories you are going to discuss or the examples in each category. If you do, use a **colon** to introduce your list, and make sure that a complete sentence comes before the colon.

> Many car names seem to be chosen simply for how they sound: Alero, Corvette, Neon, Probe, Caprice.

For information on how to use a colon to introduce a list, see 35d.

Step-by-Step Guide: Writing a Classification Essay

Now, you are ready to write a classification essay on one of the following topics (or a topic of your own).

TOPICS

Types of teachers (or bosses)
Ways to lose (or gain) weight
Items hanging on your walls
Kinds of moods
Kinds of stores in a local
    shopping mall
Kinds of learning styles

Traits of oldest children, middle
    children, and youngest children
Kinds of desserts
Kinds of workers you encounter
    in a typical day
College students' clothing choices
Kinds of tattoos

As you write your essay, follow these steps.

1. Planning
   - Make sure your topic calls for classification.
   - Find ideas to write about.
   - Identify your main idea, and write a thesis statement.

2. Organizing
   - Decide what categories you will discuss.
   - Sort examples and details into categories.
   - Arrange your categories in an effective order, making an informal outline if necessary.

3. Drafting
   - Draft your essay.

4. TESTing and Revising

 ▪ TEST your essay, referring to the TESTing a Classification Essay checklist that follows.

 ▪ Revise your essay, referring to the Self-Assessment Checklist on page 163 and the Strategies for Revising chart on page 162.

5. Editing and Proofreading

 ▪ Edit your essay, referring to the Self-Assessment Checklist on page 166.

 ▪ Proofread your essay, and make sure it follows the proper format.

TESTing a classification essay

Thesis Statement Unifies Your Essay

☐ Does your introduction include a **thesis statement** that clearly identifies the subject of your classification and the categories you will discuss?

Evidence Supports Your Essay's Thesis Statement

☐ Does all your **evidence**—examples and details—support your thesis, or should some be deleted?

☐ Do you treat each major category similarly and with equal thoroughness?

Summary Statement Reinforces Your Essay's Unity

☐ Does your conclusion include a **summary statement** that reinforces your essay's thesis?

Transitions Add Coherence to Your Essay

☐ Do you include **transitions** that introduce your categories and lead readers from one category to the next?

15h   Definition Essays

Definition explains the meaning of a term or concept. A **definition essay** presents an *extended definition*, using various patterns of development to move beyond a simple dictionary definition. (For information about writing definition paragraphs, see Chapter 11.)

When you TEST a **definition** essay, make sure it includes all these elements.

T ■ **Thesis Statement**—The introduction of a definition essay should include a **thesis statement** that communicates the essay's main idea and identifies the term you are going to define.

E ■ **Evidence**—The body paragraphs should include **evidence**—examples and details—that supports the thesis statement and defines your term. Body paragraphs may use different patterns of development.

S ■ **Summary Statement**—The conclusion of a definition essay should include a **summary statement** that reinforces the essay's thesis.

T ■ **Transitions**—A definition essay should include **transitional words and phrases** to move readers from one section of the definition to the next.

Moving from Assignment to Thesis

The wording of your assignment may suggest that you write a definition essay. For example, you may be asked to *define* or *explain* or to answer the question *What is x?* or *What does x mean?* Once you decide that your assignment calls for definition, you need to develop a thesis statement that reflects this purpose.

ASSIGNMENT	THESIS STATEMENT
Art Explain the meaning of the term *performance art*.	Unlike more conventional forms of art, *performance art* extends beyond the canvas.
Biology What did Darwin mean by the term *natural selection*?	*Natural selection*, popularly known as "survival of the fittest," is a good deal more complicated than most people think.
Psychology What is *attention-deficit hyperactivity disorder*?	*Attention-deficit hyperactivity disorder* (**ADHD**), once narrowly defined as a childhood problem, is now known to affect adults as well as children.

Organizing a Definition Essay

As the thesis statements in the chart above suggest, definition essays can be developed in various ways. For example, you can define something by telling how it occurred (narration), by describing its appearance (description), by giving a series of examples (exemplification), by explaining how it operates (process), by telling how it is similar to or different from something else (comparison and contrast), or by discussing its parts (classification).

Some definition essays use a single pattern of development; others combine several patterns of development, perhaps using a different one in each paragraph.

Essay Map: *Single Pattern of Development*

Introduction (thesis statement identifies term to be defined)

Definition by example

Additional examples

Additional examples

Conclusion (includes summary statement)

Evidence

Essay Map: *Combination of Several Different Patterns of Development*

Introduction (thesis statement identifies term to be defined)

Definition by description

Definition by example

Definition by comparison and contrast

Conclusion (includes summary statement)

Evidence

Transitions in Definition Essays

The kinds of transitions used in a definition essay depend on the specific pattern or patterns of development in the essay. For a list of transitional words and phrases that are frequently used in definition, see page 120.

Case Study: A Student Writes a Definition Essay

Kristin Whitehead, a student in a first-year writing course, was given the following assignment.

> From the attached list, choose a slang term, an abbreviation or short-hand used in text messages, or a technical term used in one of your classes. Write an essay in which you define this term, developing your definition with any patterns that seem appropriate.

Because her instructor gave the class a list of topics to choose from, Kristin was able to decide on a topic quickly. She chose to define *street smart*, a term with which she was very familiar. She was particularly interested in defining this term because she thought of herself as a street-smart person.

Kristin had learned from experience how important it was to be street smart, and she **brainstormed** about her experiences to find information to guide her as she drafted her essay. In her **thesis statement**, she indicated why she was defining this term, and in her body paragraphs she defined her term by giving examples of behavior that she considered to be (and *not* to be) street smart.

When she **TEST**ed her draft, she was satisfied with the wording of her thesis statement and her supporting evidence, but she knew that she still needed to add a summary statement that did more than just repeat the wording of her thesis statement; she also needed to add clearer topic sentences. Since she knew she was going to meet with her **peer-review** group, she decided to ask her classmates for advice about these two issues. With their help, she revised her summary statement and tied her body paragraphs together by adding the same introductory phrase to the topic sentences of paragraphs 2, 3, and 4. When she finished **revising** her essay, Kristin went on to **edit** and **proofread** it and checked her **format**.

The final draft that follows includes all the elements Kristin looked for when she **TEST**ed her essay.

Model Definition Essay

Read Kristin's finished essay, and complete the tasks in Practice 15-8.

Street Smart

1   I grew up in a big city, so I was practically born street smart. I learned the hard way how to act and what to do, and so did my friends. To us, being *street smart* meant having common sense. We wanted to be cool, but we needed to be safe, too. Now I go to college in a big city, and I realize that not everyone here grew up the way I did. Many students are from suburbs or rural areas, and they are either terrified of the city or totally ignorant of city life. The few suburban or rural students who are willing to venture downtown are not street smart—but they should be. Being street smart is a vital survival skill, one that everyone should learn.

2   For me, being street smart means knowing how to protect my possessions. Friends of mine who are not used to city life insist on wearing all their jewelry when they go downtown. I think this is asking for trouble, and I know better. I always tuck my chain under my shirt and leave my gold earrings home. Another thing that surprises me is how some of my friends wave their money around. They always seem to be standing on the street, trying to count their change or stuff dollars into their wallets. Street-smart people make sure to put their money safely away in their pockets or purses before they leave a store. A street-smart person will also carry a backpack, a purse strapped across the chest, or no purse at all. A person who is not street smart carries a purse loosely over one shoulder or dangles it by its handle. Again, these people are asking for trouble.

3   Being street smart also means protecting myself. It means being aware of my surroundings at all times and looking alert. A lot of times, I have been downtown with people who kept stopping on the street to talk about where they should go next or walking up and down the same street over and over again. A street-smart person would never do this. It is important that I look as if I know where I am going at all times, even if I don't. Whenever possible, I decide on a destination in advance, and I make sure I know how to get there. Even if I am not completely sure where I am headed, I make sure my body language conveys my confidence in my ability to reach my destination.

4   Finally, being street smart means protecting my life. A street-smart person does not walk alone, especially after dark, in an unfamiliar neighborhood.

T **E** S T

- Thesis Statement
- Evidence
- Summary Statement
- Transitions

Introduction

Topic sentence (identifies first part of definition)

Examples and details

Topic sentence (identifies second part of definition)

Body paragraphs

Examples and details

Topic sentence (identifies third part of definition)

Examples and details

A street-smart person does not ask random strangers for directions; when lost, he or she asks a shopkeeper for help. A street-smart person takes main streets instead of side streets. When faced with danger or the threat of danger, a street-smart person knows when to run, when to scream, and when to give up money or possessions to avoid violence.

Conclusion

Being street smart is vitally important—sometimes even a matter of life and death. Some people think it is a gift, but I think it is something almost anyone can learn. Probably the best way to learn how to be street smart is to hang out with people who know where they are going.

5

PRACTICE
15-8

1. Restate Kristin's thesis statement in your own words.

2. In your own words, define the term *street smart*. Why does this term require more than a one-sentence definition?

3. Where does Kristin use examples to develop her definition? Where does she use comparison and contrast?

4. What phrase does Kristin repeat in her topic sentences to tie her essay's three body paragraphs together?

5. Kristin's conclusion is quite a bit shorter than her other paragraphs. Do you think she should expand this paragraph? If so, what should she add?

6. What is this essay's greatest strength? What is its greatest weakness?

grammar in context

Definition

When you write a definition essay, you may begin with a one-sentence definition that you expand in the rest of your essay. When you write your definition sentence, do not use the phrase *is when* or *is where*.

For me, being street smart ~~is when I know~~ how to protect my
                                    means knowing

possessions.

Being street smart is also ~~where I protect~~ myself.
                          means protecting

For information on how to structure a definition sentence, see the Grammar in Context box in 11a.

Step-by-Step Guide: Writing a Definition Essay

Now, you are ready to write a definition essay on one of the following topics (or a topic of your choice).

TOPICS

Upward mobility	Responsibility	Courage
Peer pressure	Procrastination	Happiness
Success	Security	Home
Loyalty	Ambition	Family

As you write your essay, follow these steps.

1. Planning
   - Make sure your topic calls for definition.
   - Find ideas to write about.
   - Identify your main idea, and write a thesis statement.

2. Organizing
   - Decide what patterns of development to use to support your thesis.
   - Arrange supporting examples and details in an effective order, making an informal outline if necessary.

3. Drafting
   - Draft your essay.

4. TESTing and Revising
   - TEST your essay, referring to the TESTing a Definition Essay checklist that follows.
   - Revise your essay, referring to the Self-Assessment Checklist on page 163 and the Strategies for Revising chart on page 162.

5. Editing and Proofreading
   - Edit your essay, referring to the Self-Assessment Checklist on page 166.
   - Proofread your essay, and make sure it follows the proper format.

TESTing a definition essay

T hesis Statement Unifies Your Essay

☐ Does your introduction include a **thesis statement** that identifies the term your essay will define and provides a brief definition?

E vidence Supports Your Essay's Thesis Statement

☐ Is all your **evidence**—examples and details—clearly related to the term you are defining, or should some be deleted?

☐ Do you use appropriate patterns of development to support your definition, or should you explore other options?

S ummary Statement Reinforces Your Essay's Unity

☐ Does your conclusion include a **summary statement** that reinforces your essay's thesis?

T ransitions Add Coherence to Your Essay

☐ Do you include **transitions** that introduce your points and link your ideas?

15i Argument Essays

Argument takes a stand on a debatable issue—that is, an issue that has two sides (and can therefore be debated). An **argument essay** uses different kinds of *evidence*—facts, examples, and sometimes expert opinion—to persuade readers to accept a position. (For information about writing argument paragraphs, see Chapter 12.)

When you **TEST** an **argument** essay, make sure it includes all these elements.

T ▪ **Thesis Statement**—The introduction of an argument essay should include a **thesis statement** that expresses the essay's main idea: the position you will take on the issue.

E ▪ **Evidence**—The body paragraphs should include **evidence**—facts, examples, and expert opinion—to support the thesis statement convincingly. The topic sentence of each body paragraph should identify one point of support for your thesis.

S ▪ **Summary Statement**—The conclusion of an argument essay should include a strong **summary statement** that reinforces the essay's thesis.

T ▪ **Transitions**—An argument essay should include **transitional words and phrases** that show how your points are logically related and that move readers through your argument.

Moving from Assignment to Thesis

The wording of your assignment may suggest that you write an argument essay. For example, you may be asked to *debate, argue, consider, give your opinion, take a position,* or *take a stand.* Once you decide that your assignment calls for argument, you need to develop a thesis statement that takes a position on the topic you will write about in your essay.

ASSIGNMENT	THESIS STATEMENT
Composition Explain your position on a current social issue.	People should be able to invest some of their Social Security contributions in the stock market.
American history Do you believe that General Lee was responsible for the South's defeat at the Battle of Gettysburg? Why or why not?	Because Lee refused to listen to the advice given to him by General Longstreet, he is largely responsible for the South's defeat at the Battle of Gettysburg.
Ethics Should physician-assisted suicide be legalized?	Although many people think physician-assisted suicide should remain illegal, it should be legal in certain situations.

Organizing an Argument Essay

An argument essay can be organized *inductively* or *deductively*. An **inductive argument** moves from the specific to the general—that is, from a group of specific observations to a general conclusion based on these observations. An essay on the first topic in the chart on page 232, for example, could be an inductive argument. It could begin by presenting facts, examples, and expert opinion about the benefits of investing in the stock market and end with the conclusion that people should be able to invest part of their Social Security contributions in the stock market.

A **deductive argument** moves from the general to the specific. A deductive argument begins with a **major premise** (a general statement that the writer believes his or her audience will accept) and then moves to a **minor premise** (a specific instance of the belief stated in the major premise). It ends with a **conclusion** that follows from the two premises. For example, an essay on the last topic in the chart on page 232 could be a deductive argument. It could begin with the major premise that all terminally ill patients who are in great pain should be given access to physician-assisted suicide. It could then go on to state and explain the minor premise that a particular patient is both terminally ill and in great pain, offering facts, examples, and the opinions of experts to support this premise. The essay could conclude that this patient should, therefore, be allowed the option of physician-assisted suicide. The deductive argument presented in the essay would have three parts.

MAJOR PREMISE   All terminally ill patients who are in great pain should be allowed to choose physician-assisted suicide.

MINOR PREMISE   John Lacca is a terminally ill patient who is in great pain.

CONCLUSION   Therefore, John Lacca should be allowed to choose physician-assisted suicide.

Before you present your argument, think about whether your readers are likely to be hostile toward, neutral toward, or in agreement with your position. Once you understand your audience, you can decide which points to make in support of your argument. Strive for a balanced, moderate tone, and avoid name-calling or personal attacks.

Begin each paragraph of your argument essay with a topic sentence that clearly introduces a point in support of your thesis. Throughout your essay, include specific examples that will make your arguments persuasive. Keep in mind that arguments that rely just on generalizations are not as convincing as those that include vivid details and specific examples.

In addition to presenting your case, your essay should also briefly summarize arguments *against* your position and **refute** them (that is, argue against them) by identifying factual errors or errors in logic. If an opposing argument is particularly strong, concede its strength—but try to point out some weaknesses as well. If you deal with opposing arguments in this way, your audience will see you as a fair and reasonable person.

Essay Map: *Inductive Argument*

Introduction (includes thesis statement)

First point

Second point

Third point

Opposing arguments identified and refuted

Conclusion (includes summary statement)

⎤ Evidence

Essay Map: *Deductive Argument*

Introduction (includes thesis statement)

Major premise stated and explained

Minor premise stated and explained

Minor premise further explained

Opposing arguments identified and refuted

Conclusion (includes summary statement)

⎤ Evidence

Transitions in Argument Essays

Transitions are extremely important in argument essays because they not only signal the movement from one part of the argument to another but also relate specific points to one another and to the thesis statement. For a list of transitional words and phrases that are frequently used in argument, see page 130.

Case Study: A Student Writes an Argument Essay

Alex Norman, a student in a first-year writing course, was assigned to write an argument essay on a controversial issue of his choice. His instructor suggested that students find a topic by reading their campus and local newspapers, going online to read national news stories and political blogs, and watching public affairs programs on television. Alex followed this advice and also talked about his assignment with friends and family members.

The issue that most interested him was one about which he had already written an argument paragraph for an earlier assignment: the question of whether the federal government should do more to subsidize the cost of college for low-income students. Now, he thought he could do some additional work to develop some of that paragraph's ideas into an argument essay.

Alex began by **brainstorming**, recording all his ideas on this complex issue, including those he had discussed in his earlier paragraph. He also included ideas he developed as he spoke to his sister, a recent college graduate, and to his boss at the bank where he worked part-time. When he read over his brainstorming notes, he saw that he had good arguments both for and against increasing government funding for low-income students. Although Alex sympathized with students who needed help paying for school, he questioned whether taxpayers should have to foot the bill. At this point, he wasn't sure what position to take in his essay, so he scheduled an appointment for a **conference** with his instructor.

Alex's instructor pointed out that he could make a good case either for or against greater government subsidies; like many controversial issues, this one had no easy answers. She encouraged him to support the position that seemed right to him and to use the information on the opposing side to present (and refute) opposing arguments. She also recommended that Alex email his first draft to her so she could review it.

After he thought about his instructor's comments, Alex decided to argue in favor of increasing government grants to help low-income students pay for college. Before he began to draft his essay, he wrote a **thesis statement** that presented his position on the issue; then, he arranged supporting points from his brainstorming notes into an **outline** that he could follow as he wrote. As he **drafted** his essay, Alex made sure to support his thesis with evidence and to explain his position as clearly and thoroughly as possible. He paid special attention to choosing transitional words and phrases that would indicate how his points were logically connected to one another.

When Alex finished his draft, he **TEST**ed it, taking a quick inventory to make sure he had included all four necessary components of an essay. Then, he emailed the draft to his instructor. Following her suggestions, he **revised** his draft, focusing on his topic sentences, his presentation (and refutation) of opposing arguments, and his introductory and concluding paragraphs. When he was satisfied with his revisions, he **edited** and **proofread** his paper and checked his **format**.

The final draft that follows includes all the elements Alex looked for when he **TEST**ed his essay.

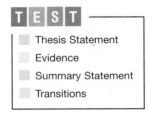

T E S T
- Thesis Statement
- Evidence
- Summary Statement
- Transitions

Model Argument Essay

Read Alex's finished essay, and complete the tasks in Practice 15-9.

Increase Grant Money for Low-Income College Students

1   The price of college tuition has more than doubled over the last two decades. Today, low-income students are finding it especially difficult (and sometimes impossible) to pay for school. Should the government help these students more than it does now? If so, what form should that help take? Rather than reducing aid or asking students to borrow more, the government should give larger grants to subsidize tuition for low-income students.

2   If this is a country that is committed to equal opportunity, then college should be affordable for all. To compete in today's high-tech job market, people need a college degree. However, students' access to college is too often determined by their parents' income. This is unfair. Therefore, the government should make it a priority to support students who are being priced out of a college education. Specifically, the government should give larger grants to low-income students. Although some critics see these grants as unnecessary "handouts," such awards are the best way for the government to invest in the future and to maintain our nation's core values. After all, the country's economy benefits when more of its citizens earn college degrees. Even more important, by giving low-income students the same opportunities to succeed as their more affluent peers, the United States keeps its promise to treat all its citizens fairly.

Introduction

Topic sentence (introduces first point)

Body paragraphs

Facts, examples, or expert opinion

Topic sentence
(introduces second
point)

Facts, examples, or
expert opinion

Topic sentence
(introduces third
point)

Body paragraphs

Facts, examples, or
expert opinion

Topic sentence
(introduces fourth
point)

Facts, examples, or
expert opinion

Conclusion

Works-cited list
(identifies sources of
facts, examples, and
expert opinions)

3   Some people argue that the best way to help students who are struggling to pay for college is to offer them more loans at a lower interest rate. However, this solution is inadequate, unfair, and shortsighted. First of all, lowering the interest rate on student loans only reduces the average monthly payments by a few dollars. Second of all, student loans already unfairly burden low-income students. Why should they have to take on more debt simply because their parents make less money? The government should be trying to reduce the amount these students have to borrow, not increase it. Finally, forcing graduates to start their careers with such a heavy financial burden is unwise for the country's economy. Although loans might cost the government less in the short term, in the long term student debt makes it more difficult for Americans to be successful and competitive.

4   The federal government does have a program in place to help students who demonstrate need, but Pell Grant funding needs to be expanded. As Joy Resmovits reports, despite the rising cost of tuition, college students actually receive proportionally less government grant money than ever before. In fact, Pell Grants are limited to $5,645 per student per year. At most, Pell Grants cover only a third of average college costs. Meanwhile, the education gap between rich and poor is growing. As education policy expert Andrew J. Rotherham observes, while 75 percent of wealthy students earn a four-year degree by age twenty-four, less than 10 percent of low-income students do. To help close this gap, the government should offer more funding to those most in need of financial assistance.

5   Some would argue, however, that the government should do just the opposite. One of the most common criticisms of government subsidies is that they are in some way to blame for the rising costs of college. Critics point out that government grants only make it easier for schools to charge more. This may be true, but as Andrew Rotherham points out, the government could do more to regulate college tuition. For example, the government could offer incentives to schools that keep their costs down or award more generous grants to students who attend affordable schools. Ultimately, withdrawing aid and abandoning students to the free market is irresponsible as well as counterproductive. Instead, the government should take steps to prevent people from taking advantage of its generosity.

6   With the cost of college continuing to rise, now is the time for the government to help the hardest-hit students by offering them more help to pay for their education. Rather than cutting spending on student aid, the government should fund more grants to low-income students. However, it must do so in ways that discourage future increases in tuition. By acting wisely and prudently, the government can improve access to higher education for all and support the country's economic future.

Works Cited

Resmovits, Joy. "Pell Grants for Poor Students Lose $170 Billion in Ryan Budget." *The Huffington Post*. TheHuffingtonPost.com, Inc., 27 Mar. 2012. Web. 19 Apr. 2014.

Rotherham, Andrew J. "How to Fix Pell Grants." *Time*. Time, Inc., 24 May 2012. Web. 19 Apr. 2014.

PRACTICE
15-9   1. In your own words, summarize the position Alex takes in his essay.

2. List the facts and examples Alex uses to support his thesis. Where does he include expert opinion?

3. Can you list any other supporting evidence that Alex should have included but didn't?

4. Review the transitional words and phrases Alex uses. How do they move his argument along? Should he add any transitions?

5. Where does Alex address opposing arguments? Can you think of other arguments he should have addressed?

6. What is this essay's greatest strength? What is its greatest weakness?

grammar in context

Argument

When you write an argument essay, you need to show the relationships between your ideas by combining sentences to create **compound sentences** and **complex sentences**.

> The federal government does have a program in place to help students who demonstrate need*, but* Pell Grant funding needs to be expanded. (compound sentence)
>
> *Although some critics* ~~Some critics~~ see these grants as unnecessary "handouts*,*" *such* ~~Such~~ awards are the best way for the government to invest in the future and to maintain our nation's core values. (complex sentence)

For information on how to create compound sentences, see Chapter 18.
For information on how to create complex sentences, see Chapter 19.

Step-by-Step Guide: Writing an Argument Essay

Now, you are ready to write an argument essay on one of the following topics (or a topic of your choice).

TOPICS

Teenagers who commit serious crimes should (or should not) be tried as adults.

Citizens without criminal records should (or should not) be permitted to carry concealed weapons.

Human beings should (or should not) be used as subjects in medical research experiments.

College financial aid should (or should not) be based solely on merit.
Government funds should (or should not) be used to support the arts.
Public high schools should (or should not) be permitted to distribute condoms to students.
The minimum wage should (or should not) be raised.
College athletes should (or should not) be paid to play.
Convicted felons should (or should not) lose the right to vote.

As you write your essay, follow these steps.

1. Planning
   - Make sure your topic calls for argument.
   - Find ideas to write about.
   - Decide on the position you will support, and write a thesis statement that clearly expresses this position.

2. Organizing
   - List the key points in support of your thesis.
   - Arrange your key supporting points in an effective order.
   - List evidence (facts, examples, and expert opinion) in support of each point.
   - List arguments against your position.
   - Make an outline that includes key supporting and opposing points.

3. Drafting
   - Draft your essay.

4. TESTing and Revising
   - TEST your essay, referring to the TESTing an Argument Essay checklist on page 239.
   - Revise your essay, referring to the Self-Assessment Checklist on page 163 and the Strategies for Revising chart on page 162.

5. Editing and Proofreading
   - Edit your essay, referring to the Self-Assessment Checklist on page 166.
   - Proofread your essay, and make sure it follows the proper format.

TESTing an argument essay

Thesis Statement Unifies Your Essay

☐ Does your introduction include a **thesis statement** that clearly expresses the stand you take on the issue you will discuss? Is this issue debatable—that is, does it really have two sides?

Evidence Supports Your Essay's Thesis Statement

☐ Does all your **evidence**—facts, examples, and expert opinion—support your thesis, or should some be deleted?

☐ Do you have enough evidence to support your points?

☐ Have you considered whether readers are likely to be hostile toward, neutral toward, or in agreement with your position—and have you chosen your points accordingly?

☐ Is your evidence presented in a clear inductive or deductive order?

Summary Statement Reinforces Your Essay's Unity

☐ Does your conclusion include a **summary statement** that reinforces your essay's thesis?

Transitions Add Coherence to Your Essay

☐ Do you include **transitions** that introduce your points?

☐ Do you include enough transitional words and phrases to help readers follow the logic of your argument?

Although this chapter presents student essays that are structured primarily according to a single pattern of development—exemplification, narration, description, process, cause and effect, comparison and contrast, classification, definition, or argument—professional writers often combine several patterns in a single essay.

The following short newspaper commentary, "Whatever Happened to Walking to School?" by Lenore Skenazy, combines several of the patterns of development that are explained and illustrated in this chapter. Read the essay carefully, and then answer the Questions for Discussion on page 241.

Whatever Happened to Walking to School?

Lenore Skenazy

If you think the first week of September means kids skipping off to school, you might want to check your calendar—for the century. The way you got to school isn't the way they do.

Take the bus. Sure, about 40% of kids still ride the cheery yellow chugger, but in many towns it doesn't stop only at the bus stops anymore. It stops at each child's house.

Often, the kids aren't waiting outside to get on. They are waiting in their parents' cars—cars the parents drove from the garage to the sidewalk so their children would be climate-controlled and safe from the predators so prevalent on suburban driveways.

Those of us who remember using our own legs for transit now run the risk of sounding Abe Lincolnesque. Today, only about one in 10 kids walks to school, says Lauren Marchetti, director of the National Center for Safe Routes to School.

The shift is so profound that the language itself has changed. "Arrival" and "dismissal" have become "drop-off and "pick-up" because an adult is almost always involved—even when it doesn't make sense.

"When we first moved to town we found a house three blocks from the school," says Annie Anderson, a mom in Corpus Christi, Texas. "The day before school started a lady knocked on my door and asked if I'd like to join the carpool."

"Carpool to where?" Ms. Anderson asked. "She proceeded to explain that not only would I pick up her kid and others every morning of my assigned week, but I would need to pick up their 'carpool seats' before Monday and pass them to the next parent on Friday." Ms. Anderson declined and allowed her second-grader to walk instead. He beat the car every day.

Driving makes sense if the bus takes forever, or if school is on the way to work. But too often drop-off in the morning means snarls and traffic, and afternoon pick-up has become the evacuation of Saigon. At schools around the country, here's how it works:

First, the "car kids" are herded into the gym. "The guards make sure all children sit still and do not move or speak during the process," reports a dad in Tennessee. Outside, "People get there 45 minutes early to get a spot. And the scary thing is, most of the kids live within biking distance," says Kim Meyer, a mom in Greensboro, N.C.

When the bell finally rings, the first car races into the pick-up spot, whereupon the car-line monitor barks into a walkie-talkie: "Devin's mom is here!"

Devin is grabbed from the gym, escorted to the sidewalk and hustled into the car as if under enemy fire. His mom peels out and the next car pulls up. "Sydney's mom is here!"

Kerry Buss, a curriculum developer in Fairfax County, Va., says her son's school does this, "And this is the same school that took out the bike racks to discourage kids from biking." It's also the school her husband attended as a child. Back then, "he and his sister walked to school like every other kid in the neighborhood. It was unheard of that there'd be a bus, much less a car line."

How did we get to this point? How did we forget that it's just a walk to school?

Simple. We bought the line that good parenting is the same as overparenting. That the more we could do for our children, the better. We forgot the joy of scuffing down the street when we were young, crunching leaves, picking up seeds, and decided we'd do it all for our kids, independence be damned!

Except independence is good. Children who walk to school are healthier, for obvious reasons. New studies suggest they may do better academically, too. "You can see the difference in the kids who walk or bike," says Jerry Flynn, principal of St. Thomas Aquinas, a Catholic school in Indianapolis that has been encouraging parents to stop driving their kids. "They're bright, chatty, ready to go."

And one day, they might even get to tell their own kids something more than: "When I was your age, I walked 10 feet to the SUV—and it was uphill both ways."

QUESTIONS FOR DISCUSSION

1. What patterns of development are used in this essay? Work with another student to decide where each pattern is used. Then, label the section of the essay where each pattern appears.

2. What is the thesis of this essay? Restate it in your own words. If you were to add this thesis statement to the essay, where would you put it?

3. How does each pattern of development that you identified in Question 1 support the essay's thesis?

4. Look again at the thesis statement you supplied in your answer to Question 2. What pattern of development does it suggest?

5. What do you think is this essay's primary pattern of development? Explain.

review checklist

Patterns of Essay Development

☐ **Exemplification** essays use specific examples to support a thesis. (See 15a.)

☐ **Narrative** essays tell a story by presenting a series of events in chronological order. (See 15b.)

☐ **Descriptive** essays use details to give readers a clear, vivid picture of a person, place, or object. (See 15c.)

☐ **Process** essays explain the steps in a procedure, telling how something is (or was) done or how to do something. (See 15d.)

☐ **Cause-and-effect** essays identify causes or predict effects. (See 15e.)

☐ **Comparison-and-contrast** essays explain how two things are alike or how they are different. (See 15f.)

☐ **Classification** essays divide a whole into categories, sorting various items into these categories. (See 15g.)

☐ **Definition** essays use various patterns to develop an extended definition. (See 15h.)

☐ **Argument** essays take a stand on a debatable issue, using evidence to persuade readers to accept a position. (See 15i.)

16 Using Research in Your Writing

write first

This chapter will guide you through the process of writing a short source-based essay on a topic of your own choosing. To begin the process, brainstorm to develop a list of topics that you would be interested in researching and writing about.

In this chapter, you will learn to

- choose a topic (16a)
- do research (16b)
- take notes (16c)
- watch out for plagiarism (16d)
- develop a thesis (16e)
- make an outline (16f)
- draft your essay (16g)
- document your sources (16h)

In some essays, you use your own ideas to support your thesis. In others—such as argument essays—your own knowledge about a subject might not be enough to support your thesis. In these situations, you will have to supplement your ideas with **research**—a careful examination of the ideas and opinions of others. Doing research gives you a number of advantages.

- It exposes you to a cross-section of opinion.
- It helps you find supporting material for your essay—for example, an expert's opinion, a memorable quotation, or a useful fact or statistic.
- It tells readers that you are someone who has gained a fuller understanding of your topic—and for this reason are worth listening to.

When you write an essay that calls for research, you find material on the Internet, in the library, and in other places. This information may be in print or electronic form, and it may be drawn from a variety of sources—for example, journals, magazines, newspapers, websites, and books.

16a Choosing a Topic

The first step in writing an essay that calls for research is finding a topic to write about. Before you choose a topic, ask the following questions.

- What is your page limit?
- When is your essay due?
- How many sources are you expected to use?
- What kinds of sources are you expected to use?

The answers to these questions will help you determine if your topic is too broad or too narrow.

When May Compton, a student in a composition course, was asked to write a three- to four-page essay that was due in five weeks, she decided that she wanted to write about the counterfeit designer goods that seemed to be for sale everywhere. May was used to seeing sidewalk vendors selling brand-name sunglasses and jewelry. Recently, she and her friends had been invited to a "purse party," where they were able to buy expensive handbags at extremely low prices. Even though these handbags were not identified as fakes, she was sure that they were. Because May was a marketing major, she wondered how these copies were marketed and sold.

She also wondered if these counterfeits had any negative effects on consumers.

May decided to explore the problem of counterfeit designer merchandise in her essay because she could discuss it in the required number of pages and would be able to finish her essay within the five-week time limit.

choose a topic

Look back at the list of topics you developed in your brainstorming, and choose a topic to write about. Keep in mind that the topic you choose should be one that you are interested in as well as one that you know something about.

16b   Doing Research

When you do research, you—like most students—probably go straight to the Internet. If you do this, however, you are shortchanging yourself. Your college library gives you access to valuable resources—for example, books, journals, and electronic databases—that are available nowhere else, including on the Internet. For this reason, when you begin your research, you should use your college library as well as the Internet.

Finding Information in the Library

For the best results, you should do your library research systematically. Once you get a sense of your topic, you should consult the library's **online catalog**—a comprehensive information system that gives you access to the resources housed in the library. A search of the online catalog is not as "open" as a search of the Internet, where anything and everything is posted. Library resources have been screened by librarians (as well as instructors) and, in many cases, conform to academic standards of reliability.

You search the online catalog just as you would search the Internet: by carrying out a *keyword search* or a *subject search*.

1. You do a **keyword search** the same way you would search using Google or About.com—by entering your keywords in a search box to retrieve a list of books, periodicals, and other materials that are relevant to your topic. The more specific your keywords are, the more focused your search will be. Thus, the keywords *Facebook privacy* will yield more specific (and useful) results than the words *social networking* would.
2. You do a **subject search** by entering a subject heading related to your topic. Unlike keywords, subject headings are predetermined and come from a list of subject headings published by the Library of Congress. Many online catalogs provide lists of subject headings you can use. A subject search is best when you want information about a general topic—for example, *rap music*, *discography*, or *Mark Twain*.

After consulting the online catalog, you should look at the **electronic databases**—such as InfoTrac and ProQuest—that your college library subscribes to. These databases enable you to obtain information from newspapers, magazines, and journals that you cannot freely access by doing a web search. Most of the library's electronic databases enable you to retrieve the full text of articles. (You can usually search them remotely, from home or from anywhere on campus.)

Most online catalogs list the databases to which the library subscribes along with descriptions of the material the databases contain. For example, a database may contain articles on a wide variety of subjects, or it may focus on a specific subject area. Unlike websites, many library databases get information from experts in a particular field. In addition, database sources usually contain full bibliographic information, sometimes in the form of a works-cited entry.

Evaluating Library Sources

In general, the sources in library databases are usually much more reliable than the sources you access on the Internet. Even so, you should still **evaluate** them—that is, determine their usefulness and reliability—before you use them in your essay.

<table>
<tr><td>WORD POWER

tabloid a newspaper that emphasizes stories with sensational content</td></tr>
</table>

- First, determine the **credibility** (believability) of a source. For example, an article in a respected periodical, such as the *New York Times* or the *Wall Street Journal*, is more credible than one in a tabloid, such as the *National Enquirer* or the *Sun*.
- Next, look at the date of publication to decide if the book or periodical is up-to-date.
- Finally, consider the author. Is he or she an expert in the subject the source explores? Does the author strive for objectivity, or does he or she seem to be advancing a particular point of view?

Your instructor or college librarian can help you select sources that are both appropriate and reliable.

Finding Information on the Internet

The Internet can give you access to a great deal of information that can help you support your ideas and develop your essay. However, you have to be very careful when using the Internet because it is an "open" source; anyone can create a website and upload material. Unlike the resources available in your college library, no one is responsible for checking the accuracy of information or the credentials of people who post on the Internet. For this reason, it is your responsibility (and obligation) to determine the trustworthiness of an Internet source and decide whether it is appropriate for your paper.

Once you are online, you need to connect to a **search engine**, which helps you find information by sorting through the millions of documents that are available on the Internet. Among the most popular search engines are Google, Yahoo!, and Bing.

There are two ways to use a search engine to access information.

1. *You can do a keyword search.* All search engines let you do a keyword search. You type a term (or terms) into a box, and the search engine looks for documents that contain the term, listing all the hits that it finds.
2. *You can do a subject search.* Some search engines, such as About .com and Yahoo!, let you do a subject search. First, you choose a broad subject from a list: *Humanities, Arts, Entertainment, Business,* and so on. Each of these general subjects then leads you to more specific subjects, until you eventually get to the subtopic that you want.

Evaluating Internet Sources

Just as you would with library sources, you should determine whether information you find on the Internet is believable and useful. With the Internet, however, you have problems that you generally don't have with the sources available in your college library. Because anyone can publish on the Internet, it is often difficult—if not impossible—to judge the credentials of an author or the accuracy of his or her claims. To make matters worse, sometimes sources have no listed author. Dates can also be missing, so it may be difficult to tell when information was originally posted and when it was updated. Finally, it is often hard to determine if a site has a purpose other than providing information. For example, is the site trying to sell something or advance a political or social agenda? If it is, it may contain information that is biased or incorrect.

You can evaluate Internet sources by asking some basic questions.

- *Who is the author of the site?* Avoid information written by unnamed authors or by authors with questionable credentials.
- *Who is the sponsoring organization?* Be especially careful of using information from websites that are sponsored by companies trying to sell something or organizations that have a particular agenda.
- *Can you verify information posted on the site?* Make sure that you are able to check the source of the information. For example, you should see if an article on a site includes documentation. Also, cross-check information you find there. Does the same information appear in other sources that are reliable?
- *Does the site contain errors?* In addition to factual errors, look out for mistakes in grammar or spelling. Errors such as these should raise a red flag about the accuracy of the information on the site you are visiting.
- *Do the links on the site work?* Make sure that the links on the site are "live." The presence of "dead" links is a good indication that a site is not being properly maintained.
- *Is the information up-to-date?* Make sure that the site's information is current. Avoid sites that contain information that seems old or outdated. A reliable site will usually include the date information was posted and the date it was revised.

When in doubt, the surest strategy for determining whether a website is reliable is to check with a reference librarian or with your instructor. Unless you can be certain that a site is reliable, do not use it as a source.

FYI

Using Wikipedia as a Source

Most college students regularly consult Wikipedia, the open-source online encyclopedia. The rationale behind Wikipedia is that if a large number of people review information, errors will eventually be discovered and corrected. Because there are no full-time editors, however, Wikipedia articles can (and do) contain inaccurate as well as biased information. In addition, anyone—not just experts—can write and edit entries. Understandably, some instructors distrust—or at least question—the accuracy of Wikipedia entries. Be sure to check the accuracy of the information you find in Wikipedia by comparing it to the information in other sources you are using. (Keep in mind that many instructors do not consider articles from any encyclopedia—print or electronic—acceptable for college research.)

May Compton began her research by doing a subject search of her college library's online catalog to find books on her topic. Under the general subject of *counterfeits*, she found the headings *counterfeit coins* and *counterfeit money*. She did not, however, find any books on counterfeit designer goods. Thinking that her topic might be too recent for any books to have been published on the subject, she turned to her library's databases.

A quick look at the InfoTrac database showed that many recent articles had been written about counterfeit designer merchandise. Although some articles just reported police raids on local counterfeiting operations, a few discussed the reasons for counterfeiting and the negative effects of counterfeit goods.

Because May's topic was so current, she found the Internet to be a good source of information. For example, using Google to search for the keywords *counterfeit designer goods*, she found a site maintained by the Resource for Security Executives that gave recent statistics of counterfeit seizures by the Department of Homeland Security. Using the same keywords on Yahoo!, May found an article in the *Arizona Republic* that discussed the purse parties that are often used to sell counterfeit designer handbags.

find information

Review the topic you chose to write about. Then, do research in the library and on the Internet to help you find information on this topic. Remember, you will be using this information to support the points you make.

16c   Taking Notes

Once you have gathered the source material you will need, read it carefully, recording any information you think you can use in your essay. Record your notes either in computer files that you have created for this purpose or on index cards.

Remember that taking notes involves more than just copying down or downloading information. As you record information, you should put it into a form that you can use when you write your paper. For this reason, you should always *paraphrase, summarize,* or *quote* relevant information from your sources.

FYI

Avoiding Plagiarism

When you transfer information from websites into your notes, you may carelessly cut and paste text without recording where the material came from. If you then copy this material into your essay without citing the source, you are committing **plagiarism**—stealing someone else's ideas. Also keep in mind that you must document *all* material that you get from the Internet, just as you document material that you get from print sources. For information on documentation, see 16h. For information on plagiarism, see 16d.

Paraphrasing

When you **paraphrase**, you use your own words to convey a source's key ideas. You paraphrase when you want to include detailed information from the source but not the author's exact words. Paraphrasing is useful when you want to make a difficult discussion easier to understand while still presenting a comprehensive overview of the original.

Writing a Paraphrase

1. Read the passage until you understand it.
2. Note the main idea of the passage, and list key supporting points.
3. Draft your paraphrase, beginning with the source's main idea and then presenting the source's most important supporting points.
4. When you revise, make sure you have used your own words and phrasing, not the words or sentence structure of the original. Use quotation marks to identify any unique or memorable phrases you have borrowed from the source.
5. Document your source.

Here is a passage from the article "Hot Fakes," by Joanie Cox, followed by a student's paraphrase.

ORIGINAL

Always pay close attention to the stitching. On a Kate Spade bag, the logo is stitched perfectly straight; it's not a sticker. Most designers stitch a simple label to the inside of their purses. On Chanel bags, however, the interior label is usually stamped and tends to match the color of the exterior. Study the material the bag is made from. A real Chanel Ligne Cambon multipocket bag, for example, is constructed from buttery lambskin leather, not vinyl.

PARAPHRASE

It is often possible to tell a fake designer handbag from a genuine one by looking at the details. For example, items such as logos should not be crooked. You should also look for the distinctive features of a particular brand of handbag. Counterfeiters will not take the time to match colors, and they may use vinyl instead of expensive leather (Cox).

Note that this paraphrase does not simply change a word here and there. Instead, the student has taken the time to fully understand the main idea and supporting points of the passage and has restated ideas in her own words.

Summarizing

Unlike a paraphrase, which presents the key points of a source in detail, a **summary** is a general restatement, in your own words, of just the main idea of a passage. For this reason, a summary is always much shorter than the original.

> ### Writing a Summary
>
> 1. Read the passage until you understand it.
> 2. Jot down the main idea of the passage.
> 3. As you write, make sure you use your own words, not those of your source.
> 4. When you revise, make sure your summary contains only the ideas of the source.
> 5. Document your source.

Here is a student's summary of the original passage at the top of this page.

SUMMARY

Buyers who want to identify fake handbags should check details such as the way the label is sewn and the material the item is made from (Cox).

Quoting

When you **quote**, you use the author's exact words as they appear in the source, including all punctuation and capitalization. Enclose all words from your source in quotation marks—*followed by appropriate documentation.*

Because quotations can distract readers, use them only when you think that the author's exact words will add something to your discussion.

> ### When to Quote
>
> 1. Quote when the words of a source are so memorable that to put them into your own words would lessen their impact.
> 2. Quote when the words of a source are so precise that a paraphrase or summary would change the meaning of the original.
> 3. Quote when the words of a source add authority to your discussion. The exact words of a recognized expert can help you make your point convincingly.

Here is how a student writer incorporated a quotation from the original passage on page 250 into her notes.

QUOTATION

Someone who wants to buy an authentic designer handbag should look carefully at the material the purse is made from. For example, there is a big difference between vinyl and Chanel's "buttery lambskin leather" (Cox).

Working Sources into Your Writing

To show readers why you are using a source and to help you blend source material smoothly into your essay, introduce paraphrases, summaries, and quotations with **identifying tags** (sometimes called *signal phrases*)—phrases that name the source or its author. You can position an identifying tag at various places in a sentence.

As one celebrity fashion columnist points out, "A real Chanel Ligne Cambon multipocket bag, for example, is constructed from buttery lambskin leather, not vinyl" (Cox).

"A real Chanel Ligne Cambon multipocket bag, for example," says one celebrity fashion columnist, "is constructed from buttery lambskin leather, not vinyl" (Cox).

"A real Chanel Ligne Cambon multipocket bag, for example, is constructed from buttery lambskin leather, not vinyl," observes one celebrity fashion columnist (Cox).

FYI

Identifying Sources

Instead of repeating the word *says*, you can use one of the following words or phrases to identify the source of a quotation, paraphrase, or summary.

admits	concludes	points out
believes	explains	remarks
claims	notes	states
comments	observes	suggests

Synthesizing

When you **synthesize**, you combine ideas from two or more sources with your own ideas. The goal of a synthesis is to use sources to develop your own point about a topic. In a synthesis, then, your own ideas, not those of your sources, should dominate the discussion. In a sense, every time you weave together paraphrase, summary, and quotation to support a point, you are writing a synthesis.

Writing a Synthesis

1. Decide on the point you want to develop.
2. Select at least two or three sources to support your point.
3. Read each source carefully, taking note of how they are alike, how they are different, and how they relate to your point.
4. Begin your synthesis by clearly stating the point you are going to develop.
5. Use specific examples (paraphrases, summaries, and quotations) from your sources to support your point.
6. When you revise, make sure that you have used appropriate transitions to indicate the movement from one source to another. Also be sure that you have clearly identified each source that you discuss.
7. Document all words and ideas that you take from your sources.

Here is a paragraph from May Compton's essay on pages 263–265 in which she incorporates material from three different sources. Notice how she uses source material (underlined) to develop her point that buying counterfeit items is really stealing.

> What most people choose to ignore is that buying counterfeit items is really stealing. Between 2002 and 2012, 325 percent more counterfeit goods were seized than in the previous decade (O'Donnell 03b). The FBI estimates that in the United States alone, companies lose about $250 billion as a result of counterfeits (Wallace). In addition, buyers of counterfeit items avoid the state and local sales taxes that legitimate companies pay. Thus, New York City alone loses about a billion dollars every year as a result of the sale of counterfeit merchandise ("Counterfeit Goods"). When this happens, everyone loses. After all, a billion dollars would pay for a lot of police officers and teachers, would fill a lot of potholes, and would pave a lot of streets. Buyers of counterfeit designer goods do not think of themselves as thieves, but that is exactly what they are.

take notes

Review the information you gathered. Then, take notes, making sure that you fairly and accurately paraphrase, summarize, quote, and synthesize your sources. (Don't forget to include full source information, including page numbers, with each note.)

16d   Watching Out for Plagiarism

As a rule, you must **document** (give source information for) all words, ideas, or statistics from an outside source. You must also document all visuals—tables, graphs, photographs, and so on—that you do not create yourself. (It is not necessary, however, to document **common knowledge**—factual information widely available in various reference works.)

When you present information from another source as if it is your own (whether you do it intentionally or unintentionally), you commit **plagiarism**—and plagiarism is theft. Although most plagiarism is accidental, the penalties can still be severe. You can avoid plagiarism by understanding what you must document and what you do not have to document.

FYI

What to Document

You should document the following.

- All quotations from a source
- All summaries and paraphrases of source material
- All ideas—opinions, judgments, and insights—of others
- All tables, graphs, charts, and statistics from a source

You do not need to document the following.

- Your own ideas
- Common knowledge
- Familiar quotations

Read the following passage from "The Facts on Fakes!," an article by Adele R. Meyer, and the four rules that follow it. This material will help you understand the most common causes of plagiarism and show you how to avoid it.

ORIGINAL

Is imitation really the sincerest form of flattery? Counterfeiting deceives the consumer and tarnishes the reputation of the genuine manufacturer. Brand value can be destroyed when a trademark is imposed on counterfeit products of inferior quality—hardly a form of flattery! Therefore, prestigious companies who are the targets of counterfeiters have begun to battle an industry that copies and sells their merchandise. They have filed lawsuits and in some cases have employed private investigators across the nation to combat the counterfeit trade. A quick search of the Internet brings up dozens of press releases from newspapers throughout the country, all reporting instances of law enforcement cracking down on sellers of counterfeit goods by confiscating bogus merchandise and imposing fines.

Rule 1. Document Ideas from Your Sources

PLAGIARISM

When counterfeits are sold, the original manufacturer does not take it as a compliment.

Even though the student writer does not quote her source directly, she must identify the article as the source of this material because it expresses the article's ideas, not her own.

CORRECT

When counterfeits are sold, the original manufacturer does not take it as a compliment (Meyer).

Rule 2. Place Borrowed Words in Quotation Marks

PLAGIARISM

It is possible to ruin the worth of a brand by selling counterfeit products of inferior quality—hardly a form of flattery (Meyer).

Although the student writer cites the source, the passage incorrectly uses the source's exact words without quoting them. She must quote the borrowed words.

CORRECT (BORROWED WORDS IN QUOTATION MARKS)

It is possible to ruin the worth of a brand by selling "counterfeit products of inferior quality—hardly a form of flattery" (Meyer).

Rule 3. Use Your Own Phrasing

PLAGIARISM

Is copying a design a compliment? Not at all. The fake design not only tries to fool the buyer but also harms the original company. It can ruin the worth of a brand. Because counterfeits are usually of poor quality, they pay the original no compliment. As a result, companies whose products are often copied have started to fight back. They have sued the counterfeiters and have even used private detectives to identify phony goods. Throughout the United States, police have fined people who sell counterfeits and have seized their products (Meyer).

Even though the student writer acknowledges Meyer as her source, and even though she does not use the source's exact words, her passage closely follows the order, emphasis, sentence structure, and phrasing of the original.

In the following passage, the student writer uses her own wording, quoting one distinctive phrase from the source.

CORRECT

According to "The Facts on Fakes!" it is not a compliment when an original design is copied by a counterfeiter. The poor quality of most fakes is "hardly a form of flattery." The harm to the image of the original manufacturers has caused them to fight back against the counterfeiters, sometimes using their own detectives. As a result, lawsuits and criminal charges have led to fines and confiscated merchandise (Meyer).

Note: The quotation does not require separate documentation because the identifying tag—According to "The Facts on Fakes!"—makes it clear that all the borrowed material in the passage is from the same source.

Rule 4. Distinguish Your Ideas from the Source's Ideas

PLAGIARISM

Counterfeit goods are not harmless. Counterfeiting not only fools the consumer but also destroys confidence in the quality of the real thing. Manufacturers know this and have begun to fight back. A number have begun to sue "and in some cases have employed private investigators across the nation to combat the counterfeit trade" (Meyer).

In this passage, it appears that only the quotation in the last sentence is borrowed from the article by Meyer. In fact, however, the ideas in the second sentence also come from Meyer's article.

In the following passage, the student writer uses an identifying tag to acknowledge the borrowed material in the second sentence.

CORRECT

Counterfeit goods are not harmless. According to the article "The Facts on Fakes!," counterfeiting not only fools the consumer but also destroys confidence in the quality of the real thing. Manufacturers know this and have begun to fight back. A number have begun to sue "and in some cases have employed private investigators across the nation to combat the counterfeit trade" (Meyer).

watch out for plagiarism

Review your notes. First, make sure that you have included documentation for all information that came from a source. Then, check your notes against the examples in 16d to make sure that you have avoided the most common types of accidental plagiarism.

16e   Developing a Thesis

After you have taken notes, review the information you have gathered, and develop a thesis statement. Your **thesis statement** is a single sentence that states the main idea of your essay and tells readers what to expect.

After reviewing her notes, May Compton came up with the following thesis statement for her essay on counterfeit designer goods.

THESIS STATEMENT

People should not buy counterfeit designer merchandise, no matter how tempted they are to do so.

develop a thesis

Review your notes again, and then draft a thesis statement for your essay.

16f Making an Outline

Once you have a thesis statement, you are ready to make an outline. Your outline, which covers just the body paragraphs of your essay, can be either a **topic outline** (in which each idea is expressed in a word or a short phrase) or a **sentence outline** (in which each idea is expressed in a complete sentence).

After reviewing her notes, May Compton wrote the following sentence outline for her essay.

I. Many people consider real designer goods too expensive.
   A. Genuine designer merchandise costs ten times more than it costs to make it.
   B. Even people who can afford it buy fakes.

II. Buying designer knockoffs is a form of stealing.
   A. The buyer is stealing the work of the original designer and manufacturer.
   B. The buyer is stealing the sales taxes that would be paid by the original designer.

III. Buying designer knockoffs supports organized crime.
   A. The production of designer knockoffs requires money and organization, which often come from organized crime.
   B. Buying knockoffs supports other illegal activities.
      1. The profits of selling knockoffs support murder, prostitution, and drug rings.
      2. Knockoffs are made in shops that violate labor and other laws.

IV. There is evidence that designer knockoffs support terrorism.
   A. The 1993 World Trade Center bombing has been connected to a counterfeit operation.
   B. The 2001 World Trade Center bombing has been connected to counterfeiting.
   C. The 2004 Madrid train bombing has been connected to counterfeiting.

make an outline

Review all your notes as well as your thesis statement. Then, make an outline of the body paragraphs of your essay.

16g Drafting Your Essay

Once you have decided on a thesis and written an outline, you are ready to write a draft of your essay. When you are finished, you will TEST, revise, edit, and proofread it.

Remember, you will probably write several drafts of your essay before you hand it in. As you draft, be sure to include parenthetical citations so that you do not lose track of your sources and accidentally commit plagiarism. After you revise and edit, you can check to make sure your documentation formats are correct. (See 16h for information on documentation.)

May Compton's completed essay on counterfeit designer goods begins on page 263.

draft your essay

Using your thesis statement and your outline to guide you, write a draft of your essay.

TEST · Revise · Edit · Proofread

TEST your draft. Then, use the Self-Assessment Checklists in 13i and 13j to help you revise, edit, and proofread. Finally, check your essay's format to make sure it conforms to your instructor's requirements.

16h Documenting Your Sources

When you **document** your sources, you tell readers where you found the information you used in your essay. The Modern Language Association (MLA) recommends the following documentation style for essays that use sources. This format consists of *parenthetical references* in the body of the paper that refer to a *works-cited list* at the end of the paper.

Parenthetical References in the Text

A parenthetical reference should include enough information to lead readers to a specific entry in your works-cited list. A typical parenthetical reference consists of the author's last name and the page number (Brown 2). Notice that there is no comma and no *p* or *p.* before the page number.

Whenever possible, introduce information from a source with a phrase that includes the author's name. (If you do this, include only the page number in parentheses.) Place documentation so that it does not interrupt the flow of your ideas, preferably at the end of a sentence.

> As Jonathan Brown observes in "Demand for Fake Designer Goods Is Soaring," as many as 70 percent of buyers of luxury goods are willing to wear designer brands alongside of fakes (2).

Here are some specific guidelines for special situations:

1. When You Are Citing a Work by Two Authors

> Instead of buying nonbranded items of similar quality, many customers are willing to pay extra for the counterfeit designer label (Grossman and Shapiro 79).

2. When You Are Citing a Work without Page Numbers

> A seller of counterfeited goods in California "now faces 10 years in prison and $20,000 in fines" (Cox).

3. When You Are Citing a Work without a Listed Author or Page Numbers

> More counterfeit goods come from China than from any other country ("Counterfeit Goods").

Note: Material from the Internet frequently lacks some publication information—for example, page or paragraph numbers. For this reason, the parenthetical references that cite it may contain just the author's name (as in example 2) or just a shortened title (as in example 3) if the article appears without an author.

4. When You Are Citing a Statement by One Author That Is Quoted in a Work by Another Author

> Speaking of consumers' buying habits, designer Miuccia Prada says, "There is a kind of an obsession with bags" (qtd. in Thomas A23).

FYI

Formatting Quotations

1. **Short quotations**   Quotations of no more than four typed lines share the same margins as the rest of your essay. End punctuation comes after the parenthetical reference, which follows the quotation marks.

   According to Dana Thomas, customers often "pick up knockoffs for one-tenth the legitimate bag's retail cost, then pass them off as real" (A23).

2. **Long quotations**   Quotations of more than four lines are set off from the text of your essay. Begin a long quotation on a new line, indented one inch from the left-hand margin, and do not enclose it in quotation marks. Do not indent the first line of a single paragraph. If a quoted passage has more than one paragraph, indent the first line of each paragraph (including the first) an extra one-quarter inch. Introduce a long quotation with a complete sentence followed by a colon, and place the parenthetical reference one space *after* the end punctuation.

The editorial "Terror's Purse Strings" describes a surprise visit to a factory that makes counterfeit purses:

> On a warm winter afternoon in Guangzhao, I accompanied Chinese police officers on a raid in a decrepit tenement. We found two dozen children, ages 8 to 13, gluing and sewing together fake luxury-brand handbags. The police confiscated everything, arrested the owner and sent the children out. Some punched their timecards, hoping to still get paid. (Thomas A23)

The Works-Cited List

The works-cited list includes all the works you **cite** (refer to) in your essay. The following sample works-cited entries cover the situations you will encounter most often.

Periodicals

JOURNALS

A **journal** is a periodical aimed at readers who know a lot about a particular subject—literature or history, for example.

When citing an article from a journal, include the journal's volume number and issue number, separating the two numbers by a period, with no space after the period. Following the date of publication in parentheses, include page numbers, if there are any. Give the medium of publication, such as *Print* or *Web*. Before the medium, include the name of the online database (such as Academic Search Premier) if you used one to find the source. For all web sources, add the date you accessed the source.

Article in a Print Journal

Gioia, Dana. "Robert Frost and the Modern Narrative." *Virginia Quarterly Review* 89.2 (2013): 185–93. Print.

Article in a Journal Accessed through a Library Database

Wineapple, Brenda. "Ladies Last." *American Scholar* 82.3 (2013): 28–38. *MasterFILEPremier*. Web. 17 Feb. 2014.

MAGAZINES

A **magazine** is a periodical aimed at general readers, rather than people who already know a lot about a subject. Frequently, an article in a magazine is not printed on consecutive pages. For example, it may begin on page 40, skip to page 47, and continue on page 49. If this is the case, your citation should include only the first page, followed by a plus sign. Include the medium of publication.

Article in a Print Magazine

Poniewozik, James. "Why I Watch Reality TV with My Kids." *Time* 17 June 2013: 54–55. Print.

Article in a Magazine Accessed through a Library Database

Dobb, Edwin. "The New Oil Landscape." *National Geographic* Mar. 2013: 28–59. *Academic Search Premier*. Web. 7 Aug. 2014.

NEWSPAPERS

List page numbers, section numbers, and any special edition information (such as "late ed.") as provided by the source. If the article falls into a special category, such as an editorial, a letter to the editor, or a review, add this label to your entry, after the title.

Article in a Print Newspaper

Shah, Neil. "More Young Adults Live with Parents." *Wall Street Journal* 28 Aug. 2013: A2. Print.

Article from a Newspaper Accessed through a Library Database

Marklein, Mary Beth. "'Caution! Student Loans Must Be Paid Back!'" *USA Today* 26 Aug. 2013, sec. A: 04. *National Newspaper Index*. Web. 9 Mar. 2014.

Books

Books by One Author

List the author with last name first. Italicize the title. Include the city of publication and a shortened form of the publisher's name—for example, *Bedford* for *Bedford/St. Martin's*. Use the abbreviation *UP* for *University Press*, as in *Princeton UP* and *U of Chicago P*. Include the date of publication. End with the medium of publication.

Mantel, Hilary. *Bring up the Bodies*. New York: Holt, 2012. Print.

Books by Two or More Authors

For books with more than one author, list second and subsequent authors with first name first, in the order in which they are listed on the book's title page.

Mooney, Chris, and Sheril Kirshenbaum. *Unscientific America: How Scientific Illiteracy Threatens Our Future*. New York: Basic, 2009. Print.

For books with more than three authors, you may list only the first author, followed by the abbreviation *et al.* ("and others").

Two or More Books by the Same Author

List two or more books by the same author in alphabetical order according to title. In each entry after the first, use three unspaced hyphens (followed by a period) instead of the author's name.

> Eggers, Dave. *The Circle*. New York: Random, 2013. Print.
>
> ---. *A Hologram for the King*. San Francisco: McSweeney's, 2012. Print.

Edited Book

> Austen, Jane. *Persuasion: An Annotated Edition*. Ed. Robert Morrison. Cambridge: Belknap-Harvard UP, 2011. Print.

Anthology

> Adler, Frances P., Debra Busman, and Diana Garcia, eds. *Fire and Ink: An Anthology of Social Action Writing*. Tucson: U of Arizona P, 2009. Print.

Essay in an Anthology or Chapter of a Book

> Weise, Matthew J. "How the Zombie Changed Videogames." *Zombies Are Us: Essays on the Humanity of the Walking Dead*. Ed. Christopher M. Moreman and Cory James Rushton. Jefferson: McFarland, 2011. 151–68. Print.

Internet Sources

Full source information is not always available for Internet sources. When citing Internet sources, include whatever information you can find—ideally, the name of the author (or authors), the title of the article or other document (in quotation marks), the title of the site (italicized), the sponsor or publisher, the date of publication or last update, and the date on which you accessed the source. Include the medium of publication (Web) between the publication date and the access date.

It is not necessary to include a web address (URL) when citing an electronic source. However, you should include a URL (in angle brackets) if your instructor requires that you do so or if you think readers might not be able to locate the source without it (see the "Personal Site" entry below).

Document within a Website

> Baker, Fred W. "Army Lab Works to Improve Soldier Health, Performance." *DefenseLINK*. U.S. Department of Defense, 25 June 2009. Web. 15 Aug. 2014.

Personal Site

> Heffernan, Margaret. Home page. Margaret Heffernan, 7 July 2014. Web. 10 July 2014. <www.mheffernan.com>.

Article in an Online Reference Book or Encyclopedia

> "Sudan." *Infoplease World Atlas and Map Library*. Pearson Education, 2009. Web. 29 Apr. 2014.

Article in an Online Newspaper

> Wilbon, Michael. "The 'One and Done' Song and Dance." *Washington Post*. The Washington Post Company, 25 June 2009. Web. 1 Sept. 2013.

FYI

Preparing the Works-Cited List

- Begin the works-cited list on a new page after the last page of your essay.

- Number the works-cited page as the next page of your essay.

- Center the heading "Works Cited" one inch from the top of the page; do not italicize the heading or place it in quotation marks.

- Double-space the list.

- List entries alphabetically according to the author's last name.

- Alphabetize unsigned articles according to the first major word of the title.

- Begin typing each entry at the left-hand margin.

- Indent second and subsequent lines of each entry one-half inch.

- Separate major divisions of each entry—author, title, and publication information—by a period and one space.

document your sources

Check to make sure you have included correct parenthetical citations for all information that requires documentation. Then, consulting the guidelines in the FYI box, prepare your works-cited list.

Sample MLA-Style Essay

On the pages that follow is May Compton's completed essay on the topic of counterfeit designer goods. The essay uses MLA documentation style and format and includes a works-cited page.

Compton 1

May Compton
Professor DiSalvo
English 100
29 Apr. 2014

The True Price of Counterfeit Goods

At purse parties in city apartments and suburban homes, customers can buy "designer" handbags at impossibly low prices. On street corners, sidewalk vendors sell name-brand perfumes and sunglasses for much less than their list prices. On the Internet, buyers can buy fine watches for a fraction of the prices charged by manufacturers. Is this too good to be true? Of course it is. All of these "bargains" are knockoffs—counterfeit copies of the real thing. What the people who buy these items do not know (or prefer not to think about) is that the money they are spending supports organized crime—and, sometimes, terrorism. For this reason, people should not buy counterfeit designer merchandise, no matter how tempted they are to do so.

People who buy counterfeit designer merchandise defend their actions by saying that designer products are very expensive. This is certainly true. According to Dana Thomas, the manufacturers of genuine designer merchandise charge ten times more than what it costs to make it (A23). A visitor from Britain, who bought an imitation Gucci purse in New York City for fifty dollars, said, "The real thing is so overpriced. To buy a genuine Gucci purse, I would have to pay over a thousand dollars" (qtd. in "Counterfeit Goods"). Even people who can easily afford to pay the full amount buy fakes. For example, movie stars like Jennifer Lopez openly wear counterfeit goods, and many customers think that if it is all right for celebrities like Lopez to buy fakes, it must also be all right for them, too (Malone). However, as the well-known designer Giorgio Armani points out, counterfeiters create a number of problems for legitimate companies because they use the brand name but do not maintain quality control.

What most people choose to ignore is that buying counterfeit items is really stealing the work of the original designer and manufacturer. Between 2002 and 2012, 325 percent more counterfeit goods were seized than in the previous decade (O'Donnell 03b). The FBI estimates that in the United States alone, companies lose about $250 billion as a result of counterfeits (Wallace). In addition, buyers of counterfeit items avoid the state and local sales taxes that legitimate companies pay. Thus, New York City alone loses about a billion dollars every year as a result of the sale of counterfeit merchandise ("Counterfeit Goods"). When this happens, everyone loses. After all, a billion dollars would pay for a lot of police officers and teachers, would fill a lot of potholes, and would pave a lot of streets. Buyers of counterfeit designer goods do not think of themselves as thieves, but that is exactly what they are.

Include your last name and the page number in the upper right-hand corner of every page.

Center your title; do not italicize or underline.

Include your name, instructor's name, course title, and date on first page.

Introduction

Thesis statement

Paragraph combines paraphrase, quotation, and May's own ideas.

Paragraph synthesizes May's own ideas with material from three articles.

Compton 2

Buyers of counterfeit merchandise also do not realize that the sale of knockoffs is a criminal activity. Most of the profits go to the criminal organization that either makes or imports the counterfeit goods—not to the person who sells the items. In fact, the biggest manufacturer and distributor of counterfeit items is organized crime (Nellis). Michael Kessler, who heads a company that investigates corporate crime, makes this connection clear when he describes the complicated organization that is needed to make counterfeit perfume:

> They need a place that makes bottles, a factory with pumps to fill the bottles, a printer to make the labels, and a box manufacturer to fake the packaging. Then, they need a sophisticated distribution network, as well as all the cash to set everything up. (qtd. in Malone)

Kessler concludes that only an organized crime syndicate—not an individual—has the money to support this illegal activity. For this reason, anyone who buys counterfeits may also be supporting activities such as prostitution, drug distribution, smuggling of illegal immigrants, gang warfare, extortion, and murder (Nellis). In addition, the people who make counterfeits often work in sweatshops where labor and environmental laws are ignored. As Dana Thomas points out, a worker in China who makes counterfeits earns only a fraction of the salary of a worker who makes the real thing (A23).

Finally, and perhaps most shocking, is the fact that some of the money earned from the sale of counterfeit designer goods also supports international terrorism. For example, Kim Wallace reports in her *Times Daily* article that during Al-Qaeda training, terrorists are advised to sell fakes to get money for their operations. According to Interpol, an international police organization, the bombing of the World Trade Center in 1993 was paid for in part by the sale of counterfeit T-shirts. Also, evidence suggests that associates of the 2001 World Trade Center terrorists may have been involved with the production of imitation designer goods (Malone). Finally, the 2004 bombing of commuter trains in Madrid was financed in part by the sale of counterfeits. In fact, an intelligence source states, "It would be more shocking if Al-Qaeda *wasn't* involved in counterfeiting. The sums involved are staggering—it would be inconceivable if money were not being raised for their terrorist activities" (qtd. in Malone).

Consumers should realize that when they buy counterfeits, they are actually breaking the law. By doing so, they are making it possible for organized crime syndicates and terrorists to earn money for their illegal activities. Although buyers of counterfeit merchandise justify their actions by saying that the low prices are impossible to resist, they might reconsider if they knew the uses to which their money was going. The truth of the matter is that counterfeit designer products, such as handbags, sunglasses, jewelry, and T-shirts, are luxuries, not necessities. By resisting the temptation to buy knockoffs, consumers could help to eliminate the companies that hurt legitimate manufacturers, exploit workers, and even finance international terrorism.

Long quotation is set off one inch from the left-hand margin. No quotation marks are used.

Paragraph contains May's own ideas as well as a paraphrase and a quotation.

Conclusion contains May's original ideas, so no documentation is necessary.

Works Cited

Armani, Giorgio. "10 Questions for Giorgio Armani." *Time*. Time, 12 Feb. 2009.
Web. 24 Mar. 2014.

"Counterfeit Goods Are Linked to Terror Groups." *International Herald Tribune*.
International Herald Tribune, 12 Feb. 2007. Web. 24 Mar. 2014.

Malone, Andrew. "Revealed: The True Cost of Buying Cheap Fake Goods."
Mail Online. Daily Mail, 29 July 2007. Web. 25 Mar. 2014.

Nellis, Cynthia. "Faking It: Counterfeit Fashion." *About.com: Women's Fashion*.
About.com, 2009. Web. 24 Mar. 2014.

O'Donnell, Jayne. "Counterfeits Are a Growing—and Dangerous—Problem."
USA Today 6 June 2012, sec. Money: 03b. Print.

Thomas, Dana. "Terror's Purse Strings." Editorial. *New York Times* 30 Aug. 2007,
late ed.: A23. *Academic One File*. Web. 25 Mar. 2014.

Wallace, Kim. "A Counter-Productive Trade." *TimesDaily.com*. Times Daily,
28 July 2007. Web. 31 Mar. 2014.

Works-cited list starts a new page.

This Internet source has no listed author, so it is alphabetized in the list by the title.

First lines of entries are set flush left; subsequent lines are indented one-half inch.

EDITING PRACTICE: AVOIDING PLAGIARISM

Read the following paragraph taken from the *New York Times* online article "The New Math on Campus," by Alex Williams. Then, read the three student paragraphs that use this article as a source. In each of these paragraphs, student writers have accidentally committed plagiarism. On the line below each student paragraph, explain the problem. Then, edit the paragraph so that it correctly documents the source and avoids plagiarism.

> North Carolina, with a student body that is nearly 60 percent female, is just one of many large universities that at times feel eerily like women's colleges. Women have represented about 57 percent of enrollments at American colleges since at least 2000, according to a recent report by the American Council on Education. Researchers there cite several reasons: women tend to have higher grades; men tend to drop out in disproportionate numbers; and female enrollment skews higher among older students, low-income students, and black and Hispanic students.

About 60% female, the University of North Carolina is an example of large universities with many more women than men. According to a report from the American Council on Education, one reason is that "female enrollment skews higher among older students, low-income students, and black and Hispanic students" (Williams). If this is true, what will this mean for the black and Hispanic communities?

_____

_____

In recent years, colleges and universities have taken on a very different atmosphere. The reason is clear to anyone who takes a casual look around at just about any college campus. Women now outnumber men, so much so that some colleges at times feel eerily like women's colleges (Williams). This situation seems likely to continue in the years to come.

_____

_____

Why do women outnumber men in today's colleges? Researchers at the American Council on Education mention a few reasons: women often have higher grades, men tend to drop out in larger numbers, and female enrollment

is especially high for some groups such as older students, low-income students,

and black and Hispanic students (Williams). These reasons may all be true at our

school, which certainly has more women than men.

COLLABORATIVE ACTIVITY: CREATING A WORKS-CITED LIST

Working in a group of three or four students, create a works-cited list for
an essay that uses the following two sources. Make sure that you arrange
the entries in alphabetical order and that you use the correct format for
each type of source.

Article in a Journal Accessed through a Library Database

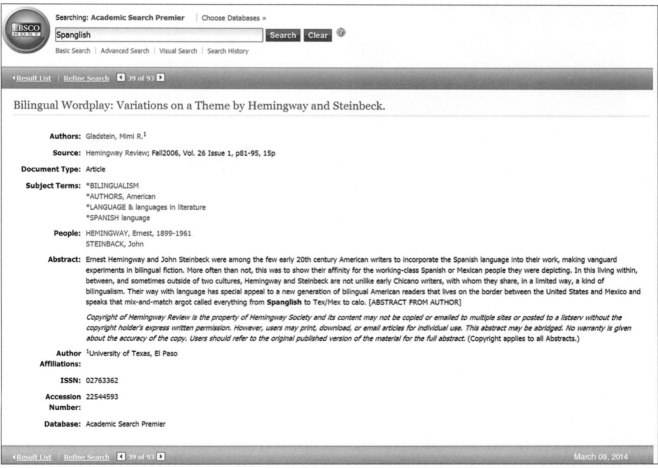

Courtesy of EBSCO Publishing, Inc.

Book (Print)

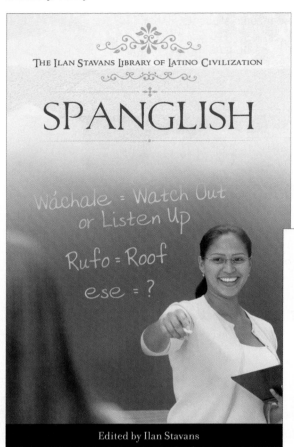

THE ILAN STAVANS LIBRARY OF LATINO CIVILIZATION

SPANGLISH

Wáchale = Watch Out
or Listen Up

Rufo = Roof

ese = ?

Edited by Ilan Stavans

Jose Luis Pelaez Inc./Blend Images/Corbis

Library of Congress Cataloging-in-Publication Data

Spanglish / edited by Ilan Stavans.
   p. cm. — (The Ilan Stavans library of Latino civilization, ISSN 1938–615X)
 Includes bibliographical references and index.
 ISBN 978–0–313–34804–4 (alk. paper)
 1. Spanish language—Foreign elements—English. 2. English language—Influence on Spanish. 3. Languages in contact—America. I. Stavans, Ilan.
 PC4582.E6S63 2008
 460'.4221—dc22   2008014855

British Library Cataloguing in Publication Data is available.

Library of Congress Catalog Card Number: 2008014855
ISBN: 978–0–313–34804–4
ISSN: 1938–615X

First published in 2008

Greenwood Press, 88 Post Road West, Westport, CT 06881
An imprint of Greenwood Publishing Group, Inc.
www.greenwood.com

Printed in the United States of America

(∞)™

The paper used in this book complies with the
Permanent Paper Standard issued by the National
Information Standards Organization (Z39.48–1984).

10 9 8 7 6 5 4 3 2 1

iv

Works Cited

_____

_____

_____

_____

17 Writing Simple Sentences

write first

This photo shows a young girl who was matched with a Skilled Companion dog through the nonprofit organization Canine Companions for Independence, which provides trained assistance dogs to people with disabilities. Imagine you had ten thousand dollars to donate to the nonprofit organization or charity of your choice. Which group would you support, and why? Write a paragraph explaining your choice.

In this chapter, you will learn to
- identify a sentence's subject (17a)
- identify prepositions and prepositional phrases (17b)
- distinguish a prepositional phrase from a subject (17b)
- identify a sentence's verb (17c)

A **sentence** is a group of words that expresses a complete thought. Every sentence includes both a subject and a verb. A **simple sentence** consists of a single **independent clause**: one <u>subject</u> and one <u>verb</u>.

Chase Utley <u>plays</u> baseball.

17a Identifying Subjects

macmillanhighered.com
/writingfirst
Additional Grammar
Exercises > Identifying
Subjects

Every sentence includes a subject. The **subject** of a sentence tells who or what is being talked about in the sentence. Without a subject, a sentence is not complete. In the following three sentences, the subject is underlined.

<u>Derek Walcott</u> won the Nobel Prize in Literature.

<u>He</u> was born in St. Lucia.

<u>St. Lucia</u> is an island in the Caribbean.

The subject of a sentence can be a noun or a pronoun. A **noun** names a person, place, or thing—*Derek Walcott, St. Lucia*. A **pronoun** takes the place of a noun—*I, you, he, she, it, we, they,* and so on.

The subject of a sentence can be *singular or plural*. A **singular subject** is one person, place, or thing (*Derek Walcott, St. Lucia, he*).

A **plural subject** is more than one person, place, or thing (*poets, people, they*).

<u>Readers</u> admire Walcott's poems.

A plural subject that joins two subjects with *and* is called a **compound subject**.

<u>St. Lucia and Trinidad</u> are Caribbean islands.

**PRACTICE
17-1** In the following paragraph, underline the subject of each sentence.

Example: <u>Amazon.com</u> is named after the Amazon River.

(1) In just twenty years, Amazon.com has become an extremely successful business. (2) Jeff Bezos founded the company in 1994. (3) In 1995, the

business made its first sale. (4) Originally, Amazon.com sold only books. (5) In 1998, music and videos became available as well. (6) Since then, the company has expanded greatly. (7) Amazon owns many other businesses. (8) It also produces its own consumer electronics. (9) The Kindle is just one example. (10) Bezos is known for his patience as well as for his smart management. (11) Amazon.com did not earn a profit until 2001. (12) Now, Bezos's company is the biggest online retailer in the world.

17b Identifying Prepositional Phrases

A **prepositional phrase** consists of a **preposition** (a word such as *on, to, in,* or *with*) and its **object** (the noun or pronoun it introduces).

macmillanhighered.com /writingfirst
LearningCurve > Prepositions and Conjunctions; Additional Grammar Exercises > Identifying Prepositional Phrases

PREPOSITION	+	OBJECT	=	PREPOSITIONAL PHRASE
on		the stage		on the stage
to		Nia's house		to Nia's house
in		my new car		in my new car
with		them		with them

Because the object of a preposition is a noun or a pronoun, it may seem to be the subject of a sentence. However, the object of a preposition can never be the subject of a sentence. To identify a sentence's true subject, cross out each prepositional phrase. (Remember, every prepositional phrase is introduced by a preposition.)

SUBJECT   PREP PHRASE
The cost ~~of the repairs~~ was astronomical.

PREP PHRASE   PREP PHRASE   PREP PHRASE   SUBJECT
~~At the end of the novel~~, ~~after an exciting chase~~, the lovers flee

PREP PHRASE
~~to Mexico~~.

Frequently Used Prepositions

about	at	during	off	under
above	before	except	on	underneath
according to	behind	for	onto	until
across	below	from	out	up
after	beneath	in	outside	upon
against	beside	inside	over	with
along	between	into	through	within
among	beyond	like	throughout	without
around	by	near	to	
as	despite	of	toward	

PRACTICE

17-2 Each of the following sentences includes at least one prepositional phrase. To identify each sentence's subject, begin by crossing out each prepositional phrase. Then, underline the subject of the sentence.

Example: Bicycling ~~on busy city streets~~ can be dangerous.

(1) In many American cities, cyclists are concerned about sharing the road with cars. (2) For this reason, people are becoming more interested in "green" lanes. (3) These bike lanes are separated from the road by curbs, planters, or parked cars. (4) For years, people in Europe have been creating and using these protected bike lanes. (5) Now, with the help of the Bikes Belong Foundation and the Federal Highway Administration, several U.S. cities are installing green lanes. (6) For their supporters, these bike lanes are a positive step toward healthier, safer cities. (7) However, some critics worry about reduced space for traffic lanes and parking. (8) Still, despite the criticism, green lanes are increasing the number of bike riders and reducing the number of bike accidents.

17c   Identifying Verbs

In addition to its subject, every sentence also includes a verb. This **verb** (also called a **predicate**) tells what the subject does or connects the subject to words that describe or rename it. Without a verb, a sentence is not complete.

macmillanhighered.com /writingfirst
LearningCurve > Verbs, Adjectives, and Adverbs; Additional Grammar Exercises > Identifying Verbs

Action Verbs

An **action verb** tells what the subject does, did, or will do.

Peyton Manning <u>plays</u> football.
Amelia Earhart <u>flew</u> across the Atlantic.
Renee <u>will drive</u> to Tampa on Friday.

Action verbs can also show mental and emotional actions.

Travis always <u>worries</u> about his job.

Sometimes the subject of a sentence performs more than one action. In this case, the sentence includes two or more action verbs that form a **compound predicate**.

He <u>hit</u> the ball, <u>threw</u> down his bat, and <u>ran</u> toward first base.

Linking Verbs

A **linking verb** does not show action. Instead, it connects the subject to a word or words that describe or rename it. The linking verb tells what the subject is (or what it was, will be, or seems to be).

A googolplex <u>is</u> an extremely large number.

Many linking verbs, like *is*, are forms of the verb *be*. Other linking verbs refer to the senses (*look*, *feel*, and so on).

The photocopy <u>looks</u> blurry.

Some students <u>feel</u> anxious about the future.

Frequently Used Linking Verbs

act	feel	seem
appear	get	smell
be (am, is, are,	grow	sound
was, were)	look	taste
become	remain	turn

PRACTICE

17-3 In each of the following sentences, underline every verb twice. Remember that a verb can be an action verb or a linking verb.

Example: Airplane pilots and investment bankers <u>use</u> checklists.

(1) In *The Checklist Manifesto*, surgeon Atul Gawande argues for using checklists in operating rooms. (2) Gawande reminds readers of the complexity of modern medicine. (3) Currently, there are six thousand drugs and four thousand medical and surgical procedures. (4) Each year, the number of drugs and procedures increases. (5) As a result, even knowledgeable and highly trained surgeons make mistakes. (6) For some types of patients, the error rate is very high. (7) For example, doctors deliver inappropriate care to 40 percent of patients with coronary artery disease. (8) Luckily, checklists make a big difference for these and other patients. (9) In fact, checklists reduce complications by more than one-third. (10) It is hard to imagine an argument against such a simple and effective tool.

Helping Verbs

Many verbs consist of more than one word. For example, the verb in the following sentence consists of two words.

Minh <u>must make</u> a decision about his future.

In this sentence, *make* is the **main verb**, and *must* is a **helping verb**.

Frequently Used Helping Verbs

does	was	must	should
did	were	can	would
do		could	will
is	have	may	
are	has	might	
am	had		

A sentence's **complete verb** is made up of a main verb plus any helping verbs that accompany it. In the following sentences, the complete verb is underlined twice, and the helping verbs are checkmarked.

Minh <u>should have gone</u> earlier.

<u>Did</u> Minh <u>ask</u> the right questions?

Minh <u>will work</u> hard.

Minh <u>can</u> really <u>succeed</u>.

FYI

Helping Verbs with Participles

Participles, such as *going* and *gone*, cannot stand alone as main verbs in a sentence. They need a helping verb to make them complete.

INCORRECT   Minh going to the library.

CORRECT   Minh <u>is going</u> to the library.

INCORRECT   Minh gone to the library.

CORRECT   Minh <u>has gone</u> to the library.

PRACTICE

17-4 The verbs in the sentences that follow consist of a main verb and one or more helping verbs. In each sentence, underline the complete verb twice, and put a check mark above each helping verb.

> **Example:** In 1954, the Salk polio vaccine ✓was given to more than a million schoolchildren.

(1) By the 1950s, polio had become a serious problem throughout the United States. (2) For years, it had puzzled doctors and researchers. (3) Thousands had become ill each year in the United States alone. (4) Children should have played happily. (5) Instead, they would get very sick. (6) Polio was sometimes called infantile paralysis. (7) In fact, it did cause paralysis in children and in adults as well. (8) Some patients could breathe only with the help of machines called iron lungs. (9) Others would remain in wheelchairs for life. (10) By 1960, Jonas Salk's vaccine had reduced the incidence of polio in the United States by more than 90 percent.

TEST · Revise · Edit · Proofread

Look back at your response to the Write First prompt on page 269. Circle every subject and every action verb. Then, try to replace some of them with more descriptive subjects (such as *charity* instead of *group*) and more specific action verbs (for example, *donated* instead of *gave*). When you have finished, TEST and revise your paragraph. Then, edit and proofread your work.

EDITING PRACTICE

Read the following student essay. Underline the subject of each sentence once, and underline the complete verb of each sentence twice. If you have trouble locating the subject, try crossing out the prepositional phrases. The first sentence has been done for you.

A New Way to Learn

Salman Khan founded the nonprofit online Khan Academy in 2009. Khan Academy promises "a free world-class education for anyone anywhere." With the help of short videos, people can learn a subject like physics or economics at their own pace. According to some, Khan Academy is in the process of revolutionizing education.

Salman Khan was born in New Orleans in 1976. His parents had moved to Louisiana from Bangladesh. Eventually, he earned three degrees from MIT and one degree from Harvard. His degrees are in math, engineering, computer science, and business. He had never considered a career in education. However, in 2004, Khan's cousin asked him for help with algebra. He made some short YouTube videos for her. To his surprise, the lessons became extremely popular. He had a talent for teaching. In 2009, with a small donation from an investor, Salman Khan started Khan Academy.

Khan Academy has succeeded well beyond Khan's expectations. Now, the organization receives millions of dollars in donations. The Khan Academy website has more than 3,200 free videos. Khan teaches many of the lessons himself. He researches his subjects. Then, without a script, he records each video in one take. These videos are not traditional lectures. The audience never sees Khan's face. Throughout each lesson, Khan's writing appears on the screen. Related images appear as well. For viewers, each lesson feels like a one-on-one tutoring session.

The site also offers exercises for students and tools for teachers. Students can practice subjects by themselves. They can progress at their own speed. Some schools are even using Khan Academy lessons in their classrooms. With the help of Khan's videos, teachers can create a "flipped" classroom. Students learn basic concepts at night on their computers. Then, during the day, students work on problems with the teacher's help. This means more time for questions. For some students, this method has been extremely effective.

Without any training in education, Salman Khan has changed people's ideas about learning. Around the world, people are using his website. They are learning new ideas. Khan is happy about this. In his view, education should be accessible for all.

COLLABORATIVE ACTIVITY

Fold a sheet of paper in half vertically. Working in a group of three or four students, spend two minutes listing as many nouns as you can in the column to the left of the fold. When your time is up, exchange papers with another group of students, and write an appropriate action verb beside each noun. (Each noun will now be the subject of a short sentence.)

Then, choose five of your sentences, and collaborate with the other students in your group to create more fully developed sentences. First, expand each subject by adding words or prepositional phrases that give more information about the subject. (For example, you could expand *boat* to *the small, leaky boat with the red sail*.) Then, expand each sentence further, adding ideas after the verb. (For example, the sentence *The boat bounced* could become *The small, leaky boat with the red sail bounced helplessly on the water*.)

review checklist

Writing Simple Sentences

☐ A sentence expresses a complete thought. The subject tells who or what is being talked about in the sentence. (See 17a.)

☐ A prepositional phrase consists of a preposition and its object (the noun or pronoun it introduces). (See 17b.)

☐ The object of a preposition cannot be the subject of a sentence. (See 17b.)

☐ An action verb tells what the subject does, did, or will do. (See 17c.)

☐ A linking verb connects the subject to a word or words that describe or rename it. (See 17c.)

☐ Many verbs are made up of more than one word. The complete verb in a sentence includes the main verb plus any helping verbs. (See 17c.)

18 Writing Compound Sentences

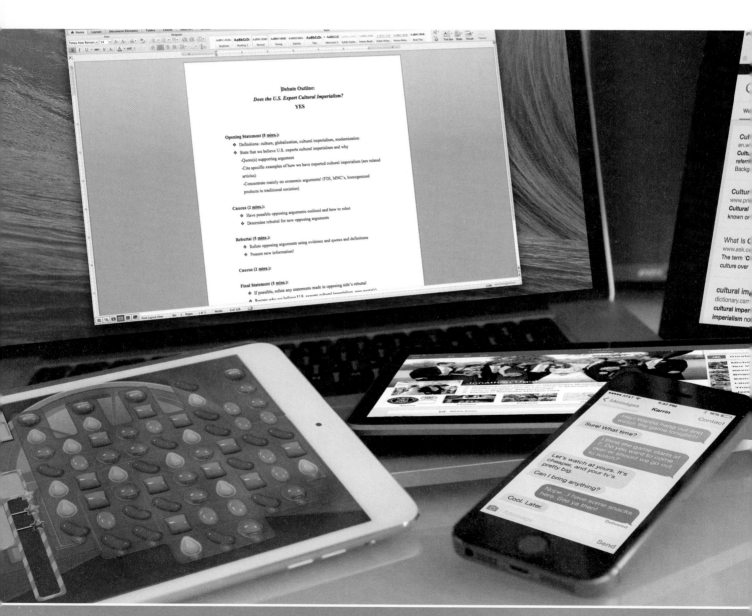

Jonathan Ugol

write first

Write a paragraph in which you explain the impact of a particular electronic device on your life or on the lives of your family members.

In this chapter, you will learn to

- form compound sentences with coordinating conjunctions (18a)
- form compound sentences with semicolons (18b)
- form compound sentences with transitional words and phrases (18c)

The most basic kind of sentence, a **simple sentence**, consists of a single **independent clause**: one <u>subject</u> and one <u>verb</u>.

European <u>immigrants</u> <u>arrived</u> at Ellis Island.

A **compound sentence** is made up of two or more simple sentences (independent clauses).

18a Using Coordinating Conjunctions

One way to form a compound sentence is by joining two independent clauses with a **coordinating conjunction** preceded by a comma.

Many European immigrants arrived at Ellis Island, <u>but</u> many Asian immigrants arrived at Angel Island.

macmillanhighered.com /writingfirst
LearningCurve > Prepositions and Conjunctions; Additional Grammar Exercises > Using Coordinating Conjunctions

Coordinating Conjunctions

and	for	or	yet
but	nor	so	

WORD POWER

coordinate (verb) to link two or more things that are equal in importance, rank, or degree

FYI

Use the letters that spell *FANBOYS* to help you remember the coordinating conjunctions.

F	for
A	and
N	nor
B	but
O	or
Y	yet
S	so

Coordinating conjunctions join two ideas of equal importance. They describe the relationship between two ideas, showing how and why the ideas are related. Different coordinating conjunctions have different meanings.

- To indicate addition, use *and*.

  He acts like a child, <u>and</u> people think he is cute.

- To indicate contrast or contradiction, use *but* or *yet*.

  He acts like a child, <u>but</u> he is an adult.

  He acts like a child, <u>yet</u> he wants to be taken seriously.

- To indicate a cause-and-effect relationship, use *so* or *for*.

  He acts like a child, <u>so</u> we treat him like one.

  He acts like a child, <u>for</u> he needs attention.

- To present alternatives, use *or*.

  He acts like a child, <u>or</u> he gets no attention.

- To eliminate alternatives, use *nor*.

  He does not act like a child, <u>nor</u> does he look like one.

FYI

Commas with Coordinating Conjunctions

When you use a coordinating conjunction to join two independent clauses into a single compound sentence, always put a comma before the coordinating conjunction.

We can stand in line all night, or we can go home now.

PRACTICE

18-1 Fill in the coordinating conjunction—*and, but, for, nor, or, so,* or *yet*—that most logically links the two parts of each compound sentence. Remember to insert a comma before each coordinating conjunction.

Example: Fairy tales have been told by many people around the world, __*but*__ the stories by two German brothers may be the most famous.

(1) Jakob and Wilhelm Grimm lived in the nineteenth century _____ they wrote many well-known fairy tales. (2) Most people think fondly of fairy tales _____ the Brothers Grimm wrote many unpleasant and violent stories. (3) In their best-known works, children are abused _____ endings are not always happy. (4) Either innocent children are brutally punished for no reason _____ they are neglected. (5) For example, in "Hansel and Gretel," the stepmother mistreats the children _____ their father abandons them in the woods. (6) In this story, the events are horrifying _____ the ending is still happy. (7) The children outwit the evil adults _____ they escape unharmed.

(8) Apparently, they are not injured physically _____ are they harmed emotionally. (9) Nevertheless, their story can hardly be called pleasant _____ it remains a story of child abuse and neglect.

PRACTICE

18-2   Add coordinating conjunctions to combine some of the simple sentences in the following paragraph. Remember to put a comma before each coordinating conjunction you add.

Example: Years ago, few Americans lived to be one hundred*/* ~~Today,~~ *, but today,*
there are over seventy thousand centenarians.

(1) Diet, exercise, and family history may explain centenarians' long lives. (2) This is not the whole story. (3) A recent study showed surprising similarities among centenarians. (4) They did not all avoid tobacco and alcohol. (5) They did not have low-fat diets. (6) In fact, they ate relatively large amounts of fat, cholesterol, and sugar. (7) Diet could not explain their long lives. (8) They did, however, share four key traits. (9) First, all the centenarians were optimistic about life. (10) All were positive thinkers. (11) They also had deep religious faith. (12) In addition, they had continued to lead physically active lives. (13) They remained mobile even as elderly people. (14) Finally, all were able to adapt to loss. (15) They had lost friends, spouses, or children. (16) They were able to get on with their lives.

PRACTICE

18-3   Write another simple sentence to follow each of the sentences below. Then, connect the sentences with a coordinating conjunction and the correct punctuation.

Example: Many patients need organ transplants*/* *, but there is a serious*
shortage of organ donors.

1. Secondhand smoke is dangerous. _____

_____

2. Dancing is good exercise. _____

_____

3. Motorcycle helmet laws have been dropped in some states. _____

_____

4. Pretzels are healthier than potato chips. _____

_____

5. People tend to resist change. _____

_____

18b   Using Semicolons

e macmillanhighered.com /writingfirst
Additional Grammar Exercises > Using Semicolons

Another way to create a compound sentence is by joining two simple sentences (independent clauses) with a **semicolon**. A semicolon connects clauses whose ideas are closely related.

> The AIDS Memorial Quilt contains thousands of panels; each panel represents a life lost to AIDS.

Also use a semicolon to show a strong contrast between two ideas.

> With new drugs, people can live with AIDS for years; many people, however, cannot get these drugs.

FYI

Avoiding Fragments

A semicolon can only join two complete sentences (independent clauses). A semicolon cannot join a sentence and a fragment.

INCORRECT   ┌──── FRAGMENT ────┐ Because millions worldwide are still dying of AIDS; more research is needed.

CORRECT   ┌──── SENTENCE ────┐ Millions worldwide are still dying of AIDS; more research is needed.

PRACTICE

18-4   Each of the following items consists of one simple sentence. Create a compound sentence for each item by changing the period to a semicolon and then adding another simple sentence.

Example: My brother is addicted to fast food/ *; he eats it every day.* _____

1. Fast-food restaurants are an American institution. _____

_____

2. Families often eat at these restaurants. _____

_____

3. Many teenagers work there. _____

_____

4. Many fast-food restaurants offer some low-fat menu items. _____

_____

5. Some offer recyclable packaging. _____

_____

6. Some even have playgrounds. _____

_____

18c Using Transitional Words and Phrases

e macmillanhighered.com
/writingfirst
Additional Grammar
Exercises > Using Transitional
Words and Phrases

Another way to create a compound sentence is by combining two simple sentences (independent clauses) with a **transitional word or phrase**. When you use a transitional word or phrase to join two sentences, always place a semicolon *before* the transitional word or phrase and a comma *after* it.

Some college students receive grants; <u>in addition,</u> they often have to take out loans.

He had a miserable time at the party; <u>besides,</u> he lost his wallet.

Frequently Used Transitional Words

also	instead	still
besides	later	subsequently
consequently	meanwhile	then
eventually	moreover	therefore
finally	nevertheless	thus
furthermore	now	
however	otherwise	

Frequently Used Transitional Phrases

after all	in comparison
as a result	in contrast
at the same time	in fact
for example	in other words
for instance	of course
in addition	on the contrary

Adding a transitional word or phrase makes the connection between ideas in a sentence clearer and more precise than it would be if the ideas were linked with just a semicolon. Different transitional words and phrases convey different meanings, as the following chart shows.

Relationship between Clauses	Transitional Word or Phrase	Example
Addition	also, besides, furthermore, in addition, moreover	I have a lot on my mind; also, I have a lot to do.
Causal connection	as a result, consequently, therefore	I have a lot on my mind; therefore, it is hard to concentrate.
Contradiction or contrast	however, in contrast, nevertheless, still	I have a lot on my mind; still, I must try to focus.
Alternatives	instead, on the contrary, otherwise	I have a lot on my mind; otherwise, I might be able to relax.
Sequence	at the same time, eventually, finally, later, meanwhile, now, then	I have a lot on my mind; meanwhile, I still have work to do.

PRACTICE

18-5 Add semicolons and commas where required to set off transitional words and phrases that join two independent clauses.

Example: Ketchup is a popular condiment, therefore, it is available in almost every restaurant.

(1) Andrew F. Smith, a food historian, wrote a book about the tomato later he wrote a book about ketchup. (2) This book, *Pure Ketchup*, was a big project in fact Smith worked on it for five years. (3) The word *ketchup* may have come from a Chinese word however Smith is not certain of the word's origins. (4) Ketchup has existed since ancient times in other words it is a very old product. (5) Ketchup has changed a lot over the years for example special dyes were developed in the nineteenth century to make it red. (6) Smith discusses many other changes for instance preservative-free ketchup was invented in 1907. (7) Ketchup is now used by people

in many cultures still salsa is more popular than ketchup in the United States. (8) Today, designer ketchups are being developed meanwhile Heinz has introduced green and purple ketchup in squeeze bottles. (9) Some of today's ketchups are chunky in addition some ketchups are spicy. (10) Ketchup continues to evolve meanwhile Smith has written a book about hamburgers.

PRACTICE
18-6 Consulting the lists of transitional words and phrases on page 283, choose a word or phrase that logically connects each pair of simple sentences in the following paragraph into one compound sentence. Be sure to punctuate appropriately.

Example: *Time*'s Person of the Year is often a prominent politician*;*
however, sometimes
~~Sometimes~~ it is not.

(1) Every year since 1927, *Time* has designated a Person of the Year. The Person of the Year has almost never been an average person—or even a "person" at all. (2) In the 1920s and 1930s, world leaders were often chosen. Franklin Delano Roosevelt was chosen twice. (3) During World War II, Hitler, Stalin, Churchill, and Roosevelt were all chosen. Stalin was featured twice. (4) Occasionally, the Person of the Year was not an individual. In 1950, it was The American Fighting Man. (5) In 1956, The Hungarian Freedom Fighter was Person of the Year. In 1966, *Time* editors chose The Young Generation. (6) In 1975, American Women were honored as a group. The Person of the Year has nearly always been male. (7) Very few people of color have been designated Person of the Year. Martin Luther King Jr. was honored in 1963. (8) The Person of the Year has almost always been one or more human beings. The Computer was selected in 1982 and Endangered Earth in 1988. (9) In 2005, *Time* wanted to honor the contributions of philanthropists. The magazine named Bill Gates, Melinda Gates, and Bono its Persons of the Year. (10) For 2010 and 2012, *Time* chose Facebook founder

WORD POWER

philanthropist
someone who tries to improve human lives through charitable aid

Mark Zuckerberg and President Barack Obama, respectively. In 2011, it chose The Protester, recognizing dissidents in the Middle East and North Africa. (11) In 2013, *Time* chose Pope Francis, the first non-European pope in 1,200 years, as its Person of the Year. Political leaders are most likely to be selected in the future.

PRACTICE

18-7 Add the suggested transitional word or phrase to each of the following simple sentences. Then, add a new independent clause after it. Be sure to punctuate correctly.

> **Example:** Commuting students do not really experience campus life. (however)
>
> *Commuting students do not really experience campus life; however, there are some*
>
> *benefits to being a commuter.*

1. Living at home gives students access to home-cooked meals. (in contrast)

   _____

   _____

2. Commuters have a wide choice of jobs in the community. (on the other hand)

   _____

   _____

3. There are also some disadvantages to being a commuter. (for example)

   _____

   _____

4. Unlike dorm students, many commuters have family responsibilities. (in fact)

   _____

   _____

5. Commuting to college has pros and cons. (therefore)

   _____

   _____

TEST · Revise · Edit · Proofread

Look back at your response to the Write First prompt on page 278.
TEST and revise what you have written. Then, edit and proofread your
work, checking each compound sentence to make sure you have used
the coordinating conjunction or transitional word or phrase that best
conveys your meaning and that you have punctuated these sentences
correctly.

EDITING PRACTICE

Read the following student essay. Then, create compound sentences by linking pairs of simple sentences where appropriate, joining them with a coordinating conjunction, a semicolon, or a transitional word or phrase. Remember to put commas before coordinating conjunctions and to use semicolons and commas correctly with transitional words and phrases. The first two sentences have been combined for you.

My Grandfather's Life

My great-grandparents were born in Ukraine/ ~~They~~ *, but they* raised my grandfather in western Pennsylvania. The ninth of their ten children, he had a life I cannot begin to imagine. To me, he was my big, strong, powerful grandfather. He was also a child of poverty.

My great-grandfather worked for the American Car Foundry. The family lived in a company house. They shopped at the company store. In 1934, my great-grandfather was laid off. He went to work digging sewer lines for the government. At that time, the family was on welfare. Every week, they were entitled to get food rations. My grandfather would go to pick up the food. The family desperately needed the prunes, beans, flour, margarine, and other things.

For years, my grandfather wore his brothers' hand-me-down clothes. He wore thrift-shop shoes with cardboard over the holes in the soles. He was often hungry. He would sometimes sit by the side of the railroad tracks, waiting for the engineer to throw him an orange. My grandfather would do any job to earn a quarter. Once, he weeded a mile-long row of tomato plants. For this work, he was paid twenty-five cents and a pack of Necco wafers.

My grandfather saved his pennies. Eventually, he was able to buy a used bicycle for two dollars. He dropped out of school at fourteen and got a job. The family badly needed his income. He woke up every day at 4 a.m. He rode his bike to his job at a meatpacking plant. He worked for fifty cents a day.

In 1943, at the age of seventeen, my grandfather joined the U.S. Navy. He discovered a new world. For the first time in his life, he had enough to eat.

He was always first in line at the mess hall. He went back for seconds and thirds before anyone else. After the war ended in 1945, he was discharged from the Navy. He went to work in a meat market in New York City. The only trade he knew was the meat business. Three years later, when he had saved enough to open his own store, Pete's Quality Meats, he knew his life of poverty was finally over.

COLLABORATIVE ACTIVITY

Working in a small group, pair each of the simple sentences in the left-hand column with a sentence in the right-hand column to create ten compound sentences. Use as many different coordinating conjunctions as you can to connect the independent clauses. Be sure each coordinating conjunction you choose conveys a logical relationship between ideas, and remember to put a comma before each one. You may use some of the listed sentences more than once. *Note:* Many different combinations—some serious and factually accurate, some humorous—are possible.

Some dogs wear little sweaters.	Many are named Hamlet.
Pit bulls are raised to fight.	They live in groups.
Bonobos are pygmy chimpanzees.	One even sings Christmas carols.
Many people fear Dobermans.	They can wear bandannas.
Leopards have spots.	They can play Frisbee.
Dalmatians can live in firehouses.	Many live in equatorial Zaire.
Horses can wear blankets.	Some people think they are gentle.
All mules are sterile.	They don't get cold in winter.
Great Danes are huge dogs.	They are half horse and half donkey.
Parrots can often speak.	They can be unpredictable.

review checklist

Writing Compound Sentences

☐ A compound sentence is made up of two simple sentences (independent clauses).

☐ A coordinating conjunction—*and, but, for, nor, or, so,* or *yet*—can join two independent clauses into one compound sentence. A comma always comes before the coordinating conjunction. (See 18a.)

☐ A semicolon can join two independent clauses into one compound sentence. (See 18b.)

☐ A transitional word or phrase can also join two independent clauses into one compound sentence. When it joins two independent clauses, a transitional word or phrase is always preceded by a semicolon and followed by a comma. (See 18c.)

19 Writing Complex Sentences

write first

This picture shows cigarette packages from the United Kingdom, which have larger, more explicit warning labels than those sold in the United States. (Some European warning labels are even more explicit, showing pictures of diseased lungs.) Write a paragraph about whether you think cigarette companies in the United States should have similar explicit warning labels. Explain why you think such a change is (or is not) necessary.

In this chapter, you will learn to
- identify complex sentences (19a)
- use subordinating conjunctions to form complex sentences (19b)
- use relative pronouns to form complex sentences (19c)

19a Identifying Complex Sentences

As you learned in Chapter 18, an **independent clause** can stand alone as a sentence.

INDEPENDENT CLAUSE   The exhibit was controversial.

However, a **dependent clause** cannot stand alone as a sentence.

DEPENDENT CLAUSE   Because the exhibit was controversial

What happened because the exhibit was controversial? To answer this question, you need to add an independent clause that completes the idea begun in the dependent clause. The result is a **complex sentence**—a sentence that consists of one independent clause and one or more dependent clauses.

COMPLEX SENTENCE   ┌──── DEPENDENT CLAUSE ────┐ ┌─ INDEPENDENT CLAUSE ─┐
Because the exhibit was controversial, many people came to see it.

PRACTICE

19-1   In the blank after each of the following items, indicate whether the group of words is an independent clause (*IC*) or a dependent clause (*DC*).

Example: When novelist Toni Morrison was born in Ohio in 1931.

_____DC_____

1. As a young reader, Toni Morrison liked the classic Russian novelists.

   _____

2. After she graduated from Howard University with a bachelor's degree in English. _____

3. Morrison based her novel *The Bluest Eye* on a childhood friend's prayers to God for blue eyes. _____

4. While she raised two sons as a single mother and worked as an editor at Random House. _____

5. As her reputation as a novelist grew with the publication of *Song of Solomon* and *Tar Baby*. _____

6. Her picture appeared on the cover of *Newsweek* in 1981. _____

7. Before her novel *Beloved* won the 1988 Pulitzer Prize for Fiction. _____

8. *Beloved* was made into a film starring Oprah Winfrey. _____

9. In 1993, Morrison became the first African-American woman to win the Nobel Prize in Literature. _____

10. Who published the novel *A Mercy* in 2008 to favorable reviews. _____

19b Using Subordinating Conjunctions

macmillanhighered.com
/writingfirst
LearningCurve > Prepositions
and Conjunctions; Additional
Grammar Exercises > Using
Subordinating Conjunctions

WORD POWER

subordinate (adj)
lower in rank or position;
secondary in importance

One way to form a complex sentence is to use a **subordinating conjunction**—a word such as *although* or *because*—to join two simple sentences (independent clauses). When the subordinating conjunction is added to the beginning of the simple sentence, the sentence becomes dependent for its meaning on the other simple sentence.

TWO SIMPLE SENTENCES	Muhammad Ali was stripped of his heavyweight title for refusing to go into the army. Many people admired his antiwar position.

DEPENDENT CLAUSE

COMPLEX SENTENCE	Although Muhammad Ali was stripped of his heavyweight title for refusing to go into the army, many people admired his antiwar position.

Frequently Used Subordinating Conjunctions

after	even though	since	whenever
although	if	so that	where
as	if only	than	whereas
as if	in order that	that	wherever
as though	now that	though	whether
because	once	unless	while
before	provided that	until	
even if	rather than	when	

As the chart below shows, different subordinating conjunctions express different relationships between dependent and independent clauses.

Relationship between Clauses	Subordinating Conjunction	Example
Time	after, before, since, until, when, whenever, while	When the whale surfaced, Ahab threw his harpoon.
Reason or cause	as, because	Scientists scaled back the project because the government cut funds.
Result or effect	in order that, so that	So that students' math scores will improve, many schools have begun special programs.
Condition	even if, if, unless	The rain forest may disappear unless steps are taken immediately.
Contrast	although, even though, though	Although Thomas Edison had almost no formal education, he was a successful inventor.
Location	where, wherever	Pittsburgh was built where the Allegheny and Monongahela Rivers meet.

PRACTICE

19-2 In the blank in each of the following sentences, write an appropriate subordinating conjunction. Be sure to choose a conjunction that expresses the logical relationship between the two clauses it links.

Example: _Although_ many actual cowboys were African American, movie cowboys are usually portrayed as white.

(1) _____ they were once common, few people today know about black cowboys. (2) _____ the transcontinental railroad was built, cowboys were in high demand. (3) The ranchers hired cowboys to drive their cattle to the Midwest, _____ the cows were loaded on

trains headed to eastern cities. (4) Many former slaves became cowboys _____ they wanted a new start. (5) Many African Americans also became cowboys _____ they had experience working with horses and cattle on southern plantations or farms. (6) _____ almost one-fourth of cowboys were black, few writers wrote about them. (7) The myth of the white-only cowboy was spread in novels, films, and television shows _____ black cowboys never existed. (8) Black cowboys did appear in some films of the 1970s, _____ by this time Westerns were no longer popular. (9) Things started to change in the 1970s, _____ several museums honored black, Indian, and Mexican cowboys. (10) _____ African-American cowboys have finally received some recognition, their history can now be more fully understood.

19c Using Relative Pronouns

macmillanhighered.com
/writingfirst
LearningCurve > Nouns and
Pronouns; Additional Grammar
Exercises > Using Relative
Pronouns

Another way to form a complex sentence is to use **relative pronouns** (*who, that, which,* and so on) to join two simple sentences (independent clauses).

TWO SIMPLE SENTENCES	Harry Potter is an adolescent wizard. He attends Hogwarts School of Witchcraft and Wizardry.

COMPLEX SENTENCE	DEPENDENT CLAUSE Harry Potter, who attends Hogwarts School of Witchcraft and Wizardry, is an adolescent wizard.

Note: The relative pronoun always refers to a word or words in the independent clause. (In the complex sentence above, *who* refers to *Harry Potter.*)

Relative Pronouns

| that | which | whoever | whomever |
| what | who | whom | whose |

A relative pronoun indicates the relationship between the ideas in the independent and dependent clauses it links.

TWO SIMPLE SENTENCES	Nadine Gordimer lived in South Africa. She won the Nobel Prize in Literature in 1991.

COMPLEX SENTENCE	Nadine Gordimer, who won the Nobel Prize in Literature in 1991, lived in South Africa.
TWO SIMPLE SENTENCES	Last week I had a job interview. It went very well.
COMPLEX SENTENCE	Last week I had a job interview that went very well.
TWO SIMPLE SENTENCES	Transistors have replaced vacuum tubes in radios and televisions. They were invented in 1948.
COMPLEX SENTENCE	Transistors, which were invented in 1948, have replaced vacuum tubes in radios and televisions.

PRACTICE

19-3 In each of the following complex sentences, underline the dependent clause once, and underline the relative pronoun twice. Then, draw an arrow from the relative pronoun to the word or words to which it refers.

Example: MTV, which was the first television network devoted to popular music videos, began in 1981.

1. MTV's very first music video, which was performed by a group called the Buggles, contained the lyric "Video killed the radio star."

2. The earliest videos on MTV were simple productions that recorded live studio performances.

3. Music videos eventually became complicated productions that featured special effects and large casts of dancers.

4. Music video directors gained recognition at MTV's Video Music Awards presentation, which first aired in September 1984.

5. *The Real World*, a reality series that featured a group of young people living together in New York City, was introduced by MTV in 1992.

6. MTV's later reality shows featured celebrities such as Jessica Simpson, who starred in *Newlyweds: Nick and Jessica* in 2003.

7. Today, MTV, which devotes less and less time to music videos, produces many hours of original programming.

8. One of MTV's most popular reality shows, which featured cast members at the beach, was *Jersey Shore*.

9. Another popular but controversial show is *16 and Pregnant*, which presents the stories of pregnant high school girls.

10. Needless to say, these shows have their critics, who claim that the shows undermine society's most basic values.

TEST · Revise · Edit · Proofread

Look back at your response to the Write First prompt on page 290. TEST and revise what you have written. Then, edit and proofread your work, checking carefully to make sure that you have used subordinating conjunctions and relative pronouns correctly and that your complex sentences are punctuated correctly.

EDITING PRACTICE

Read the following student essay. Then, revise it by combining pairs of simple sentences with subordinating conjunctions or relative pronouns that indicate the relationship between them. The first two sentences have been combined for you.

Community Art

When a
A city has a crime problem, ~~The~~ *, the* police and the courts try to solve it. Some cities have come up with creative ways to help young people stay out of trouble. One example is the Philadelphia Mural Arts Program. It offers free art education for high school students.

In the 1960s, Philadelphia had a serious problem. The problem was graffiti. Graffiti artists had painted on buildings all over the city. A solution to the problem was the Philadelphia Anti-Graffiti Network. This offered graffiti artists an alternative. The artists would give up graffiti. They would not be prosecuted. The artists enjoyed painting. They could paint murals on public buildings instead. They could create beautiful landscapes, portraits of local heroes, and abstract designs. The graffiti artists had once been lawbreakers. They could now help beautify the city.

The Mural Arts Program began in 1984 as a part of the Philadelphia Anti-Graffiti Network. By 1996, the Philadelphia Anti-Graffiti Network was focusing on eliminating graffiti, and its Mural Arts Program was working to improve the community. It no longer worked with graffiti offenders. It ran after-school and summer programs for students. The Mural Arts Program got national recognition in 1997. That is when President Bill Clinton helped paint a mural. So far, the Mural Arts Program has completed more than 2,800 murals. This is more than any other public art program in the country.

Over twenty thousand students have taken part in the Mural Arts Program. The students come from all parts of the city. In one part of the program, students work alongside professional artists. The students get to paint parts of the artists' murals themselves. The artwork is on public buildings. The artwork can be seen by everyone.

The Mural Arts Program continues to build a brighter future for students and their communities. It is now over thirty years old. Students help bring people together to create a mural. They feel a stronger connection to their community and more confidence in themselves. They leave the program. They are equipped to make a positive difference in their communities and in their own lives.

COLLABORATIVE ACTIVITY

Working in a group of four students, make a list of three or four of your favorite television shows. Then, divide into pairs, and with your partner, write two simple sentences describing each show. Next, use subordinating conjunctions or relative pronouns to combine each pair of sentences into one complex sentence. With your group, discuss how the ideas in each complex sentence are related, and make sure you have used the subordinating conjunction or relative pronoun that best conveys this relationship.

> **Example:** *Downton Abbey* is a period drama set in the early twentieth century. It appeals to many of today's viewers.
>
> Although *Downton Abbey* is a period drama set in the early twentieth century, it appeals to many of today's viewers.

review checklist

Writing Complex Sentences

☐ A complex sentence consists of one independent clause (simple sentence) combined with one or more dependent clauses. (See 19a.)

☐ Subordinating conjunctions—dependent words such as *although, after, when, while,* and *because*—can join two independent clauses into one complex sentence. (See 19b.)

☐ Relative pronouns—dependent words such as *who, which,* and *that*—can also join two independent clauses into one complex sentence. The relative pronoun shows the relationship between the ideas in the two independent clauses that it links. (See 19c.)

20 Writing Varied Sentences

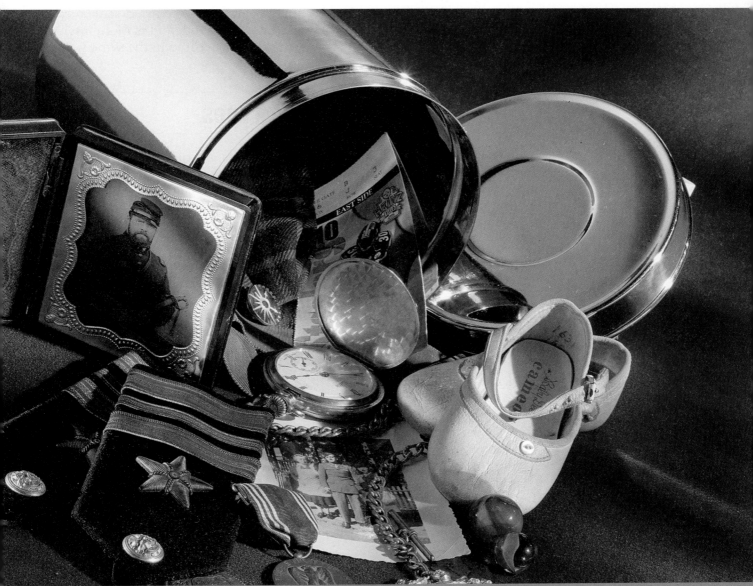

write first

This picture shows items about to be preserved in a time capsule at the History Center in Pittsburgh. Write a paragraph about a time capsule you might construct for your children to open when they are adults. What items would you include? How would you expect each item to communicate to your children what you and your world were like? Be sure to include explanations for your decisions.

In this chapter, you will learn to
- vary sentence types (20a)
- vary sentence openings (20b)
- combine sentences (20c)
- mix long and short sentences (20d)

ⓔ macmillanhighered.com
/writingfirst
Additional Grammar
Exercises > Identifying
Sentence Types

Sentence variety is important because a paragraph of varied sentences flows more smoothly, is easier to read and understand, and is more interesting than one in which all the sentences are structured in the same way.

20a Varying Sentence Types

Most English sentences are **statements**. Others are **questions** or **exclamations**. One way to vary your sentences is to use an occasional question or exclamation where it is appropriate.

In the following paragraph, a question and an exclamation add variety.

> Jacqueline Cochran, the first woman pilot to break the sound barrier, was one of the most important figures in aviation history. In 1996, the United States Postal Service issued a stamp honoring Cochran; the words "Pioneer Pilot" appear under her name. <u>What did she do to earn this title and this tribute?</u> Cochran broke more flight records than anyone else in her lifetime and won many awards, including the United States Distinguished Service Medal in 1945 and the United States Air Force Distinguished Flying Cross in 1969. During World War II, she helped form the WASPs—the Women's Air Force Service Pilots program—so that women could fly military planes to their bases (even though they were not allowed to go into combat). Remarkably, she accomplished all this with only three weeks of flying instruction. She only decided to get her pilot's license in the first place because she wanted to start her own cosmetics business and flying would enable her to travel quickly around the country. Although she never planned to be a pilot, once she discovered flying she quickly became the best. <u>Not surprisingly, when the Postal Service honored Jacqueline Cochran, it was with an airmail stamp!</u>

Question (margin label)

Exclamation (margin label)

PRACTICE
20-1

Revise the following paragraph by changing one of the statements into a question and one of the statements into an exclamation.

Example: The cell phone may be making the wristwatch obsolete. (statement)

Is the cell phone making the wristwatch obsolete? (question)

(1) As cell phones and other small electronic devices are becoming more common, fewer people are wearing watches. (2) Most cell phones,

iPads, and MP3 players display the time. (3) Moreover, cell-phone clocks give very accurate time. (4) This is because they set themselves with satellite signals. (5) They also adjust automatically to time-zone changes. (6) Typical wristwatches cannot compete with these convenient features. (7) After all, unlike the newer devices, watches are not computers. (8) However, watches do remain appealing for other reasons. (9) For many people, they are fashion accessories or status symbols. (10) For some, watches are still essential for telling time.

20b   Varying Sentence Openings

When all the sentences in a paragraph begin the same way, your writing is likely to seem dull and repetitive. In the following paragraph, for example, every sentence begins with the subject.

> Scientists have been observing a disturbing phenomenon. The population of frogs, toads, and salamanders has been declining. This decline was first noticed in the mid-1980s. Some reports blamed chemical pollution. Some biologists began to suspect that a fungal disease was killing these amphibians. The most reasonable explanation seems to be that the amphibians' eggs are being threatened by solar radiation. This radiation penetrates the thinned ozone layer, which used to shield them from the sun's rays.

> **WORD POWER**
>
> **amphibians** cold-blooded vertebrates, such as frogs, that live both in the water and on land

Beginning with Adverbs

Instead of opening every sentence in a paragraph with the subject, you can try beginning some sentences with one or more **adverbs**.

> Scientists have been observing a disturbing phenomenon. <u>Gradually but steadily</u>, the population of frogs, toads, and salamanders has been declining. This decline was first noticed in the mid-1980s. Some reports blamed chemical pollution. Some biologists began to suspect that a fungal disease was killing these amphibians. <u>However</u>, the most reasonable explanation seems to be that the amphibians' eggs are being threatened by solar radiation. This radiation penetrates the thinned ozone layer, which used to shield them from the sun's rays.

PRACTICE

20-2 Underline the adverb in each of the following sentences, and then rewrite the sentence so that the adverb appears at the beginning. Be sure to punctuate correctly.

Example: An internship is <u>usually</u> a one-time work or service experience related to a student's career plans.

Usually, an internship is a one-time work or service experience related to a student's

career plans.

1. Internships are sometimes paid or counted for academic credit.

_____

2. A prospective student intern should first talk to an academic adviser.

_____

3. The student should next write a résumé listing job experience, education, and interests.

_____

4. The student can then send the résumé to organizations that are looking for interns.

_____

5. Going to job fairs and networking are often good ways to find internships.

_____

PRACTICE

20-3 In each of the following sentences, fill in the blank with an appropriate adverb. Be sure to punctuate correctly.

Example: ___*Slowly,*___ the sun crept over the horizon.

1. _____ the speeding car appeared from out of nowhere.
2. _____ it crashed into the guardrail.
3. _____ the car jackknifed across the highway.
4. _____ drivers behind the car slammed on their brakes.
5. _____ someone called 911.
6. _____ the ambulance arrived.
7. _____ emergency medical technicians went to work.
8. _____ no one was badly hurt in the accident.

Beginning with Prepositional Phrases

Another way to create sentence variety is to begin some sentences with prepositional phrases. A **prepositional phrase** (such as *along the river* or *near the diner*) is made up of a preposition and its object.

In recent years, scientists have observed a disturbing phenomenon. Gradually but steadily, the population of frogs, toads, and salamanders has been declining. This was first noticed in the mid-1980s. At first, some reports blamed chemical pollution. After a while, some biologists began to suspect that a fungal disease was killing them. However, the most reasonable explanation seems to be that the amphibians' eggs are being threatened by solar radiation. This radiation penetrates the thinned ozone layer, which used to shield them from the sun's rays.

PRACTICE
20-4
Underline the prepositional phrase in each of the following sentences, and then rewrite the sentence so that the prepositional phrase appears at the beginning. Be sure to punctuate correctly.

Example: Very few American women did factory work before the 1940s.

Before the 1940s, very few American women did factory work.

1. Many male factory workers became soldiers during World War II.

   _____

2. The U.S. government encouraged women to take factory jobs in the war's early years.

   _____

   _____

3. Over six million women took factory jobs between 1942 and 1945.

   _____

4. A new female image emerged with this greater responsibility and independence.

   _____

   _____

5. Many women wore pants for the first time.

   _____

6. Most women lost their factory jobs after the war and returned to "women's work."

   _____

PRACTICE
20-5
In each of the following sentences, fill in the blank with an appropriate prepositional phrase. Be sure to punctuate correctly.

Example: *At the start of the New York Marathon,*   Justin felt as if he could run forever.

1. _____ he warmed up by stretching and bending.

2. _____ all the runners were crowded together.

3. _____ they crossed a bridge over the Hudson River.

4. _____ the route became more and more challenging.

5. _____ Justin grabbed some water from a helpful onlooker.

6. _____ he staggered across the finish line.

PRACTICE
20-6

Every sentence in the following paragraph begins with the subject, but several contain prepositional phrases or adverbs that could be moved to the beginning. To vary the sentence openings, move prepositional phrases to the beginnings of four sentences, and move adverbs to the beginnings of two other sentences. Be sure to place a comma after these introductory phrases.

Example: Spain ~~by the end of the 1800s~~ had lost most of its colonies.
By the end of the 1800s,

(1) People in the Cuban-American community often mention José Julián Martí as one of their heroes. (2) José Martí was born in Havana in 1853, at a time when Cuba was a colony of Spain. (3) He had started a newspaper demanding Cuban freedom by the time he was sixteen years old. (4) The Spanish authorities forced him to leave Cuba and go to Spain in 1870. (5) He published his first pamphlet calling for Cuban independence while in Spain, openly continuing his fight. (6) He then lived for fourteen years in New York City. (7) He started the journal of the Cuban Revolutionary Party during his time in New York. (8) Martí's essays and poems argued for Cuba's freedom and for the individual freedom of Cubans. (9) He died in battle against Spanish soldiers in Cuba, passionately following up his words with actions.

macmillanhighered.com
/writingfirst
Additional Grammar
Exercises > Combining
Sentences

20c Combining Sentences

You can also create sentence variety by experimenting with different ways of combining sentences.

Using *-ing* Modifiers

A **modifier** identifies or describes other words in a sentence. You can use an *-ing* modifier to combine two sentences.

TWO SENTENCES	Duke Ellington composed more than a thousand songs. He worked hard to establish his reputation.
COMBINED WITH -*ING* MODIFIER	Composing more than a thousand songs, Duke Ellington worked hard to establish his reputation.

When the two sentences are combined, the -*ing* modifier (*composing more than a thousand songs*) describes the new sentence's subject (*Duke Ellington*).

PRACTICE

20-7 Use an -*ing* modifier to combine each of the following pairs of sentences into a single sentence. Eliminate any unnecessary words, and place a comma after each -*ing* modifier.

Example: Many American colleges are setting an example for the rest of the country. They are going green.

Setting an example for the rest of the country, many American colleges are going green.

1. Special lamps in the dorms of one Ohio college change from green to red. They warn of rising energy use.

   _____

   _____

2. A Vermont college captures methane from dairy cows. It now needs less energy from other sources.

   _____

   _____

3. Student gardeners at a North Carolina college tend a campus vegetable plot. They supply the cafeteria with organic produce.

   _____

   _____

4. A building on a California campus proves that recycled materials can be beautiful. It is built from redwood wine casks.

   _____

   _____

5. Some colleges offer courses in sustainability. They are preparing students to take the green revolution beyond campus.

   _____

   _____

Using *-ed* Modifiers

You can also use an *-ed* modifier to combine two sentences.

TWO SENTENCES	Nogales is located on the border between Arizona and Mexico. It is a bilingual city.
COMBINED WITH *-ED* MODIFIER	<u>Located on the border between Arizona and Mexico,</u> Nogales is a bilingual city.

When the two sentences are combined, the *-ed* modifier (*located on the border between Arizona and Mexico*) describes the new sentence's subject (*Nogales*).

PRACTICE

20-8   Use an *-ed* modifier to combine each of the following pairs of sentences into a single sentence. Eliminate any unnecessary words, and use a comma to set off each *-ed* modifier. When you are finished, underline the *-ed* modifier in each sentence.

Example: Potato chips and cornflakes were invented purely by accident. They are two of America's most popular foods.

<u>Invented purely by accident</u>, potato chips and cornflakes are two of America's most

popular foods.

1. George Crum was employed as a chef in a fancy restaurant. He was famous for his French fries.

   _____

2. A customer was dissatisfied with the fries. He complained and asked for thinner fries.

   _____

3. The customer was served thinner fries. He was still not satisfied and complained again.

   _____

4. Crum was now very annoyed. He decided to make the fries too thin and crisp to eat with a fork.

   _____

5. The customer was thrilled with the extra-thin and crisp potatoes. He ate them all.

   _____

6. Potato chips were invented to get even with a customer. They are the most popular snack food in America today.

   _____

   _____

7. Dr. John Kellogg was concerned about the diet of patients at his hospital. He and his brother set out to make healthy foods.

   _____

   _____

8. The brothers were called away on an urgent matter. They left a pot of boiled wheat on the stove.

   _____

9. The wheat had hardened by the time they returned. It broke into flakes when they rolled it.

   _____

10. The brothers were delighted with the results. They came up with a new flake made of corn.

    _____

Using a Series of Words

Another way to vary your sentences is to combine a group of sentences into one sentence that includes a **series** of words (nouns, verbs, or adjectives). Combining sentences in this way eliminates a boring string of similar sentences and repetitive phrases and also makes your writing more concise.

GROUP OF SENTENCES	College presidents want to improve athletes' academic performance. Coaches, too, want to improve athletes' academic performance. The players themselves also want to improve their academic performance.
COMBINED (SERIES OF NOUNS)	College <u>presidents</u>, <u>coaches</u>, and the <u>players</u> themselves want to improve athletes' academic performance.
GROUP OF SENTENCES	In 1997, first-time novelist Arundhati Roy published *The God of Small Things*. She won the Pulitzer Prize. She became a literary sensation.
COMBINED (SERIES OF VERBS)	In 1997, first-time novelist Arundhati Roy <u>published</u> *The God of Small Things*, <u>won</u> the Pulitzer Prize, and <u>became</u> a literary sensation.
GROUP OF SENTENCES	As the tornado approached, the sky grew dark. The sky grew quiet. The sky grew threatening.
COMBINED (SERIES OF ADJECTIVES)	As the tornado approached, the sky grew <u>dark</u>, <u>quiet</u>, and <u>threatening</u>.

PRACTICE

20-9   Combine each of the following groups of sentences into one sentence that includes a series of nouns, verbs, or adjectives.

Example: Many years ago, Pacific Islanders from Samoa settled in Hawaii. Pacific Islanders from Fiji also settled in Hawaii. Pacific Islanders from Tahiti settled in Hawaii, too.

Many years ago, Pacific Islanders from Samoa, Fiji, and Tahiti settled in Hawaii.

_____

1. In the eighteenth century, the British explorer Captain Cook came to Hawaii. Other explorers also came to Hawaii. European travelers came to Hawaii, too.

_____

_____

2. Explorers and traders brought commerce to Hawaii. They brought new ideas. They brought new cultures.

_____

_____

3. Missionaries introduced the Christian religion. They introduced a Hawaiian-language bible. Also, they introduced a Hawaiian alphabet.

_____

_____

4. In the mid-nineteenth century, pineapple plantations were established in Hawaii. Sugar plantations were established there as well. Other industries were also established.

_____

_____

5. By 1900, Japanese people were working on the plantations. Chinese people were also working on the plantations. In addition, native Hawaiians were working there.

_____

_____

6. People of many different races and religions now live in Hawaii. People of many different races and religions now go to school in Hawaii. People of many different races and religions now work in Hawaii.

_____

_____

7. Schoolchildren still study the Hawaiian language. They learn about the Hawaiian kings and queens. They read about ancient traditions.

_____

_____

8. Today, Hawaii is well known for its tourism. It is also well known for its weather. It is especially well known for its natural beauty.

_____

_____

9. Tourists can swim. They can surf. They can play golf. They can ride in outrigger canoes.

_____

_____

10. Today, the state of Hawaii remains lively. It remains culturally diverse. It remains very beautiful.

_____

_____

Using Appositives

An **appositive** is a word or word group that identifies, renames, or describes an adjacent noun or pronoun. Creating an appositive is often a good way to combine two sentences about the same subject.

> **WORD POWER**
> **adjacent** next to

TWO SENTENCES   C. J. Walker was the first American woman to become a self-made millionaire. She marketed a line of hair-care products for black women.

COMBINED WITH APPOSITIVE   C. J. Walker, the first American woman to become a self-made millionaire, marketed a line of hair-care products for black women.

In the example above, the appositive appears in the middle of a sentence. However, an appositive can also come at the beginning or at the end of a sentence.

The first American woman to become a self-made millionaire, C. J. Walker marketed a line of hair-care products for black women. (appositive at the beginning)

Several books have been written about C. J. Walker, the first American woman to become a self-made millionaire. (appositive at the end)

PRACTICE
20-10   Combine each of the following pairs of sentences into one sentence by creating an appositive. Note that the appositive may appear at the beginning, in the middle, or at the end of the sentence. Be sure to use commas appropriately.

Example: Wikipedia is a popular online information source. It is available in more than two hundred languages.

(1) Wikipedia is one of the largest reference sites on the web. It is different from other encyclopedias in many ways. (2) This site is a constant

work in progress. It allows anyone to add, change, or correct information in its articles. (3) For this reason, researchers have to be careful when using information from Wikipedia. Wikipedia is a source that may contain factual errors. (4) The older articles are the ones that have been edited and corrected the most. These often contain the most trustworthy information. (5) Despite some drawbacks, Wikipedia has many notable advantages. These advantages include free and easy access, up-to-date information, and protection from author bias.

20d   Mixing Long and Short Sentences

A paragraph of short, choppy sentences—or a paragraph of long, rambling sentences—can be monotonous. By mixing long and short sentences, perhaps combining some simple sentences to create **compound** and **complex** sentences, you can create a more interesting paragraph.

In the following paragraph, the sentences are all short, and the result is boring and hard to follow.

> The world's first drive-in movie theater opened on June 6, 1933. This drive-in was in Camden, New Jersey. Automobiles became more popular. Drive-ins did, too. By the 1950s, there were more than four thousand drive-ins in the United States. Over the years, the high cost of land led to a decline in the number of drive-ins. So did the rising popularity of television. Soon, the drive-in movie theater had almost disappeared. It was replaced by the multiplex. In 1967, there were forty-six drive-ins in New Jersey. Today, only one is still open. That one is the Delsea Drive-in in Vineland, New Jersey.

The revised paragraph that follows is more interesting and easier to read. (Note that the final short sentence is retained for emphasis.)

> The world's first drive-in movie theater opened on June 6, 1933, in Camden, New Jersey. As automobiles became more popular, drive-ins did, too, and by the 1950s, there were more than four thousand drive-ins in the United States. Over the years, the high cost of land and the rising popularity of television led to a decline in the number of drive-ins. Soon, the drive-in movie theater had almost disappeared, replaced by the multiplex. In 1967, there were forty-six drive-ins in New Jersey, but today, only one is still open. That one is the Delsea Drive-in in Vineland, New Jersey.

PRACTICE

20-11   The following paragraph contains a series of short, choppy sentences that can be combined. Revise the paragraph so that it mixes long and short sentences. Be sure to use commas and other punctuation appropriately.

Example: Kente cloth has special significance for many African
Americans./ ~~Some~~ *, but some* other people do not understand this significance.

(1) Kente cloth is made in western Africa. (2) It is produced primarily by the Ashanti people. (3) It has been worn for hundreds of years by African royalty. (4) They consider it a sign of power and status. (5) Many African Americans wear kente cloth. (6) They see it as a link to their heritage. (7) Each pattern on the cloth has a name. (8) Each color has a special significance. (9) For example, red and yellow suggest a long and healthy life. (10) Green and white suggest a good harvest. (11) African women may wear kente cloth as a dress or head wrap. (12) African-American women, like men, usually wear strips of cloth around their shoulders. (13) Men and women of African descent wear kente cloth as a sign of racial pride. (14) It often decorates college students' gowns at graduation.

TEST · Revise · Edit · Proofread

Look back at your response to the Write First prompt on page 299. TEST what you have written. Then, using the strategies discussed in this chapter that seem most appropriate, revise your writing so that your sentences are varied, interesting, and smoothly connected. Finally, edit and proofread your work.

EDITING PRACTICE

The following student essay lacks sentence variety. All of its sentences begin with the subject, and the essay includes a number of short, choppy sentences. Using the strategies discussed in this chapter as well as strategies for creating compound and complex sentences, revise the essay to achieve greater sentence variety. The first sentence has been edited for you.

Toys by Accident

Many popular toys and games are the result of accidents. *when people* ~~People~~ try to invent one thing but discover something else instead. Sometimes they are not trying to invent anything at all. They are completely surprised to find a new product.

Play-Doh is one example of an accidental discovery. Play-Doh is a popular preschool toy. Play-Doh first appeared in Cincinnati. A company made a compound to clean wallpaper. They sold it as a cleaning product. The company then realized that this compound could be a toy. Children could mold it like clay. They could use it again and again. The new toy was an immediate hit. Play-Doh was first sold in 1956. Since then, more than two billion cans of Play-Doh have been sold.

The Slinky was discovered by Richard James. He was an engineer. At the time, he was trying to invent a spring to keep ships' instruments steady at sea. He tested hundreds of springs of varying sizes, metals, and tensions. None of them worked. One spring fell off the desk and "walked" down a pile of books. It went end over end onto the floor. He thought his children might enjoy playing with it. James took the spring home. They loved it. Every child in the neighborhood wanted one. The first Slinky was demonstrated at Gimbel's Department Store in Philadelphia in 1945. All four hundred Slinkys were sold within ninety minutes. The Slinky is simple and inexpensive. The Slinky is still popular with children today.

The Frisbee was also discovered by accident. According to one story, a group of Yale University students were eating pies from a local bakery. The bakery was called Frisbies. They finished eating the pies. They started throwing the empty pie tins around. A carpenter in California made a plastic version. He called it the Pluto Platter. The Wham-O company bought the patent on the product. Wham-O renamed it the Frisbee after the bakery. This is how the Frisbee came to be.

Some new toys are not developed by toy companies. Play-Doh, the Frisbee, and the Slinky are examples of very popular toys that were discovered by accident. Play-Doh started as a cleaning product. The Slinky was discovered by an engineer who was trying to invent something else. The Frisbee was invented by students having fun. The toys were discovered unexpectedly. All three toys have become classics.

COLLABORATIVE ACTIVITY

Read the following list of sentences. Working in a small group, change one sentence to a question and one to an exclamation. Then, add adverbs or prepositional phrases at the beginning of several of the sentences in the list.

Many well-known African-American writers left the United States in the years following World War II.

Many went to Paris.

Richard Wright was a novelist.

He wrote *Native Son* and *Black Boy*.

He wrote *Uncle Tom's Children*.

He left the United States for Paris in 1947.

James Baldwin wrote *Another Country*, *The Fire Next Time*, and *Giovanni's Room*.

He also wrote essays.

He came to Paris in 1948.

Chester Himes wrote detective stories.

He arrived in Paris in 1953.

William Gardner Smith was a novelist and a journalist.

He also left the United States for Paris.

These expatriates found Paris more hospitable than America.

They also found it less racist.

Finally, use the strategies discussed and illustrated in 20c and 20d to help you combine your sentences into a paragraph.

review checklist

Writing Varied Sentences

- [ ] Vary sentence types. (See 20a.)
- [ ] Vary sentence openings. (See 20b.)
- [ ] Combine sentences. (See 20c.)
- [ ] Mix long and short sentences. (See 20d.)

21 Using Parallelism

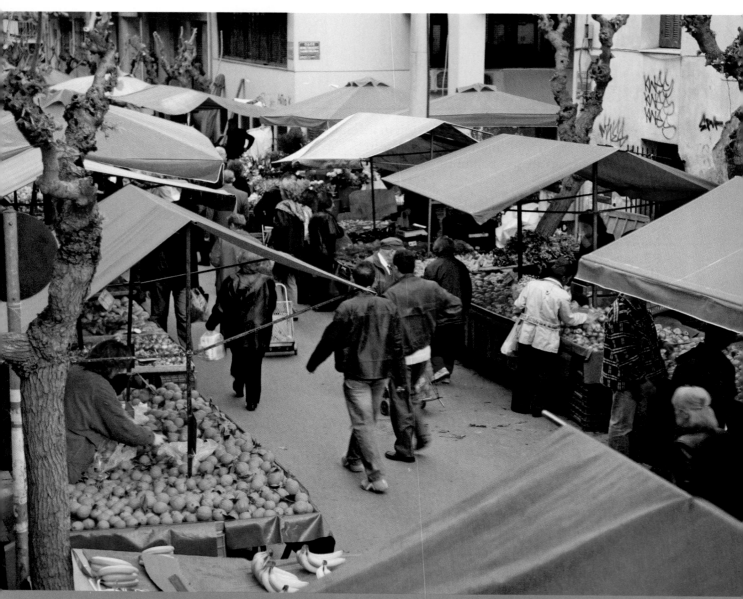

© Vasiliki Varvaki/iStockphoto

write first

This picture shows a green market in an urban neighborhood, part of a growing trend that many people think is making U.S. cities more livable. Write a paragraph discussing three positive things about your own neighborhood, school, or workplace. Support your statements with specific examples.

In this chapter, you will learn to
• recognize parallel structure (21a)
• use parallel structure (21b)

macmillanhighered.com
/writingfirst
LearningCurve > Parallelism;
Additional Grammar Exercises
> Recognizing Parallel
Structure

21a Recognizing Parallel Structure

Parallelism is the use of matching words, phrases, clauses, and sentence structure to highlight similar ideas in a sentence. When you use parallelism, you are telling readers that certain ideas are related and have the same level of importance. By repeating similar grammatical patterns to express similar ideas, you create sentences that are clearer, more concise, and easier to read.

In the following examples, the parallel sentences highlight similar ideas; the other sentences do not.

PARALLEL

Please leave your name, your number, and your message.

I plan to graduate from high school and become a nurse.

The grass was soft, green, and sweet smelling.

Making the team was one thing; staying on it was another.

We can register for classes in person, or we can register by email.

NOT PARALLEL

Please leave your name, your number, and you should also leave a message.

I plan to graduate from high school, and then becoming a nurse would be a good idea.

The grass was soft, green, and the smell was sweet.

Making the team was one thing, but it was very difficult to stay on it.

We can register for classes in person, or registering by email is another option.

PRACTICE

21-1 In the following sentences, decide whether the underlined words and phrases are parallel. If so, write *P* in the blank. If not, rewrite the sentences so that the underlined ideas are presented in parallel terms.

Examples

The missing dog had brown fur, a red collar, and a long tail. _____P_____

Signs of drug abuse in teenagers include falling grades, mood swings, and ~~they lose~~ weight, *loss.* _____

1. The food in the cafeteria is varied, tasty, and it is healthy. _____

2. Do you want the job done <u>quickly</u>, or do you want it done <u>well</u>? _____

3. Last summer I <u>worked at the library</u>, <u>babysat for my neighbor's daughter</u>, and <u>there was a soup kitchen where I volunteered</u>. _____

4. <u>Pandas eat bamboo leaves</u>, and <u>eucalyptus leaves are eaten by koalas</u>. _____

5. Skydiving is <u>frightening</u> but <u>fun</u>. _____

6. A number of interesting people work at the co-op with me, including <u>an elderly German man</u>, <u>there is a middle-aged Chinese woman</u>, and <u>a teenaged Mexican boy</u>. _____

7. <u>The bell rang</u>, and <u>the students stood up</u>. _____

8. To conserve energy while I was away, I <u>unplugged the television</u>, <u>closed the curtains</u>, and <u>the thermostat was set at 65 degrees</u>. _____

9. <u>I put away the dishes</u>; will you <u>put away the laundry</u>? _____

10. For several weeks after the storm, the supermarkets had <u>no eggs</u>, <u>they were out of milk</u>, and <u>they did not have any bread</u>. _____

ie macmillanhighered.com
/writingfirst
Additional Grammar Exercises
> Using Parallel Structure

21b Using Parallel Structure

Parallel structure is especially important in *paired items, items in a series,* and *items in a list or in an outline.*

Paired Items

Use parallel structure when you connect ideas with a **coordinating conjunction**—*and, but, for, nor, or, so,* or *yet.*

George believes in <u>doing a good job</u> and <u>minding his own business</u>.

You can <u>pay me now</u> or <u>pay me later</u>.

You should also use parallel structure for paired items joined by *both . . . and, not only . . . but also, either . . . or, neither . . . nor,* and *rather . . . than.*

Jan is both <u>skilled in writing</u> and <u>fluent in French</u>.

The group's new recording not only has a dance beat but also has thought-provoking lyrics.

I'd rather eat one worm by itself than eat five worms with ice cream.

Items in a Series

Use parallel structure for items in a series—words, phrases, or clauses. (Be sure to use commas to separate three or more items in a series. Never put a comma after the final item.)

Every Wednesday I have English, math, and psychology. (three words)

Increased demand, high factory output, and a strong dollar will help the economy. (three phrases)

She is a champion because she stays in excellent physical condition, puts in long hours of practice, and has an intense desire to win. (three clauses)

Items in a List or in an Outline

Use parallel structure for items in a numbered or bulleted list.

There are three reasons to open an individual retirement account (IRA):
1. To save money
2. To reduce taxes
3. To be able to retire

Use parallel structure for the elements in an outline.

A. Types of rocks
   1. Igneous
   2. Sedimentary
   3. Metamorphic

PRACTICE

21-2   Fill in the blanks in the following sentences with parallel words, phrases, or clauses of your own that make sense in context.

Example: At the lake, we can _____*go for a swim*_____, _____*paddle a canoe*_____, and _____*play volleyball*_____.

1. When I get too little sleep, I am _____, _____, and _____.

2. I am good at _____ but not at _____.

3. My ideal mate is _____ and _____.

4. I personally define success not only as _____ but also as

_____.

5. I use my computer for both _____ and _____.

PRACTICE
21-3   Rewrite the following sentences so that matching ideas are presented in parallel terms. Add punctuation as needed.

Example: Some experts believe homework is harmful to learning, and also it is harmful to children's health and to family life.

Some experts believe homework is harmful to learning, to children's health,

and to family life.

1. Experts who have objected to homework include Dorothy Rich and Harris Cooper, and another expert, Alfie Kohn, has also objected to homework.

_____

_____

2. Harris Cooper of Duke University says that middle school students do not benefit from more than one and a half hours of homework, and more than two hours of homework does not benefit high school students.

_____

_____

_____

_____

3. In his book *The Homework Myth*, Alfie Kohn says that homework creates family conflict, and stress is also created in children.

_____

_____

4. Kohn suggests that children could do other things after school to develop their bodies and minds, and they could also do some things to develop their family relationships.

_____

_____

_____

5. Kohn believes that instead of doing homework, children could interview parents about family history and also chemistry could be learned through cooking.

_____

_____

_____

.

TEST · **Revise · Edit · Proofread**

Look back at your response to the Write First prompt on page 314. **TEST** what you have written. Then, revise your paragraph, checking carefully to make sure you used parallel structure to highlight similar ideas or items in your sentences. If you used parallel structure to present three or more items in a series, make sure you used commas to separate the items. Finally, edit and proofread your work.

EDITING PRACTICE

Read the following student essay, which contains examples of faulty parallelism. Identify the sentences you think need to be corrected, and make the changes required to achieve parallelism. Be sure to supply all words necessary for clarity, grammar, and sense. Add punctuation as needed. The first error has been edited for you.

Self-Made Men and Women Helping Others

Many self-made people go from poverty to ~~achieving~~ success. Quite a few of them not only achieve such success but also they help others. Three of these people are Oprah Winfrey, Alfredo Quiñones-Hinojosa, and Geoffrey Canada. Their lives are very different, but all possess great strength, being determined, and concern for others.

Oprah is one of the most influential people in the world, and she has more money than almost anyone in the world. She came from a very poor family. At first, she lived with her grandmother on a Mississippi farm, and then her mother in Milwaukee. During this time, she was abused by several relatives. When she was thirteen, she was sent to Nashville to live with her father. He used strict discipline, and she was taught by him to value education. Through her own determination and because she was ambitious, Winfrey got a job at a local broadcasting company. This started her career. However, Oprah was not satisfied with being successful. Through Oprah's Angel Network and the Oprah Winfrey Leadership Academy, she helps others and making the world a better place.

Today, Alfredo Quiñones-Hinojosa is a top brain surgeon and conducting research on new ways to treat brain cancer. At age nineteen, he was an illegal immigrant from Mexico, worked in the fields, and without any English. When he told his cousin he wanted to learn English and get a better job, his cousin told him he was crazy. Then, while a welder on a railroad crew, he fell into an empty petroleum tank and was almost dying from the fumes. However, Alfredo overcame these hardships. He enrolled in a community college, and with determination and by working hard, he began to change his life. He won a scholarship to Berkeley, went on to medical school at Harvard, and eventually winding up as director of the brain tumor program at Johns Hopkins University. In 1997, he became a citizen of the United States. At each step along the way, he has made a special effort to reach out to students from low-income backgrounds and to inspire others.

Geoffrey Canada grew up in a New York City neighborhood that was poor, dangerous, and where violence was not uncommon. His mother was a single parent who struggled to support Geoffrey and his three brothers. Geoffrey learned to survive on the streets, but he also studied a lot in school. Thanks to his hard work, he won a scholarship to college in Maine and went on to a career in education. Deciding to leave his neighborhood in New York was not hard, but to decide to come back was not hard either. He wanted to help children in poor families succeed in school and so they could have better lives. With this in mind, he started the Harlem Children's Zone (HCZ). HCZ includes (1) workshops for parents, (2) a preschool and three charter schools, and (3) running health programs for children and families. President Obama has said he would like to see more programs like HCZ.

Oprah Winfrey, Alfredo Quiñones-Hinojosa, and Geoffrey Canada have very different careers—in entertainment, in medicine, and educating children. However, all three overcame great adversity, all three have achieved enormous success, and chose to help others. They have helped their communities, their country, and have contributed to the world.

COLLABORATIVE ACTIVITY

Working in a group, list three or four qualities that you associate with each word in the following pairs.

Brothers/sisters
Teachers/students
Parents/children
City/country
Fast food/organic food
Movies/TV shows
Work/play

Then, write a compound sentence comparing the two words in each pair. Use a coordinating conjunction to join the clauses, and make sure each sentence uses clear parallel structure, mentions both words, and includes the qualities you listed for the word pairs.

_____

_____

e macmillanhighered.com /writingfirst LearningCurve > Parallelism

review checklist

Using Parallelism

☐ Use matching words, phrases, clauses, and sentence structure to high-light similar items or ideas. (See 21a.)

☐ Use parallel structure with paired items. (See 21b.)

☐ Use parallel structure for items in a series. (See 21b.)

☐ Use parallel structure for items in a list or in an outline. (See 21b.)

22 Using Words Effectively

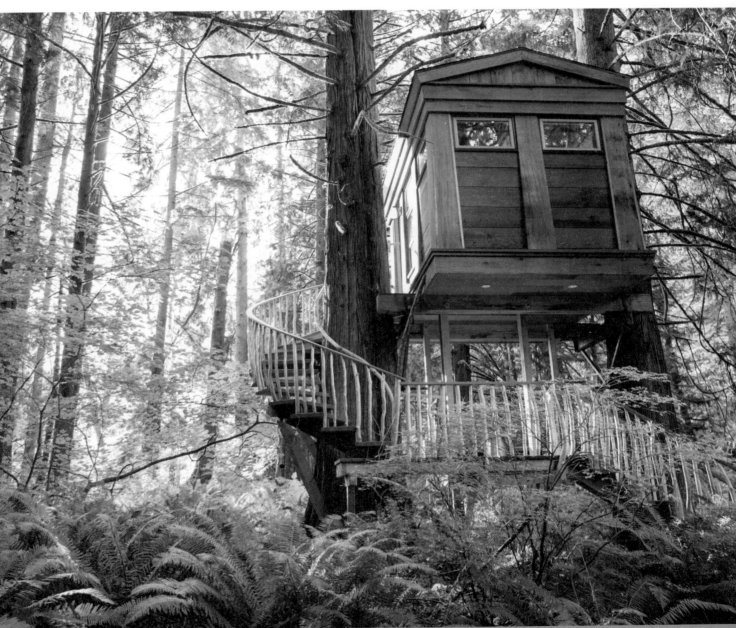

Adam Crowley/Getty Images

write first

This picture shows a luxury tree house. Look at the house carefully, and then write a paragraph in which you describe your dream house. Would it resemble the house in the picture, or would it be different? How? What would be inside the house? Be as specific as possible.

In this chapter, you will learn to

- use specific words (22a)
- use concise language (22b)
- avoid slang (22c)
- avoid clichés (22d)
- use similes and metaphors (22e)
- avoid sexist language (22f)
- recognize commonly confused words (22g)

22a Using Specific Words

macmillanhighered.com /writingfirst

LearningCurve > Word Choice and Appropriate Language; Additional Grammar Exercises > Using Specific Words

Specific words refer to particular people, places, things, ideas, or qualities. **General words** refer to entire classes or groups. Sentences that contain specific words are more precise and vivid than those that contain only general words.

SENTENCES WITH GENERAL WORDS	SENTENCES WITH SPECIFIC WORDS
While walking in the woods, I saw an <u>animal</u>.	While walking in the woods, I saw a <u>baby skunk</u>.
<u>Someone</u> decided to run for Congress.	<u>Rebecca</u> decided to run for Congress.
<u>Weapons</u> are responsible for many murders.	<u>Unregistered handguns</u> are responsible for many murders.
Denise bought new <u>clothes</u>.	Denise bought a new <u>blue dress</u>.
I really enjoyed my <u>meal</u>.	I really enjoyed my <u>pepperoni pizza with extra cheese</u>.
Darrell had always wanted a <u>classic car</u>.	Darrell had always wanted a <u>black 1969 Chevrolet Camaro</u>.

FYI

Using Specific Words

One way to strengthen your writing is to avoid general words like *good*, *nice*, or *great*. Take the time to think of more specific words. For example, when you say the ocean looked *pretty*, do you really mean that it *sparkled*, *glistened*, *rippled*, *foamed*, *surged*, or *billowed*?

PRACTICE
22-1 In the following passage, underline the specific words that help you imagine the scene the writer describes. The first sentence has been done for you.

Last summer, I spent three weeks backpacking through <u>the remote rural province of Yunnan in China</u>. One day, I came across <u>four farm</u>

women playing a game of mahjong on a patch of muddy ground. Squatting on rough wooden stools around a faded green folding table, the women picked up and discarded the smooth ivory mahjong tiles as if they were playing cards. In the grassy field around them, their chestnut-colored horses grazed with heavy red and black market bags tied to their backs. A veil of shimmering white fog hung over a nearby hill, and one woman sat under a black umbrella to shelter herself from the sun. A fifth woman watched, with her wrinkled hands on her hips and a frown on her face. The only sound was the sharp click of the tiles and the soft musical talk of the women as they played.

PRACTICE

22-2 The following one-paragraph job-application letter uses many general words. Rewrite the paragraph, substituting specific words and adding details where necessary. Start by making the first sentence, which identifies the job, more specific: for example, "I would like to apply for the <u>dental technician</u> position you advertised on <u>March 15</u> in the *Post*." Then, add information about your background and qualifications. Expand the original paragraph into a three-paragraph letter.

> I would like to apply for the position you advertised in today's paper. I graduated from high school and am currently attending college. I have taken several courses that have prepared me for the duties the position requires. I also have several personal qualities that I think you would find useful in a person holding this position. In addition, I have had certain experiences that qualify me for such a job. I would appreciate the opportunity to meet with you to discuss your needs as an employer. Thank you.

22b   Using Concise Language

Concise language says what it has to say in as few words as possible. Too often, writers use words and phrases that add nothing to a sentence's meaning. A good way to test a sentence for these words is to see if crossing them out changes the sentence's meaning. If the sentence's meaning does not change, you can assume that the words you crossed out are unnecessary.

~~It is clear that the~~ *The* United States was not ready to fight World War II.

~~In order to~~ *To* follow the plot, you must make an outline.

Sometimes you can replace several unnecessary words with a single word.

~~Due to the fact that~~ *Because* I was tired, I missed my first class.

FYI

Using Concise Language

The following wordy phrases add nothing to a sentence. You can usually delete or condense them with no loss of meaning.

WORDY	CONCISE
It is clear that	(delete)
It is a fact that	(delete)
The reason is because	Because
The reason is that	Because
It is my opinion that	I think / I believe
Due to the fact that	Because
Despite the fact that	Although
At the present time	Today/Now
At that time	Then
In most cases	Usually
In order to	To
In the final analysis	Finally
Subsequent to	After

Unnecessary repetition—saying the same thing twice for no reason—can also make your writing wordy. When you revise, delete repeated words and phrases that add nothing to your sentences.

My instructor told me the book was ~~old-fashioned and~~ outdated. (An old-fashioned book *is* outdated.)

The ~~terrible~~ tragedy of the fire could have been avoided. (A tragedy is *always* terrible.)

PRACTICE

 To make the following sentences more concise, eliminate any unnecessary repetition, and delete or condense wordy expressions.

Example: ~~It is a fact that each individual~~ Each production of *Sesame Street* around the world is geared toward the local children ~~in that region.~~

(1) In order to meet the needs of international children all over the world, Sesame Workshop helps produce versions of its popular show *Sesame Street* in other countries outside the United States. (2) Due to the fact that each country has different issues and concerns, the content of

these shows varies. (3) In most cases, the producers focus on and con-centrate on the cultural diversity in their country. (4) In order to develop the most appropriate material for their shows, producers also consult with and talk to local educators and child development experts, people who are experts in the field. (5) At the present time, versions of *Sesame Street* exist in a wide variety of places and countries, including Mexico, Russia, South Africa, Bangladesh, and Egypt.

22c Avoiding Slang

Slang is nonstandard language that calls attention to itself. It is usually associated with a particular social group—instant message users or skate-boarders, for example. Some slang eventually spreads beyond its original context and becomes widely used. Often, it is used for emphasis or to pro-duce a surprising or an original effect. In any case, because it is very infor-mal, slang is not acceptable in college writing.

easy.
My psychology exam was really ~~sweet.~~

relax ^
On the weekends, I like to ~~chill~~ and watch movies on my laptop.
^

If you have any question about whether a term is slang or not, look it up in a dictionary. If the term is identified as *slang* or *informal*, find a more suitable term.

FYI

Avoiding Abbreviations and Shorthand

While abbreviations and shorthand such as *LOL*, *BTW*, *IMO*, and *2day* are acceptable in informal electronic communication, they are not acceptable in your college writing, in emails to your instructors, or in online class discussions.

In my opinion,
~~IMO~~ your essay needs a strong thesis statement.
^

you   *today.*
I would like to meet with ~~u~~ for a conference ~~2day.~~
^   ^

PRACTICE

22-4 Edit the following sentences, replacing the slang expressions with clearer, more precise words and phrases.

yelled at me
Example: My father ~~lost it~~ when I told him I crashed the car.
^

1. Whenever I get bummed, I go outside and jog.

2. Tonight I'll have to leave by eleven because I'm wiped out.

3. I'm not into movies or television.

4. Whenever we argue, my boyfriend knows how to push my buttons.

5. I really lucked out when I got this job.

e macmillanhighered.com
/writingfirst
Additional Grammar Exercises >
Avoiding Clichés and Sexist
Language

22d Avoiding Clichés

Clichés are expressions—such as "easier said than done" and "last but not least"—that have been used so often they have lost their meaning. These worn-out expressions get in the way of clear communication.

When you identify a cliché in your writing, replace it with a direct statement—or, if possible, with a fresher expression.

CLICHÉ   When school was over, she felt free ~~as a bird~~.

CLICHÉ   These days, you have to be ~~sick as a dog~~ *seriously ill* before you are

admitted to a hospital.

FYI

Avoiding Clichés

Here are examples of some clichés you should avoid in your writing.

back in the day	play God
better late than never	pushing the envelope
break the ice	raining cats and dogs
cutting edge	selling like hotcakes
face the music	the bottom line
give 110 percent	think outside the box
hard as a rock	touch base
it goes without saying	tried and true
it is what it is	water under the bridge
keep your eye on the ball	what goes around comes around

PRACTICE
22-5   Cross out any clichés in the following sentences. Then, either substitute a fresher expression or restate the idea more directly.

Example: Lottery winners often think they will be ~~on easy street~~ *free of financial worries* for

the rest of their lives.

(1) Many people think that a million-dollar lottery jackpot allows the winner to stop working like a dog and start living high on the hog. (2) All things considered, however, the reality for lottery winners is quite different. (3) For one thing, lottery winners who hit the jackpot do not always receive their winnings all at once; instead, yearly payments—for example, $50,000—can be paid out over twenty years. (4) Of that $50,000 a year, close to $20,000 goes to taxes and anything else the lucky stiff already owes the government, such as student loans. (5) Next come relatives and friends with their hands out, leaving winners between a rock and a hard place. (6) They can either cough up gifts and loans or wave bye-bye to many of their loved ones. (7) Adding insult to injury, many lottery winners lose their jobs because employers think that now that they are "millionaires," they no longer need to draw a salary. (8) Many lottery winners wind up way over their heads in debt within a few years. (9) In their hour of need, many might like to sell their future winnings to companies that offer lump-sum payments of forty to forty-five cents on the dollar. (10) This is easier said than done, however, because most state lotteries do not allow winners to sell their winnings.

22e Using Similes and Metaphors

A **simile** is a comparison of two unlike things that uses *like* or *as*.

His arm hung at his side <u>like</u> a broken branch.

He was <u>as</u> content <u>as</u> a cat napping on a windowsill.

A **metaphor** is a comparison of two unlike things that does not use *like* or *as*.

Invaders from another world, the dandelions conquered my garden.

He was a beast of burden, hauling cement from the mixer to the building site.

The impact of similes and metaphors comes from the surprise of seeing two seemingly unlike things being compared. Used in moderation, similes and metaphors can make your writing more lively and more interesting.

PRACTICE
22-6   Use your imagination to complete each of the following items by creating three original similes.

Example: A boring class is like ___*toast without jam.*___

___*a four-hour movie.*___

___*a bedtime story.*___

1. A good friend is like _____

_____

_____

2. A thunderstorm is like _____

_____

_____

3. A workout at the gym is like _____

_____

_____

macmillanhighered.com
/writingfirst
Additional Grammar Exercises >
Avoiding Clichés and Sexist
Language

22f Avoiding Sexist Language

Sexist language refers to men and women in insulting terms. Sexist language is not just words such as *stud* or *babe*, which people may find objectionable. It can also be words or phrases that unnecessarily call attention to gender or that suggest a job or profession is held only by a man (or only by a woman) when it actually is not.

You can avoid sexist language by using a little common sense. There is always an acceptable nonsexist alternative for a sexist term.

SEXIST	NONSEXIST
man, mankind	humanity, humankind, the human race
businessman	executive, businessperson
fireman, policeman, mailman	firefighter, police officer, letter carrier
male nurse, woman engineer	nurse, engineer
congressman	member of Congress, representative
stewardess, steward	flight attendant
man and wife	man and woman, husband and wife
man-made	synthetic
chairman	chair, chairperson
anchorwoman, anchorman	anchor
actor, actress	actor

FYI

Avoiding Sexist Language

Do not use *he* when your subject could be either male or female.

> **SEXIST** Everyone should complete his assignment by next week.

You can correct this problem in three ways.

- *Use* he or she *or* his or her.

  Everyone should complete his or her assignment by next week.

- *Use plural forms.*

  Students should complete their assignments by next week.

- *Eliminate the pronoun.*

  Everyone should complete the assignment by next week.

PRACTICE

22-7 Edit the following sentences to eliminate sexist language.

                  or her (or omit "his")

Example: A doctor should be honest with his patients.

1. Many people today would like to see more policemen patrolling the streets.

2. The attorneys representing the plaintiff are Geraldo Diaz and Mrs. Barbara Wilkerson.

3. Every soldier picked up his weapons.

4. Christine Fox is the female mayor of Port London, Maine.

5. Travel to other planets will be a significant step for man.

22g Recognizing Commonly Confused Words

Accept/Except *Accept* means "to receive something." *Except* means "with the exception of."

> "I <u>accept</u> your challenge," said Alexander Hamilton to Aaron Burr.
> Everyone <u>except</u> Darryl visited the museum.

:e macmillanhighered.com
/writingfirst
Additional Grammar Exercises >
Commonly Confused Words

Affect/Effect   *Affect* is a verb meaning "to influence." *Effect* is a noun meaning "result."

> Carmen's job could <u>affect</u> her grades.

> Overexposure to sun can have a long-term <u>effect</u> on skin.

All ready/Already   *All ready* means "completely prepared." *Already* means "previously, before."

> Serge was <u>all ready</u> to take the history test.

> Gina had <u>already</u> been to Italy.

Brake/Break   *Brake* is a noun that means "a device to slow or stop a vehicle." *Break* is a verb meaning either "to smash" or "to exceed" and sometimes a noun meaning "a gap" or "an interruption" or "a stroke of luck."

> Peter got into an accident because his foot slipped off the <u>brake</u>.

> Babe Ruth thought no one would ever <u>break</u> his home run record.

> The baseball game was postponed until there was a <u>break</u> in the bad weather.

Buy/By   *Buy* means "to purchase." *By* is a preposition meaning "close to," "next to," or "by means of."

> The Stamp Act forced colonists to <u>buy</u> stamps for many public documents.

> He drove <u>by</u> but did not stop.

> He stayed <u>by</u> her side all the way to the hospital.

> Malcolm X wanted "freedom <u>by</u> any means necessary."

Conscience/Conscious   *Conscience* is a noun that refers to the part of the mind that urges a person to choose right over wrong. *Conscious* is an adjective that means "aware" or "deliberate."

> After he cheated at cards, his <u>conscience</u> started to bother him.

> As she walked through the woods, she became <u>conscious</u> of the hum of insects.

> Elliott made a <u>conscious</u> decision to stop smoking.

Everyday/Every day   *Everyday* is a single word that means "ordinary" or "common." *Every day* is two words that mean "occurring daily."

> *Friends* was a successful comedy show because it appealed to <u>everyday</u> people.

> <u>Every day</u>, the six friends met at the Central Perk café.

Fine/Find   *Fine* means "superior quality" or "a sum of money paid as a penalty." *Find* means "to locate."

> He sang a <u>fine</u> solo at church last Sunday.

> Demi had to pay a <u>fine</u> for speeding.

> Some people still use a willow rod to <u>find</u> water.

Hear/Here   *Hear* means "to perceive sound by ear." *Here* means "at or in this place."

> I moved to the front so I could <u>hear</u> the speaker.
>
> My great-grandfather came <u>here</u> in 1883.

Its/It's   *Its* is the possessive form of *it*. *It's* is the contraction of either *it is* or *it has*.

> The airline canceled <u>its</u> flights because of the snow.
>
> <u>It's</u> twelve o'clock, and we are late.
>
> Ever since <u>it's</u> been in the accident, the car has rattled.

Know/No/Knew/New   *Know* means "to have an understanding of" or "to have fixed in the mind." *No* means "not any," "not at all," or "not one." *Knew* is the past tense form of the verb *know*. *New* means "recent or never used."

> I <u>know</u> there will be a lunar eclipse tonight.
>
> You have <u>no</u> right to say that.
>
> He <u>knew</u> how to install a <u>new</u> light switch.

Lie/Lay   *Lie* means "to rest or recline." The past tense of *lie* is *lay*. *Lay* means "to put or place something down." The past tense of *lay* is *laid*.

> Every Sunday, I <u>lie</u> in bed until noon.
>
> They <u>lay</u> on the grass until it began to rain, and then they went home.
>
> Tammy told Carl to <u>lay</u> his cards on the table.
>
> Brooke and Cassia finally <u>laid</u> down their hockey sticks.

Loose/Lose   *Loose* means "not fixed or rigid" or "not attached securely." *Lose* means "to mislay" or "to misplace."

> In the 1940s, many women wore <u>loose</u>-fitting pants.
>
> I never gamble because I hate to <u>lose</u>.

Passed/Past   *Passed* is the past tense of the verb *pass*. It means "moved by" or "succeeded in." *Past* is a noun or an adjective meaning "earlier than the present time."

> The car that <u>passed</u> me was doing more than eighty miles an hour.
>
> David finally <u>passed</u> his driving test.
>
> The novel was set in the <u>past</u>.
>
> The statement said that the bill was <u>past</u> due.

Peace/Piece   *Peace* means "the absence of war" or "calm." *Piece* means "a part of something."

> The British prime minister tried to achieve <u>peace</u> with honor.
>
> My <u>peace</u> of mind was destroyed when the flying saucer landed.
>
> "Have a <u>piece</u> of cake," said Marie.

Principal/Principle   *Principal* means "first" or "highest" or "the head of a school." *Principle* means "a law or basic assumption."

> She had the <u>principal</u> role in the movie.
>
> I'll never forget the day the <u>principal</u> called me into his office.
>
> It was against his <u>principles</u> to lie.

Quiet/Quit/Quite   *Quiet* means "free of noise" or "still." *Quit* means "to leave a job" or "to give up." *Quite* means "actually" or "very."

> Jane looked forward to the <u>quiet</u> evenings at the lake.
>
> Sammy <u>quit</u> his job and followed the girls into the parking lot.
>
> "You haven't <u>quite</u> got the hang of it yet," she said.
>
> After practicing all summer, Tamika got <u>quite</u> good at tennis.

Raise/Rise   *Raise* means "to elevate" or "to increase in size, quantity, or worth." The past tense of *raise* is *raised*. *Rise* means "to stand up" or "to move from a lower position to a higher position." The past tense of *rise* is *rose*.

> Carlos <u>raises</u> his hand whenever the teacher asks for volunteers.
>
> They finally <u>raised</u> the money for the down payment.
>
> The crowd <u>rises</u> every time the home team scores a touchdown.
>
> Kim <u>rose</u> before dawn so she could see the eclipse.

Sit/Set   *Sit* means "to assume a sitting position." The past tense of *sit* is *sat*. *Set* means "to put down or place" or "to adjust something to a desired position." The past tense of *set* is *set*.

> I usually <u>sit</u> in the front row at the movies.
>
> They <u>sat</u> at the clinic, waiting for their names to be called.
>
> Elizabeth <u>set</u> the mail on the kitchen table and left for work.
>
> Every semester I <u>set</u> goals for myself.

Suppose/Supposed   *Suppose* means "to consider" or "to assume." *Supposed* is both the past tense and the past participle of *suppose*. *Supposed* also means "expected" or "required." (Note that when *supposed* has this meaning, it is always followed by *to*.)

> <u>Suppose</u> researchers were to find a cure for cancer.
>
> We <u>supposed</u> the movie would be over by ten o'clock.
>
> You were <u>supposed</u> to finish a draft of the report by today.

Their/There/They're   *Their* is the possessive form of the pronoun *they*. *There* means "at or in that place." *There* is also used in the phrases *there is* and *there are*. *They're* is the contraction of *they are*.

> They wanted poor people to improve <u>their</u> living conditions.
>
> I put the book over <u>there</u>.
>
> <u>There</u> are three reasons I will not eat meat.
>
> <u>They're</u> the best volunteer firefighters I've ever seen.

Then/Than   *Then* means "at that time" or "next in time." *Than* is used in comparisons.

>He was young and naive <u>then</u>.

>I went to the job interview and <u>then</u> stopped off for coffee.

>My dog is smarter <u>than</u> your dog.

Threw/Through   *Threw* is the past tense of *throw*. *Through* means "in one side and out the opposite side" or "finished."

>Satchel Paige <u>threw</u> a baseball more than ninety-five miles an hour.

>It takes almost thirty minutes to go <u>through</u> the tunnel.

>"I'm <u>through</u>," said Clark Kent, storming out of Perry White's office.

To/Too/Two   *To* means "in the direction of." *Too* means either "also" or "more than enough." *Two* denotes the numeral 2.

>During spring break, I am going <u>to</u> Disney World.

>My roommates are coming, <u>too</u>.

>The microwave popcorn is <u>too</u> hot to eat.

>"If we get rid of the Tin Man and the Cowardly Lion, the <u>two</u> of us can go to Oz," said the Scarecrow to Dorothy.

Use/Used   *Use* means "to put into service" or "to consume." *Used* is both the past tense and the past participle of *use*. *Used* also means "accustomed." (Note that when *used* has this meaning, it is followed by *to*.)

>I <u>use</u> a soft cloth to clean my glasses.

>"Hey! Who <u>used</u> all the hot water?" he yelled from the shower.

>Marisol had <u>used</u> all the firewood during the storm.

>After two years in Alaska, they got <u>used</u> to the short winter days.

Weather/Whether   *Weather* refers to temperature, humidity, precipitation, and so on. *Whether* is used to introduce alternative possibilities.

>The *Farmer's Almanac* says that the <u>weather</u> this winter will be severe.

><u>Whether</u> or not this prediction will be correct is anyone's guess.

Where/Were/We're   *Where* means "at or in what place." *Were* is the past tense of *are*. *We're* is the contraction of *we are*.

><u>Where</u> are you going, and <u>where</u> have you been?

>Charlie Chaplin and Mary Pickford <u>were</u> popular stars of silent movies.

><u>We're</u> doing our back-to-school shopping early this year.

Whose/Who's   *Whose* is the possessive form of *who*. *Who's* is the contraction of either *who is* or *who has*.

>My roommate asked, "<u>Whose</u> book is this?"

>"<u>Who's</u> there?" squealed the second little pig as he leaned against the door.

><u>Who's</u> been blocking the driveway?

Your/You're *Your* is the possessive form of *you*. *You're* is the contraction of *you are*.

"You should have worn <u>your</u> running shoes," said the hare as he passed the tortoise.

"<u>You're</u> too kind," said the tortoise sarcastically.

TEST · Revise · Edit · Proofread

Look back at your response to the Write First prompt on page 323. TEST what you have written. Then, revise and edit your paragraph, making sure that your language is specific as well as concise; that you have avoided slang, clichés, and sexist language; and that you have not made any errors in word usage. Try adding a simile or metaphor to add interest to your writing. Finally, proofread your work.

EDITING PRACTICE

Read the following student essay carefully, and then revise it. Make sure that your revision uses specific words; is concise; and includes no slang, clichés, sexist language, or confused words. Add an occasional simile or metaphor if you like. The first sentence has been edited for you.

Unexpected Discoveries

When we ~~here~~ *hear* the word *accident*, we think of bad things, *like dented fenders and broken glass.* But accidents can be good, too. Modern science has made advances as a result of accidents. It is a fact that a scientist sometimes works like a dog for years in his laboratory, only to make a weird discovery because of a mistake.

The most famous example of a good, beneficial accident is the discovery of penicillin. Alexander Fleming, a scientist, had seen many soldiers die of infections after being wounded in World War I. All things considered, many more soldiers died due to the fact that infections occurred then from wounds. Fleming wanted to find a drug that could put an end to these terrible, fatal infections. One day in 1928, Fleming went on vacation, leaving a pile of dishes in the lab sink. As luck would have it, he had been growing bacteria in those dishes. When he came back, he noticed that one of the dishes looked moldy. What was strange was that the bacteria near the mold were dead as a doornail. It was crystal clear to Fleming that the mold had killed the bacteria. He had discovered penicillin, the first antibiotic.

Everyone has heard the name *Goodyear*. It was Charles Goodyear who made a discovery that changed and revolutionized the rubber industry. In the early nineteenth century, rubber products became thin and runny in hot weather and cracked in cold weather. One day in 1839, Goodyear accidentally dropped some rubber mixed with sulfur on a hot stove. It changed color and turned black. After being cooled, it could be stretched, and it would return to its original size and shape. This kind of rubber is now used in tires and in many other products.

Another thing was also discovered because of a lab accident involving rubber. In 1953, Patsy Sherman, a female chemist for the 3M company, was trying to find a new type of rubber. She created a batch of man-made liquid rubber. Some of the liquid accidentally spilled onto a lab assistant's new white canvas sneaker. Her assistant used everything but the kitchen sink to clean the shoe, but nothing worked. Over time, the rest of the shoe became dirty, but the part where the spill had hit was still clean as a whistle. Sherman new that she had found something that could actually keep fabrics clean by doing a number on dirt. The 3M Corporation named it's brand new product Scotchgard.

A scientist can be clumsy and careless, but sometimes his mistakes lead to great and important discoveries. Penicillin, better tires, and Scotchgard are examples of products that were the result of scientific accidents.

COLLABORATIVE ACTIVITY

Photocopy two or three paragraphs of description from a romance novel, a western novel, or a mystery novel, and bring your paragraphs to class. Working in a group, choose one paragraph that seems to need clearer, more specific language. As a group, revise the paragraph you chose, making it as specific as possible and eliminating any clichés or sexist language. Then, exchange your revised paragraph with that of another group, and check the other group's work. Make any additional changes you think the paragraph needs.

review checklist

macmillanhighered.com /writingfirst
LearningCurve > Word Choice and Appropriate Language

Using Words Effectively

- [ ] Use specific words that convey your ideas clearly and precisely. (See 22a.)
- [ ] Use concise language that says what it has to say in the fewest possible words. (See 22b.)
- [ ] Avoid slang. (See 22c.)
- [ ] Avoid clichés. (See 22d.)
- [ ] When appropriate, use similes and metaphors to make your writing more lively and more interesting. (See 22e.)
- [ ] Avoid sexist language. (See 22f.)
- [ ] Recognize commonly confused words. (See 22g.)

Read the following student essay. Then, edit it by creating more effective sentences and correcting any misspelled words. Combine simple sentences into compound or complex sentences; create varied sentences; use parallelism; and use words that are specific, concise, and original. The first editing change has been made for you.

Eating Street Food

Street food—food cooked and served at portable carts or trucks—is extremely popular in the United States. *Usually, street* ~~Street~~-food customers ~~usually~~ get ~~there~~ *their* food quickly^*and*^ ~~They~~ do not pay much. Some regional or ethnic foods are sold as street food. Then, they become popular There are concerns about the cleanliness and freshness of street food. These problems can be avoided. It is a fact that street food has many advantages.

Street food is the original fast food. Street food is both fast and cheap. Customers usually do not have much time to wait for it to be cooked. Vendors have to offer food that can be made beforehand or prepared quickly. The original U.S. street food is the hot dog. It can be steamed ahead of time and quickly be put into a bun. Some customers want things like relish, onions, and chili. They can be added. Street food does not cost as much as restaurant food. Vendors usually have to by a license in order to sell food at a particular location. They do not have to rent a store, pay waiters and waitresses, or supply tablecloths and dishes therefore they can charge much less then a restaurant. Street-food customers do not have to make the commitment of time and money required at a sit-down restaurant. They do not have to tip the server. Customers cannot sit at tables, however. There are no tables. They have to eat while standing or walking. Customers often do not have much time. This situation suits them. Students need fast and cheap food, especially on college campuses. Food trucks make them happy as a clam.

Street food is often regional or ethnic. Vendors sell cheese steaks and soft pretzels in Philadelphia. They sell reindeer sausages in Alaska. They sell tacos and tamales in Mexican neighborhoods. In Chicago, customers can buy kielbasa sandwiches and pierogies. Often, food carts and trucks offer ethnic foods to customers who are tasting them for the first time. A person can see if he likes Indian curry, Israeli falafel, Italian panini, or a gyro from Greece. Because of the success of street vendors, many ethnic foods have gone mainstream and are now widely offered in sit-down restaurants.

There is some concern about the safety of street food. Refrigeration may be limited or nonexistent. Cleanliness can sometimes be a problem. Food from a street-corner cart or truck may be safer than food cooked in a restaurant kitchen. In the restaurant, it may sit for a long time. Also, due to the fact that food carts and trucks may lack refrigeration, very fresh ingredients are often used. Still, customers should follow some tips for buying street food. The food should be kept covered until it is cooked. The money and food should not be touched by the same individual. Local customers are a good guide to the best street food. They know where the food is freshest. A long line usually indicates a good and safe source of street food.

In the United States, street food is especially varied. In the United States, there are many immigrants. Food is an important part of culture. The popularity of a particular kind of ethnic street food can be a sign that the immigrants' culture has been accepted.

23 Run-Ons

AP Photo/Chris Pietsch

write first

This picture shows children in a physical education class. Such classes are becoming rarer in American schools, and this could be one reason why many American children are physically out of shape. What other factors do you think could be to blame? What do you think can be done about this problem? Write a paragraph that answers these questions.

In this chapter, you will learn to

- recognize run-ons (23a)
- correct run-ons in five different ways (23b)

e macmillanhighered.com
/writingfirst
LearningCurve > Run-Ons;
Additional Grammar Exercises >
Recognizing Run-Ons

WORD POWER

fused joined together

splice (verb) to join together at the ends

23a Recognizing Run-Ons

A **sentence** consists of at least one independent clause—one subject and one verb.

College costs are rising.

A **run-on** is an error that occurs when two sentences are joined incorrectly. There are two kinds of run-ons: *fused sentences* and *comma splices*.

- A **fused sentence** occurs when two sentences are joined without any punctuation.

    FUSED SENTENCE   [College costs are rising] [many students are worried.]

- A **comma splice** occurs when two sentences are joined with just a comma.

    COMMA SPLICE   [College costs are rising], [many students are worried.]

PRACTICE
23-1

Some of the sentences in the following paragraph are correct, but others are run-ons. In the answer space after each sentence, write *C* if the sentence is correct, *FS* if it is a fused sentence, and *CS* if it is a comma splice.

Example: Using a screen reader is one way for blind people to access the web, two popular programs are JAWS for Windows and Window-Eyes. ____*CS*____

(1) The Internet should be accessible to everyone, this is not always the case. _____ (2) Many blind computer users have trouble finding information on the web. _____ (3) Often, this is the result of poor web design it is the designer's job to make the site accessible. _____ (4) Most blind people use special software called screen readers, this technology translates text into speech or Braille. _____ (5) However, screen readers do not always work well the information is sometimes hard to access. _____ (6) Websites need to be understandable to all Internet users. _____ (7) The rights of blind Internet users may be protected by the Americans with Disabilities Act (ADA). _____ (8) We will have to wait for more cases

to come to trial then we will know more. _____ (9) Meanwhile, we have to rely on software companies to make the necessary changes, this will take some time. _____ (10) However, there are incentives for these companies, the 1.5 million blind computer users are all potential customers. _____

23b   Correcting Run-Ons

macmillanhighered.com /writingfirst
Additional Grammar Exercises > Correcting Run-Ons

FYI

Correcting Run-Ons

You can correct run-ons in the following five ways.

1. *Use a period to create two separate sentences.*

   College costs are rising. Many students are worried.

2. *Use a coordinating conjunction (and, but, for, nor, or, so, or yet) to connect ideas.*

   College costs are rising, and many students are worried.

3. *Use a semicolon to connect ideas.*

   College costs are rising; many students are worried.

4. *Use a semicolon followed by a transitional word or phrase to connect ideas.*

   College costs are rising; as a result, many students are worried.

5. *Use a dependent word (although, because, when, and so on) to connect ideas.*

   Because college costs are rising, many students are worried.

The pages that follow explain and illustrate the five different ways to correct run-ons.

1. *Use a period to create two separate sentences.* Be sure each sentence begins with a capital letter and ends with a period.

   INCORRECT (FUSED SENTENCE) Gas prices are very high some people are buying hybrid cars.

   INCORRECT (COMMA SPLICE) Gas prices are very high, some people are buying hybrid cars.

   CORRECT Gas prices are very high. Some people are buying hybrid cars. (two separate sentences)

PRACTICE

23-2 Correct each of the following run-ons by using a period to create two separate sentences. Be sure both of your new sentences begin with a capital letter and end with a period.

> **Example:** Stephen Colbert used to appear on Comedy Central's *The Daily Show with Jon Stewart* and *The Colbert Report,* ~~in~~ . In 2014, he replaced David Letterman as host of CBS's *The Late Show*.

1. In 2010, David Cameron became prime minister of the United Kingdom, he replaced Gordon Brown.

2. New York–style pizza usually has a thin crust Chicago-style "deep-dish pizza" has a thick crust.

3. Last week, Soraya won a text-messaging contest the prize for texting the fastest was five hundred dollars.

4. In some parts of Canada's Northwest Territory, the only way to transport supplies is over frozen lakes, being an ice road trucker is one of the most dangerous jobs in the world.

5. In 1961, the first Six Flags opened in Arlington, Texas, the six flags represent the six governments that have ruled the area that is now Texas.

2. **Use a coordinating conjunction to connect ideas.** If you want to indicate a particular relationship between ideas—for example, cause and effect or contrast—you can connect two independent clauses with a coordinating conjunction that makes this relationship clear. Always place a comma before the coordinating conjunction.

Coordinating Conjunctions			
and	for	or	yet
but	nor	so	

INCORRECT (FUSED SENTENCE)	Some schools require students to wear uniforms other schools do not.
INCORRECT (COMMA SPLICE)	Some schools require students to wear uniforms forms, other schools do not.
CORRECT	Some schools require students to wear uniforms, but other schools do not. (clauses connected with the coordinating conjunction *but*, preceded by a comma)

PRACTICE

23-3 Correct each of the following run-ons by using a coordinating conjunction (*and, but, for, nor, or, so,* or *yet*) to connect ideas. Be sure to put a comma before each coordinating conjunction.

Example: Many college students use Facebook to keep up with old
, and
friends they also use the site to find new friends.
  ^

1. A car with soft tires gets poor gas mileage, keeping tires inflated is a good way to save money on gas.

2. It used to be difficult for football fans to see the first-down line on television, the computer-generated yellow line makes it much easier.

3. Indonesia has more volcanoes than any other country in the world the United States has the biggest volcano in the world, Hawaii's Mauna Loa.

4. Chefs can become famous by cooking at popular restaurants they can gain fame by hosting television shows.

5. Overcrowded schools often have to purchase portable classrooms or trailers this is only a temporary solution.

3. *Use a semicolon to connect ideas.* If you want to indicate a particularly close connection—or a strong contrast—between two ideas, use a semicolon.

> INCORRECT
> (FUSED SENTENCE) Most professional basketball players go to college most professional baseball players do not.

> INCORRECT
> (COMMA SPLICE) Most professional basketball players go to college, most professional baseball players do not.

> CORRECT Most professional basketball players go to college; most professional baseball players do not. (clauses connected with a semicolon)

PRACTICE

23-4 Correct each of the following run-ons by using a semicolon to connect ideas. Do not use a capital letter after the semicolon unless the word that follows it is a proper noun.

Example: From 1930 until 2006, Pluto was known as a planet it is
                                                              ;
                                                              ^
now known as a "dwarf planet."

1. Of all the states, Alaska has the highest percentage of Native American residents 16 percent of Alaskans are of Native American descent.

2. Satellites and global positioning systems (GPS) can help farmers to better understand the needs of their crops, these new tools are part of a trend called "precision agriculture."

3. Enforcing traffic laws can be difficult some cities use cameras to photograph cars that run red lights.

4. Old landfills can sometimes be made into parks, César Chávez Park in Berkeley, California, is one example.

5. Freestyle motocross riders compete by doing jumps and stunts some famous FMX riders are Carey Hart, Nate Adams, and Travis Pastrana.

4. *Use a semicolon followed by a transitional word or phrase to connect ideas.* To show how two closely linked ideas are related, add a transitional word or phrase after the semicolon. The transition will indicate the specific relationship between the two clauses.

INCORRECT (FUSED SENTENCE)	Finding a part-time job can be challenging sometimes it is even hard to find an unpaid internship.
INCORRECT (COMMA SPLICE)	Finding a part-time job can be challenging, sometimes it is even hard to find an unpaid internship.
CORRECT	Finding a part-time job can be challenging; in fact, sometimes it is even hard to find an unpaid internship. (clauses connected with a semicolon followed by the transitional phrase *in fact*)

Some Frequently Used Transitional Words and Phrases

after all	for this reason	now
also	however	still
as a result	in addition	then
eventually	in fact	therefore
finally	instead	thus
for example	moreover	unfortunately
for instance	nevertheless	

For more complete lists of transitional words and phrases, see 18c.

PRACTICE
23-5   Correct each of the following run-ons by using a semicolon followed by the transitional word or phrase in parentheses to connect ideas. Be sure to put a comma after the transitional word or phrase.

Example: When babies are first born, they can only see black and white most baby clothes and blankets are made in pastel colors. (still)

; still,

1. Restaurant goers can expect to see different condiments in different regions of the country, few tables in the Southwest are without a bottle of hot sauce. (for example)

2. Every April, millions of people participate in TV-Turnoff Week by not watching television they read, spend time with family and friends, and generally enjoy their free time. (instead)

3. Today, few people can count on company pension plans, thirty years ago, most people could. (however)

4. Many people see bottled water as a waste of money tap water is free. (after all)

5. Dog breeders who run "puppy mills" are only concerned with making money they are not particularly concerned with their dogs' well-being. (unfortunately)

FYI

Connecting Ideas with Semicolons

Run-ons often occur when you use a transitional word or phrase to join two independent clauses *without also using a semicolon.*

INCORRECT (FUSED SENTENCE)	It is easy to download information from the Internet however it is not always easy to evaluate the information.
INCORRECT (COMMA SPLICE)	It is easy to download information from the Internet, however it is not always easy to evaluate the information.

To avoid this kind of run-on, always put a semicolon before the transitional word or phrase and a comma after it.

CORRECT	It is easy to download information from the Internet; however, it is not always easy to evaluate the information.

5. ***Use a dependent word to connect ideas.*** When one idea is dependent on another, you can connect the two ideas by adding a dependent word, such as *when, who, although,* or *because.*

INCORRECT (FUSED SENTENCE)	American union membership was high in the mid-twentieth century it has declined in recent years.
INCORRECT (COMMA SPLICE)	American union membership was high in the mid-twentieth century, it has declined in recent years.
CORRECT	Although American union membership was high in the mid-twentieth century, it has declined in recent years. (clauses connected with the dependent word *although*)

CORRECT   American union membership, which was high in the mid-twentieth century, has declined in recent years. (clauses connected with the dependent word *which*)

Some Frequently Used Dependent Words

after	even though	until
although	if	when
as	since	which
because	that	who
before	unless	

For more complete lists of dependent words, including subordinating conjunctions and relative pronouns, see 19b and 19c.

PRACTICE
23-6   Correct each run-on in the following paragraph by adding a dependent word. Consult the list above to help you choose a logical dependent word. Be sure to add correct punctuation where necessary.

Example: Harlem was a rural area ˄*until* improved transportation linked it to lower Manhattan.

(1) Contemporary historians have written about the Harlem Renaissance, its influence is still not widely known. (2) Harlem was populated mostly by European immigrants at the turn of the last century, it saw an influx of African Americans beginning in 1910. (3) This migration from the South continued Harlem became one of the largest African-American communities in the United States. (4) Many black artists and writers settled in Harlem during the 1920s. African-American art flourished. (5) This "Harlem Renaissance" was an important era in American literary history it is not even mentioned in some textbooks. (6) Scholars recognize the great works of the Harlem Renaissance, they point to the writers Langston Hughes and Countee Cullen and the artists Henry Tanner and Sargent Johnson. (7) Zora Neale Hurston moved to Harlem from her native Florida in 1925, she began a book of African-American folklore. (8) Harlem was an exciting place in the 1920s people from all over the city went there to listen to jazz and to dance. (9) The white playwright Eugene O'Neill went

to Harlem to audition actors for his play *The Emperor Jones*, he made an international star of the great Paul Robeson. (10) The Great Depression occurred in the 1930s it led to the end of the Harlem Renaissance.

PRACTICE

23-7 Correct each of the following run-ons in one of these four ways: by creating two separate sentences, by using a coordinating conjunction, by using a semicolon, or by using a semicolon followed by a transitional word or phrase. Remember to put a semicolon before, and a comma after, each transitional word or phrase.

> **Example:** Some fish-and-chip shops in Scotland sell deep-fried
> . Children
> Mars bars ~~children~~ are the biggest consumers of these calorie-rich
> bars.

1. Twenty-five percent of Americans under the age of fifty have one or more tattoos 50 percent of Americans under the age of twenty-five have one or more tattoos.

2. The ancient Greeks built their homes facing south this practice took advantage of light and heat from the winter sun.

3. In 1985, a team of musical artists recorded "We Are the World" in support of African famine relief in 2010, artists recorded the same song in support of Haitian earthquake relief.

4. Flamenco—a Spanish style of dancing, singing, and clapping—was traditionally informal and unplanned it has been compared to improvisational American jazz.

5. In Acadia National Park in Maine, large stones line the edges of steep trails the stones are called "Rockefeller's teeth" in honor of the trails' patron.

PRACTICE

23-8 Correct each run-on in the following paragraph in the way that best indicates the relationship between ideas. Be sure to use appropriate punctuation.

> **Example:** E. L. Doctorow's *Homer and Langley* tells the story of two ec-
> , and
> centric brothers it shows that truth can be stranger than fiction.

(1) The Collyer brothers were wealthy and educated they lived and died alone in a filthy apartment. (2) Langley and Homer Collyer were the

sons of a doctor and an opera singer the brothers seemed to be as talented and motivated as their parents. (3) Langley played piano and studied engineering Homer had a law degree. (4) However, in their twenties and thirties, the brothers did not have jobs they lived with their parents in a Manhattan apartment. (5) Their parents died Langley and Homer inherited the apartment. (6) Gradually, they became frightened of outsiders they boarded up the windows and set traps for burglars. (7) They stopped paying their bills their heat, water, and electricity were shut off. (8) They also became compulsive hoarders, they could not throw anything away. (9) They accumulated thousands and thousands of books, numerous bundles of old newspapers, and fourteen pianos, they saved tons of garbage. (10) They got their water from a public park they collected discarded food from grocery stores and butcher shops. (11) Eventually, Langley was caught in one of his own burglar traps, the trap sent three bundles of newspapers and a suitcase tumbling on top of him. (12) Langley died of his injuries Homer died by his side, surrounded by mountains of trash.

TEST · Revise · Edit · Proofread

Look back at your response to the Write First prompt on page 341. TEST and revise what you have written. Then, edit and proofread your work, making sure to identify and correct any run-ons.

EDITING PRACTICE: PARAGRAPH

Read the following student paragraph, and revise it to eliminate run-ons. Correct each run-on in the way that best indicates the relationship between ideas. Be sure to use appropriate punctuation. The first error has been corrected for you.

Cold Cases

Cold cases are criminal investigations that have not been solved, *so* they are not officially closed. New evidence is found, cold cases may be reexamined. DNA tests might provide new clues, a witness may come forward with new testimony. The new evidence might lead to new suspects it might change the nature of the crime. In some cases, an accident might be reclassified a homicide, in other cases a murder might be ruled a suicide. Sometimes a person who was convicted of a crime is found to be innocent. Cold cases usually involve violent crimes, rape and murder are two examples. Investigators sometimes reopen very old cold cases, they usually focus on more recent cases with living suspects. For serious crimes, there is no limit on how much time may pass before a suspect is brought to justice, a criminal may be convicted many years after the crime was committed. When cold cases are solved, the crime is not undone, nevertheless victims' families feel that justice has finally been served.

EDITING PRACTICE: ESSAY

Read the following student essay, and revise it to eliminate run-ons. Correct each run-on in the way that best indicates the relationship between ideas, and be sure to punctuate correctly. The first error has been corrected for you.

Comic-Book Heroes

Comic-book heroes have a long history. *They* ~~they~~ originated in comic strips and radio shows. In the "Golden Age" of comic books, individual superheroes were the most popular characters, then teams and groups of superheroes were introduced. Today, some of these superheroes can be found in movies and in longer works of graphic fiction. Over the years, superheroes have remained very popular.

One of the first comic-book heroes was Popeye. Popeye had no supernatural powers, he battled his enemy, Bluto, with strength supplied by spinach. Another early comic-book hero was the Shadow he fought crime while wearing a cape and mask. The Shadow first appeared in comic books in 1930 later the character had his own radio show.

The late 1930s and 1940s are considered the Golden Age of comic books, many famous comic-book heroes were introduced at that time. The first Superman comic appeared in 1939. Superman came out from behind his secret identity as Clark Kent, he could fly "faster than a speeding bullet." Superman was the first comic-book hero who clearly had a superhuman ability to fight evil. Batman was different from Superman he had no real superpowers. Wonder Woman appeared in 1941, she truly had superhuman qualities. For example, she could catch a bullet in one hand. She could also regrow a limb, she could tell when someone was not telling the truth.

Superheroes sometimes had help. Batman had Robin, Wonder Woman had her sister, Wonder Girl. Sometimes there were superhero teams, these were groups of superheroes who helped each other fight evil. The first team was the Justice League of America it included Superman, Batman, and Wonder Woman. Eventually, the Justice League fought against threats to the existence of the earth these threats even included alien invasions. Another superhero team was the X-Men they were mutants with supernatural abilities.

Now, comic books are not as popular as they used to be, however, superheroes can still be found in popular movies. Superman has been the main character in many movies there have also been several successful Batman, Spider-Man, Iron Man, and Fantastic Four movies. In longer works of graphic fiction, Superman, Batman, and the Fantastic Four are still heroes, some works of graphic fiction feature Captain America and the Runaways. Apparently, people still want to see superheroes fight evil and win.

COLLABORATIVE ACTIVITY

Find an interesting paragraph in a newspaper or magazine article or on the web. Working in a small group, copy the paragraph onto a separate sheet of paper, creating run-ons. Exchange paragraphs with another group. Then, working in your own group, correct each fused sentence and comma splice in the other group's paragraph. When you have finished, return the paragraph to the group that created it. Finally, continuing to work with members of your group, evaluate the other group's work on your paragraph, comparing it to the original newspaper, magazine, or online paragraph.

review checklist

Run-Ons

☐ A run-on is an error that occurs when two sentences are joined incorrectly. There are two kinds of run-ons: fused sentences and comma splices. (See 23a.)

☐ A fused sentence occurs when two sentences are incorrectly joined without any punctuation. (See 23a.)

☐ A comma splice occurs when two sentences are joined with just a comma. (See 23a.)

☐ Correct a run-on in one of the following ways. (See 23b.)

1. By creating two separate sentences

   _____. _____.

2. By using a coordinating conjunction

   _____, [coordinating conjunction] _____.

3. By using a semicolon

   _____; _____.

4. By using a semicolon followed by a transitional word or phrase

   _____; [transitional word or phrase], _____.

5. By using a dependent word

   [Dependent word] _____, _____.

   _____ [dependent word] _____.

macmillanhighered.com /writingfirst
LearningCurve > Run-Ons

24 Fragments

Erick W. Rasco/Getty Images

write first

Imagine you are writing a magazine ad for your favorite beverage, footwear, or health or beauty product. Write a paragraph that describes the product as persuasively as possible. Try to include a few memorable advertising slogans.

In this chapter, you will learn to
- recognize fragments (24a)
- correct missing-subject fragments (24b)
- correct phrase fragments (24c)
- correct *-ing* fragments (24d)
- correct dependent-clause fragments (24e)

24a Recognizing Fragments

A **fragment** is an incomplete sentence. Every sentence must include at least one subject and one verb, and every sentence must express a complete thought. If a group of words does not do *both* these things, it is a fragment and not a sentence—even if it begins with a capital letter and ends with a period.

The following is a complete sentence.

macmillanhighered.com /writingfirst
LearningCurve > Fragments; Additional Exercises > Recognizing Fragments

SENTENCE	The <u>actors</u> in the play <u>were</u> very talented. (The sentence includes both a subject and a verb and expresses a complete thought.)

Because a sentence must have both a subject and a verb and express a complete thought, the following groups of words are not complete sentences; they are fragments.

FRAGMENT (NO VERB)	The actors in the play. (What point is being made about the actors?)
FRAGMENT (NO SUBJECT)	Were very talented. (Who were very talented?)
FRAGMENT (NO SUBJECT OR VERB)	Very talented. (Who was very talented?)
FRAGMENT (DOES NOT EXPRESS COMPLETE THOUGHT)	Because the actors in the play were very talented. (What happened because they were very talented?)

FYI

Spotting Fragments

Fragments almost always appear next to complete sentences.

┌─── COMPLETE SENTENCE ───┐ ┌─────── FRAGMENT ───────┐
Celia took two electives. Physics 320 and Spanish 101.

The fragment above does not have a subject or a verb. The complete sentence that comes before it, however, has both a subject (*Celia*) and a verb (*took*).

Often, you can correct a fragment by attaching it to an adjacent sentence that supplies the missing words. (This sentence will usually appear right before the fragment.)

Celia took two electives, Physics 320 and Spanish 101.

WORD POWER

adjacent next to

355

PRACTICE

24-1 Some of the following items are fragments, and others are complete sentences. On the line following each item, write *F* if it is a fragment and *S* if it is a complete sentence.

    Example: Star formations in the night sky. _____*F*_____

1. To save as much as possible for college. _____

2. The judge gave her a two-year sentence. _____

3. A birthday on Christmas Day. _____

4. Because he lost ten pounds on his new diet. _____

5. Working in the garden and fixing the roof. _____

6. Sonya flew to Mexico. _____

7. Starts in August in many parts of the country. _____

8. And slept in his own bed last night. _____

9. Famous for her movie roles. _____

10. A phone that also plays music and takes photos. _____

PRACTICE

24-2 In the following paragraph, some of the numbered groups of words are missing a subject, a verb, or both. First, underline each fragment. Then, decide how each fragment could be attached to a nearby word group to create a complete new sentence. Finally, rewrite the entire paragraph, using complete sentences, on the lines provided.

    Example: Gatorade was invented at the University of Florida. <u>To help the Florida Gators fight dehydration.</u>

    Rewrite: *Gatorade was invented at the University of Florida to help the*
Florida Gators fight dehydration.

    (1) Doctors discovered that football players were losing electrolytes and carbohydrates. (2) Through their sweat. (3) They invented a drink. (4) That replaced these important elements. (5) Gatorade tasted terrible. (6) But did its job. (7) The Florida Gators survived a very hot season. (8) And won most of their games. (9) Now, Gatorade is used by many college and professional football teams. (10) As well as baseball, basketball, tennis, and soccer teams.

Rewrite:

_____

_____

_____

_____

_____

24b   Missing-Subject Fragments

Every sentence must include both a subject and a verb. If the subject is left out, the sentence is incomplete. In the following example, the first word group is a sentence. It includes both a subject (*He*) and a verb (*packed*). However, the second word group is a fragment. It includes a verb (*took*), but it does not include a subject.

|— SENTENCE —————————|— FRAGMENT —————|

He <u>packed</u> his books and papers. And also took an umbrella.

The best way to correct this kind of fragment is to attach it to the sentence that comes right before it. This sentence will usually contain the missing subject.

CORRECT   He packed his books and papers and also took an umbrella.

Another way to correct this kind of fragment is to add the missing subject.

CORRECT   He packed his books and papers. He also took an umbrella.

PRACTICE

24-3   Each of the following items includes a missing-subject fragment. Revise each item using one of the two methods for correcting fragments.

Example: Back-to-school sales are popular with students. And with their parents.

Back-to-school sales are popular with students and with their parents.   or

Back-to-school sales are popular with students. The sales are also popular

with their parents.

1. Some retailers give a lot of money to charity. And even donate part of their profits.

   _____

   _____

2. Geography bees resemble spelling bees. But instead test the contestants' knowledge of countries around the world.

   _____

   _____

3. School uniforms are often preferred by parents. And also favored by many school principals.

_____

_____

4. Pro-football linemen can weigh more than three hundred pounds. But are still able to run fast.

_____

_____

5. Using an electric toothbrush can be good for the teeth. And promotes healthy gums.

_____

_____

24c   Phrase Fragments

Every sentence must include a subject and a verb. A **phrase** is a group of words that is missing a subject or a verb or both. When you punctuate a phrase as if it were a sentence, you create a fragment.

If you spot a phrase fragment in your writing, you can often correct it by attaching it to the sentence that comes directly before it.

Appositive Fragments

An **appositive** identifies, renames, or describes an adjacent noun or pronoun. An appositive cannot stand alone as a sentence.

To correct an appositive fragment, attach it to the sentence that comes right before it. (This sentence will contain the noun or pronoun that the appositive describes.)

┌─ FRAGMENT ─┐

INCORRECT   He decorated the room in his favorite colors. Brown and black.

CORRECT   He decorated the room in his favorite colors, brown and black.

Sometimes a word or an expression—like *especially, except, including, such as, for example,* or *for instance*—introduces an appositive. Even if an appositive is introduced by one of these words or expressions, it is still a fragment.

┌─FRAGMENT─┐

INCORRECT   A balanced diet should include high-fiber foods. Such as leafy vegetables, fruits, beans, and whole-grain bread.

CORRECT   A balanced diet should include high-fiber foods, such as leafy vegetables, fruits, beans, and whole-grain bread.

Prepositional Phrase Fragments

A **prepositional phrase** consists of a preposition and its object. A prepositional phrase cannot stand alone as a sentence. To correct a prepositional phrase fragment, attach it to the sentence that comes immediately before it.

┌──────── FRAGMENT ────────┐

INCORRECT   She promised to stand by him. In sickness and in health.

CORRECT   She promised to stand by him in sickness and in health.

Infinitive Fragments

An **infinitive** consists of *to* plus the base form of the verb (*to be, to go, to write*). An infinitive phrase (*to be free, to go home, to write a novel*) cannot stand alone as a sentence. You can usually correct an infinitive fragment by attaching it to the sentence that comes directly before it.

┌──── FRAGMENT ────┐

INCORRECT   Eric considered dropping out of school. To start his own

business.

CORRECT   Eric considered dropping out of school to start his own

business.

You can also add the words needed to complete the sentence.

CORRECT   Eric considered dropping out of school. He wanted to

start his own business.

PRACTICE

24-4   In the following paragraph, some of the numbered groups of words are phrase fragments. First, underline each fragment. Then, decide how each fragment could be attached to an adjacent sentence to create a complete new sentence. Finally, rewrite the entire paragraph, using complete sentences, on the lines provided.

Example: Florence Nightingale worked as a nurse. During the

Crimean War.

Rewrite: *Florence Nightingale worked as a nurse during the Crimean War.*

(1) Nurses' uniforms have changed a lot. (2) Over the years. (3) Originally, nurses' uniforms looked like nuns' habits because nuns used to provide care. (4) To sick people. (5) In the late 1800s, a student of Florence Nightingale created a brown uniform. (6) With a white apron and cap. (7) This uniform was worn by student nurses at her school. (8) The Florence Nightingale School of Nursing and Midwifery. (9) Eventually, nurses began to wear white uniforms, white stockings, white shoes, and starched white caps. (10) To

stress the importance of cleanliness. (11) Many older people remember these uniforms. (12) With affection. (13) Today, most nurses wear bright, comfortable scrubs. (14) To help patients (especially children) feel more at ease.

Rewrite:

_____

_____

_____

_____

_____

_____

_____

_____

_____

**PRACTICE
24-5** Each of the following items is a phrase fragment, not a sentence. Correct each fragment by adding any words needed to turn the fragment into a complete sentence. (You may add words before or after the fragment.)

Example: During World War I. _A flu epidemic killed millions of people during_
World War I.   or   _During World War I, a flu epidemic killed millions of people._

1. To be the best player on the team. _____

_____

2. From a developing nation in Africa. _____

_____

3. Such as tulips or roses. _____

_____

4. Behind door number 3. _____

_____

5. Including my parents and grandparents. _____

_____

6. With a new car in the driveway. _____

_____

7. To make a difficult career decision. _____

_____

8. For a long time. _____

_____

9. Turkey, stuffing, mashed potatoes, and cranberry sauce. _____

_____

10. In less than a year. _____

_____

24d   *-ing* Fragments

Every sentence must include a subject and a verb. If the verb is incomplete, a word group is a fragment, not a sentence.

An *-ing* verb cannot be a complete verb; it needs a **helping verb** to complete it. An *-ing* verb, such as **looking**, cannot stand alone in a sentence without a helping verb (*is looking, was looking, were looking,* and so on). When you use an *-ing* verb without a helping verb, you create a fragment.

┌─────────────── FRAGMENT ───────────────┐

INCORRECT   The twins are full of mischief. Always looking for trouble.

The best way to correct an *-ing* fragment is to attach it to the sentence that comes right before it.

CORRECT   The twins are full of mischief, always looking for trouble.

Another way to correct an *-ing* fragment is to add a subject and a helping verb.

CORRECT   The twins are full of mischief. They are always looking for trouble.

FYI

Being

As you write, be careful not to use the *-ing* verb *being* as if it were a complete verb.

INCORRECT   I decided to take a nap. The outcome being that I slept through calculus class.

To correct this kind of fragment, substitute a form of the verb *be* that can serve as the main verb in a sentence—for example, *is, was, are,* or *were*.

CORRECT   I decided to take a nap. The outcome was that I slept through calculus class.

PRACTICE

24-6 Each of the following items includes an *-ing* fragment. In each case, correct the fragment by attaching it to the sentence before it.

Example: Certain tips can help grocery shoppers. Saving them a lot of money.

Certain tips can help grocery shoppers, saving them a lot of money.

1. Always try to purchase a store brand. Costing less than the well-known and widely advertised brands.

   _____

   _____

2. Look for a product's cost per pound. Comparing it to the cost per pound of similar products.

   _____

   _____

3. Examine sale-priced fruits and vegetables. Checking carefully for damage or spoilage.

   _____

   _____

4. Buy different brands of the same product. Trying each one to see which brand you like best.

   _____

   _____

5. Use coupons whenever possible. Keeping them handy for future shopping trips.

   _____

   _____

PRACTICE

24-7 Each of the following items is an *-ing* fragment. Turn each fragment into a complete sentence by adding a subject and a helping verb. Write your revised sentence on the line below each fragment.

Example: Running up and down the stairs.

Revised: *Jane and her dog are always running up and down the stairs.*

1. Trying to decide where to live.

   Revised: _____

   _____

2. Really feeling optimistic about the future.

   Revised: _____

   _____

3. Always complaining about the lab manual.

   Revised: _____

   _____

4. Deciding whether or not to get a new cell phone.

   Revised: _____

   _____

5. Minding their own business.

   Revised: _____

   _____

24e Dependent-Clause Fragments

Every sentence must include a subject and a verb. Every sentence must also express a complete thought.

A **dependent clause** is a group of words that is introduced by a dependent word, such as *although*, *because*, *that*, or *after*. A dependent clause includes a subject and a verb, but it does not express a complete thought. Therefore, it cannot stand alone as a sentence. To correct a dependent-clause fragment, you must complete the thought.

The following dependent clause is incorrectly punctuated as if it were a sentence.

   FRAGMENT   After Simon won the lottery.

This fragment includes both a subject (*Simon*) and a complete verb (*won*), but it does not express a complete thought. What happened after Simon won the lottery? To turn this fragment into a sentence, you need to complete the thought.

   SENTENCE   After Simon won the lottery, <u>he quit his night job.</u>

Some dependent clauses are introduced by dependent words called **subordinating conjunctions**.

   FRAGMENT   Although Marisol had always dreamed of visiting America.

This fragment includes a subject (*Marisol*) and a complete verb (*had dreamed*), but it is not a sentence; it is a dependent clause introduced by the subordinating conjunction *although*.

To correct this kind of fragment, attach it to an **independent clause** (a simple sentence) to complete the idea. (You can often find the independent clause you need right before or right after the fragment.)

SENTENCE   Although Marisol had always dreamed of visiting America, <u>she did not have enough money for the trip until 2005.</u>

Subordinating Conjunctions

after	even though	since	whenever
although	if	so that	where
as	if only	than	whereas
as if	in order that	that	wherever
as though	now that	though	whether
because	once	unless	while
before	provided that	until	
even if	rather than	when	

For information on how to use subordinating conjunctions, see 19b.

FYI

Correcting Dependent-Clause Fragments

The simplest way to correct a dependent-clause fragment is to cross out the dependent word that makes the idea incomplete.

~~Although~~ Marisol had always dreamed of visiting America.

However, when you delete the dependent word, readers may have trouble seeing the connection between the new sentence and the one before or after it. A better way to revise is to attach the dependent-clause fragment to an adjacent independent clause, as illustrated in the example at the top of this page.

Some dependent clauses are introduced by dependent words called **relative pronouns**.

FRAGMENT   Novelist Richard Wright, <u>who</u> came to Paris in 1947.

FRAGMENT   A quinceañera, <u>which</u> celebrates a Latina's fifteenth birthday.

FRAGMENT   A key World War II battle <u>that</u> was fought on the Pacific island of Guadalcanal.

Each of these sentence fragments includes a subject (*Richard Wright, quinceañera, battle*) and a complete verb (*came, celebrates, was fought*). However, they are not sentences because they do not express complete thoughts. In each case, a relative pronoun creates a dependent clause.

To correct each of these fragments, add the words needed to complete the thought.

SENTENCE   Novelist Richard Wright, who came to Paris in 1947, <u>spent the rest of his life there.</u>

SENTENCE   A quinceañera, which celebrates a Latina's fifteenth birthday, <u>signifies her entrance into womanhood.</u>

SENTENCE   A key World War II battle that was fought on the
Pacific island of Guadalcanal <u>took place in 1943.</u>

Relative Pronouns

that	who	whomever
what	whoever	whose
which	whom	

For information on how to use relative pronouns, see 19c.

PRACTICE

24-8   Correct each of the following dependent-clause fragments by attaching it to the sentence before or after it. If the dependent clause comes at the beginning of a sentence, place a comma after it.

Example: Before it became a state. West Virginia was part of Virginia.

Before it became a state, West Virginia was part of Virginia.

1. Because many homeless people are mentally ill. It is hard to find places

   for them to live. _____

   _____

2. Even though they can be found in many parts of the United States.

   People do not realize how dangerous raccoons can be. _____

   _____

   _____

3. I make plans to be a better student. Whenever a new semester begins.

   _____

4. Until something changes. We will just have to accept the situation.

   _____

5. Because it is a very controversial issue. My parents and I have agreed

   not to discuss it. _____

   _____

PRACTICE
24-9 Correct each of these dependent-clause fragments by adding the words needed to complete the idea.

Example: Many minor species of animals, which are rapidly disappearing.

Many minor species of animals, which are rapidly disappearing, need to be _____

protected. _____

1. The film that frightened me. _____

_____

2. People who drink and drive. _____

_____

3. Some parents who are very strict with their children. _____

_____

4. The Vietnam War, which many Americans did not support. _____

_____

5. Animals that are used in medical research. _____

_____

PRACTICE
24-10 Each of the following is a fragment. Turn each fragment into a complete sentence, writing the revised sentence on the line below the fragment. Whenever possible, try creating two different revisions.

Example: Waiting in the dugout.

Revised: *Waiting in the dugout, the players chewed tobacco.* _____

Revised: *The players were waiting in the dugout.* _____

1. Going around in circles.

Revised: _____

_____

Revised: _____

_____

2. To win the prize for the most unusual costume.

Revised: _____

_____

Revised: _____

_____

3. Students who thought they could afford to go to college.

Revised: _____

_____

Revised: _____

_____

4. Because many instructors see cheating as a serious problem.

Revised: _____

_____

Revised: _____

_____

5. The rule that I always felt was the most unfair.

Revised: _____

_____

Revised: _____

_____

6. And finished in record time.

Revised: _____

_____

Revised: _____

_____

TEST · Revise · Edit · Proofread

Look back at your response to the Write First prompt on page 354. Reread each word group you have punctuated as a sentence, starting with the last one and working your way back; make sure that each one contains a subject and a verb. Then, underline any words ending in *-ing*; any subordinating conjunctions; and the words *which*, *that*, and *who*, making sure that the word groups they appear in are complete sentences. When you have finished, TEST and revise your paragraph. Then, edit and proofread your work.

EDITING PRACTICE: PARAGRAPH

Read the following student paragraph, which includes incomplete sentences. Underline each fragment. Then, correct the fragment by attaching it to a nearby sentence that completes the thought. Be sure to punctuate correctly. The first fragment has been underlined and corrected for you.

Committed to Education

Teach for America is a nonprofit organization, *that* aims to improve education in poor communities. Teach for America hires recent college graduates and professionals. To teach in underserved schools. These teachers are not officially certified. But do receive intensive training. Working in these schools can be very challenging. It can also be very rewarding. For both the teachers and the students. Admission into the Teach for America program is very competitive. Even for graduates of Ivy League schools. Only 11 percent of applicants are accepted. These talented people become members of the teaching corps. Bringing with them a variety of experiences and backgrounds. Corps members commit to teach for two years. Although many choose to stay longer.

EDITING PRACTICE: ESSAY

Read the following student essay, which includes incomplete sentences. Underline each fragment. Then, correct the fragment by attaching it to an adjacent sentence that completes the idea. Be sure to punctuate correctly. The first fragment has been underlined and corrected for you.

Bad Behavior at the Movies

Some people have completely stopped, *going* ~~Going~~ to the movies. They have not stopped because they dislike the movies but because they dislike the rude moviegoers. Who ruin their experience. One big problem is irritating cell-phone use. There are also problems with noise. And with sharing the theater space with strangers. All these issues can make going to the movies seem like more trouble than it is worth.

Cell phones cause all sorts of problems. In movie theaters. People are told to turn off their phones. But do not always do so. Loud cell-phone conversations can be infuriating. To people who want to hear the movie. When a phone rings during an important scene in the movie. It is especially annoying. Some moviegoers even complain that bright text-message screens distract them. From the movie. Of course, theaters could use jammers. To block all cell-phone signals. Unfortunately, they would also block incoming emergency calls.

Noise in the movies also comes from other sources. Such as crying babies. People pay money to watch a movie. Not to listen to a baby screaming. Crinkling candy wrappers are also annoying. In addition, some moviegoers insist on talking to each other. During the movie. In fact, they may make watching a movie an interactive event. Talking to the actors and telling them what they should do next. If they have seen the movie before, they may recite lines of dialogue before the actors do. Spoiling the suspense for everyone else. In all these cases, the noise is a problem. For anyone who wants to watch the movie and hear the actors on the screen.

Finally, going to the movies requires sharing the theater with other people. Who are neither relatives nor friends. Unfortunately, many people behave in movie theaters the same way they behave at home. When they are watching television. They may put their feet up on the seats in front of them. Making it impossible for others to sit there. Moviegoers become very annoyed if someone sits right in front of them. And blocks their view of the screen. Of course, these issues do not come up at home. Where friends and relatives can easily work out any problems.

Irritating movie behavior has driven many people to stop going to movie theaters. To end this rude behavior, moviegoers need to become aware of the needs of others. And make a real effort to change their behavior. Selfishness is the problem; thinking about other people is the solution.

COLLABORATIVE ACTIVITY

Working in a group of three or four students, build as many sentences as you can from the following list of fragments. Use your imagination to come up with as many creative sentences as you can.

Example

FRAGMENT Knowing that he has an incredible memory

SENTENCES Zack, knowing that he has an incredible memory, wonders how he managed to forget everything he learned about chemistry.

Knowing that he has an incredible memory, Monty the Magnificent is confident that he can amaze his audience.

FRAGMENTS

1. Wandering in the desert
2. Never worrying about anything
3. Looking for his ideal mate
4. Always using as much ketchup as possible
5. Starting a new job

review checklist

Fragments

☐ A fragment is an incomplete sentence. Every sentence must include a subject and a verb and express a complete thought. (See 24a.)

☐ Every sentence must include a subject. (See 24b.)

☐ Phrases cannot stand alone as sentences. (See 24c.)

☐ Every sentence must include a complete verb. (See 24d.)

☐ Dependent clauses cannot stand alone as sentences. (See 24e.)

ᴇ **macmillanhighered.com /writingfirst**
LearningCurve > Fragments; Additional Grammar Exercises > Correcting Fragments

25 Subject-Verb Agreement

Estate of Ralph Fasanella/Andrew Edlin Gallery

write first

This painting by self-taught twentieth-century American artist Ralph Fasanella is called *Baseball Panorama*. In a paragraph, describe what is happening on the field and in the stands. (Use present tense verbs.)

In this chapter, you will learn to avoid agreement problems
- with compound subjects (25b)
- with *be*, *have*, and *do* (25c)
- when words come between the subject and the verb (25d)
- with collective noun subjects (25e)
- with indefinite pronoun subjects (25f)
- when verbs come before subjects (25g)

e macmillanhighered.com
/writingfirst
LearningCurve > Subject-Verb
Agreement

25a Understanding Subject-Verb Agreement

A sentence's subject (a noun or a pronoun) and its verb must **agree**: singular subjects take singular verbs, and plural subjects take plural verbs.

The <u>museum</u> <u>opens</u> at ten o'clock. (singular noun subject *museum* takes singular verb *opens*)

Both <u>museums</u> <u>open</u> at ten o'clock. (plural noun subject *museums* takes plural verb *open*)

<u>She</u> always <u>watches</u> the eleven o'clock news. (singular pronoun subject *she* takes singular verb *watches*)

<u>They</u> always <u>watch</u> the eleven o'clock news. (plural pronoun subject *they* takes plural verb *watch*)

Subject-Verb Agreement with Regular Verbs

	SINGULAR	PLURAL
First person	I play	Molly and I/we play
Second person	you play	you play
Third person	he/she/it plays	they play
	Molly plays	Molly and Sam play
	the man plays	the men play

WORD POWER

locavore a person who eats only locally produced foods

**PRACTICE
25-1** Underline the correct form of the verb in each of the following sentences. Make sure that the verb agrees with its subject.

Example: Sometimes local farmers (<u>grow</u>/grows) unusual vegetables.

(1) Locavores (choose/chooses) to eat locally grown food for a number of reasons. (2) Some locavores (eat/eats) local food simply because

they (like/likes) the taste. (3) When food (travel/travels) a long distance, it (lose/loses) some of its flavor and freshness. (4) By eating locally grown food, locavores also (hope/hopes) to decrease the use of fossil fuels. (5) After all, food transportation (require/requires) a lot of energy. (6) In addition, locavores (visit/visits) farmers' markets to support local producers. (7) Local farmers (need/needs) their community's support to survive. (8) In some cases, local food supporters (buy/buys) only food produced within 50 or 100 miles. (9) In colder or drier regions, however, the climate (make/makes) such a strict policy difficult. (10) More often, a locavore diet (contain/contains) a mix of food from local and faraway places.

25b Compound Subjects

The subject of a sentence is not always a single word. It can also be a **compound subject**, made up of two or more subjects joined by *and* or *or*. To avoid subject-verb agreement problems with compound subjects, follow these rules.

1. When the parts of a compound subject are connected by *and*, the compound subject takes a plural verb.

> John and Marsha share an office.

2. When the parts of a compound subject are connected by *or*, the verb agrees with the part of the subject that is closer to it.

> The mayor or the council members meet with community groups.

> The council members or the mayor meets with community groups.

PRACTICE

25-2 Underline the correct form of the verb in each of the following sentences. Make sure that the verb agrees with its compound subject.

Example: Every summer, wind and rain (pound/pounds) the small shack on the beach.

1. Trophies and medals (fill/fills) my sister's bedroom.

2. Mashed potatoes and gravy (come/comes) with all our chicken dinners.

3. The instructor or his graduate students (grade/grades) the final exams.

4. A voice coach and a piano instructor (teach/teaches) each of the gifted students.

5. Pollen or cat hair (trigger/triggers) allergies in many people.

25c Be, Have, and Do

The irregular verbs *be, have,* and *do* can present problems with subject-verb agreement. Memorizing their forms is the only sure way to avoid such problems.

Subject-Verb Agreement with Be

	SINGULAR	PLURAL
First person	I am	we are
Second person	you are	you are
Third person	he/she/it is	they are
	Tran is	Tran and Ryan are
	the boy is	the boys are

Subject-Verb Agreement with Have

	SINGULAR	PLURAL
First person	I have	we have
Second person	you have	you have
Third person	he/she/it has	they have
	Shana has	Shana and Robert have
	the student has	the students have

Subject-Verb Agreement with Do

	SINGULAR	PLURAL
First person	I do	we do
Second person	you do	you do
Third person	he/she/it does	they do
	Ken does	Ken and Mia do
	the book does	the books do

PRACTICE

25-3   Fill in the blank with the correct present tense form of the verb *be*, *have*, or *do*.

Example: Sometimes people _____*do*_____ damage without really meaning to. (do)

(1) Biologists _____ serious worries about the damage that invading species of animals can cause. (have) (2) The English sparrow _____ one example. (be) (3) It _____ a role in the decline in the number of bluebirds. (have) (4) On the Galapagos Islands, cats _____ another example. (be) (5) Introduced by early explorers, they currently _____ much damage to the eggs of the giant tortoises that live on the islands. (do) (6) Scientists today _____ worried now about a new problem. (be) (7) This _____ a situation caused by wildlife agencies that put exotic fish into lakes and streams. (be) (8) They _____ this to please those who enjoy fishing. (do) (9) Although popular with people who fish, this policy _____ major drawbacks. (have) (10) It _____ one drawback in particular: many native species of fish have been pushed close to extinction. (have)

25d   Words between Subject and Verb

Keep in mind that a verb must always agree with its subject. Don't be confused when a group of words (for example, a prepositional phrase) comes between the subject and the verb. These words do not affect subject-verb agreement.

     CORRECT   High <u>levels</u> of mercury <u>occur</u> in some fish.
     CORRECT   <u>Water</u> in the fuel lines <u>causes</u> an engine to stall.
     CORRECT   <u>Food</u> between the teeth <u>leads</u> to decay.

An easy way to identify the subject of the sentence is to cross out the words that come between the subject and the verb.

High levels ~~of mercury~~ occur in some fish.

Water ~~in the fuel lines~~ causes an engine to stall.

Food ~~between the teeth~~ leads to decay.

FYI

Words between Subject and Verb

Look out for words such as *in addition to, along with, together with, as well as, except,* and *including.* Phrases introduced by these words do not affect subject-verb agreement.

> ...St. Thomas, ~~along with St. Croix and St. John,~~ is part of the
>
> United States Virgin Islands.

PRACTICE

25-4   In each of the following sentences, cross out the words that separate the subject and the verb. Then, underline the subject of the sentence once and the verb that agrees with the subject twice.

Example: The messages ~~on the phone~~ (say/says) that Carol is out of town.

1. Each summer, fires from lightning (cause/causes) great damage.

2. Books downloaded onto an eReader usually (cost/costs) less than print books.

3. One out of ten men (gets/get) prostate cancer.

4. The woodstove in the living room (heat/heats) the entire house.

5. Trans fat in a variety of foods (lead/leads) to increased rates of heart disease.

25e   Collective Noun Subjects

Collective nouns are words (such as *family* and *audience*) that name a group of people or things but are singular. Because they are singular, they always take singular verbs.

> The team practices five days a week in the gym.

Frequently Used Collective Nouns

army	club	family	jury
association	committee	gang	mob
band	company	government	team
class	corporation	group	union

PRACTICE
25-5 Fill in the blank with the correct present tense form of the verb.

Example: Our government ___*is*___ democratically elected by the people. (be)

1. The Caribbean Culture Club _____ on the first Thursday of every month. (meet)

2. The company no longer _____ health insurance for part-time employees. (provide)

3. The basketball team _____ competing in the division finals next week. (be)

4. After two days, the jury _____ been unable to reach a verdict. (have)

5. The union _____ guaranteed raises for its members. (want)

25f Indefinite Pronoun Subjects

Indefinite pronouns—*anybody, everyone,* and so on—do not refer to a particular person, place, or idea.

Most indefinite pronouns are singular and take singular verbs.

No one likes getting up early.

Everyone likes to sleep late.

Somebody likes beets.

macmillanhighered.com
/writingfirst
Additional Grammar
Exercises > Indefinite
Pronoun Subjects

Singular Indefinite Pronouns

another	either	neither	somebody
anybody	everybody	nobody	someone
anyone	everyone	no one	something
anything	everything	nothing	
each	much	one	

A few indefinite pronouns (*both, many, several, few, others*) are plural and take plural verbs.

Many were left homeless by the flood.

FYI

Indefinite Pronouns as Subjects

If a prepositional phrase comes between the indefinite pronoun and the verb, cross out the prepositional phrase to help you identify the sentence's subject.

Each of the boys has a bike.

Many of the boys have bikes.

PRACTICE
25-6 Underline the correct verb in each sentence.

Example: As my friends and I know, anything (helps/help) when it comes to paying for college.

1. One of my friends (has/have) an academic scholarship.

2. Another (relies/rely) entirely on loans.

3. Everybody (says/say) that work-study jobs are best.

4. Many of the most interesting work-study jobs (is/are) located on campus.

5. Some of the work-study jobs (tends/tend) to be better than a regular job.

e macmillanhighered.com
/writingfirst
Additional Grammar
Exercises > Verbs
before Subjects

25g Verbs before Subjects

A verb always agrees with its subject—even if the verb comes *before* the subject. In questions, for example, word order is reversed, with the verb coming before the subject or with the subject coming between two parts of the verb.

Where is the bank?
Are you going to the party?

If you have trouble identifying the subject of a question, answer the question with a statement. (In the statement, the subject will come before the verb.)

Where is the bank? The bank is on Walnut Street.

FYI

There Is and *There Are*

When a sentence begins with *there is* or *there are*, the word *there* is not the subject of the sentence. The subject comes after the form of the verb *be*.

> There <u>is</u> one <u>chief justice</u> on the Supreme Court.

> There <u>are</u> nine <u>justices</u> on the Supreme Court.

PRACTICE

25-7 Underline the subject of each sentence, and circle the correct form of the verb.

Example: Who (is/are) the baseball <u>player</u> who broke Hank Aaron's home-run record?

1. How (has/have) the citrus crop been affected by the freezing temperatures?

2. Why (do/does) people who cannot afford them buy lottery tickets?

3. (Is/Are) there any states that do not follow daylight saving time?

4. How (do/does) an immigrant become a citizen?

5. There (is/are) three branches of government in the United States.

TEST · Revise · Edit · Proofread

Look back at your response to the Write First prompt on page 371. TEST and revise what you have written. Then, edit and proofread your work, making sure that all your verbs agree with their subjects. Pay particular attention to agreement problems described in this chapter.

EDITING PRACTICE: PARAGRAPH

Read the following student paragraph, which includes errors in subject-verb agreement. Decide whether each of the underlined verbs agrees with its subject. If it does not, cross out the verb, and write in the correct form. If it does, write *C* above the verb. The first sentence has been done for you.

Conflict Diamonds

Today, many people *C* know about conflict diamonds, and most *want* wants this violent trade to end. These illegal diamonds comes from countries where there are civil war. Most often, the origin of these stones is an unstable central or west African nation. Rebel groups in these countries mines the diamonds and sells them to raise money for weapons. In the process, local people, who does not benefit from the sale of the diamonds, often gets hurt or killed. How does a person who wants to buy a diamond avoid buying a conflict diamond? Once a diamond reach a store, neither a customer nor a gem expert have the ability to determine its history just by looking at it. However, a consumer can ask for proof that the diamond is "conflict-free." Each of the diamonds in a store are supposed to have an official certificate to prove that it is legal.

EDITING PRACTICE: ESSAY

Read the following student essay, which includes errors in subject-verb agreement. Decide whether each of the underlined verbs agrees with its subject. If it does not, cross out the verb, and write in the correct form. If it does, write *C* above the verb. The first sentence has been done for you.

Party in the Parking Lot

Fun at football games *is* are not limited to cheering for the home team. Many people arrives four or five hours early, sets up grills in the parking lot, and start cooking. Typically, fans drives to the stadium in a pickup truck, a station wagon, or an SUV. They open up the tailgate, puts out the food, and enjoys the fun with their friends. In fact, tailgating is so popular that for some fans, it is more important than the game itself.

What <u>do</u> it take to tailgate? First, most tailgaters <u>plan</u> their menus in advance. To avoid forgetting anything, they <u>makes</u> lists of what to bring. Paper plates, along with a set of plastic cups, <u>make</u> it unnecessary to bring home dirty dishes. Jugs of water <u>is</u> essential, and damp towels <u>helps</u> clean up hands and faces. Also, light-weight chairs or another type of seating <u>is</u> important.

At the game, parking near a grassy area or at the end of a parking row <u>are</u> best. This location <u>give</u> tailgaters more space to cook and eat. If the food <u>are</u> ready two hours before the game <u>start</u>, there <u>is</u> plenty of time to eat and clean up.

Some tailgaters <u>buys</u> expensive equipment. The simple charcoal grill <u>have</u> turned into a combination grill, cooler, and foldout table with a portable awning. There <u>is</u> grills with their own storage space. Other grills <u>swings</u> out from the tailgate to provide easy access to the vehicle's storage area. Some deluxe grills even <u>has</u> their own beer taps, stereo systems, and sinks.

Whatever equipment tailgaters <u>brings</u> to the game, the most important factors <u>is</u> food and companionship. There <u>is</u> a tradition of sharing food and swapping recipes with other tailgaters. Most tailgaters <u>loves</u> to meet and to compare recipes. For many, the tailgating experience <u>is</u> more fun than the game itself.

COLLABORATIVE ACTIVITY

Working in a group of four students, list ten nouns (five singular and five plural)—people, places, or things—along the left-hand side of a sheet of paper. Beside each noun, write the present tense form of a verb that could logically be used with the noun. Then, expand each noun-and-verb combination you listed into a complete sentence. Next, write a sentence that could logically follow each of these sentences, using a pronoun as the subject of the new sentence. Make sure the pronoun you choose refers to the noun in the previous sentence, as in this example: *Alan watches three movies a week. <u>He</u> is addicted to films.* Check to be certain the subjects in your sentences agree with the verbs.

review checklist

Subject-Verb Agreement

- [ ] Singular subjects (nouns and pronouns) take singular verbs, and plural subjects take plural verbs. (See 25a.)

- [ ] Special rules govern subject-verb agreement with compound subjects. (See 25b.)

- [ ] The irregular verbs *be, have,* and *do* often present problems with subject-verb agreement. (See 25c.)

- [ ] Words that come between the subject and the verb do not affect subject-verb agreement. (See 25d.)

- [ ] Collective nouns are singular and take singular verbs. (See 25e.)

- [ ] Most indefinite pronouns, such as *no one* and *everyone,* are singular and take a singular verb when they serve as the subject of a sentence. A few are plural and take plural verbs. (See 25f.)

- [ ] A sentence's subject and verb must always agree, even if the verb comes before the subject. (See 25g.)

26 Illogical Shifts

write first

This picture shows elementary school students at the annual Washington State Elementary Chess Championship. Do you believe that after-school chess clubs and similar programs can help students succeed? Write a paragraph in which you express your ideas on this subject.

In this chapter, you will learn to avoid illogical shifts in

- tense (26a)
- person (26b)
- voice (26c)

A **shift** occurs whenever a writer changes **tense**, **person**, or **voice**. As you write and revise, be sure that any shifts you make are **logical**—that is, that they occur for a reason.

macmillanhighered.com
/writingfirst
Learning Curve > Verbs;
Additional Grammar
Exercises > Shifts in Tense

26a Shifts in Tense

Tense is the form a verb takes to show when an action takes place or when a situation occurs. Some shifts in tense are necessary—for example, to indicate a change from past time to present time.

LOGICAL SHIFT   When they first came out, cell phones were large and bulky, but now they are small and compact.

An **illogical shift in tense** occurs when a writer shifts from one tense to another for no apparent reason.

ILLOGICAL SHIFT IN TENSE   The dog walked to the fireplace. Then, he circles twice and lies down in front of the fire. (shift from past tense to present tense)

REVISED   The dog walked to the fireplace. Then, he circled twice and lay down in front of the fire. (consistent use of past tense)

REVISED   The dog walks to the fireplace. Then, he circles twice and lies down in front of the fire. (consistent use of present tense)

PRACTICE 26-1

Edit the sentences in the following paragraph to correct illogical shifts in tense. If a sentence is correct, write *C* in the blank.

Example: The 100th Battalion of the 442nd Infantry is the only remaining United States Army Reserve ground combat unit that fought in World War II. _____*C*_____

(1) During World War II, the 100th Battalion of the 442nd Combat Infantry Regiment was made up of young Japanese Americans who are eager to serve in the U.S. Army. _____ (2) At the start of World War II, 120,000 Japanese Americans were sent to relocation camps because

the government feared that they might be disloyal to the United States.

_____ (3) However, in 1943, the United States needed more soldiers, so it sends recruiters to the camps to ask for volunteers. _____ (4) The Japanese-American volunteers are organized into the 442nd Combat Infantry Regiment. _____ (5) The soldiers of the 442nd Infantry fought in some of the bloodiest battles of the war, including the invasion of Italy at Anzio and a battle in Bruyères, France, where they capture over two hundred enemy soldiers. _____ (6) When other U.S. troops are cut off by the enemy, the 442nd Infantry soldiers were sent to rescue them. _____ (7) The Japanese-American soldiers suffered the highest casualty rate of any U.S. unit and receive over eighteen thousand individual decorations.

26b Shifts in Person

macmillanhighered.com /writingfirst Learning Curve > Pronoun Agreement and Pronoun Reference

Person is the form a pronoun takes to show who is speaking, spoken about, or spoken to.

Person	SINGULAR	PLURAL
First person	I	we
Second person	you	you
Third person	he, she, it	they

An **illogical shift in person** occurs when a writer shifts from one person to another for no apparent reason.

ILLOGICAL SHIFT IN PERSON	The hikers were told that you had to stay on the trail. (shift from third person to second person)
REVISED	The hikers were told that they had to stay on the trail. (consistent use of third person)
ILLOGICAL SHIFT IN PERSON	Anyone can learn to cook if you practice. (shift from third person to second person)
REVISED	You can learn to cook if you practice. (consistent use of second person)
REVISED	Anyone can learn to cook if he or she practices. (consistent use of third person)

**PRACTICE
26-2**   The sentences in the following paragraph contain illogical shifts in person. Edit each sentence so that it uses pronouns consistently. Be sure to change any verbs that do not agree with the new subjects.

Example: Before a person finds a job in the fashion industry, ~~you have~~ *he or she has* to have some experience.

(1) Young people who want careers in the fashion industry do not always realize how hard you will have to work. (2) They think that working in the world of fashion will be glamorous and that you will make a lot of money. (3) In reality, no matter how talented you are, recent college graduates entering the industry are paid only about $22,000 a year. (4) The manufacturers who employ new graduates expect you to work at least three years at this salary before getting a raise. (5) A young designer may get a big raise if you are very talented, but this is unusual. (6) New employees have to pay their dues, and you soon realize that most of your duties are boring. (7) An employee may land a job as an assistant designer but then find that you have to color in designs that have already been drawn. (8) Other beginners discover that you spend most of your time typing up orders. (9) If a person is serious about working in the fashion industry, you have to be realistic. (10) For most newcomers to the industry, the ability to do what you are told to do is more important than your talent.

ⓔ macmillanhighered.com
/writingfirst
Additional Grammar
Exercises > Shifts in
Person and Voice

26c Shifts in Voice

Voice is the form a verb takes to indicate whether the subject is acting or is acted upon. When the subject is acting, the sentence is in the **active voice**. When the subject is acted upon, the sentence is in the **passive voice**.

ⓔ macmillanhighered.com
/writingfirst
Learning Curve > Active
and Passive Voice

ACTIVE VOICE	Nat Turner organized a slave rebellion in August 1831. (Subject *Nat Turner* is acting.)
PASSIVE VOICE	A slave rebellion was organized by Nat Turner in 1831. (Subject *rebellion* is acted upon.)

An **illogical shift in voice** occurs when a writer shifts from active to passive voice or from passive to active voice for no apparent reason.

ILLOGICAL SHIFT IN VOICE	J. D. Salinger wrote *The Catcher in the Rye*, and *Franny and Zooey* was also written by him. (shift from active to passive)
REVISED	J. D. Salinger wrote *The Catcher in the Rye*, and he also wrote *Franny and Zooey*. (consistent use of active voice)
ILLOGICAL SHIFT IN VOICE	Radium was discovered by Marie Curie in 1910, and she won a Nobel Prize in Chemistry in 1911. (shift from passive to active)
REVISED	Marie Curie discovered radium in 1910, and she won a Nobel Prize in Chemistry in 1911. (consistent use of active voice)

FYI

Correcting Illogical Shifts in Voice

You should usually use the active voice in your college writing because it is stronger and more direct than the passive voice.

To change a sentence from the passive to the active voice, determine who or what is acting, and make this noun the subject of a new active-voice sentence.

PASSIVE VOICE	The campus escort service is used by my friends.
ACTIVE VOICE	My friends use the campus escort service. (*My friends* are acting.)

PRACTICE

26-3 The following sentences contain illogical shifts in voice. Revise each sentence by changing the underlined passive-voice verb to the active voice.

Example: Two teachers believed they could help struggling students in New York City schools, so Chess in the Schools was founded by them.

Two teachers believed they could help struggling students in New York City

schools, so they founded Chess in the Schools.

1. Chess develops critical-thinking skills, and self-discipline and self-esteem are developed by players, too.

_____

_____

2. Because players face complicated chess problems, good problem-solving skills <u>are developed</u> by them.

_____

_____

3. Student chess players improve their concentration, and reading and math skills <u>can be improved</u> through this better concentration.

_____

_____

4. Chess teaches students how to lose as well as win, and that ability <u>will be needed</u> by students throughout their lives.

_____

_____

5. Chess in the Schools also helps keep students out of trouble because of the conflict-resolution skills <u>developed</u> by them.

_____

_____

TEST · Revise · Edit · Proofread

Look back at your response to the Write First prompt on page 383. TEST and revise what you have written. Then, edit and proofread your work, paying particular attention to illogical shifts in tense, person, or voice.

EDITING PRACTICE: PARAGRAPH

Read the following student paragraph, which includes illogical shifts in tense, person, and voice. Edit the passage to eliminate the illogical shifts, making sure subjects and verbs agree. The first error has been corrected for you.

The Origin of Baseball Cards

The first baseball cards appeared in the late 1800s. These cardboard pictures *were* ~~are~~ inserted in packs of cigarettes. Some people collected the cards, and the cigarette companies use the cards to encourage people to buy their products. By the early twentieth century, it was found by candy makers that one could use baseball cards to sell candy to children, so they developed new marketing plans. For example, each Cracker Jack box contains a baseball card. In 1933, gum manufacturers packaged bubble gum with baseball cards to make "bubble gum cards." Children could trade these cards. Sometimes children would put cards in the spokes of their bike wheels. The cards made noise when the wheels turns. Eventually, the bubble gum is dropped by the card manufacturers, and people just bought the cards. Still, collecting baseball cards was seen as a hobby for children until the 1970s, when dealers began to sell their rarest cards at high prices. Today, baseball-card collectors were mainly adults who are interested in investment, not baseball. For example, in 2007, a rare Honus Wagner baseball card sells for a record $2.8 million.

EDITING PRACTICE: ESSAY

Read the following student essay, which includes illogical shifts in tense, person, and voice. Edit the passage to eliminate the illogical shifts, making sure subjects and verbs agree. The first sentence has been edited for you.

A Different Kind of Vacation

During our upcoming winter break, my sister and I *are* ~~were~~ going to Belize to help build a school. Like many people, we want to travel and see new places, but we did not want to be tourists who only see what is in a guidebook. We also want to help people who are less fortunate than we were. Volunteering gives us the opportunity to combine travel with community service and to get to know a different culture at the same time.

These days, many people are using his or her vacation time to do volunteer work. Lots of charitable organizations offer short-term projects during school or holiday breaks. For most projects, no experience was necessary. All people need is his or her interest in other people and a desire to help.

For example, last year my aunt goes to Tanzania to work in a health clinic. She loved her experience volunteering in a poor rural community, where you help local doctors. She also loved the host family who shared their modest house with her. Before she left Tanzania, she and some of the other volunteers climb Mount Kilimanjaro. She said it was the best vacation she had ever had.

Although many volunteer vacations focus on improving schools or health care, a wide range of projects was available. Everyone can find work that suits their interests. For instance, people can volunteer to help preserve the environment, or you can work to protect women's rights. Countries all over the world welcome volunteers because help is needed by a lot of people.

My sister and I decided to help with the school in Belize because we believe a clean and safe place to learn is deserved by everyone. We are also eager to do some construction, get to know the local people, and enjoy the warm weather. If we have enough time, we hoped to visit some Mayan ruins as well. All in all, we are looking forward to a rewarding and unforgettable experience.

COLLABORATIVE ACTIVITY

Working in a group of three or four students, make up a test with five sentences containing illogical shifts in tense, person, and voice. Exchange tests with another group in the class. After you have taken the other group's test, compare answers with the other group.

review checklist

Illogical Shifts

☐ An illogical shift in tense occurs when a writer shifts from one tense to another for no apparent reason. (See 26a.)

☐ An illogical shift in person occurs when a writer shifts from one person to another for no apparent reason. (See 26b.)

☐ An illogical shift in voice occurs when a writer shifts from active to passive voice or from passive to active voice for no apparent reason. (See 26c.)

macmillanhighered.com /writingfirst
Additional Grammar Exercises > Illogical Shifts

27 Misplaced and Dangling Modifiers

write first

Write a one-paragraph recipe explaining how to prepare your favorite food. Begin by describing the food; then, list the ingredients, and explain how to make it.

In this chapter, you will learn to recognize and correct
- misplaced modifiers (27a)
- dangling modifiers (27b)

PREVIEW

A **modifier** is a word or word group that identifies or describes another word or word group in a sentence. Many word groups that act as modifiers are introduced by *-ing* (present participle) or *-ed* (past participle) modifiers. To avoid confusion, a modifier should be placed as close as possible to the word it modifies—ideally, directly before or directly after it.

Working in his garage, Steve Jobs invented the personal computer.

Rejected by Hamlet, Ophelia goes mad and drowns herself.

Used correctly, *-ing* and *-ed* modifiers provide useful information. Used incorrectly, however, these types of modifiers can be very confusing.

The two most common problems with modification are *misplaced modifiers* and *dangling modifiers*.

27a Correcting Misplaced Modifiers

A **misplaced modifier** appears to modify the wrong word or word group because it is placed incorrectly in the sentence. To correct this problem, move the modifier so it is as close as possible to the word it is supposed to modify (usually directly before or after it).

INCORRECT   Sarah fed the dog wearing her pajamas. (Was the dog wearing Sarah's pajamas?)

CORRECT   Wearing her pajamas, Sarah fed the dog.

INCORRECT   Dressed in a raincoat and boots, I thought my son was prepared for the storm. (Who was dressed in a raincoat and boots?)

CORRECT   I thought my son, dressed in a raincoat and boots, was prepared for the storm.

macmillanhighered.com /writingfirst
Additional Grammar Exercises > Correcting Misplaced Modifiers

PRACTICE
27-1   Underline the modifier in each of the following sentences. Then, draw an arrow to the word or words it modifies.

Example: Helping people worldwide, Doctors Without Borders is a group of volunteer medical professionals.

1. Suffering from famine and other disasters, some people are unable to help themselves.

2. Feeding and healing those in need, Doctors Without Borders improves people's lives.

3. Responding to a recent earthquake, doctors arrived within three days to help with the relief effort.

4. Setting up refugee camps in Thailand, the group quickly helped its first survivors.

5. Some doctors, chartering a ship called *The Island of Light*, once provided medical aid to people escaping Vietnam by boat.

PRACTICE

27-2   Rewrite the following sentences, which contain misplaced modifiers, so that each modifier clearly refers to the word or words it logically modifies.

Example: Mark ate a pizza standing in front of the refrigerator.

Standing in front of the refrigerator, Mark ate a pizza.
_____

1. Running across my bathroom ceiling, I saw two large, hairy bugs.

_____

_____

2. Lori looked at the man sitting in the chair with red hair.

_____

_____

3. The deer was hit by a car running across the street.

_____

_____

4. Dressed in a beautiful wedding gown, the groom watched the bride walk down the aisle.

_____

_____

5. The exterminator sprayed the ants wearing a mask.

_____

_____

27b   Correcting Dangling Modifiers

A **dangling modifier** "dangles" because the word it modifies does not appear in the sentence. Often, a dangling modifier comes at the beginning of a sentence and appears to modify the noun or pronoun that follows it.

macmillanhighered.com /writingfirst
Additional Grammar Exercises > Correcting Dangling Modifiers

Using my computer, the report was finished in two days.

In this sentence, the modifier *Using my computer* seems to be modifying *the report*. But this makes no sense. (How can the report use a computer?) The word the modifier should logically refer to is missing. To correct this sentence, you need to supply the missing word.

Using my computer, I finished the report in two days.

To correct a dangling modifier, supply a word to which the modifier can logically refer.

INCORRECT   Moving the microscope's mirror, the light can be directed

onto the slide. (Can the light move the mirror?)

CORRECT   Moving the microscope's mirror, you can direct the light

onto the slide.

INCORRECT   Paid in advance, the furniture was delivered. (Was the

furniture paid in advance?)

CORRECT   Paid in advance, the movers delivered the furniture.

PRACTICE
27-3

Each of the following sentences contains a dangling modifier. To correct each sentence, add a word to which the modifier can logically refer.

Example: Waiting inside, my bus passed by.

Waiting inside, I missed my bus.

1. Pushing on the brakes, my car would not stop for the red light.

_____

_____

2. Working overtime, his salary almost doubled.

_____

_____

3. Angered by the noise, the concert was called off.

_____

_____

4. Using the correct formula, the problem was easily solved.

_____

_____

5. Tired and hungry, the assignment was finished by midnight.

_____

_____

PRACTICE
27-4   Complete the following sentences, making sure to include a word or word group to which each modifier can logically refer.

Example: Dancing with the man of her dreams, *she decided it was* _____

time to wake up. _____

1. Blocked by the clouds, _____

_____

2. Applying for financial aid, _____

_____

3. Settled into his recliner, _____

_____

4. Fearing that they might catch a cold, _____

_____

5. Hearing strange noises through the wall, _____

_____

TEST · Revise · Edit · Proofread

Look back at your response to the Write First prompt on page 392. TEST and revise what you have written. Then, edit and proofread your work, paying particular attention to *-ing* and *-ed* modifiers. Check your work to make sure that you do not have any misplaced or dangling modifiers.

EDITING PRACTICE: PARAGRAPH

Read the following student paragraph, which includes modification errors. Rewrite sentences where necessary to correct misplaced and dangling modifiers. In some cases, you will need to supply a word or word group to which the modifier can logically refer. The first error has been corrected for you.

Beyond Mickey Mouse

For more than twenty years, Pixar computer animation studios have produced

movies. Sketched by hand before Pixar, *thousands of pictures were provided by artists* ~~artists provided thousands of pictures~~

for traditional animated films. Led by Steve Jobs, animation was revolutionized

by Pixar. With computers, special software was used by animators to create speech

and movement. Invented by Pixar, animators were able to achieve startling lifelike

effects. The typical Pixar plot shows characters growing as they move into the

world. Encouraging this growth, the characters' friends offer advice and guidance.

The first commercially successful Pixar film was *Toy Story*. Completed in 1995,

the use of computer animation made *Toy Story* a success. *Toy Story* was followed by

A Bug's Life, *Finding Nemo*, and *The Incredibles*. Bringing in more than $525 million,

audiences made these movies very successful. In 2006, Disney bought Pixar

for $7.4 billion. Now, the company that pioneered traditional animation eighty

years ago owns Pixar.

EDITING PRACTICE: ESSAY

Read the following student essay, which includes modification errors. Rewrite sentences where necessary to correct misplaced and dangling modifiers. In some cases, you will need to supply a word or word group to which the modifier can logically refer. The first error has been corrected for you.

Eating as a Sport

After eating a big meal, ~~the food often makes~~ *often* you feel stuffed. Imagine how

someone participating in competitive eating feels. To win, you have to eat more

food faster than anyone else. Training for days, many different kinds of food

are eaten in these contests. For example, contestants eat chicken wings, pizza, ribs, hot dogs, and even matzo balls. Training for events, competitive eating is considered a sport by participants. By winning, a good living can be made by a competitive eater. Considered dangerous by some, competitive eaters and their fans nevertheless continue to grow.

The way it works is that each competitor eats the same weight or portion of food. Giving the signal, the competitors begin eating. Breaking the food in pieces or just eating the food whole, any technique can be used. The competitors, soaked in water, can make the food softer. They can even eat hot dogs separately from their buns. Good competitors are usually not overweight. In fact, some are quite thin. Keeping the stomach from expanding, competitors are hurt by extra fat. By drinking large amounts of water, their stomachs stretch and increase their chances of winning. This is one technique many competitors use when they train.

The International Federation of Competitive Eating watches over the contests to make sure they are fair and safe. Providing the dates and locations, contests are listed on its Web site. Often, contests are held at state fairs. Also listing participants, prizes, and rankings of winners, new participants are invited. Before entering the contests, their eating specialty and personal profile must be indicated by new participants. Competitors must also be at least eighteen years old.

Many competitive eaters participate in lots of contests. For example, weighing only 100 pounds, 8.1 pounds of sausage was eaten in only 10 minutes by Sonya Thomas. At another contest, she ate 46 crab cakes in 10 minutes. Held in the United States, some participants come from other countries. For instance, Takeru Kobayashi, who comes from Japan, once ate 18 pounds of cow brains in 15 minutes. Winners usually get cash prizes. The largest prize, $20,000, was awarded in a hot dog–eating contest at Coney Island, which was televised by ESPN. By eating 66 hot dogs and their buns in 12 minutes, the contest was won by Joey Chestnut, a professional speed eater. Almost 50,000 people attended the contest in person, and millions watched on television.

There is some concern about competitive eating. By stretching the stomach, a person's health may be affected. There is also concern about obesity and overeating. Worried about choking, events should have doctors present some people argue. Still, many people like to watch these contests, and they seem to be getting more popular each year.

COLLABORATIVE ACTIVITY

Working in a group of five or six students, make a list of five modifiers that end in *-ing* and five modifiers that end in *-ed*. Exchange your list with another group, and complete the other group's sentences.

Examples

Typing as fast as he could, _John could not wait to finish his screenplay._

Frightened by a snake, _the horse ran away._

review checklist

Misplaced and Dangling Modifiers

☐ Correct a misplaced modifier by placing the modifier as close as possible to the word it modifies. (See 27a.)

☐ Correct a dangling modifier by supplying a word to which the modifier can logically refer. (See 27b.)

Read the following student essay, which contains run-ons, fragments, errors with subject-verb agreement, illogical shifts, and misplaced and dangling modifiers. Edit the essay to correct the errors. The first error has been corrected for you.

Not in My Back Yard

NIMBY, a term that was coined in 1980, stands for "not in my back yard." *even*
"NIMBYs" are people who are against certain changes in their communities, ~~Even~~ though these changes will benefit the general population. For example, NIMBYs may oppose new public housing, "big box" stores, prisons, airports, or highways. Because they may harm the community. These people also fear the presence in their neighborhoods of certain groups. Such as people with certain disabilities. They did not want these people. To live anywhere near them. NIMBYs have raised important issues. About the conflict between the rights of the individual and the rights of the population as a whole.

NIMBYs are suspicious of the government, they worry that the government will ignore their community's needs. For example, the government may say new jobs will be available, however, what if the jobs pay low wages? What if the new employers force locally owned small stores out of business? Low-income housing may be badly needed, but what if one of the results are a reduction in the value of nearby property? What if the strains on schools and traffic is unacceptable? NIMBYs always ask these questions.

NIMBYs understand that certain facilities must be built or improved nevertheless, they worry that each change may have their own negative effects. For example, needing new airport runways to reduce delays, NIMBYs object to the increased noise it causes. Although new sources of energy is badly needed, NIMBYs oppose the noise pollution. That windmills would bring to their community. New sites may be needed to dispose of hazardous waste, but NIMBYs are afraid of leaking waste containers. That may contaminate homes and neighborhoods.

Finally, there is always going to be fears. Of the unknown. Group homes for people with physical disabilities and mental illness is often a problem for NIMBYs.

They are also opposed to having sex offenders living in their community. Of course, no one wants a dangerous criminal living in their neighborhood. However, if someone has completed the required prison sentence, they have to live somewhere. Some of these negative attitudes is a result of lack of information others are based on a parent's real concerns about the safety of their children. Parents did not quarrel with the right of sex offenders to find a place to live they just do not want them to live anywhere near their children. NIMBYs feel that they have to protect themselves and their families.

The conflicts of NIMBY involve a real moral dilemma. On the one hand, belief in the importance of individuals mean that people should rely on themselves, not on the government. On the other hand, belief in social responsibility means that people should think about the well-being of others. The conflict between these two positions may be very difficult to resolve. Because sometimes the needs of the individual is in conflict with the needs of the general community.

28 Verbs: Past Tense

AP Photo/Jeff Chiu

write first

The obituary on the following page provides a short recap of the life of Apple cofounder Steve Jobs. Read the obituary, and then write one that summarizes your own life. (Refer to yourself by name or by *he* or *she*.) As you write, assume that you have led a long life and have achieved everything you hoped you would. Be sure to include the accomplishments for which you would most like to be remembered. Don't forget to use transitional words and phrases that clearly show how one event in your life relates to another.

In this chapter, you will learn to

- understand regular verbs in the past tense (28a)
- understand irregular verbs in the past tense (28b)
- deal with problem verbs in the past tense (28c and 28d)

Apple's Visionary Redefined Digital Age

New York Times
October 5, 2011

Steven P. Jobs, the visionary co-founder of Apple who helped usher in the era of personal computers and then led a cultural transformation in the way music, movies and mobile communications were experienced in the digital age, died Wednesday. He was 56.

The death was announced by Apple, the company Mr. Jobs and his high school friend Stephen Wozniak started in 1976 in a suburban California garage. A friend of the family said the cause was complications of pancreatic cancer. . . .

Mr. Jobs had largely come to define the personal computer industry and an array of digital consumer and entertainment businesses centered on the Internet. He had also become a very rich man, worth an estimated $8.3 billion.

Mr. Jobs was neither a hardware engineer nor a software programmar, nor did he think of himself as a manager. He considered himself a technology leader, choosing the best people possible, encouraging and prodding them, and making the final call on product design. . . .

He put much stock in the notion of "taste," a word he used frequently. It was a sensibility that shone in products that looked like works of art and delighted users. Great products, he said, were a triumph of taste, of "trying to expose yourself to the best things humans have done and then trying to bring those things into what you are doing."

Tense is the form a verb takes to show when an action or situation takes place. The **past tense** indicates that an action occurred in the past.

28a Regular Verbs

macmillanhighered.com /writingfirst
LearningCurve > Verbs; Additional Grammar Exercises > Regular Verbs

Regular verbs form the past tense by adding either *-ed* or *-d* to the **base form** of the verb (the present tense form of the verb that is used with *I*).

We register<u>ed</u> for classes yesterday.

Walt Disney produce<u>d</u> short cartoons in 1928.

Regular verbs that end in *-y* form the past tense by changing the *y* to *i* and adding *-ed*.

tr<u>y</u>	tr<u>ied</u>
appl<u>y</u>	appl<u>ied</u>

PRACTICE

28-1 Change the regular verbs in the following paragraph to the past tense.

Example: Every year, my mother ~~visits~~ *visited* her family in Bombay.

(1) My mother always returns from India with henna designs on her hands and feet. (2) In India, henna artists create these patterns. (3) Henna originates in a plant found in the Middle East, India, Indonesia, and northern Africa. (4) Many women in these areas use henna to color their hands, nails, and parts of their feet. (5) Men dye their beards as well as the manes and hooves of their horses. (6) They also color animal skins with henna. (7) In India, my mother always celebrates the end of the Ramadan religious fast by going to a "henna party." (8) A professional henna artist attends the party to apply new henna decorations to the women. (9) After a few weeks, the henna designs wash off. (10) In the United States, my mother's henna designs attract the attention of many people.

28b Irregular Verbs

**macmillanhighered.com
/writingfirst**
Additional Grammar
Exercises > Irregular Verbs

Unlike regular verbs, whose past tense forms end in *-ed* or *-d*, **irregular verbs** have irregular forms in the past tense. In fact, their past tense forms may look very different from their present tense forms.

The following chart lists the base form and past tense form of many of the most commonly used irregular verbs. (The past tense of other irregular verbs can be found in a dictionary.)

Irregular Verbs in the Past Tense

BASE FORM	PAST	BASE FORM	PAST
awake	awoke	break	broke
be (am, are)	was (were)	bring	brought
beat	beat	build	built
become	became	buy	bought
begin	began	catch	caught
bet	bet	choose	chose
bite	bit	come	came
blow	blew	cost	cost

BASE FORM	PAST	BASE FORM	PAST
cut	cut	quit	quit
dive	dove (dived)	read	read
do	did	ride	rode
draw	drew	ring	rang
drink	drank	rise	rose
drive	drove	run	ran
eat	ate	say	said
fall	fell	see	saw
feed	fed	sell	sold
feel	felt	send	sent
fight	fought	set	set
find	found	shake	shook
fly	flew	shine	shone (shined)
forgive	forgave	sing	sang
freeze	froze	sit	sat
get	got	sleep	slept
give	gave	speak	spoke
go	went	spend	spent
grow	grew	spring	sprang
have	had	stand	stood
hear	heard	steal	stole
hide	hid	stick	stuck
hold	held	sting	stung
hurt	hurt	swear	swore
keep	kept	swim	swam
know	knew	take	took
lay (to place)	laid	teach	taught
lead	led	tear	tore
leave	left	tell	told
let	let	think	thought
lie (to recline)	lay	throw	threw
light	lit	understand	understood
lose	lost	wake	woke (waked)
make	made	wear	wore
meet	met	win	won
pay	paid	write	wrote

PRACTICE

28-2 Fill in the correct past tense form of each irregular verb in parentheses, using the chart above to help you.

Example: Security on Campus ___*was*___ (be) founded in 1987.

(1) After their daughter, Jeanne, _____ (be) murdered at Lehigh University, Connie and Howard Cleary _____ (begin) a movement to improve safety on college campuses. (2) Jeanne _____ (think) she

was safe. (3) However, her attacker _____ (get) into her dorm room through three different doors that had all been left unlocked. (4) Shockingly, Jeanne's attacker actually _____ (go) to Lehigh. (5) Shattered by the loss of their daughter, Jeanne's parents _____ (do) not withdraw into their pain. (6) Instead, they _____ (feel) that the best memorial to their daughter would be the prevention of similar crimes, so they founded Security on Campus, Inc. (SOC). (7) SOC _____ (make) legal information available to victims of crimes on college campuses. (8) Because of the efforts of SOC, Congress _____ (write) a law that forced colleges to disclose their crime statistics. (9) Colleges also _____ (have) to explain the steps they _____ (take) to protect their students. (10) Because of this law, the number of campus crimes _____ (fall).

macmillanhighered.com
/writingfirst
Additional Grammar
Exercises > Problem Verbs: *Be*

28c   Problem Verbs: *Be*

The irregular verb *be* causes problems because it has two different past tense forms—*was* for singular subjects and *were* for second-person singular subjects as well as for plural subjects. (All other English verbs have just one past tense form.)

> Carlo was interested in becoming a city planner. (singular)
> They were happy to help out at the school. (plural)

Past Tense Forms of the Verb *Be*

	SINGULAR	PLURAL
First person	I was tired.	We were tired.
Second person	You were tired.	You were tired.
Third person	He was tired.	
	She was tired.	They were tired.
	It was tired.	
	The man was tired.	Frank and Billy were tired.

PRACTICE

28-3   Edit the following passage for errors in the use of the verb *be*. Cross out any underlined verbs that are incorrect, and write the correct forms above them. If a verb form is correct, label it *C*.

> **Example:**   Before 1990, there <u>was</u> *were* no female Hispanic astronauts in the
>
> NASA program.

(1) Although there had never been a Hispanic woman astronaut, it <u>was</u> impossible for NASA to ignore Ellen Ochoa's long career in physics and engineering. (2) When Ochoa <u>was</u> young, her main interests <u>was</u> music, math, and physics. (3) After getting a degree in physics at San Diego State University, she <u>were</u> considering a career in music or business. (4) However, she <u>was</u> convinced by her mother to continue her education. (5) In 1983, Ochoa <u>was</u> studying for a doctorate in electrical engineering at Stanford University when the first female astronaut, Sally Ride, flew on the space shuttle. (6) Ochoa <u>were</u> inspired by Sally Ride to become an astronaut. (7) More than two thousand people <u>was</u> also inspired to apply for the astronaut program. (8) In 1990, Ochoa <u>was</u> picked to fly into space. (9) On one of her flights, she <u>was</u> a mission specialist and used a remote-controlled robotic arm to catch a satellite. (10) After four space flights, Ochoa <u>were</u> made director of flight crew operations.

28d   Problem Verbs: *Can/Could* and *Will/Would*

The helping verbs *can/could* and *will/would* present problems because their past tense forms are sometimes confused with their present tense forms.

Can/Could

Can, a present tense verb, means "is able to" or "are able to."

> First-year students <u>can</u> apply for financial aid.

Could, the past tense of *can*, means "was able to" or "were able to."

> Escape artist Harry Houdini claimed that he <u>could</u> escape from any prison.

e macmillanhighered.com
/writingfirst
Additional Grammar
Exercises > Problem Verbs:
Can/Could and *Will/Would*

Will/Would

Will, a present tense verb, talks about the future from a point in the present.

> A solar eclipse <u>will</u> occur in ten months.

Would, the past tense of *will*, talks about the future from a point in the past.

> I told him yesterday that I <u>would</u> think about it.

Would is also used to express a possibility or wish.

> If we stuck to our budget, we <u>would</u> be better off.
> Laurie <u>would</u> like a new stuffed animal.

FYI

Will and Would

Note that *will* is used with *can* and that *would* is used with *could*.

> I will feed the cats if I can find their food.

> I would feed the cats if I could find their food.

**PRACTICE
28-4** Circle the appropriate helping verb from the choices in parentheses.

Example: People who don't want to throw things away (can, could) rent a self-storage unit.

(1) In the past, warehouse storage (will, would) provide a place to store excess items. (2) However, people (will, would) have to hire moving vans and (can, could) hardly ever have access to their stored items. (3) They (will, would) have to sign an expensive long-term contract. (4) Now, however, they (can, could) take advantage of another option. (5) They (can, could) store possessions in a space as small as a closet or as large as a house. (6) With self-storage, people (can, could) easily move their belongings in and out of the storage unit. (7) When they need more space, they (will, would) be able to get it. (8) In fact, the managers of self-storage facilities (can, could) suggest how much space owners (will, would) need. (9) The only person who (can, could) get into the self-storage unit is the person who has rented it. (10) If people need a hand truck to move their

belongings, they (can, could) usually borrow one. (11) All in all, using self-storage (can, could) solve a lot of problems for people with too many possessions.

TEST · Revise · Edit · Proofread

Look back at your response to the Write First prompt on page 402. TEST and revise what you have written. Then, edit and proofread your work, making sure that you have used the correct past tense form for each of your verbs.

EDITING PRACTICE

Read the following student essay, which includes errors in past tense verb forms. Decide whether each of the underlined past tense verbs is correct. If the verb is correct, write *C* above it. If it is not, cross out the verb, and write in the correct past tense form. The first sentence has been corrected for you. (If necessary, consult the list of irregular verbs on pages 404–405.)

Healing

The window seat ~~were~~ *was* our favorite place to sit. I piled pillows on the ledge and spended several minutes rearranging them. Then, my friend and I lied on our backs and propped our feet on the wall. We sat with our arms around our legs and thinked about the mysteries of life.

We stared at the people on the street below and wonder who they was and where they was going. We imagined that they can be millionaires, foreign spies, or drug smugglers. We believed that everyone except us leaded wonderful and exciting lives.

I heard a voice call my name. Reluctantly, I standed up, tearing myself away from my imaginary world. My dearest and oldest friend—my teddy bear—and I came back to the real world. I grabbed Teddy and brung him close to my chest. Together, we go into the cold dining room, where twelve other girls sit around a table eating breakfast. None of them looked happy.

In the unit for eating disorders, meals was always tense. Nobody wants to eat, but the nurses watched us until we eated every crumb. I set Teddy on the chair beside me and stared gloomily at the food on our plate. I closed my eyes and taked the first bite. I feeled the calories adding inches of ugly fat. Each swallow were like a nail being ripped from my finger. At last, it was over. I had survived breakfast.

Days passed slowly. Each passing minute was a victory. After a while, I learned how to eat properly. I learned about other people's problems. I also learned that people loved me. Eventually, even Teddy stopped feeling sorry for me. I begun to smile—and laugh. Sometimes I even considered myself happy. My doctors challenged me—and, surprisingly, I rised to the occasion.

COLLABORATIVE ACTIVITY

Form a group with three other students. What national or world events do you remember most clearly? Take ten minutes to list news events that you think have defined the last five years. On your own, write a few paragraphs in which you discuss the significance of the three or four events that the members of your group agree were the most important.

review checklist

Verbs: Past Tense

☐ The past tense is the form a verb takes to show that an action occurred in the past.

☐ Regular verbs form the past tense by adding either -*ed* or -*d* to the base form of the verb. (See 28a.)

☐ Irregular verbs have irregular forms in the past tense. (See 28b.)

☐ *Be* has two different past tense forms—*was* for singular subjects and *were* for second-person singular subjects as well as for plural subjects. (See 28c.)

☐ *Could* is the past tense of *can. Would* is the past tense of *will.* (See 28d.)

e macmillanhighered.com /writingfirst
LearningCurve > Verbs

29 Verbs: Past Participles

write first

This still from the film *Mad Hot Ballroom* shows children practicing ballroom dancing. Write a paragraph about an activity—a hobby or a sport, for example—that you have been involved in for a relatively long time. Begin by identifying the activity and stating why it has been important to you. Then, describe the activity, paying particular attention to what you have gained from it over the years.

In this chapter, you will learn to
- identify regular past participles (29a)
- identify irregular past participles (29b)
- use the present perfect tense (29c)
- use the past perfect tense (29d)
- use past participles as adjectives (29e)

29a Regular Past Participles

Every verb has a past participle form. The **past participle** form of a regular verb is identical to its past tense form. Both are formed by adding either *-ed* or *-d* to the **base form** of the verb (the present tense form of the verb that is used with the pronoun *I*).

PAST TENSE
He earned a fortune.

PAST PARTICIPLE
He has earned a fortune.

PAST TENSE
He created a work of art.

PAST PARTICIPLE
He has created a work of art

 macmillanhighered.com
/writingfirst
LearningCurve > Verbs;
Additional Grammar
Exercises > Regular Past
Participles

PRACTICE

29-1 Fill in the correct past participle form of each regular verb in parentheses.

Example: For years, volunteer vacationers have __*visited*__ (visit) remote areas to build footpaths, cabins, and shelters.

(1) Recently, vacationers have _____ (discover) some new opportunities to get away from it all and to do good at the same time. (2) Groups such as Habitat for Humanity, for example, have _____ (offer) volunteers a chance to build homes in low-income areas. (3) Habitat's Global Village trips have _____ (raise) awareness about the lack of affordable housing in many countries. (4) Participants in Sierra Club programs have _____ (donate) thousands of work hours all over the United States. (5) Sometimes these volunteers have _____ (join) forest service workers to help restore wilderness areas. (6) They have _____ (clean) up trash at campsites. (7) They have also _____ (remove) nonnative plants. (8) Some volunteer vacationers have _____ (travel) to countries such as Costa Rica, Russia, and Thailand to help with local projects. (9) Other vacationers have _____ (serve) as English teachers. (10) Volunteering vacations have _____ (help) to strengthen cross-cultural understanding.

29b Irregular Past Participles

macmillanhighered.com
/writingfirst
Additional Grammar
Exercises > Irregular Past
Participles

Irregular verbs nearly always have irregular past participles. Irregular verbs do not form the past participle by adding -ed or -d to the base form of the verb.

The following chart lists the base form, the past tense form, and the past participle of the most commonly used irregular verbs.

Irregular Past Participles

BASE FORM	PAST TENSE	PAST PARTICIPLE
awake	awoke	awoken
be (am, are)	was (were)	been
beat	beat	beaten
become	became	become
begin	began	begun
bet	bet	bet
bite	bit	bitten
blow	blew	blown
break	broke	broken
bring	brought	brought
build	built	built
buy	bought	bought
catch	caught	caught
choose	chose	chosen
come	came	come
cost	cost	cost
cut	cut	cut
dive	dove (dived)	dove (dived)
do	did	done
draw	drew	drawn
drink	drank	drunk (drank)
drive	drove	driven
eat	ate	eaten
fall	fell	fallen
feed	fed	fed
feel	felt	felt
fight	fought	fought
find	found	found
fly	flew	flown
forgive	forgave	forgiven
freeze	froze	frozen
get	got	got (gotten)
give	gave	given
go	went	gone
grow	grew	grown
have	had	had
hear	heard	heard
hide	hid	hidden
hold	held	held

BASE FORM	PAST TENSE	PAST PARTICIPLE
hurt	hurt	hurt
keep	kept	kept
know	knew	known
lay (to place)	laid	laid
lead	led	led
leave	left	left
let	let	let
lie (to recline)	lay	lain
light	lit	lit
lose	lost	lost
make	made	made
meet	met	met
pay	paid	paid
quit	quit	quit
read	read	read
ride	rode	ridden
ring	rang	rung
rise	rose	risen
run	ran	run
say	said	said
see	saw	seen
sell	sold	sold
send	sent	sent
set	set	set
shake	shook	shaken
shine	shone (shined)	shone (shined)
sing	sang	sung
sit	sat	sat
sleep	slept	slept
speak	spoke	spoken
spend	spent	spent
spring	sprang	sprung
stand	stood	stood
steal	stole	stolen
stick	stuck	stuck
sting	stung	stung
swear	swore	sworn
swim	swam	swum
take	took	taken
teach	taught	taught
tear	tore	torn
tell	told	told
think	thought	thought
throw	threw	thrown
understand	understood	understood
wake	woke (waked)	woken (waked)
wear	wore	worn
win	won	won
write	wrote	written

PRACTICE

29-2 Edit the following paragraph for errors in irregular past participles. Cross out any underlined past participles that are incorrect, and write in the correct form above them. If the verb form is correct, label it *C.*

Example: In recent years, some people have ~~standed~~ up against overseas sweatshops.
(stood)

(1) Buying products from overseas sweatshops has <u>became</u> controversial over the last few decades. (2) American manufacturers have <u>sended</u> their materials to developing countries where employees work under terrible conditions for very low wages. (3) Violations of basic U.S. labor laws—such as getting extra pay for overtime and being paid on time—have <u>lead</u> to protests. (4) Low-wage workers in developing countries have <u>finded</u> themselves facing dangerous working conditions as well as verbal and sexual abuse. (5) Even well-known retailers—such as Walmart, Nike, Reebok, Tommy Hilfiger, and Target—have <u>gotten</u> in trouble for selling items made in sweatshops. (6) Recently, colleges have <u>be</u> criticized for using overseas sweatshops to make clothing featuring school names. (7) Students have <u>spoke</u> out against such practices, and schools have <u>had</u> to respond. (8) While some manufacturers may have <u>losed</u> money by increasing wages for overseas workers, they have <u>understanded</u> that this is the right thing to do. (9) They have <u>made</u> a promise to their customers that they will not employ sweatshop labor. (10) Critics have <u>argue</u>, however, that in developing countries, sweatshop jobs are often an improvement over other types of employment.

29c The Present Perfect Tense

The past participle can be combined with the present tense forms of *have* to form the **present perfect tense**.

The Present Perfect Tense

(*have* or *has* + past participle)

SINGULAR

I have gained.
You have gained.
He has gained.
She has gained.
It has gained.

PLURAL

We have gained.
You have gained.
They have gained.

■ Use the present perfect tense to indicate an action that began in the past and continues into the present.

> **PRESENT PERFECT**   The nurse has worked at the Welsh Mountain clinic for two years. (The working began in the past and continues into the present.)

■ Use the present perfect tense to indicate that an action has just occurred.

> **PRESENT PERFECT**   I have just eaten. (The eating has just occurred.)

PRACTICE

29-3   Fill in the appropriate tense (past or present perfect) of the verb in parentheses.

Example: Now, cell phones fit easily into a pocket, but the first mobile-phone users _____*carried*_____ (carry) devices that were more than a foot long.

(1) In recent years, the size of many everyday items _____ (change) considerably. (2) Cell phones and computers _____ (undergo) the biggest changes. (3) There was a time, not long ago, when a single computer _____ (fill) an entire room and a cell phone weighed as much as two pounds. (4) Since then, we _____ (invent) smaller and smaller devices. (5) Now, we _____ (become) accustomed to tiny devices that act as both phone and computer yet weigh only a few ounces. (6) However, while these items have shrunk, other things _____ (get) bigger. (7) For example, flat-screen TVs now come in sizes up to 100 inches. (8) Moreover, as Americans _____ (grow) heavier, hospital

equipment has had to get sturdier. (9) Ten years ago, manufacturers _____ (build) operating tables that supported a maximum of 700 pounds. (10) Now, medical supply companies _____ (develop) a standard table that supports up to 1,200 pounds. (11) To accommodate the growing number of overweight people, movie theater seats and caskets _____ (increase) in size as well. (12) Whereas moviegoers in the 1980s _____ (sit) in 20-inch seats, today's viewers sit in 26-inch seats. (13) Similarly, standard-size caskets have expanded in width from 24 to 28 inches, and some companies _____ (start) making plus-size caskets as large as 52 inches across. (14) Clearly, consumers prefer some items to be smaller even as they themselves _____ (get) bigger.

macmillanhighered.com
/writingfirst
Additional Grammar
Exercises > Present Perfect
and Past Perfect Tenses

29d The Past Perfect Tense

The past participle can also be used to form the **past perfect tense**, which consists of the past tense of *have* plus the past participle.

The Past Perfect Tense

(*had* + past participle)

SINGULAR	PLURAL
I had returned.	We had returned.
You had returned.	You had returned.
He had returned.	They had returned.
She had returned.	
It had returned.	

Use the past perfect tense to show that an action occurred before another past action.

PAST PERFECT TENSE   PAST TENSE
Chief Sitting Bull had fought many battles before he defeated General Custer. (The fighting was done before Sitting Bull defeated Custer.)

PRACTICE

29-4 Underline the appropriate verb tense (present perfect or past perfect) from the choices in parentheses.

Example: Although he (has missed/<u>had missed</u>) his second free throw, the crowd cheered for him anyway.

1. Meera returned to Bangladesh with the money she (has raised/had raised).

2. Her contributors believe that she (has shown/had shown) the ability to spend money wisely.

3. The planner told the commission that she (has found/had found) a solution to the city's traffic problem.

4. It seems clear that traffic cameras (have proven/had proven) successful in towns with similar congestion problems.

5. Emily says she (has saved/had saved) a lot of money by driving a motor scooter instead of a car.

6. She sold the car she (has bought/had bought) three years before.

7. Because they are huge fans, Esteban and Tina (have camped/had camped) out in front of the theater to buy tickets.

8. The people who (have waited/had waited) all night were the first to get tickets.

9. Sam and Ryan volunteer at Habitat for Humanity, where they (have learned/had learned) many useful skills.

10. After they (have completed/had completed) five hundred hours of work, they were eligible to get their own house.

29e Past Participles as Adjectives

In addition to functioning as verbs, past participles can function as adjectives modifying nouns that follow them.

I cleaned up the broken glass.

The exhausted runner finally crossed the finish line.

Past participles are also used as adjectives after **linking verbs**, such as *seemed* or *looked*.

Jason seemed surprised.

He looked shocked.

PRACTICE

29-5 Edit the following passage for errors in past participle forms used as adjectives. Cross out any underlined participles that are incorrect, and write the correct form above them. If the participle form is correct, label it *C*.

Example: College students are often <u>worried</u> about money.   *C*

(1) College students are <u>surprise</u> when they get <u>preapprove</u> applications for credit cards in the mail. (2) Credit-card companies also recruit <u>targeted</u> students through booths that are <u>locate</u> on or near college campuses. (3) The booths are <u>design</u> to attract new customers with offers of gifts. (4) Why have companies gone to all this trouble to attract <u>qualified</u> students? (5) Most older Americans already have at least five credit cards that are <u>stuff</u> in their wallets. (6) Banks and credit-card companies see younger college students as a major <u>untapped</u> market. (7) According to experts, students are a good credit risk because <u>concern</u> parents usually bail them out when they cannot pay a bill. (8) Finally, people tend to feel emotionally <u>tie</u> to their first credit card. (9) Companies want to be the first card that is <u>acquire</u> by a customer. (10) For this reason, credit-card companies target <u>uninform</u> college students.

TEST · Revise · Edit · Proofread

Look back at your response to the Write First prompt on page 412. TEST and revise what you have written. Then, edit and proofread your work, paying particular attention to present perfect and past perfect verb forms and to past participles used as adjectives.

EDITING PRACTICE

Read the following student essay, which includes errors in the use of past participles and perfect tenses. Decide whether each of the underlined verbs or participles is correct. If it is correct, write *C* above it. If it is not, write in the correct verb form. The first error has been corrected for you.

The Flash Mob Phenomenon

The first flash mob <u>had take</u> [*took*] place in 2003, when two hundred people assembled in a New York City Macy's store. Since then, these strange spontaneous gatherings <u>had popped</u> up in cities around the world and <u>have involve</u> all kinds of unusual behaviors. Occasionally, a group <u>has organized</u> a flash mob for criminal purposes, but in most cases, flash mobs <u>had been</u> harmless acts of group expression.

Organizer Bill Wasik <u>had</u> actually <u>intend</u> the first flash mob to be a social commentary. Wasik <u>has wanted</u> to make fun of "hipster" New Yorkers who showed up at events simply because other people did. However, almost no one <u>had saw</u> the first flash mob that way. In fact, people mostly <u>have thought</u> it was cool. As a result, admirers started organizing their own flash mobs.

So far, few flash mobs <u>had have</u> a political or social purpose. Typically, people <u>had participate</u> simply because these gatherings are fun. For example, over the years, people <u>have gathered</u> in cities around the world to dance to Michael Jackson's "Thriller." People <u>had</u> also <u>enjoyed</u> getting together in public spaces for massive pillow fights. In addition, several groups <u>have coordinated</u> group "freeze frames," in which participants all "freeze" at the same moment. Organized quietly by text messages or social media, most flash mobs <u>have</u> not <u>publicize</u> their plans in traditional media. Consequently, passersby <u>have enjoyed</u> the feeling that the group <u>had gathered</u> spontaneously.

Although the majority of flash mob organizers <u>have create</u> these brief performances to entertain, people <u>have</u> occasionally <u>use</u> flash mobs to commit crimes. Over the last few years, several groups <u>have robbed</u> stores by entering in large numbers, stealing merchandise, and then separating quickly. Worse, several groups <u>have came</u> together to commit violent acts or destroy property. Most of today's flash mobs, however, are peaceful.

Over the last decade, flash mobs <u>have became</u> more popular than anyone could have imagined. Although they have not had the impact that early enthusiasts <u>had hoped</u> for, they <u>given</u> many people a lot of enjoyment. Flash mobs allow people to be creative, to work together, and to have fun. Although a few flash mobs <u>have done</u> harm, most <u>have offer</u> people a way to be a part of something memorable.

COLLABORATIVE ACTIVITY

Assume that you are a restaurant employee who has been nominated for the Employee-of-the-Year Award. To win this award (along with a thousand-dollar prize), you have to explain in writing what you have done during the past year to deserve this honor. Write a letter to your supervisor and the awards committee. When you have finished, trade papers with another student and edit his or her letter.

macmillanhighered.com /writingfirst
LearningCurve > Verbs

review checklist

Verbs: Past Participles

☐ The past participle of regular verbs is formed by adding *-ed* or *-d* to the base form. (See 29a.)

☐ Irregular verbs usually have irregular past participles. (See 29b.)

☐ The past participle is combined with the present tense forms of *have* to form the present perfect tense. (See 29c.)

☐ The past participle is used to form the past perfect tense, which consists of the past tense of *have* plus the past participle. (See 29d.)

☐ The past participle can function as an adjective. (See 29e.)

30 Nouns and Pronouns

AP Photo/NASA/Neil A. Armstrong

write first

Write a paragraph about a significant local, national, or international event you remember. Begin by explaining what happened. Then, tell why the event was important to you.

In this chapter, you will learn to
- identify nouns (30a) and pronouns (30c)
- form plural nouns (30b)
- understand (30d) and solve special problems with (30e) pronoun-antecedent agreement
- avoid vague and unnecessary pronouns (30f)
- understand (30g) and solve special problems with (30h) pronoun case
- identify reflexive and intensive pronouns (30i)

macmillanhighered.com
/writingfirst
LearningCurve > Nouns and Pronouns

30a Identifying Nouns

A **noun** is a word that names a person (*singer, Jay-Z*), an animal (*dolphin, Flipper*), a place (*downtown, Houston*), an object (*game, Scrabble*), or an idea (*happiness, Darwinism*).

A **singular noun** names one thing. A **plural noun** names more than one thing.

30b Forming Plural Nouns

Most nouns that end in consonants add *-s* to form plurals. Other nouns add *-es* to form plurals. For example, most nouns that end in *-o* add *-es* to form plurals. Other nouns, whose singular forms end in *-s, -ss, -sh, -ch, -x*, or *-z*, also add *-es* to form plurals. (Some nouns that end in *-s* or *-z* double the *s* or *z* before adding *-es*.)

SINGULAR	PLURAL
street	streets
tomato	tomatoes
gas	gases
class	classes
bush	bushes
church	churches
fox	foxes
quiz	quizzes

Irregular Noun Plurals

Some nouns form plurals in unusual ways.

- Nouns whose plural forms are the same as their singular forms

SINGULAR	PLURAL
a deer	a few deer
this species	these species
a television series	two television series

- Nouns ending in *-f* or *-fe*

SINGULAR	PLURAL
each half	both halves
my life	our lives
a lone thief	a gang of thieves
one loaf	two loaves
the third shelf	several shelves

Exceptions: *roof* (plural *roofs*), *proof* (plural *proofs*), *belief* (plural *beliefs*)

- Nouns ending in *-y*

SINGULAR	PLURAL
another baby	more babies
every worry	many worries

Note that when a vowel (*a, e, i, o, u*) comes before the *y*, the noun has a regular plural form: *monkey* (plural *monkeys*), *day* (plural *days*).

- Hyphenated compound nouns

SINGULAR	PLURAL
Lucia's sister-in-law	Lucia's two favorite sisters-in-law
a mother-to-be	twin mothers-to-be
the first runner-up	all the runners-up

Note that the plural ending is attached to the compound's first word: *sister, mother, runner*.

- Miscellaneous irregular plurals

SINGULAR	PLURAL
that child	all children
a good man	a few good men
the woman	lots of women
my left foot	both feet
a wisdom tooth	my two front teeth
this bacterium	some bacteria

30c Identifying Pronouns

A **pronoun** is a word that refers to and takes the place of a noun or another pronoun. In the following sentence, the pronouns *she* and *her* take the place of the noun *Michelle*.

Michelle was excited because <u>she</u> had finally found a job that made <u>her</u> happy. (*She* refers to *Michelle*; *her* refers to *she*.)

Pronouns, like nouns, can be singular or plural.

- Singular pronouns (*I*, *he*, *she*, *it*, *him*, *her*, and so on) always take the place of singular nouns or pronouns.

  Geoff left his jacket at work, so <u>he</u> went back to get <u>it</u> before <u>it</u> could be stolen. (*He* refers to *Geoff*; *it* refers to *jacket*.)

- Plural pronouns (*we*, *they*, *our*, *their*, and so on) always take the place of plural nouns or pronouns.

  Jessie and Dan got up early, but <u>they</u> still missed <u>their</u> train. (*They* refers to *Jessie and Dan*; *their* refers to *they*.)

- The pronoun *you* can be either singular or plural.

  When the volunteers met the mayor, they said, "We really admire <u>you</u>." The mayor replied, "I admire <u>you</u>, too." (In the first sentence, *you* refers to *the mayor*; in the second sentence, *you* refers to *the volunteers*.)

FYI

Demonstrative Pronouns

Demonstrative pronouns—*this*, *that*, *these*, and *those*—point to one or more items.

- *This* and *that* point to one item: <u>This</u> is a work of fiction, and <u>that</u> is a nonfiction book.

- *These* and *those* point to more than one item: <u>These</u> are fruits, but <u>those</u> are vegetables.

PRACTICE

30-1 In the following sentences, fill in each blank with an appropriate pronoun.

Example: Ever since _____*I*_____ had my first scuba-diving experience, _____*I*_____ have wanted to search for sunken treasure.

(1) Three friends and _____ decided to explore an area off the Florida coast where a shipwreck had occurred almost three hundred years ago. (2) The first step was to buy a boat; _____ all agreed on a used rubber boat with a fifteen-horsepower engine. (3) _____ had

hardly been used and was in very good condition. (4) _____ also needed some equipment, including an anchor and metal detectors. (5) If there was treasure on the bottom of the ocean, _____ would find it. (6) _____ stayed in the boat while my friends made the first dive. (7) At first, _____ found only fish and sea worms, but _____ didn't give up. (8) Finally, one of the metal detectors started beeping because _____ had located a cannon and two cannonballs. (9) Then, it started beeping again; this time, _____ had found some pieces of pottery and an old pistol. (10) Although our group didn't find any coins, _____ all enjoyed our search for sunken treasure.

30d   Pronoun-Antecedent Agreement

The word that a pronoun refers to is called the pronoun's **antecedent**. In the following sentence, the noun *leaf* is the antecedent of the pronoun *it*.

> The leaf turned yellow, but it did not fall.

A pronoun must always agree with its antecedent. If an antecedent is singular, as it is in the preceding sentence, the pronoun must also be singular. If an antecedent is plural, as it is in the following sentence, the pronoun must also be plural.

> The leaves turned yellow, but they did not fall.

If an antecedent is feminine, the pronoun that refers to it must also be feminine.

> Melissa passed her driver's exam with flying colors.

If an antecedent is masculine, the pronoun that refers to it must also be masculine.

> Matt wondered what courses he should take.

If an antecedent is **neuter** (neither masculine nor feminine), the pronoun that refers to it must also be neuter.

> The car broke down, but they decided not to fix it again.

e macmillanhighered.com
/writingfirst
Additional Grammar
Exercises > Identifying
Antecedents; Pronoun–
Antecedent Agreement

PRACTICE 30-2

In the following sentences, circle the antecedent of each underlined pronoun. Then, draw an arrow from the pronoun to its antecedent.

Example: College (students) today often fear <u>they</u> will be the victims of crime on campus.

(1) Few campuses are as safe as <u>they</u> should be, experts say. (2) However, crime on most campuses is probably no worse than <u>it</u> is in any other community. (3) Still, students have a right to know how safe <u>their</u> campuses are. (4) My friend Joyce never walks on campus without <u>her</u> can of Mace. (5) Joyce believes <u>she</u> must be prepared for the worst. (6) Her boyfriend took a self-defense course that <u>he</u> said was very helpful. (7) My friends do not let fear of crime keep <u>them</u> from enjoying the college experience. (8) We know that our school is doing all <u>it</u> can to make the campus safe.

PRACTICE 30-3

Fill in each blank in the following passage with an appropriate pronoun.

Example: Americans celebrate July 4 because ____*it*____ is Independence Day.

(1) For some Germans, November 9 is a day to celebrate positive change; for others, _____ recalls the human potential for violence and destruction. (2) November 9, designated "World Freedom Day," is important because _____ is the day in 1989 when the Berlin Wall fell. (3) However, Germans have mixed feelings about this date because November 9 also reminds _____ of a dark moment in their history. (4) On the night of November 9, 1938, Nazis took sledgehammers and axes to as many Jewish businesses, synagogues, and homes as _____ could find. (5) In German, this violent event is called *Kristallnacht*; in English, _____ is known as "the Night of Broken Glass." (6) Coincidentally, Albert Einstein, a German Jew, received the Nobel Prize on November 9, 1921; the theories _____ described have changed how scientists think. (7) Thus, November 9 in Germany is a day of opposites; like so many dates in human history, _____ marks both triumph and tragedy.

30e Special Problems with Agreement

e macmillanhighered.com
/writingfirst
Additional Grammar
Exercises > Revising for
Pronoun-Antecedent
Agreement

Certain kinds of antecedents can cause problems for writers because they cannot be easily identified as singular or plural.

Compound Antecedents

A **compound antecedent** consists of two or more words connected by *and* or *or*.

- Compound antecedents connected by *and* are plural, and they are used with plural pronouns.

  During World War II, Belgium and France tried to protect their borders.

- Compound antecedents connected by *or* may take a singular or a plural pronoun. The pronoun always agrees with the word that is closer to it.

  Is it possible that European nations or Russia may send its [not *their*] troops?

  Is it possible that Russia or European nations may send their [not *its*] troops?

**PRACTICE
30-4** In each of the following sentences, underline the compound antecedent, and circle the connecting word (*and* or *or*). Then, circle the appropriate pronoun in parentheses.

Example: Marge (and) Homer Simpson love (his or her/(their)) children very much in spite of the problems they cause.

1. Either *24* or *Lost* had the highest ratings for any television show in (its/their) final episode.

2. In *South Park*, Geek 1 and Geek 2 help create a time machine out of (his/their) friend Timmy's wheelchair.

3. Recent movies and documentaries about penguins have delighted (its/their) audiences.

4. In baseball, pitchers and catchers communicate (his or her/their) plays with hand signals.

5. Either PlayStation 4 or Xbox One gives (its/their) players many hours of gaming fun.

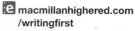 macmillanhighered.com
/writingfirst
Additional Grammar
Exercises > Indefinite Pronoun
Antecedents

Indefinite Pronoun Antecedents

Most pronouns refer to a specific person or thing. However, **indefinite pronouns** do not refer to any particular person or thing.

Most indefinite pronouns are singular.

Singular Indefinite Pronouns

another	everybody	no one
anybody	everyone	nothing
anyone	everything	one
anything	much	somebody
each	neither	someone
either	nobody	something

When an indefinite pronoun antecedent is singular, use a singular pronoun to refer to it.

Everything was in its place. (*Everything* is singular, so it is used with the singular pronoun *its*.)

FYI

Indefinite Pronouns with *Of*

The singular indefinite pronouns *each*, *either*, *neither*, and *one* are often used in phrases with *of*—*each of, either of, neither of,* or *one of*—followed by a plural noun. Even in such phrases, these indefinite pronoun antecedents are always singular and take singular pronouns.

Each of the routes has its [not *their*] own special challenges.

A few indefinite pronouns are plural.

Plural Indefinite Pronouns

both
few
many
others
several

When an indefinite pronoun antecedent is plural, use a plural pronoun to refer to it.

They all wanted to graduate early, but few received their diplomas in January. (*Few* is plural, so it is used with the plural pronoun *their*.)

FYI

Using *His* or *Her* with Indefinite Pronouns

Even though the indefinite pronouns *anybody, anyone, everybody, everyone, somebody, someone,* and so on are singular, many people use plural pronouns to refer to them.

> Everyone must hand in <u>their</u> completed work before 2 p.m.

This usage is widely accepted in spoken English. Nevertheless, indefinite pronouns like *everyone* are singular, and written English requires a singular pronoun.

However, using the singular pronoun *his* to refer to *everyone* suggests that *everyone* refers to a male. Using *his or her* is more accurate because the indefinite pronoun can refer to either a male or a female.

> Everyone must hand in <u>his or her</u> completed work before 2 p.m.

When used over and over again, *he or she, him or her,* and *his or her* can create wordy or awkward sentences. Whenever possible, use plural forms.

> All students must hand in <u>their</u> completed work before 2 p.m.

PRACTICE

 In each of the following sentences, first circle the indefinite pronoun. Then, circle the pronoun in parentheses that refers to the indefinite pronoun antecedent.

Example: (Each) of the lacrosse players will have (his or her)/their)

own locker at training camp.

1. Everyone likes to choose (his or her/their) own class schedule.

2. Somebody left (his or her/their) iPod on the bus.

3. Most of the *American Idol* contestants did (his or her/their) best for the

   judges.

4. Someone in the audience forgot to turn off (his or her/their) cell phone

   before the performance.

5. Neither of the dogs wanted to have (its/their) coat brushed.

6. Coach Reilly personally gave each of the players (his or her/their)

   trophy.

7. Both of the soldiers donated (his or her/their) cars to Purple Heart, an

   organization that helps veterans.

8. No one should ever give (his or her/their) Social Security number to a telephone solicitor.

9. Anyone who works hard in college can usually receive (his or her/their) degree.

10. Everyone loves receiving presents on (his or her/their) birthday.

PRACTICE

30-6 Edit the following sentences for errors in pronoun-antecedent agreement. When you edit, you have two options: either substitute *its* or *his or her* for *their* to refer to the singular antecedent, or replace the singular antecedent with a plural word.

Examples: Everyone is responsible for ~~their~~ own passport.
his or her

~~Each~~ of the children took their books out of their backpacks.
All

1. Either of the hybrid cars comes with their own tax rebate.

2. Anyone who loses their locker key must pay five dollars for a new one.

3. Everyone loves seeing their home team win.

4. Somebody left their scarf and gloves on the subway.

5. Almost everyone waits until the last minute to file their tax returns.

6. Each student returned their library books on time.

7. Everything we need to build the model airplane comes in their kit.

8. Anyone who wants to succeed needs to develop their public-speaking skills.

9. One of the hockey teams just won their first Olympic medal.

10. No one leaving the show early will get their money back.

Collective Noun Antecedents

Collective nouns are words (such as *band* and *team*) that name a group of people or things but are singular. Because they are singular, collective noun antecedents are used with singular pronouns.

The band played on, but it never played our song.

> **Frequently Used Collective Nouns**
>
> | | | | |
> |---|---|---|---|
> | army | club | gang | mob |
> | association | committee | government | posse |
> | band | company | group | team |
> | class | family | jury | union |

PRACTICE

30-7   Circle the collective noun antecedent in each of the following sentences. Then, circle the correct pronoun in parentheses.

   Example: The (jury) returned with ((its)/their) verdict.

1. The company offers good benefits to (its/their) employees.

2. All five study groups must hand in (its/their) projects by Tuesday.

3. Any government should be concerned about the welfare of (its/their) citizens.

4. Every family has (its/their) share of problems.

5. Even the best teams have (its/their) bad days.

PRACTICE

30-8   Edit the following passage for correct pronoun-antecedent agreement. First, circle the antecedent of each underlined pronoun. Then, cross out any pronoun that does not agree with its antecedent, and write the correct form above it. If the pronoun is correct, write *C* above it.

   Example: Many Americans believe that the (country) is ready for its *(C)* first female president.

(1) The history of woman suffrage in the United States shows that women were determined to achieve her equal rights. (2) Before 1920, most American women were not allowed to vote for the candidates they preferred. (3) However, in the mid-1800s, women began to demand her right to vote—or "woman suffrage." (4) Supporters of woman suffrage believed that everyone, regardless of their gender, should be able to vote. (5) At the first woman suffrage convention, Elizabeth Cady Stanton and Lucretia Mott gave speeches explaining his or her views. (6) The first state to per-

mit women to vote was Wyoming, and soon other states became more friendly to her cause. (7) Many women participated in marches, where he or she carried banners and posters for their cause. (8) Finally, in 1919, the House of Representatives and the states gave its approval to the Nineteenth Amendment, which gave American women the right to vote.

30f   Vague and Unnecessary Pronouns

Vague and unnecessary pronouns clutter up your writing and make it hard to understand. Eliminating them will make your writing clearer and easier for readers to follow.

Vague Pronouns

A pronoun should always refer to a specific antecedent. When a pronoun—such as *they* or *it*—has no antecedent, readers will be confused.

VAGUE PRONOUN	On the news, they said baseball players would strike. (Who said baseball players would strike?)
VAGUE PRONOUN	It says in today's paper that our schools are overcrowded. (Who says schools are overcrowded?)

If a pronoun does not refer to a specific word in the sentence, replace the pronoun with a noun.

REVISED	On the news, the sportscaster said baseball players would strike.
REVISED	An editorial in today's paper says that our schools are overcrowded.

Unnecessary Pronouns

When a pronoun comes directly after its antecedent, it is unnecessary.

UNNECESSARY PRONOUN	The librarian, he told me I should check the database.

In this sentence, the pronoun *he* serves no purpose. Readers do not need to be directed back to the pronoun's antecedent (the noun *librarian*) because it appears right before the pronoun. The pronoun should therefore be deleted.

REVISED	The librarian told me I should check the database.

PRACTICE

30-9   The following sentences contain vague or unnecessary pronouns. Revise each sentence on the line below it.

Example: On their website, they advertised a special offer.

On its website, the Gap advertised a special offer.

1. In Jamaica, they love their spectacular green mountains.

_____

2. My hamster, he loves his exercise wheel.

_____

3. On *Jeopardy!* they have to give the answers in the form of questions.

_____

4. On televisions all over the world, they watched the moon landing.

_____

5. In Sociology 320, they do not use a textbook.

_____

30g   Pronoun Case

A **personal pronoun** refers to a particular person or thing. Personal pronouns change form according to their function in a sentence. Personal
pronouns can be *subjective*, *objective*, or *possessive*.

**macmillanhighered.com
/writingfirst**
Additional Grammar
Exercises > Personal
Pronouns

Personal Pronouns

SUBJECTIVE	OBJECTIVE	POSSESSIVE
I	me	my, mine
he	him	his
she	her	her, hers
it	it	its
we	us	our, ours
you	you	your, yours
they	them	their, theirs
who	whom	whose
whoever	whomever	

Subjective Case

When a pronoun is a subject, it is in the **subjective case**.

Finally, <u>she</u> realized that dreams could come true.

macmillanhighered.com /writingfirst
Additional Grammar
Exercises > Pronoun Case

Objective Case

When a pronoun is an object, it is in the **objective case**.

If Joanna hurries, she can stop <u>him</u>. (The pronoun *him* is the object of the verb *can stop*.)

Professor Miller sent <u>us</u> information about his research. (The pronoun *us* is the object of the verb *sent*.)

Marc threw the ball to <u>them</u>. (The pronoun *them* is the object of the preposition *to*.)

Possessive Case

When a pronoun shows ownership, it is in the **possessive case**.

Hieu took <u>his</u> lunch to the meeting. (The pronoun *his* indicates that the lunch belongs to Hieu.)

Debbie and Kim decided to take <u>their</u> lunches, too. (The pronoun *their* indicates that the lunches belong to Debbie and Kim.)

PRACTICE

30-10 In the following passage, fill in the blank after each pronoun to indicate whether the pronoun is subjective (*S*), objective (*O*), or possessive (*P*).

Example: Famous criminals Bonnie and Clyde committed their _____*P*_____ crimes in broad daylight.

(1) Bonnie Parker and Clyde Barrow are remembered today because they _____ were the first celebrity criminals. (2) With their _____ gang, Bonnie and Clyde robbed a dozen banks as well as many stores and gas stations. (3) In small towns, they _____ terrorized the police. (4) Capturing them _____ seemed impossible. (5) To many Americans, however, their _____ crimes seemed exciting. (6) Because Bonnie was a woman, she _____ was especially fascinating to them _____. (7) During their _____ crimes, Bonnie and Clyde would often carry a camera, take photographs of themselves, and then send them _____ to the newspapers, which were happy to publish them _____. (8) By the time they _____ were killed in an ambush by Texas and Louisiana law officers, Bonnie and Clyde were famous all over the United States.

30h   Special Problems with Pronoun Case

When you are trying to determine which pronoun case to use in a sentence, three kinds of pronouns can cause problems: pronouns in compounds, pronouns in comparisons, and the pronouns *who* and *whom* (or *whoever* and *whomever*).

Pronouns in Compounds

Sometimes a pronoun is linked to a noun or to another pronoun with *and* or *or* to form a **compound**.

> The teacher and I met for an hour.

> He or she can pick up Jenny at school.

To determine whether to use the subjective or objective case for a pronoun in the second part of a compound, follow the same rules that apply for a pronoun that is not part of a compound.

- If the compound is a subject, use the subjective case.

  > Toby and I [not *me*] like jazz.

  > He and I [not *me*] went to the movies.

- If the compound is an object, use the objective case.

  > The school sent my father and me [not *I*] the financial-aid forms.

  > This argument is between Kate and me [not *I*].

FYI

Choosing Pronouns in Compounds

To determine which pronoun case to use in a compound that joins a noun and a pronoun, rewrite the sentence with just the pronoun.

> Toby and [*I* or *me*?] like jazz.
> I like jazz. (not *Me like jazz*)
> Toby and I like jazz.

PRACTICE

30-11   In the following sentences, the underlined pronouns are parts of compounds. Check them for correct subjective or objective case. If the pronoun is incorrect, cross it out, and write the correct form above it. If the pronoun is correct, write *C* above it.

Example: My classmates and I were surprised by the results of a study on listening.

(1) According to a recent study, the average listener remembers only 50 percent of what <u>him</u> or <u>her</u> hears. (2) Two days later, <u>he</u> or <u>she</u> can correctly recall only 25 percent of the total message. (3) My friend Alyssa and <u>me</u> decided to ask our school to sponsor a presentation about listening in the classroom. (4) One point the speaker made was especially helpful to Alyssa and <u>I</u>. (5) We now know that <u>us</u> and the other students in our class each have four times more mental "room" than we need for listening. (6) The presenter taught the other workshop participants and <u>we</u> how to use this extra space. (7) Now, whenever one of our professors pauses to write on the board or take a sip of water, Alyssa and <u>I</u> remember to silently summarize the last point <u>he</u> or <u>she</u> made. (8) Throughout the lecture, we pay attention to the big ideas and overall structure that the professor wants the other students and <u>us</u> to take away. (9) Also, to keep ourselves actively thinking about the topic, we try to predict where the professor will lead our peers and <u>us</u> next.

Pronouns in Comparisons

Sometimes a pronoun appears after the word *than* or *as* in the second part of a **comparison**.

> John is luckier <u>than I</u>.
> The inheritance changed Raymond as much <u>as her</u>.

- If the pronoun is a subject, use the subjective case.

  > John is luckier <u>than I</u> [am].

- If the pronoun is an object, use the objective case.

  > The inheritance changed Raymond as much <u>as</u> [it changed] <u>her</u>.

FYI

Choosing Pronouns in Comparisons

Sometimes the pronoun you use can change your sentence's meaning. For example, if you say, "I like Cheerios more than *he*," you mean that you like Cheerios more than the other person likes them.

> I like Cheerios more than he [does].

If, however, you say, "I like Cheerios more than *him*," you mean that you like Cheerios more than you like the other person.

> I like Cheerios more than [I like] him.

PRACTICE

30-12 Each of the following sentences includes a comparison with a pronoun following the word *than* or *as*. In each blank, write the correct form (subjective or objective) of the pronoun in parentheses. In brackets, add the word or words needed to complete the comparison.

Example: Many people are better poker players than ____*I [am]*____ (I/me).

1. The survey showed that most people like the candidate's wife as much

   as _____ (he/him).

2. No one enjoys shopping more than _____ (she/her).

3. My brother and Aunt Cecile were very close, so her death affected him

   more than _____ (I/me).

4. No two people could have a closer relationship than _____

   (they/them).

5. My neighbor drives better than _____ (I/me).

6. He may be as old as _____ (I/me), but he does not have as much

   work experience.

7. That jacket fits you better than _____ (I/me).

8. The other company had a lower bid than _____ (we/us), but we

   were awarded the contract.

Who and *Whom, Whoever* and *Whomever*

To determine whether to use *who* or *whom* (or *whoever* or *whomever*), you need to know how the pronoun functions within the clause in which it appears.

■ When the pronoun is the subject of the clause, use *who* or *whoever*.

> I wonder <u>who</u> wrote that song. (*Who* is the subject of the clause *who wrote that song.*)

macmillanhighered.com
/writingfirst
Additional Grammar
Exercises > Pronoun Case:
Who/Whom

I will vote for <u>whoever</u> supports the youth center. (*Whoever* is the subject of the clause *whoever supports the youth center.*)

■ When the pronoun is the object of the clause, use *whom* or *whomever*.

<u>Whom</u> do the police suspect? (*Whom* is the direct object of the verb *suspect*.)

I wonder <u>whom</u> the song is about. (*Whom* is the object of the preposition *about* in the clause *whom the song is about*.)

Vote for <u>whomever</u> you prefer. (*Whomever* is the object of the verb *prefer* in the clause *whomever you prefer*.)

FYI

Who and *Whom*

To determine whether to use *who* or *whom*, try substituting another pronoun for *who* or *whom* in the clause. If you can substitute *he* or *she*, use *who*; if you can substitute *him* or *her*, use *whom*.

[Who/Whom] wrote a love song? <u>He</u> wrote a love song.
[Who/Whom] was the song about? The song was about <u>her</u>.

The same test will work for *whoever* and *whomever*.

PRACTICE

30-13   Circle the correct form—*who* or *whom* (or *whoever* or *whomever*)—in parentheses in each sentence.

Example: With (who/whom) did Rob collaborate?

1. The defense team learned (who/whom) was going to testify for the prosecution.

2. (Who/Whom) does she think she can find to be a witness?

3. The runner (who/whom) crosses the finish line first will be the winner.

4. They will argue their case to (whoever/whomever) will listen.

5. It will take time to decide (who/whom) is the record holder.

6. Take these forms to the clerk (who/whom) is at the front desk.

7. We will have to penalize (whoever/whomever) misses the first training session.

8. (Who/Whom) did Kobe take to the prom?

9. We saw the man (who/whom) fired the shots.

10. To (who/whom) am I speaking?

30i Reflexive and Intensive Pronouns

Two special kinds of pronouns, *reflexive pronouns* and *intensive pronouns*, end in *-self* (singular) or *-selves* (plural). Although the functions of the two kinds of pronouns are different, their forms are identical.

macmillanhighered.com /writingfirst
Additional Grammar Exercises > Reflexive Pronouns

Reflexive and Intensive Pronouns

Singular Forms

ANTECEDENT	REFLEXIVE OR INTENSIVE PRONOUN
I	myself
you	yourself
he	himself
she	herself
it	itself

Plural Forms

ANTECEDENT	REFLEXIVE OR INTENSIVE PRONOUN
we	ourselves
you	yourselves
they	themselves

Reflexive Pronouns

Reflexive pronouns indicate that people or things did something to themselves or for themselves.

Rosanna lost herself in the novel.

You need to watch yourself when you mix those solutions.

Mehul and Paul made themselves cold drinks.

Intensive Pronouns

Intensive pronouns always appear directly after their antecedents, and they are used for emphasis.

I myself have had some experience in sales and marketing.

The victim himself collected the reward.

They themselves were uncertain of the significance of their findings.

PRACTICE

30-14 Fill in the correct reflexive or intensive pronoun in each of the following sentences.

Example: The opening act was exciting, but the main attraction ___*itself*___ was boring.

1. My aunt welcomed her visitors and told them to make _____ at home.

2. Migrating birds can direct _____ through clouds, storms, and moonless nights.

3. The First Lady _____ gave a speech at the rally.

4. We all finished the marathon without injuring _____.

5. Even though the government offered help to flood victims, the residents _____ did most of the rebuilding.

6. Sometimes he finds _____ daydreaming in class.

7. The guide warned us to watch _____ on the slippery path.

8. The senators were not happy about committing _____ to vote for lower taxes.

9. She gave _____ a manicure.

10. Although everyone else in my family can sing or play a musical instrument, I _____ am tone-deaf.

TEST · **Revise · Edit · Proofread**

Look back at your response to the Write First prompt on page 423. TEST and revise what you have written. Then, edit and proofread your work, paying special attention to your use of nouns and pronouns.

EDITING PRACTICE

Read the following student essay, which includes noun and pronoun errors. Check for errors in plural noun forms, pronoun case, and pronoun-antecedent agreement. Then, make any editing changes you think are necessary. The first sentence has been edited for you.

Cell-Phone Misbehavior

Good ~~manneres~~ *manners* used to mean using the right fork and holding the door open for others. Today, however, people may find that good manners are more complicated than it used to be. Cell phones, in particular, have created some challenges.

One problem is the "cell yell," which is the tendency of a person to shout while they are using their cell phones. Why do they do this? Maybe they do not realize how loudly they are talking. Maybe they yell out of frustration. Anyone can become angry when they lose a call. Dead batterys can be infuriating. Unfortunately, the yeller annoys everyone around them.

Even if cell-phone users theirselves speak normally, other people can hear them. My friends and me are always calling each other, and we do not always pay attention to whom can hear us. The result is that other people are victims of "secondhand conversations." These conversations are not as bad for people's health as secondhand smoke, but it is just as annoying. Whom really wants to hear about the private lifes of strangers? Restrooms used to be private; now, whomever is in the next stall can overhear someone's private cell-phone conversation and learn their secrets.

Also, some cell-phone user seem to think that getting his calls is more important than anything else that might be going on. Phones ring, chirp, or play silly tunes at concertes, in classrooms, at weddings, in churchs, and even at funerals. Can you picture a grieving family at a cemetery having their service interrupted by a ringing phone? People should have enough sense to turn off his or her cell phones at times like these.

In the United States, there are more than 150 million cell phones. Some people hate being tied to cell phones, but they do not think they can live without it. The problem is that cell phones became popular before there were any rules for its use. However, even if the government passed laws about cell-phone behavior, they would have a tough time enforcing it. In any case, cell-phone users should not need laws to make them behave theirself.

COLLABORATIVE ACTIVITY

Working in a group, fill in the following chart, writing one noun on each line. If the noun is a proper noun, be sure to capitalize it.

CARS	TREES	FOODS	FAMOUS COUPLES	CITIES
____	____	____	____	____
____	____	____	____	____
____	____	____	____	____
____	____	____	____	____
____	____	____	____	____
____	____	____	____	____
____	____	____	____	____

Now, using as many of the nouns listed in the chart as you can, write a one-paragraph news article that describes an imaginary event. Exchange your work with another group, and check the other group's article to be sure the correct pronoun refers to each noun. Return the article to its original group for editing.

review checklist

Nouns and Pronouns

macmillanhighered.com /writingfirst
LearningCurve > Nouns and Pronouns

☐ A noun is a word that names something. A singular noun names one thing; a plural noun names more than one thing. (See 30a.)

☐ Most nouns add -s or -es to form plurals. Some nouns have irregular plural forms. (See 30b.)

☐ A pronoun is a word that refers to and takes the place of a noun or another pronoun. (See 30c.)

☐ The word a pronoun refers to is called the pronoun's antecedent. A pronoun and its antecedent must always agree. (See 30d.)

☐ Compound antecedents connected by *and* are plural and are used with plural pronouns. Compound antecedents connected by *or* may take singular or plural pronouns. (See 30e.)

☐ Most indefinite pronoun antecedents are singular and are used with singular pronouns; some are plural and are used with plural pronouns. (See 30e.)

☐ Collective noun antecedents are singular and are used with singular pronouns. (See 30e.)

☐ A pronoun should always refer to a specific antecedent. (See 30f.)

☐ Personal pronouns can be in the subjective, objective, or possessive case. (See 30g.)

☐ Pronouns present special problems when they are used in compounds and comparisons. The pronouns *who* and *whom* and *whoever* and *whomever* can also cause problems. (See 30h.)

☐ Reflexive and intensive pronouns must agree with their antecedents. (See 30i.)

31 Adjectives and Adverbs

Zuma Press, Inc./Alamy

write first

This picture shows children being homeschooled by their mother. Write a paragraph about the advantages and disadvantages of being educated at home by parents instead of at school by professional teachers.

In this chapter, you will learn to
- understand the difference between adjectives and adverbs (31a)
- identify demonstrative adjectives (31a)
- form comparatives and superlatives of adjectives and adverbs (31b)

PREVIEW

31a Identifying Adjectives and Adverbs

Adjectives and adverbs are words that modify (identify or describe) other words. They help make sentences more specific and more interesting.

An **adjective** answers the question *What kind? Which one?* or *How many?* Adjectives modify nouns or pronouns.

The Turkish city of Istanbul spans two continents. (*Turkish* modifies the noun *city*, and *two* modifies the noun *continents*.)

It is fascinating because of its location and history. (*Fascinating* modifies the pronoun *it*.)

:e: **macmillanhighered.com /writingfirst**
LearningCurve > Verbs, Adjectives, and Adverbs; Additional Grammar Exercises > Identifying Adjectives and Adverbs

FYI

Demonstrative Adjectives

Demonstrative adjectives—*this, that, these,* and *those*—do not describe other words. They simply identify particular nouns.

This and *that* identify singular nouns and pronouns.

This website is much more up-to-date than that one.

These and *those* identify plural nouns.

These words and phrases are French, but those expressions are Creole.

An **adverb** answers the question *How? Why? When? Where?* or *To what extent?* Adverbs modify verbs, adjectives, or other adverbs.

Traffic moved steadily. (*Steadily* modifies the verb *moved*.)

Still, we were quite impatient. (*Quite* modifies the adjective *impatient*.)

Very slowly, we moved into the center lane. (*Very* modifies the adverb *slowly*.)

FYI

Distinguishing Adjectives from Adverbs

Many adverbs are formed when *-ly* is added to an adjective form.

ADJECTIVE	ADVERB
slow	slowly
nice	nicely
quick	quickly
real	really

ADJECTIVE   Let me give you one <u>quick</u> reminder. (*Quick* modifies the noun *reminder*.)

ADVERB   He <u>quickly</u> changed the subject. (*Quickly* modifies the verb *changed*.)

PRACTICE

   In the following sentences, circle the correct form (adjective or adverb) from the choices in parentheses.

Example: Beatles enthusiasts all over the world have formed tribute bands devoted to the (famous/famously) group's music.

(1) To show appreciation for their favorite musicians, tribute bands go to (great/greatly) lengths. (2) Fans who have a (real/really) strong affection for a particular band may decide to play its music and copy its style. (3) Sometimes they form their own groups and have successful careers (simple/simply) performing that band's music. (4) These groups are (usual/usually) called "tribute bands." (5) Most tribute bands are (passionate/passionately) dedicated to reproducing the original group's work. (6) They not only play the group's songs but (careful/carefully) imitate the group's look. (7) They study the band members' facial expressions and body movements and create (exact/exactly) copies of the band's costumes and instruments. (8) Some more (inventive/inventively) tribute bands take the original band's songs and interpret them (different/differently). (9) For example, by performing Beatles songs in the style of Metallica, the tribute band Beatallica has created a (unique/uniquely) sound.

(10) Some people believe such tributes are the (ultimate/ultimately) compliment to the original band; others feel (sure/surely) that tribute bands are just copycats who (serious/seriously) lack imagination.

FYI

Good and *Well*

Be careful not to confuse *good* and *well*. Unlike regular adjectives, whose adverb forms add -*ly*, the adjective *good* is irregular. Its adverb form is *well*.

> ADJECTIVE   Fred Astaire was a good dancer. (*Good* modifies the noun *dancer*.)

> ADVERB   He danced especially well with Ginger Rogers. (*Well* modifies the verb *danced*.)

Always use *well* when you are describing a person's health.

> He really didn't feel well [not *good*] after eating the entire pizza.

macmillanhighered.com /writingfirst
Additional Grammar Exercises > *Good* and *Well*

PRACTICE
31-2

Circle the correct form (*good* or *well*) in the following sentences.

Example: It can be hard for some people to find a (good)/ well) job that they really like.

(1) Some people may not do (good/well) sitting in an office. (2) Instead, they may prefer to find jobs that take advantage of their (good/well) physical condition. (3) Such people might consider becoming smoke jumpers—firefighters who are (good/well) at parachuting from small planes into remote areas to battle forest fires. (4) Smoke jumpers must be able to work (good/well) even without much sleep. (5) They must also handle danger (good/well). (6) They look forward to the (good/well) feeling of saving a forest or someone's home. (7) As they battle fires, surrounded by smoke and fumes, smoke jumpers may not feel very (good/well). (8) Sometimes things go wrong; for example, when their parachutes fail to work (good/well), jumpers may be injured or even killed. (9) Smoke jumpers do not get paid particularly (good/well). (10) However, they are proud of their strength and endurance and feel (good/well) about their work.

31b Comparatives and Superlatives

The **comparative** form of an adjective or adverb compares two people or things. Adjectives and adverbs form the comparative with *-er* or *more*. The **superlative** form of an adjective or adverb compares more than two things. Adjectives and adverbs form the superlative with *-est* or *most*.

ADJECTIVES	This film is <u>dull</u> and <u>predictable</u>.
COMPARATIVE	The film I saw last week was even <u>duller</u> and <u>more predictable</u> than this one.
SUPERLATIVE	The film I saw last night was the <u>dullest</u> and <u>most predictable</u> one I've ever seen.
ADVERBS	For a beginner, Jane did needlepoint <u>skillfully</u>.
COMPARATIVE	After she had watched the demonstration, Jane did needlepoint <u>more skillfully</u> than Rosie.
SUPERLATIVE	Of the twelve beginners, Jane did needlepoint the <u>most skillfully</u>.

macmillanhighered.com
/writingfirst
Additional Grammar
Exercises > Comparatives and
Superlatives

Forming Comparatives and Superlatives

Adjectives

■ One-syllable adjectives generally form the comparative with *-er* and the superlative with *-est*.

great   greater   greatest

■ Adjectives with two or more syllables form the comparative with *more* and the superlative with *most*.

wonderful   more wonderful   most wonderful

Exception: Two-syllable adjectives ending in *-y* add *-er* or *-est* after changing the *y* to an *i*.

funny   funnier   funniest

Adverbs

■ All adverbs ending in *-ly* form the comparative with *more* and the superlative with *most*.

efficiently   more efficiently   most efficiently

■ Some other adverbs form the comparative with *-er* and the superlative with *-est*.

soon   sooner   soonest

Solving Special Problems with Comparatives and Superlatives

The following rules will help you avoid errors with comparatives and superlatives.

- Never use both *-er* and *more* to form the comparative or both *-est* and *most* to form the superlative.

    Nothing could have been <u>more awful</u>. (not *more awfuller*)

    Space Mountain is the <u>most frightening</u> (not *most frighteningest*) ride at Disney World.

- Never use the superlative when you are comparing only two things.

    This is the <u>more serious</u> (not *most serious*) of the two problems.

- Never use the comparative when you are comparing more than two things.

    This is the <u>worst</u> (not *worse*) day of my life.

PRACTICE

31-3 Fill in the correct comparative form of the word supplied in parentheses.

Example: Children tend to be _____*noisier*_____ (noisy) than adults.

1. Traffic always moves _____ (slowly) during rush hour than late at night.

2. The weather report says temperatures will be _____ (cold) tomorrow.

3. Some elderly people are _____ (healthy) than younger people.

4. It has been proven that pigs are _____ (intelligent) than dogs.

5. When someone asks you to repeat yourself, you usually answer _____ (loudly).

6. The _____ (tall) of the two buildings was damaged by the earthquake.

7. They want to teach their son to be _____ (respectful) of women than many young men are.

8. Las Vegas is _____ (famous) for its casinos than for its natural resources.

9. The WaterDrop is _____ (wild) than any other ride in the amusement park.

10. You must move _____ (quickly) if you expect to catch the ball.

PRACTICE

31-4 Fill in the correct superlative form of the word supplied in parentheses.

Example: The first remote controls came with only the

most expensive (expensive) televisions.

(1) The invention of the remote control in the 1950s was one of the _____ (important) moments in television history. (2) The remote was especially welcomed by lazy viewers, who were the _____ (empowered) by the new device. (3) Even the _____ (lazy) people could now change channels without getting off the couch. (4) However, as remote controls developed, even the _____ (simple) devices could sometimes confuse the _____ (skilled) users. (5) The large number of buttons became one of the _____ (irritating) features. (6) Even today, remotes remain one of the _____ (unnecessarily) complicated electronic devices. (7) According to one critic, the TV remote is one of the _____ (poorly) designed inventions of all time. (8) Improving the remote is one of the _____ (challenging) projects for inventors. (9) Already, the _____ (innovative) companies are adding voice and motion control to the _____ (late) remotes. (10) One of the _____ (astonishing) possible new developments may be a remote control operated entirely by the viewer's mind.

FYI

Good/Well and *Bad/Badly*

Most adjectives and adverbs form the comparative with *-er* or *more* and the superlative with *-est* or *most*. The adjectives *good* and *bad* and their adverb forms *well* and *badly* are exceptions.

ADJECTIVE	COMPARATIVE FORM	SUPERLATIVE FORM
good	better	best
bad	worse	worst

ADVERB	COMPARATIVE FORM	SUPERLATIVE FORM
well	better	best
badly	worse	worst

ⓔ macmillanhighered.com /writingfirst
Additional Grammar Exercises > *Good/Well* and *Bad/Badly*

PRACTICE

31-5   Fill in the correct comparative or superlative form of *good*, *well*, *bad*, or *badly*.

Example: My sister is a ___*better*___ (good) runner than I am.

1. Neela was certain she was the _____ (good) chef in the competition.

2. Because he studied more, Helio earned _____ (good) grades than his sister.

3. An optimist, Mara always thinks she will do _____ (well) next time.

4. Many people drive the _____ (badly) when they are in a hurry.

5. Of all the mortgage companies Ramon researched, Plains Bank had the _____ (good) interest rate.

6. I feel bad when I get rejected, but I feel _____ (bad) when I do not try.

7. For nontraditional students, access to education is _____ (good) than it used to be.

8. Jamie sings badly, but Simon sings _____ (badly).

9. I learn the _____ (well) when I am not distracted.

10. After looking at every painting in the gallery, they decided that the landscapes were definitely the _____ (bad) paintings there.

TEST · Revise · Edit · Proofread

Look back at your response to the Write First prompt on page 446. TEST and revise what you have written. Then, edit and proofread your work, paying special attention to your use of adjectives and adverbs.

EDITING PRACTICE

Read the following student essay, which includes errors in the use of adjectives and adverbs. Make any changes necessary to correct adjectives incorrectly used for adverbs and adverbs incorrectly used for adjectives. Also, correct any errors in the use of comparatives and superlatives and in the use of demonstrative adjectives. Finally, try to add some adjectives and adverbs that you feel would make the writer's ideas clearer or more specific. The first sentence has been edited for you.

Starting Over

A wedding can be the ~~joyfullest~~ *most joyful* occasion in two people's lives, the beginning of a couple's ~~most~~ happiest years. For some unlucky women, however, a wedding can be the worse thing that ever happens; it is the beginning not of their happiness but of their battered lives. As I went through the joyful day of my wedding, I wanted bad to find happiness for the rest of my life, but what I hoped and wished for did not come true.

I was married in the savannah belt of the Sudan in the eastern part of Africa, where I grew up. I was barely twenty-two years old. The first two years of my marriage progressed peaceful, but problems started as soon as our first child was born.

Many American women say, "If my husband hit me just once, that would be it. I'd leave." But those attitude does not work in cultures in which tradition has overshadowed women's rights and divorce is not accepted. All women can do is accept their sadly fate. Battered women give many reasons for staying in their marriages, but fear is the commonest. Fear immobilizes these women, ruling their decisions, their actions, and their very lives. This is how it was for me.

Of course, I was real afraid whenever my husband hit me. I would run to my mother's house and cry, but she would always talk me into going back and being more patiently with my husband. Our tradition discourages divorce, and wife beating is taken for granted. The situation is really quite ironic: the religion I practice sets harsh punishments for abusive husbands, but tradition has so overpowered religion that the laws do not work very good.

One night, I asked myself whether life had treated me fair. True, I had a high school diploma and two of the beautifullest children in the world, but all this was not enough. I realized that to stand up to the husband who treated me so bad, I would have to achieve a more better education than he had. That night, I decided to get a college education in the United States. My husband opposed my decision, but with the support of my father and mother, I was able to begin to change my life. My years as a student and single parent in the United States have been real difficult for me, but I know I made the right choice.

COLLABORATIVE ACTIVITY

Working in a small group, write a plot summary for an imaginary film. Begin with one of the following three sentences.

- Dirk and Clive were sworn enemies, but that night on Boulder Ridge they vowed to work together just this once, for the good of their country.
- Genevieve entered the room in a cloud of perfume, and when she spoke, her voice was like velvet.
- The desert sun beat down on her head, but Susanna was determined to protect what was hers, no matter what the cost.

Now, exchange summaries with another group, and add as many adjectives and adverbs as you can to the other group's summary. Finally, reread your own group's plot summary, and edit it carefully, paying special attention to the way adjectives and adverbs are used.

review checklist

Adjectives and Adverbs

- [ ] Adjectives modify nouns or pronouns. (See 31a.)
- [ ] Demonstrative adjectives—*this, that, these,* and *those*—identify particular nouns. (See 31a.)
- [ ] Adverbs modify verbs, adjectives, or other adverbs. (See 31a.)
- [ ] To compare two people or things, use the comparative form of an adjective or adverb. To compare more than two people or things, use the superlative form of an adjective or adverb. (See 31b.)
- [ ] The adjectives *good* and *bad* and their adverb forms *well* and *badly* have irregular comparative and superlative forms. (See 31b.)

e macmillanhighered.com /writingfirst
LearningCurve > Verbs, Adjectives, and Adverbs

32 Grammar and Usage for ESL Writers

Christie's Images/Superstock

write first

This painting by Frederick Childe Hassam shows American flags displayed on the Fourth of July, Independence Day. Using the present tense, write a paragraph explaining how you and your family celebrate this holiday or any other holiday that is important to you.

In this chapter, you will learn to

- understand how subjects are used in sentences (32a)
- understand (32b) and use determiners with count and noncount nouns (32c)
- understand articles (32d)
- form negative statements and questions (32e)
- indicate verb tense (32f)
- recognize stative verbs (32g)
- understand gerunds (32h)
- choose correct prepositions (32i)
- use prepositions in phrasal verbs (32j)

32a Subjects in Sentences

e macmillanhighered.com
/writingfirst
LearningCurve > Multilingual
Writers: Sentence Structure;
Additional Grammar Exercises >
Special Problems with
Subjects

English requires that every sentence state its subject. Every independent clause and every dependent clause must also have a subject.

INCORRECT Elvis Presley was only forty-two years old when died. (When who died?)

CORRECT Elvis Presley was only forty-two years old when he died.

When the real subject follows the verb and the normal subject position before the verb is empty, it must be filled by a "dummy" subject, such as *it* or *there*.

INCORRECT Is hot in this room.

CORRECT It is hot in this room.

INCORRECT Are many rivers in my country.

CORRECT There are many rivers in my country.

Standard English also does not permit a two-part subject in which the second part of the subject is a pronoun referring to the same person or thing as the first part.

INCORRECT The Caspian Sea it is the largest lake in the world.

CORRECT The Caspian Sea is the largest lake in the world.

PRACTICE

32-1 Each of the following sentences is missing a subject. On the lines provided, rewrite each sentence, adding an appropriate subject. Then, underline the subject you have added.

Example: Because college students often have very little money, are always looking for inexpensive meals.

Because college students often have very little money, they are always looking

for inexpensive meals.

1. Ramen noodles are a popular choice for students because are cheap, tasty, and easy to prepare.

   _____

   _____

2. In minutes, a student can enjoy hot noodles flavored with chicken, shrimp, or beef, and sell vegetarian versions, too.

   _____

   _____

3. Although high in carbohydrates (a good source of energy), also contain saturated and trans fats and few vitamins or minerals.

   _____

   _____

4. Ramen noodles are not just popular with American college students; are also popular in upscale restaurants and in many other countries around the world.

   _____

   _____

5. The noodles have even found their way to the International Space Station, where enjoy them in space.

   _____

   _____

PRACTICE

32-2 The following sentences contain unnecessary two-part subjects. Cross out the unnecessary pronoun. Then, rewrite each sentence correctly on the lines provided.

Example: Travelers to China ~~they~~ often visit the Great Wall.

Travelers to China often visit the Great Wall.

1. The first parts of the Great Wall they were built around AD 200.

   _____

   _____

2. The Great Wall it was built to keep out invading armies.

   _____

   _____

3. The sides of the Great Wall they are made of stone, brick, and earth.

_____

_____

4. The top of the Great Wall it is paved with bricks, forming a roadway for horses.

_____

_____

5. The Great Wall it is so huge that it can be seen by astronauts in space.

_____

_____

32b Count and Noncount Nouns

macmillanhighered.com /writingfirst
LearningCurve > Multilingual Writers: Articles and Nouns; Additional Grammar Exercises > Count and Noncount Nouns

A **count noun** names one particular thing or a group of particular things that can be counted: *a teacher, a panther, a bed, an ocean, a cloud, an ice cube*; *two teachers, many panthers, three beds, two oceans, several clouds, some ice cubes*. A **noncount noun** names things that cannot be counted: *gold, cream, sand, blood, smoke, water*.

Count nouns usually have a singular form and a plural form: *cube, cubes*. Noncount nouns usually have only a singular form: *water*. Note how the nouns *cube* and *water* differ in the way they are used in sentences.

CORRECT   The glass is full of ice cubes.

CORRECT   The glass is full of water.

INCORRECT   The glass is full of waters.

CORRECT   The glass contains five ice cubes.

CORRECT   The glass contains some water.

INCORRECT   The glass contains five waters.

Often, the same idea can be expressed with either a count noun or a noncount noun.

COUNT	NONCOUNT
people (plural of *person*)	humanity [*not* humanities]
tables, chairs, beds	furniture [*not* furnitures]
letters	mail [*not* mails]
supplies	equipment [*not* equipments]
facts	information [*not* informations]
guns	ammunition [*not* ammunitions]

Some words can be either count or noncount, depending on the meaning intended.

COUNT He had many interesting <u>experiences</u> at his first job.

NONCOUNT It is often difficult to get a job if you do not have <u>experience</u>.

FYI

Guidelines for Using Count and Noncount Nouns

■ Use a count noun to refer to a living animal, but use a noncount noun to refer to the food that comes from that animal.

COUNT There are three live lobsters in the tank.

NONCOUNT This restaurant specializes in lobster.

■ If you use a noncount noun for a substance or class of things that can come in different varieties, you can often make that noun plural if you want to talk about those varieties.

NONCOUNT Cheese is a rich source of calcium.

COUNT Many different cheeses come from Italy.

■ If you want to shift attention from a concept in general to specific examples of it, you can often use a noncount noun as a count noun.

NONCOUNT You have a great deal of talent.

COUNT My talents do not include singing.

PRACTICE

32-3 In each of the following sentences, decide if the underlined word is being used as a count or a noncount noun. If it is being used as a noncount noun, circle the *N* following the sentence. If it is being used as a count noun, circle the *C*.

Examples: As a Peace Corps <u>volunteer</u> in Ecuador, Dave Schweidenback realized how important bicycles could be.   N Ⓒ

Using his <u>imagination</u>, Dave figured out an effective way to recycle America's unwanted bicycles. Ⓝ C

1. Pedals for Progress is an American nonprofit <u>organization</u>. N C

2. Founded in 1991 by Dave Schweidenback, the <u>group</u> collects and re-pairs old bicycles and sends them to countries where they are needed.   N   C

3. Pedals for Progress aims to reduce the amount of bicycle <u>waste</u> that ends up in American landfills.   N   C

4. People in the United States throw away millions of bikes and bike parts every <u>year</u>.   N   C

5. At the same time, lack of <u>transportation</u> is a serious problem for many people in developing countries.   N   C

6. Without an efficient and affordable way to get to work, a person can-not hold a <u>job</u>.   N   C

7. A working bicycle provides an easy and environmentally friendly <u>way</u> to get around.   N   C

8. Bicycles from Pedals for Progress cost the user only a small amount of <u>money</u>.   N   C

9. To help maintain these recycled bikes, the organization also helps to establish local repair <u>shops</u>.   N   C

10. By making it easier for people to work, Pedals for Progress hopes to reduce <u>poverty</u>.   N   C

32c Determiners with Count and Noncount Nouns

Determiners are adjectives that *identify* rather than describe the nouns they modify. Determiners may also *quantify* nouns (that is, indicate an amount or a number).

Determiners include the following words.

macmillanhighered.com /writingfirst
LearningCurve > Multilingual Writers: Articles and Nouns; Additional Grammar Exercises > Determiners with Count and Noncount Nouns

- Articles: *a, an, the*
- Demonstrative adjectives: *this, these, that, those*
- Possessive adjectives: *my, our, your, his, her, its, their*
- Possessive nouns: *Sheila's, my friend's,* and so on
- *Whose, which, what*
- *All, both, each, every, some, any, either, no, neither, many, most, much, a few, a little, few, little, several, enough*
- All numerals: *one, two,* and so on

When a determiner is accompanied by one or more other adjectives, the determiner always comes first. For example, in the phrase *my expensive new digital watch*, *my* is a determiner; you cannot put *expensive, new, digital*, or any other adjective before *my*.

A singular count noun must always be accompanied by a determiner—for example, *my watch* or *the new digital watch*, not just *watch* or *new digital watch*. However, noncount nouns and plural count nouns sometimes have determiners but sometimes do not. *This honey is sweet* and *Honey is sweet* are both acceptable, as are *These berries are juicy* and *Berries are juicy*. (In each case, the meaning is different.) You cannot say *Berry is juicy*, however; say instead *This berry is juicy*, *Every berry is juicy*, or *A berry is juicy*.

FYI

Determiners

Some determiners can be used only with certain types of nouns.

- *This* and *that* can be used only with singular nouns (count or noncount): *this berry, that honey*.

- *These, those, a few, few, many, both*, and *several* can be used only with plural count nouns: *these berries, those apples, a few ideas, few people, many students, both sides, several directions*.

- *Much, little*, and *a little* can be used only with noncount nouns: *much affection, little time, a little honey*.

- *Some, enough, all*, and *most* can be used only with noncount or plural count nouns: *some honey, some berries; enough trouble, enough problems; all traffic, all roads; most money, most coins*.

- *A, an, every, each, either*, and *neither* can be used only with singular count nouns: *a berry, an elephant, every possibility, each citizen, either option, neither candidate*.

PRACTICE

32-4 In each of the following sentences, circle the more appropriate choice from each pair of words or phrases in parentheses.

Examples: Volcanoes are among the most destructive of (all/every) natural forces on earth.

People have always been fascinated and terrified by (this/these) force of nature.

1. Not (all/every) volcano is considered a danger.

2. In (major some/some major) volcanic eruptions, huge clouds rise over the mountain.

3. In 2010, ash from a volcano in Iceland caused (many/much) disruption for airline passengers throughout Europe.

4. (A few violent/Violent a few) eruptions are so dramatic that they blow the mountain apart.

5. (Most/Much) volcanic eruptions cannot be predicted.

6. Since the 1400s, (many/much) people—almost 200,000—have lost their lives in volcanic eruptions.

7. When a volcano erupts, (little/a little) can be done to prevent property damage.

8. By the time people realize an eruption is about to take place, there is rarely (many/enough) time to escape.

9. Volcanoes can be dangerous, but they also produce (a little/some) benefits.

10. For example, (a few/a little) countries use energy from underground steam in volcanic areas to produce electric power.

32d Articles

The **definite article** *the* and the **indefinite articles** *a* and *an* are determiners that tell readers whether the noun that follows is one they can identify (*the book*) or one they cannot yet identify (*a book*).

macmillanhighered.com
/writingfirst
LearningCurve > Multilingual
Writers: Articles and Nouns;
Additional Grammar
Exercises > Articles

The Definite Article

When the definite article *the* is used with a noun, the writer is saying to readers, "You can identify which particular thing or things I have in mind. The information you need to make that identification is available to you. Either you have it already, or I am about to give it to you."

Readers can find the necessary information in the following ways.

■ By looking at other information in the sentence

   Meet me at <u>the</u> corner of Main Street and Lafayette Road.

In this example, *the* is used with the noun *corner* because other words in the sentence tell readers which particular corner the writer has in mind: the one located at Main and Lafayette.

■ By looking at information in other sentences

> Aisha ordered a slice of pie and a cup of coffee. <u>The</u> pie was delicious. She asked for a second slice.

Here, *the* is used before the word *pie* in the second sentence to indicate that it is the same pie identified in the first sentence. Notice, however, that the noun *slice* in the third sentence is preceded by an indefinite article (*a*) because it is not the same slice referred to in the first sentence.

■ By drawing on general knowledge

> <u>The</u> earth revolves around <u>the</u> sun.

Here, *the* is used with the nouns *earth* and *sun* because readers are expected to know which particular things the writer is referring to.

FYI

The Definite Article

Always use *the* (rather than *a* or *an*) in the following situations.

- ■ Before the word *same*: *the same day*
- ■ Before the superlative form of an adjective: *the youngest son*
- ■ Before a number indicating order or sequence: *the third time*

Indefinite Articles

When an indefinite article is used with a noun, the writer is saying to readers, "I don't expect you to have enough information right now to identify a particular thing that I have in mind. I do, however, expect you to recognize that I'm referring to only one item."

Consider the following sentences.

> We need <u>a</u> table for our computer.

> I have <u>a</u> folding table; maybe you can use that.

In the first sentence, the writer is referring to a hypothetical table, not an actual one. Because the table is indefinite to the writer, it is clearly indefinite to the reader, so *a* is used, not *the*. The second sentence refers to an actual table, but because the writer does not expect the reader to be able to identify the table specifically, it is also used with *a* rather than *the*.

WORD POWER

hypothetical
assumed or supposed; not supported by evidence

FYI

Indefinite Articles

Unlike the definite article (*the*), the indefinite articles *a* and *an* occur only with singular count nouns. *A* is used when the next sound is a consonant, and *an* is used when the next sound is a vowel. In choosing *a* or *an*, pay attention to sound rather than to spelling: *a house*, *a year*, *a union*, but *an hour*, *an uncle*.

No Article

Only noncount and plural count nouns can stand without articles: *butter*, *chocolate*, *cookies*, *strawberries* (but *a cookie* or *the strawberry*).

Nouns without articles can be used to make generalizations.

<u>Infants</u> need <u>affection</u> as well as <u>food</u>.

Here, the absence of articles before the nouns *infants*, *affection*, and *food* indicates that the statement is not about particular infants, affection, or food but about infants, affection, and food in general. Remember not to use *the* in such sentences; in English, a sentence like *The infants need affection as well as food* can only refer to particular, identifiable infants, not to infants in general.

Articles with Proper Nouns

Proper nouns can be divided into two classes: names that take *the* and names that take no article.

- Names of people usually take no article unless they are used in the plural to refer to members of a family, in which case they take *the*: *Napoleon, Mahatma Gandhi* (but *the Parkers*).
- Names of places that are plural in form usually take *the*: *the Andes, the United States*.
- The names of most places on land (cities, states, provinces, and countries) take no article: *Salt Lake City, Mississippi, Alberta, Japan*. The names of most bodies of water (rivers, seas, and oceans, although not lakes or bays) take *the*: *the Mississippi, the Mediterranean, the Pacific* (but *Lake Erie, San Francisco Bay*).
- Names of streets take no article: *Main Street*. Names of unnumbered highways take *the*: *the Belt Parkway*.

PRACTICE

32-5 In the following passage, decide whether each blank needs a definite article (*the*), an indefinite article (*a* or *an*), or no article. If a definite or an indefinite article is needed, write it in the space provided. If no article is needed, leave the space blank.

Example: A sundial can be _____*an*_____ attractive addition to _____ backyard gardens.

(1) Sundials take many forms, and they have come _____ long way from their origins. (2) Today's backyard sundials usually feature _____ small, circular table with _____ triangular fin that casts _____ shadow. (3) Two hundred years ago, however, _____ most popular sundials were small enough to be carried in _____ pocket. (4) Even though _____ first watch was made in 1504, pocket sundials were used instead of _____ watches until _____ 1800s.

(5) It took watchmakers centuries to get _____ tiny parts inside _____ watch to run smoothly. (6) For this reason, _____ rich European during _____ Renaissance might have bought _____ watch as _____ fancy toy but used _____ pocket sundial to tell time. (7) Pocket sundials are certainly _____ thing of _____ past, but larger sundials continue to be built for _____ variety of purposes. (8) _____ large sundial is often much more than _____ attractive decoration for _____ garden. (9) It might be _____ sophisticated timekeeper, _____ architectural wonder, or _____ symbol. (10) For example, at _____ Jantar Mantar observatory in Jaipur, India, _____ three-hundred-year-old disk dial tells time as accurately as _____ cell phone equipped with GPS. (11) At _____ university in Hong Kong, _____ red, flame-shaped sundial is a startling sculpture for _____ main entrance to its campus. (12) In California, _____ bridge that spans _____ Sacramento River is held up by _____ enormous sundial.

macmillanhighered.com
/writingfirst
LearningCurve > Multilingual
Writers: Verbs; Additional
Grammar Exercises > Negative
Statements

32e Negative Statements and Questions

Negative Statements

To form a negative statement, add the word *not* directly after the first helping verb of the complete verb.

> Global warming has been getting worse.
> Global warming has <u>not</u> been getting worse.

When there is no helping verb, a form of the verb *do* must be inserted before *not*.

> Automobile traffic contributes to pollution.
> Automobile traffic <u>does not</u> contribute to pollution.

However, if the main verb is *am, is, are, was,* or *were*, do not insert a form of *do* before *not*: *Harry was late. Harry was <u>not</u> late.*

Remember that when *do* is used as a helping verb, the form of *do* used must match the tense and number of the original main verb. Note that in the negative statement, the main verb loses its tense and appears in the base form (*contribute*, not *contributes*).

Questions

To form a question, move the helping verb that follows the subject to the position directly before the subject.

> The governor <u>is</u> trying to compromise.
>
> <u>Is</u> the governor trying to compromise?
>
> The governor <u>is</u> working on the budget.
>
> <u>Is</u> the governor working on the budget?

The same rule applies even when the verb is in the past or future tense.

e macmillanhighered.com
/writingfirst
Additional Grammar
Exercises > Questions

> The governor <u>was</u> trying to lower state taxes.
>
> <u>Was</u> the governor trying to lower state taxes?
>
> The governor <u>will</u> try to get reelected.
>
> <u>Will</u> the governor try to get reelected?

As with negatives, when the verb does not include a helping verb, you must supply a form of *do*. To form a question, put the correct form of *do* directly before the subject.

> The governor <u>works</u> hard.
>
> <u>Does</u> the governor <u>work</u> hard?
>
> The governor <u>improved</u> life in his state.
>
> <u>Did</u> the governor <u>improve</u> life in his state?

However, if the main verb is *am, is, are, was,* or *were,* do not insert a form of *do* before the verb. Instead, move the main verb to precede the subject: *Harry was late. <u>Was</u> Harry late?*

Note: The helping verb never comes before the subject if the subject is a question word, such as *who* or *which.*

> <u>Who</u> is talking to the governor?
>
> <u>Which</u> bills have been vetoed by the governor?

PRACTICE

32-6 Rewrite each of the following sentences in two ways: first, turn the sentence into a question; then, rewrite the original sentence as a negative statement.

Example: Her newest album is selling as well as her first one.

Question: <u>Is her newest album selling as well as her first one?</u>

Negative statement: <u>Her newest album is not selling as well as her first one.</u>

1. Converting metric measurements to the system used in the United States is difficult.

Question: _____

_____

Negative statement: _____

_____

2. That family was very influential in the early 1900s.

Question: _____

_____

Negative statement: _____

_____

3. Most great artists are successful during their lifetimes.

Question: _____

_____

Negative statement: _____

_____

4. American cities are as dangerous as they were thirty years ago.

Question: _____

_____

Negative statement: _____

_____

5. Segregation in the American South ended with the Civil War.

Question: _____

_____

Negative statement: _____

_____

32f Verb Tense

In English, a verb's form must indicate when an action took place (for instance, in the past or in the present). Always use the appropriate tense of the verb—even if the time is obvious or if the sentence includes other indications of time (such as *two years ago* or *at present*).

INCORRECT Albert Einstein emigrate from Germany in 1933.

CORRECT Albert Einstein emigrated from Germany in 1933.

32g Stative Verbs

macmillanhighered.com
/writingfirst
LearningCurve > Multilingual
Writers: Verbs; Additional
Grammar Exercises > Stative
Verbs

Stative verbs usually tell that someone or something is in a state that will not change, at least for a while.

> Hiro <u>knows</u> American history very well.

Most English verbs show action, and these action verbs can be used in the progressive tenses. The **present progressive** tense consists of the present tense of *be* plus the present participle (*I am going*). The **past progressive** tense consists of the past tense of *be* plus the present participle (*I was going*). Unlike most verbs, however, stative verbs are rarely used in the progressive tenses.

> INCORRECT Hiro is knowing American history very well.

> CORRECT Hiro knows American history very well.

FYI

Stative Verbs

Verbs that are stative—such as *know, understand, think, believe, want, like, love,* and *hate*—often refer to mental states. Other stative verbs include *be, have, need, own, belong, weigh, cost,* and *mean*. Certain verbs of sense perception, like *see* and *hear*, are also stative (even though they can refer to momentary events as well as to unchanging states).

Many verbs have more than one meaning, and some of these verbs are active with one meaning but stative with another. An example is the verb *weigh*.

> ACTIVE The butcher <u>weighs</u> the meat.

> STATIVE The meat <u>weighs</u> three pounds.

In the first sentence, the verb *weigh* means "to put on a scale"; it is active, not stative. In the second sentence, however, the same verb means "to have weight," so it is stative, not active. It would be unacceptable to say "The meat is weighing three pounds," but "The butcher is weighing the meat" would be correct.

PRACTICE

32-7 In each of the following sentences, circle the verb or verbs. Then, correct any problems with stative verbs by crossing out the incorrect verb tense and writing the correct verb tense above the line. If the verb is correct, write *C* above it.

> **Example:** Police officers ~~are knowing~~ *know* that fingerprint identification *is* one of the best ways to catch criminals.

1. As early as 1750 BC, ancient Babylonians were signing their identities with fingerprints on clay tablets.

2. By AD 220, the Chinese were becoming aware that ink fingerprints could identify people.

3. However, it was not until the late 1800s that anyone was believing that criminal identification was possible with fingerprints.

4. Today, we know that each person is having unique patterns on the tips of his or her fingers.

5. When police study a crime scene, they want to see whether the criminals have left any fingerprint evidence.

6. There is always a layer of oil on the skin, and police are liking to use it to get fingerprints.

7. Crime scene experts are often seeing cases in which the criminals are touching their hair and pick up enough oil to leave a good fingerprint.

8. The police are needing to judge whether the fingerprint evidence has been damaged by sunlight, rain, or heat.

9. In the courtroom, juries often weigh fingerprint evidence before they are deciding on their verdict.

10. The FBI is collecting millions of fingerprints, which police departments can compare with the fingerprints they find at crime scenes.

32h Gerunds

macmillanhighered.com /writingfirst
LearningCurve > Multilingual Writers: Verbs

A **gerund** is a verb form ending in *-ing* that acts as a noun.

<u>Reading</u> the newspaper is one of my favorite things to do on Sundays.

Just like a noun, a gerund can be used as a subject, a direct object, a subject complement, or the object of a preposition.

- A gerund can be a subject.

    Playing tennis is one of my hobbies.

- A gerund can be a direct object.

    My brother influenced my racing.

- A gerund can be a subject complement.

    The most important thing is winning.

- A gerund can be the object of a preposition.

    The teacher rewarded him for passing.

PRACTICE

32-8   To complete the following sentences, fill in the blanks with the gerund form of the verb provided in parentheses.

Example: ___*Typing*___ (type) is a skill that used to be taught in high school.

1. _____ (eat) five or six small meals throughout the day is healthier than eating two or three big meals.

2. The household task I dread the most is _____ (clean).

3. Her parents praised her for _____ (remember) their anniversary.

4. I did not like his _____ (sing).

5. The best way to prepare for the concert is by _____ (practice).

32i   Choosing Prepositions

A **preposition** introduces a noun or pronoun and links it to other words in the sentence. The word the preposition introduces is called the **object** of the preposition.

A preposition and its object combine to form a **prepositional phrase**: *on the table, near the table, under the table*.

    I thought I had left the book on the table or somewhere near the table, but I found it under the table.

The prepositions *at, in,* and *on* sometimes cause problems for non-native speakers of English. For example, to identify the location of a place or an event, you can use *at, in,* or *on.*

- The preposition *at* specifies an exact point in space or time.

    The museum is at 1000 Fifth Avenue. Let's meet there at 10:00 tomorrow morning.

- Expanses of space or time are treated as containers and therefore require *in.*

    Women used to wear long skirts in the early 1900s.

■ *On* must be used in two cases: with names of streets (but not with exact addresses) and with days of the week or month.

> We will move into our new office <u>on</u> 18th Street either <u>on</u> Monday or <u>on</u> March 12.

FYI

Using Prepositions in Familiar Expressions

Below is a list of familiar expressions that have similar meanings. They are often used in the same contexts.

acquainted with/familiar with	interested in/fascinated by
addicted to/hooked on	interfere with/disrupt
angry with (a person)/upset with	meet with/get together with
bored with/tired of	object to/oppose
capable of/able to	pleased with/happy with
consist of/have/contain/include	protect against/guard against
deal with/address (a problem)	reply to/answer
depend on/rely on	responsible for/accountable for
differ from (something else)/be different from	similar to/almost the same as
differ with (someone else)/disagree	succeed in/attain success in
emigrate from/move from (another country)	take advantage of/use an opportunity to
grateful for (a favor)/thankful for	wait for (something to happen)/expect
immigrate to/move to (another country)	wait on (in a restaurant)/serve

**PRACTICE
32-9** In the following paragraph, fill in each blank with the correct preposition.

Example: Like other struggling artists, writers often make a living

working ____*in*____ restaurants and waiting ____*on*____ customers.

(1) Most writers, even those who succeed _____ the literary world,

need day jobs to help pay _____ food and rent. (2) Many _____

them work _____ related fields—for example, _____ bookstores,

_____ publishing houses, or _____ newspapers. (3) Some take ad-

vantage _____ their talents and devote themselves _____ teaching

others _____ language and literature. (4) For example, _____ the

1990s, Harry Potter author J. K. Rowling worked as a teacher _____ Portugal and _____ Britain. (5) _____ the 1960s and 1970s, students _____ Howard University _____ Washington, D.C., could enroll _____ classes taught _____ Nobel Prize winner Toni Morrison. (6) Other writers work _____ fields unrelated _____ writing. (7) For instance, poet William Carlos Williams was a medical doctor who wrote poetry only _____ the evenings. (8) Science fiction writer Isaac Asimov worked _____ Boston University _____ the department _____ biochemistry. (9) Occasionally, an aspiring writer has friends and family who approve _____ his or her goals, and he or she can depend _____ them _____ financial help. (10) However, many family members, wanting to protect young writers _____ poverty, encourage them to focus _____ other goals.

32j   Prepositions in Phrasal Verbs

A **phrasal verb** consists of two words, a verb and a preposition, that are joined to form an idiomatic expression. Many phrasal verbs are **separable**. This means that a direct object can come between the verb and the preposition. However, some phrasal verbs are **inseparable**; that is, the preposition must always come immediately after the verb.

Separable Phrasal Verbs

In many cases, phrasal verbs may be split, with the direct object coming between the two parts of the verb. With these types of phrasal verbs, when the direct object is a noun, the second word of the phrasal verb can come either before or after the object.

In the following sentences, *fill out* is a phrasal verb. Because the object of the verb *fill out* is a noun (*form*), the second word of the verb can come either before or after the verb's object.

> CORRECT   Please fill out the form.

> CORRECT   Please fill the form out.

When the object is a pronoun, however, these phrasal verbs must be split, and the pronoun must come between the two parts of the verb.

> INCORRECT   Please fill out it.

> CORRECT   Please fill it out.

Some Common Separable Phrasal Verbs

ask out	give away	put back	throw away
bring up	hang up	put on	try out
call up	leave out	set aside	turn down
carry out	let out	shut off	turn off
drop off	make up	take down	wake up
fill out	put away	think over	

Remember, when the object of the verb is a pronoun, these phrasal verbs must be split, and the pronoun must come between the two parts (for example, *take it down*, *put it on*, *let it out*, and *make it up*).

Inseparable Phrasal Verbs

Some phrasal verbs, however, cannot be separated; that is, the preposition cannot be separated from the verb. This means that a direct object cannot come between the verb and the preposition.

INCORRECT   Please go the manual over carefully.

CORRECT   Please go over the manual carefully.

Notice that in the correct sentence, the direct object (*manual*) comes right after the preposition (*over*).

Some Common Inseparable Phrasal Verbs

come across	run across	show up
get along	run into	stand by
go over	see to	stay away

PRACTICE

32-10 In each of the following sentences, look closely at the phrasal verb, and decide whether the preposition is placed correctly in the sentence. If it is, write *C* in the blank after the sentence. If the preposition needs to be moved, edit the sentence.

Example: People who live in American suburbs are often surprised to come across wild animals in their neighborhoods. _____ *C* _____

1. Although it is a good idea to stay from bears away, most wild bears are timid. _____

2. When there is a drought, people are more likely to run into bears and other wild animals. _____

3. Bears need to put on weight before the winter, so they may have to find food in suburban garbage cans. _____

4. It is a good idea for families to go their plans over to safeguard their property against bears. _____

5. People should not leave pet food out overnight, or else their dog may find that a hungry bear has eaten its dinner. _____

6. If people have a bird feeder in the yard, they should put away it during the autumn. _____

7. As the human population grows, more and more houses are built in formerly wild areas, so bears and people have to learn to get along with each other. _____

TEST · Revise · Edit · Proofread

Look back at your response to the Write First prompt on page 456. TEST and revise what you have written. Then, edit and proofread your work, paying special attention to the grammar and usage issues discussed in this chapter.

EDITING PRACTICE

Read the following student essay, which includes errors in the use of subjects, nouns, articles and determiners, and stative verbs, as well as errors with prepositions in familiar expressions and phrasal verbs. Check each underlined word or phrase. If it is not used correctly, write in any necessary changes. If the underlined word or phrase is correct, write *C* above it. The title of the essay has been edited for you.

How to Succeed ~~on~~ *in* Multinational Business

Success in multinational business often <u>depends in</u> the ability to understand other countries' cultures. Understanding how cultures <u>differ to</u> our own, however, is only one key to <u>these</u> success. Also, <u>is</u> crucial that businesses learn to adapt to different cultures. <u>The ethnocentrism</u> is the belief that one's own culture has <u>a</u> best way of doing things. In international business, <u>is</u> necessary to set aside this belief. A company cannot <u>be using</u> the same methods or sell the same products overseas as it does at home. Though making these changes requires a lot of work, companies that choose to adjust to new markets are usually <u>happy with</u> their decision.

<u>It is</u> many aspects of a country that must be understood before successful international business can be <u>carried out</u>. To protect itself <u>from</u> legal errors, a company needs to understand the country's legal system, which may be very different from its home country's legal system. <u>May be</u> necessary to get licenses to export products <u>onto</u> other countries. The role of women is also likely to be different; without knowing this, businesspeople might unintentionally offend people. Also, <u>much</u> personal interactions in other countries may give the wrong impression to someone who is inexperienced. For example, in Latin American countries, people <u>are often standing</u> close together and touch each other when they are talking. Americans may feel uncomfortable in such a situation <u>unless understand</u> it.

To <u>succeed in</u> international business, companies <u>are also needing</u> to understand what people buy and why. To avoid problems, a company that wants to sell its product internationally <u>it</u> should do <u>a few</u> market research. For example, when McDonald's opened restaurants <u>on</u> India, <u>realized</u> that beef burgers would not work in a country where many people believe that cows are sacred. Instead, burgers were made from ground chickens. For India's many vegetarians, McDonald's created several different vegetable patties. McDonald's understood that both the religious and the cultural characteristic of India had to be considered if its new restaurants were going to succeed.

Looking to attract new customers in today's international market, companies they are noticing a growing demand for *halal* goods and services. The word *halal* indicates an object or action that is permissible by Islamic law. Businesses are realizing that world's Muslims depend in companies to provide acceptable *halal* foods, banks, hotels, magazines, and other services. Nestlé, Kentucky Fried Chicken, Subway, LG, and Nokia are just a few of the well-known companies that have been successfully remaking their products to appeal in Muslim consumers. Because these high-quality items also appeal to non-Muslims, many of this companies are discovering that meeting cultural needs and desires are simply good business.

Over time, the marketplace is becoming more global. In those setting, individuals from numerous cultures come together. To take advantage from opportunities and perform effectively, an international company must hire people with the right experiences. To deal with other cultures, multinational companies inside today's global market must have good informations and show other cultures the highest respects.

COLLABORATIVE ACTIVITY

Working in a small group, make a list of ten prepositional phrases that include the prepositions *above, around, at, between, from, in, on, over, under,* and *with*. Use appropriate nouns as objects of these prepositions, and use as many modifying words as you wish. (Try, for example, to write something like *above their hideous wedding portrait*, not just *above the picture*.) Now, work together to compose a list of ten sentences, each including one of your ten prepositional phrases.

review checklist

Grammar and Usage for ESL Writers

☐ English sentences must state their subjects. (See 32a.)

☐ English nouns may be count nouns or noncount nouns. A count noun names one particular thing or a group of particular things (*a teacher*, *oceans*). A noncount noun names something that cannot be counted (*gold*, *sand*). (See 32b.)

☐ Determiners are adjectives that identify rather than describe the nouns they modify. Determiners may also indicate amount or number. (See 32c.)

☐ The definite article *the* and the indefinite articles *a* and *an* are determiners that indicate whether the noun that follows is one readers can identify (*the book*) or one they cannot yet identify (*a book*). (See 32d.)

☐ To form a negative statement, add the word *not* directly after the first helping verb of the complete verb. To form a question, move the helping verb that follows the subject to the position directly before the subject. (See 32e.)

☐ A verb's form must indicate when an action took place. (See 32f.)

☐ Stative verbs indicate that someone or something is in a state that will not change, at least for a while. Stative verbs are rarely used in the progressive tenses. (See 32g.)

☐ A gerund is a verb form ending in *-ing* that is always used as a noun. (See 32h.)

☐ The prepositions *at*, *in*, and *on* sometimes cause problems for nonnative speakers of English. (See 32i.)

☐ A phrasal verb consists of two words, a verb and a preposition, that are joined to form an idiomatic expression. (See 32j.)

Read the following student essay, which includes errors in the use of verbs, nouns, pronouns, adjectives, and adverbs, as well as ESL errors. Make any changes necessary to correct the basic grammar of the sentences. The first sentence has been edited for you.

The Mystery of the Bermuda Triangle

The Bermuda Triangle is an area in the Atlantic Ocean also ~~know~~ *known* as the Devil's Triangle. Its size, between 500,000 and 1.5 million square miles, depends on who you are believing. Strange events happen there.

During the past century, more than fifty ships and twenty airplanes have disappeared to these area. According to some people, a mysterious force causes ships and planes to vanish in the Bermuda Triangle. Everyone who hears about the mystery has to decide what to believe. However, according to the U.S. Coast Guard, the explanations are not mysterious.

The stories about odd these occurrences they may have started as early as 1492. When Columbus sailed through the area, him and his crew seen unusual lights in the sky. In addition, his compass reacted strangely. Now is believed that the lights came from a meteor that crashed into the ocean. The peculiar compass readings were probably cause from the fact that in this area, magnetic compasses point toward true north rather than magnetic north. These variation can cause navigators to sail off course.

The modern Bermuda Triangle legend started in 1945, when Flight 19, compose of five U.S. Navy Avenger torpedo bombers, disappeared while on a routine training mission. Rescue plane that has been sent to search for them also disappeared. Six aircraft and twenty-seven man vanished. Not only were their lifes lost, but no bodies were ever found. Were a mysterious force responsible? Although the events themselves seem strange, there are several good explanation. First, all the crew members except his leader were trainees. It is quite possibly that they flied through a magnetic storm or that the leader's compass was not working. If so, they would have become confused of their location. Radio transmissions were unreliable because of a bad weather and a broken receiver in one of the planes. The crew leader was not functioning very good. The leader told his pilots to head east; he thinked that they were over the Gulf of Mexico. However, they were flying up the Atlantic coastline, so his instructions sent him farther out to sea. If the planes crashed into the ocean at night, it is not likely there would have been any survivors. No wreckage was ever recover.

After Flight 19 disappeared, storys start to appear about the events that have occurred. The odd compass readings, the problems with radio transmissions, and the missing wreckage lead to strange tales. Some people believed that the missing ships and planes were taken by UFOs (unidentified flying objects) to a different dimension. Others thought that those whom disappeared were kidnapped from aliens from other planets. However, there are most logical explanations. The fact that magnetic compasses point toward true north in this area is now well known. It is also well known that the weather patterns in the southern Atlantic and Caribbean is unpredictable. In addition, human error may have been involved. For these reason, the tales of the Bermuda Triangle are clearly science fiction, not fact.

33 Using Commas

Mario Tama/Getty Images & Joshua Lutz/Redux Pictures

write first

One of these pictures shows public housing in disrepair; the other shows new affordable housing units. Write a paragraph that explains your idea of ideal affordable housing. Where should complexes for low-income families be located? What should they look like? What facilities and services should be offered to residents?

In this chapter, you will learn to

- use commas in a series (33a)
- use commas to set off introductory phrases and transitional words and phrases (33b)
- use commas to set off appositives (33c)
- use commas to set off nonrestrictive clauses (33d)
- use commas in dates and addresses (33e)
- avoid unnecessary commas (33f)

A **comma** is a punctuation mark that separates words or groups of words within sentences. In this way, commas keep ideas distinct from one another.

33a   Commas in a Series

Use commas to separate all elements in a **series** of three or more words, phrases, or clauses.

> Leyla, Zack, and Kathleen campaigned for Representative Lewis.
>
> Leyla, Zack, or Kathleen will be elected president of Students for Lewis.
>
> Leyla made phone calls, licked envelopes, and ran errands for the campaign.
>
> Leyla is president, Zack is vice president, and Kathleen is treasurer.

e macmillanhighered.com
/writingfirst
LearningCurve > Commas;
Additional Grammar
Exercises > Commas
in a Series

FYI

Using Commas in a Series

Newspapers and magazines usually omit the comma before the coordinating conjunction in a series. However, in college writing, you should always use a comma before the coordinating conjunction.

> Leyla, Zack, and Kathleen worked on the campaign.

Exception: Do not use *any* commas if all the items in a series are separated by coordinating conjunctions.

> Leyla or Zack or Kathleen will be elected president of Students for Lewis.

PRACTICE
33-1   Edit the following sentences for the use of commas in a series. If the sentence is correct, write *C* in the blank.

Examples

Costa Rica produces bananas, cocoa, and sugarcane. _____*C*_____

The pool rules state that there is no running/ or jumping/ or diving.

_____

1. The musician plays guitar bass and drums. _____

2. The organization's goals are feeding the hungry, housing the homeless and helping the unemployed find work. _____

3. In native Hawaiian culture, yellow was worn by the royalty red was worn by priests and a mixture of the two colors was worn by others of high rank. _____

4. Most coffins manufactured in the United States are lined with bronze, or copper, or lead. _____

5. California's capital is Sacramento, its largest city is Los Angeles and its oldest settlement is San Diego. _____

33b Commas with Introductory Phrases and Transitional Words and Phrases

Introductory Phrases

Use a comma to set off an **introductory phrase** from the rest of the sentence.

> In the event of a fire, proceed to the nearest exit.
> Walking home, Nelida decided to change her major.

PRACTICE

33-2 Edit the sentences in the following paragraph for the use of commas with introductory phrases. If a sentence is correct, write *C* in the blank.

macmillanhighered.com
/writingfirst
Additional Grammar
Exercises > Commas
with Introductory Phrases

Examples

For some medical conditions, effective treatments are hard to find.

_____

After taking placebos, some depressed patients experience relief from their symptoms. _____C_____

(1) Also known as sugar pills placebos contain no actual medicine. _____ (2) Despite this fact, placebos sometimes have positive effects on patients who take them. _____ (3) For years researchers have used placebos in experiments. _____ (4) To evaluate the effectiveness of a

medication scientists test the drug on volunteers. _____ (5) To ensure that the experiment's results are reliable, researchers always have a control group. _____ (6) Instead of taking the drug the control group takes a placebo. _____ (7) Thinking they are taking an actual medicine patients in the control group may experience the "placebo effect." _____ (8) After receiving treatment with a placebo, they feel better. _____ (9) In some cases patients feel better even when they know they have taken a placebo. _____ (10) Puzzling to researchers, this "honest placebo effect" is the subject of several new scientific studies. _____

Transitional Words and Phrases

Also use commas to set off **transitional words or phrases**, whether they appear at the beginning, in the middle, or at the end of a sentence.

> In fact, Thoreau spent only one night in jail.
> He was, of course, bailed out by a friend.
> He did spend more than two years at Walden Pond, however.

ie macmillanhighered.com
/writingfirst
Additional Grammar
Exercises > Commas with
Transitional Words and
Phrases

FYI

Using Commas in Direct Address

Always use commas to set off the name of someone whom you are addressing (speaking to) directly, whether the name appears at the beginning, in the middle, or at the end of a sentence.

> Molly, come here and look at this.
> Come here, Molly, and look at this.
> Come here and look at this, Molly.

PRACTICE

33-3 Edit the following sentences for the use of commas with transitional words and phrases. If the sentence is correct, write *C* in the blank.

Example: Eventually, most people build a personal credit history.

(1) Often establishing credit can be difficult. _____ (2) College students for example often have no credit history of their own, especially if their parents pay their bills. _____ (3) Similarly some married women have no personal credit history. _____ (4) In fact their

credit cards may be in their husbands' names. _____ (5) As a result, they may be unable to get their own loans. _____ (6) Of course one way to establish credit is to apply for a credit card at a local department store. _____ (7) Also, it is relatively easy to get a gas credit card. _____ (8) It is important to pay these credit-card bills promptly however. _____ (9) In addition having checking and savings accounts can help to establish financial reliability. _____ (10) Finally, people who want to establish a credit history can sign an apartment lease and pay the rent regularly to show that they are good credit risks. _____

33c Commas with Appositives

Use commas to set off an **appositive**—a word or word group that identifies, renames, or describes a noun or a pronoun.

> I have visited only one country, Canada, outside the United States. (*Canada* is an appositive that identifies the noun *country*.)
>
> Carlos Santana, leader of the group Santana, played at Woodstock in 1969. (*Leader of the group Santana* is an appositive that identifies *Carlos Santana*.)
>
> A really gifted artist, he is also a wonderful father. (*A really gifted artist* is an appositive that describes the pronoun *he*.)

e macmillanhighered.com /writingfirst
Additional Grammar Exercises > Commas with Appositives

FYI

Using Commas with Appositives

Most appositives are set off by commas, whether they fall at the beginning, in the middle, or at the end of a sentence.

> A dreamer, he spent his life thinking about what he could not have.
>
> He always wanted to build a house, a big white one, overlooking the ocean.
>
> He finally built his dream house, a log cabin.

PRACTICE

33-4 Underline the appositive in each of the following sentences. Then, check each sentence for the correct use of commas to set off appositives, and add any missing commas. If the sentence is correct, write *C* in the blank.

Example: Wendy Kopp, a college student developed the Teach For America program to help minority students get a better education. _____

1. Guglielmo Marconi a young Italian inventor, sent the first wireless message across the Atlantic Ocean in 1901. _____

2. A member of the boy band 'N Sync Justin Timberlake went on to establish a successful career as a solo musician and an actor. _____

3. HTML hypertext markup language, is the set of codes used to create web documents. _____

4. William Filene, founder of Filene's Department Store, invented the "bargain basement." _____

5. Known as NPR National Public Radio presents a wide variety of programs. _____

6. On the southwest coast of Nigeria lies Lagos a major port. _____

7. Home of the 2008 Olympics, Beijing continues to have serious problems with its air quality. _____

8. Lightning a strong electrical charge can be both beautiful and dangerous. _____

9. A plant that grows on mountains and in deserts, the fern is surprisingly adaptable. _____

10. Golf a game developed in Scotland, is very popular in the United States. _____

33d Commas with Nonrestrictive Clauses

WORD POWER

restrict to keep within limits

restrictive limiting

Clauses are often used to add information within a sentence. In some cases, you need to add commas to set off these clauses; in other cases, commas are not required.

Use commas to set off **nonrestrictive clauses**—clauses that are not essential to a sentence's meaning. Do not use commas to set off **restrictive clauses**.

■ **A nonrestrictive clause** does *not* contain essential information. Nonrestrictive clauses are set off from the rest of the sentence by commas.

Telephone calling-card fraud, which cost consumers and phone companies four billion dollars last year, is increasing.

Here, the clause between the commas (underlined) provides extra information to help readers understand the sentence, but the sentence would still communicate the same idea without this information.

> Telephone calling-card fraud is increasing.

■ A **restrictive clause** contains information that is essential to a sentence's meaning. Restrictive clauses are *not* set off from the rest of the sentence by commas.

> Many rock stars who recorded hits in the 1950s made little money from their songs.

macmillanhighered.com /writingfirst
Additional Grammar Exercises > Commas with Nonrestrictive Clauses

In this sentence, the clause *who recorded hits in the 1950s* supplies specific information that is essential to the idea the sentence is communicating: it tells readers which group of rock stars made little money. Without the clause, the sentence does not communicate the same idea because it does not tell which rock stars made little money.

> Many rock stars made little money from their songs.

Compare the meanings of the following pairs of sentences with nonrestrictive and restrictive clauses.

NONRESTRICTIVE   Young adults, who text while driving, put themselves and others in danger. (This sentence says that all young adults text while driving and all pose a danger.)

RESTRICTIVE   Young adults who text while driving put themselves and others in danger. (This sentence says that only those young adults who text and drive pose a danger.)

NONRESTRICTIVE   Student loans, which are based on need, may not be fair to middle-class students. (This sentence says that all student loans are based on need and all may be unfair to middle-class students.)

RESTRICTIVE   Student loans that are based on need may not be fair to middle-class students. (This sentence says that only those student loans that are based on need may be unfair to middle-class students.)

FYI

Which, That, and *Who*

■ *Which* always introduces a nonrestrictive clause.

> The job, which had excellent benefits, did not pay well. (clause set off by commas)

■ *That* always introduces a restrictive clause.

> He accepted the job that had the best benefits. (no commas)

(continued)

(continued from previous page)

■ *Who* can introduce either a restrictive or a nonrestrictive clause.

RESTRICTIVE   Many parents who work feel a lot of stress. (no commas)

NONRESTRICTIVE   Both of my parents, who have always wanted the best for their children, have worked two jobs for years. (clause set off by commas)

PRACTICE

33-5   Edit the following sentences so that commas set off all non-restrictive clauses. (Remember, commas are *not* used to set off restrictive clauses.) If a sentence is correct, write *C* in the blank.

Example: A museum exhibition that celebrates the Alaska highway tells the story of its construction. _____*C*_____

(1) During the 1940s, a group of African-American soldiers who would defy the forces of nature and human prejudice were shipped to Alaska. _____ (2) They built the Alaska highway which stretches twelve hundred miles across Alaska. _____ (3) The troops who worked on the highway have received little attention in most historical accounts. _____ (4) The highway which cut through some of the roughest terrain in the world was begun in 1942. _____ (5) The Japanese had just landed in the Aleutian Islands which lie west of the tip of the Alaska Peninsula. _____ (6) Military officials, who oversaw the project, doubted the ability of the African-American troops. _____ (7) As a result, they made them work under conditions, that made construction difficult. _____ (8) The troops who worked on the road proved their commanders wrong by finishing the highway months ahead of schedule. _____ (9) In one case, white engineers, who surveyed a river, said it would take two weeks to bridge. _____ (10) To the engineers' surprise, the soldiers who worked on the project beat the estimate. _____ (11) A military report that was issued in 1945 praised them. _____ (12) It said the goals that the African-American soldiers achieved would be remembered through the ages. _____

33e Commas in Dates and Addresses

e macmillanhighered.com /writingfirst
Additional Grammar Exercises > Commas in Dates and Addresses

Dates

Use commas in dates to separate the day of the week from the month and the day of the month from the year.

> The first Cinco de Mayo we celebrated in the United States was Tuesday, May 5, 1998.

When a date that includes commas does not fall at the end of a sentence, place a comma after the year.

> Tuesday, May 5, 1998, was the first Cinco de Mayo we celebrated in the United States.

Addresses

Use commas in addresses to separate the street address from the city and the city from the state or country.

> The office of the famous fictional detective Sherlock Holmes was located at 221b Baker Street, London, England.

When an address that includes commas falls in the middle of a sentence, place a comma after the state or country.

> The office at 221b Baker Street, London, England, belonged to the famous fictional detective Sherlock Holmes.

PRACTICE

33-6 Edit the following sentences for the correct use of commas in dates and addresses. Add any missing commas, and cross out any unnecessary commas. If the sentence is correct, write *C* in the blank.

Examples

Usher's album *Looking 4 Myself* was released on June 8, 2012. _____

The entertainer grew up in Chattanooga, Tennessee. _____

1. On Tuesday June 5, 2012, people around the world witnessed the rare astronomical phenomenon known as the transit of Venus. _____

2. For traditional Venezuelan food, locals go to Café Casa Veroes on Avenida Norte in Caracas Venezuela. _____

3. Stefani Joanne Angelina Germanotta, more commonly known as Lady Gaga, was born on March 28 1986 in New York New York. _____

4. Mets pitcher Johan Santana threw the team's first no-hitter on June 1, 2012. _____

5. Donations can be sent to the American Red Cross at PO Box 4002018 in Des Moines, Iowa. _____

6. To visit the New York Transit Museum, visitors must travel to 130 Livingston Street in Brooklyn New York. _____

7. The Anne Frank House in Amsterdam the Netherlands became a museum on May 3 1960. _____

8. First released on November 1 1997, *Titanic* remains one of the highest-grossing movies of all time. _____

9. Fans from around the world travel to visit Ernest Hemingway's houses in Key West Florida and San Francisco de Paula, Cuba. _____

10. Oprah addressed the graduating class at Spelman College on Sunday May 20, 2012 in College Park Georgia. _____

33f Unnecessary Commas

In addition to knowing where commas are required, it is also important to know when *not* to use commas.

■ Do not use a comma before the first item in a series.

    INCORRECT *Duck Soup* starred, Groucho, Chico, and Harpo Marx.

    CORRECT *Duck Soup* starred Groucho, Chico, and Harpo Marx.

■ Do not use a comma after the last item in a series.

    INCORRECT Groucho, Chico, and Harpo Marx, starred in *Duck Soup*.

    CORRECT Groucho, Chico, and Harpo Marx starred in *Duck Soup*.

■ Do not use a comma between a subject and a verb.

    INCORRECT Students and teachers, should try to respect each other.

    CORRECT Students and teachers should try to respect each other.

■ Do not use a comma before the coordinating conjunction that separates the two parts of a compound predicate.

    INCORRECT The transit workers voted to strike, and walked off the job.

    CORRECT The transit workers voted to strike and walked off the job.

■ Do not use a comma before the coordinating conjunction that separates the two parts of a compound subject.

INCORRECT   The transit workers, and the sanitation workers voted to strike.

CORRECT   The transit workers and the sanitation workers voted to strike.

■ Do not use a comma to set off a restrictive clause.

INCORRECT   People, who live in glass houses, should not throw stones.

CORRECT   People who live in glass houses should not throw stones.

■ Finally, do not use a comma before a dependent clause that follows an independent clause.

INCORRECT   He was exhausted, because he had driven all night.

CORRECT   He was exhausted because he had driven all night.

PRACTICE

33-7   Some of the following sentences contain unnecessary commas. Edit to eliminate unnecessary commas. If the sentence is correct, write *C* in the blank following it.

Example: Both the Dominican Republic/ and the republic of Haiti occupy the West Indian island of Hispaniola. _____

1. The country's tropical climate, generous rainfall, and fertile soil, make the Dominican Republic suitable for many kinds of crops. _____

2. Some of the most important crops are, sugarcane, coffee, cocoa, and rice. _____

3. Mining is also important to the country's economy, because the land is rich in many ores. _____

4. Spanish is the official language of the Dominican Republic, and Roman Catholicism is the state religion. _____

5. In recent years, resort areas have opened, and brought many tourists to the country. _____

6. Because the republic's economy has not always been strong, many Dominicans have immigrated to the United States. _____

7. However, many Dominican immigrants maintain close ties to their home country, and return often to visit. _____

TEST · Revise · Edit · Proofread

Look back at your response to the Write First prompt on page 481. TEST and revise what you have written. Then, complete the following tasks.

1. Add a sentence that includes a series of three or more words or word groups.
2. Add introductory phrases to two of your sentences.
3. Add an appositive to one of your sentences.
4. Add a transitional word or phrase to one of your sentences (at the beginning, in the middle, or at the end).
5. Add a nonrestrictive clause to one of your sentences.

When you have made all the additions, edit and proofread your work, carefully checking your use of commas.

EDITING PRACTICE

Read the following student essay, which includes errors in comma use. Add commas where necessary between items in a series and with introductory phrases, transitional words and phrases, appositives, and nonrestrictive clauses. Cross out any unnecessary commas. The first sentence has been edited for you.

Brave Orchid

One of the most important characters in *The Woman Warrior*, Maxine Hong Kingston's autobiographical work, is Brave Orchid, Kingston's mother. Brave Orchid was a strong woman, but not a happy one. Through Kingston's stories about her mother, readers learn a lot about Kingston herself.

Readers are introduced to Brave Orchid, a complex character as an imaginative storyteller, who tells her daughter vivid tales of China. As a young woman she impresses her classmates with her intelligence. She is a traditional woman. However she is determined to make her life exactly what she wants it to be. Brave Orchid strongly believes in herself; still, she considers herself a failure.

In her native China Brave Orchid trains to be a midwife. The other women in her class envy her independence brilliance and courage. One day Brave Orchid bravely confronts the Fox Spirit, and tells him he will not win. First of all, she tells him she can endure any pain that he inflicts on her. Next she gathers together the women in the dormitory to burn the ghost away. After this event the other women admire her even more.

Working hard Brave Orchid becomes a midwife in China. After coming to America however she cannot work as a midwife. Instead she works in a Chinese laundry, and picks tomatoes. None of her classmates in China would have imagined this outcome. During her later years in America Brave Orchid becomes a woman, who is overbearing and domineering. She bosses her children around, she tries to ruin her sister's life and she criticizes everyone and everything around her. Her daughter, a straight-A student is the object of her worst criticism.

Brave Orchid's intentions are good. Nevertheless she devotes her energy to the wrong things. She expects the people around her to be as strong as she is. Because she bullies them however she eventually loses them. In addition she is too busy criticizing her daughter's faults to see all her accomplishments. Brave Orchid an independent woman and a brilliant student never achieves her goals. She is hard on the people around her, because she is disappointed in herself.

COLLABORATIVE ACTIVITY

Bring a homemaking, sports, or fashion magazine to class. Working in a small group, look at the people pictured in the ads. In what roles are men most often depicted? In what roles are women presented? Identify the three or four most common roles for each sex, and give each kind of character a descriptive name—*athlete* or *mother*, for example.

Working on your own, choose one type of character, and write a paragraph in which you describe his or her typical appearance and habits. Then, circle every comma in your paragraph, and work with your group to explain why each comma is used. If no one in your group can explain why a particular comma is used, cross it out.

review checklist

macmillanhighered.com /writingfirst
LearningCurve > Commas; Additional Grammar Exercises > Correct Comma Use; Types of Comma Use

Using Commas

☐ Use commas to separate all elements in a series of three or more words or word groups. (See 33a.)

☐ Use commas to set off introductory phrases and transitional words and phrases from the rest of the sentence. (See 33b.)

☐ Use commas to set off appositives from the rest of the sentence. (See 33c.)

☐ Use commas to set off nonrestrictive clauses. (See 33d.)

☐ Use commas to separate parts of dates and addresses. (See 33e.)

☐ Avoid unnecessary commas. (See 33f.)

34 Using Apostrophes

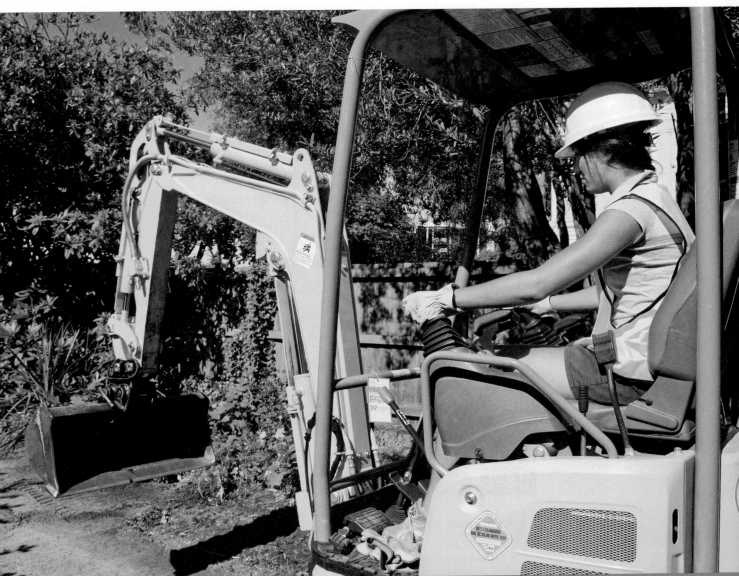

Jinny Goodman/Alamy

write first

Certain jobs have traditionally been considered "men's work," and others have been viewed as "women's work." Although the workplace has changed considerably in recent years, some things have remained the same. Write a paragraph about the tasks that are considered "men's work" and "women's work" at your job or in your current household. Be sure to give examples of the kinds of tasks you discuss. (*Note:* Contractions, such as *isn't* or *don't*, are acceptable in this informal response.)

In this chapter, you will learn to
• use apostrophes to form contractions (34a)
• use apostrophes to form possessives (34b)
• revise incorrect use of apostrophes (34c)

An **apostrophe** is a punctuation mark that is used in two situations: to form a contraction and to form the possessive of a noun or an indefinite pronoun.

ⓔ macmillanhighered.com
/writingfirst
LearningCurve > Apostrophes

34a Apostrophes in Contractions

A **contraction** is a word that uses an apostrophe to combine two words. The apostrophe takes the place of omitted letters.

I didn't (*did not*) realize how late it was.

It's (*it is*) not right for cheaters to go unpunished.

Frequently Used Contractions

I + am = I'm	are + not = aren't
we + are = we're	can + not = can't
you + are = you're	do + not = don't
it + is = it's	will + not = won't
I + have = I've	should + not = shouldn't
I + will = I'll	let + us = let's
there + is = there's	that + is = that's
is + not = isn't	who + is = who's

PRACTICE
34-1   In the following sentences, add apostrophes to contractions if needed. If the sentence is correct, write *C* in the blank.

Example: *What's*
~~Whats~~ the deadliest creature on earth? _____
          ^

(1) Bacteria and viruses, which we cant see without a microscope, kill many people every year. _____ (2) When we speak about the deadliest creatures, however, were usually talking about creatures that cause illness or death from their poison, which is called venom. _____ (3) After your bitten, stung, or stuck, how long does it take to die? _____ (4) The fastest killer is a creature called the sea wasp, but it isn't a wasp at all. _____ (5) The sea wasp is actually a fifteen-foot-long jellyfish, and

although its not aggressive, it can be deadly. _____ (6) People who've gone swimming off the coast of Australia have encountered this creature. _____ (7) While jellyfish found off the Atlantic coast of the United States can sting, they arent as dangerous as the sea wasp, whose venom is deadly enough to kill sixty adults. _____ (8) A person whos been stung by a sea wasp has anywhere from thirty seconds to four minutes to get help or die. _____ (9) Oddly, it's been found that something as thin as pantyhose worn over the skin will prevent these stings. _____ (10) Also, theres an antidote to the poison that can save victims. _____

macmillanhighered.com
/writingfirst
Additional Grammar
Exercises > Apostrophes in
Contractions and Possessives

34b Apostrophes in Possessives

Possessive forms of nouns and pronouns show ownership. Nouns and indefinite pronouns do not have special possessive forms. Instead, they use apostrophes to indicate ownership.

Singular Nouns and Indefinite Pronouns

To form the possessive of **singular nouns** (including names) and **indefinite pronouns**, add an apostrophe plus an *s*.

Cesar Chavez's goal (*the goal of Cesar Chavez*) was justice for American farmworkers.

The strike's outcome (*the outcome of the strike*) was uncertain.

Whether it would succeed was anyone's guess (*the guess of anyone*).

FYI

Singular Nouns Ending in *-s*

Even if a singular noun already ends in *-s*, add an apostrophe plus an *s* to form the possessive.

The class's next assignment was a research paper.

Dr. Ramos's patients are participating in a clinical trial.

Plural Nouns

Most plural nouns end in *-s*. To form the possessive of **plural nouns ending in *-s*** (including names), add just an apostrophe (not an apostrophe plus an *s*).

The two <u>drugs'</u> side effects (*the side effects of the two drugs*) were quite different.

The <u>Johnsons'</u> front door (*the front door of the Johnsons*) is red.

Some irregular noun plurals do not end in *-s*. If a plural noun does not end in *-s*, add an apostrophe plus an *s* to form the possessive.

The <u>men's</u> room is right next to the <u>women's</u> room.

PRACTICE

34-2   Rewrite the following phrases, changing the noun or indefinite pronoun that follows *of* to the possessive form. Be sure to distinguish between singular and plural nouns.

Examples

the mayor of the city   *the city's mayor* _____

the uniforms of the players   *the players' uniforms* _____

1. the video of the singer _____

2. the scores of the students _____

3. the favorite band of everybody _____

4. the office of the boss _____

5. the union of the players _____

6. the specialty of the restaurant _____

7. the bedroom of the children _____

8. the high cost of the tickets _____

9. the dreams of everyone _____

10. the owner of the dogs _____

34c   Incorrect Use of Apostrophes

Be careful not to confuse a plural noun (*boys*) with the singular possessive form of the noun (*boy's*). Never use an apostrophe with a plural noun unless the noun is possessive.

Termites can be dangerous <u>pests</u> [not *pest's*].

The <u>Velezes</u> [not *Velez's*] live on Maple Drive, right next door to the <u>Browns</u> [not *Brown's*].

Also remember not to use apostrophes with possessive pronouns that end in *-s*: *theirs* (not *their's*), *hers* (not *her's*), *its* (not *it's*), *ours* (not *our's*), and *yours* (not *your's*).

Be especially careful not to confuse possessive pronouns with sound-alike contractions. Possessive pronouns never include apostrophes.

POSSESSIVE PRONOUN

The dog bit its master.

The choice is theirs.

Whose house is this?

Is this your house?

CONTRACTION

It's (*it is*) time for breakfast.

There's (*there is*) no place like home.

Who's (*who is*) on first base?

You're (*you are*) late again.

PRACTICE

34-3   Check the underlined words in the following sentences for correct use of apostrophes. If a correction needs to be made, cross out the word and write the correct version above it. If the noun or pronoun is correct, write *C* above it.

> **Example:**   The president's views were presented after several other *speakers* *theirs.* speaker's presented their's.

1. Parent's should realize that when it comes to disciplining children, the responsibility is there's.

2. It's also important that parents offer praise for a child's good behavior.

3. In it's first few week's of life, a dog is already developing a personality.

4. His and her's towels used to be popular with couple's, but it's not so common to see them today.

5. All the Ryan's spent four year's in college and then got good jobs.

6. From the radio came the lyrics "You're the one who's love I've been waiting for."

7. If you expect to miss any class's, you will have to make arrangements with someone who's willing to tell you you're assignment.

8. No other school's cheerleading squad tried as many stunts as our's did.

9. Surprise test's are common in my economics teacher's class.

10. Jazz's influence on many mainstream musician's is one of the book's main subject's.

TEST · Revise · Edit · Proofread

Look back at your response to the Write First prompt on page 495. TEST and revise what you have written. Then, edit and proofread your work, checking to make sure that you have used apostrophes correctly in contractions and possessive forms. (Remember, because this is an informal exercise, contractions are acceptable.)

EDITING PRACTICE

Read the following student essay, which includes errors in the use of apostrophes. Edit it to eliminate errors by crossing out incorrect words and writing corrections above them. (Note that this is an informal response paper, so contractions are acceptable.) The first sentence has been edited for you.

The Women of Messina

In William ~~Shakespeares'~~ *Shakespeare's* play *Much Ado about Nothing*, the women of Messina, whether they are seen as love objects or as ~~shrew's,~~ *shrews,* have very few options. A womans role is to please a man. She can try to resist, but she will probably wind up giving in.

The plays two women, Hero and Beatrice, are very different. Hero is the obedient one. Heroes cousin, Beatrice, tries to challenge the rules of the mans world in which she lives. However, in a place like Messina, even women like Beatrice find it hard to get the respect that should be their's.

Right from the start, we are drawn to Beatrice. Shes funny, she has a clever comment for most situation's, and she always speaks her mind about other peoples behavior. Unlike Hero, she tries to stand up to the men in her life, as we see in her and Benedicks conversations. But even though Beatrice's intelligence is obvious, she often mocks herself. Its clear that she doesn't have much self-esteem. In fact, Beatrice is'nt the strong woman she seems to be.

Ultimately, Beatrice does get her man, and she will be happy—but at what cost? Benedicks' last word's to her are "Peace! I will stop your mouth." Then, he kisses her. The kiss is a symbolic end to their bickering. It is also the mark of Beatrices defeat. She has lost. Benedick has silenced her. Now, she will be Benedick's wife and do what he wants her to do. Granted, she will have more say in her marriage than Hero will have in her's, but she is still defeated.

Shakespeares audience might have seen the plays ending as a happy one. For contemporary audience's, however, the ending is disappointing. Even Beatrice, the most rebellious of Messinas women, finds it impossible to achieve anything of importance in this male-dominated society.

COLLABORATIVE ACTIVITY

Bring to class a book, magazine, or newspaper whose style is informal—for example, a romance novel, *People*, your school newspaper, or even a comic book. Working in a group, circle every contraction you can find on one page of each publication, and substitute for each contraction the words it combines. Are your substitutions an improvement? (You may want to read a few paragraphs aloud before you reach a conclusion.)

review checklist

Using Apostrophes

- ☐ Use apostrophes to form contractions. (See 34a.)

- ☐ Use an apostrophe plus an *s* to form the possessive of singular nouns (including names) and indefinite pronouns, even when a noun ends in *-s*. (See 34b.)

- ☐ Use an apostrophe alone to form the possessive of plural nouns ending in *-s* (including names). If a plural noun does not end in *-s*, add an apostrophe plus an *s*. (See 34b.)

- ☐ Do not use apostrophes with plural nouns unless they are possessive. Do not use apostrophes with possessive pronouns. (See 34c.)

macmillanhighered.com /writingfirst
LearningCurve > Apostrophes

35 Understanding Mechanics

Photofest

write first

This picture shows a familiar scene from the classic 1939 film *The Wizard of Oz*. Write a paragraph describing a memorable scene from your favorite movie. Begin by giving the film's title and listing the names of the major actors and the characters they play. Then, tell what happens in the scene, quoting a few words of dialogue, if possible.

In this chapter, you will learn to

- capitalize proper nouns (35a)
- punctuate direct quotations (35b)
- set off titles (35c)
- use minor punctuation marks correctly (35d)

PREVIEW

35a Capitalizing Proper Nouns

macmillanhighered.com
/writingfirst
LearningCurve >
Capitalization; Additional
Grammar Exercises >
Capitalizing Proper Nouns

A **proper noun** names a particular person, animal, place, object, or idea. Proper nouns are always capitalized. The list that follows explains and illustrates specific rules for capitalizing proper nouns.

- Always capitalize names of **races, ethnic groups, tribes, nationalities, languages, and religions**.

    The census data revealed a diverse community of Caucasians, African Americans, and Asian Americans, with a few Latino and Navajo residents. Native languages included English, Korean, and Spanish. Most people identified themselves as Catholic, Protestant, or Muslim.

- Capitalize names of **specific people and the titles that accompany them**. In general, do not capitalize titles used without a name.

    In 1994, President Nelson Mandela was elected to lead South Africa.

    The newly elected fraternity president addressed the crowd.

- Capitalize names of **specific family members and their titles**. Do not capitalize words that identify family relationships, including those introduced by possessive pronouns.

    The twins, Aunt Edna and Aunt Evelyn, are Dad's sisters.

    My aunts, my father's sisters, are twins.

- Capitalize names of **specific countries, cities, towns, bodies of water, streets, and so on**. Do not capitalize words that do not name specific places.

    The Seine runs through Paris, France.

    The river runs through the city.

- Capitalize names of **specific geographical regions**. Do not capitalize such words when they specify direction.

    William Faulkner's novels are set in the South.

    Turn right at the golf course, and go south for about a mile.

- Capitalize names of **specific groups, clubs, teams, and associations**. Do not capitalize general references to such groups.

> The Teamsters Union represents workers who were at the stadium for the Republican Party convention, the Rolling Stones concert, and the Phillies-Astros game.

> The union represents workers who were at the stadium for the political party's convention, the rock group's concert, and the baseball teams' game.

- Capitalize **brand names**. Do not capitalize general references to kinds of products.

> While Jeff waited for his turn at the Xerox machine, he drank a can of Coke.

> While Jeff waited for his turn at the copier, he drank a can of soda.

- Capitalize **titles of specific academic courses**. Do not capitalize names of general academic subject areas, except for proper nouns—for example, a language or a country.

> Are Introduction to American Government and Biology 200 closed yet?

> Are the introductory American government course and the biology course closed yet?

- Capitalize **days of the week, months of the year, and holidays**. Do not capitalize the names of seasons.

> The Jewish holiday of Passover usually falls in April.

> The Jewish holiday of Passover falls in the spring.

Note: Also capitalize names of specific buildings and monuments; names of specific historical periods, events, and documents; and names of businesses, government agencies, schools, and other institutions.

PRACTICE

35-1 Edit the following sentences, capitalizing letters or changing capitals to lowercase where necessary.

Example: The third-largest ₵ity in the ᵁnited ₴tates is ₵hicago, ᴵllinois.

(1) Located in the midwest on lake Michigan, chicago is an important port city, a rail and highway hub, and the site of o'hare international airport, one of the Nation's busiest. (2) The financial center of the city is Lasalle street, and the lakefront is home to Grant park, where there

are many Museums and monuments. (3) To the North of the city, soldier field is home to the chicago bears, the city's football team, and wrigley field is home to the chicago cubs, a national league Baseball Team. (4) In the mid-1600s, the site of what is now Chicago was visited by father jacques marquette, a catholic missionary to the ottawa and huron tribes, who were native to the area. (5) By the 1700s, the city was a trading post run by john kinzie. (6) The city grew rapidly in the 1800s, and immigrants included germans, irish, italians, poles, greeks, and chinese, along with african americans who migrated from the south. (7) Today, Chicago's skyline has many Skyscrapers, built by such businesses as the john hancock company, sears, and amoco.

35b Punctuating Direct Quotations

macmillanhighered.com /writingfirst
Additional Grammar Exercises > Punctuating Direct Quotations

A **direct quotation** shows the *exact* words of a speaker or writer. Direct quotations are always placed in quotation marks.

A direct quotation is usually accompanied by an **identifying tag**—a phrase (such as "she said") that names the person being quoted. In the following sentences, the identifying tag is underlined.

> <u>Lauren said</u>, "My brother and Tina have gotten engaged."

> A <u>famous advertising executive wrote</u>, "Don't sell the steak; sell the sizzle."

When a quotation is a complete sentence, it begins with a capital letter and ends with a period (or a question mark or an exclamation point). When a quotation falls at the end of a sentence (as in the two preceding examples), the period is placed *before* the quotation marks.

If the quotation is a question or an exclamation, the question mark or exclamation point is also placed *before* the closing quotation mark.

> The instructor asked, "Has anyone read *Sula*?"

> Officer Warren shouted, "Hold it right there!"

If the quotation itself is not a question or an exclamation, the question mark or exclamation point is placed *after* the closing quotation mark.

> Did Joe really say, "I quit"?

> I can't believe he really said, "I quit"!

FYI

Indirect Quotations

A direct quotation shows someone's *exact* words, but an **indirect quotation** simply summarizes what was said or written. Do not use quotation marks with indirect quotations.

DIRECT QUOTATION	Martin Luther King Jr. said, "I have a dream."
INDIRECT QUOTATION	Martin Luther King Jr. said that he had a dream.

The rules for punctuating direct quotations with identifying tags are summarized here.

Identifying Tag at the Beginning

When the identifying tag comes *before* the quotation, it is followed by a comma.

Alexandre Dumas wrote, "Nothing succeeds like success."

Identifying Tag at the End

When the identifying tag comes at the *end* of the quoted sentence, it is followed by a period. A comma (or, sometimes, a question mark or an exclamation point) inside the closing quotation mark separates the quotation from the identifying tag.

"Life is like a box of chocolates," stated Forrest Gump.

"Is that so?" his friends wondered.

"That's amazing!" he cried.

Identifying Tag in the Middle

When the identifying tag comes in the *middle* of the quoted sentence, it is followed by a comma. The first part of the quotation is also followed by a comma, placed inside the closing quotation mark. Because the part of the quotation that follows the identifying tag is not a new sentence, it does not begin with a capital letter.

"This is my life," Bette insisted, "and I'll live it as I please."

Identifying Tag between Two Sentences

When the identifying tag comes *between two* quoted sentences, it is preceded by a comma and followed by a period. (The second quoted sentence begins with a capital letter.)

"Producer Berry Gordy is an important figure in the history of music," Tony explained. "He was the creative force behind Motown records."

PRACTICE

35-2 The following sentences contain direct quotations. First, underline the identifying tag. Then, punctuate the quotation correctly, adding capital letters as necessary.

Example: "Why, <u>Darryl asked</u>, "are teachers so strict about deadlines?"

1. We who are about to die salute you said the gladiators to the emperor.

2. When we turned on the television, the newscaster was saying ladies and gentlemen, we have a new president-elect.

3. The bigger they are said boxer John L. Sullivan the harder they fall.

4. When asked for the jury's verdict, the foreperson replied we find the defendant not guilty.

5. I had felt for a long time that if I was ever told to get up so a white person could sit Rosa Parks recalled I would refuse to do so.

6. Yabba dabba doo Fred exclaimed this brontoburger looks great.

35c Setting Off Titles

macmillanhighered.com /writingfirst
Additional Grammar Exercises > Setting Off Titles

Some titles are typed in *italics*. Others are enclosed in quotation marks. The following box shows how to set off different kinds of titles.

Italics or Quotation Marks?

ITALICIZED TITLES

Books: *How the García Girls Lost Their Accents*
Newspapers: *Miami Herald*
Magazines: *People*
Long poems: *John Brown's Body*
Plays: *Death of a Salesman*
Films: *The Rocky Horror Picture Show*
Television or radio series: *Battlestar Galactica*
Paintings and sculpture: *American Gothic*
Video Games: *Call of Duty*

TITLES IN QUOTATION MARKS

Book chapters: "Understanding Mechanics"
Short stories: "The Tell-Tale Heart"
Essays and articles in newspapers and magazines: "The Suspected Shopper"
Short poems: "Richard Cory"
Songs and speeches: "America the Beautiful"; "I Have a Dream"
Individual episodes of television or radio series: "The Montgomery Bus Boycott" (an episode of the PBS series *Eyes on the Prize*)

FYI

Capital Letters in Titles

Capitalize the first letters of all important words in a title. Do not capitalize an **article** (*a, an, the*), a **preposition** (*to, of, around,* and so on), the *to* in an infinitive, or a **coordinating conjunction** (*and, but,* and so on)—unless it is the first or last word of the title or subtitle (*On the Road*; "To an Athlete Dying Young"; *No Way Out*; *And Quiet Flows the Don*).

PRACTICE

35-3 Edit the following sentences, capitalizing letters as necessary in titles.

Example: *New york times* best-seller *gone girl* has been made into a feature film staring Ben Affleck.

1. When fans of the television show *lost* voted for their favorite episodes, "through the looking glass," "the shape of things to come," and "the incident" were in the top ten.

2. In 1948, Eleanor Roosevelt delivered her famous speech "the struggle for human rights" and published an article titled "toward human rights throughout the world."

3. Before being elected president, Barack Obama wrote and published two books: *dreams from my father* and *the audacity of hope*.

4. English actor Daniel Craig plays secret agent James Bond in the films *casino royale* and *quantum of solace*.

5. *janis joplin's greatest hits* includes songs written by other people, such as "piece of my heart," as well as songs she wrote herself, such as "mercedes benz."

PRACTICE

35-4 In the following sentences, underline titles to indicate italics or place them in quotation marks. (Remember that titles of books and other long works are italicized, and titles of stories, essays, and other short works are enclosed in quotation marks.)

Example: An article in the <u>New York Times</u> titled "Whoopi Goldberg Joins <u>The View</u>" talks about a television talk show hosted by women.

1. Oprah Winfrey publishes a magazine called O.

2. At the beginning of most major American sporting events, the crowd stands for The Star Spangled Banner.

3. People who want to purchase new cars often compare the different models in Consumer Reports magazine.

4. U2's song Pride (in the Name of Love) is about Martin Luther King Jr.

5. Edgar Allan Poe wrote several mysterious short stories, two of which are called The Tell-Tale Heart and The Black Cat.

6. The popular Broadway show Fela! was based on the life of the Nigerian musician Fela Kuti.

7. Tina Fey, who won two Golden Globes for her role in the TV show 30 Rock, wrote a best-selling autobiography called Bossypants.

8. In a college textbook called Sociology: A Brief Introduction, the first chapter is titled The Essence of Sociology.

35d Using Minor Punctuation Marks

macmillanhighered.com /writingfirst
Additional Grammar Exercises > Minor Punctuation Marks

The Semicolon

Use a **semicolon** to join independent clauses in a compound sentence.

> Twenty-five years ago, smartphones did not exist; today, many people cannot imagine life without them.

The Colon

▪ Use a **colon** to introduce a quotation.

> Our family motto is a simple one: "Accept no substitutes."

▪ Use a colon to introduce an explanation, a clarification, or an example.

> Only one thing kept him from climbing Mt. Everest: fear of heights.

▪ Use a colon to introduce a list.

> I left my job for four reasons: boring work, poor working conditions, low pay, and a terrible supervisor.

The Dash

Use **dashes** to set off important information.

> She parked her car—a red Firebird—in a tow-away zone.

Parentheses

Use **parentheses** to enclose material that is relatively unimportant.

The weather in Portland (a city in Oregon) was overcast.

PRACTICE

35-5 Add semicolons, colons, dashes, and parentheses to the following sentences where necessary.

Example: Megachurches (churches with more than two thousand worshippers at a typical service) have grown in popularity since the 1950s.

1. Megachurches though they are Protestant are not always affiliated with the main Protestant denominations.

2. Services in megachurches are creative preaching is sometimes accompanied by contemporary music and video presentations.

3. Although many of these churches are evangelical actively recruiting new members, people often join because of friends and neighbors.

4. Megachurches tend to keep their members because they encourage a variety of activities for example, hospitality committees and study groups.

5. Worshippers say that their services are upbeat they are full of joy and spirituality.

6. Megachurches in nearly all cases use technology to organize and communicate with their members.

7. The largest of these churches with ten thousand members would be unable to function without telecommunications.

8. Some even offer services in a format familiar to their younger members the podcast.

9. Critics of megachurches and there are some believe they take up too much tax-exempt land.

10. Other critics fear that smaller churches already struggling to keep members will lose worshippers to these huge congregations and eventually have to close.

TEST · Revise · Edit · Proofread

Look back at your response to the Write First prompt on page 502. TEST and revise what you have written.

   If you have quoted any dialogue from the film you wrote about, try varying the placement of the identifying tags you have used. If you did not include any lines of dialogue, try adding one or two. Then, add an example or a list to your writing, introducing this new material with a colon. Make sure that a complete sentence comes before the colon.

   Finally, edit and proofread your work, paying special attention to the issues covered in this chapter.

EDITING PRACTICE

Read the following student essay, which includes errors in capitalization and punctuation and in the use of direct quotations and titles. Correct any errors you find. The first sentence has been edited for you.

A Threat to Health

Pandemics are like Épidemics, only more widespread, perhaps even spreading throughout the Ẃorld. In a pandemic, a serious Disease spreads very easily. In the past, there have been many pandemics. In the future, in spite of advances in Medicine, there will still be pandemics. In fact, scientists agree that not every pandemic can be prevented, so pandemics will continue to be a threat.

Probably the best-known pandemic is the bubonic plague. It killed about one-third of the Population of europe during the middle ages. Some areas suffered more than others. According to Philip ziegler's book the black Death, at least half the people in florence, Italy, died in one year. Many years later, in 1918, a flu pandemic killed more than 50 million people worldwide, including hundreds of thousands in the United states.

Unfortunately, pandemics have not disappeared. AIDS, for example, is a current pandemic. Philadelphia the 1993 movie starring denzel washington and tom hanks is still one of the most moving depictions of the heartbreak of AIDS. The rate of AIDS infection is over 30 percent in parts of africa, the disease continues to spread on other Continents as well. So far, efforts to find an AIDS vaccine have failed. Dr. anthony s. Fauci acknowledged this when he discussed AIDS research on NPR's series All things considered in a program called Search for an HIV vaccine expands.

Although some pandemic diseases, such as Smallpox, have been wiped out by Vaccination, new pandemics remain a threat. Many viruses and Bacteria change in response to treatment, so they may become resistant to Vaccination and Antibiotics. Also, with modern transportation, a disease can move quickly from Country to Country. For example, the disease known as severe acute respiratory syndrome (SARS) began in china but was spread to other countries by travelers. Hundreds died as a result of the SARS pandemic between November 2002 and july 2003. Birds also remain a threat because they can transmit disease. It is obviously impossible to prevent birds from flying from one country to another. Markos kyprianou, when he was health commissioner of the European union, said that I am concerned that birds in Turkey have been found with the bird flu Virus. He said, There is a direct relationship with viruses found in Russia, Mongolia and china. If this Virus ever changes so that it can move easily from birds to Humans, bird flu could become the next pandemic.

Public Health Officials are always on the lookout for diseases with three characteristics they are new, they are dangerous, and they are very contagious. Doctors try to prevent them from becoming Pandemics. However, they continue to warn that some Pandemics cannot be prevented.

COLLABORATIVE ACTIVITY

Working in pairs, write a conversation between two characters, real or fictional, who have very different positions on a particular issue. Place all direct quotations within quotation marks, and include identifying tags that clearly indicate which character is speaking. (Begin a new paragraph each time a new person speaks.)

Exchange your conversation with another pair, and check their work to see that directly quoted speech is set within quotation marks and that capital letters and other punctuation are used correctly.

review checklist

Understanding Mechanics

- [ ] Capitalize proper nouns. (See 35a.)
- [ ] Always place direct quotations within quotation marks. (See 35b.)
- [ ] In titles, capitalize all important words. Use italics or quotation marks to set off titles. (See 35c.)
- [ ] Use semicolons to join independent clauses in a compound sentence. (See 35d.)
- [ ] Use colons, dashes, and parentheses to set off material from the rest of the sentence. (See 35d.)

Read the following student essay, which contains errors in the use of punctuation and mechanics. Identify the sentences that need to be corrected, and edit the faulty sentences. (Underline to indicate italics where necessary.) The first sentence has been edited for you.

Telenovelas

What is the most-watched kind of television program in Spanish-speaking countries It's the telenovela, a Spanish-language soap opera. Televised on Weeknights in the prime evening hour's; telenovelas started in the early 1950s and are still popular today. In fact more telenovelas are shown in central America and South america than any other type of TV drama. In a recent study more than half the population of Latin American countries said "that they watch these shows." Telenovelas are different from american soap operas in the way they are planned and scheduled. Also they dont have the same kinds of plots. Telenovela's popularity can be seen in their websites, and by their growth in countries whose residents dont speak spanish.

Telenovelas are quite different from. American Soap Operas. In the United States, there have been some evening soap-opera dramas (dallas and dynasty are good examples but they have usually been televised only once a week, however telenovelas usually appear Monday through Friday. In the United States soap operas generally continue until viewers stop watching, and ratings fall. The writers of an american soap opera, do not know how the plot will develop; or when it will end. In contrast telenovela's are usually completely mapped out at the beginning. In general a telenovela continues for about eight months and then the short-lived drama is over. A new telenovela takes it's place.

The plots may seem strange to american viewers. In a typical telenovela the beautiful Heroine is a girl—who has no money but has a good heart. The hero—a rich, handsome man, rejects his rich but evil girlfriend in favor of the heroine. Eventually the heroine may turn out to be the secret child of a wealthy family. The unhappy villain's may wind up in the cemetery and the heroine and her hero will live "happily ever after." Other telenovelas occur in the past, or may deal with modern social problems such as drug abuse, or prejudice. Some telenovelas are really serial comedies and are more, like American sitcoms.

Telenovelas are becoming more and more popular. There are even websites dedicated to: popular telenovelas and their actors. For example viewers can go to the website called topnovelas to access: plot summaries lists of the most popular shows and downloads of episodes'. Although telenovelas started in Spanish-speaking countries they have spread to other countries. The first telenovela to be translated into another language was The Rich Cry too (Los Ricos También Lloran) which was first produced in Mexico in 1979 and was brought to, China, the Soviet Union and the United States. Other places where telenovelas are popular include the following countries; france israel japan, malaysia Singapore and indonesia.

The popularity of the telenovela in the United states is only partly a reflection of its' millions of spanish-speaking viewers. Although it is true that Networks want to attract hispanic viewers it is also true that the format, and subject matter interest English-Speaking viewers. Its quite possible that one day, telenovelas in English will appear every night?

36 Reading Critically

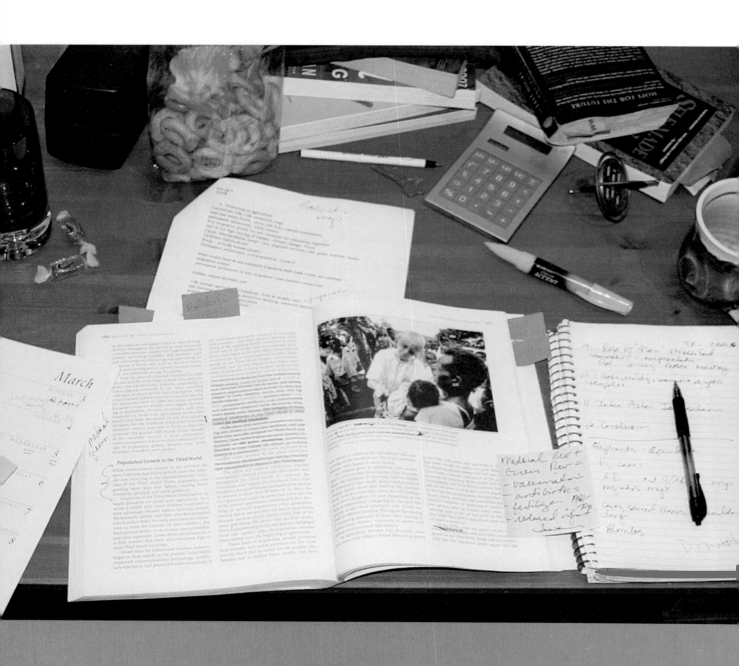

Reading is essential in all your college courses. To get the most out of your reading, you should approach the books, articles, and web pages you read in a practical way, always asking yourself what information they can offer you. You should also approach assigned readings critically, just as you approach your own writing when you revise.

Reading critically does not mean challenging or arguing with every idea; rather, it means considering, commenting, questioning, and assessing. Most of all, it means being an active rather than a passive reader. Being an **active reader** means participating in the reading process: approaching a reading assignment with a clear understanding of your purpose, previewing a selection, highlighting and annotating it, and perhaps outlining it—all *before* you begin to respond in writing to what you have read.

To gain an understanding of your **purpose**—your reason for reading—you should start by answering some questions.

QUESTIONS ABOUT YOUR PURPOSE

- Why are you reading?
- Will you be expected to discuss what you are reading? If so, will you discuss it in class or in a conference with your instructor?
- Will you have to write about what you are reading? If so, will you be expected to write an informal response (for example, a journal entry) or a more formal one (for example, an essay)?
- Will you be tested on the material?

Once you understand your purpose, you are ready to begin reading.

36a Previewing

Your first step is to *preview* the material you have been assigned to read. When you **preview**, you do not read a passage word for word; instead, you **skim** it, reading it quickly to get a sense of the writer's main idea and key supporting points as well as the general emphasis. This strategy is particularly useful when you need to read many pages in a short amount of time. (Skimming can also help you determine if a particular text will be useful to you.) When you skim, you focus on just the key ideas, skipping details and examples. You look at the title, the author's name, the first paragraph (which often contains a thesis statement or an overview), and the last paragraph (which often contains a summary of the writer's points). You also look at each paragraph's first sentence. As you skim a text, you should also look for clues to content and emphasis in **visual signals**, such as headings, boxed text, and images.

Guidelines for Previewing

- Look at the title.
- Look at the author's name.
- Look at the opening paragraph, searching for the sentence that best expresses the main idea.
- Look at the closing paragraph, searching for a summary of the writer's ideas.
- Look at each paragraph's first sentence.
- Look at headings and subheadings.
- Look at *italicized* and **boldfaced** words.
- Look at numbered lists.
- Look at bulleted lists (like this one).
- Look at graphs, charts, tables, diagrams, photographs, and other visuals.
- Look at any information that is boxed.
- Look at any information that is in color.

When you have finished previewing, you should have a general sense of what the writer wants to communicate.

PRACTICE

36-1   "No Comprendo" ("I Don't Understand") is a newspaper opinion article by Barbara Mujica, a professor of Spanish at Georgetown University in Washington, D.C. In this article, which was published in the *New York Times*, Mujica argues against bilingual education (teaching students in their native language as well as in English).

In preparation for class discussion and for other activities that will be assigned later in this chapter, preview the article. As you skim, identify the writer's main idea and key supporting points. Then, write them on the lines that follow the article.

NO COMPRENDO

Barbara Mujica

Last spring, my niece phoned me in tears. She was graduating from high school and had to make a decision. An outstanding soccer player, she was offered athletic scholarships by several colleges. So why was she crying?   1

My niece came to the United States from South America as a child. 2 Although she had received good grades in her schools in Miami, she spoke English with a heavy accent, and her comprehension and writing skills were deficient. She was afraid that once she left the Miami environment, she would feel uncomfortable and, worse still, have difficulty keeping up with class work.

Programs that keep foreign-born children in Spanish-language 3 classrooms for years are only part of the problem. During a visit to my niece's former school, I observed that all business, not just teaching, was conducted in Spanish. In the office, secretaries spoke to the administrators and the children in Spanish. Announcements over the public-address system were made in an English so fractured that it was almost incomprehensible.

I asked my niece's mother why, after years in public schools, her 4 daughter had poor English skills. "It's the whole environment," she replied. "All kinds of services are available in Spanish or Spanglish. Sports and after-school activities are conducted in Spanglish. That's what the kids hear on the radio and in the street."

WORD POWER

Spanglish A mixture of Spanish and English

Until recently, immigrants made learning English a priority. But even 5 when they didn't learn English themselves, their children grew up speaking it. Thousands of first-generation Americans still strive to learn English, but others face reduced educational and career opportunities because they have not mastered this basic skill they need to get ahead.

According to the 1990 census, 40 percent of the Hispanics born in the 6 United States do not graduate from high school, and the Department of Education says that a lack of proficiency in English is an important factor in the drop-out rate.

People and agencies that favor providing services only in foreign 7 languages want to help people who do not speak English, but they may be doing these people a disservice by condemning them to a linguistic ghetto from which they cannot easily escape.

And my niece? She turned down all of her scholarship opportunities, 8 deciding instead to attend a small college in Miami, where she will never have to put her English to the test.

Writer's main idea

_____

_____

Key supporting points

1. _____

2. _____

3. _____

4. _____

36b   Highlighting

After you preview the assigned material, read it carefully, *highlighting* as you read. **Highlighting** means using underlining and symbols to identify key ideas. This active reading strategy will help you understand the writer's ideas and make connections among them when you reread. Be selective when you highlight. Because you will eventually be rereading every high-lighted word, phrase, and sentence, highlight only the most important, most useful information.

Using Highlighting Symbols

- <u>Underline</u> key ideas—for example, topic sentences.
- Box or circle words or phrases you want to remember.
- Place a check mark (✓) or star (✳) next to an important idea.
- Place a double check mark (✓✓) or double star (✳✳) next to an especially significant idea.
- Draw lines or arrows to connect related ideas.
- Put a question mark (?) beside a word or an idea that you need to look up.
- Number the writer's key supporting points or examples.

FYI

Knowing What to Highlight

You want to highlight what's important—but how do you *know* what's important?

- *Look for visual signals.* As a general rule, you should look for the same **visual signals** you looked for when you did your preview-ing. Many of the ideas you will need to highlight will probably be found in material that is visually set off from the rest of the text—opening and closing paragraphs, lists, and so on.

- *Look for verbal signals.* Also look for **verbal signals**—words and phrases that often introduce key points. (Some of these verbal signals are listed in the box on page 521.)

Together, these visual and verbal signals will give you clues to the writer's meaning and emphasis.

Recognizing Verbal Signals

- Phrases that signal emphasis ("The *primary* reason"; "The *most important* idea")
- Repeated words and phrases
- Words that signal addition (*also, in addition, furthermore*)
- Words that signal time sequence (*first, after, then, next, finally*)
- Words that identify causes and effects (*because, as a result, for this reason*)
- Words that introduce examples (*for example, for instance*)
- Words that signal comparison (*likewise, similarly*)
- Words that signal contrast (*unlike, although, in contrast*)
- Words that signal contradiction (*however, on the contrary*)
- Words that signal a narrowing of the writer's focus (*in fact, specifically, in other words*)
- Words that signal summaries or conclusions (*to sum up, in conclusion*)

Here is how one student highlighted a passage from a newspaper column, "Barbie at Thirty-Five" by Anna Quindlen.

But consider the recent study at the University of Arizona investigating the attitudes of white and black teenage girls toward body image. The attitudes of the white girls were a nightmare. Ninety percent expressed dissatisfaction with their own bodies, and many said they saw dieting as a kind of all-purpose panacea. "I think the reason I would diet would be to gain self-confidence," said one. "I'd feel like it was a way of getting control," said another. And they were curiously united in their description of the perfect girl. She's 5 feet 7 inches, weighs just over 100 pounds, has long legs and flowing hair. The researchers concluded, "The ideal girl was a living manifestation of the Barbie doll."

While white girls described an impossible ideal, black teenagers talked about appearance in terms of style, attitude, pride, and personality. White respondents talked "thin," black ones "shapely." Seventy percent of the black teenagers said they were satisfied with their weight, and there was little emphasis on dieting. "We're all brought up and taught to be realistic about life," said one, "and we don't look at things the way you want them to be. You look at them the way they are."

The student who highlighted the passage was preparing to write an essay about eating disorders. Because the passage included no visual signals apart from the paragraph divisions, she looked carefully for verbal signals.

The student began her highlighting by underlining and starring the writer's main idea. She then boxed the names of the two key groups the passage compares—*white girls* and *black teenagers*—and underlined two phrases that illustrate how the attitudes of the two groups differ (*dissatisfaction with their own bodies* and *satisfied with their weight*). Check marks in the margin remind the student of the importance of these two phrases, and arrows connect each phrase to the appropriate group of girls.

The student also circled three related terms that characterize white girls' attitudes—*perfect girl*, *Barbie doll*, and *impossible ideal*—drawing lines to connect them. Finally, she circled the unfamiliar word *panacea* and put a question mark beside it to remind herself to look up the word's meaning.

PRACTICE

36-2 Review the highlighted passage. How would your own highlighting of this passage be similar to or different from the sample student highlighting?

PRACTICE

36-3 Reread "No Comprendo" (pp. 518–519). As you reread, highlight the article by underlining and starring main ideas, boxing and circling key words, checkmarking important points, and drawing lines and arrows to connect related ideas. Be sure to circle each unfamiliar word and to put a question mark beside it.

36c Annotating

As you highlight, you should also *annotate* what you are reading. **Annotating** a passage means reading critically and making notes—of questions, reactions, reminders, and ideas for writing or discussion—in the margins or between the lines. (If you run out of room on the page, you can use sticky notes.) Keeping an informal record of ideas as they occur to you will prepare you for class discussion and for writing.

As you read, thinking about the following questions will help you make useful annotations.

Questions for Critical Reading

- What is the writer saying? What do you think the writer is suggesting or implying? What makes you think so?
- What is the writer's purpose (his or her reason for writing)?
- What kind of audience is the writer addressing?
- Is the writer responding to another writer's ideas?
- What is the writer's main idea?
- How does the writer support his or her points? Does the writer use facts? Opinions? Both?
- What kind of supporting details and examples does the writer use?
- Does the writer include enough supporting details and examples?
- What pattern of development does the writer use to arrange his or her ideas? Is this pattern the best choice?

- Does the writer seem well informed? Reasonable? Fair?
- Do you understand the writer's vocabulary?
- Do you understand the writer's ideas?
- Do you agree with the points the writer is making?
- How are the ideas presented in this reading selection like (or unlike) those presented in other selections you have read?

FYI

Making Useful Annotations

As you annotate, be careful not to write too much or too little; good annotations fit in the margins or between the lines or on a small sticky note on the page. You should *not* write your annotations on a separate sheet of paper. If you do, you will be tempted to write too much, and you can easily lose track of where a particular note belongs or what point it comments on. (And if you lose the sheet of paper, you will lose all of your notes and thoughts.) Think of your annotations as a study aid that you can consult when you return to the text a few days later. If you have made useful annotations, they will help you follow the writer's ideas and remember what is most important in the text.

The following passage, which reproduces the student's highlighting from page 521, also illustrates her annotations.

But consider the recent study at the University of Arizona investigating the

attitudes of white and black teenage girls toward body image. The attitudes of the

white girls were a nightmare. Ninety percent expressed dissatisfaction with their   ✓

own bodies, and many said they saw dieting as a kind of all-purpose panacea.   = cure-all

"I think the reason I would diet would be to gain self-confidence," said one. "I'd feel   Need for control, perfection. Why? Media? Parents?

like it was a way of getting control," said another. And they were curiously united

in their description of the perfect girl. She's 5 feet 7 inches, weighs just over 100

pounds, has long legs and flowing hair. The researchers concluded, "The ideal girl   Barbie doll = plastic, unreal

was a living manifestation of the Barbie doll."

While white girls described an impossible ideal, black teenagers talked about

appearance in terms of style, attitude, pride, and personality. White respondents

talked "thin," black ones "shapely." Seventy percent of the black teenagers   "Thin"vs. "shapely"

said they were satisfied with their weight, and there was little emphasis on dieting.   Only 30% dissatisfied—but 90% of white girls

"We're all brought up and taught to be realistic about life," said one, "and we don't

look at things the way you want them to be. You look at them the way they are."

overgeneralization?   vs. Barbie doll (= unrealistic)

In her annotations, this student wrote down the meaning of the word *panacea*, put the study's conclusions and the contrasting statistics into her own words, and recorded questions she intended to explore further.

PRACTICE 36-4 Reread "No Comprendo" (pp. 518–519). As you reread, refer to the Questions for Critical Reading (pp. 522–523), and use them to guide you as you write down your own thoughts and questions in the margins of the article. Note where you agree or disagree with the writer, and briefly explain why. Quickly summarize any points you think are particularly important. Take time to look up any unfamiliar words you have circled and to write brief definitions. Think of these annotations as your preparation for discussing the article in class and eventually writing about it.

36d Outlining

Outlining is another technique you can use to help you understand a reading assignment. Unlike a **formal outline**, which follows strict conventions, an **informal outline** enables you to record a passage's ideas in the order in which they are presented. After you have made an informal outline of a passage, you should be able to see the writer's emphasis (which ideas are more important than others) as well as how the ideas are related.

FYI

Constructing an Informal Outline

To construct an informal outline, follow these guidelines.

1. Write or type the passage's main idea at the top of a sheet of paper. (This will remind you of the writer's focus and help keep your outline on track.)

2. At the left margin, write down the most important idea of the first body paragraph or first part of the passage.

3. Indent the next line a few spaces, and list the examples or details that support this idea. (You can use your computer's Tab key to help you set up your outline.)

4. As ideas become more specific, indent farther. (Ideas that have the same degree of importance are indented the same distance from the left margin.)

5. Repeat the process with each body paragraph or part of the passage.

The student who highlighted and annotated the excerpt from Anna Quindlen's "Barbie at Thirty-Five" (pp. 521–523 and) made the following informal outline to help her understand the writer's ideas.

<u>Main idea</u>: White and African–American teenage girls have very different attitudes about their body images.

<u>White girls dissatisfied</u>
    90% dissatisfied with appearance
    Dieting = cure-all
        –self-confidence
        –control
    Ideal = unrealistic
        –tall and thin
        –Barbie doll

<u>African–American girls satisfied</u>
    70% satisfied with weight
    Dieting not important
    Ideal = realistic
        –shapely
        –not thin

PRACTICE

36-5 Working on your own or in a small group, make an informal outline of "No Comprendo" (pp. 518–519). Refer to your highlighting and annotations as you construct your outline. When you have finished, check to make certain your outline accurately represents the writer's emphasis and the relationships among her ideas.

36e Summarizing

Once you have previewed, highlighted, annotated, and outlined a passage, you may want to *summarize* it to help you understand it better. A **summary** retells, *in your own words*, what a passage is about. A summary condenses a passage, so it leaves out all but the main idea and perhaps the key supporting points. A summary omits supporting examples and details, and it does *not* include your own ideas or opinions.

To summarize a reading assignment, follow these guidelines.

1. Review your outline.
2. Consulting your outline, restate the passage's main idea *in your own words*.
3. Consulting your outline, restate the passage's key supporting points. Add transitional words and phrases between sentences where necessary.
4. Reread the original passage to make sure you have not left out anything significant.

FYI

To avoid accidentally using the exact language of the original, do not look at the passage while you are writing your summary. If you want to use a distinctive word or phrase from the original passage, put it in quotation marks.

The student who highlighted, annotated, and outlined the excerpt from "Barbie at Thirty-Five" (pp. 521, 523, and 525) wrote the following summary.

> As Anna Quindlen reports in "Barbie at Thirty-Five," a University of Arizona study found that white and African-American teenage girls have very different attitudes about their body images. Almost all white girls said they were dissatisfied with their appearance; African-American girls in the study, however, were generally happy with their weight.

PRACTICE

36-6 Write a brief summary of "No Comprendo" (pp. 518–519). Use your outline to guide you, and keep your summary short and to the point. Your summary should be about one-quarter to one-third the length of the original article.

36f   Writing a Response Paragraph

Once you have highlighted and annotated a reading selection, you are ready to write about it—perhaps in a **response paragraph** in which you record your informal reactions to the writer's ideas.

Because a response paragraph is informal, no special guidelines or rules govern its format or structure. As in any paragraph, however, you should include a topic sentence and supporting evidence, use complete sentences, and link sentences with appropriate transitions. In a response paragraph, informal style and personal opinions are acceptable.

The student who highlighted, annotated, outlined, and summarized "Barbie at Thirty-Five" wrote the following response paragraph.

> Why are white and African–American girls' body images so different? Why do African–American girls think it's okay to be "shapely" while white girls want to be thin? Maybe it's because music videos and movies and fashion magazines show so many more white models, all half-starved, with perfect hair and legs. Or maybe white girls get different messages from their parents or from the people they date. Do white and African–American girls' attitudes about their bodies stay the same when they get older? And what about <u>male</u> teenagers' self-images? Do white and African–American <u>guys</u> have different body images, too?

The process of writing this paragraph was very helpful to the student. The questions she asked suggested some interesting ideas that she could explore in class discussion or in a more fully developed piece of writing.

PRACTICE

37-7 Write a response paragraph expressing your reactions to "No Comprendo" (pp. 518–519) and to the issue of bilingual education.

36g   Reading in the Classroom, in the Community, and in the Workplace

In college, in your life as a citizen of your community, and in the workplace, you will read material in a variety of formats—for example, textbooks, newspapers, web pages, and job-related documents.

Although the active reading process you have just reviewed can be applied to all types of material, various kinds of reading require slightly different strategies during the previewing stage. One reason for this is that different kinds of reading may have different purposes (for example, to present information or to persuade). Another reason is that the various documents you read are aimed at specific audiences, and different readers require different signals about content and emphasis. For these reasons, you need to look for specific kinds of verbal and visual signals when you preview different kinds of reading material.

Reading Textbooks

Much of the reading you do in college is in textbooks (like this one). The purpose of a textbook is to present information, and when you read a textbook, your goal is to understand that information. To do this, you need to figure out which ideas are most important as well as which points support those ideas and which examples illustrate them.

checklist

Reading Textbooks

Look for the following features as you preview.

- [ ] **Boldfaced** and *italicized* words, which can indicate terms to be defined
- [ ] Boxed checklists or summaries, which may appear at the ends of sections or chapters
- [ ] Bulleted or numbered lists, which may list key reasons or examples or summarize important material
- [ ] Diagrams, charts, tables, graphs, photographs, and other visuals that illustrate the writer's points
- [ ] Marginal quotations and definitions
- [ ] Marginal cross-references
- [ ] Web links

PRACTICE

36-8   Using the checklist for reading textbooks as a guide, preview the page from the textbook *Psychology*, Sixth Edition (2013), by Don H. Hockenbury and Sandra E. Hockenbury, on page 528. When you have finished, highlight and annotate it.

Hearing

From Vibration to Sound

███ **KEY THEME**

> Auditory sensation, or hearing, results when sound waves are collected in the outer ear, amplified in the middle ear, and converted to neural messages in the inner ear.

███ **KEY QUESTIONS**

> How do sound waves produce different auditory sensations?

> What are the key structures of the ear and their functions?

> How do place theory and frequency theory explain pitch perception?

We have hiked in a desert area that was so quiet we could hear the whir of a single grasshopper's wings in the distance. And we have waited on a subway platform where the screech of metal wheels against metal rails forced us to cover our ears.

The sense of hearing, or **audition,** is capable of responding to a wide range of sounds, from faint to blaring, simple to complex, harmonious to discordant. The ability to sense and perceive very subtle differences in sound is important to physical survival, social interactions, and language development. Most of the time, all of us are bathed in sound—so much so that moments of near-silence, like our experience in the desert, can seem almost eerie.

What We Hear

The Nature of Sound

Whether it's the ear-splitting screech of metal on metal or the subtle whir of a grasshopper's wings, *sound waves* are the physical stimuli that produce our sensory experience of sound. Usually, sound waves are produced by the rhythmic vibration of air molecules, but sound waves can be transmitted through other media, such as water, too. Our perception of sound is directly related to the physical properties of sound waves (see Figure 3.7).

One of the first things that we notice about a sound is how loud it is. **Loudness** is determined by the intensity, or **amplitude,** of a sound wave and is measured in units called **decibels.** Zero decibels represents the loudness of the softest sound that humans can hear, or the absolute threshold for hearing. As decibels increase, perceived loudness increases.

Pitch refers to the relative "highness" or "lowness" of a sound. Pitch is determined by the frequency of a sound wave. **Frequency** refers to the rate of vibration, or number of waves per second, and is measured in units called *hertz.* Hertz simply refers to the number of wave peaks per second. The faster the vibration, the higher the frequency, the closer together the waves are—and the higher the tone produced. If you pluck the high E and the low E strings on a guitar, you'll notice that the low E vibrates far fewer times per second than does the high E.

Most of the sounds we experience do not consist of a single frequency but are *complex,* consisting of several sound-wave frequencies. This combination of frequencies produces the distinctive quality, or **timbre,** of a sound, which enables us to distinguish easily between the same note played on a saxophone and on a piano. Every human voice has its own distinctive timbre, which is why you can immediately identify a friend's voice on the telephone from just a few words, even if you haven't talked to each other for years.

■ **audition** The technical term for the sense of hearing.

■ **loudness** The intensity (or amplitude) of a sound wave, measured in decibels.

■ **amplitude** The intensity or amount of energy of a wave, reflected in the height of the wave; the amplitude of a sound wave determines a sound's loudness.

■ **decibel** (DESS-uh-bell) The unit of measurement for loudness.

■ **pitch** The relative highness or lowness of a sound, determined by the frequency of a sound wave.

■ **frequency** The rate of vibration, or the number of sound waves per second.

■ **timbre** (TAM-ber) The distinctive quality of a sound, determined by the complexity of the sound wave.

FIGURE 3.7 Characteristics of Sound Waves The length of a wave, its height, and its complexity determine the loudness, pitch, and timbre that we hear. The sound produced by (a) would be high-pitched and loud. The sound produced by (b) would be soft and low. The sound in (c) is complex, like the sounds we usually experience in the natural world.

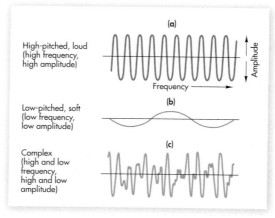

Reading News Articles

As a student, as a citizen, and as an employee, you read school, community, local, and national newspapers in print and online. Like textbooks, news articles communicate information. In addition, newspapers publish editorials (which aim to persuade) as well as feature articles (which may be designed to entertain as well as to inform).

Many people read news articles online rather than in print form. If this is what you usually do, keep in mind that newspaper web pages tend to be very busy and crowded, so you may need to work hard to distinguish important information from not-so-important material. For example, a news article that you read online may be surrounded by advertising and include links to irrelevant (and potentially distracting) material. For this reason, it is very important to read online material with care.

checklist

Reading News Articles

Look for the following features as you preview.

- [ ] Headlines

- [ ] **Boldfaced** headings within articles

- [ ] Labels like *editorial*, *commentary*, or *opinion*, which indicate that an article communicates the writer's own views

- [ ] Brief biographical information at the end of an opinion piece

- [ ] Phrases or sentences in **boldface** (to emphasize key points)

- [ ] The article's first sentence, which often answers the questions *who*, *what*, *why*, *where*, *when*, and *how*

- [ ] The **dateline**, which tells you the date and the city the writer is reporting from

- [ ] Photographs, charts, graphs, and other visuals

- [ ] In *print news articles*, related articles that appear on the same page, such as boxed information and **sidebars**—short related articles that provide additional background on people and places mentioned in the article

- [ ] In *online news articles*, links to related articles, reader comments, and other useful material

PRACTICE

36-9

Using the checklist for reading news articles as a guide, preview the online news article on page 530. Then, highlight and annotate it.

Reading on the Job

In your workplace, you may be called on to read email messages, memos, letters, and reports. These documents, which may be designed to convey information or to persuade, are often addressed to a group rather than to a single person. (Note that the most important information is often presented *first*—in a subject line or in the first paragraph.)

checklist

Reading on the Job

Look for the following features as you preview.

☐ Numbered or bulleted lists of tasks or problems (numbers indicate the order of the items' importance)

☐ The first and last paragraphs and the first sentence of each body paragraph, which often contain key information

☐ **Boldfaced**, underlined, or *italicized* words

☐ In a report, visuals that illustrate key concepts

☐ In electronic communications, the person(s) addressed, the subject line, and links to the web

☐ In a memo or a report, headings that highlight key topics or points

PRACTICE

36-10 Using the checklist for reading on the job as a guide, preview the email message on page 532. What is the writer's purpose? What is the most important piece of information she wants to communicate? Highlight and annotate the email, and then write a two-sentence summary of it.

To...   ⊞ **Work-Study - New Students**

Cc...

Send   Bcc...

Subject: Reminder: First-Day Orientation tomorrow morning

Dear students,

Don't forget to report to the campus café on the south quad tomorrow at 8:00 am for our First-Day Orientation to welcome you to the work-study program.

We will spend the first half of the hour getting you acquainted with the kinds of work you'll be doing and going over some important safety information. During the second half hour, we will schedule your work shifts in the dining hall and campus café, so be sure to bring a copy of your course schedule with you.

I look forward to meeting you all tomorrow morning.

Best regards,
Mina

Mina M. Raine
Work-Study Program Coordinator
Bedford Community College
(121) 126-1212
mraine@bedfordcc.edu

---

review checklist

Reading Critically

- [ ] Preview the material. (See 36a.)

- [ ] Highlight the material. (See 36b.)

- [ ] Annotate the material. (See 36c.)

- [ ] Outline the material. (See 36d.)

- [ ] Summarize the material. (See 36e.)

- [ ] Write a response paragraph. (See 36f.)

- [ ] Use active reading strategies when reading textbooks, news articles, and workplace communications. (See 36g.)

37 Readings for Writers

The following essays by professional writers offer interesting material to read, react to, think critically about, discuss, and write about. In addition, these essays illustrate some of the ways you can organize ideas in your own writing.

The essays in this chapter use the nine patterns of development you learned about in Units 2 and 3 of this book: exemplification, narration, description, process, cause and effect, comparison and contrast, classification, definition, and argument. Of course, these patterns are not your only options for arranging ideas in essays; in fact, many essays combine several patterns of development. Still, understanding how each of these nine patterns works will help you choose the most effective organization strategy when you are writing for a particular purpose and audience.

In this chapter, two essays by professional writers illustrate each pattern of development. (For argument, three model essays are included.) For process, classification, definition, and argument, one reading is offered online as an e-reading—part of LaunchPad Solo for *Writing First*. Each essay is preceded by a short **headnote**—an introduction that tells you something about the writer and suggests what to look for as you read. Following each essay are three sets of questions and two writing prompts. (Questions that you can work on in collaboration with other students are marked with an **asterisk** [*].)

- **Reacting to Language** questions focus on the writer's words.
- **Reacting to Ideas** questions encourage you to respond critically to the writer's ideas and perhaps to consider his or her audience or purpose.
- **Reacting to the Pattern** questions ask you to consider how ideas are arranged within the essay and how they are connected to one another.
- **Writing Practice** prompts give you opportunities to explore writing ideas and organizational strategies related to the chapter's readings.

As you read each of the following essays, **preview**, **highlight**, and **annotate** it to help you understand the writer's ideas and emphasis. (See pp. 517–524 for advice on previewing, highlighting, and annotating.) Then, read the essay again carefully in preparation for class discussion and writing.

EXEMPLIFICATION
"Don't Call Me a Hot Tamale," Judith Ortiz Cofer 534
"No, I Do Not Want to Pet Your Dog," Farhad Manjoo 537

:e These e-readings are available online at **macmillan .com/writingfirst**

37a Exemplification

An **exemplification** essay uses specific examples to support a thesis statement. The two selections that follow, "Don't Call Me a Hot Tamale" by Judith Ortiz Cofer and "No, I Do Not Want to Pet Your Dog" by Farhad Manjoo, are exemplification essays.

Don't Call Me a Hot Tamale

Judith Ortiz Cofer

Award-winning poet, novelist, and essayist Judith Ortiz Cofer often writes about her experiences as a Latina—a Hispanic woman—living in a non-Hispanic culture. In 1998, Cofer received the Christ-Janner Award in Creative Research from the University of Georgia, where she is now the Regents' and Franklin Professor of English and Creative Writing, Emerita. In "Don't Call Me a Hot Tamale," an excerpt from her book *The Latin Deli: Prose and Poetry* (1993), she discusses how being Puerto Rican has affected her in the world beyond Puerto Rico. As you read, note how her examples illustrate the stereotypes she encounters in reaction to both her heritage and her gender.

On a bus to London from Oxford University, where I was earning some graduate credits one summer, a young man, obviously fresh from a pub, approached my seat. With both hands over his heart, he went down on his knees in the aisle and broke into an Irish tenor's rendition of "Maria" from *West Side Story*. I was not amused. "Maria" had followed me to London, reminding me of a prime fact of my life: You can leave the island of Puerto Rico, master the English language, and travel as far as you can, but if you're a Latina, especially one who so clearly belongs to Rita Moreno's[1] gene pool, the island travels with you. 1

Growing up in New Jersey and wanting most of all to belong, I lived in two completely different worlds. My parents designed our life as a microcosm of their *casas* on the island—we spoke in Spanish, ate Puerto Rican food bought at the *bodega*, and practiced strict Catholicism complete with Sunday mass in Spanish. 2

> **WORD POWER**
> **microcosm** Something seen as a small version of something larger

I was kept under tight surveillance by my parents, since my virtue and modesty were, by their cultural equation, the same as their honor. As teenagers, my friends and I were lectured constantly on how to behave as proper *señoritas*. But it was a conflicting message we received, since our Puerto Rican mothers also encouraged us to look and act like women by dressing us in clothes our Anglo schoolmates and their mothers found too "mature" and flashy. I often felt humiliated when I appeared at an American friend's birthday party wearing a dress more suitable for a semiformal. At Puerto Rican festivities, neither the music nor the colors we wore could be too loud. 3

I remember Career Day in high school, when our teachers told us to come dressed as if for a job interview. That morning, I agonized in front of my closet, trying to figure out what a "career girl" would wear, because the only model I had was Marlo Thomas[2] on TV. To me and my Puerto Rican girl-friends, dressing up meant wearing our mother's ornate jewelry and clothing. 4

At school that day, the teachers assailed us for wearing "everything at once"—meaning too much jewelry and too many accessories. And it was painfully obvious that the other students in their tailored skirts and silk blouses thought we were hopeless and vulgar. The way they looked at us was a taste of the cultural clash that awaited us in the real world, where prospective employers and men on the street would often misinterpret our tight skirts and bright colors as a come-on. 5

It is custom, not chromosomes, that leads us to choose scarlet over pale pink. Our mothers had grown up on a tropical island where the natural environment was a riot of primary colors, where showing your skin was one way to keep cool as well as to look sexy. On the island, women felt freer to dress and move provocatively since they were protected by 6

---

1. A Puerto Rican actress, dancer, and singer. She is well known for her role in the movie musical *West Side Story*, a version of Shakespeare's *Romeo and Juliet* featuring Anglos and Puerto Ricans in New York City.
2. Star of a 1966–71 television comedy about a young woman living on her own in New York City.

WORD POWER

machismo a strong sense of masculine pride

the traditions and laws of a Spanish/Catholic system of morality and machismo, the main rule of which was: *You may look at my sister, but if you touch her I will kill you.* The extended family and church structure provided them with a circle of safety on the island; if a man "wronged" a girl, everyone would close in to save her family honor.

Off-island, signals often get mixed. When a Puerto Rican girl who is 7 dressed in her idea of what is attractive meets a man from the mainstream culture who has been trained to react to certain types of clothing as a sexual signal, a clash is likely to take place. She is seen as a Hot Tamale, a sexual firebrand. I learned this lesson at my first formal dance when my date leaned over and painfully planted a sloppy, overeager kiss on my mouth. When I didn't respond with sufficient passion, he said in a resentful tone: "I thought you Latin girls were supposed to mature early." It was only the first time I would feel like a fruit or vegetable—I was supposed to *ripen*, not just grow into womanhood like other girls.

These stereotypes, though rarer, still surface in my life. I recently 8 stayed at a classy metropolitan hotel. After having dinner with a friend, I was returning to my room when a middle-aged man in a tuxedo stepped directly into my path. With his champagne glass extended toward me, he exclaimed, "Evita!"[3]

Blocking my way, he bellowed the song "Don't Cry for Me, Argentina." 9 Playing to the gathering crowd, he began to sing loudly a ditty to the tune of "La Bamba"[4]—except the lyrics were about a girl named Maria whose exploits all rhymed with her name and gonorrhea.

I knew that this same man—probably a corporate executive, even 10 worldly by most standards—would never have regaled a white woman with a dirty song in public. But to him, I was just a character in his universe of "others," all cartoons.

Still, I am one of the lucky ones. There are thousands of Latinas with- 11 out the privilege of the education that my parents gave me. For them every day is a struggle against the misconceptions perpetuated by the myth of the Latina as whore, domestic worker or criminal.

Rather than fight these pervasive stereotypes, I try to replace them 12 with a more interesting set of realities. I travel around the U.S. reading from my books of poetry and my novel. With the stories I tell, the dreams and fears I examine in my work, I try to get my audience past the particulars of my skin color, my accent or my clothes.

I once wrote a poem in which I called Latinas "God's brown daugh- 13 ters." It is really a prayer, of sorts, for communication and respect. In it, Latin women pray "in Spanish to an Anglo God / with a Jewish heritage," and they are "fervently hoping / that if not omnipotent, / at least He be bilingual."

WORD POWER

perpetuated made to last indefinitely
pervasive existing in every part of something
omnipotent all-powerful

Reacting to Language

*What is a tamale? What does the phrase *hot tamale* suggest to you? What do you think Cofer intends it to suggest? Can you think of another word or phrase that might be more effective?

---

3. Eva Perón, wife of Juan Perón, president of Argentina in the 1940s and 1950s. She is the subject of the musical *Evita*.
4. A song with Spanish lyrics popular in the late 1950s.

Reacting to Ideas

*1. Cofer states her thesis in paragraph 1: "You can leave the island of Puerto Rico, master the English language, and travel as far as you can, but if you're a Latina, . . . the island travels with you." Restate this thesis in your own words. Do you think this statement applies only to Latinas or to members of other ethnic groups as well? Explain.

 2. How, according to Cofer, are the signals sent by dress and appearance interpreted differently in Puerto Rico and "off-island" (paragraph 7)? How does this difference create problems for Cofer? Do you think there is anything she can do to avoid these problems?

Reacting to the Pattern

 1. What examples does Cofer use to support her thesis? Do you think she supplies enough examples to convince readers that her thesis is reasonable?

 2. Cofer begins her essay with an example. Do you think this is an effective opening strategy? Why or why not? How else might she have begun her essay?

 3. All of Cofer's examples are drawn from her own experiences. Are these personal examples as convincing as statistics or examples from current news articles would be? Are they *more* convincing? Explain.

Writing Practice

 1. What positive examples can you think of to respond to the stereotype of the Latina as "whore, domestic worker or criminal" (paragraph 11)? Write a letter to a television network in which you propose the addition of several different Latina characters to actual programs in which they might appear.

 2. Do you think others stereotype you because of your heritage—or because of your age, your gender, your dress, or where you live? Write an essay in which you discuss some specific instances of such stereotyping, and explain why it is troublesome to you.

No, I Do Not Want to Pet Your Dog

Farhad Manjoo

Farhad Manjoo was born in South Africa in 1978 and moved with his family to the United States when he was a young boy. He graduated from Cornell University, where he served as the editor of the student newspaper. He has worked as a staff writer for *Slate* and has been a regular contributor to National Public Radio. He currently writes a technology column for the *Wall Street Journal* and is the author of *True Enough: Learning to Live in a Post-Fact Society* (2008). In "No, I Do Not Want to Pet Your Dog," which first appeared in *Slate*, Manjoo responds to an everyday irritation by describing an America in which dogs have "achieved dominion" over spaces from which they were once barred. As you read, note how he uses examples to poke fun at the way dog owners talk about and treat their beloved pets.

The other day I walked into my gym and saw a dog. A half-dozen people 1
were crowding around him, cooing and petting. He was a big dog, a lean
and muscular Doberman with, I later learned, the sort of hair-trigger bark
you'd prize if you wanted to protect a big stash of gold bullion.

"This is Y.," the dog's owner said. No explanation was offered for the 2
pooch's presence, as if it were the most natural thing in the world to have
a dog in a place usually reserved for human beings. *Huh*, I thought.

The dog came up to me, because in my experience that's what dogs 3
do when you don't want them to come up to you. They get up real close,
touching you, licking you, theatrically begging you to respond. The dog
pushed his long face toward my hand, the canine equivalent of a high five.
And so—in the same way it's rude to leave a high-fiver hanging, especially
if the high-fiver has big teeth and a strong jaw—I was expected to pet him.
I ran my hand across his head half-heartedly. I guess I was fairly sure he
wouldn't snap and bite me, but stranger things have happened—for instance, dogs snapping and biting people all the time.

Anyway, happily, I survived. 4

But wait a second. Come on! Why was this dog here? And why was 5
no one perturbed that this dog was here? When this beast was barking at
passersby through the window as we were all working out, why did no one
go, *Hey, just throwing this out there, should we maybe not have this distracting, possibly dangerous animal by the free weights?*

No one was asking because no one could ask. Sometime in the last de- 6
cade, dogs achieved dominion over urban America. They are everywhere
now, allowed in places that used to belong exclusively to humans, and
sometimes only to human adults: the office, restaurants, museums, buses,
trains, malls, supermarkets, barber shops, banks, post offices. Even at the
park and other places where dogs belong, they've been given free rein.
Dogs are frequently allowed to wander off leash, to run toward you and
around you, to run across the baseball field or basketball court, to get up
in your grill. Even worse than the dogs are the owners, who seem never
to consider whether there may be people in the gym/office/restaurant/
museum who do not care to be in close proximity to their dogs. After all,
what kind of monster would have a problem with a poor innocent widdle
doggie? It's a dog's world. We just live in it. And it's awful. Bad dogs!

Not everyone agrees with me on this issue. Some people—or maybe 7
even most people, since dogs, like zombies, have an insidious way of turning opponents into allies—love that dogs abound. If you adore dogs but
aren't able to keep one, the world is now your dog park, with pooches
everywhere to pet and nuzzle and otherwise brighten your day.

I am not a dog person. (Could you tell?) It's not that I actively despise 8
mutts; I just don't have much time for them, in the same way I don't have
time for crossword puzzles or Maroon 5. Now imagine if, everywhere you
went, whatever you did, Maroon 5 was always playing and everyone pretended it was totally normal—that this permanent new situation was not
in any way offensive, distracting, dirty, and potentially dangerous.

OK, bad example. 9

But here's my problem: There's now a cultural assumption that every- 10
one must love dogs. Dog owners are rarely forced to reckon with the idea
that there are people who aren't enthralled by their furry friends, and that
taking their dogs everywhere might not be completely pleasant for these
folks.

WORD POWER

dominion the power to
rule

WORD POWER

proximity nearness

WORD POWER

insidious harmful but
enticing

Example: If you're in the office and someone has brought her dog in 11 for the day—because, *fun*!—the dog is sure to come around you, get between your legs, rub against your thigh, take a nap on your feet, or do some other annoying thing.

If the dog's owner notices these antics, I can promise you she won't 12 apologize for the imposition. Nor will she ask you if you mind her dog doing what he's doing. Nor will she pull on its leash, because there won't be a leash, this being an office, where dogs are as welcome as Wi-Fi and free coffee.

Instead, if the owner says anything, it will be on the order of, "Don't 13 worry, he loves people!" Oh, OK then! I guess I'll just take your word for it, and forget for the moment that 1,000 Americans a day go to emergency rooms because of dog bites. More Americans seek medical attention for dog bites than for choking or falls. You're more likely to have to go to a doctor for a bite than to call the fire department for a home fire. Like it or not, American dog owner, your pet is a hazard.

But let's leave aside the possibility that I'm scared (maybe legitimately!) 14 of your dog, since you've assured me your dog loves people, and there's no chance you could be wrong. What if I'm allergic? Or what if I just plain hate your dog? What if I think he's dirty, since after all he did just put his nose in another dog's butt? And what if I just want to go through my workday without being slobbered on by an animal?

I know this sounds curmudgeonly. You want to shake me and tell me 15 to snap out of it, to get over myself and just love dogs already. But that's because you like dogs and don't see anything but good in them. For you, a dog is like ice cream. What churl doesn't like ice cream? Well, I'm that churl—I'm canine intolerant.

To give you a sense of how I feel when I'm accosted by your dog, let's 16 replace that animal with my 2½-year-old son. Now, I love my son, but on any objective scale of socially acceptable behavior, he is the worst. He's loud. He's inconsiderate of people's personal space—if he's left free he won't watch where he's walking and will run into you, either on purpose or accidentally. He's jumpy and fidgety in confined spaces; in an airplane it is physically impossible to restrain him from kicking the seat in front of him. He scratches himself often, sometimes picks his nose, sometimes offers to pick yours. He will constantly say inappropriate things. The other day at Target, he noticed a little person and commented, for pretty much everyone to hear, "That lady is short!" On top of all this, he may be packing a diaper full of urine and feces.

Weirdly, irrationally, despite all this, I feel the same way about my son 17 as you do about your dog: I love him unconditionally and just don't understand why even strangers wouldn't want him around all the time. Indeed, I think almost everything he does, even the inappropriate things, is the cutest behavior ever exhibited in human history.

And yet, still, I rein him in. I realize that, although he's impossibly cute, 18 it's possible he might aggravate some people. For this reason, whenever I go into public spaces with my toddler, I treat him as if I were handling nuclear waste or a dangerous animal. I keep him confined. I shush him. If he does anything out of turn—screams, touches people—I make a show of telling him to quit it and I apologize profusely. And, finally, there are some places that are completely off-limits to my son: nice restaurants, contemplative adult spaces like grown-up museums and coffee shops, the gym, and the office. Especially the office.

WORD POWER

curmudgeonly bad tempered

WORD POWER

accosted approached in an aggressive way

Yes, there are parents who don't act this way, awful parents who let 19 their terrible kids run free. The rest of us hate those people because they give all parents a bad name. But I'll submit there are many more such dog owners than there are overindulgent parents. Most parents I know are mortified by the thought that their children might be causing anguish for others. This is evident in the world around you: It's why your co-workers rarely bring their toddlers to work. It's why 2-year-olds don't approach you in the park and lick your leg or ask you whether you need to visit the potty. It's why, when a child is being unruly in a supermarket or restaurant, you'll usually see his parents strive to get him to knock it off.

But dog owners? They seem to suffer few qualms about their animals' 20 behavior. That's why there are so many dogs running around at the park, jumping up on the bench beside you while you're trying to read a book, the owner never asking if it's OK with you. That's why, when you're at a café, the dog at the neighboring table feels free to curl up under your seat. That's why there's a dog at your office right at this moment and you're having to pretend that he's just the cutest.

Well, no more, my fellow doggie skeptics. Let's take back the peace 21 we're owed. The next time your young, happy co-worker brings in his dog for the day, tell him the office is not a canine playpen. It's time to take that dog home.

Reacting to Language

*In paragraph 5, Manjoo uses the word *beast* to refer to a dog. What other words (nouns and adjectives) does he use to characterize dogs? Are these words generally neutral, positive, or negative?

Reacting to Ideas

1. What main idea does Manjoo want to get across in this essay? Do you think that his title (or his essay's last line) is his essay's thesis? Why or why not?

2. Manjoo says that dogs "are everywhere now" (paragraph 6). Do your own observations support this claim? If so, do you see the presence of dogs "everywhere" as a problem?

*3. In paragraph 16, Manjoo begins explaining the similarities he sees between being "accosted" by a dog and being confronted with a young child. Does this extended comparison seem reasonable to you? Explain.

Reacting to the Pattern

1. What examples does Manjoo give to support his claim that dogs "are everywhere now" (6)? What evidence does he give to support his belief that this is a problem?

2. In paragraph 10, Manjoo says, "There's now a cultural assumption that everyone must love dogs." Does he give examples to support this statement? If so, where? If not, can you think of any supporting examples?

Writing Practice

1. Do you agree with Manjoo? Write an exemplification essay that illustrates the problems dogs cause in your own life—for example, in your workplace or on the streets of your community.

2. Do you disagree with Manjoo? Write an exemplification essay that illustrates the benefits of a policy of welcoming dogs in your community, in your workplace, or on your campus.

37b Narration

A **narrative** essay tells a story by presenting a series of events in chronological order. In the first of the two essays that follow, "The Sanctuary of School," Lynda Barry tells readers about her home and family. In the second essay, "My Grandfather the Outlaw," Frank Bruni traces the experiences of his Italian immigrant grandfather.

The Sanctuary of School

Lynda Barry

In her many illustrated works—including graphic novels, comic books, and a weekly cartoon strip, *Ernie Pook's Comeek*, which appears in a number of newspapers and magazines—Lynda Barry looks at the world through the eyes of children. Her characters remind adult readers of the complicated world of young people and of the clarity with which they see social situations. In "The Sanctuary of School," first published in the *Baltimore Sun* in 1992, Barry tells a story from her own childhood. As you read this essay, note how Barry relates her personal experience to a broader issue.

I was 7 years old the first time I snuck out of the house in the dark. It was winter and my parents had been fighting all night. They were short on money and long on relatives who kept "temporarily" moving into our house because they had nowhere else to go.

My brother and I were used to giving up our bedroom. We slept on the couch, something we actually liked because it put us that much closer to the light of our lives, our television.

At night when everyone was asleep, we lay on our pillows watching it with the sound off. We watched Steve Allen's mouth moving. We watched Johnny Carson's mouth moving.[1] We watched movies filled with gangsters shooting machine guns into packed rooms, dying soldiers hurling a last grenade and beautiful women crying at windows. Then the sign-off finally came and we tried to sleep.

The morning I snuck out, I woke up filled with a panic about needing to get to school. The sun wasn't quite up yet but my anxiety was so fierce that I just got dressed, walked quietly across the kitchen and let myself out the back door.

---

1. Steve Allen and Johnny Carson were late-night television hosts.

It was quiet outside. Stars were still out. Nothing moved and no one 5
was in the street. It was as if someone had turned the sound off on the
world.

I walked the alley, breaking thin ice over the puddles with my shoes. I 6
didn't know why I was walking to school in the dark. I didn't think about
it. All I knew was a feeling of panic, like the panic that strikes kids when
they realize they are lost.

That feeling eased the moment I turned the corner and saw the dark 7
outline of my school at the top of the hill. My school was made up of
about 15 nondescript portable classrooms set down on a fenced concrete
lot in a rundown Seattle neighborhood, but it had the most beautiful view
of the Cascade Mountains. You could see them from anywhere on the
playfield and you could see them from the windows of my classroom—
Room 2.

I walked over to the monkey bars and hooked my arms around the cold 8
metal. I stood for a long time just looking across Rainier Valley. The sky
was beginning to whiten and I could hear a few birds.

In a perfect world my absence at home would not have gone un- 9
noticed. I would have had two parents in a panic to locate me, instead of
two parents in a panic to locate an answer to the hard question of survival
during a deep financial and emotional crisis.

But in an overcrowded and unhappy home, it's incredibly easy for any 10
child to slip away. The high levels of frustration, depression and anger
in my house made my brother and me invisible. We were children with
the sound turned off. And for us, as for the steadily increasing number of
neglected children in this country, the only place where we could count on
being noticed was at school.

"Hey there, young lady. Did you forget to go home last night?" It was 11
Mr. Gunderson, our janitor, whom we all loved. He was nice and he was
funny and he was old with white hair, thick glasses and an unbelievable
number of keys. I could hear them jingling as he walked across the playfield. I felt incredibly happy to see him.

He let me push his wheeled garbage can between the different por- 12
tables as he unlocked each room. He let me turn on the lights and raise
the window shades and I saw my school slowly come to life. I saw Mrs.
Holman, our school secretary, walk into the office without her orange lipstick on yet. She waved.

I saw the fifth-grade teacher Mr. Cunningham, walking under the 13
breezeway eating a hard roll. He waved.

And I saw my teacher, Mrs. Claire LeSane, walking toward us in a red 14
coat and calling my name in a very happy and surprised way, and suddenly
my throat got tight and my eyes stung and I ran toward her crying. It was
something that surprised us both.

It's only thinking about it now, 28 years later, that I realize I was crying 15
from relief. I was with my teacher, and in a while I was going to sit at my
desk, with my crayons and pencils and books and classmates all around
me, and for the next six hours I was going to enjoy a thoroughly secure,
warm and stable world. It was a world I absolutely relied on. Without it, I
don't know where I would have gone that morning.

Mrs. LeSane asked me what was wrong and when I said "Nothing," 16
she seemingly left it at that. But she asked me if I would carry her purse
for her, an honor above all honors, and she asked if I wanted to come into
Room 2 early and paint.

She believed in the natural healing power of painting and drawing 17 for troubled children. In the back of her room there was always a drawing table and an easel with plenty of supplies, and sometimes during the day she would come up to you for what seemed like no good reason and quietly ask if you wanted to go to the back table and "make some pictures for Mrs. LeSane." We all had a chance at it—to sit apart from the class for a while to paint, draw and silently work out impossible problems on 11 × 17 sheets of newsprint.

Drawing came to mean everything to me. At the back table in Room 2, 18 I learned to build myself a life preserver that I could carry into my home.

We all know that a good education system saves lives, but the people 19 of this country are still told that cutting the budget for public schools is necessary, that poor salaries for teachers are all we can manage and that art, music and all creative activities must be the first to go when times are lean.

Before- and after-school programs are cut and we are told that pub- 20 lic schools are not made for baby-sitting children. If parents are neglectful temporarily or permanently, for whatever reason, it's certainly sad, but their unlucky children must fend for themselves. Or slip through the cracks. Or wander in a dark night alone.

WORD POWER

fend to try to get along without help

We are told in a thousand ways that not only are public schools not 21 important, but that the children who attend them, the children who need them most, are not important either. We leave them to learn from the blind eye of a television, or to the mercy of "a thousand points of light"[2] that can be as far away as stars.

I was lucky. I had Mrs. LeSane. I had Mr. Gunderson. I had an abun- 22 dance of art supplies. And I had a particular brand of neglect in my home that allowed me to slip away and get to them. But what about the rest of the kids who weren't as lucky? What happened to them?

By the time the bell rang that morning I had finished my drawing and 23 Mrs. LeSane pinned it up on the special bulletin board she reserved for drawings from the back table. It was the same picture I always drew—a sun in the corner of a blue sky over a nice house with flowers all around it.

Mrs. LeSane asked us to please stand, face the flag, place our right 24 hands over our hearts and say the Pledge of Allegiance. Children across the country do it faithfully. I wonder now when the country will face its children and say a pledge right back.

Reacting to Language

*Look up the word *sanctuary* in a dictionary. Which of the listed definitions do you think comes closest to Barry's meaning?

Reacting to Ideas

1. In paragraph 10, Barry characterizes herself and her brother as "children with the sound turned off." What do you think she means?
*2. List the ways in which Barry's home and school worlds are different.

---

2. Phrase used by former president George Herbert Walker Bush to promote volunteerism.

3. What is the main point of Barry's essay—the idea that she wants to convince readers to accept? Is this idea actually stated in her essay? If so, where? If not, do you think it should be?

Reacting to the Pattern

1. Paragraphs 9–10 and 19–22 interrupt Barry's narrative. What purpose do these paragraphs serve? Do you think the essay would be more effective if paragraphs 9 and 10 came earlier? If paragraphs 19–22 came after paragraph 24? Explain.
2. What transitional words and phrases does Barry use to move readers from one event to the next? Do you think her essay needs more transitions? If so, where should they be added?

Writing Practice

1. Did you see elementary school as a "sanctuary" or as something quite different? Write a narrative essay that conveys to readers what school meant to you when you were a child.
2. In addition to school, television was a sanctuary for Barry and her brother. Did television watching (or some other activity) serve this function for you when you were younger? Is there some activity that fills this role now? In a narrative essay, write about your own "sanctuary."

My Grandfather the Outlaw

Frank Bruni

Frank Bruni has been a writer for the *New York Times* since 2004, serving first as chief restaurant critic and now as an op-ed columnist. In 2012, Bruni received the GLAAD Media Award for Outstanding Newspaper Columnist. Additionally, he has written two *New York Times* best-sellers: a chronicle of George W. Bush's campaign for the presidency, *Ambling into History* (2002), and a memoir, *Born Round*: A Story of Family, Food, and a Ferocious Appetite (2009). He is also coauthor of *A Gospel of Shame: Children, Sexual Abuse, and the Catholic Church* (1993). As you read, notice how Bruni uses the narrative of his grandfather's immigrant life in America to comment on broader immigration issues.

> **WORD POWER**
>
> **embodied** represented in a clear way

1   My father's father embodied the American dream. His is the kind of story trumpeted from the stages of our political conventions, the kind of life held up as an affirmation of the rewards this country holds for people willing to take chances, work like crazy and insist on something better for their children than they themselves ever knew.

2   He left Southern Italy in his early 20s, alone, with only enough cash to make it to the United States and last a short time here. It was 1929. He arrived just months before Black Tuesday and the dawn of the Great Depression and found himself scrounging for day labor as a stonemason.

3   And somehow, just barely, he stayed afloat and pressed on until the Depression began to lift. Until his luck turned. Until he could make a down payment on a small grocery store—a bodega, really—where he, his wife and

my father, the eldest of their three sons, toiled so late into the night that the family dinner was often eaten in a stark, sad room in the back. Until his sons went off to Ivy League colleges and became great successes in their respective fields. And until he saw his grandchildren growing up in spacious homes in leafy suburbs, our charmed youths utterly unrecognizable from his own.

Did I mention that he was an illegal alien? 4

He took a ship to Canada from France, then entered the United States 5 across a border that immigration historians tell me was famously porous then. A train deposited him in Manhattan, and soon after he settled in the nearby city of White Plains, which had a populous Italian community. He was undocumented, living off the books and outside the law, and remained so for about a decade before finally becoming a citizen.

WORD POWER

porous capable of being penetrated

The details of all of this are fuzzy: he died in 1980, and his wife—my 6 grandmother, also an Italian immigrant—is long gone as well. What remains are their sons' imperfect memories. But my dad and his brothers know that for a long time, like the estimated 11 million illegal immigrants at the center of our current political debate, Mauro Bruni wasn't supposed to be here. He was trespassing in the country he came to love more fiercely than the one he'd left, the country in which his children and their children would lead highly productive lives, pay many millions of dollars in taxes over time, and get to be a small part of the decision, as voters, about how we were going to treat his spiritual descendants, who traveled here as he did: without explicit invitations or official authorization but with such ferocious energy, such enormous hope.

More Americans than admit or even know it have roots like mine and 7 are the flowers of illegal immigration. And while that doesn't diminish our need to make clear-eyed and sometimes difficult assessments about how many newcomers we can accommodate and what degree of present forgiveness equals future enticement, it must inform our understanding of the people whose tomorrows are in the balance. Their countries of origin tend to be different from those of the illicit arrivals in my grandfather's day. Their skin might be darker. But they're really his kin. My kin. And to see them as some new breed of takers or moochers is to deny history and indulge in a cynical generalization, tinged with an insidious racism, whose targets simply change over time.

WORD POWER

illicit unlawful or illegal

The uncertain journeys that wave after wave of immigrants have under- 8 taken and the daily sacrifices that such transplants have made reflect a degree of grit that many of the American-born people I know have never been forced to muster, a magnitude of drive that we don't possess. It wasn't necessary for us. Wasn't make or break. And these qualities have contributed in a mighty and essential way to this country's dynamism, to its competitiveness.

Coming from southern Europe, Mauro Bruni was considered different 9 from, and less desirable than, an immigrant from northern Europe. Donna Gabaccia, the former director of the Immigration History Research Center at the University of Minnesota, noted that in some circles back then, "Italians and others were 'not quite white' or 'in between' people." From 1899 to 1924, she said, immigration officials even made distinctions among Italians. Those from the country's north were more welcomed than those, like Mauro, from its south.

He spoke no English. The one person he knew in America couldn't give 10 him financial support or, for that matter, even put him up for the night. He had no safety net—and wasn't looking to the government for one, because he couldn't have the government looking his way. His health, his trade, his determination: these were his only assets.

On his first nights here, he paid by the night for a bed in a communal 11 room. He took what masonry jobs he could get, whether they lasted just days or weeks. One of the best was at West Point, where he constructed a long stone wall. His sweat and that of other illegal immigrants went into the gilding of the United States Military Academy, if the accounts that he gave his sons are correct.

In White Plains he met my grandmother, who had managed to come 12 here legally and was a citizen. They married in 1933, and in part because of that, he was later able to declare himself and, through a kind of amnesty, be anointed an American. This had happened by 1941, which was around the time he bought his market.

Were there taxes evaded before he was documented? No doubt, but 13 they couldn't have amounted to much, given his income. The long view is this: he was a taxpayer for more years than he wasn't, and he was the sire of many taxpayers to come. Among his children and grandchildren, there is no one on the dole, no one behind bars, a range of contributions to the vibrancy of this country, a panoply of professions: partner in an international accounting firm, college dean, owner of a plumbing company, investment banker, journalist, management consultant, headhunter, theater director, teacher, professional figure skater.

My grandfather and my grandmother Adelina indeed wanted to wring 14 America for all it was worth. That was selfish, but also very fruitful. And their patriotism was all the stronger because America wasn't their birthright but their choice. Their wager. They were invested in seeing it as the best possible decision, the only right call.

When I recently asked my uncle Jim, their middle son, how intent they 15 were on weaving their children into the fabric of this land, he told me about my grandmother's early relationship with my own mother, whose Irish-English-Scottish family had been here for generations. Adelina Bruni would keep Leslie Jane Frier up late at night, just to prolong the conversation and listen awhile longer to my mother, who didn't sound like any of Grandma's friends. Grandma loved the music of Mom's precise, unaccented English. It was the music of assimilation.

> **WORD POWER**
> **assimilation** the act of adopting the ways of a different culture

Reacting to Language

*1. Consider Bruni's use of the word *outlaw* in his title. What does this word mean to you? Do you think it accurately describes Bruni's grandfather? Why or why not?

2. What does the term *illegal alien* (paragraph 4) mean to you? What other terms could be used to define people in Bruni's grandfather's situation?

Reacting to Ideas

1. Besides Bruni's grandfather, what is this essay about? What main idea does the narrative support?

*2. What does Bruni hope to accomplish in the sections of his essay that are not part of the narrative—for example, paragraphs 7–8 and 13–15?

3. Why do you think Bruni decided to isolate the sentence, "Did I mention that he was an illegal alien?" (4) in its own paragraph? Do you think this was a good decision?

Reacting to the Pattern

1. List the events that make up Bruni's narrative. Where does the actual narrative begin? Where does it end?
*2 Although his essay is a narrative, Bruni also uses other patterns of development. Where, for example, does he use description? Where does he use comparison?

Writing Practice

1. Write a narrative that traces the life story of someone in your own family whose life you believe has "embodied the American dream" (1).
2. Write a narrative that tells the story of your own life—or a part of your life—so far.

37c   Description

A **descriptive** essay tells what something looks, sounds, smells, tastes, or feels like. It uses details to give readers a clear, vivid picture of a person, a place, or an object. In "Fish Cheeks," Amy Tan describes a family meal. In "Rice," Jhumpa Lahiri describes her father as well as his *pulao*, a rice dish.

Fish Cheeks

Amy Tan

Born in California shortly after her parents immigrated there from China, Amy Tan started writing at an early age. Author of the best-selling novel *The Joy Luck Club* (1989) and the more recent *Saving Fish from Drowning* (2006) and *The Valley of Amazement* (2013), Tan is known for exploring Chinese-American mother-daughter relationships. In "Fish Cheeks," originally published in 1987 in *Seventeen* magazine, Tan describes her family's Christmas dinner and the lessons she learned about sharing and appreciating her Chinese heritage. As you read, note how her descriptions reflect her mixed feelings about the dinner.

I fell in love with the minister's son the winter I turned fourteen. He was 1 not Chinese, but as white as Mary in the manger. For Christmas I prayed for this blond-haired boy, Robert, and a slim new American nose.

When I found out that my parents had invited the minister's family over 2 for Christmas Eve dinner, I cried. What would Robert think of our shabby *Chinese* Christmas? What would he think of our noisy *Chinese* relatives who lacked proper American manners? What terrible disappointment would he feel upon seeing not a roasted turkey and sweet potatoes but *Chinese* food?

On Christmas Eve I saw that my mother had outdone herself in creat- 3 ing a strange menu. She was pulling black veins out of the backs of fleshy prawns. The kitchen was littered with appalling mounds of raw food: a slimy rock cod with bulging fish eyes that pleaded not to be thrown into a pan of hot oil. Tofu, which looked like stacked wedges of rubbery white sponges. A bowl soaking dried fungus back to life. A plate of squid, their backs crisscrossed with knife markings so they resembled bicycle tires.

WORD POWER

appalling inspiring horror or disgust

WORD POWER

clamor a loud, continuous noise

WORD POWER

grimaced made a face expressing disgust

And then they arrived—the minister's family and all my relatives in a clamor of doorbells and rumpled Christmas packages. Robert grunted hello, and I pretended he was not worthy of existence. 4

Dinner threw me deeper into despair. My relatives licked the ends of their chopsticks and reached across the table, dipping them into the dozen or so plates of food. Robert and his family waited patiently for platters to be passed to them. My relatives murmured with pleasure when my mother brought out the whole steamed fish. Robert grimaced. Then my father poked his chopsticks just below the fish eye and plucked out the soft meat. "Amy, your favorite," he said, offering me the tender fish cheek. I wanted to disappear. 5

At the end of the meal my father leaned back and belched loudly, thanking my mother for her fine cooking. "It's a polite Chinese custom to show you are satisfied," explained my father to our astonished guests. The minister managed to muster up a quiet burp. I was stunned into silence the rest of the night. 6

After everyone had gone, my mother said to me, "You want to be the same as American girls on the outside." She handed me an early gift. It was a miniskirt in beige tweed. "But inside you must always be Chinese. You must be proud you are different. Your only shame is to have shame." 7

And even though I didn't agree with her then, I knew that she understood how much I had suffered during the evening's dinner. It wasn't until many years later—long after I had gotten over my crush on Robert—that I was able to fully appreciate her lesson and the true purpose behind our particular menu. For Christmas Eve that year, she had chosen all my favorite meals. 8

Reacting to Language

*Look carefully at each use of the word *Chinese* in this essay. What does the word suggest in each case? Does it suggest something positive, negative, or neutral?

Reacting to Ideas

1. Tan is very nervous about the encounter between her family and Robert's. What do you think she is really afraid of?
*2. What does Tan's mother mean by "Your only shame is to have shame" (paragraph 7)?
3. Why does Tan's mother give her the tweed miniskirt?

Reacting to the Pattern

*1. In paragraph 2, Tan asks, "What would Robert think of our shabby *Chinese* Christmas?" How does this question help to establish the dominant impression Tan wants to convey?
2. In paragraph 3, Tan describes the food that was served; in paragraphs 5 and 6, she describes the people. How do the descriptive details she chooses support the essay's dominant impression?
3. Is this essay primarily a subjective or an objective description? Explain.

Writing Practice

1. Describe a family meal of your own—either a typical breakfast, lunch, or dinner or a "company" or holiday meal.
2. Describe the Tan family's meal from Robert's point of view. What does he see? How does the scene (and the food) look to him?

Rice

Jhumpa Lahiri

Born in London to Bengali Indian parents and raised in the United States, Jhumpa Lahiri is a writer whose first short-story collection, *Interpreter of Maladies* (1999), won the 2000 Pulitzer Prize for Fiction and whose first novel, *The Namesake* (2003), was made into a popular film. Her most recent novel is *The Lowland* (2013). In her fiction, Lahiri examines the culture shock Indian immigrants experience when they move to America. Lahiri's "Rice" first appeared in the *New Yorker* magazine in 2009. As you read, consider the kinds of details Lahiri includes to give readers a clear picture of her father and the way he makes his famous *pulao*.

My father, seventy-eight, is a methodical man. For thirty-nine years, he has had the same job, cataloguing books for a university library. He drinks two glasses of water first thing in the morning, walks for an hour every day, and devotes almost as much time, before bed, to flossing his teeth. "Winging it" is not a term that comes to mind in describing my father. When he's driving to new places, he does not enjoy getting lost.

In the kitchen, too, he walks a deliberate line, counting out the raisins that go into his oatmeal (fifteen) and never boiling even a drop more water than required for tea. It is my father who knows how many cups of rice are necessary to feed four, or forty, or a hundred and forty people. He has a reputation for *andaj*—the Bengali word for "estimate"—accurately gauging quantities that tend to baffle other cooks. An oracle of rice, if you will.

But there is another rice that my father is more famous for. This is not the white rice, boiled like pasta and then drained in a colander, that most Bengalis eat for dinner. This other rice is pulao, a baked, buttery, sophisticated indulgence, Persian in origin, served at festive occasions. I have often watched him make it. It involves sautéing grains of basmati in butter, along with cinnamon sticks, cloves, bay leaves, and cardamom pods. In go halved cashews and raisins (unlike the oatmeal raisins, these must be golden, not black). Ginger, pulverized into a paste, is incorporated, along with salt and sugar, nutmeg and mace, saffron threads if they're available, ground turmeric if not. A certain amount of water is added, and the rice simmers until most of the water evaporates. Then it is spread out in a baking tray. (My father prefers disposable aluminum ones, which he recycled long before recycling laws were passed.) More water is flicked on top with his fingers, in the ritual and cryptic manner of Catholic priests. Then the tray, covered with foil, goes into the oven, until the rice is cooked through and not a single grain sticks to another.

Despite having a superficial knowledge of the ingredients and the technique, I have no idea how to make my father's pulao, nor would I ever dare attempt it. The recipe is his own, and has never been recorded. There has never been an unsuccessful batch, yet no batch is ever identical to any

WORD POWER
methodical working in a careful and organized way

WORD POWER
oracle a person giving wise or authoritative opinions

WORD POWER
indulgence something that is enjoyed as a special pleasure

WORD POWER
cryptic mysterious

other. It is a dish that has become an extension of himself, that he has perfected, and to which he has earned the copyright. A dish that will die with him when he dies.

In 1968, when I was seven months old, my father made pulao for the first time. We lived in London, in Finsbury Park, where my parents shared the kitchen, up a steep set of stairs in the attic of the house, with another Bengali couple. The occasion was my *annaprasan*, a rite of passage in which Bengali children are given solid food for the first time; it is known colloquially as a *bhath*, which happens to be the Bengali word for "cooked rice." In the oven of a stove no more than twenty inches wide, my father baked pulao for about thirty-five people. Since then, he has made pulao for the *annaprasans* of his friends' children, for birthday parties and anniversaries, for bridal and baby showers, for wedding receptions, and for my sister's Ph.D. party. For a few decades, after we moved to the United States, his pulao fed crowds of up to four hundred people, at events organized by Prabasi, a Bengali cultural institution in New England, and he found himself at institutional venues—schools and churches and community centers—working with industrial ovens and stoves. This has never unnerved him. He could probably rig up a system to make pulao out of a hot-dog cart, were someone to ask.

There are times when certain ingredients are missing, when he must use almonds instead of cashews, when the raisins in a friend's cupboard are the wrong color. He makes it anyway, with exacting standards but a sanguine hand.

When my son and daughter were infants, and we celebrated their *annaprasans*, we hired a caterer, but my father made the pulao, preparing it at home in Rhode Island and transporting it in the trunk of his car to Brooklyn. The occasion, both times, was held at the Society for Ethical Culture, in Park Slope. In 2002, for my son's first taste of rice, my father warmed the trays on the premises, in the giant oven in the basement. But by 2005, when it was my daughter's turn, the representative on duty would not permit my father to use the oven, telling him that he was not a licensed cook. My father transferred the pulao from his aluminum trays into glass baking dishes, and microwaved, batch by batch, rice that fed almost a hundred people. When I asked my father to describe that experience, he expressed no frustration. "It was fine," he said. "It was a big microwave."

Reacting to Language

*Suggest an alternative one-word title for this essay.

Reacting to Ideas

*1. Do you think the subject of this essay is really rice (as its title suggests), or do you think the real subject is Lahiri's father? Explain.

2. What role has *pulao* played in Lahiri's life? What do you think it means to her now?

Reacting to the Pattern

1. Lahiri describes both *pulao* and ordinary white rice. How are they different?
2. Is this essay primarily a subjective or an objective description? Explain.
*3. What dominant impression does this essay give readers of Lahiri's father? Of his rice?

Writing Practice

1. Write a subjective description of a food you loved when you were a child. Try to describe the smell, taste, and feel of the food as well as its appearance.
2. How have your tastes in food changed since you were a child? Describe the foods that defined each stage of your life. Your thesis should convey how (and perhaps why) your preferences changed over time.

37d   Process

A **process** essay explains the steps in a procedure, telling how something is (or was) done. In "Slice of Life," Russell Baker gives a set of instructions for carving a turkey. In "My Grandmother's Dumpling"—available online at **macmillanhighered.com/writingfirst**—Amy Ma explains the stages in the process of making dumplings with her family.

macmillanhighered.com /writingfirst
e-readings > Amy Ma, "My Grandmother's Dumpling"

Slice of Life

Russell Baker

Pulitzer Prize—winning columnist and author Russell Baker was known for his keen political insight and sharp social commentary. He was also known for being funny. The source of much of Baker's humor is his deadpan approach, in which he pretends to be completely serious. In "Slice of Life," first published in the *New York Times* in 1974, Baker uses this approach to turn what seems to be a straightforward set of instructions into a humorous discussion of a holiday ritual. As you read, think about your family's Thanksgivings.

How to carve a turkey: 1

Assemble the following tools—carving knife, stone for sharpening   2
carving knife, hot water, soap, wash cloth, two bath towels, barbells, meat cleaver. If the house lacks a meat cleaver, an ax may be substituted. If it is, add bandages, sutures, and iodine to above list.

Begin by moving the turkey from the roasting pan to a suitable carving   3
area. This is done by inserting the carving knife into the posterior stuffed area of the turkey and the knife-sharpening stone into the stuffed area under the neck.

Thus skewered, the turkey may be lifted out of the hot grease with rela-   4
tive safety. Should the turkey drop to the floor, however, remove the knife

WORD POWER

gingerly very cautiously
or carefully

WORD POWER

execute to do or perform

and stone, roll the turkey gingerly into the two bath towels, wrap them several times around it and lift the encased fowl to the carving place.

You are now ready to begin carving. Sharpen the knife on the stone 5 and insert it where the thigh joins the torso. If you do this correctly, which is improbable, the knife will almost immediately encounter a barrier of bone and gristle. This may very well be the joint. It could, however, be your thumb. If not, execute a vigorous sawing motion until satisfied that the knife has been defeated. Withdraw the knife and ask someone nearby, in as testy a manner as possible, why the knives at your house are not kept in better carving condition.

Exercise the biceps and forearms by lifting barbells until they are 6 strong enough for you to tackle the leg joint with bare hands. Wrapping one hand firmly around the thigh, seize the turkey's torso in the other hand and scream. Run cold water over hands to relieve pain of burns.

Now, take a bath towel in each hand and repeat the above maneuver. 7 The entire leg should snap away from the chassis with a distinct crack, and the rest of the turkey, obedient to Newton's law[1] about equal and opposite reactions, should roll in the opposite direction, which means that if you are carving at the table the turkey will probably come to rest in someone's lap.

Get the turkey out of the lap with as little fuss as possible, and con- 8 centrate on the leg. Use the meat cleaver to sever the sinewy leather which binds the thigh to the drumstick.

If using the alternate, ax method, this operation should be performed 9 on a cement walk outside the house in order to preserve the table.

Repeat the above operation on the turkey's uncarved side. You now 10 have two thighs and two drumsticks. Using the wash cloth, soap and hot water, bathe thoroughly and, if possible, go to a movie. Otherwise, look each person in the eye and say, "I don't suppose anyone wants white meat."

If compelled to carve the breast anyhow, sharpen the knife on the stone 11 again with sufficient awkwardness to tip over the gravy bowl on the person who started the stampede for white meat.

While everyone is rushing about to mop the gravy off her slacks, hack at 12 the turkey breast until it starts crumbling off the carcass in ugly chunks.

The alternative method for carving white meat is to visit around the 13 neighborhood until you find someone who has a good carving knife and borrow it, if you find one, which is unlikely.

This method enables you to watch the football game on neighbors' 14 television sets and also creates the possibility that somebody back at your table will grow tired of waiting and do the carving herself.

In this case, upon returning home, cast a pained stare upon the mound 15 of chopped white meat that has been hacked out by the family carving knife and refuse to do any more carving that day. No one who cares about the artistry of carving can be expected to work upon the mutilations of amateurs, and it would be a betrayal of the carver's art to do so.

Reacting to Language

*In paragraph 14, Baker uses *herself* to refer to *somebody*. What is your reaction to this pronoun use? What other options did Baker have? Why do you think he chose to use *herself*?

1. Sir Isaac Newton, seventeenth-century physicist and mathematician known for formulating the laws of gravity and light and for inventing calculus.

Reacting to Ideas

1. Baker does not expect readers to take his instructions seriously or to follow them exactly. How can you tell?
*2. List the steps in Baker's process of carving a turkey. Then, cross out all nonessential or humorous material. Are the remaining instructions logically ordered? Clear? Accurate?

Reacting to the Pattern

1. How can you tell that this essay is a set of instructions and not an explanation of a process?
*2. Do you think the phrase "How to carve a turkey" is an adequate introduction for this essay? What other kind of introduction might Baker have written?
3. Identify the various cautions and warnings that Baker provides for readers. Are they all necessary? Explain.

Writing Practice

1. Write a new introductory paragraph for this essay. Then, turn Baker's instructions into a straightforward process explanation, deleting any material you consider irrelevant to your purpose. Be sure to include all necessary articles (*a, an, the*) and transitions.
2. List the steps in a recipe for preparing one of your favorite dishes. Then, expand your recipe into an essay, adding transitions and cautions and reminders. Finally, add opening and closing paragraphs that describe the finished product and tell readers why the dish is worth preparing.

37e Cause and Effect

A **cause-and-effect** essay identifies causes or predicts effects; sometimes, it does both. In "How Facebook Is Making Friending Obsolete," Julia Angwin considers how Facebook has changed the nature of friendship. In "The Seat Not Taken," John Edgar Wideman considers the possible motives of train passengers who choose not to sit beside him.

How Facebook Is Making Friending Obsolete

Julia Angwin

Raised in Silicon Valley by parents who both worked in technology, Julia Angwin acquired an interest in digital technology at an early age. Before taking up her post at the *Wall Street Journal* as a technology editor and columnist (2000–2013), Angwin covered technology at the *San Francisco Chronicle*. In 2009, she published the book *Stealing MySpace*, which examines the cultural phenomenon of MySpace and other social-networking sites. Currently, she works at ProPublica. In "How Facebook Is Making Friending Obsolete," first published in the *Wall Street Journal* in 2009, Angwin comments on the potential consequences of Facebook's efforts to make it harder to keep profiles private. As you read, consider your own feelings about Facebook and privacy.

"Friending" wasn't used as a verb until about five years ago, when social networks such as Friendster, MySpace and Facebook burst onto the scene. 1

Suddenly, our friends were something even better—an audience. If blogging felt like shouting into the void, posting updates on a social network felt more like an intimate conversation among friends at a pub. 2

Inevitably, as our list of friends grew to encompass acquaintances, friends of friends and the girl who sat behind us in seventh-grade homeroom, online friendships became devalued. 3

Suddenly, we knew as much about the lives of our distant acquaintances as we did about the lives of our intimates—what they'd had for dinner, how they felt about Tiger Woods and so on. 4

Enter Twitter with a solution: no friends, just followers. These one-way relationships were easier to manage—no more annoying decisions about whether to give your ex-boyfriend access to your photos, no more fussing over who could see your employment and contact information. 5

Twitter's updates were also easily searchable on the Web, forcing users to be somewhat thoughtful about their posts. The intimate conversation became a talent show, a challenge to prove your intellectual prowess in 140 characters or less. 6

This fall, Twitter turned its popularity into dollars, inking lucrative deals to allow its users' tweets to be broadcast via search algorithms on Google and Bing. 7

Soon, Facebook followed suit with deals to distribute certain real-time data to Google and Bing. (Recall that despite being the fifth-most-popular Web site in the world, Facebook is barely profitable.) Facebook spokesman Barry Schnitt says no money changed hands in the deals but says there was "probably an exchange of value." 8

Just one catch: Facebook had just "exchanged" to Google and Microsoft something that didn't exist. 9

The vast majority of Facebook users restrict updates to their friends, and do not expect those updates to appear in public search results. (In fact, many people restrict their Facebook profile from appearing at all in search results.) 10

So Facebook had little content to provide to Google's and Bing's real-time search results. When Google's real-time search launched earlier this month, its results were primarily filled with Twitter updates. 11

Coincidentally, Facebook presented its 350 million members with a new default privacy setting last week. For most people, the new suggested settings would open their Facebook updates and information to the entire world. Mr. Schnitt says the new privacy suggestions are an acknowledgement of "the way we think the world is going." 12

Facebook Chief Executive Mark Zuckerberg led by example, opening up his previously closed profile, including goofy photos of himself curled up with a teddy bear. 13

Facebook also made public formerly private info such as profile pictures, gender, current city and the friends list. (Mr. Schnitt suggests that users are free to lie about their hometown or take down their profile picture to protect their privacy; in response to users' complaints, the friends list can now be restricted to be viewed only by friends.) 14

Of course, many people will reject the default settings on Facebook and keep on chatting with only their Facebook friends. (Mr. Schnitt said more than 50% of its users had rejected the defaults at last tally.) 15

But those who want a private experience on Facebook will have to 16 work harder at it: if you inadvertently post a comment on a friend's profile page that has been opened to the public, your comment will be public too.

Just as Facebook turned friends into a commodity, it has likewise 17 gathered our personal data—our updates, our baby photos, our endless chirping birthday notes—and readied it to be bundled and sold.

So I give up. Rather than fighting to keep my Facebook profile private, 18 I plan to open it up to the public—removing the fiction of intimacy and friendship.

But I will also remove the vestiges of my private life from Facebook 19 and make sure I never post anything that I wouldn't want my parents, employer, next-door neighbor or future employer to see. You'd be smart to do the same.

We'll need to treat this increasingly public version of Facebook with 20 the same hard-headedness that we treat Twitter: as a place to broadcast, but not a place for vulnerability. A place to carefully calibrate, sanitize and bowdlerize our words for every possible audience, now and forever. Not a place for intimacy with friends.

> **WORD POWER**
>
> **calibrate** to adjust precisely for a particular function
>
> **bowdlerize** to remove material that could offend people

Reacting to Language

*Write a one-sentence definition of the verb *to friend*.

Reacting to Ideas

*1. Angwin claims that online friendships have been "devalued" (paragraph 3). What does she mean? Do you agree with her? Why or why not?

*2. How, according to Angwin, is Facebook "making friending obsolete"? In your opinion, is Facebook also making *friendship* obsolete—or at least changing its meaning?

Reacting to the Pattern

1. What actions has Facebook taken to make its information increasingly more public? What has led to these actions? What has been the result of these actions?

2. Is this essay's emphasis on causes, on effects, or on both causes and effects? Explain.

Writing Practice

1. Angwin states that she plans to open her Facebook profile to the public. Would you do—or have you already done—the same? Why or why not? Write a cause-and-effect essay in which you give your reasons for either making your profile public or keeping it private.

2. How would your life change if you lost access to social networking? Write an essay explaining the possible results of this loss of access.

The Seat Not Taken

John Edgar Wideman

John Edgar Wideman has published numerous books, both fiction and nonfiction, as well as articles in publications such as the *New York Times*, the *New Yorker*, *Vogue*, *Emerge*, and *Esquire*. Wideman has received the O. Henry Award, the American Book Award for Fiction, the Lannan Literary Fellowship for Fiction, the PEN/Faulkner Award for Fiction (twice—the first person so honored), and a MacArthur Fellowship. He is currently professor of Africana Studies and English at Brown University. In "The Seat Not Taken," an op-ed article first published in the *New York Times* in 2010, Wideman reflects on his weekly train commute and raises questions about the motives his fellow commuters have for not sitting in the empty seat beside him. As you read, think about how you would react in Wideman's situation.

WORD POWER

disquieting making worried or nervous

WORD POWER

shun to avoid

1   At least twice a week I ride Amtrak's high-speed Acela train from my home in New York City to my teaching job in Providence, R.I. The route passes through a region of the country populated by, statistics tell us, a significant segment of its most educated, affluent, sophisticated and enlightened citizens.

2   Over the last four years, excluding summers, I have conducted a casual sociological experiment in which I am both participant and observer. It's a survey I began not because I had some specific point to prove by gathering data to support it, but because I couldn't avoid becoming aware of an obvious, disquieting truth.

3   Almost invariably, after I have hustled aboard early and occupied one half of a vacant double seat in the usually crowded quiet car, the empty place next to me will remain empty for the entire trip.

4   I'm a man of color, one of the few on the train and often the only one in the quiet car, and I've concluded that color explains a lot about my experience. Unless the car is nearly full, color will determine, even if it doesn't exactly clarify, why 9 times out of 10 people will shun a free seat if it means sitting beside me.

5   Giving them and myself the benefit of the doubt, I can rule out excessive body odor or bad breath; a hateful, intimidating scowl; hip-hop clothing; or a hideous deformity as possible objections to my person. Considering also the cost of an Acela ticket, the fact that I display no visible indications of religious preference and, finally, the numerous external signs of middle-class membership I share with the majority of the passengers, color appears to be a sufficient reason for the behavior I have recorded.

6   Of course, I'm not registering a complaint about the privilege, conferred upon me by color, to enjoy the luxury of an extra seat to myself. I relish the opportunity to spread out, savor the privacy and quiet and work or gaze at the scenic New England woods and coast. It's a particularly appealing perk if I compare the train to air travel or any other mode of transportation, besides walking or bicycling, for negotiating the mercilessly congested Northeast Corridor. Still, in the year 2010, with an African-descended, brown president in the White House and a nation confidently asserting its passage into a postracial era, it strikes me as odd to ride beside a vacant seat, just about every time I embark on a three-hour journey each way, from home to work and back.

I admit I look forward to the moment when other passengers, searching for a good seat, or any seat at all on the busiest days, stop anxiously prowling the quiet-car aisle, the moment when they have all settled elsewhere, including the ones who willfully blinded themselves to the open seat beside me or were unconvinced of its availability when they passed by. I savor that precise moment when the train sighs and begins to glide away from Penn or Providence Station, and I'm able to say to myself, with relative assurance, that the vacant place beside me is free, free at last, or at least free until the next station. I can relax, prop open my briefcase or rest papers, snacks or my arm in the unoccupied seat.   7

But the very pleasing moment of anticipation casts a shadow, because   8
I can't accept the bounty of an extra seat without remembering why it's empty, without wondering if its emptiness isn't something quite sad. And quite dangerous, also, if left unexamined. Posters in the train, the station, the subway warn: if you see something, say something.

> **WORD POWER**
> **bounty** something that is given generously

Reacting to Language

*In paragraph 1, Wideman suggests that his fellow passengers are some of the United States' "most educated, affluent, sophisticated and enlightened citizens." What impression does he intend to convey by using these words to characterize the other passengers?

Reacting to Ideas

*1. Why does Wideman see the empty seat beside him as not simply sad but also dangerous? Do you think he is right to see it this way, or do you think he is overreacting? Explain your views.

*2. Why does Wideman close the essay with "if you see something, say something"? In what context(s) does this sentence usually appear these days? What is the "something" that Wideman wants people to say in this case?

Reacting to the Pattern

*1. This essay examines causes. What do you think might be the *effects* (on Wideman and on society in general) of the behavior Wideman describes?

2. Write a one-sentence thesis statement for this essay, including at least one word or phrase (for example, *because*, *for this reason*, or *as a result*) that indicates it is a cause-and-effect essay.

Writing Practice

1. How do you account for the empty seat beside Wideman on so many train trips? Do you agree with his analysis of the situation, or can you think of other explanations that he has not considered? Write a cause-and-effect essay responding to Wideman's article and its reflections on race.

2. What kinds of people would you try to avoid sitting next to on a train? Why? Do you see your objections as reasonable, or do you think some of your objections might be viewed as prejudice? Write an essay in which you explain your objections as clearly and thoughtfully as possible.

37f   Comparison and Contrast

A **comparison-and-contrast** essay explains how two things are alike or how they are different. In "Environmentalism as Religion," Paul H. Rubin considers the similarities between environmentalism and "a religious belief system." In "Songs of the Summer of 1963 . . . and 2013," Juan Williams looks at the differences between popular music in the early 1960s and contemporary rap music.

Environmentalism as Religion

Paul H. Rubin

Paul H. Rubin, a professor of economics at Emory University, has published widely in the fields of economics, law, and politics and has written op-eds and essays for a number of newspapers, including the *Wall Street Journal* and the *Washington Times*. Rubin is the author of *Darwinian Politics: The Evolutionary Origin of Freedom* (2002) and coauthor of *Privacy and the Commercial Use of Personal Information* (2001). In "Environmentalism as Religion," originally published in 2010 in the *Wall Street Journal*, Rubin draws comparisons between the environmental movement and organized religion. As you read, note any points of comparison that you find surprising.

WORD POWER

adherents people who give support or maintain loyalty

WORD POWER

criterion a standard on which a judgment or decision may be based

Many observers have made the point that environmentalism is eerily close   1
to a religious belief system, since it includes creation stories and ideas of original sin. But there is another sense in which environmentalism is becoming more and more like a religion: It provides its adherents with an identity.

Scientists are understandably uninterested in religious stories because   2
they do not meet the basic criterion for science: They cannot be tested. God may or may not have created the world—there is no way of knowing, although we do know that the biblical creation story is scientifically incorrect. Since we cannot prove or disprove the existence of God, science can't help us answer questions about the truth of religion as a method of understanding the world.

But scientists, particularly evolutionary psychologists, have identified   3
another function of religion in addition to its function of explaining the world. Religion often supplements or replaces the tribalism that is an innate part of our evolved nature.

Original religions were tribal rather than universal. Each tribe had its   4
own god or gods, and the success of the tribe was evidence that their god was stronger than others.

But modern religions have largely replaced tribal gods with univer-   5
sal gods and allowed unrelated individuals from outside the tribe to join. Identification with a religion has replaced identification with a tribe. While many decry religious wars, modern religion has probably net reduced human conflict because there are fewer tribal wars. (Anthropologists have shown that tribal wars are even more lethal per capita than modern wars.)

It is this identity-creating function that environmentalism provides. As   6
the world becomes less religious, people can define themselves as being Green rather than being Christian or Jewish.

Consider some of the ways in which environmental behaviors echo 7
religious behaviors and thus provide meaningful rituals for Greens:

- There is a holy day—Earth Day.

- There are food taboos. Instead of eating fish on Friday, or avoiding pork, Greens now eat organic foods and many are moving towards eating only locally grown foods.

- There is no prayer, but there are self-sacrificing rituals that are not particularly useful, such as recycling. Recycling paper to save trees, for example, makes no sense since the effect will be to reduce the number of trees planted in the long run.

- Belief systems are embraced with no logical basis. For example, environmentalists almost universally believe in the dangers of global warming but also reject the best solution to the problem, which is nuclear power. These two beliefs co-exist based on faith, not reason.

- There are no temples, but there are sacred structures. As I walk around the Emory campus, I am continually confronted with recycling bins, and instead of one trash can I am faced with several for different sorts of trash. Universities are centers of the environmental religion, and such structures are increasingly common. While people have worshipped many things, we may be the first to build shrines to garbage.

- Environmentalism is a proselytizing religion. Skeptics are not merely people unconvinced by the evidence: They are treated as evil sinners. I probably would not write this article if I did not have tenure.

> **WORD POWER**
> **proselytizing** trying to persuade others to join

Some conservatives spend their time criticizing the way Darwin is 8
taught in schools. This is pointless and probably counterproductive. These
same efforts should be spent on making sure that the schools only teach
those aspects of environmentalism that pass rigorous scientific testing. By
making the point that Greenism is a religion, perhaps we environmental
skeptics can enlist the First Amendment on our side.

> **WORD POWER**
> **counterproductive** not helpful
> **skeptics** people who question or doubt something

Reacting to Language

*In this essay, Rubin often uses language that is associated with religion—
for example, *holy day* (paragraph 7). Can you identify other examples of
such words and expressions? How does this kind of language help Rubin
make his point?

Reacting to Ideas

*1. According to Rubin, how is environmentalism like religion? Do all the similarities he identifies make sense to you? Can you think of ways in which environmentalism and religion are different?

2. In your own words, paraphrase Rubin's thesis.

3. In paragraph 8, Rubin says that it is "pointless and probably counterproductive" for "some conservatives" to criticize the way schools teach Darwin. Why? What does he think conservatives should focus on instead?

Reacting to the Pattern

1. Is this a point-by-point or a subject-by-subject comparison? How can you tell?

*2. The actual comparison between environmentalism and religion—the list of ways in which they are similar—begins in paragraph 7. What does Rubin do in paragraphs 1–6?

Writing Practice

1. Write an essay in which you explain how being environmentally conscious has changed the way you live. Be sure to compare your behavior before you became environmentally conscious with your life now.

2. Write an essay in which you consider how something else—for example, a sport or a job—is like a religion. Give your essay a title that makes your comparison clear—for example, "Football as Religion." Your essay can be humorous or serious.

Songs of the Summer of 1963 . . . and 2013

Juan Williams

Born in Panama, Juan Williams is an American journalist who has been published in the *New York Times*, the *Washington Post*, the *Atlantic Monthly*, and *Time* magazine. He is the author of *Thurgood Marshall: American Revolutionary* (2000) and *Enough* (2006), which addresses what Williams refers to as the "culture of failure." Williams has received several awards for his work, including an Emmy. In this essay, originally published in the *Wall Street Journal* in 2013, Williams contrasts the "uplifting" music of the 1960s, during the March on Washington, with the "degrading" lyrics of contemporary rap songs. As you read, consider your own opinions of today's popular rap music and note places where you agree or disagree with Williams.

WORD POWER

seminal very important and influential

1   Fifty years after the March on Washington, mystical memories of that seminal moment in the civil-rights era are less likely to focus on movement politics than on the great poetry and great music.

2   The emotional uplift of the monumental march is a universe of time away from today's degrading rap music—filled with the n-word, bitches and "hoes"—that confuses and depresses race relations in America now.

3   The poetry of Aug. 28, 1963, is best on view when Martin Luther King Jr. went off his speech script and started using a musical, chanting reprise—"I have a dream." The transforming insight born of the power of the interracial gathering at that time of turmoil, combined with the power of the spoken word, created an emotional message that still grips the American mind.

4   "I have a dream that one day on the red hills of Georgia, sons of former slaves and the sons of former slave owners will be able to sit down together at the table of brotherhood," King said, in verse that somehow spanned a history of slavery and the Founding Fathers' uniquely American promise of equality.

5   "I have a dream that one day even the state of Mississippi, a state sweltering with the heat of injustice, sweltering with the heat of oppression,

will be transformed into an oasis of freedom and justice. I have a dream that my four little children will one day live in a nation where they will not be judged by the color of their skin but [by] the content of their character. I have a dream today!"

That poetry rose above the reality that as King spoke the civil-rights   6 movement was stalled. Few schools had integrated after the Supreme Court's *Brown v. Board of Education* decision nine years earlier. One hundred years after the Emancipation Proclamation, the Civil Rights Act was stuck in Congress. NAACP leader Medgar Evers had been killed in June. After a violent April in Alabama, in which protest marchers were beaten and set upon by police dogs, an estimated 15,000 more civil-rights activists had been arrested at protests across the country that summer.

King sailed past all those sad realities to invoke his soaring vision of   7 the nation at racial peace. When he finished speaking, the crowd spontaneously broke into singing "We Shall Overcome," holding hands and swaying as if in communal prayer.

That sense of unity, promise and purpose was also evident in the music   8 of the march. It's music that still stirs emotions to this day.

Bob Dylan's "Blowin' in the Wind," written in 1962, hit No. 2 on the   9 Billboard charts just before the crowd gathered in Washington. When the folk-music trio Peter, Paul and Mary sang the song for the 250,000 people in front of the Lincoln Memorial that day, it became an interracial anthem for change. The song itself drew inspiration from two others: The lyrics brought to mind Woody Guthrie's "Bound for Glory," which included an allegory about newspapers blowing down city streets, and its melody came from a slave protest song called "No More Auction Block."

And so they sang in Washington: "Yes, how many years can some people exist before they're allowed to be free? Yes, how many times can a man turn his head, pretending that he just doesn't see? The answer my friend is blowin' in the wind, the answer is blowin' in the wind."   10

Sam Cooke, the black gospel and rhythm-and-blues singer, began performing the Dylan song immediately after the march. He had been working on a song about the hurt he felt as a black man living with racism yet also with hope for better times. In December 1963, Cooke recorded "A Change Is Gonna Come." The song became a hit on black radio, another anthem of yearning for a nation without racial rancor.   11

"I go to the movie and I go downtown, somebody keep telling me don't   12 hang around," Cooke wrote. "It's been a long time coming but I know a change is gonna come, oh yes it will."

The next year, in 1964, Curtis Mayfield—also openly inspired by the   13 music of the march—wrote an even more hopeful song: "People Get Ready." It, too, picked up on a frequent image of American folklore, the train of salvation.

Just as Woody Guthrie and Johnny Cash had sung "This Train's Bound   14 for Glory," Mayfield, a black Chicago singer steeped in church gospel music and the blues, sang about faith in the American struggle for racial justice.

"People get ready, there's a train a comin'; you don't need no baggage   15 you just get on board . . . there ain't no room for the hopeless sinner who would hurt all mankind just to save his own. Have pity on those whose chances grow thinner. For there's no hiding place against the Kingdom's throne."

WORD POWER

anthem a song that is important to a particular group of people

WORD POWER

rancor a feeling of hatred or dislike for someone who has treated you unfairly

The uplifting lyrics made "People Get Ready" one of the earliest hits 16 on both black and white radio. Bob Marley later used some of the words in his poignant song "One Love." Bruce Springsteen used the song as a healing anthem at concerts after the 9/11 terror attacks.

The songs by Dylan, Cooke and Mayfield have been ranked 14th, 12th 17 and 24th on Rolling Stone magazine's list of greatest songs of all time. All three have roots in the March on Washington.

Now, half a century after the lyrical promise of that inspiring music 18 and poetry, there is the inescapable and heartbreaking contrast with the malignant, self-aggrandizing rap songs that define today's most popular music.

In Jay-Z's current hit, "Holy Grail," he sings about "psycho bitches" and 19 uses the n-word seven times while bragging that he is "Living the life . . . Illest [n-word] alive." Another top rapper, Lil Wayne, released a song in the spring with an obscenity *in the title*, using the n-word repeatedly and depicting himself as abusing "hoes" and "bitches."

Similar examples abound in the rap-music world and have persisted 20 for years with scarcely any complaint from today's civil-rights leaders. Their failure to denounce these lyrics for the damage they do to poor and minority families—words celebrating tattooed thugs and sexually indiscriminate women as icons of "keeping it real"—is a sad reminder of how long it has been since the world heard the sweet music of the March on Washington.

> **WORD POWER**
>
> **self-aggrandizing**
> making oneself appear
> great or greater

Reacting to Language

*In paragraph 19, Williams refers to rappers' use of "the n-word." How do you feel about the use of this word by rap artists? How do you feel about the use of the phrase *the n-word* in place of the actual word?

Reacting to Ideas

1. Williams states his thesis in paragraph 2. Restate this thesis in your own words.
*2. Do you agree with Williams's assessment of today's popular music? Why or why not?
3. Do you think Williams should have included more examples in paragraph 19—or included additional paragraphs about contemporary music? Explain.

Reacting to the Pattern

1. This essay is a subject-by-subject comparison. What two subjects is Williams comparing? How does he indicate to readers that he is moving from one subject to the next?
2. Why do you think Williams organized his essay as a subject-by-subject comparison instead of as a point-by-point comparison?
*3. Williams devotes much more space to one subject than to the other. Why do you think he does this? Do you see this imbalance as a flaw in his essay? Why or why not?

Writing Practice

1. Building on the two examples in paragraph 19, write an essay comparing what Williams calls today's "malignant, self-aggrandizing rap songs" with contemporary popular music that you consider to be inspiring or uplifting.

2. Write a comparison-and-contrast essay in which you compare the lyrics of any two popular songs.

37g Classification

A **classification** essay divides a whole into parts and sorts various items into categories. In "The Men We Carry in Our Minds," Scott Russell Sanders classifies the workingmen he has known. In "The Dog Ate My Flash Drive, and Other Tales of Woe"—available online at **macmillanhighered.com /writingfirst**—Carolyn Foster Segal classifies students' excuses for late work.

macmillanhighered.com /writingfirst
e-readings > Carolyn Foster Segal, "The Dog Ate My Flash Drive, and Other Tales of Woe"

The Men We Carry in Our Minds

Scott Russell Sanders

Scott Russell Sanders is a professor of English and an essayist. His essays are personal reflections that include social and philosophical commentary and are often set in the Midwest, where he was born and raised. In "The Men We Carry in Our Minds," first published in the *Milkweed Chronicle* in 1984, Sanders reflects on the working lives of the men he knew when he was a boy and classifies them according to the kind of work they do. His essay discusses not only his boyhood impressions of the work these men did but also the direction his own professional life has taken. As you read, notice how Sanders moves from classifying men's work to comparing men's lives to women's lives.

The first men, besides my father, I remember seeing were black convicts and white guards, in the cottonfield across the road from our farm on the outskirts of Memphis. I must have been three or four. The prisoners wore dingy gray-and-black zebra suits, heavy as canvas, sodden with sweat. Hatless, stooped, they chopped weeds in the fierce heat, row after row, breathing the acrid dust of boll-weevil poison. The overseers wore dazzling white shirts and broad shadowy hats. The oiled barrels of their shotguns flashed in the sunlight. Their faces in memory are utterly blank. Of course those men, white and black, have become for me an emblem of racial hatred. But they have also come to stand for the twin poles of my early vision of manhood—the brute toiling animal and the boss. 1

When I was a boy, the men I knew labored with their bodies. They were marginal farmers, just scraping by, or welders, steelworkers, carpenters; they swept floors, dug ditches, mined coal, or drove trucks, their forearms ropy with muscle; they trained horses, stoked furnaces, built tires, stood on assembly lines wrestling parts onto cars and refrigerators. They got up before light, worked all day long whatever the weather, and when they came home at night they looked as though somebody had been whipping them. In the evenings and on weekends they worked on their own places, 2

WORD POWER

sodden heavy and wet

acrid bitter and unpleasant in taste or smell

overseers people who supervise the work of others

tilling gardens that were lumpy with clay, fixing broken-down cars, hammering on houses that were always too drafty, too leaky, too small.

The bodies of the men I knew were twisted and maimed in ways visible and invisible. The nails of their hands were black and split, the hands tattooed with scars. Some had lost fingers. Heavy lifting had given many of them finicky backs and guts weak from hernias. Racing against conveyor belts had given them ulcers. Their ankles and knees ached from years of standing on concrete. Anyone who had worked for long around machines was hard of hearing. They squinted, and the skin of their faces was creased like the leather of old work gloves. There were times, studying them, when I dreaded growing up. Most of them coughed, from dust or cigarettes, and most of them drank cheap wine or whiskey, so their eyes looked bloodshot and bruised. The fathers of my friends always seemed older than the mothers. Men wore out sooner. Only women lived into old age.

As a boy I also knew another sort of men, who did not sweat and break down like mules. They were soldiers, and so far as I could tell they scarcely worked at all. During my early school years we lived on a military base, an arsenal in Ohio, and every day I saw GIs in the guardshacks, on the stoops of barracks, at the wheels of olive drab Chevrolets. The chief fact of their lives was boredom. Long after I left the Arsenal I came to recognize the sour smell the soldiers gave off as that of souls in limbo. They were all waiting—for wars, for transfers, for leaves, for promotions, for the end of their hitch—like so many braves waiting for the hunt to begin. Unlike the warriors of older tribes, however, they would have no say about when the battle would start or how it would be waged. Their waiting was broken only when they practiced for war. They fired guns at targets, drove tanks across the churned-up fields of the military reservation, set off bombs in the wrecks of old fighter planes. I knew this was all play. But I also felt certain that when the hour for killing arrived, they would kill. When the real shooting started, many of them would die. This was what soldiers were *for*, just as a hammer was for driving nails.

Warriors and toilers: those seemed, in my boyhood vision, to be the chief destinies for men. They weren't the only destinies, as I learned from having a few male teachers, from reading books, and from watching television. But the men on television—the politicians, the astronauts, the generals, the savvy lawyers, the philosophical doctors, the bosses who gave orders to both soldiers and laborers—seemed as removed and unreal to me as the figures in tapestries. I could no more imagine growing up to become one of these cool, potent creatures than I could imagine becoming a prince.

A nearer and more hopeful example was that of my father, who had escaped from a red-dirt farm to a tire factory, and from the assembly line to the front office. Eventually he dressed in a white shirt and tie. He carried himself as if he had been born to work with his mind. But his body, remembering the earlier years of slogging work, began to give out on him in his fifties, and it quit on him entirely before he turned sixty-five. Even such a partial escape from man's fate as he had accomplished did not seem possible for most of the boys I knew. They joined the Army, stood in line for jobs in the smoky plants, helped build highways. They were bound to work as their fathers had worked, killing themselves or preparing to kill others.

A scholarship enabled me not only to attend college, a rare enough feat in my circle, but even to study in a university meant for the children of the

3

4

5

6

7

rich. Here I met for the first time young men who had assumed from birth that they would lead lives of comfort and power. And for the first time I met women who told me that men were guilty of having kept all the joys and privileges of the earth for themselves. I was baffled. What privileges? What joys? I thought about the maimed, dismal lives of most of the men back home. What had they stolen from their wives and daughters? The right to go five days a week, twelve months a year, for thirty or forty years to a steel mill or a coal mine? The right to drop bombs and die in war? The right to feel every leak in the roof, every gap in the fence, every cough in the engine, as a wound they must mend? The right to feel, when the layoff comes or the plant shuts down, not only afraid but ashamed?

I was slow to understand the deep grievances of women. This was 8 because, as a boy, I had envied them. Before college, the only people I had ever known who were interested in art or music or literature, the only ones who read books, the only ones who ever seemed to enjoy a sense of ease and grace were the mothers and daughters. Like the menfolk, they fretted about money, they scrimped and made do. But, when the pay stopped coming in, they were not the ones who had failed. Nor did they have to go to war, and that seemed to me a blessed fact. By comparison with the narrow, ironclad days of fathers, there was an expansiveness, I thought, in the days of mothers. They went to see neighbors, to shop in town, to run errands at school, at the library, at church. No doubt, had I looked harder at their lives, I would have envied them less. It was not my fate to become a woman, so it was easier for me to see the graces. Few of them held jobs outside the home, and those who did filled thankless roles as clerks and waitresses. I didn't see, then, what a prison a house could be, since houses seemed to me brighter, handsomer places than any factory. I did not realize—because such things were never spoken of—how often women suffered from men's bullying. I did learn about the wretchedness of abandoned wives, single mothers, widows; but I also learned about the wretchedness of lone men. Even then I could see how exhausting it was for a mother to cater all day to the needs of young children. But if I had been asked, as a boy, to choose between tending a baby and tending a machine, I think I would have chosen the baby. (Having now tended both, I know I would choose the baby.)

So I was baffled when the women at college accused me and my sex 9 of having cornered the world's pleasures. I think something like my bafflement has been felt by other boys (and by girls as well) who grew up in dirt-poor farm country, in mining country, in black ghettos, in Hispanic barrios, in the shadows of factories, in Third World nations—any place where the fate of men is as grim and bleak as the fate of women. Toilers and warriors. I realize now how ancient these identities are, how deep the tug they exert on men, the undertow of a thousand generations. The miseries I saw, as a boy, in the lives of nearly all men I continue to see in the lives of many—the body-breaking toil, the tedium, the call to be tough, the humiliating powerlessness, the battle for a living and for territory.

When the women I met at college thought about the joys and privileges 10 of men, they did not carry in their minds the sort of men I had known in my childhood. They thought of their fathers, who were bankers, physicians, architects, stockbrokers, the big wheels of the big cities. These fathers rode the train to work or drove cars that cost more than any of my childhood houses. They were attended from morning to night by female helpers, wives and nurses and secretaries. They were never laid off, never short of cash at month's end, never lined up for welfare. These fathers made decisions that mattered. They ran the world.

The daughters of such men wanted to share in this power, this glory. 11 So did I. They yearned for a say over their future, for jobs worthy of their abilities, for the right to live at peace, unmolested, whole. Yes, I thought, yes yes. The difference between me and these daughters was that they saw me, because of my sex, as destined from birth to become like their fathers, and therefore as an enemy to their desires. But I knew better. I wasn't an enemy, in fact or in feeling. I was an ally. If I had known, then, how to tell them so, would they have believed me? Would they now?

Reacting to Language

*Suggest two or three alternative names for the categories *warriors* and *toilers* (paragraph 5). Do you think any of your suggestions are better than Sanders's choices?

Reacting to Ideas

1. When Sanders was young, what did he see as his destiny? How did he escape his fate? How else do you think he might have escaped?
2. What were the grievances of the women Sanders met at college? Why did Sanders have trouble understanding these grievances?
*3. Who do you believe has an easier life—men or women? Explain.

Reacting to the Pattern

1. What two types of men did Sanders know when he was young? How are they different? What do they have in common?
2. What kinds of men discussed in the essay do not fit into the two categories Sanders identifies in paragraphs 2–4? Why don't they fit?
*3. Sanders does not categorize the women he discusses. Can you think of a few categories into which these women could fit?

Writing Practice

1. Write a classification essay in which you identify and discuss three or four categories of workers (females as well as males) you observed in your community when you were growing up. In your thesis statement, draw a conclusion about the relative status and rewards of these workers' jobs.
2. Write an essay in which you categorize the workers in your current place of employment or on your college campus.

37h Definition

A **definition** essay presents an extended definition, using other patterns of development to move beyond a simple one-sentence formal definition. In "What Happiness Is," Eduardo Porter defines the "slippery concept" of happiness. In "I Want a Wife"—available online at **macmillanhighered.com /writingfirst**—Judy Brady defines a wife.

macmillanhighered.com /writingfirst
e-readings > Judy Brady, "I Want a Wife"

What Happiness Is

Eduardo Porter

Eduardo Porter was born in Phoenix, Arizona, of a Mexican mother and an American father. Porter started his career in journalism at Notimex, a Mexican news agency, where he wrote mostly in Spanish about the stock market and the financial world. He has written for popular publications such as the *Wall Street Journal* and the *New York Times*, and in 2011, he published *The Price of Everything: Solving the Mystery of Why We Pay What We Do.* The selection that follows is an excerpt from a chapter in that book. As you read, consider your own understanding of what happiness is.

1   Happiness is a slippery concept, a bundle of meanings with no precise, stable definition. Lots of thinkers have taken a shot at it. "Happiness is when what you think, what you say, and what you do are in harmony," proposed Gandhi. Abraham Lincoln argued "most people are about as happy as they make up their minds to be." Snoopy, the beagle-philosopher in *Peanuts*, took what was to my mind the most precise stab at the underlying epistemological problem. "My life has no purpose, no direction, no aim, no meaning, and yet I'm happy. I can't figure it out. What am I doing right?"

2   Most psychologists and economists who study happiness agree that what they prefer to call "subjective well-being" comprises three parts: satisfaction, meant to capture how people judge their lives measured up against their aspirations; positive feelings like joy; and the absence of negative feelings like anger.

WORD POWER
aspirations things a person wants to achieve

3   It does exist. It relates directly to objective measures of people's quality of life. Countries whose citizens are happier on average report lower levels of hypertension in the population. Happier people are less likely to come down with a cold. And if they get one, they recover more quickly. People who are wounded heal more quickly if they are satisfied with their lives. People who say they are happier smile more often, sleep better, report themselves to be in better health, and have happier relatives. And some research suggests happiness and suicide rates move in opposite directions. Happy people don't want to die.

4   Still, this conceptual mélange can be difficult to measure. Just ask yourself how happy you are, say, on a scale of one to three, as used by the General Social Survey. Then ask yourself what you mean by that. Answers wander when people are confronted with these questions. We entangle gut reactions with thoughtful analysis, and confound sensations of immediate pleasure with evaluations of how life meshes with our long-term aspirations. We might say we know what will make us happy in the future—fame,

WORD POWER
mélange a mixture of different things
confound confuse

fortune, or maybe a partner. But when we get to the future, it rarely does. While we do seem to know how to tell the difference between lifelong satisfaction and immediate well-being, the immediate tends to contaminate the ontological.

During an experiment in the 1980s, people who found a dime on top 5 of a Xerox machine before responding to a happiness survey reported a much higher sense of satisfaction with life than those who didn't. Another study found that giving people a chocolate bar improved their satisfaction with their lives. One might expect that our satisfaction with the entire span of our existence would be a fairly stable quantity—impervious to day-to-day joys and frustrations. Yet people often give a substantially different answer to the same question about lifetime happiness if it is asked again one month later.

Sigmund Freud argued that people "strive after happiness; they want 6 to become happy and to remain so." Translating happiness into the language of economics as "utility," most economists would agree. This simple proposition gives them a powerful tool to resist Bobby Kennedy's proposal to measure not income but something else. For if happiness is what people strive for, one needn't waste time trying to figure out what makes people happy. One must only look at what people do. The fact of the matter is that people mostly choose to work and make money. Under this optic, economic growth is the outcome of our pursuit of well-being. It is what makes us happy.

This approach has limitations. We often make puzzling choices that do 7 not make us consistently happier. We smoke despite knowing about cancer and emphysema. We gorge on chocolate despite knowing it will make us unhappy ten pounds down the road. Almost two thirds of Americans say they are overweight, according to a recent Gallup poll. But only a quarter say they are seriously trying to lose weight. In the 1980s a new discipline called Prospect Theory—also known as behavioral economics—deployed the tools of psychology to analyze economic behavior. It found all sorts of peculiar behaviors that don't fit economics' standard understanding of what makes us happy. For instance, losing something reduces our happiness more than winning the same thing increases it—a quirk known as loss aversion. We are unable to distinguish between choices that have slightly different odds of making us happy. We extrapolate from a few experiences to arrive at broad, mostly wrong conclusions. We herd, imitating successful behaviors around us.

Still, it remains generally true that we pursue what we think makes us 8 happy—and though some of our choices may not make us happy, some will. Legend has it that Abraham Lincoln was riding in a carriage one rainy evening, telling a friend that he agreed with economists' theory that people strove to maximize their happiness, when he caught sight of a pig stuck in a muddy riverbank. He ordered the carriage to stop, got out, and pulled the pig out of the muck to safety. When the friend pointed out to a mud-caked Lincoln that he had just disproved his statement by putting himself through great discomfort to save a pig, Lincoln retorted: "What I did was perfectly consistent with my theory. If I hadn't saved that pig I would have felt terrible."

So perhaps the proper response to Bobby Kennedy's angst is to agree 9 that pursuing economic growth often has negative side effects—carbon

WORD POWER

impervious not allowing something to pass through

WORD POWER

quirk an unusual habit
extrapolate to form an opinion from known facts

WORD POWER

angst strong feeling of being nervous or worried

emissions, environmental degradation—that are likely to make us unhappy down the road. Still, it remains true that American citizens—and the citizens of much of the world—expend enormous amounts of time and energy pursuing more money and a bigger GDP because they think it will improve their well-being. And that will make them happy.

Reacting to Language

Porter opens his essay with the statement, "Happiness is a slippery concept, a bundle of meanings with no precise, stable definition." What do the words *slippery*, *bundle*, and *stable* mean in this context.

Reacting to Ideas

*1. Do you agree with Porter's claim that "people mostly choose to work and make money. . . . It is what makes us happy" (paragraph 6)? Explain why you agree or disagree.
*2. What point does Porter make with the story about Abraham Lincoln and the pig (8)?

Reacting to the Pattern

1. How does Porter illustrate the generalization he makes in the opening sentence of the essay?
2. How does Porter use economics to explain what he thinks happiness is? What are the limitations, if any, of his economic model?

Writing Practice

1. How do you define *happiness*? Develop your own definition of the word, citing examples from your own experiences.
2. Who is the happiest person you know? Write a definition essay using narration, description, and exemplification to define *happy person*.

37i Argument

An **argument** essay takes a stand on one side of a debatable issue, using facts, examples, and expert opinion to persuade readers to accept a position. The writers of the two essays that follow—Mark Edmundson in "The Trouble with Online Education" and Roma Downey and Mark Burnett in "Why Public Schools Should Teach the Bible"—try to convince readers to accept their positions (or at least to acknowledge that they are reasonable). An additional example of an argument essay, "Tweet Less, Kiss More" by Bob Herbert, is available online at **macmillanhighered.com/writingfirst**.

macmillanhighered.com /writingfirst
e-readings > Bob Herbert, "Tweet Less, Kiss More"

The Trouble with Online Education

Mark Edmundson

Mark Edmundson, a professor of English at the University of Virginia, is the author of several books, including *Why Read*? (2004) and *Why Teach*? (2013), and has written numerous essays for publications including *Harper's* and *The Chronicle of Higher Education*. He has also been the recipient of many honors and awards, including the *New York Times* Notable Book of the Year for *Teacher: The One Who Made the Difference* (2002). In "The Trouble with Online Education," originally published in 2012 as an op-ed in the *New York Times*, Edmundson argues for the value of a classroom education over online education. As you read, think about your own experiences with online education.

WORD POWER

latent used to describe something that exists but cannot be seen

vexing causing trouble, worry, or annoyance

"AH, you're a professor. You must learn so much from your students."   1

This line, which I've heard in various forms, always makes me cringe.   2
Do people think that lawyers learn a lot about the law from their clients?
That patients teach doctors much of what they know about medicine?

Yet latent in the sentiment that our students are our teachers is an   3
important truth. We do in fact need to learn from them, but not about the
history of the Roman Empire or the politics of *Paradise Lost*. Understanding what it is that students have to teach teachers can help us to deal with
one of the most vexing issues now facing colleges and universities: online
education. At my school, the University of Virginia, that issue did more
than vex us; it came close to tearing the university apart.

A few weeks ago our president, Teresa A. Sullivan, was summarily dis-   4
missed and then summarily reinstated by the university's board of visitors.
One reason for her dismissal was the perception that she was not moving
forward fast enough on Internet learning. Stanford was doing it, Harvard,
Yale and M.I.T. too. But Virginia, it seemed, was lagging. Just this week,
in fact, it was announced that Virginia, along with a number of other universities, signed on with a company called Coursera to develop and offer
online classes.

But can online education ever be education of the very best sort?   5

It's here that the notion of students teaching teachers is illuminating.   6
As a friend and fellow professor said to me: "You don't just teach students,
you have to learn 'em too." It took a minute—it sounded like he was chan-
neling Huck Finn—but I figured it out.

With every class we teach, we need to learn who the people in front   7
of us are. We need to know where they are intellectually, who they are as
people and what we can do to help them grow. Teaching, even when you
have a group of a hundred students on hand, is a matter of dialogue.

In the summer Shakespeare course I'm teaching now, I'm constantly   8
working to figure out what my students are able to do and how they can
develop. Can they grasp the contours of Shakespeare's plots? If not, it's
worth adding a well-made film version of the next play to the syllabus.
Is the language hard for them, line to line? Then we have to spend more
time going over individual speeches word by word. Are they adept at understanding the plot and the language? Time to introduce them to the
complexities of Shakespeare's rendering of character.

Every memorable class is a bit like a jazz composition. There is the basic melody that you work with. It is defined by the syllabus. But there is also a considerable measure of improvisation against that disciplining background.

Something similar applies even to larger courses. We tend to think that the spellbinding lecturers we had in college survey classes were gifted actors who could strut and fret 50 amazing minutes on the stage. But I think that the best of those lecturers are highly adept at reading their audiences. They use practical means to do this—tests and quizzes, papers and evaluations. But they also deploy something tantamount to artistry. They are superb at sensing the mood of a room. They have a sort of pedagogical sixth sense. They feel it when the class is engaged and when it slips off. And they do something about it. Their every joke is a sounding. It's a way of discerning who is out there on a given day.

A large lecture class can also create genuine intellectual community. Students will always be running across others who are also enrolled, and they'll break the ice with a chat about it and maybe they'll go on from there. When a teacher hears a student say, "My friends and I are always arguing about your class," he knows he's doing something right. From there he folds what he has learned into his teaching, adjusting his course in a fluid and immediate way that the Internet professor cannot easily match.

Online education is a one-size-fits-all endeavor. It tends to be a monologue and not a real dialogue. The Internet teacher, even one who responds to students via e-mail, can never have the immediacy of contact that the teacher on the scene can, with his sensitivity to unspoken moods and enthusiasms. This is particularly true of online courses for which the lectures are already filmed and in the can. It doesn't matter who is sitting out there on the Internet watching; the course is what it is.

Not long ago I watched a pre-filmed online course from Yale about the New Testament. It was a very good course. The instructor was hyperintelligent, learned and splendidly articulate. But the course wasn't great and could never have been. There were Yale students on hand for the filming, but the class seemed addressed to no one in particular. It had an anonymous quality. In fact there was nothing you could get from that course that you couldn't get from a good book on the subject.

A truly memorable college class, even a large one, is a collaboration between teacher and students. It's a one-time-only event. Learning at its best is a collective enterprise, something we've known since Socrates. You can get knowledge from an Internet course if you're highly motivated to learn. But in real courses the students and teachers come together and create an immediate and vital community of learning. A real course creates intellectual joy, at least in some. I don't think an Internet course ever will. Internet learning promises to make intellectual life more sterile and abstract than it already is—and also, for teachers and for students alike, far more lonely.

WORD POWER

improvisation the act of speaking or performing without preparation

WORD POWER

tantamount equal to something in value, meaning, or effect
pedagogical relating to teachers or education

WORD POWER

collaboration the act of working with others

Reacting to Language

Edmundson uses relatively formal language in this essay. Choose a paragraph that includes some elevated language, and rewrite it using less formal language. What do you think is gained and lost by rewriting this passage?

Reacting to Ideas

1. What does Edmundson think instructors can (and should) learn from their students?

*2. In paragraph 9, Edmundson says, "Every memorable class is a bit like a jazz composition." What do you think he means? Do you agree?

3. According to Edmundson, online education is "a one-size-fits-all endeavor" (paragraph 12). Do you believe, as Edmundson does, that an online course can never be "a collective enterprise" (14)? Explain.

Reacting to the Pattern

1. In paragraph 5, Edmundson states his thesis in the form of a question. Rewrite this thesis as a statement. Which version of his thesis is more effective? Why?

*2. Most of the evidence that Edmundson uses to support his thesis is from his own experience. Does this evidence provide enough support for his thesis? What other kinds of evidence could he have used?

3. What preconceived ideas does Edmundson assume his readers have about online education? About traditional classroom instruction? How do you know?

Writing Practice

1. Assume that your school is considering replacing all traditional classes with online instruction. Write a letter to the president of your college or university in which you argue for or against this policy. Be specific, and use your own experience as well as Edmundson's piece to support your points.

2. In paragraph 5, Edmundson asks, "Can online education ever be education of the very best sort?" Write an essay in which you answer this question. Make sure that your essay not only answers Edmundson's question but also refutes one or two opposing arguments.

Why Public Schools Should Teach the Bible

Roma Downey and Mark Burnett

Roma Downey is an actress and Emmy-nominated producer from Northern Ireland. She is perhaps best known for her leading role on the CBS series *Touched by an Angel*. Her husband, Mark Burnett, is an award-winning producer who is best known for producing the reality show *Survivor*. Both were raised in Christian households and maintain their faith today. Together they produced the biblical drama *Son of God* (2014), which was based on their 2013 miniseries for the History Channel called *The Bible*. In the following essay, which originally appeared in the *Wall Street Journal*, Downey and Burnett argue for the teaching of the Bible in public schools. As you read, consider how you feel about this issue and whether this essay changes your mind or reinforces your position.

Have you ever sensed in your own life that "the handwriting was on the   1
wall"? Or encouraged a loved one to walk "the straight and narrow"?

Have you ever laughed at something that came "out of the mouths of 2
babes"? Or gone "the extra mile" for an opportunity that might vanish "in
the twinkling of an eye"?

If you have, then you've been thinking of the Bible. 3

These phrases are just "a drop in the bucket" (another biblical phrase) 4
of the many things we say and do every day that have their origins in the
most read, most influential book of all time. The Bible has affected the
world for centuries in innumerable ways, including art, literature, philosophy, government, philanthropy, education, social justice and humanitari-
anism. One would think that a text of such significance would be taught
regularly in schools. Not so. That is because of the "stumbling block" (the
Bible again) that is posed by the powers that be in America.

It's time to change that, for the sake of the nation's children. It's time 5
to encourage, perhaps even mandate, the teaching of the Bible in public
schools as a primary document of Western civilization.

We know firsthand of its educational value, having grown up in 6
Europe—Mark in England, Roma in Ireland—where Bible teaching was
viewed as foundational to a well-rounded education. Now that we are nat-
uralized U.S. citizens, we want to encourage public schools in America to
give young people the same opportunity.

This is one of the reasons we created *The Bible*, a 10-part miniseries 7
premiering March 3 on the History Channel that dramatizes key stories
from Scriptures. It will encourage audiences around the world to open or
reopen Bibles to understand and enjoy these stories.

Without the Bible, Shakespeare would read differently—there are 8
more than 1,200 references to Scripture in his works. Without the Bible,
there would be no Sistine Chapel and none of the biblically inspired
masterpieces that hang in countless museums worldwide.

In movies, without biblical allegories, there would be no *Les Misérables*, 9
no *Star Wars*, no *Matrix*, no *Lord of the Rings* trilogy, no *Narnia* and no
Ben-Hur. There would be no Alcoholics Anonymous, Salvation Army or
Harvard University—all of which found their roots in Scripture. And really,
what would Bono sing about if there were no Bible?

Teaching the Bible is of course a touchy subject. One can't broach it 10
without someone barking "separation of church and state" and "forcing
religion down my throat."

Yet the Supreme Court has said it's perfectly OK for schools to do 11
so, ruling in 1963 (*Abington School District v. Schempp*) that "the Bible is
worthy of study for its literary and historic qualities. Nothing we have said
here indicates that such study of the Bible or of religion, when presented
objectively as a part of a secular (public school) program of education,
may not be effected consistently with the First Amendment."

The Supreme Court understood that we're not talking about religion 12
here, and certainly not about politics. We're talking about knowledge. The
foundations of knowledge of the ancient world—which informs the understanding of the modern world—are biblical in origin. Teddy Roosevelt,
the 26th president known more as a cigar-chomping Rough Rider than
a hymn-signing Bible-thumper, once said: "A thorough knowledge of the
Bible is worth more than a college education."

Can you imagine students not reading the Constitution in a U.S. gov- 13
ernment class? School administrators not sharing the periodic table of
the elements with their science classes? A driver's ed course that expected

young men and women to pass written and road tests without having access to a booklet enumerating the rules of the road?

It would be the same thing, we believe, to deny America's sons and   14
daughters the benefits of an education that includes a study of the Bible. Although we are both Christians, the list is long of ardent atheists who appreciate the Bible's educational heft while rejecting its spiritual claims. It is possible to have education without indoctrination. On this point, believers and nonbelievers should be able to "see eye to eye." (More Bible goodness.)

Interestingly enough, the common desktop reference guide *The*   15
Dictionary of Cultural Literacy best sums up the Bible's value as a tool of cultural literacy. Its first page declares: "No one in the English speaking world can be considered literate without a basic knowledge of the Bible."

Can we hear an amen?   16

Reacting to Language

*A *cliché* is a word or phrase that has been used so often that it is no longer interesting or effective. Choose two or three of the phrases that Downey and Burnett identify as clichés, and rewrite them, making the same point in a more original way.

Reacting to Ideas

1. Why do Downey and Burnett think that it is a good idea to teach schoolchildren the Bible? Do you agree? Why or why not?
2. Why do Downey and Burnett make a point of saying that they both grew up in Europe? Why do they mention that they created a miniseries based on the Bible?
3. Downey and Burnett conclude their argument with a quotation from *The Dictionary of Cultural Literacy*: "No one in the English speaking world can be considered literate without a basic knowledge of the Bible." Do you agree with this statement?

Reacting to the Pattern

1. Downey and Burnett open their essay with a series of questions. Why do they use this strategy? Do you think it is effective? Why or why not?
2. Paragraphs 10–14 refute objections to teaching the Bible. Why do the authors devote so much space to addressing opposing arguments?
3. Do Downey and Burnett provide enough support for their point that the Bible is a "primary document of Western civilization" (paragraph 5)? Should they have given more examples? Different types of examples? Explain.

Writing Practice

1. Do you think that the Bible should be taught to children in public schools? Take a position on this issue, using your own experience to support your points.

2. In paragraph 14, Downey and Burnett say, "It is possible to have education without indoctrination." Do you agree? Do you think that it is possible to teach the Bible without its "spiritual claims" (14)? Write an essay in which you support your position on this subject.

Acknowledgments

Index

Note: Page numbers in **bold** type indicate pages on which terms are defined.

Inside LaunchPad Solo for *Writing First with Readings*

LearningCurve Activities

Active and Passive Voice

Apostrophes

Capitalization

Commas

Fragments

Multilingual Writers: Articles and Nouns

Multilingual Writers: Sentence Structure

Multilingual Writers: Verbs

Nouns and Pronouns

Parallelism

Prepositions and Conjunctions

Pronoun Agreement and Pronoun Reference

Run-Ons

Subject-Verb Agreement

Verbs

Verbs, Adjectives, and Adverbs

Word Choice and Appropriate Language

Additional Grammar Exercises

Chapter 17 Writing Simple Sentences

Chapter 18 Writing Compound Sentences

Chapter 19 Writing Complex Sentences

Chapter 20 Writing Varied Sentences

Chapter 21 Using Parallelism

Chapter 22 Using Words Effectively

Chapter 23 Run-Ons

Chapter 24 Fragments

Chapter 25 Subject-Verb Agreement

Chapter 26 Illogical Shifts

Chapter 27 Misplaced and Dangling Modifiers

Chapter 28 Verbs: Past Tense

Chapter 29 Verbs: Past Participles

Chapter 30 Nouns and Pronouns

Chapter 31 Adjectives and Adverbs

Chapter 32 Grammar and Usage for ESL Writers

Chapter 33 Using Commas

Chapter 34 Using Apostrophes

Chapter 35 Understanding Mechanics

e-readings

Process: *Amy Ma*, "My Grandmother's Dumpling"

Classification: *Carolyn Foster Segal*, "The Dog Ate My Flash Drive, and Other Tales of Woe"

Definition: *Judy Brady*, "I Want a Wife"

Argument: *Bob Herbert*, "Tweet Less, Kiss More"